Essentials of Production and Operations Management

Text and Cases

FOURTH EDITION

Ray Wild
Henley Management College, UK

CASSELL

Cassell
Wellington House
125 Strand
London WC2R 0BB

215 Park Avenue South
New York
NY 10003, USA

British Library Cataloguing-in-Publication Data

A catalogue record for this book is available from the British Library.

ISBN 0–304–33130–9

Typeset by Falcon Oast Graphic Art
Printed and bound in Great Britain by Redwood Books Limited, Trowbridge, Wiltshire

Contents

Preface

This is an introductory book on production and operations management.[1] The production and operating functions within businesses are concerned with the processes which provide goods and/or 'services'. Production and operations managers are responsible for these processes. This book therefore deals with the management of both goods-producing and service-producing processes.

The definitions and ideas presented later in this book are based on a wide view of production and operations management. This approach views the production operations function as the core—the essential part—of any business. Furthermore, taking this view it will be shown that we are all production and operations managers. All types of business depend on production or operating systems and therefore require good production/operations management. Our subject, therefore, is of importance to *all* managers, whatever their title and whatever their job.

The book introduces some theories, ideas and concepts. It deals also with principles, procedures and techniques. It is intended as a teaching text. It is intended as an economic, straightforward volume, and aims to provide maximum value for minimum effort, for both student and teacher.

FOURTH EDITION

In preparing this edition, I have again stuck closely to three principles which have guided the previous editions, i.e.:

1. This is a book about operations—broadly defined—in which I try to deal with the subject as a whole. I have, in particular, tried to avoid separate treatment of production/manufacture and service operations. I have tried throughout to ensure that everything relates to both 'aspects'. I have tried to bring things together—to integrate, not differentiate.
2. This is a book for anybody. It is not specifically for engineers or for those with a technical background. It is not aimed specifically at those with analytical skills/interests, nor at those who are already in production/operations management jobs. All such people, but also all others with an interest in the subject will, I hope, find it valuable—but nothing by way of background, experience, skills etc. is pre-supposed.

[1] The parent text for this book is *Production and Operations Management* 5th edition, 1995, Ray Wild, Cassell. It covers everything in this edition and more, and in greater detail.

3. The 'incremental change' approach, has again been used. I take the view that lecturers do not want new editions of books which they use to be massively different. They don't want to start again with them. They do, however, want to think that adapting to a new edition is worthwhile, so they want to see some changes. In short, they value familiarity but of course want to be up-to-date—in the interests of both their own and their students' development.

Within this framework, several significant changes have been made. Coverage of Policy/Strategic aspects has been increased, and extended; the treatment of work systems has been restructured; the section on Quality has been changed substantially; there is new material in many other areas. The inclusion of a large number of *International case studies* in Part 9 is a major change. Also more case examples are used throughout the text.

However, the overall structure remains the same—even though the format, size, presentation, and a significant part of the content is changed.

TUTOR'S GUIDE

Finally, and of interest to Tutors only, the introduction of a major *Tutor's Guide* is a new development. It serves this book—and the 'parent' text—*Production and Operations Management*. (5th edn). It contains all of the additional material that should be required by those who are using this text as a core teaching text. It is available, free of charge, to tutors who adopt the text. To obtain the text tutors should write, on university/college letterhead, also enclosing their business card, to the publishers.

ACKNOWLEDGEMENTS

I am grateful to the many users of the previous edition of this book, worldwide, who have offered comments, advice and suggestions. I hope that they will find the 4th edition to be of value.

I am grateful also to several people from around the world who have helped me put together the set of international case studies contained in Part 9. Their contributions are acknowledged, individually, in that section. I am grateful to Virginia Wild for some typing and also to Joan Walker for her assistance with parts of the manuscript.

Ray Wild
Henley-on-Thames
March 1995

Operating Systems and Operations Management

INTRODUCTION TO PART I

This part of the book is the principal foundation for subsequent chapters. Here we take a broad view of operations management. Definitions are developed and a categorization of types of operating system is provided. Operations objectives are identified. The major problem areas, or decisions required of operations managers, are considered and three principal problem areas are identified. A model is presented to identify the factors influencing the operations manager's decision-making and role.

The chapter introduces several concepts and ideas, and aims to encourage the reader to think about the fundamental nature of operating systems and the role of the operations manager.

Chapter 1

The nature of operating systems and operations management

ISSUES

What is an operating system?
What is the function or purpose of operations?
What is the role of operations management?
What are the basic operations management objectives?
Why is the structure of operating systems important?
What are the basic operating system structures?
What are the main problem areas for operations management?

THE NATURE OF OPERATING SYSTEMS

Definition:

An operating system is a configuration of resources combined for the provision of goods or services.

Bus and taxi services, motels and dentists, tailors and mines, fire services and refuse collectors, retail organizations, hospitals and builders are all operating systems. They all convert inputs in order to provide outputs which are required by a customer.

Resources in operating systems

Operations managers are principally concerned with the use of physical resources; therefore we shall take a physical view of operating systems and concentrate on the physical resources used by the system, which for convenience will be categorized as follows:

(a) *Materials*, i.e. the physical items consumed or converted by the system, e.g. raw materials, fuel, indirect materials.

(b) *Machines*, i.e. the physical items used by the system, e.g. plant, tools, vehicles, buildings.

(c) *Labour*, i.e. the people who provide or contribute to the operation of the system, without whom neither machines nor materials are effectively used.

Functions of operating systems

A large variety of systems may be considered as operating systems, so some form of categorization of systems would be of value, if only for descriptive purposes. If we distinguish between goods-producing and service-producing systems, we have a simple categorization of operating systems. However, a more useful categorization is afforded by a consideration of system function.

The function of an operating system is a reflection of the purpose it serves for its customer, i.e. the utility of its output to the customer. Four principal functions can be identified:

(a) *Manufacture*, in which the principal common characteristic is that something is physically created, i.e. the output consists of goods which differ physically, e.g. in form or content, from those materials input to the system. Manufacture therefore requires some physical transformation, or a change in *form utility* of resources.

(b) *Transport*, in which the principal common characteristic is that a customer, or something belonging to the customer, is moved from place to place, i.e. the location of someone or something is changed. The system uses its resources primarily to this end, and such resources will not normally be substantially physically changed. There is no major change in the form of resources, and the system provides primarily a change in *place utility*.

(c) *Supply*, in which the principal common characteristic is that the ownership or possession of goods is changed. Unlike manufacture, goods output from the system are physically the same as those input. There is no physical transformation and the system function is primarily one of change in *possession utility* of a resource.

(d) *Service*, in which the principal common characteristic is the treatment or accommodation of something or someone. There is primarily a change in *state utility* of a resource. Unlike in supply systems, the state or condition of physical outputs will differ from inputs by virtue of having been treated in some way.

Most organizations comprise several systems—often with different functions. For example, an airline will have operating systems for transport, supply and service, and a typical manufacturing organization will also have internal transport and service systems. So, if we want to describe an organization in any detail we will need to consider its parts—or sub-systems.

The four principal functions can together be used in describing all operating systems and their sub-systems. They provide a basic language for operations management and permit the development of a slightly more detailed definition of an operating system:

Redefinition:[1]

An operating system is a configuration of resources combined for the function of manufacture, transport, supply or service.

---

[1] This, deliberately, is a wide definition. The approach employed throughout this book is equally wide. It derives from the belief that operating systems are at the centre of all types of enterprise and that running all types of enterprise can be seen to be the task of operations management.

Each of these four basic functions is considered briefly, with examples, below.

Manufacture

Considering business or organizations as a whole, a tailor, coal mine and builder would be categorized as manufacturing systems since their *overall* purpose is that of creating goods. Whether we consider large systems and therefore describe their function in over-all terms, or much smaller systems and therefore take account of more detail, will depend on our purpose. But whatever our level of description it should be possible to identify different types of manufacturing system. The classical way to categorize manufacture is as follows:

1. Process. The 'ongoing' production of a commodity or 'bulk' product, e.g. petrochemicals.
2. Mass. Similar to 'process' but for discrete items, e.g. consumer products.
3. Batch. The processing of 'lots' or batches of identical or similar items at intervals, i.e. so that after one batch has been processed, another batch of different types of item are processed through the system.
4. Jobbing. The manufacture of 'one-offs' e.g. major construction work.

Process and Mass, at least in their pure forms, are both types of continuous manufacture. Batch and jobbing are intermittent.

Each of these types of manufacture is characteristic of several different industries, but nevertheless no industry consists exclusively of any one type of manufacture. Increasing demand for products at present manufactured by means of a jobbing-type arrangement may enable a form of batch production to be introduced; and, similarly, increased demand for products at present manufactured in batches may indicate the desirability of mass production.

Transport

The principal function of transport systems is that of changing the location of someone or something. Taxi or bus services, ambulance services, furniture removers and refuse disposal systems can be categorized as transport systems. Within manufacturing organizations, transport systems may be employed for moving work-in-progress between manufacturing departments, removing waste materials, etc.

Supply

The principal function of supply systems is to change the ownership or possession of item(s) which are otherwise physically unchanged. At an organization level, a retail shop, warehouse, petrol station and broker may be seen to have the principal function of supply. Within organizations, supply systems may be evident as internal stores, etc.

Service

Dentists, fire services, launderettes, hospital wards and motels may be considered to have the principal function of service, i.e. the function of treating or accommodating something or someone. Within organizations a similar function may be performed by systems such as welfare departments and rest rooms.

THE NATURE OF OPERATIONS MANAGEMENT

Definition:

Operations management is concerned with the design and the operation of systems for manufacture, transport, supply or service.

Operations managers are 'decision takers'. The need for decisions implies the existence of problems. Operations managers must deal with a host of problems. Some are 'one-offs' or infrequent, others are recurrent. Many are interrelated.

We will consider the nature of operations problems and decisions later in this chapter. For the present it is sufficient to note that several key problem areas exist. They are inescapable. Tackling them and making decisions in these areas is central to the job of the operations manager.

This decision-making, is influenced by three major factors:

1. What should be achieved?

2. What can be done?

3. What would we like to do?

These are the *desirability, feasibility* and *preference* factors of operations management. Desirability is associated with *objectives*. Feasibility is associated with the nature of the operating *system*. Preference is associated with the *manager*.

Putting these factors together provides us with our basic model for operations management. It is outlined in Figure 1.1 and discussed below.

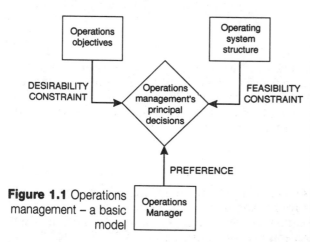

Figure 1.1 Operations management – a basic model

The way in which the operations manager tackles certain key or principal problems, i.e. his or her decision-making strategy, will be greatly influenced by the need to achieve given objectives. These objectives may have been determined by others, jointly, or largely by the operations manager. Whatever their origin, their influence on the operations manager and his or her job will be great. How the operations manager tackles certain problems must also reflect what is possible. That, in turn, may be influenced by the nature of the system which the manager must run. The magnitude of these two constraints will largely determine the scope that the operations manager has for exercising choice, i.e. the 'freedom of movement'. Given choice, the manager will have preferences about the way in which things are done. Methods that have been used before and found to be successful may be attractive. Familiarity will be a factor. The perceived expectations of others, e.g. superiors, may lead operations managers to choose a particular strategy for tackling certain problems. Habit, training, even personality may predispose the manager to do things in particular ways. The greater the desirability and feasibility constraints, the less the choice . . . and the tougher the job — and vice versa.

OPERATIONS MANAGEMENT OBJECTIVES

Customer service

The purpose of operating systems is the conversion of input for the satisfaction of customer wants. Customer service is therefore a key objective of operations management.

Customers should want the particular output of the operating system; this is a primary condition of their being customers. In other words the system must provide something to a *specification* which can satisfy the customer. Other considerations, however, will exist

Table 1.1   The three aspects of customer service

Primary consideration	Other considerations
To satisfy customers in respect of *specifications*, i.e. to provide what customers want or expect or will accept	To satisfy customers in respect of *costs*, i.e. to minimize the cost to the customer and To satisfy customers in respect of *timing*, i.e. to provide goods or services when required or expected (and in the case of service and transport with an acceptable duration)

Table 1.2   Aspects of customer service

Principal function	Principal customer wants	
	Primary considerations	Other considerations
Manufacture	Goods of a given, requested or acceptable *specification*	Cost, i.e. purchase price or cost of obtaining goods Timing, i.e. delivery delay from order or request to receipt of goods
Transport	Movement of a given, requested or acceptable *specification*	Cost, i.e. cost of movement Timing, i.e. (1) duration or time to move (2) wait, or delay from requesting to its commencement
Supply	Goods of a given, requested or acceptable *specification*	Cost, i.e. purchase price or cost of obtaining goods Timing, i.e. delivery delay from order or request to supply, to receipt of goods
Service	Treatment of a given, requested or acceptable *specification*	Cost, i.e. cost of treatment Timing, i.e. (1) duration or time required for treatment (2) wait, or delay from requesting treatment to its provision

and for simplicity these can be considered in terms of *cost* and *timing*. Thus, one objective of operations management is to ensure customer satisfaction by providing the 'right thing at the right price and at the right time'.

These three aspects of customer satisfaction—specification, cost and timing—are summarized in Table 1.1 and described in a little more detail for the four functions in Table 1.2. They are the principal sources of customer satisfaction and must therefore be the principal dimensions of the customer service objective for operations managers.

Generally an organization will aim reliably and consistently to achieve certain standards, or levels, on these three aspects, and operations managers will be influential in attempting to achieve these aims. Normally an organization will not aim to maximize customer service in all three areas. Particular emphasis will be placed on some and less on others, and in this way an organization will distinguish itself from others in the market place. So, an operations manager in one organization will not necessarily be working to the same mix of customer service objectives as a colleague in another organization. But in all cases, the objective will influence the operations manager's decisions since the actions the manager takes must be designed to achieve the required customer service.

Resource utilization

Given infinite resources any system should be able to provide adequate customer service. Problems for operations management arise from the fact that operating systems must satisfy multiple objectives. Customer service must be provided simultaneously with the efficient use of resources.

Operations management is concerned with the utilization of resources. The extent of their utilization might be expressed in terms of the proportion of available time used or occupied, space utilization, levels of activity, etc. Each measure indicates the extent to which the potential or capacity of such resources is utilized. We shall refer to this as the objective of *resource utilization*.

Few organizations will aim to maximize the utilization of all resources. Different emphasis will be placed on materials, machines and labour. But in all cases this objective, whatever the balance, will influence the operations manager's decisions, since the actions the manager takes must be designed to achieve the required levels of efficiency, as well as effectiveness.

The balancing of objectives

Figure 1.2 summarizes the twin objectives. Operations management is concerned with the achievement of both satisfactory customer service and resource utilization. Often both cannot be maximized, hence a satisfactory performance must be achieved on both, and sub-optimization must be avoided. All of the activities of operations management must be tackled with these two objectives in mind, and it is from the 'conflict' between them that many of the problems faced by operations managers derive.

The type of balance established, both between and within these two basic objectives, will be influenced by market considerations, competition, the strengths and weaknesses of the organization etc. The operations manager should have some influence when these objectives are set, but such decisions rarely rest entirely within the operations function. This balance will generally differ between organizations (and may change over time).

Figure 1.2 The twin (often conflicting) objectives of operations management.

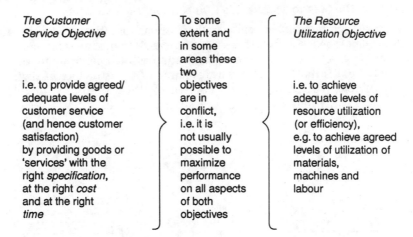

The Customer Service Objective	To some extent and in some areas these two	*The Resource Utilization Objective*
i.e. to provide agreed/ adequate levels of customer service (and hence customer satisfaction) by providing goods or 'services' with the right *specification*, at the right *cost* and at the right *time*	objectives are in conflict, i.e. it is not usually possible to maximize performance on all aspects of both objectives	i.e. to achieve adequate levels of resource utilization (or efficiency), e.g. to achieve agreed levels of utilization of materials, machines and labour

The fact of this difference is one reason why the operations management job is not the same in different organizations. A comparison of operations objectives for two organizations with the same function is given in Figure 1.3.

Figure 1.3 Operations objectives for two organizations

	Resource utilization			Customer service		
	Machines[1]	Materials[2]	Labour	Specification	Cost[3]	Timing
Luxury Goods Shop				✓		✓
Mail Order Co.	✓	✓	✓		✓	

Notes:
1. Display areas and equipment, check-out facilities, etc.
2. 'Intermediate' materials, e.g. wrappings etc. (not the goods themselves)
3. Maximizing customer service on cost, i.e. minimizing cost

✓ = Relatively important

THE STRUCTURE OF OPERATING SYSTEMS

Our original categorization of systems by function (manufacture, transport, supply and service) tells us something about their scope and purpose, but little about their nature. The categorization by function is an external perspective. It enables us to describe systems—as seen by the customer. Given that the nature of the system influences how operations managers tackle problems, we need a managerial perspective, i.e., a way of categorizing operating systems, which enables us to distinguish between them from an internal, managerial viewpoint. One way to achieve this is to consider their structure.

Using simple systems terminology, all operating systems comprise inputs, processes and outputs in the manner of Figure 1.4. This simple system structure can represent any operating system at any level of detail, e.g., an organization as a whole, or some part of it. As a descriptive device it is limited, so we must examine system structure in slightly more detail. The terminology of Figure 1.5 will be used for this purpose. With this simple approach we can identify four simple structures for *manufacture*:

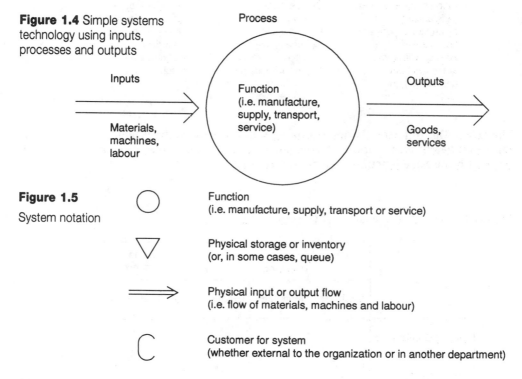

Figure 1.4 Simple systems technology using inputs, processes and outputs

Process

Inputs

Function
(i.e. manufacture,
supply, transport,
service)

Materials,
machines,
labour

Outputs

Goods,
services

Figure 1.5

System notation

Function
(i.e. manufacture, supply, transport or service)

Physical storage or inventory
(or, in some cases, queue)

Physical input or output flow
(i.e. flow of materials, machines and labour)

Customer for system
(whether external to the organization or in another department)

(a) *'Make from stock, to stock, to customer'*, i.e. all input resources are stocked and the customer is served from a stock of finished goods.

(b) *'Make from source, to stock, to customer'*, i.e. no input resource stocks are held, but goods are produced to stock.

(c) *'Make from stock, direct to customer'*, i.e. all input resources are stocked but goods are made only against and on receipt of customers' orders.

(d) *'Make from source, direct to customer'*, i.e. no input resource stocks are held and all goods are made only against and on receipt of customers' orders.

Each structure shows how a system will provide for future output. Structure (d), for example, indicates that, in order to provide the next output for a customer, resources must first be acquired, whereas in (c) the next customer order will be satisfied through the use of already existing resources.

Now consider *supply* systems in a similar manner. Both structures (a) and (b) require function in anticipation of order, i.e. structure (a) depicts 'supply from stock, to stock, to customer' and structure (b) depicts 'supply from source, to stock, to customer'. Neither case is common in supply operations, but both can exist. Normally structures (c) or (d) will exist. Structure (c) depicts 'supply from stock direct to customer', and structure (d) 'supply from source direct to customer'.

These four basic structures for manufacture and supply systems are shown in Figure 1.6.

Figure 1.6 Basic system structures for manufacture and supply

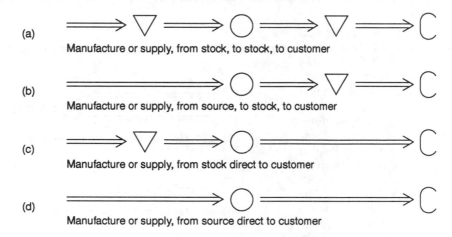

(a)   Manufacture or supply, from stock, to stock, to customer

(b)   Manufacture or supply, from source, to stock, to customer

(c)   Manufacture or supply, from stock direct to customer

(d)   Manufacture or supply, from source direct to customer

A slightly different situation applies in both *transport* and *service*. Those structures which require function in anticipation or in advance of receipt of a customer's order are not feasible, since no physical output stock is possible. Consider transport. A taxi service cannot satisfy a customer's relocation or movement requirements before receiving the customer's order. Similarly, an ambulance, refuse collection or furniture removal service cannot build up a stock of outputs to satisfy future customer demands. Nor can a bus service perform its function of transporting individuals before those individual customers arrive. Looking at this a slightly different way—since the function of transport and service is to 'treat' the customers (whether a thing or a person), the customer is a resource input to the system, i.e. *the beneficiary of the function is or provides a major physical resource input to the function.* Thus transport and service systems are dependent on customers for the supply of major physical input(s) to the function without which the function would not be achieved. For example in transport, a taxi, ambulance or bus service moves customers or something supplied by them, e.g. pieces of luggage. In service systems, e.g. hospitals or motels, the customer is treated in person, while launderettes and fire services treat items which might themselves be considered as customers or whose supply is controlled by the customer.

In other words, unlike manufacture and supply, transport and service systems are activated or 'triggered' by an input or supply. The customers exert some 'push' on the system. In manufacture and supply they 'pull' the system, in that they pull goods out of the system whether direct from the function (structures (c) and (d)) or from output stock (structures (a) and (b)). In transport and service the customers push the system: they act directly on input. In such systems, therefore, some part of the resource input is not directly under the control of operations management. In these 'push' systems the customers control an input channel, and we must therefore distinguish this channel when developing models of systems.

Somewhat different structures are therefore required to represent transport and service systems. Three structures would seem to exist, as illustrated in Figure 1.7.

(e) *'Function from stock, and from customer'*, i.e. input resources are stocked, except in the case of customer inputs where no *queuing* exists.

(f) *'Function from source, and from customer queue'*, i.e. no input resources are stocked although customer inputs accumulate in a queue.

(g) *'Function from stock, and from customer queue'*, in which inputs are stocked and customers queue.

Customer queues are physical stocks in the customer input channel, although they cannot be utilized by operations management in the same way as other resource stocks, for they are usually beyond their direct control. Queues comprise those customers who have 'arrived' at the system and await service or transport. They are the customers who at any one time have asked to be 'treated' by the system. The queue therefore represents known and committed future demand.

In total, therefore, we have seven basic structures for operating systems. Listed in Figure 1.8, they are simple system descriptions. For example, they deal only with single channels for outputs and only with physical flows. However, this type of approach can be used to describe more complex systems. Furthermore, these basic system models can be used to describe operating systems at any level of detail—the organization, a division, a department, a section, etc.—depending on our particular focus.

The principal differences between these basic system types derive from the location and existence of stocks. The presence or absence of output stocks and customer queues is a straightforward aspect, but input stocks can comprise ma-

Figure 1.7 Basic system structures for transport and service

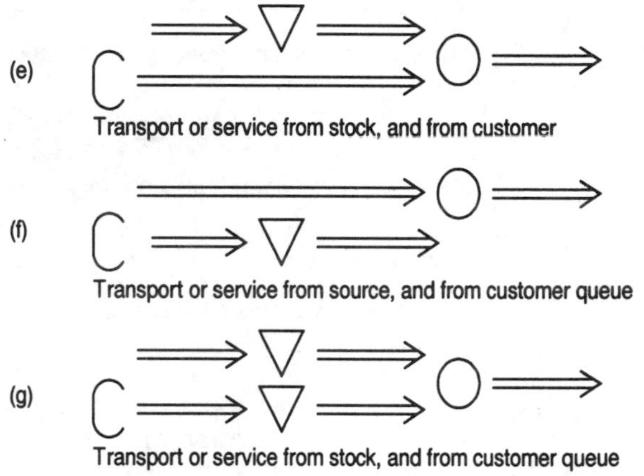

(e) Transport or service from stock, and from customer

(f) Transport or service from source, and from customer queue

(g) Transport or service from stock, and from customer queue

Figure 1.8 Seven basic operating system structures

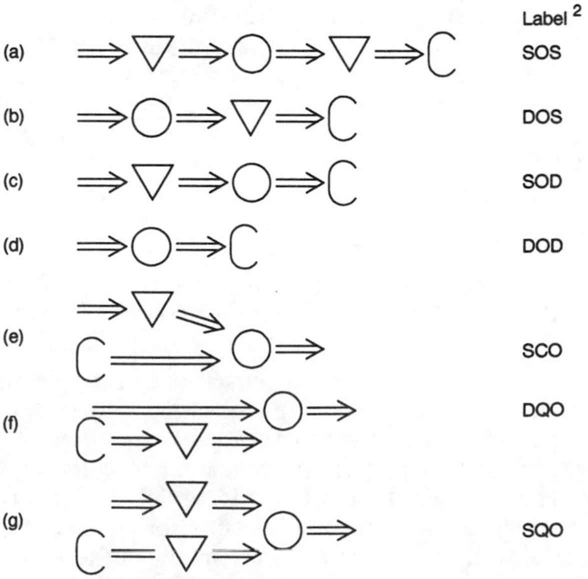

		Label [2]
(a)		SOS
(b)		DOS
(c)		SOD
(d)		DOD
(e)		SCO
(f)		DQO
(g)		SQO

[2] It is sometimes convenient to have a 'label' for each structure, so as not to have to refer to diagrams. In these labels, O = operation, S = stock, D = direct, Q = customer queue, C = customer direct input.

terials, machines and labour (our three types of physical resource). We can regard an input stock of resources to exist if some or all of the necessary resources are available. If any of the required resources are not available in stock awaiting use then in effect the system cannot operate for no capacity exists, and for our purposes we can consider stock to be absent.

Examples of system structures

At their simplest level, i.e., described as a single system, we might model operations in the manner shown in Figure 1.9. We could go into more details and describe operations as comprising certain sub-systems: Figure 1.10 is an example. The amount of detail will depend upon our purpose. If we aim to understand the nature of a single operation, managed by a single operations manager, then a simple model would suffice. If there are identifiable sub-systems, each with its own operations manager, we would need more detail. Whatever the level, being able to identify the type of system in this way will help us understand how that system must be managed. For this reason, structure is important to the operations manager. Simply knowing the function is not enough.

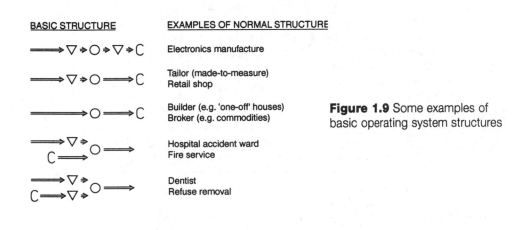

Figure 1.9 Some examples of basic operating system structures

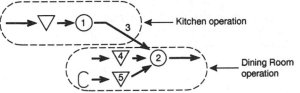

Figure 1.10 Operating systems structures for a restaurant

Notes:
1. Kitchen function = manufacture
2. Dining room function = service
3. Output from kitchen = meals
4. Dining room resources
5. Customer queue (i.e. waiting). N.B. Might be 'concealed' by a bar operation

Overall structures
Kitchen = SOD
Dining Room = DQO (Because whilst some resources are stocked, not all are, i.e. meals, hence no capacity exists, in advance, to serve customers)

OPERATIONS PROBLEMS AND DECISIONS

Having established the type of context in which operations decisions are taken, we should now identify, and catalogue, the decisions, i.e. the problem areas which must be dealt with by operations managers.

The scope of the operations manager's job is indicated by the list of problem areas given in 'life-cycle' order in Table 1.3.

Table 1.3	The scope of operations management
	Problem areas
Design and planning	Involvement in design/specification of the goods/service
	Design/specification of process/system
	Location of facilities
	Layout of facilities/resources and materials handling
	Determination of capacity
	Design of work or jobs
	Involvement in determination of remuneration system and work standards
Operation and control	Planning and scheduling of activities
	Control and planning of inventories
	Control of quality
	Scheduling and control of maintenance
	Replacement of facilities
	Involvement in performance measurement

Principal problem areas

Although each of these problem areas is important in the effective planning and operation of the system, we can identify *three areas* which have a particular significance for operations management. These are the principal problem areas of operations management; they are the problems of *capacity management*, *scheduling* and *inventory management*. The type of problem faced by operations management in each of these three principal problem areas will be influenced by the operating systems structure and operations objectives, as shown in Figure 1.1.

Capacity management

The determination of capacity is the key system planning problem and the adjustment of capacity is the key problem area in system control. Capacity decisions will have a direct influence on system performance in respect of both resource utilization and customer service. It is difficult to see how any organization can operate effectively without good capac-

---

[3] Throughout we shall use the term 'goods and services' to include all outputs from operating systems, i.e. items, transports and the services defined at the beginning of the chapter.

ity management. Excess capacity inevitably gives rise to low resource productivity, while inadequate capacity may mean poor customer service. Decisions made in other areas are unlikely to offset errors in this area.

Scheduling

Scheduling is concerned with the timing of occurrences. *Operations scheduling* in its widest sense may be considered to be concerned with the specification in advance of the timing of occurrences within the system, arrivals to and departures from the system including arrivals to and departures from inventories within the system. Thus we can consider the inventory management problem to be a part of a wider operations scheduling problem. Conventionally we take a narrower view of the scheduling problem. We normally focus on *activity scheduling*, which is concerned only with activities directly related to the function. The timing of such activities may have a significant impact on resource utilization and customer service.

Inventory management

The existence of output stocks may facilitate the provision of high customer service, at least in terms of availability or 'timing'. However, they may be costly. The provision of input resource stocks may benefit customer service, yet resource productivity may be adversely affected because more resources are idle. Few organizations can exist entirely without stocks of raw materials, work in progress or, where appropriate, output goods. The planning of inventory levels, the control of inventories and the maintenance of such stocks are expensive but necessary. Inventories will normally tie up considerable amounts of capital, so there is a balance to be struck between obtaining the benefits of inventories such as flexibility, high customer service and insulation against demand fluctuations, and minimizing the cost of such stocks.

One factor adding considerably to the complexity of inventory, capacity and scheduling problems is their close interdependence. Decisions made in one will have a direct impact on performance in the others. Such interdependence is less evident in the other problem areas, a fact which tends to 'underline' the central importance of these three problem areas in the management of operations. In many respects the problems of inventory management and scheduling are subsidiary to the problem of capacity management. Capacity management decisions will determine how the operating system accommodates customer demand level fluctuations. Capacity management decisions will provide a context within which inventories and activities will be both planned and controlled. They will to some extent reflect operating policy decisions, while inventory and scheduling problems might be considered as more tactical issues.

COMMON PROBLEM AREAS

Unlike the three 'principal' problem areas of operations management, many of the others identified in Table 1.3 are not so substantially influenced by both system structures and operations objectives. They do not differentiate systems in quite the same way. They are important, of course, but are less inter-related.

OPERATIONS MANAGEMENT IN HOSPITAL OUTPATIENT CLINICS

EXAMPLE

An operations management-style approach was used to improve management of outpatient clinics at the Royal Lancaster Infirmary in the UK. The clinics involved were those that check the progress of patients who had previously been treated in the Accident and Emergency department. Each clinic suffered from a high degree of congestion, with patients often waiting well over 30 minutes for a consultation that lasted less than two to three minutes. Hospital management wanted to investigate two areas with a view to improvement: the appointment systems, and the occurrence of what seemed to be an excessive number of repeat visits. Several scenarios were investigated before new systems were decided upon. It was clear that operations could be improved and that there was considerable scope for reducing patients' waiting times without increasing doctors' idle times significantly.

Source: Worthington, D. and Brahimi, M. (1993) Improving out-patient appoint systems. *International Journal of Health Care Quality Assurance*, **6**(1), pp. 18–23.

KEY POINTS FOR CHAPTER 1

Operating systems serve the functions of manufacture, transport, supply and service.

The principal, physical resources of operating systems are materials, machines and labour.

Operations management is concerned with the design and operation of such systems.

Three factors influence the operations manager's decision making:

1. operations objectives
2. operating systems
3. manager's preferences

Operations objectives relate to both customer service and resource utilization.

Customer service concerns specification, cost and timing.

Resource utilization concerns the use of physical resources.

Operations managers must achieve an appropriate objectives balance.

The structure of operating systems influences operations decisions.

There are seven basic operating system structures: 4 for manufacture and supply, and 3 for transport and service.

The main differentiating features of system structures are the existence and location of stocks and the influence of the customer.

There are 3 principal operations management problem areas: capacity management, scheduling and inventory management.

The 3 principal problem areas are interrelated.

FURTHER READING

Waters, C.D.I. (1991) *An introduction to Operations Management.* Addison-Wesley, Chapter 1.

Meredith, J.R. (1992) *The Management of Operations: A Conceptual Emphasis*, 4th edition, Chichester: Wiley, Chapter 1.

Foggarty, D.W. Hoffman, T.R. Stonebraker, P.W. (1989) *Production and Operations Management*, South Western, Chapter 1.

CASE STUDY

The following case, from Part 9 of the book, is relevant to the topics covered in this chapter.

No.	Name	Country
1	Carreras SL	Spain

QUESTIONS

1.1 How far is it possible for the operations function within the organization to operate independently of the other main functional areas? Which functions, in particular, experience interlocking problems?

1.2 Describe the principal types or classes of manufacture. What are the prerequisites for each of these types of manufacture and what are the principal operations management problems associated with each type? Illustrate your answers by describing actual industrial situations with which you are familiar.

1.3 Identify seven basic operating system structures and give examples of each, making the simplifying assumption, if necessary, of single-channel inputs and outputs.

1.4 Using the basic operating structures in series and/or in parallel, with multiple input and output channels if necessary, describe (i.e. model) the following operating systems:

(a) a typical 'take-away' or 'fast food' shop (e.g. a hamburger house);

(b) a taxi service.

Identify and explain any assumptions you make.

PART 2

The Context of Operations Management

INTRODUCTION TO PART 2

Here we consider the business context of operations management. As we take the view that the operating system and operations management are the heart of any enterprise, we must recognize that there must be relationships with other functions in the business. We look at business policy decision-making, the nature of its influence on operations management, and the nature of the influence of operations management on it. We look at operations policy formulation, and then consider the nature of the relationships between operations management and marketing, organizational, financial control and design decisions. Throughout we shall concentrate on basic concepts and ideas, so that the nature of and reasons for these relationships are clear. Similarly in Chapter 4 we look at some basic aspects of operations economics and costs.

Chapter 2

Business and operations policy

ISSUES

How are Business policies formulated?
How do Business policies impact on Operations?
What are Business Policy options?
How do these options relate to operations objectives?
What are the key elements of operations policy?
What are the main operations Policy decisions?
How is operations policy implemented?

Although operations managers will have a considerable degree of control over decisions within their own area of responsibility, they will not in general be able, or wish, to ignore the actions of others. There exists an external 'framework' for their actions, and marketing, financial, personal and other decisions are the components of this framework.

This is the business policy context for operations. Before considering operations management decision-making we must consider the manner in which this works, for it is essential that we are aware of those factors which influence operations decisions and the manner in which this influence is exerted. This chapter will therefore consider business policy and its influence on operations management, while Chapter 3 will examine some important components of the framework of operations management decisions.

THE NATURE OF BUSINESS POLICY

Business policy planning is a continuous and systematic activity aimed not only at identifying purposes for the organization but also at defining procedures, organizing efforts to achieve these purposes and measuring results against expectations. It is a systematic approach to both the formulation and the implementation of total business plans.

Formal systematic planning is essential, since detailed forecasts and action plans are required to allow co-ordinated action throughout the organization and adequate evaluation of performance. Such planning necessitates co-operation between functional specialists, subdivisions, etc., and therefore brings about a degree of co-ordination and a perspective which might not otherwise have existed within the organization. The existence of detailed plans facilitates delegation and permits the establishment of relatively autonomous divisions, while ensuring that overall control remains. It provides a set of goals and criteria for assessing the merits of new opportunities and proposals, whether for concentration or diversification of the business. Two important and interrelated aspects are evident in the business policy process: *formulation* (or planning) and *implementation*.

Formulation of business policy

Classically, four steps must be taken in formulating a business policy:

1 the identification of *opportunities* for, and threats to, the organization, together with the estimation of the degree of risk associated with each;

2 the assessment of the organization's present and potential *strengths* and *weaknesses*, particularly in respect of its material, financial, technical and personnel resources, i.e. its potential capacity to pursue identified opportunities and/or to deal with threats;

3 consideration of the personal *values* and aspirations of the organization's major stakeholders and its managers;

4 clarification and acknowledgement of the major social *responsibilities* and objectives of the organization.

Consideration of (1) and (2) above can give rise to the development of a rational *economic policy* for an organization through the matching of opportunities to capabilities. This is rarely the total perspective for the development of business policy, for it will often be necessary to consider personal aspirations and preferences (3). It will be necessary to identify what an organization will 'want to do' as distinct from, or as a sub-set of, what it 'can or might do'. Finally, the inclusion of (4) above—a largely non-economic dimension—raises the question of what the organization 'should do', i.e. having regard to its responsibilities and social objectives. This four-part perspective is illustrated in Figure 2.1,

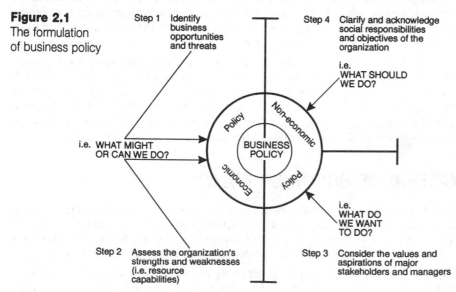

Figure 2.1
The formulation
of business policy

Step 1 Identify business opportunities and threats

Step 4 Clarify and acknowledge social responsibilities and objectives of the organization

i.e. WHAT SHOULD WE DO?

i.e. WHAT MIGHT OR CAN WE DO?

BUSINESS POLICY

i.e. WHAT DO WE WANT TO DO?

Step 2 Assess the organization's strengths and weaknesses (i.e. resource capabilities)

Step 3 Consider the values and aspirations of major stakeholders and managers which identifies the economic and non-economic aspects of the process.

The culmination of this policy formulation stage is the statement of policies on:

I   the nature of the goods or services to be provided by the organization;

II the nature of the markets/demand to be served;

III the manner in which these markets are to be served.

These are all aspects of considerable direct significance to operations management.

Implementation of business policy

Implementation of an agreed policy is concerned with the acquisition and mobilization of resources, the creation of appropriate structures and processes, and monitoring and control. Again four aspects can be identified:

1   use of physical resources, e.g. equipment, machinery and labour, and the development of appropriate technology;

2   the creation of appropriate organization structures and relationships, e.g. the roles and responsibilities of individuals, departments and functions, and the use of appropriate information systems, etc.;

3   organizational processes and behaviour, e.g. the development of individuals, their motivation and rewards, performance measurement, and the establishment of standards;

4   top leadership, i.e. the provision, monitoring and updating of overall objectives, inter-function and inter-division co-ordination, overall resources allocation, etc.

It is through the effective implementation of an appropriate business policy that an organization will 'make its mark'. Success or failure derives from these decisions and actions, and the whole nature of management in and of the organization, including operations management, is influenced by and reflects the policies of the organization.

Relationships of business policy and operations management decisions

We will look at the relationship of Business Policy and Operations in both 'directions'.

Influence of business policy on operations management decisions

Policy decisions on the nature of the goods or services to be provided, the nature of the market/demand to be served, and the manner in which these markets are to be served, will influence:

A   operations management's choice of operating structure;

B   the formulation of operations management objectives;

C   operations management's choice of decision-making strategies.

The way in which these influences are exerted is shown diagrammatically in Figure 2.2 and is discussed below.

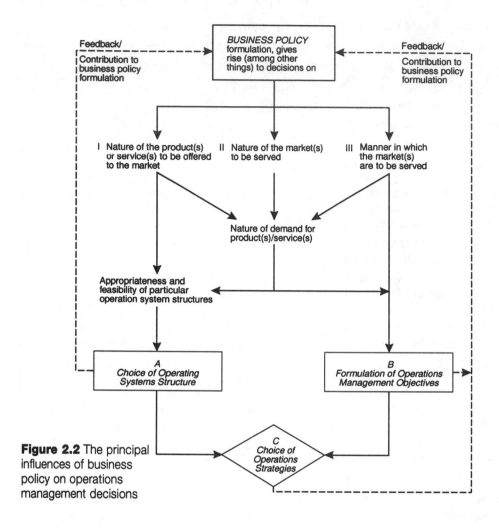

Figure 2.2 The principal influences of business policy on operations management decisions

Business policy influences on choice of operating systems structure (A) and the formulation of management objectives (B)

The structure of the operating system influences the role and problems of operations management; however, operations managers are unlikely to have a free *choice of system structure*, since the nature of the function and the customers' influence on the system are major external factors influencing the appropriateness of a system structure. For example, an organization may have some scope for influencing the customer, and thus the 'pull' or 'push' on the operating system. Such influence may derive from advertising and marketing activities, pricing, etc. An organization may therefore have some influence on the structure of the operating system, but such influence will normally be external to the operations manager. From the operations manager's point of view the nature of the function and the customer influence on the system are constraints, deriving in part from decisions relating to the nature of the product or service and the nature of the market, i.e. the goods/services and market/demand characteristics determined through business policy decisions.

Taking a slightly different viewpoint, the operations manager will recognize that in some circumstances certain system structures cannot be adopted, i.e. they are infeasible, since the factors which permit their existence are absent. There are certain prerequisites for the existence of an operating system structure. Certain factors will permit, and in exceptional conditions cause, one or more of the structures to exist. Such prerequisites or enabling factors are essentially of an external nature and are mainly related to the predictability of the nature of demand. The feasibility of system structures is dependent on the predictability of the nature of the demands of the customer on the system. Such predictability is an enabling factor, hence it does not follow that the existence of predictable customer demand will necessarily give rise to the existence of a certain structure. For example, the nature of the demand for the output of a power station is known, yet output is not stocked. This condition is, however, one prerequisite—a further external factor—without which certain structures cannot in reality exist. It will limit the extent to which operations management can choose, or change, structures, and again this constraint will be largely influenced by decisions relating to the nature of the product or service and the nature of the market, i.e. the goods/market and market/demand characteristics determined through business policy decisions.

Given the feasibility of certain operating system structures, the choice between them will be influenced by the *objectives of operations management*. These will reflect management's view of what the customer wants or will be prepared to accept by way of service, and the need within this constraint to maximize resource utilization. While the general objectives of operations management are clear, the manner in which those objectives are pursued, and certainly the emphasis placed on each, may be influenced by broader business policy decisions. To some extent, therefore, operations management will be required to pursue a stipulated policy as effectively as possible. Policy on customer service may be influenced to some considerable degree by broader business policy considerations. Although a mail order firm, a luxury store and a supermarket are all concerned with the function of supply, they each have a different approach to the objective of customer service, so operations management will not be required to achieve the same standards of service in each case. Often standards or objectives for customer service will be influenced by other functions in the organization.

Business policy influences on choice of operations management decision-making strategies (C)

In Chapter 1 we considered how system structure and operations management objectives influenced certain 'principal' operations management problems and the way in which decisions are taken. We saw that the nature of the problems to be tackled by operations management is influenced by system structure. The manner in which these problems are tackled will also be influenced by the objectives which exist. In other words, a problem may be tackled in a particular manner in order to achieve a particular outcome given one set of objectives, and in a different manner for a different end given a different set of objectives. Thus the decision strategies adopted by operations management i.e. the general approaches employed, will be influenced by the nature of the problems which exist and the objectives which are to be pursued. The selection of strategies is therefore influenced by business policy decisions in two ways: through the influences on the selection of system structure in the manner discussed above, and through the influence on operations management objectives.

Contribution of operations management to business policy decisions

The principal means by which operations management contributes to or influences business policy decisions is through the provision of information on:

(a) the existing operating system structure, objectives and decision strategies;

(b) the implications for operations management of the goods/service and market/demand strategies which are proposed or being considered by the business policy makers.

Change situations may occur when a change or modification of the existing goods or service(s) is under consideration and/or when new markets are being investigated. In such situations an operating system is in existence and changes are being considered which might affect or necessitate a change of system objectives and strategies. Clearly some knowledge of the nature of the existing system, its characteristics and performance will be of value in making business policy considerations in such circumstances. The alternative is the situation in which business policy decisions will lead to the establishment of *new* operating systems. Here operations management must interpret alternative goods/services and market/demand strategies into implications for operations management, since the nature of the system structure, operations management objectives and strategies required to meet given goods/service and market/demand characteristics will influence the choice between alternatives. The main factor in both cases is the need to match operating system structures, operations management objectives and strategies to given goods or service and demand conditions, or vice versa. If it is intended to change goods or service and/or demand specifications, then a knowledge of the characteristics and capabilities of the existing operating system, existing operations management objectives and strategies, and the effectiveness of existing systems and strategies, is important. Equally, it is important when considering alternative goods or service and/or demand specifications to know what system structures, objectives and strategies will be required for effective operation.

Business policy for competitive advantage

One aspect of business policy formulation is of particular relevance to operations management. It relates primarily to decisions on (iii), the manner in which markets are to be served, and has implications especially for B, the formulation of operations objectives (see Fig. 2.2).

Policy options

In determining its policy a business will normally be seeking to secure competitive advantages. In other words a business will be aiming to put itself in a position in which it will be able to serve its customers in some way better than its competitors are able to do. Frequently this will involve an organization in identifying its distinctive competencies in order to deploy them, whilst also avoiding its weaknesses.

Generally, there is no single obvious, secure source of sufficient competitive advantage; thus businesses must consider the policy options available to them in order to construct a policy which when taken as a whole gives some competitive strength. Figure 2.3 identifies some of these options, and their interrelationships. They are explained below.

(a) *Flexibility*. The ability to supply customers with different types of goods or services;

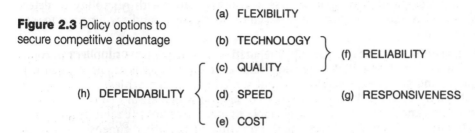

Figure 2.3 Policy options to secure competitive advantage

(a) FLEXIBILITY

(b) TECHNOLOGY

(c) QUALITY

(d) SPEED

(e) COST

(f) RELIABILITY

(g) RESPONSIVENESS

(h) DEPENDABILITY

to offer different variants on a basic portfolio, i.e. to customize, adapt and tailor, can be a major strategic advantage. This capability may help build long-term, more secure relationships with customers, whose needs may change over time. Such flexibility may enable organizations to command a higher price, to secure more profitable sectors of a market, etc.

(b) *Technology.* Organizations with strong research and development will often be in a position to market products/services which are more advanced, more sophisticated or more capable than others. They may be able to get such items to the market earlier than their customers, create new markets and win large market shares. In some sectors technological superiority may be a critical success factor (e.g. aerospace, health care); the ability to compete by innovating provides advantages which might be secured through patent protection. For some it is a major strength, and an advantage beyond that available to organizations who seek, or are able only to exploit existing, established technologies.

(c) *Quality.* For most organizations, product/service quality is important. Few customers will willingly acquire low-quality items or services. However, the ability to provide products or services of outstanding quality, when compared to those of competitors, can afford a major strategic advantage. Quality is a variable. It is often related to price. Having the organizational capabilities to deliver high quality can be a major source, or one source, of competitive advantage.

(d) *Speed.* Doing things quickly can mean quicker delivery to customers, shorter queuing or waiting time for customers, and quicker processing of customers, than can be achieved by competitors. 'Speed is of essence' for many customers. The ability to satisfy a customer now rather than tomorrow can be a major strength in manufacturing transport, supply and service businesses.

(e) *Cost.* Some organizations choose to compete on cost, e.g. price to the customer. High volume operations providing a limited range of goods or services may have a cost and price advantage.

(f) *Reliability.* The fact that something (whether product or service) is always available, serviceable, and satisfactory—doing what it was intended to do and in the intended manner—can be a major attraction to certain customers in certain circumstances. The ability to provide outputs having such high reliability conveys considerable competitive advantage to organizations in industries such as aerospace, motor vehicles, health care, emergency services, etc. The factor relates in some ways to quality, the two often being interdependent, and also technology.

(g) *Responsiveness.* This has to do with speed. Advantage may be secured by an organization which is able to respond quickly to changes in customer requirements, e.g. the need for new types of product or service, and which can most quickly satisfy those needs. Thus getting new 'offerings' to the market place can put an organization in an advantageous position. Responsiveness is also associated with an ability to detect and/or understand a customer's need—even to anticipate it—and a willingness to seek ways to satisfy it.

(h) *Dependability*. To have a record and a reputation as a dependable supplier can count for a great deal. The ability to provide, time after time, what is required when it is required and at the expected price is not something all can achieve. Such dependability alone, even for the supply of goods or services which are available from others, and at the same price, can be a considerable strength. It is not the same as speed. It is to do with consistency and repeatability on three of the other dimensions: quality, speed and cost.

Focus and position

The determination of the competitive stance of the organization, i.e. which of the above options to concentrate on, should give a focus to the organization's efforts and a character to the organization. An organization which has chosen to compete on flexibility, quality and responsiveness will neither behave nor feel like one that is competing on speed and cost. Each will have positioned itself in the market, and in respect of its competitors. Each will have sought to differentiate itself from others in the eyes of the customer.

The management roles in each, not least the roles of operations managers, will be different, for amongst other things the operations objectives will be different. Certainly the weight attached to the three customer service objectives for operations will be different.

EXAMPLE

Walden Paddlers

Walden Paddlers has designed, produced and marketed a technically sophisticated rowing kayak made from recycled plastic. It significantly undercuts its competition on price and outmanoeuvres in its performance. Walden Paddlers, despite its low-tech appearance, is what is increasingly known as a 'virtual corporation'—a company that outsources just about everything in the pursuit of flexibility, low price and product innovation to secure its chosen market position.

Source: Welles, E.O. (1993) Virtual realities. *Inc.* **15**(8), pp. 50–58.

OPERATIONS POLICY

Achieving competitive advantage

Operations managers will aim to influence the policy options chosen by businesses in their pursuit of competitive advantage. Once those decisions are made, the nature of one part of the operations objectives to be pursued by operations managers is fixed, for the policy options followed by a business will largely determine the customer service objectives of operations managers. This relationship is illustrated by Fig. 2.4. We should also remind ourselves of one other point made in our discussion of objectives in

Figure 2.4 The relationship of policy options and operations objectives

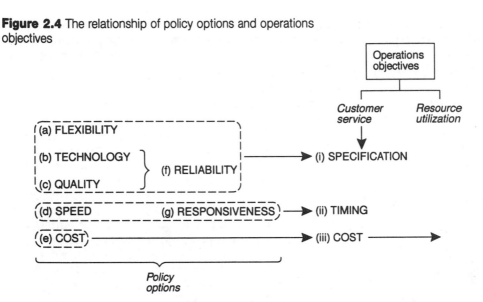

Table 2.1	Policy options and operations implications	
Competitive advantage	**Policy option**	**Typical operations requirements**
Products/services to satisfy a wide range of customer needs	Flexibility	Versatile facilities and labour Rapid change-overs Broad range Flexible work systems
Most sophisticated and advanced products/services	Technology	High process and product technology Substantial R&D Good new-project management
High-quality products/services	Quality	Error-free processes and systems Substantial quality assurance/control Adequate systems capability
Fastest delivery or service with minimum waiting time	Speed	Fast throughput Adequate capacity Short queues Dedicated/specialized work systems
Lowest price	Cost	High productivity/resource utilization Limited range/standardization Low inventories
Unfailing serviceability of products/services	Reliability	Good systems/resources maintenance Rapid 'de-bugging' of new products/services High process quality
Fastest response to new customer requirements	Responsiveness	Rapid new product/service development
Consistently good service	Dependability	High repeatability of processes and systems High reliability of resources

chapter 1, i.e. that customers will have some interest in the reliability of operations in delivering goods and services to agreed specifications, cost and timing. So the 'dependability' and 'reliability' options (Figure 2.3) also relate to the customer service objectives of operations.

Policy implications for operations

Pursuit of each of the policy options will have implications for operations managers. They will need to achieve certain things in order that the business policy be achieved. The implications are outlined in Table 2.1. Notice that they relate largely to resources and the manner in which the operating system must be used. For example, to achieve competitive advantage on cost, the operation must be highly productive, intensive, and efficient. To achieve flexibility, the operating system must be versatile, readily changed, and adaptable. To compete on speed, there must be fast throughput, low in-process inventories, short lead times, etc. In each case a policy option can be perceived as a customer service objective, from which certain resource management and utilization objectives are evident; so, business policies aimed to achieve competitive advantage, which influence the way in which the business serves its markets, must be translated into customer service objectives for operations—which therefore is one critical aspect of operations policy decision-making.

EXAMPLE

Sleep Inn

CASE

Choice Hotels International wanted to return to the days of no-frills rooms at bargain prices. The company also needed to find a way to deal with the unexpected labour shortages and declining employee productivity in the service industry. The solution was the 'labour-lean' Sleep Inn, which won Personnel Journal's 1991 Human Resources Award in the 'competitive advantage' category. Sleep Inns are less expensive to operate and require half as many employees as a comparable budget hotel. The rooms are smaller and designed for cleaning efficiency, enabling housekeepers to service them in 2/3 the time it takes to clean the average room. This strategy, with its prime objective of labour-saving and efficiency, resulted in profit margins 10% better than the average budget hotel. A Choice Hotels study shows that 97% of Sleep Inn guests rated their stay either excellent or good, while 99% indicated that the rooms had high value for the price paid.

ANALYSIS

Here the business priorities are to achieve competitive advantage in the market, and also to minimize labour needs and increase labour efficiency. So, the strategy of providing a low-cost service, for a market which attaches importance to cost reliability and dependability, is established. From an operations viewpoint this can be interpreted as implying an emphasis on:

Customer Service:

Specification   low but reliable and consistent
Cost   low
Timing   rapid

The implications for operations management are that there is the need to achieve the following:

(a) High labour productivity, e.g. through
    Efficient work scheduling
    Flexible labour
    Good training
    Appropriate facilities design.

(b) Consistent and dependable quality, e.g. through
    Standardized work procedures
    Appropriate quality controls
    Good maintenance of facilities and equipment
    Error-free work.

(c) Short cycle-time operations, e.g. through
    Close facilities monitoring
    Adequate materials stocks
    Good labour supervision and control.

Source: Schember, J. (1991) Sleep Inn wakes up to new labor, *Personnel* **70**(8), pp. 71–73.

Operations policy decisions

We can now reflect on policy for the operations function in the business. First we will identify the general framework for operations policy based on our previous discussion; then we will look at policy implementation for operations.

The nature of operations policy decisions

We have seen that three major operations management decisions are influenced by prior business policy decisions, i.e.

A selection/choice of system structure;

B selection/formulation of operations management objectives;

C selection/formulation of strategies for the management of the operating system.

These are key operations management decision areas. They are all concerned with planning. Operations management must determine system structure and objectives and contribute to the determination of objectives before anything can be manufactured, supplied, transported or serviced. They are key decisions, since wrong decisions in these areas will inevitably affect the performance of the system and the organization. Together they will determine the nature and character of the operating system. They are in fact operations management *policy* decisions. The choice of operating system structure, the objectives of the system, and the strategies which will be employed in the management of the system are the principal ingredients in the formulation of an operations management policy.

We have seen that operations management contributes to business policy decisions by providing information on:

(a) the existing system structure, objectives and strategy, in order that the characteristics and capabilities of the system might be considered in the selection/change of goods or service and demand characteristics;

(b) the implications of proposed or alternative goods or service and demand characteristics for system structure, objectives and strategy.

This contribution of operations management to business policy decision-making therefore derives from the three operations management policy decision areas. In fact, therefore, as would have been expected, it is principally the policy decisions of operations management which both are influenced by and contribute to business policy decisions.

Implementing operations policies

To achieve operations policies, managers must make decisions and take action in particular areas. It is these decisions and subsequent actions which link operations policies to the day-to-day running of the operation. The principal 'linkages' are listed in Table 2.2. Decisions such as these will determine the character of operations and the role of operations managers.

Table 2.2	Principal 'linkage' decision areas for operations
1.	**Capacity and facilities:** Amount and location of resources
2.	**Scheduling and control:** Methods for planning and controlling flows
3.	**Inventories:** Locations and quantities
4.	**Technology:** Types of processes, degree of automation
5.	**Workforce:** Skills, payment
6.	**Organization:** Structure, roles, authority
7.	**Integration:** Links with suppliers, etc.

KEY POINTS FOR CHAPTER 2

A Business Policy

Identifies the long term purposes of an organization.

The Business Policy process involves formulation and implementation.

The formulation of a Business Policy requires consideration of opportunities; strengths and weaknesses, values, and responsibilities.

A Business Policy will stipulate

the nature of the goods/services

the nature of the markets

the manner in which markets are to be served.

Implementation of a Business Policy

Requires consideration of resources, structures, processes and leadership.

Business Policy decisions influence Operations Management on their

  choice of system structures

  choice of objectives

  choice of strategies.

Operations Managers

Must contribute to Business Policy formulations through seeking to match policy aims with operations capabilities.

Business Policy formulation often seeks to secure a competitive advantage through some of the following policy options:

  flexibility, technology, quality, speed, cost, dependability, reliability, responsiveness.

Achieving competitive advantage through these options will impact on the operations manager, as the choice of options influences the nature of the operations manager's customer service objective.

Operations Managers' own policy decisions relate to

  selection/choice of system structures

  selection/formulation of objectives

  selection/formulation of strategies.

FURTHER READING

Harrison, M. (1993), *Operations Management Strategy*. London, Pitman.

Berry, W.L. and Hill, T. (1992), Linking Systems to Strategy. *International Journal of Operations and Production Management* **12** (10), pp. 3–15.

Garvin, D.A. (1992) *Operations Strategy—Text and Cases*. London, Prentice Hall.

CASE STUDY

The following case, from Part 9 of the book, is relevant to the topics covered in this chapter.

Case No.	Name	Country
9	America Burger & Pasta	Brazil

QUESTIONS

2.1 How might business policy decisions influence operations management decision-making? How might operations management contribute to the formulation of business policy?

2.2 Discuss the relationship of operating system structure and (a) the characteristics of the goods or services provided by the system, and (b) the nature of the market(s) and demand(s) for the goods or services.

2.3 What are the main policy decision areas of operations management? How are these related to business policy decisions?

Chapter 3

Operations management and other business functions

ISSUES

What is the relationship of Operations and Marketing?
How do Marketing decisions affect the Operations manager?
How are goods or services designed or specified?
What is the contribution of operations to this process?

Chapter 2 showed that certain decisions which are largely 'external' to the operations function have a considerable influence on decisions within the function. These external policy-related decisions are largely concerned with the organization's relationship with its market(s). They are

I. decisions on the nature of the goods or services to be provided by the organization, i.e. the *market offering*;

II. decisions on the nature of the markets to be served, i.e. the *market/demand characteristics*; and

III. the manner in which these markets are to be served, i.e. the *market relationship*.

Operations management must therefore recognize a close relationship with the marketing function in the business. This chapter will focus initially on the nature of the marketing function and its relationship with operations management. We then look at the way in which products or services are designed and how operations relationships function with the design.

MARKETING DECISIONS

The marketing function of the business is concerned primarily with the nature of the 'offering' (the goods/service characteristics) and the methods by which the 'offering' is made (the advertising and distribution methods, etc.). Conventionally such decisions are considered to comprise the elements of the *marketing mix* of goods/services, cost, distribution, and promotion. While all businesses must make decisions on each of these four elements of the marketing mix, different types of business will employ different mixes, since they will attach different importance to each element.

(a) *goods/service*, i.e. goods/service characteristics—the actual item, transport or service provided to the customer, its attributes and characteristics, the features and provisions surrounding it and the essential benefits it provides;

(b) *cost*, i.e. the purchase price of the goods or service and any additional costs or allowances;

(c) *distribution*, i.e. the location of the market, channels of distribution, outlets, territories, etc., involved in the provision of the offering to the customer;

(d) *promotion*, i.e. the publicity, selling and advertising practices employed to bring the goods or services to the notice of the intended customer.

These *market decisions* influence, but do not determine, the nature of the demand faced by the organization, i.e. the demand felt by the operating system. In addition, other factors only partially influenced by the organization will influence demand, i.e.

(e) **environmental variables:** factors (largely beyond the control of the enterprise) that have broad effects on demand, e.g. the economic situation, public policy and culture;

(f) **competitive variables:** factors under the control of competitors.

Figure 3.1 Factors influencing demand and operations management

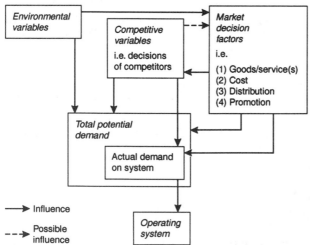

Figure 3.1 indicates the manner in which environmental, competitive and market decision variables influence demand. The introduction of a new product or service may affect the total actual demand for products or services of that type and will also attract a part of that total. Environmental variables, the action of competitors and the market decisions of the enterprise may all affect the size of the total potential and actual market. Certain actions of competitors, e.g. advertising or price changes, may affect the size of the actual market, and of course market decisions by an organization, particularly promotion decisions, will directly affect actual market share. The nature of the environment will be known and may therefore influence market decisions. The actions of competitors

will be uncertain but nevertheless may be considered by an enterprise when making decisions on goods/services, cost, promotion and distribution.

Within this framework we shall focus on market decision variables, i.e. those decisions required of the business. In so doing we shall look more closely at the market-related policy decisions identified at the beginning of this chapter in order to try to identify how these decisions, which directly influence operations management, are made, and thus to identify the means by which operations managers might influence them.

Factors influencing decisions on goods/service characteristics

Here we are dealing with one market decision variable (1 in Figure 3.1). We shall identify some of the factors that influence this decision.

Growth is a common, corporate policy. Goods/service(s) decisions are an important ingredient in the formulation and implementation of each of four possible policies for growth; i.e.

(a) *Market penetration* is the expansion of sales of existing offerings in existing markets by selling more to existing customers, and/or gaining new customers in existing markets.

(b) *Market development* is the creation of new markets by discovering new applications for existing offerings.

(c) *Product development* is the launching of new offerings on to existing markets.

(d) *Diversification* or lateral integration is the development of new offerings for new markets.

For reasons of diversification and goods/service development, most enterprises will offer a range of goods and/or services. This market decision may therefore require consideration of the characteristics of a particular offering or the number and mix of the whole range of offerings. It may be concerned with the addition, change or abandonment of one offering or one group of offerings from the whole range, and/or with the nature, consistency and mix of the whole range. The following factors will be of relevance.

Life-cycles

It has been found that products and services have a life-cycle over which demand increases, stabilizes and falls.

Four stages in the life-cycle of offerings can be identified: incubation, growth, maturity and decline. The span of the life-cycle may be determined by such factors as:

(a) the degree of technological progress;

(b) changes in customer habits;

(c) ease of entry to the market.

Different actions or market decisions may be required at each stage of a life-cycle. Price decisions will be required before or at the launch time, while during the incubation period the emphasis will be on promotion. Distribution is all-important during the growth period. The maturity period may see the introduction of price changes or changes in specifications to prevent decline, and/or the introduction of new offerings.

The development process

Goods/service development involves the search for new offerings as well as the improvement of the existing. Since the number of entirely new offerings is normally small, development is concerned largely with the introduction of variants through adaptations and improvements.

At least six stages of development can be identified. These are:

1. Exploration, including research, i.e. the continual search for new ideas.
2. Systematic, rapid screening to eliminate less promising ideas.
3. Business analysis, including market research and cost analysis.
4. Development of the remaining possibilities.
5. Testing the offerings developed.
6. Launching on a commercial scale.

Development, testing and launching (4, 5 and 6) are the most time-consuming and most costly stages. Few new ideas are eventually launched, and of these only a small proportion succeed.

Market policies

Three main methods are available to the enterprise to exploit the market.

Market aggregation is the penetration of the market to the greatest possible width and depth with a single offering or a very limited range. This approach relies on a uniform pattern of consumption and an appeal to the needs which customers have in common in order to win sales.

Market segmentation is concerned with placing an extensive range of offerings each of which is suited to the needs of a different submarket or market segment. Here a conscious search is made to determine the essential differences between buyer groups in order that they can be clearly separated into different segments, each varying in size, buying power and buyer behaviour.

Product differentiation is the deliberate attempt to encourage demand to adjust itself to the manner in which supply has been segmented. Unlike market segmentation, product differentiation may be employed where segments are not clearly defined and where segments must therefore be *created* by emphasizing the presence of product differences between the enterprise's own offerings and those of competitors, in particular by emphasizing product differences which promote a social–psychological segmentation of the market, favouring the product concerned.

Quality, brand and brand policy

Quality is the extent to which an offering satisfies a need. Improving the quality of an offering or a line is known as 'trading up', and the reverse as 'trading down'. Quality may be changed. For example, it may be appropriate to adjust the range in response to economic developments such as the trade cycle, and/or to raise or lower both the quality and the price of offerings in the range. Trading up or down in the long term may help the enterprise to gain access, from its traditional market position, to other higher or lower segments of the market.

A brand is used to identify offerings and distinguish them from those of competitors. For brand policy to be successful the offering must lend itself to differentiation, to facilitate advertising and promotion. The aim of branding is to facilitate, improve and simplify control of the market process. A successful brand image will help secure a market. A brand suggests consistency in the quality and origin of the offering.

Factors influencing decisions on market/demand characteristics

Here, in effect, we are concerned with three market decision variables (2, 3 and 4 in Figure 3.1). Two aspects are of particular importance to the operations manager. First, there are those decisions which influence or determine the nature of the market for the offering and the nature of the demand felt by the organization. The operations manager will, of course, have some interest in these decisions and will wish to make some contribution to them. Second, given these decisions, the operations manager will be particularly concerned with the nature of the demand which is to be met. He or she will wish to measure or estimate demand, and may seek to predict future demand, all as a means to facilitate his or her own decision-making on capacity, schedules and inventories.

Here we shall consider the three market decision variables—cost, distribution and promotion—all of which will influence market/demand characteristics.

Cost

Price is normally the most important, but not the only, cost factor.

Price is clearly important as a regulator of demand and a component of customer service. It:

(a) regulates sales volume;

(b) determines revenue;

(c) influences the rate of return on investment through its influence on sales profitability;

(d) has an impact on unit costs.

The principal decisions in pricing derive from four main problems:

(a) How should the relative importance and the relative emphasis of price and non-price variables within marketing decisions be determined?

(b) To which pricing policy is a particular price geared? Pricing policy, in a broad sense, should answer two questions:

1. What are the objectives for pricing?

2. How will these objectives be attained?

(c) How should prices (i.e. price levels) for offerings be determined (and redetermined)?

(d) How should pricing policy be implemented, e.g. the timing and extent of price changes and deviations such as discounts?

Distribution

As the purpose of distribution is to move items from the point of provision to the point of consumption, market decisions on the nature of distribution are primarily the concern of *manufacture* and *supply* systems. Manufacture must rely upon a distribution system to ensure that goods reach the final customers or users. A supply system will form part of the distribution system for a manufacturer and may itself rely on subsequent distribution to the final user. For example, wholesalers will form part of the chain of distribution for a manufacturer and will themselves supply retailers.

Two aspects of decision-making for distribution can be identified: (a) distribution channel decisions, and (b) physical distribution management decisions. The latter, involving decisions on stock levels, etc., are more likely to influence operations management directly.

Promotion

Promotion is concerned primarily with persuasion, aimed largely at securing and increasing the share of the actual market. Four promotional activities can be identified:

(a) *advertising*—any paid form of non-personal presentation and promotion of products or services by an identified sponsor;

(b) *personal selling*—oral presentation with one or more prospective purchasers for the purpose of making sales;

(c) *publicity*—non-personal stimulation of demand for a product or service, by planting commercially significant news about it in a published medium or obtaining favourable presentation of it that is not paid for by the sponsor;

(d) *sales promotion*—those marketing activities, other than personal selling, advertising and publicity, that stimulate consumer purchasing and dealer effectiveness, such as displays, shows and exhibitions, demonstrations, and various non-recurrent selling efforts not in the ordinary routine.

An enterprise must decide how much promotional effort to make, and the relative mix or importance of each of the above within that total effort. The importance of promotion will, among other things, depend on the merits of alternative non-promotional expenditure, the nature of the product or service offered by the enterprise and its competitors, and the stage in the product or service life-cycle.

Promotion is one way to secure and stimulate demand. Given limited resources, promotion competes for funds with the other three market decision variables. The more impersonal the method of distribution and the greater the similarity to the products or services offered by competitors, the greater is the need for promotional effort. Products and services which are at an early stage in their life-cycle, where exposure and customer awareness are important, may also need relatively high promotion.

THE RELATIONSHIPS OF OPERATIONS MANAGEMENT AND MARKETING DECISIONS

Marketing managers are primarily responsible for the four 'marketing mix' decisions discussed above. These decisions are of substantial interest to operations managers, for they will determine the products/services to be provided by the operating system and the nature of demand for those outputs. Operations managers will often wish to exercise some influence on these decisions to ensure that marketing managers do not make decisions which give rise to circumstances which operations managers cannot adequately accommodate. It would be appropriate for them, therefore, to have in mind a 'checklist' of those decisions which influence the nature of the product/service, the market for that 'offering' and the manner in which that market is to be satisfied. Table 3.1 provides such a checklist.

Table 3.1 A checklist of some marketing decisions which influence operations management	
Product/service characteristics: The development philosophy Market policy The nature and quality of the product/service	**Cost:** Pricing policy The price of the offering Price variations
Distribution: Level of service Inventory decisions	**Promotion:** Advertising – amount – scheduling Selling – size of sales force

EXAMPLE

MARKETING AND OPERATIONS:
The Need for Synergy

Marketers need to understand 7 key factors that may be critical to achieving a productive and smoothly running service operation. The ideal strategy is one that achieves synergy between marketing and operational objectives and the seven issues that are as relevant to marketers as they are to operations managers. They are:

1 productivity improvement
2 standardization versus customization
3 batch versus unit processing
4 facilities layout and design
5 job design
6 capacity management
7 management of service queues

Both market and operational managers should be searching for ways to work together: Marketers may be able to develop customer-oriented strategies designed to make the operation run more smoothly, while operations concepts can be used to provide better service to customers.

Source: Lovelock, C. (1992), Seeking synergy in service operations: seven things marketers need to know about service operations. *European Management Journal* **10**(1), pp. 22–29.

THE DESIGN FUNCTION

The nature of the 'offering', i.e. the product or service for the market, was discussed in Chapter 2. We know that there is a need for offering(s) with potential competitive advantages. We have considered pricing, promotion, quality and other market-related issues earlier in this chapter. Here we will look briefly at the process by which such offerings are designed or specified, for operations managers must contribute to that process, if only to ensure that the final specification can in fact be delivered or achieved in practice.

The design process

Whilst some of the procedures and techniques in this area have been evolved primarily in connection with product design, the basic ideas that we shall discuss apply equally to products and services.

The traditional design process involves many steps from initial design though to final provision. Traditionally these will involve several functions or departments in the orginization. This can be a long process, so it is often difficult to get new products/services quickly to market—and thus achieve competitive advantage on 'responsiveness' or 'speed'.

Figure 3.2 p. looks at this traditional 'design to provision' process. It shows also that many initial ideas can be lost at each stage, and so the number surviving the whole process is very small. An outline description of the stages in process is given in Table 3.2.

The role of operations

Operations has a contribution to make in stages 2, 3, 4, 5, 6 and 7 in the above process—for there is little benefit in conceiving a product or service which cannot be efficiently, fully or economically provided. So operations must enter into the design dialogue as follows:

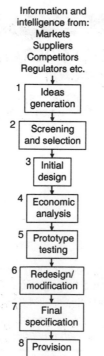

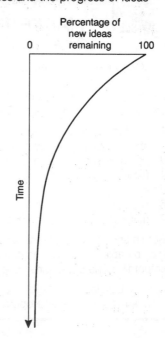

Figure 3.2 The 'design to provision' process and the progress of ideas

Stage 2: Screening and selection
Can the product/service be provided by the operating system?

Do we have the processes, technology, and skills?

Do we have the capacity?

Stage 3: Initial design
What is the most appropriate design for providability, at the required quality and probable cost required?

Stage 4: Economic analysis
How much would it cost to provide the appropriate volumes and at the required quality?

Table 3.2	Stages in the design process

1. Ideas generation
Market- or technology-oriented ideas
New concepts or incremental developments
Internally or externally generated

2. Screening and selection
Market analysis test
Technological feasibility
Competitive advantage
Risk assessments

3. Initial design
Specification of major aspects/features
Initial model/'mock-up'

4. Economic analysis
Estimate of development cost

Estimate of provision cost, thus:
Estimate of final cost
Estimate of price

5. Prototype testing
Performance/function testing
Consumer tests
Test of 'providability'

6. Redesign/modification
Improvements, corrections and modifications
Retesting if necessary
Approval for final design

7. Final specification
Full detailed specification of content, structure, function and performance

Stage 5: Prototype testing
Check providability through operating systems

Stage 6: Redesign/modification
Introduce modifications to improve providability

Stage 7: Final specifications
Ensure appropriate quality specifications
Begin process specifications

In making the above contribution, operations must have regard to the following.

Quality *(see also Chapter 19)*

In Chapter 19 we shall show that the quality of a product or service, and hence its reliability, is invested during two stages: design and operation/provision. During the design stage, quality is determined by the specification of appropriate standards on dimensions, content, etc. The quality level obtained is, of course, a function of cost. While nothing can be designed to have perfect quality or perfect reliability, the expenditure of more money on materials, testing, operations and control will, of course, improve quality levels. In practice, quality will be determined not only by the availability of suitable resources but also by the quality of competitors' offerings, the elasticity of demand and the planned price.

Purchasing *(see also Chapter 16)*

Since no organization is completely independent of suppliers, the purchasing function will influence design. Not only will the new design depend on the ready availability of certain purchased items or services but also on the redesign, i.e. modification, replacement or improvement of existing items. The purchasing department will play an important part because of its knowledge of such factors in the development of new or improved items and services.

Make or buy decision *(see also Chapter 16)*

Theoretically, every item or service which is currently purchased from an outside supplier is a candidate for internal provision and vice versa. In reality the problem is not quite so extensive as this, since there will always be many things which it would just not be in our interest to provide ourselves. Similarly, there will always be many things which it would not be in our interest to purchase. By making an item or providing a service ourselves we reduce our dependence on other companies, we are able to determine our own quality levels and we preserve our trade secrets. Conversely, to purchase rather than provide ourselves may enable us to obtain them more quickly, and to obtain the benefits of a continual development programme which we ourselves could not sustain. Additionally, purchase instead of self-production may reduce costs such as those associated with storage, handling, paperwork, etc. as well as releasing our facilities for jobs on which they might be more suitably and profitably employed.

Standardization

Specifications provide details of product or service requirements in terms of content, performance, and so on, while standards are rules, models or criteria against which comparisons can be made. Standardization is therefore concerned with the concept of variety, and, more specifically with the control of necessary variety. Company standardization begins to operate once unnecessary variety has been eliminated. The elimination of unnecessary variety (variety reduction) can be defined as 'the process of eliminating the unnecessary diversity' which frequently exists in the various stages from design to provision and is undertaken in anticipation of obtaining some or all of the following advantages:

(a) Increased interchangeability of items or services.

(b) Provision of goods/services, or parts of them, in larger quantities, with better resource utilization.

(c) Staff training is simplified.

(d) Record-keeping and inventory control is simplified.

(e) Greater flexibility is possible.

(f) Reduced cost and price.

Simultaneous development

Many companies have discovered that their competitors can get new items or services to the market far quicker that they are able to do. In other words they cannot compete on 'responsiveness'—their 'time to market' was too long.

In order to improve 'time to market', organizations have sought to 'streamline' and thus speed up the design/development process by achieving simultaneous rather that sequential activity.

'Simultaneous development' aims to optimize the process to achieve reduced lead time, improved quality and cost, by integrating the stages of the process through maximum parallelisms of working practice. Critical elements of this revised process include.

the use of multi-disciplinary/multi-departmental task forces or project teams in design and development;

improved communications between functions/disciplines;

simultaneous development of the product/service, the process, quality control and marketing processes;

design for 'provability' and performance.

EXAMPLE

A.T. & T

AT & T's Consumer Products Division needed to improve its lengthy new-product-development cycle. Currently it could take two years to introduce a design change because it had to pass through a lengthy product-development cycle. Benchmarking studies revealed that competitors' development cycles were between 40% and 75% shorter than AT & T's. The strategy for improving the development cycle was to adopt time as the critical element. Three phases were developed: 1. definition phase, 2. development phase, and 3. production phase. Throughout the development cycle dialogue among the cross-functional members of the product team strengthens the information flow. To accelerate product development 'platforms', or previously established capabilities, are provided to support the development team's work.

Source: Sansone, P and Singer, M. (1993) AT & T's 3-phase plan rings in results. *Appliance Manufacturer* **41** (2), pp. 71–74.

Designing 'services'—the differences

All of the concepts outlined above apply to the 'design through to provision' process for goods and for services. However, there are some distinctive aspects in 'service' design which should be noted. These will be of particular relevance to those involved in supply, transport and service type operations as defined in chapter 1.

The first thing to note is that, as far as the customer is concerned, there is no physical product involved in transport and service systems. That is not to say that no products are used, but rather that they are the products of other organizations, acquired and used by the system rather than being designed and provided by it. Supply systems do bring products into contact with customers, but, again, they are the products of other organizations—designed by them.

In general, in designing the offerings of supply, transport and service systems more emphasis will be placed on the process, i.e. the operation itself, in which the customer takes some part. Thus the relative effort required and the time devoted to initial idea generation are less. The main task is to design the process which delivers the service idea. For this reason operations managers will probably be more involved, and from an early stage. However there will still exist opportunities for achieving economies through simultaneous development.

The provision of supply, transport and service will usually be a labour-intensive process, so labour will be a critical factor in evaluating whether a system can deliver services of adequate quality, etc.

The lead time for the design and development of such offerings will often be shorter than for product design and development. 'Prototype' testing will often be more difficult to achieve, and of course such offerings when finalized cannot be protected with patents.

The equivalent to a design 'blueprint' for a service is usually a flow chart which shows, in detail, the processes through which a customer will pass. Examination of that flow chart will often show that there are some activities which, whilst essential for the delivery of the offering, are nevertheless separated from the customers—a type of 'technical care' which for the customer remains in the background. Often, securing efficiency and effectiveness in supply, transport and service systems involves separating that care, or decoupling it from the 'up-front' system, so as to be able to operate an efficient, repetitive, high-volume activity whilst exposing the customer to the minimal actual contact with the organization to deliver the required benefit. The 'behind the scenes' activities in freight companies, hospitals, etc. are good examples.

Finally we must note that, as with product design and development, it is often the customer who specifies the design, through an expressed need. Nevertheless, in all types of operation there is always the possibility of developing something entirely new which customers will be found to want, even though they could not express a prior need.

KEY POINTS FOR CHAPTER 3

Marketing decisions are a major part of the 'external' policy framework within which operations exist.

Marketing decisions focus on the marketing mix—goods/services; cost; distribution; promotion.

Marketing mix decisions influence demand, as do environmental and competitor factors.

Marketing decisions, and how they are implemented, influence both the nature of the goods/services to be provided and the markets to be served.

The key marketing decisions which influence operations are.

    product/service decisions

    cost/price decisions

    distribution decisions

    promotion decisions

The design function is concerned with the specification of products and services.

The design process traditionally involves many sequential steps. Operations contribute to most of these.

Efforts to speed up the design to market cycle have led to the evolution of the simultaneous development approach.

The design or specification of services focuses on the process rather than on products.

The customer is often particularly influential in the specification of services.

FURTHER READING

Cannon, T. (1995) *Basic Marketing* (4th edn) London: Cassell.

Lovelock, C. (1992) Seeking synergy in service operations—seven things marketing needs to know about service operations. *European Journal of Management*, 10 (1), pp.22–29.

CASE STUDY

The following case, from Part 9 of the book, is relevant to the topics covered in this chapter.

Case No	Name	Country
13	Food Concept Sdn Bhd	Malaysia

QUESTIONS

3.1 In what way can 'marketing mix', decisions influence the customer demand on the operating system?

3.2 How does the performance of the operating system influence decisions on the 'marketing mix' variables?

3.3 Identify and discuss the principal considerations and factors which will be taken into account in determining the nature of the goods or services to be provided by the organization.

3.4 What factors or variables can be manipulated in order to create particular market/demand conditions and how might decisions on these factors/variables be made?

3.5 Select a particular type of service and describe how a 'simultaneous development' approach might shorten the time required to develop a replacement service and get that service to the market.

Chapter 4

Operations economics and costs

ISSUES

What are operations costs?
What factors influence operations costs?
What are economies of 'scale' and 'scope'?
What is a 'break even' point?
How are costs controlled?

The transformation process within any business adds value and cost to the goods or services provided by the system. In manufacturing the cost of physical conversion, e.g. materials processing, will often represent a major part of the total cost of the items produced. In transport, the cost of moving the customer, comprising the cost of the equipment used and the labour employed, as well as any overheads, will often be a major ingredient determining the total cost. Similarly, in supply and service systems the operations function will add significant cost to the total cost of the items or services provided for the eventual customer. Given this responsibility for 'cost contribution', the operations manager must be familiar with the factors contributing to the cost of operations, the factors influencing these costs, and the means available for the measurement and control of the cost of operations.

OPERATIONS COSTS

The components of operations costs may be direct or indirect. *Direct costs* (or the prime cost) comprise those which may be identified separately for each good or service provided, e.g. the cost of the direct materials consumed or incorporated and the cost of the direct labour involved.

Indirect costs (or operations overheads) are all other expenses which cannot be charged specifically to particular output items, services or transports. Indirect costs include the cost of indirect materials, indirect labour and all other charges involved in operating the

Figure 4.1 Operations and total cost

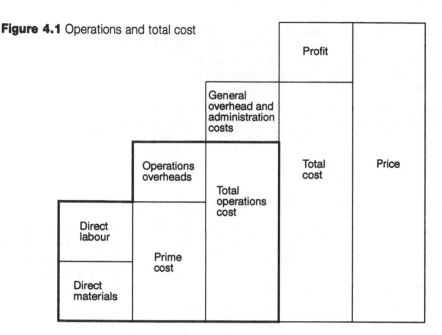

system where such charges cannot be allocated realistically or accurately to particular goods or service.

Together these costs add up to the *total operations cost* and thus, with the general and administrative costs and the profit, to the total cost to the customer, i.e. the selling or purchase price, in the manner shown in Figure 4.1. Notice that while the prime cost is normally considered to comprise the sum of direct labour and materials, no provision is made for direct costs associated with the third of the major resource inputs to the operating system—the machinery employed. The assumption here is that machinery is used for multiple purposes and its costs therefore cannot normally be seen as a direct charge; they must be allocated as part of the overheads associated with the operation. Although in some cases expenses other than those associated with labour and materials can be charged directly to particular outputs, other expenses are normally seen as part of the operations overheads. The operations overheads can, in turn, be subdivided into material, labour and other expenses in the manner outlined in Table 4.1.

Table 4.1	Operations overheads		
			Other expenses
Indirect materials	**Indirect labour**	**Standing costs**	**General costs**
Tools	Supervision	Rent	Management
Consumed materials	Technical services	Depreciation	Welfare costs
	Transport	Insurance	Planning
	Quality control	Rates	Services
	Operations control		Power
			Maintenance

Operations managers are responsible for the total operations cost. They will be interested in the components of this cost, and also in the distinction between *fixed* and *variable* costs. Over a fairly short period of time certain of the organization's costs, in particular those associated with the operating system, can be seen to be fixed; they will not be affected by changes in the scale of the operation, i.e. changes in the throughput rate or output rate. These fixed costs will include many of the operations overheads, e.g. rent and rates on premises, depreciation on significant items of equipment, and insurance. Certain other costs, e.g. direct costs, in particular wages and the cost of consumer materials, will vary in the short term in that they will increase roughly in proportion to increased throughput or output, and vice versa.

Factors influencing operations costs

The specification of the item to be produced, or in the case of non-manufacturing systems the specification of the service or transport to be provided, has significant implications for the cost of operations. The way in which the operating system is managed, e.g. the choice of batch sizes and the scheduling of operations, must also have cost implications. The productivity of the resources employed will clearly affect unit operations costs.

In certain industries the value added to inputs is very much greater. Such differences cannot be attributed solely to the productivity of the various operations resources, but rather to the nature and mixture of these resources. For example, the greater the quantity of machinery the lower the labour charges per unit of output. Thus where labour charges are high there will be some benefit in substituting machinery for labour, despite the fact that the additional machinery incurs depreciation, maintenance and other costs. Comparisons between industries will provide the opportunity only for long-term control and not enough opportunity for day-to-day control of costs within the operations function. For this reason certain budgeting and cost control systems must be employed (see below).

Note also that certain scale factors are associated with the cost of operations, so that with increasing throughput or output rates unit costs might be reduced. These are discussed in the following section.

OPERATIONS ECONOMICS

Figure 4.2 illustrates some aspects of the relationship between operations cost and output (or throughput) rate. Over a short period certain of the operations costs are fixed while others, the variable costs, will increase as output or the scale of operations increases. Initially this increase will be fairly rapid, then will become more stable, and eventually become rapid as the maximum possible output or throughput rate is reached, and as bottlenecks are experienced and overtime working/subcontracting, etc. become necessary. The sum of the fixed and variable costs is shown in Figure 4.2 as the total operations costs.

Also shown in Figure 4.2 is a curve representing revenue, i.e. the income generated from customers in payment for the goods or services provided by the operating system. It also shows a curve representing the profit associated with that output, i.e. revenue less total costs. Total revenue rises as the organization is able to expand its scale of operations and thus its sales, although eventually revenue will reach a maximum point as price is lowered in order to stimulate further sales. The profits are maximized at a point where the difference between the total revenue and total cost curve is greatest. Notice that in most cases this profit maximization point occurs at a lower level than the point of maximum

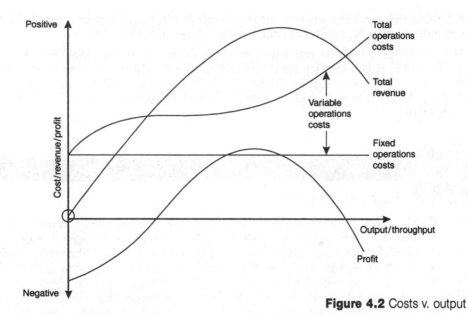

Figure 4.2 Costs v. output

revenue, which in turn occurs at less than maximum output/sales.

The relationship which will be of particular interest to the operations manager is that between the cost per unit throughput and the level or scale of throughput.

In the short term the operations manager might alter output by varying the amount of variable factors employed, e.g. materials and labour, whereas in the longer term all factors can be varied. In the short term the unit cost structure might appear as in Figure 4.3. As fixed costs remain the same the fixed cost per unit will fall as output or throughput increases. The variable cost per unit will fall at first and then rise as further variable factors are employed in order to expand output or throughput. Figure 4.4 shows the long-run average total cost/output relationship. Superimposed on this long-run average total cost curve is an average total cost curve for a short-run period. Thus while in the short term increasing output or throughput from Q_1 to Q_2 will give rise to a U-shaped curve representing falling unit total cost followed by increasing total costs, in the long run, since the 'fixed' factors can also be varied, the unit total cost curve should continue to

Figure 4.3 Short-term unit cost/output relationship

Figure 4.4 Long-term unit cost/output relationship

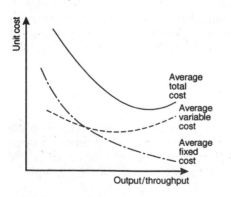

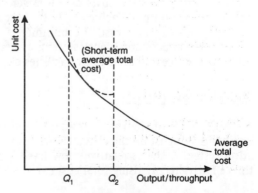

51

fall. Thus in the long term, since all the factors can be considered variable, increasing output should result in economies of scale reflected in reduced unit costs.

It follows that while the operations manager might, by clever combination of the resources at his or her disposal, effect a reduction in unit cost in the short term, continued increase in the scale of operations can be undertaken economically only by the manipulation of the mix of all of the factors involved, including those which in the short term are fixed.

EXAMPLE

Corona Extra

Grupo Modelo, maker of world-renowed Corona Extra beer, has a presence in more than 50 countries, with significant success in countries such as the US, Japan and Australia. The Company, known for its tall clear bottle, has helped Mexico become the 10th-largest brewer in the world. The Company has formed, in areas where it manufactures, so-called 'beer clusters' which group together raw material providers and factories in the agro-industrial, glass, aluminium and cardboard industries. With this approach, economies of scale have translated into immediate availability of inputs, lower costs, and quality control. Computerization and mechanization have modernized bottling, packaging and inventory control.

Source: Shuey, M. (1994) 'Liquid gold: Corona conquers market share'. *Business Mexico* **4** (1, 2), pp. 56-59.

Economics of scale and scope

This is an appropriate point at which to contrast economies of scale and of scope. Economies of scale derive from the factors discussed above. The achievement of such economies has been one of the objectives behind the development of operations in many sectors. In other words, the drive for reduced costs has tended to encourage organizations to try to deal with larger volumes, which in turn tended to reduce variety. Volume and variety have, traditionally, been seen as somewhat incompatible.

Market pressures on organizations to provide a variety of types of output or service, at competitive cost, and with minimum delay, have focused attention on how best to achieve economies of scope. This has led to the development of operating systems which are efficient and flexible. We will consider this again in Chapter 14. In fact the real basis for achieving such economies differs little from that of economies of scale, i.e. the possibility of spreading fixed costs over a larger output. The only fundamental difference is how this larger output is achieved. In the case of economies of scale it is achieved through repetition whilst in the case of economies of scope it is achieved by making the processing requirements of non-identical items as similar as possible, which in turn requires careful design, process planning and facilities design.

Breakeven point

A breakeven point chart also shows the relationship between output or throughput on the one hand and cost on the other. Figure 4.5 shows two breakeven charts. A chart for operating system A shows relatively low fixed costs but fairly substantial variable costs and thus a fairly steeply rising total cost curve, albeit one starting from a relatively low point.

The cost structure for operating system B shows higher fixed costs with relatively low variable costs, thus a less steeply rising total cost curve, albeit one starting from a substantially higher initial total cost point than in system A. The cost structure for operating system B might reflect the higher capital investment of that system, whereas operating system A may be more dependent on the use of overtime work, double staffing, etc. to achieve increased output. Notice that because of the differing cost structures the breakeven point, i.e. the point at which income begins to exceed total costs, is lower for operating system A

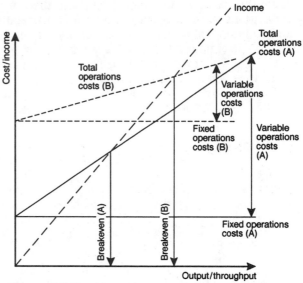

Figure 4.5 Breakeven charts

than it is for B but that the excess of income over total cost increases more rapidly beyond the breakeven point in the case of operating system B. A point worth noting therefore is that for systems dependent on greater fixed costs greater output must be achieved before a breakeven point is reached but that thereafter, rewards are likely to increase at a greater rate.

EXAMPLE

Unconventional banks

Many banks are introducing untraditional methods of delivering services. For example, there are currently about 1,200 full-service bank branches in supermarkets in the USA. International Bank Technologies, which operates 400 of these branches, estimate that such branches reach breakeven 5 times faster than conventional branches. Premium Federal Savings Bank of Gibbsboro, New Jersey is one bank which operates entirely by mail and telephone. With only one office, overheads are kept to a minimum. The simplicity of the branchless operations requires a staff of only 13, about 1/4 the number of employers in a conventional $136-million institution.

Source: Smart, J. (1992) A Dozen Eggs, a Quart of Milk and the IRA? *Bank Marketing* **24** (12) pp. 18–21.

COST CONTROL SYSTEMS

Some form of cost accounting or cost control system will be essential within an organization and will be of considerable importance to the operations manager. As with all such managerial control systems the operations manager will seek to employ the cost control mechanisms to sustain and improve the efficiency of the operating system, whereas his or her superiors will use the same cost information, albeit analysed somewhat differently, as a means of establishing objectives for and maintaining control over the operations manager.

From the operations manager's viewpoint, therefore, the cost control mechanism provides a means of assessing the efficiency of the operating system, noting significant variations from normal or budgeted performance, assessing the efficiency of new operating methods, determining the relative allocation of resources, determining the capacity required, etc. The cost control or cost accounting system adopted by an organization, and thus by the operations manager, will depend largely on the scale and nature of the organization, in particular on the type of operating system employed and the type of goods/services provided.

Job costing

Job costing is often employed by organizations which produce goods or provide services, transport, etc., to the specific requirements of the customer. In job costing, items or customers passing through the system remain identifiable and are associated with particular costs. All costs specific to particular jobs, items or customers will be accumulated, while all indirect costs will be apportioned or allocated to jobs so that on completion the total cost of each job is ascertained.

Process costing

Process costing is used by organizations engaged in more repetitive activities, i.e. where the operating system is devoted to the provision of a relatively small variety of goods, services or transport on a fairly repetitive basis. Since in such situations it is not practical to identify separate items of throughput, unit costs are determined by dividing the total costs of each process by the number of units, i.e. goods or customer's output or throughput, making allowances for items partially completed or customers partially serviced at the beginning and the end of the costing period.

Budgeting

The long-range plans formulated for the organization must be translated into detailed short-term plans or budgets for individual departments. The performance of departments, including the operating system, will be evaluated against these departmental budgets. The operations budget will specify the output or throughput required as well as the planned direct and indirect costs, broken down into appropriate detail. Preparation of this budget will involve apportioning or allocating operations overheads on some equitable basis between departments and/or 'jobs'. Overheads might be apportioned in proportion to the direct wages or direct materials costs, etc. The budget will make a distinction between current costs and revenue items and capital expenditure items. The former comprises such things as wages, salaries and material costs. The latter group includes expenditure on equipment and building.

Once budgets have been established and the periods to which they relate have commenced, the actual costs incurred during each period must be collected for subsequent comparison.

Standard costing

Standard costing is widely used in industries where rapid cost feedback information is required, i.e. where operations take place on a relatively short cycle time. In such circumstances costs are estimated and compared with actual costs on a month-by-month basis. The estimate is referred to as the 'standard cost'. Standard costs for items or services are established by category, e.g. labour, materials and overheads, based on predicted prices, labour rates and other expenses for the given period. Variations from predicted costs can be assessed and the necessary action taken to prevent their recurrence without having to wait for the end of the costing period, e.g. one year, before the necessary cost control information is available.

Marginal costing

Accurate standard costs necessitate the use of realistic means and bases for the apportionment of overhead costs to departments, cost centres, jobs, etc., and accurate pre-estimation of throughput or output volumes as bases for establishing cost rates. The use of marginal costing avoids these problems. After distinguishing direct from overhead costs, marginal costing divides overheads into those which vary with output and those which are fixed. Direct costs are also divided into the categories 'variable' and 'fixed'. All variable costs are then related to units of throughput/output while fixed costs are not charged to separate units but kept as a single block to be set against revenues earned by the throughputs of the system. Thus with marginal costing the cost of unit throughput or output is considered to comprise direct material, direct labour and direct expenses plus their variable overheads only, the total being the variable cost per unit output/throughput. This variable cost is in fact the marginal cost, since it is the amount by which total cost would increase as a result of the processing of one extra unit. Marginal costing provides a convenient way of assessing the effects of volume on profits and can be used in conjunction with the breakeven chart approach.

Activity-based costing

An activity-based costing (ABC) system generates costs by relating consumption of resources to activities, with greater discrimination than does a system of traditional account methods such as those described above. The system accomplishes this by identifying and differentiating the various types of activities that support operations. It is based on the premise that outputs consume activities, activities consume resources, and resources consume cost. There are 2 types of activities in an ABC system:

1. direct or conversion activities, which are consumed directly at the point of operation, and

2. indirect or sustained activities, which support operations but are not directly consumed by the process. An ABC system must be designed for a specific operations environment. It is partly this custom approach which gives ABC its strength.

CASE EXAMPLE

British Telecom

British Telecom's (BT) existing costing systems were already based on some of the key principles underlying Activity Based Costing (ABC) and had been in use long before the ABC theories were propounded. The fundamental principle underlying BT's method—'cost causation'—states that costs should be apportioned on the basis of what caused them to be incurred. BT's cost apportionments use a variety of non-financial data taken from all parts of the business. Throughout, the goal is to identify the most appropriate determinant of cost causation, whether or not this leads to a service analysis. A multi-staged cascading model has been developed to accommodate these apportionments.

Source: Bussey, B. A. (1993) ABC within a service organization. *Management Accounting— London* **71** (11), pp. 40–41.

KEY POINTS FOR CHAPTER 4

The sum of the direct costs = prime costs

Prime cost plus operations overhead = total operations cost

Total operations cost + general overhead = total cost

Total cost + profit = Price

Operations managers are responsible for Total Operations costs—comprising fixed and variable costs.

Quality, scheduling, resource, utilization and the mix of resources used: all affect cost.

Profits are often maximized at output/throughput levels which are lower than the maximum revenue level, which in turn is lower than the maximum output level.

In the short term there will probably be a minimum total cost level of output/throughput.

In the long term total costs may continue to fall as output/throughput increases.

Traditionally organizations have sought economies of scale, which has led to attempts to increase volume and reduce variety.

Now, because of the development of inherently flexible operating systems it is possible also to achieve economies of scope.

The breakeven point is reached at which total income or revenue equals total cost.

Cost control systems are used to control costs, measure efficiency, and measure performance against targets.

There are several types of cost control systems, e.g.:

   job costing

   process costing

   budgeting

   standard costing

   marginal costing

   activity-based costing

FURTHER READING

Drury, C. (1990) *Costing: An Introduction* (2nd edition). Chapman Hall.

Kaplan, R.S. (1992) 'In defence of activity based cost management'. *Management Accounting* 74, pp. 58–63.

The following case, from Part 9 of the book, is relevant to the topics covered in this chapter.

No.	Name	Country
4	Bourg Breton	France

QUESTIONS

4.1 Within organizations overheads are usually divided between operations overheads and general and administrative overheads and costs (including administrative overheads and selling and distribution overheads). Explain why this distinction is made and suggest methods by which each class of overhead can be absorbed or allocated to units of throughput/output.

4.2 The following data relate to a company:

Total capacity, 75 000 units

Fixed costs, £12 000 per annum

Variable expenses, 75p per unit

Sales prices, up to 4000 units £1.5 per unit and then over 4000 units £1.0 per unit

Draft a breakeven chart incorporating these data.

4.3 Throughput volumes (or output volumes) can affect unit operating costs. In addition, batch volumes can affect unit costs. Both output/throughput volumes and costs are related to profits. Outline the nature of these relationships, illustrating your answer with simple graphs.

4.4 How, in the long term, might a transport organization seek to reduce unit total operations costs beyond the level available in the short term?

The Arrangement of Facilities

INTRODUCTION TO PART 3

This part deals with locational and layout decisions. We look at the problem of locating an entirely new facility. We also deal with the problem of locating an additional new facility for an organization, to provide access to existing facilities, suppliers and markets. In Chapter 6 we look at layout decisions—themselves a form of layout problem—and at materials handling. We look at the problem of arranging an entirely new layout for a facility, and consider also the modification of existing facilities and the addition of new departments or items of equipment to existing facilities. Throughout we consider the nature of the problems involved and introduce some relevant procedures and techniques.

Chapter 5

Location of facilities

ISSUES

Why and when do we need to select a location?
What factors will influence that decision?
What are the different types of locational choice problem?
How are locations evaluated and chosen?

The facilities location problem is of major importance in all types of business. Whether we are concerned with manufacture, supply, transport or service we must consider the problem of where to base our operations. Certainly the location problem for a transport operation is slightly different since, by definition, transport moves. However, even in such cases there will normally be a 'home base' or centre of operations at which certain facilities are provided. Throughout this chapter, when referring to facilities we mean the collection of *geographically static resources* required for the operation.

We can consider the location problem as applying in two basic situations, i.e. the case of the entirely new business and the case of the existing business. For the *new* organization, the locational choice decision will be critical, for it will affect all future operations. The *existing* firm will seek new facility locations in order to either expand capacity or replace existing facilities. An increase in demand, if it is to be satisfied by the organization, gives rise to one or more of three decisions.

(a) whether to expand the present capacity and facilities;

(b) whether to seek locations for additional facilities;

(c) whether to close down existing facilities in favour of larger premises elsewhere.

The need to replace existing facilities may result from one or more of the following:

(a) the movement of markets, i.e. changes in the location of demand;

(b) changes in the cost or availability of local labour;

(c) changes in the availability of materials;

(d) demolition or compulsory purchase of premises;

(e) changes in the availability or effectiveness of transport;

(f) relocation of associated industries or plants;

(g) national legislation.

For our purposes, it makes little difference whether we consider the problem as applying to a new business or to an existing one. However, since the latter tends to be the more complex, we shall focus on it.

An increase in demand will, unless associated with increased productivity, result in pressure for additional capacity. On the other hand, a reduction in demand will often result in the under-utilization of existing capacity and encourage a move to smaller premises. Figure 5.1 outlines some of the forces within a company which give rise to the pressure for either an increase or a decrease in the amount of space available. While the main forces are associated with demand, and hence with the operations and marketing functions, it is worth noting that both finance and labour management might also be instrumental. Changes in interest rates may affect the cost of holding stock and cause a change in stock-holding policy, which in turn may affect space requirements.

Legislation relating to investment allowances, employment tax, depreciation, etc. may influence company financial policy enough to affect the scale or the nature of the undertaking; similarly, legislation relating to labour may necessitate a change in the nature or extent of facilities, e.g. the addition of extensive training facilities and welfare facilities. Scientific discoveries or developments, new fields of technology, increasing competition,

Figure 5.1 Pressures for change in space (which must give rise to the need to select a facility location). Adapted with permission from Townroe, P.M. (1969) Locational choice and the individual firm. *Regional Studies* **3**(1), pp. 15-24

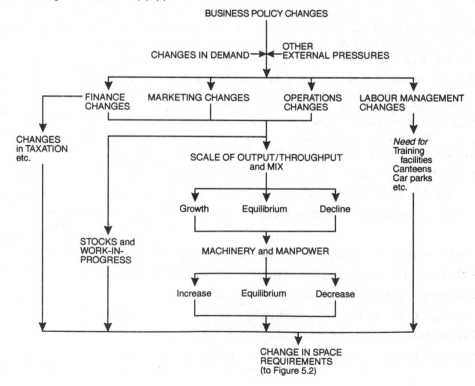

Figure 5.2 Pressures for a new location. Adapted with permission from Townroe (1969), as for Figure 5.1

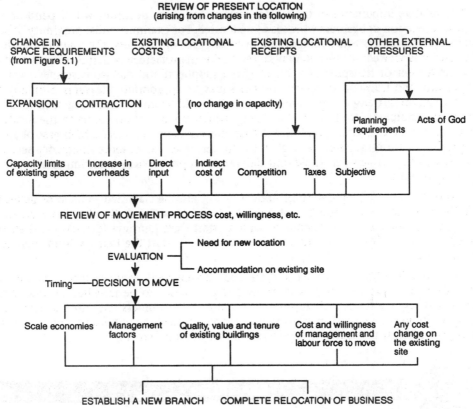

licensing or patent arrangements all may affect company research and development effort, which in turn will influence space requirements, as will changes in operations technology, the obsolescence of equipment, etc.

A change in space requirements is only one of several possible reasons for the need to consider the acquisition of an additional facility location. Figure 5.2 identifies other reasons. The need to seek smaller or larger premises may arise without the occurrence of a change in demand and thus of capacity. For example, the cost associated with the present location may change through increases in the cost of labour caused, perhaps, by increasing employment opportunities in the area. The price of raw materials or indirect materials may change through changes in the cost of transport or changes within associated industries. Indirect costs such as those associated with communications, education, housing, etc. may change. Also, new competition or changes in local taxation may prompt the decision to seek alternative premises, as may other external pressures such as labour dispute. These forces may prompt the consideration of a complete move or the acquisition of one or more additional sites.

FACTORS INFLUENCING LOCATIONAL CHOICE

Theoretically, both new and existing businesses have a vast range of alternative new locations. The selection of the site of the facility will be the final stage of a sequence of decisions which begins with the selection of an appropriate region, the selection of an appropriate area in that region, etc.

The relative importance of the factors influencing these decisions will depend on the type of operation or business which is to be located. For example whilst proximity to suppliers and customers will be important in most types of business, the manner in which this factor is viewed or assessed may differ. So for manufacture which is a **fixed** activity the movement or transport of items in (from suppliers) and out (to customers) will be important, and transport distances and costs may be appropriate measures. Similarly for supply activities, transport in from other locations will be important. In such cases, proximity to customers is to do with the ease by which customers can come to the location. Similarly for fixed services, proximity to customers is likely to focus on their ease of access to the facility unless the service is taken by the customer—as in some emergency services. So the distinction between **fixed** and **delivered** supply/services is an important one in locational choice.

Although transport, by definition moves, it can also be classified as fixed or delivered for the purposes of locational choice. This of course is the distinction between those transport systems to which customers come to start their journeys (e.g. ferry and air services) and those which go to the customers in order to start the journey from there (e.g. ambulances).

In general fixed supply, service and transport systems will evaluate locational alternatives in terms of accessibility by customers (e.g. distance to be travelled by customers) whilst delivered systems will consider accessibility to customers (e.g. time to reach customers). In both cases, customer density in a given area will be important, and in the case of supply systems proximity to suppliers will also be important.

EXAMPLE

Mercedes

Alabama was chosen by Mercedes out of 34 other states for its $300-million US assembly plant. The new plant and the vehicle scheduled for production there in 1997 are key elements of Mercedes' bid to redevelop itself. The company has a 30% cost disadvantage in the USA against Japanese and US competitors and has seen its share of the luxury market slip over several years. In selecting a new site, the company's biggest concern was transportation costs. Since it plans to export at least half the vehicles, it focused on areas near Atlantic or Gulf seaports, major highways, and rail lines. The age distribution and mix of skilled and semi-skilled workers were also important.

Source: Woodruff, D. and Templeman, J. (1993) Why Mercedes is Alabama bound. *Business Week* **3340** (11), pp. 138–139.

Costs versus revenue strategies

Another way of looking at locational choice—in particular the different concerns of manufacturing (or industrial) operations and those in the 'service' sector (especially service and supply)—is to contrast cost and revenue objectives.

Manufacturing type operations tend to focus on cost minimization in making location decisions, but revenue maximization is of equal, if not greater, concern for many 'service' type operations. The reason for this difference in focus, which is summarized in Table 5.1,

Table 5.1   Location strategies: 'service' versus manufacture operations

'Service'-type operations Revenue: Objective	Manufacturing-type operations Cost: Objective
Volume/revenue 　Drawing area 　Purchasing power 　Competition 　Advertising/promotion/pricing Physical quality 　Parking/access 　Security/lighting 　Appearance/image 　Associated business Cost determinants 　Management calibre 　Operation policies Assumptions 　Location is a major determinant of revenue 　Issues manifesting from high customer contact dominate 　Costs are relatively constant for a given area: therefore, the revenue function is critical	Tangible costs 　Transportation cost of raw material 　Shipment cost of finished goods 　Energy cost per BTU 　Utility costs 　Labour 　Raw material 　Taxes, etc. Intangible and future costs 　Attitude towards union 　Quality of life 　Education expenditures by state 　Quality of state and local government Assumptions 　Location is a major determinant of cost 　Most major costs can be identified explicitly for each site 　Low customer contact allows focus on the identifiable costs 　Intangible costs can be objectively evaluated

Source: *Based on Jay Heizer and Barry Render*, Production and Operations Management, p. 344. Copyright © 1988 by Allyn & Bacon. Reprinted with permission.

is that costs can differ significantly between locations for manufacturing or industrial operations, but may vary little for 'service' type operations. The latter, therefore, may tend to focus on revenue-related factors, e.g. the likely volume of business.

Principal factors in locational choice

The principal factors which are likely to influence locational choice are summarized in Table 5.2. Figure 5.3 examines in more detail some further factors which will generally be important in locational choice. These can be summarized as four sets of factors:

(a) variable costs;

(b) fixed costs;

(c) revenue factors;

(d) subjective factors.

Variable costs

Perhaps the main factor here is the 'accessibility' of the proposed location in terms of both inputs and outputs. As regards input, accessibility to labour is important; not merely sufficient labour, but labour of the correct type and at a correct price. Accessibility of raw materials, sub-assemblies and components is important, the cost of such input being mainly a function of transport. Access to technical advice and to other services such as warehousing and maintenance is often essential. With regard to output, a location must clearly have easy access to adequate markets, as well as public services and associated industries.

Table 5.2	Principal factors influencing locational choice	
Type of operation/ organization	**Principal factors**	
Manufacture	Movement/transport of items (e.g. goods, materials) from suppliers and to customers (possibly including other facilities within the organization)	
Supply	Accessibility by and visibility to customers (e.g. distance from markets) Accessibility from suppliers Market density in area	Accessibility to markets (e.g. time to reach customers) Accessibility from suppliers Market density in area
Service	Accessibility by and visibility to customers (e.g. distance from markets) Market density in area (e.g. no. of potential customers in area)	Accessibility to markets (e.g. time to reach customers) Market density in area (e.g. no. of potential customers in area)
Transport	Accessibility by customers (e.g. distance from markets) Market density in area (e.g. no. of potential customers in area)	Accessibility to markets (e.g. time to reach customers) Market density in area (e.g. no. of potential customers in area)
	'Fixed' operation	'Delivered' operation

Fixed costs

These are associated with the provision and maintenance of facilities. The design of buildings and the layout of facilities will influence such costs. The cost of erecting and maintaining buildings, the cost of access roads, the cost of transportation of machinery, rates, rent and so on will all influence the choice of location. We should also consider as fixed costs the cost of inventories of materials and finished items which may depend on the plant location.

Revenue factors

Often the principal economic differences between alternative locations for a service type operation relate to revenues rather than to costs. Proximity to customers/potential customers, accessibility, usability, etc. are all likely to influence demand, and therefore revenue, by influencing either the number of customers or the extent to which each makes use of the service, or both.

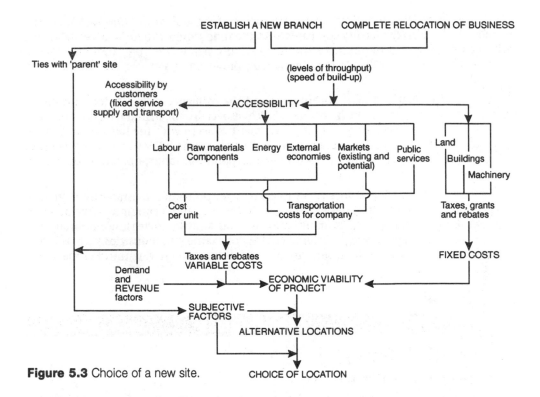

Figure 5.3 Choice of a new site.

Locating an ATM

Usage is a key factor when considering the deployment of an automated teller machine (ATM). One bank thoroughly analysed potential usage when deploying its eighth ATM. As a result, the machine's first full month of operation generated transaction volumes that significantly exceeded the average machine use within the entire network. Population density was the most important aspect and one of the easiest to examine. Where people live, and how they move around within the area, provided the best placement information. By applying basic knowledge of local street systems, it was possible to devise a general traffic flow pattern. As consumers viewed convenience as their top concern, ingress/egress as well as traffic flow had to be considered. Further, when ATM users have to leave their automobiles to use a machine, safety becomes a primary concern.

Source: Adams, P. (1991) Choosing a choice ATM site: ATM buyer's guide. *Credit Union Management* **14**(3) pp.15–20.

Subjective or largely non-quantitative assessments

Individual preferences, congeniality of the district, attitudes of present employees, etc. may all be important. National and regional data relating to the various factors influencing the facility location decision are available from a variety of sources. Data on population change, average wage levels, unemployment, industrial disputes, absenteeism, labour turnover, etc. may be relevant.

A further factor which will influence the choice of location is the *time factor*, i.e. the urgency of acquiring the facility compared with the time required to make it available, the latter being influenced by the necessity for planning permission, preparation of plans, purchase of land, availability of building labour, provision of services, electricity, water, roads, etc.

The role of central and local government and the influence of legislation and incentives can be of importance in locational choice, especially for manufacturing organizations. There may be several reasons for government concern with the location of companies and industry, e.g. regional unemployment costs associated with the congestion of major conurbations, problems of environmental pollution, and population drift from rural areas.

These are often substantial incentives to encourage companies to establish facilities in certain parts of a country designated for industrial and economic development. Furthermore, with the growth of multinational firms and the increasing importance of the international dimension in locational choice, for example in industries such as motor vehicles and chemicals, similar factors at an international level (e.g. within Europe) are of considerable significance.

EXAMPLE

Euro-Disney

Locating 'Disneyland' in Europe

Disney chooses a location 32 km east of Paris for its fourth theme park—after considering alternatives across Europe.

The site had been designated for such development by the French Government.

The location is accessible within two hours by road to 17 million Europeans.

The regional railway express network connects the area with the Paris Metro system. The journey from Centre Paris will take 23 minutes.

Major road access is good with direct motorway connection into all western European countries.

The French Government plans to make the resort the nucleus of an entire new town.

The park—operating year round—is scheduled to attract 11 million visitors in the first year: 50% from France, 40% from other western European countries and 10% from the rest of the world.

Euro-Disney: 2 years later [1]

Euro-Disney opened in 1992.

The effects of poor northern European weather, and cultural 'opposition' to the development in a region full of real historic sites probably discouraged people from visiting Disney's American-originated fantasy world in France.

Fewer than 10 million people visited the park in the first year.

Many people from Europe still preferred to visit Disney World in Florida, USA, because of the weather, cheap air fares, and cheap hotels.

Euro-Disney lost Fr5.3 billion in its first year of operation.

[1]Source: Steward T. (1992) The mouse isn't roaring *Business Week*, 24 August, p. 38.

Table 5.3	Some types of location problems	
	Type of problem	**Example – location of:**
A. Single facility		
1. Single facility with *no* connections to other locations	Locate a self-contained facility to serve a local community	Single new cinema for a small community
2. Single facility with connections *in* from other locations	Locate a facility to serve a local community taking into account the need for the facility to be supplied from elsewhere	Single new retail shop for a small community
3. Single facility with connections *out* to other locations	Locate a facility to serve customers elsewhere	Market garden to serve an area of several towns
4. Single facility with connections *in* from and *out* to other locations	Locate a facility to serve customers elsewhere, with supplies also being received from elsewhere	Single new manufacturing plant; single new wholesale distributor or warehouse
B. Multi-facility		
1. Addition(s) to an existing 'set' of facilities, with *no* connections to others in the set or to other locations	Effectively, as A1	Additional new cinema for a small community, but part of a national 'chain'
2. Addition(s) to an existing set of facilities, the 'set' having connections *in* from other locations	Effectively, as A2 (but possibly with the need to consider the distribution of capacity within the set)	Additional new retail shop for a small community, but part of a national 'chain'
3. Addition(s) to an existing set of facilities, the set having connections *out* to other locations	Effectively, as A3 (but with need to consider the distribution of capacity within the set)	Additional market garden for national organization
4. Addition(s) to an existing set of facilities, the set having connections *in* and *out* with other locations	Effectively, as A4 (but with the need to consider the distribution of capacity within the set)	Additional manufacturing plant for a company, where there is no flow between plants
5. Addition(s) to an existing set of facilities with connections *in* from within the set	Effectively, as B2	Retail shop for company to sell items supplied from elsewhere within the company
6. Addition(s) to an existing set of facilities with connections *out* to elsewhere in the set	Effectively, as B3	Additional market garden for a company to supply goods to other company locations, e.g. for packaging or processing
7. Addition(s) to an existing set of facilities with connections *in* and *out* within the set	Effectively, as B4	Additional manufacturing plant for a company, to be supplied from other plants in the company and to supply items for other company plants

Note: In many cases combinations will exist, particularly B2 and 5, B3 and 6, and B4 and 7.

TYPES OF LOCATION PROBLEMS

As we have seen, the need to select a location or site for a facility can arise for many reasons. The cause is perhaps less important to the operations manager than the nature of the locational choice problem. For example, if it is necessary to select the location of a

Table 5.4   Checklist: some factors influencing locational choice

	Of region (international)	Of area (national)	Of community (city)	Of site
Political stability	√			
Relevant legislation, e.g. industrial relations	√			
Unionization of labour	√			
Industrial relations 'climate'	√			
Feasibility of joint operations	√			
Capital restrictions	√			
Transfer of earnings restrictions	√			
Taxation for foreign firms	√			
Currency restrictions	√			
GNP trends	√			
Foreign investment trends	√			
Restrictions of foreign labour/staff	√			
Climate	√			
Language	√			
Management preference	√	√	√	?
Location of company's existing facilities	√	√	√	?
Availability of 'suitable' areas	√			
Cost of living	√			
Standard of living	√			
Location of markets/customers	√	√	√	√
Location of suppliers	√	√	√	
Proximity to related industries	√	√	√	
Labour/staff availability and skills	√	√	√	
Unemployment, turnover and absenteeism	?	√	√	
Pay levels and scales	?	√	√	
Planning and development restrictions	?	√	√	?
Tax structures and incentives	?	√	?	
Environmental (e.g. pollution) controls	?	√	?	
Communications: international	√			
national		√		
local			√	
Transport: air	√	√	√	
rail	√	√	√	
road	√	√	√	
other	√	√	√	
Availability of suitable communities		√	√	
Land availability and costs		√	√	
Availability of premises		√	√	
Cost of land		√	√	
Cost of building			√	
Rents for premises		√	√	
Cost of services			√	
Zoning and planning restrictions		√	√	
Availability of utilities		√	√	
Availability of amenities			√	
Availability of education and training		√	√	
Community attitudes and culture			√	
Energy availability		√	√	
Energy costs		√	√	
Impact on environment			√	
Development plans			√	
Availability of subcontractors			√	
Availability of suitable sites			√	
Site characteristics				√
Availability of adjacent space				√
Transport access				√
Parking space				√
Local transport provisions				√
Facilities for waste disposal				√

new single-facility business which is entirely self-contained, with no dependence on suppliers, the problem will be relatively straightforward and the choice wide. In contrast, in the choice of a site of a new facility for a company which has several existing facilities which have some supply interdependence and which together supply a particular market, the problem will be more complex and the choice more limited.

In order to understand how best to try to solve locational choice problems we must first appreciate the range of types of problems which might be encountered. Some of the common types of locational choice problems are identified in Table 5.3, and of course combinations of these basic types can exist.

The single-facility location problem *(Table 5.3, categories A1, 2, 3 and 4 and B1, with relevance also to B2, 3 and 4)*

Here we are concerned with the location of a single facility, e.g. the new single plant firm or single-facility service organization, or the location of a new facility for a larger organization where the facility has no significant dependence on or relationship with the other facilities in the business (e.g. Table 5.3 category B1).

Unlike for the multi-facility location problem, the existing or future locations of other facilities within the business will be of little relevance.

Checklists

Given a choice of possible locations, perhaps the simplest but least rigorous means for decision-making involves their comparison against a checklist of relevant factors. Such a checklist is shown in Table 5.4 which also gives some indication of the relevance of each factor at each of the four 'levels' of decision-making discussed earlier. If not an adequate means of decision-making, such a checklist at least provides a means of initially narrowing down the range of alternative regions and/or areas and/or communities and/or sites.

Location factor comparisons

Most locational decisions will at some stage involve the preparation of tabular comparisons of the type shown in Table 5.5. In some cases it will be possible and appropriate to draw up such comparisons entirely in cost terms, in which case addition of columns provides a means of comparing alternatives and therefore of choosing a location. Frequently, however, it will be necessary to consider cost and non-cost factors, and some of the latter may be represented only as 'yes' or 'no'. This ensures that this type of approach, while

Table 5.5	Comparison of factors for three possible locations for a retail shop		
Location factor	**Location A**	**Location B**	**Location C**
Site rental per year	£1 000	£1200	£800
Car parking spaces within ¹/₂ km	110	30	205
Shop frontage	4m	3m	4m
Cost of services per year	£750	£275	£800

providing a means of summarizing the factors to be considered, or providing a checklist against which to assess alternatives, must normally be employed along with more rigorous procedures of the type discussed below.

Dimensional analysis

Even if we are able to identify the various factors influencing locational choice, the problem of quantification remains. How, for example, do we determine, for various potential locations, the cost of moving or the cost of labour? Furthermore, having quantified such factors, what weight or importance do we attach to each?

Consider a simple example in which we are faced with two possible locations. We have decided that the choice between these locations will be made on the basis of the following factors:

(a) the cost of land;

(b) the cost of buildings;

(c) the cost of labour (fixed investment cost for the total required labour force for a location).

We have further found that the cost associated with each of these three factors for each of the possible locations is as shown in Table 5.6.

Table 5.6		
Factor	**Location A** **£**	**Location B** **£**
Land	10000	15000
Buildings	25000	30000
Labour	15000	10000

We might compare the relative merits of the two locations merely by summing the relevant costs, i.e.

$$\text{Total for A} = £50\,000$$

$$\text{Total for B} = £55\,000$$

Using this method of comparison we would choose location A, since it is the cheaper of the two. This method assumes that each of the factors is of equal importance, which may be far from true. For example, suppose we decide that, while the costs of land and buildings are equally important to our decisions, the cost associated with labour is twice as important as the two other costs. Then we may assess the alternatives by introducing this weighting factor:

£	£
Location A: 10000	Location B: 15000
25000	30000
+2(15000)	+2(10000)
= £65000	= £65000

Now it appears that each location is equally attractive.

Let us take this type of argument a little further by introducing two more factors into our examination of the two locations. Now, as well as the costs associated with land, buildings and labour, we need to consider the influence of community relations and the cost of moving. We find it difficult to place an accurate cost on either of these factors for the two locations, so we settle for a system of rating using a scale of 1 to 100. A rating of 1 indicates that a location scores very highly, i.e. it is the best possible result, whereas a rating of 100 is the worst possible result.

Suppose the five factors for the two locations are quantified as shown in Table 5.7; then we might again compare locations by adding together the figures to obtain the totals shown in Table 5.7. This comparison would lead us to select location A.

Table 5.7		
	Location A	**Location B**
Land (cost)	10000	15000
Buildings (cost)	25000	30000
Labour (cost)	15000	10000
Community relations (score)	60	30
Cost of moving (score)	80	40
Total	50140	55070

However, this type of analysis is quite wrong, because we have indiscriminately mixed together two dimensions: cost and ratings. To illustrate the inadequacies of the procedure, suppose we alter the scale of the first three factors and perform our calculations in £000s rather than £s, i.e.

Location A	10	Location B	15
	25		30
	15		10
	60		30
	80		40
	190		125

Such an analysis would lead us to select location B, since the change of scale has distorted our analysis.

So that such an anomaly does not occur, we must take care to treat such multi-dimensional analysis in a more satisfactory manner. Such a method was developed by Bridgeman,[1] and is referred to as dimensional analysis. Using the following notation.

$$O_{i_1}, O_{i_2}, O_{i_3}, \ldots O_{i_m} = \text{costs, scores, etc. associated with factors}$$
$$1, 2, 3, \ldots m, \text{ for location } i$$

$$W_1, W_2, W_3, \ldots W_m = \text{the weight to be attached to factors}$$
$$1, 2, 3, \ldots m$$

The merit of the various locations should be assessed as follow.

For location i, merit $= (O_{i_1})^{W_1} \times (O_{i_2})^{W_2} \times (O_{i_3})^{W_3} \ldots \times (O_{i_m})^{W_m}$

---

[1] Bridgeman, P. W. (1963) *Dimensional Analysis*. New Haven, Conn.: Yale University Press.

In the case of two possible locations the merit might be compared as follow.

$$\frac{\text{Merit of A}}{\text{Merit of B}} = \left(\frac{O_{A_1}}{O_{B_1}}\right)^{w_1} \times \left(\frac{O_{A_2}}{O_{B_2}}\right)^{w_2} \ldots \times \left(\frac{O_{A_n}}{O_{B_n}}\right)^{w_m}$$

If > 1, select B.

If < 1, select A.

EXAMPLE

A retail shop

Several factors are identified as being important in choosing one of two available locations for a new retail shop. Wherever possible the factors have been costed; otherwise a score from 1 to 10 has been given, 1 representing the best possible result and 10 the worst possible. The factors are of different importance, so they have been weighted from 1 to 10 (weight of 1 indicating least importance and 10 most importance).

Factor		Location A	Location B	Weight
Cost	=	£10 000	£15 000	1
Score	=	3	7	2
Score	=	6	2	3
Cost	=	£1 500 000	£1 000 000	4
Score	=	4	7	4
Score	=	5	5	3

The merit of location A is represented by:

$(10\,000)^1 \times (3)^2 \times (6)^3 \times (1\,500\,000)^4 \times (4)^4 \times (5)^3$

and that of location B by:

$(15\,000)^1 \times (7)^2 \times (2)^3 \times (1\,000\,000)^4 \times (7)^4 \times (5)^3$

To simplify the calculations we can change the scales for the cost factors for both locations. Hence:

Merit of A: $(1)^1 \times (3)^2 \times (6)^3 \times (150)^4 \times (5)^3$

Merit of B: $(1.5)^1 \times (7)^2 \times (2)^3 \times (100)^4 \times (7)^4 \times (5)^3$

$$\therefore \frac{\text{Merit of A}}{\text{Merit of B}} = 1.79$$

Such an analysis indicates that location B is superior on the basis of the six factors considered.

In this example we have considered only factors which should be minimized, i.e. costs. Such an analysis might also be undertaken even where some factors are to be maximized (e.g. profits, revenue) while others are to be minimized. In such a case the powers would be positive for factors to be minimized and negative for factors to be maximized.

EXAMPLE

A Cinema

Compare the merit of two locations X and Y on the basis of factors with different weights, i.e.

	Cinema location X	Cinema location Y	Weight
Costs (£)	10 000	12 000	4
Benefits (score, 1–10)	8	6	3

$$\frac{\text{Merit of X}}{\text{Merit of Y}} = \frac{(10\,000)^4(8)^{-3}}{(12\,000)^4(6)^{-3}}$$

$$= \frac{(10)^4(8)^{-3}}{(12)^4(6)^{-3}}$$

$$= 0.203$$

∴ Select location X for the cinema

EXAMPLE

Sonic Industries

At Oklahoma-based Sonic Industries Inc.—a chain of 1043 fast-food drive-ins—hunting for a superior location used to be unscientific. To choose a site today, Sonic studies demographic data to find neighbourhoods that fit the profile of the best customers—blue-collar workers who earn $11 000–$22 000 a year, drive pickup trucks, and have no more than an hour to eat their lunch. Once a business knows who its best customers are, it should start looking for neighbourhoods where many of them live. The quest can be begun at the local chamber of commerce, city planning commission, economic development agency, or local office of the US Census Bureau. Ideally, a location should be sought that includes the maximum number of choice neighbourhoods within the trade area's radius. Chosen properties should then be compared according to basic real estate criteria, including: 1. cost versus value, 2. access and traffic patterns, and 3. leasing terms.

Source: Wang, P. (1991) Finding the right location for your business. *Money*, Summer, pp. 26–33.

Minimization of transport costs

It is clear from our previous discussion that many factors other than transport cost are likely to affect locational choice. Nevertheless, minimization of transport costs may provide a suitable first solution which might then form a basis for further discussion, analysis and modifications. Such an approach might be relevant in selecting the location of a warehouse relative to its principal customers or markets, or a manufacturing plant relative to its supplies and customers. At a different level (considered in Chapter 6), this approach to the location problem resembles an approach employed in determining the layout of facilities within an area (e.g. a factory or office) where movement and travel is also an important criterion for efficient layout.

The multi-facility location problem

Whereas in the case of the single-facility location problem we have been concerned with selecting, for example, the minimum-cost single location, in the multi-facility location problem we must select the location which, when added to existing locations, minimizes the cost of the *entire system*. Each of the potential locations must be assessed not on its own merits alone, as was the case previously, but in the context of a multi-facility situation. Multi-facility location problems are considerably more complex than the single-facility problem not only because the entire system must be considered but also because, since more than one facility is to be considered, the question of size arises. Thus there are in fact two basic factors in the general multi-facility location problem.

(a) the need to identify locations for facilities relative to suppliers and customers;

(b) the need to determine the appropriate size or capacity of each such facility.

To deal with both aspects simultaneously would necessitate the use of extremely complex procedures. In many cases, therefore, the two aspects are treated separately. Again the procedures which are available apply equally to problems involving the location of manufacturing facilities, supply establishments, etc. One of the better-known approaches involves the use of the transportation method of linear programming.

Note that the factors influencing location decisions are liable to change. The logical location at the present time may, at a later date, appear inferior because of change in one of the many factors which influenced the original choice.

Conceptually, the problem of the location of facilities abroad does not differ from the problems discussed in this chapter. In practice, such a problem will often be more complex and will assume greater proportions, if only because more investment may be involved. In such situations the identification and quantification of factors may be more difficult; nevertheless, the decision is amenable to the type of technique discussed earlier.

KEY POINTS FOR CHAPTER 5

There are 2 basic types of layout problem: new businesses, and additions/changes to existing businesses.

Location decisions in existing businesses can result from changes in demand, markets, products or services, etc.

The factors which influence locational choice include:

proximity to suppliers/customers

availability of resources and services

cost of facilities

The location problem will differ for supply or service systems which are fixed, and those which deliver their services.

The distinction between cost and revenue strategies is important—manufacturing location tends to be concerned with cost, whilst service system location is often focused on revenue factors.

The principal factors influencing locational choice include:

- variable costs
- fixed costs
- revenues
- subjective factors

There are two types of location problem:

- single facility
- multi facility

Single facility location problems are often tackled, using

- checklists
- factor comparisons
- dimensional analysis

Multi-facility location problems involve consideration of the effect of new/changed locations on a longer system, and the distribution of capacity in that system.

FURTHER READING

Love, R. F. *et al.* (1986) *Facilities Location: Models and Methods.* Elsevier.

Domschke, W. and Drexl, A. (1985) *Location and Layout Planning* Springer-Verlag. (Deals with the topics of this chapter and the next.)

Haigh, R. W. (1990) Selecting a US plant location: the management decision process in foreign companies. *Columbia Journal of World Business* 25(3) pp. 22–31.

CASE STUDY

The following case, from part 9 of the book, is relevant to the topics covered in this chapter.

No.	Name	Country
7	Fotoprint Pronto	Italy

Questions

5.1 Briefly, what changes might result in the need for additional space for a service operation (of your own choice)? Under what circumstances might such changes lead to the need for an entirely new site, and what would influence the choice of such a site?

5.2 The following information is available on two possible locations for a new office. Which location would you choose? What assumptions have you made?

	Location A	Location B
Site rental/year (£)	7000	6500
Cost of services/year (£)	500	950
Cost of modifying buildings (£)	2400	1900
Local housing cost index (%)[a]	50	75

[a]Average cost of a four-bedroom house as a percentage of national average cost.

5.3 'The locational choice problem is complex mainly because multiple objectives and criteria are normally evident.' Discuss and illustrate.

5.4 Show, using numerical examples, that the simple addition of costs in the evaluation of alternative locations might lead to different decisions in different circumstances.

Chapter 6

The layout of facilities and materials handling

ISSUES

What types of layout planning problems can occur?
What are the objectives in planning or layout?
What methods and procedures are available?
How can we evaluate alternative layouts?
Why is transport and handling important?
What methods are there for moving things and people?
What is automated storage and retrieval?

The layout problem is to do with the arrangement of facilities in a given space. It is important, common and complex. All types of organization will face this problem to some extent and at some time. Objectives will differ. Even simple situations can result in much complexity. There are no simple, sufficient procedures for solving such problems.

Materials handling is to do with movement within the layout. Providing efficient and safe movement is important. Further, the need for such movement is often an important consideration in planning a layout.

THE NEED FOR LAYOUT PLANNING

We often tend to think in terms of planning complete layouts and designing entirely new sets of departments but, although such occasions undoubtedly do arise, the following are the types of problems we are much more likely to encounter.

Enlarging or reducing existing departments

The addition or removal of facilities, the trading of areas between departments, or a complete relayout may be necessary because of increases or decreases in demand for goods or services, changes in the nature of goods and services, or changes in the scope or capability of processes.

Movement of a department

The need to move a department because of a change in the specification or nature of the goods or service, or because of changes in demand or operating processes, may constitute a simple exercise. Alternatively, if the existing layout is inadequate, it may present the opportunity for a major change, the extent of which bears little relationship to the primary cause.

Adding or removing a department

Adding a department may be the result of a desire to undertake work never before done on the site, or the desire to centralize work previously undertaken in several separate departments. Conversely, the removal of a department which is no longer required may facilitate or obviate the need for a rearrangement of other departments.

Replacing equipment and adding new equipment

Frequently, even equipment designed to perform exactly the same function as its predecessors is physically different and its installation necessitates a certain amount of reorganization.

OBJECTIVES IN LAYOUT PLANNING

Some of the advantages of good facilities layouts and hence some possible objectives in planning layouts are as follows.

Cost of movement

In most operating systems there will be physical flows. The extent and cost of these flows will be affected by the layout of facilities. In manufacturing, the movement of materials, components and the finished product, as well as the movement of labour, are primarily dependent on the location of the production and service facilities. The movement of customers in a retail store or in a service system such as a hotel or restaurant will be influenced by the layout of facilities. Improved layout will result in a reduction in the distance moved by items and/or customers, in the time consumed, and hence in the cost of such movement whether to the organization or to the customer.

Congestion and delay

No value is added and nothing is contributed to profits by delays or storage during operations. Poor facilities layout may necessitate high work in progress and hence increase throughput time. Time spent by the customer waiting in a system generates no turnover. In all such cases an objective will be to minimize congestion and delay and thus provide for the more intensive use of facilities *and* the more efficient use of capacity.

Utilization of space, facilities and labour

The cost of space is high. Wasted space may be eliminated and the total area required minimized by adequate facilities layout. Effective arrangement of facilities may reduce idle time and cut down investment in both direct (e.g. plant) and indirect (e.g. support) equipment. Adequate layout also facilitates operation, maintenance, service and supervision, and therefore permits a better utilization of resources.

We have identified the importance of movement and flows and thus the handling of physical items and/or customers as factors or criteria in layout planning. Much of our discussion of layout planning techniques will reflect the importance of minimizing physical movement and handling. We have also referred to *capacity*—one objective of layout planning being the maximization of capacity utilization. When planning a new layout we must know the extent or quantity of each type of facility to be provided: we must know what capacity is to be provided. Layout planning is therefore contingent upon capacity planning, which is discussed in Chapter 11.

FACILITIES LAYOUT PROBLEMS

There are three levels of layout planning problem:

(a) the layout of 'departments' within the site;

(b) the layout of 'facilities' within the 'departments';

(c) the layout of individual 'workplaces'.

In this chapter we are concerned explicitly with level (a) but implicitly the discussion relates to level (b) also. We shall use the term 'department' to mean an area containing several (perhaps interrelated) facilities. A 'facility' will be considered as a single (perhaps large and complex) piece of equipment.

BASIC TYPES OF LAYOUT

Manufacture

There are several types of manufacturing layout, each with individual characteristics and each appropriate to some form of manufacture, depending on the output rate and the range of products involved.

Layout by process or functional layout

In a process or functional layout all operations of a similar nature are grouped together in the same department or part of the factory. Layout by process is appropriate where small quantities of a large range of products are to be manufactured, perhaps the best example being jobbing production. The nature of the layout permits flexibility in production, i.e. complex products requiring processing in every one of the functional departments may be made alongside simple products requiring processing in only a few departments. This flexibility, however, brings disadvantages. Process layouts normally operate with a comparatively high level of work-in-progress, and throughput time is high. Specialist supervision is possible. The provision of services is simpler than in other forms of layout, but the cost of materials handling is high.

Layout by product

Layout by product is appropriate for the production of a small range of products in large quantities. Ideally, only one standardized product is involved and processing should be continuous. Facilities are arranged according to the needs of the product and in the same sequence as the operations necessary for processing. Such layouts are relatively inflexible. Enough stable demand to ensure a high utilization of equipment is essential, as is a regular supply of the right quantities of materials and components.

The provision of services is difficult, since different pieces of equipment with different characteristics and requirements may be located adjacent to one another. A mixture of skills and tasks often occurs, resulting in difficulties in payment and supervision, but usually little specialized supervision is required, since the work performance is often highly rationalized. Minimum floor space is required, work-in-progress is minimized and the throughput is high. The requirements for handling materials are small and facility utilization is high.

Layout by fixed position

In the two previous layout systems the product moves past stationary production equipment. In this case the reverse applies. In the extreme case, e.g. civil engineering, neither the partly completed nor the finished product moves. Alternatively, as in ship building, the product remains stationary only until it is completed.

Historically, a large proportion of production was undertaken in this manner by artisans in their own homes. Layout by fixed position is now comparatively unimportant, except where large items are produced.

Group layout (or cell)

Process, product and fixed position layouts are the traditional forms in manufacturing industry. Recently, however, in batch production, configurations known as group layouts have begun to emerge as distinctive arrangements. In effect, group layout is a hybrid form which provides a type of product arrangement of facilities for the manufacture of similar items, each of which, if taken individually, would normally be manufactured through a process configuration. This approach is used as a means of achieving some of the benefits of layout by product in the batch manufacture of products. Given a large enough group it is practical to arrange in one area all the facilities required for their production. Group layouts differ from layout by product, therefore, in that they are used for the manufacture of final products. In most cases all items passing through a group layout will not require the use of all facilities, so flow patterns will differ, but because of the similarity of items utilization will be high. The most advanced application of group-type layouts can be found in computer controlled flexible manufacturing systems.

Hybrids and mixed layouts

Most practical manufacturing layouts are mixtures of process and product layouts. Rarely are companies in the situation where they are able to produce continuously large quantities of an absolutely standard product. Similarly, even the largest range of products normally uses certain common components, and firms obliged to concentrate on process layouts are normally able to support some product layouts as well. A common mixed layout in manufacture would involve an arrangement which was predominantly by process, but with subsidiary areas arranged by product or as group layouts. Such an arrangement might exist in engineering production where, although products differ substantially, it has been possible to identify a group of similar subassemblies or components which taken together permit the use of a more specialized layout with adequate volume throughput.

Non-manufacturing systems

The main types of layout described above also exist in non-manufacturing situations. With the exception of transport systems, these layout types encompass most of what will be encountered in planning the layout of non-manufacturing systems. Some examples are given in Table 6.1. Mixed layouts are also used, for example in service systems such as restaurants (layout by product for buffets, and layout by process for waiter-service dining).

Table 6.3	Types of layout: examples			
Type of operating system	**Type of layout**			
	Process layout	**Product layout**	**Fixed-position layout**	**Group layout**
Service systems	1. Hotel 2. Reference library	1. Automatic carwash 2. Medical screening and diagnosis	Hospital operating theatre	–
Supply systems	1. Supermarket 2. Warehouse	1. Restaurant self-service	Restaurant dining room	–
Manufacturing systems	1. Jobbing production 2. Small batch production	1. Motor-vehicle assembly line 2. Chemical process plant	1. Shipyard 2. Civil engineering	Batch production of components for a variety of products
Transport systems	See text	See text	–	–

Supply and service systems

Similar configurations can be identified in supply and service systems. In supply the principal flows and movements will resemble those of manufacturing systems, since again goods are involved. In service systems the principal flows may involve people, often customers. In a warehouse, for example, a functional layout may be employed in which particular areas are used for the storage of particular product lines or goods. In such situations flow patterns will be relatively simple in that goods will be received into the warehouse and placed into storage, from where eventually they will be transferred to customers. In such cases therefore there will be little flow or movement between areas, and thus the layout problem is considerably simplified.

A similar situation may exist in a retail store. In these situations, however, the 'picking' problem will exist in that warehouse or counter staff may be required to collect together all items required for a particular customer by travelling between the appropriate areas within the facility. Thus movement problems are of importance and minimization of movement becomes a relevant criterion for layout planning. In service systems such as hospitals, the process or functional layout will often be found, since particular wards and particular parts of the hospital will be devoted to particular types of activity, e.g. general surgery, medicine, geriatrics. Here again there may be substantial movement between areas, since customers, i.e. patients, may need attention from several areas, and staff will have to move between and work in several of these areas. In certain medical facilities the layout by product or flow-type layout may be used. For example, in certain cases a series of fairly elaborate medical tests will be made on patients as part of screening or diagnostic procedures. These tests may be arranged sequentially and facilities provided to minimize throughput time and maximize resource utilization. In both these functions it is possible to envisage a layout by fixed position, particularly in the service sector, where facilities might be brought to a customer; for example in the case of a road accident, medical facilities would be brought to the injured patient.

Thus the three traditional layouts may exist in supply and service organizations and the movement and flows of items and people between areas within the layout may be a principal feature in determining the configuration.

EXAMPLE

Herbst

Each of the 11 newest Herbst fuel filling station locations in Las Vegas has 7 profit centres. Each location features:

1 fuel pumps/fillers

2 an 'am-pm' mini market

3 a full-service car wash

4 a self-service car wash

5 a quick lube

6 a detailing shop

7 slot machines.

The building cost of each station is about $1.25 million. At one of the new stations, the am-pm mini market broke the Company's record for monthly store sales. The high store volume could largely be attributed to layout, which ensured that everybody who gets a full-service car wash walks through the convenience store.

Source: Edmond, M. (1992) Diversification Las Vegas style: Lucky seven profit centers in one. *National Petroleum News* **84**(1), pp. 44–45.

Transport systems

The essential feature of transport systems is movement. In many such systems the principal facilities employed are mobile. In this chapter we are concerned with the arrangement of essentially static facilities, so a somewhat different situation applies as regards facilities layout for transport systems, since in this context we are concerned only with the arrangement of a portion (perhaps in a way the least important portion) of the facilities of the system, namely the fixed facilities, e.g. garage, service bays. Given this, however, much the same situation might be found, and again it will be possible to identify at least two of the three traditional configurations, namely layout by process and layout by product. As with manufacture, supply and service, movement and physical flows may again be seen to be the principal criteria in establishing the layout.

LAYOUT PLANNING PROCEDURE

The planning of an entirely new layout is the most comprehensive problem and, although comparatively rare, this case is being considered here in order to cover the subject adequately.

Suppose we are proposing to establish a new set of facilities in one location. It is assumed that the precise nature of the goods or service to be provided and the demand for them either are known or may be determined. Given this information, the required capacity and hence the number and nature of facilities can be determined (see Chapter 11).

Facilities required = f (nature of goods/services and demand)

In addition to the principal facilities, other equipment will be needed; hence additional space must be provided. Storage space will be required. Departments such as personnel must be accommodated.

Space required = f (nature of facilities, and nature of additional facilities required)

The layout planning procedure therefore involves consideration of demand, capacity, work methods and standards, resource requirements, handling and movement, and space requirements, among other factors. We consider these factors below.

Demand

Normally an operation will be established to meet an existing demand. If we are building a new hospital ward to increase the total throughput of patients and reduce waiting lists, then the extent of the demand for that type of treatment will be known. If we are building a new warehouse to supply a particular area with existing items we will again know something of expected demand. Otherwise we will rely on market research to help determine the capacity required.

Capacity

The determination of capacity requires not only the estimation of steady state or average demand levels but also decisions on how best to deal with demand level fluctuations. In Chapter 11 it will be seen that the accommodation of demand fluctuations may necessitate the provision of 'storage' space for goods or customers, over-capacity, etc.; thus detailed capacity planning is essential before layout planning is begun.

Work methods and standards

Method study (see Chapter 7) will establish the sequence of operations to be performed and the types of equipment to be used. Given work methods, work measurement (see Chapter 8) will be used to establish work content.

Resource equipment

Given an estimate of capacity, and work content, it will be possible to calculate resource requirements in terms of both labour and equipment. Some allowances must be made for breakdowns, holidays, stoppages, etc.

Handling and movement

The nature of any handling equipment must be known. The equipment required to provide movement and handling will itself require space both for operation and for maintenance, repair, etc. Furthermore, in certain industries movement and handling may be achieved only in particular ways because of the particular requirements of the process.

Space requirements

In addition to the space necessary to accommodate the machinery and materials required for the operation, allowances must be made for the movement of personnel and for service and repair, etc.

Other factors affecting layout

Even more factors affect layout, for example the removal, reprocessing or use of waste materials; noise; safety legislation; customer areas; anticipated development and the necessity for change.

LAYOUT PLANNING METHODS

Traditional methods

Traditional layout planning procedures appear quite mundane beside current theory, but nevertheless they are proven, accepted and valuable. Visual aids play an important part e.g. some form of scale representation: scale drawings, templates, three-dimensional models etc. Flow diagrams, charts, etc. are also used.

The main criticism of such methods is that they are unstructured and depend on the knowledge, experience and insight of the planner. This same fact, however, can be interpreted as their main advantage; it is possible, while planning the layout, to take into account all relevant constraints. Their merit, therefore, is the breadth of their approach rather than their rigour.

If we attempt to develop analytical methods of layout planning, we must determine precisely what our objective is. The common concern in all layouts, whether in manufacturing, supply, service or transport, is the need for movement. Thus the need to minimize movement is usually the first consideration, and only after the initial layout has been obtained are additional objectives allowed to intervene.

Cross and relationship charts

These are traditional procedures in layout planning. They provide no solutions, but simply help organize data in order to help in the layout planning process. One deals with movement. The other is only a way of expressing relative locational preferences.

Figure 6.1 Cross chart showing the nature and extent of the movement of items between departments over a given period of time

FROM \ TO Dept no.	1	2	3	4	5	6	7	8	9	10	TOTAL
Dept no. 1		15				12	8	5			40
2			10	5							15
3				10							10
4					5	7		3			15
5						5					5
6							12				12
7								12	8		20
8									12	8	20
9										20	20
10											
TOTAL		15	10	15	5	24	20	20	20	28	

The *cross chart* shown in Figure 6.1 indicates the pattern and amount of movement of items among ten departments. In the case of a new layout the routeing will have been obtained from routeing instructions, e.g. flow process charts, and the quantities from output/throughput requirements. The figures in the matrix are the numbers of items or loads which in a given period of time must move from one department to another. In the case of the existing layouts this information may be obtained by sampling of the activity taking place within the area.

Notice that the row and the column totals are not necessarily equal. Where some of the items are consumed or combined, row totals may be less than column totals.

Absence of any figures below the diagonal means that none of the items backtrack between departments, but the scatter above the diagonal indicates a varied movement pattern characteristic of the processing of several types of product or customer. Some of the items follow a path through from department 1 to department 10, but, judging from these data alone, a 'product layout' seems impractical.

Various elaborations on the cross chart have been suggested, but the simple principle remains the same. For example, a *weighted cross chart* may on occasions offer sufficient

Figure 6.2   Dept no.

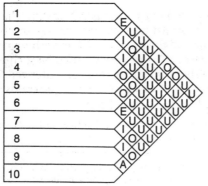

Code	Closeness
A	Essential
E	V. important
I	Important
O	Ordinary close
U	Unimportant

advantages to justify the extra effort. Here, unlike the procedure of Figure 6.1, the movements of items between departments are not given equal weight, but each movement is weighted according to that item's importance, e.g. in terms of its contribution to profit, etc. An alternative approach either with a weighted or with an unweighted cross chart is to consider only the principal goods or services.

Cross charts are a means of collecting and presenting information from which preferable departmental relationships can be obtained. This information can then be summarized on a relationship chart. For example, the *relationship chart* shown in Figure 6.2 is partly derived from the previous cross chart (Figure 6.1).

The required closeness of departments summarized by a relationship chart may reflect needs other than the minimization of movement; indeed, a relationship chart can be used to summarize proximity requirements where the minimization of movement is not of overriding importance.

COMPUTER-AIDED LAYOUT PLANNING

In all but the simplest of situations, layout planning 'by hand' can be a long and tedious process. It is partly for this reason that computer-based approaches have been developed. There are, however, other benefits of this type of approach, notably:

1. alternative layouts can be generated quickly for comparison and evaluation;

2. an interactive design procedure can be used, allowing a designer to influence the development of a layout during the design process, rather than waiting to see what is produced and then having to modify it to accommodate practical requirements, etc.;

3. Computer-based layout planning procedures can be linked with computer-based procedures for planning materials handling, maintenance, services management, etc.

The first computer programs for layout planning were developed in the early 1960s. Much has changed since then, but these origins are important, because many current software packages are direct descendants.

There are two basic methodologies behind most of today's computer-based layout planning procedures.

1. Proximity maximization

2. Movement minimization

Proximity maximization

This approach derives directly from the methodology of the Relationship Chart, as shown in Figure 6.2. Required or desired interdepartmental closeness ratings or codes, usually expressed numerically, are one type of input to the program, along with department sizes and overall building dimensions or constraints. The procedures used by such programs are often based on those first developed for either the CORELAP[1] (Computerized Relationship Layout Planning) or ALDEP[2] (Automated Layout Design Program) programs. The former has the more complex procedure, which is basically as follows:

a) Place first in the layout the department which has the highest total closeness rating (using numerical values for the closeness codes);

---

[1]Lee, R.C. and Moore, J.M. (1967) CORELAP— Computerized relationship layout planning. *Journal of Industrial Engineering*, 18(3), pp.195–200.

[2]Seehof, J.M. and Evans, W.O. (1967) Automated layout design program. *Journal of Industrial Engineering*, 18(12), pp.690–695.

b) Add other departments in descending order of total closeness rating so that they achieve, as far as possible, proximity to those departments with which they have a high closeness rating.

This, of course, is all done subject to overall space/dimension limitations, and various rules are used to determine the order in which departments are placed into the layout and to ensure appropriate relationships between pairs of departments, etc. The overall object is to maximize the total closeness score.

The ALDEP procedure also utilizes a closeness/proximity rating approach. The program either generates a series of largely random layouts and selects that with the best total closeness score, or generates one layout and then seeks incrementally to improve on it by moving/exchanging departments.

EXAMPLE

Comlad 11

COMLAD 11 is a microcomputer-based layout design program, developed from COMLAD and based on a methodology developed by Sule. The program aims to place into the layout first those departments with the strongest 'closeness' relationships with others, before placing departments with weaker relationships. Up to 20 departments can be dealt with. Besides developing an efficient layout, COMLAD 11 has useful features that allow fixing departments, changing the shape of departments, and changing the length and width dimensions of the overall layout. After the layout has been generated it is evaluated by computing a score that represents the total 'closeness' rating. The score not only is a function of the relative position of each department but also is influenced by their shape. The designer can modify the layout and the resultant closeness score is calculated.

Source: Ziai, M. R. and Sute, D. R. (1991) Computerised Facilities Layout Design. *Computers in Industrial Engineering* **21**(1–4) pp. 385–389.

Movement minimization

The proximity maximization approach, built on the relationship chart concept, will often take account of the need to minimize interdepartmental movement or traffic, because the required closeness ratings or codes will often take account of movement alongside other factors. The movement minimization approach, however, deals primarily with this criterion. It aims to minimize total interdepartmental movement, e.g. the total number of journeys over a period of time, or the total traffic density (i.e. journeys × loads) or the total cost of movement.

Most of the more widely used computer procedures are based on the CRAFT[3] program first developed in 1963. An outline of the basic procedure follows: The procedure requires an initial layout to be input at the beginning. It can therefore be considered as an 'improvement' or 'modification' *procedure*; however, it is in fact intended for the design of new layouts, since the initial layout can be an arbitrary one. A simplified flow diagram for the program is shown in Figure 6.3.

---

[3]Armour, G. C. and Buffa, E. S. (1963) A heuristic algorithm and computer simulation approach to the relative location of facilities. *Management Science*, **9**(1), pp. 294–309.

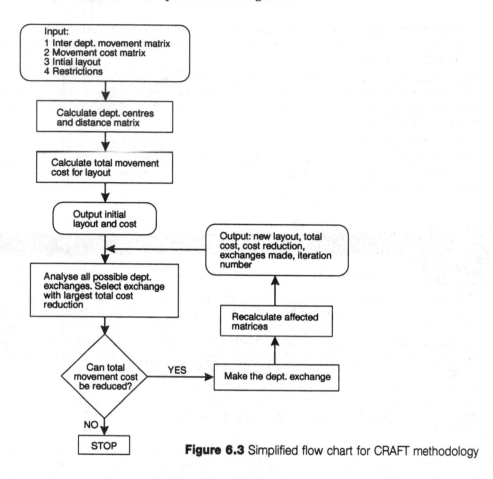

Figure 6.3 Simplified flow chart for CRAFT methodology

The necessary input is:

(a) interdepartmental flow matrix, which gives the number of unit loads moving between all departments over a given period of time;

(b) interdepartmental movement cost matrix, giving the cost per unit distance of movement between all departments;

(c) initial layout configuration showing the size of departments;

(d) any restrictions, i.e. fixed departments which cannot be moved.

The procedure then seeks to improve on the initial layout by interchanging pairs of departments. Every pair of departments is examined and the effect of their interchange on the total movement cost for the layout is calculated. The pair change giving the greatest reduction in total movement cost is effected and the process is repeated until no further interchange of departments will provide any additional reduction in the total movement cost associated with the layout.

The algorithm by which the program operates is as follows:

(a) Determine which pairs of departments may be interchanged. Departments are considered for interchange when they are adjacent, of equal area, or bordering on a common third department.

(b) Calculate the distance between departments, the distances being taken as those between the centres of the departments.

(c) Calculate the reduction in total movement costs resulting from the interchange of all possible pairs of departments.

(d) Interchange the two departments which provide the greatest saving in total movement costs.

(e) Calculate the total movement cost and print out the revised layout.

This procedure is repeated until no further cost saving is possible, and then the final layout is printed.

Several of the better known software packages embody the CRAFT methodology, often enhanced or extended for specific types of application.

PLANNING OTHER TYPES OF LAYOUT

Product layout

The approaches discussed above are concerned primarily with minimizing movement, whether of materials or of people. They are of particular relevance in planning functional/process layouts, and can be used for planning layouts in which facilities are organized on a product or group basis. As such, therefore, they are relevant in certain types of manufacturing and non-manufacturing situations. The planning of product-type layouts, whether in manufacture or service systems (e.g. flow or assembly lines, or flow-processing customers through specialist service systems), may require a somewhat different approach, and this is discussed in some detail in Chapter 15.

Fixed-position layouts

A somewhat different situation exists in the planning of fixed-position layouts. Here the principal item or customer does not move, but all necessary parts and facilities move to and from it. Such a situation might be visualized as several fixed departments or areas within a site, one of which is the customer of all others. This 'customer' area is the fixed location of the item being manufactured or the customer being serviced, while all other areas are the permanent locations of the facilities required in this process.

The layout problem therefore involves the arrangement of these areas around the main 'customer' area. Again, movement cost can be important, so it will be desirable to place close to the customer area those departments which must supply major items, while areas providing smaller quantities or smaller items might be located further away. Taking this approach the problem must be tackled by one of the methods outlined above, since in effect we are planning a process-type layout in which the flow pattern is largely one in which all departments communicate with a supply department.

Supply and storage layouts

The facilities layout problem in supply systems often involves the location of display and/or storage areas to which customers have direct access. The arrangement of display and shelving areas in a supermarket is a good example of the type of problem. In such cases there will be a need to minimize total movement for most customers. Thus the procedures referred to above will be of relevance providing that those responsible for lay-out planning have some data concerning the average or typical customer's needs in terms of goods or items to be acquired. Given this information, shelving and passageways can be arranged so that, with a knowledge of the layout, customers may collect their goods with the minimum of movement.

Other factors, however, are of relevance in the planning of the layout and should be introduced at this point. For example, the arrangement of displays and storage in supply systems such as supermarkets is also a function of display-type considerations. It is, for example, well known that 'traffic' patterns in supermarkets follow a particular form, with most customers preferring, initially at least, to travel around the edges of the area rather than along intermediate aisles and passageways. It is known that goods displayed at the end of the aisle tend to sell better than those placed in the middle of an aisle, and that goods stored in such a way that they can be seen from the entrance or through windows attract the customer to the store. Thus it might be argued that the arrangement of such facilities must take into account certain customer-oriented factors rather than simply concentrating on retailer-oriented factors such as maximum use of space, minimum transport, etc.

The arrangement of storage areas such as warehouses also necessitates the consideration of factors other than movement. In such cases there is often a conflict between the need to obtain maximum space utilization and the need to minimize the cost of movement. For example, maximum space utilization often involves high stacking, whereas the storage of items in this manner often necessitates the use of expensive materials handling equipment and therefore gives rise to high movement costs. The arrangement of passageways is also of considerable importance, while the possibility of future expansion, the need to accommodate new items which may have different dimensions or different weight, the need to locate items associated with one another in the same area, the need to provide secure areas for other items, etc., are all of some importance in layout planning.

EVALUATION OF ALTERNATIVE LAYOUTS

The comparison of alternative layouts is a necessity in many of the procedures described above. The emphasis there was on movement criteria, but it will be appropriate here to look at this need from a broader perspective.

Determining which of many alternative layouts to adopt is often a very difficult problem. If we consider all the possible features and characteristics, our list is likely to be very long indeed. If, on the other hand, we consider only the problem of movement and evaluate the alternative layouts only in this light, we shall very probably neglect certain quite important considerations and be guilty of sub-optimization. One factor should be common to whatever considerations we adopt: *cost*. We must, as a rule, aim to minimize the total cost involved in establishing and using the layout. It has been suggested that layouts should be evaluated on the basis of the following types of cost:

(a) Investment:

    1. Initial cost of new facilities of all kinds.

       (i)   buildings

       (ii)   construction

       (iii) machinery

       (iv) equipment

2. Accessory costs:

   (i)   handling equipment

   (ii)   containers

   (iii) shelves, bins, racks

3. Installation costs:

   (i)   building changes

   (ii)   machinery and equipment

   (iii) services and supporting facilities

   (iv) auxiliary service lines

(b) Operating costs:

1. Labour:

   (i)   handling and storerooms

2. General:

   (i)   floor space.

The comparison and evaluation of designs for completely new layouts is a difficult problem, and, while such factors as movement, cost of equipment, space required, etc. are normally the principal components of comparison, they are by no means the only components.

The evaluation or rearrangement of parts of factories or departments constitutes an easier problem only because of the relative lack of size of the layouts, and not because fewer factors need be considered.

MATERIALS HANDLING

The fact that we have considered the minimization of total movement cost as one principal objective in planning facilities layout is sufficient evidence of the importance of efficient handling and the efficient management of movement in most operating systems. Although we have adopted the title 'materials handling' we should emphasize that the management, i.e. the efficient planning and control of movement in all types of systems, is of considerable importance, whether that movement relates to raw materials, finished goods, customers or indirect materials. Movement of materials, work-in-progress and finished goods is of crucial importance in all manufacturing operations. The movement of customers and goods is clearly of ultimate importance in transport systems, while the handling, i.e. the organization of the movement of customers and items, is of considerable importance also in supply and service systems. Here, therefore, we are concerned with the movement of customers or items (whether materials or finished goods) into or out of stores, during processing, into the operating system, and from the operating system to the final customer.

Efficient materials handling (i.e. the movement of items or customers) can bring considerable cost benefit to operating systems. Work-in-progress might be reduced; accidents or losses might be reduced; the capacity of the operating system might be increased; speed of processing, i.e. the throughput time, might be improved; level of service to the customer, e.g. the waiting time and the number of stockout situations, might be improved; total space required by the operation might be reduced; etc. Naturally there are equally substantial costs involved in designing, installing, staffing and maintaining an efficient system, including both recurrent and capital costs, so the design and planning of the system must be undertaken with a full awareness of, and therefore after, detailed analysis of movement needs, conditions, requirements and constraints, both present and future.

Materials handling objectives

The principles of efficient materials handling are listed in Table 6.1, from which it will be seen that an early objective should be the elimination of the need for handling or movement, or, failing that, a reduction in the need for such handling or movement. This might be achieved by more appropriate layout of the operating facilities, by combining operations with movement, etc. The *necessary* handling/movement should be organized in as efficient a manner as possible. This will often involve the minimization of 'pick-up/put-down' movements, the use of unit loads and pallets, the use of straight line movement, the use of mechanical rather than manual movement, and the separation of items which require subsequent separate processing.

Table 6.1	Principles of efficient materials handling
1.	Eliminate need for handling/movement (e.g. by eliminating unnecessary movement and by suitable arrangement of processes)
2.	Combine processing and movement
3.	Plan layout of operations together with planning of materials handling to minimize handling/movement
4.	(In general) use mechanical handling where regular high-volume movement is required or where safety hazards exist
5.	Arrange handling/movement to minimize number of 'pick-up/put down' movements
6.	Use unit loads and use pallets and containers to avoid damage, reduce subsequent handling, etc.
7.	Avoid mixing items/materials which subsequently need to be separated
8.	Use straight line movement

Methods for materials handling

Table 6.2 identifies the principal classes of materials handling equipment and suggests some of the normal applications for such equipment. In this table the applications are considered in terms of the type of movement required, i.e. whether predominantly overhead, vertical, a combination of vertical or horizontal, or largely horizontal (having a fixed route, or with a variable, i.e. non-fixed, route). Certain types of equipment conventionally operate at a constant speed, although often on an intermittent basis. Conveyors normally fall into this category. Other types of equipment, e.g. trucks or cranes, are able to operate at variable speeds.

The selection of appropriate materials handling equipment will be determined by the types of applications required as well as by factors of the type listed in Table 6.2. Principal among these (see Table 6.3) are the types of materials/items/customers to be moved, their volume or weight, the frequency and regularity of movement and of course the extent to which this movement requirement is temporary or 'permanent'. The movement route,

Table 6.2	Methods for materials handling and their applications					

Class of equipment	Type of equipment	Speed (v = variable; c = constant)	Normal applications (type of movement)				
			Overhead	Vertical	Vertical/horizontal	Horizontal fixed route	Horizontal non-fixed route
Cranes	Gantry	v	√	√	√		
	Mobile (e.g. truck)	v	√	√	√		
	Revolving	v	√	√	√		
Lifts	Elevator	v		√			
	Escalator	v		√			
	Bucket	c		√			
Trucks	Fork	v					√
	Hand	v					√
	Tractor	v					√
	Sideloader	v					√
	Platform	v					√
	Pallet	v					√
	Straddle	v					√
Conveyor	Belt	c				√	
	Roller	c				√	
	Flight	c			√	√	
	Pneumatic	c			√	√	
	Screw	c				√	
	Slatted	c				√	
	Vibrating	c				√	
	Drag chain	c	√			√	
Towing	Overhead chain	c	√			√	
	Overhead monorail	v	√				
	Floor	c				√	√
Chute	Gravity	c			√	√	
	Spiral lift	c		√			

particularly whether fixed or variable, and the extent to which this route is influenced by existing constraints such as the location of equipment, the shape of buildings, etc. will be of considerable importance. In certain cases the speed of movement is determined; for example, the handling of hot items may require a speed of movement differing from that needed for the handling of fragile items. In certain cases the speed of movement required is low, since some form of processing is associated with the movement; for example, in the brewing industry, movement, storage and maturing often occur simultaneously. The type of storage employed, both before and after movement, will influence the type of materials handling equipment envisaged, as will considerations of safety and the needs of concurrent and subsequent processes.

Type of operating system	Type of layout			
	Process layout	Product layout	Fixed-position layout	Group layout
Service systems	1. Hotel 2. Reference library	1. Automatic carwash 2. Medical screening and diagnosis	Hospital operating theatre	–
Supply systems	1. Supermarket 2. Warehouse	1. Restaurant self-service	Restaurant dining room	–
Manufacturing systems	1. Jobbing production 2. Small batch production	1. Motor-vehicle assembly line 2. Chemical process plant	1. Shipyard 2. Civil engineering	Batch production of components for a variety of products
Transport systems	See text	See text	–	–

Table 6.3   Types of layout: examples

AUTOMATED STORAGE AND RETRIEVAL

Systems which provide for the automated storage of items, and automated retrieval of items from stock, are now commonplace in manufacturing, distribution and supply systems. Automated storage and retrieval (ASR) enables organizations to provide for better space utilization, and to offer greater flexibility and responsiveness in the management of stocks. ASR systems are of importance therefore in the context of flexible manufacturing, and just-in-time manufacture. They are also found in mail-order organizations, food warehouses (especially where low temperatures must be maintained), and in large retail organizations where rapid stock turnover and rapid replenishment of retail shelf space from an adjacent warehouse is important. Certain types of automated car-parking are, in effect, a form of ASR. Automated storage and retrieval systems are used alongside assembly activities in the electronics industry, and are of value in holding and managing parts stocks in maintenance organizations.

The nature of ASR systems

Whilst the size of such systems varies considerably, the same four basic components are to be found in most applications, namely:

(a) storage area(s);

(b) storage and retrieval machine(s);

(c) conveying devices;

(d) control computers.

These are shown diagrammatically in Figure 6.4.

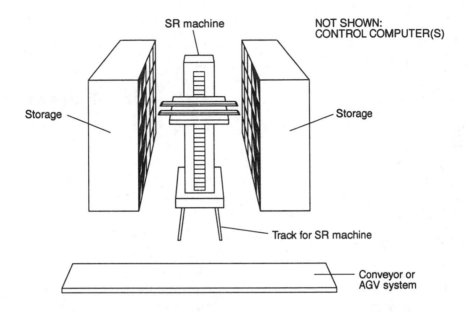

Figure 6.4 Elements of an automated storage and retrieval system (two storage areas with a single SR machine)

EXAMPLE

Terumo Medical

An $11-million automated materials handling system was installed at Terumo Medical Corp. for raw materials, work-in-process, and finished products. The system consists of an automated storage and retrieval system and two automatic guided vehicle systems. In the summer of 1988, this system helped in tripling Terumo's manufacturing capacity for syringes, medical tubing, and blood collection test kits. By 1989, the company's six-aisle 10,000-plus storage location AS/RS handled approximately 100 putaways/retrievals daily. Bar coded pallets travel by AGV to a sizing station before being put away in the AS/RS. The central computer then calls raw materials out of the AS/RS when they are needed for delivery to the assembly and sterilization areas by the 12-vehicle AGVs. The combination of bar code labels and sophisticated inventory tracking software ensures that unsterilized loads are not shipped.

Source: Forger, G. (1989) How an AS/RS and two AGV systems saved the day at Terumo. *Modern Mats Handling.* **44**(14), pp. 44–46.

KEY POINTS FOR CHAPTER 6

There are two types of layout planning problem: new layouts, and modifications to existing layouts.

The needs for layout planning include:

changing department size
moving a department
adding/removing a department
replacing/changing equipment

The objectives in layout planning include:

minimizing cost of movement
minimizing congestion and delay
maximizing space and facilities utilization

Layout problems occur at three levels:

departments in an area
facilities in a department
items in a work-area

Evaluation of alternative layouts involves comparison on factors including

investment
operating cost

Effective materials handling and movement is important in all types of operation.

There are eight principles for efficient materials handling.

Factors such as the following will affect the

The basic types of layout are:

process/functional
product
fixed position
group/cell
hybrid

Layout planning requires consideration of

demand
capacity
work methods
resources
movement

Layout planning procedures include:

Traditional e.g. cross charts, relationship charts
Computer e.g. proximity maximization and movement minimization methods

choice of materials handling equipment:

type of items/materials
volumes/ratios
routes
speed
storage needs
safety

Automated storage and retrieval is increasingly important in many types of operation.

FURTHER READING

Domeschke, W. and Drexl, A. (1985) *Location and Layout Planning.* Springer-Verlag.

Ziai, M.R. and Sute, D.R. (1989) Computerized Materials Handling and Facility Layout Design. *Computers and Industrial Engineering,* V17, (1–4), pp. 55–60.

Brown, J. (1989) AGVs in action. *Plant Engineering and Maintenance* 12, (5), pp. 24–27.

Ketcham R.L., Malstron, E.M. and McRoberts, K.L. (1989) A comparison of three computer assisted facilities design algorithms. *Computers and Industrial Engineering,* **16**,(3) pp. 375–386.

CASE STUDIES

The following case, from Part 9 of the book, is relevant to the topics covered in this chapter.

No.	Name	Country
3	Sahil Tea Garden	Turkey

QUESTIONS

6.1 The following cross chart has been constructed by means of observations of all movement between the seven production departments of a factory over a typical one-month period. In addition to these seven production departments, there are three other departments: the general office, the drawing office and the personnel department. The general office should preferably be close to the assembly department but not close to the test department. The drawing office should preferably be close to assembly, stores and the general office, but must not be close to the test area. The location of the personnel department is comparatively unimportant; however, it should not be too far away from any of the production departments. The relative location of the production departments depends on materials flow only, as shown in the figure.

Construct a relationship chart showing the desirable relative locations of each of these ten departments. Use an appropriate notation to indicate the desired proximities.

	R	S	T	M	G	A	T
Receiving		40				3	3
Stores			20	20			
Turning				18	2		
Milling					18	20	
Grinding						10	10
Assembly							38
Testing						5	

6.2 'Visual or graphical minimization is the only satisfactory and practical method of designing facility layouts, and the minimization of total movement costs is the most appropriate objective function during layout planning.' Discuss.

6.3 What factors, other than the cost of movement, need

to be considered during the planning of a new layout, and how is the consideration of these factors included in the whole layout planning procedure?

6.4 Discuss the requirements of the handling systems and identify appropriate types of handling equipment for the following applications:

(a) the handling of passengers' baggage (other than hand baggage) in an airport terminal;

(b) the movement of metal waste from the machine shop of a mass-production engineering company;

(c) the movement of goods from the goods receiving department through stores, on to shelves, and to customers in a large supermarket.

PART 4

Work and Work Systems

INTRODUCTION TO PART 4

In this part of the book we concentrate on work systems. We focus on human work, i.e. the execution of tasks by people within the operating system, and in so doing we look at some traditional and established areas of responsibility of operations management as well as at some newer topics. We shall look at work methods, work standards, the rewards for work, the problems of learning, people's attitudes to work, the design of the workplace, health and safety considerations, etc. All these topics are interrelated. For our purposes we can perhaps identify four sets of considerations which must be taken into account in the design of work systems.

Chapter 7

Work and work methods

ISSUES

Why study work methods and procedures?

What is the objective of method study?

What are the main steps involved in developing a good work method?

How can a work method be described and recorded?

How can work methods be improved?

How do we deal with learning?

In this chapter, after a brief discussion of *Work Study* we shall concentrate on the design of work methods. Chapter 8 will focus on the measurement of work. These are two of the traditional areas of responsibility of operations managers. In the next two chapters we shall focus on other related topics.

The structure and purposes of work study

Throughout these two chapters we shall use the British terminology and, where possible, the British Standard definitions. The British Standards Institution defines work study as 'a generic term for those techniques, particularly method study and work measurement, which are used in the examination of human work in all its contexts, and which lead systematically to the investigation of all the factors which affect the efficiency and economy of the situations being reviewed, in order to effect improvements.'

The aims of work study are, by analysis of work methods and the materials and equipment used, to:

(a) establish the most economical way of doing the work;

(b) standardize this method, and the materials and equipment involved;

(c) establish the time required by a qualified and adequately trained worker to do the job, while working at a defined level of performance;

(d) install this work method as standard practice.

Work study, then, is a way of either designing work for high productivity or improving productivity in existing work by improving current work methods and reducing ineffective or wasted time. In each case the design or improvements are sought within the context of existing resources and equipment; consequently work study is an immediate tool and is not dependent on the redesign of goods or services, research and development of operating processes, or extensive rearrangement of facilities.

The economic results of the study, whether they are increases in throughput reduction in waste, improved safety, reduction in training time, or better use of equipment or labour, should outweigh the cost of the investigation. To ensure this we should consider:

(a) the anticipated life of the job;

(b) whether manual work is an important part of the job, e.g. (1) the wage rate for the job, (2) the ratio of machine time to manual time in the work cycle;

(c) utilization of equipment, machines, tools, etc., the cost of such equipment, and whether the utilization is dependent on the work method;

(d) the importance of the job to the organization.

We should distinguish between work study of existing jobs and that of proposed or anticipated jobs. Whenever new products or services are to be provided or new equipment used, jobs must be designed. Consequently the question is to what extent work study should be used and how much effort is justified by the importance of the job. Some investigations may be necessary on existing jobs, not necessarily because they were inadequately designed in the first place, but perhaps because there has been a change in the process or service, new equipment is being used, etc. Examinations of existing work methods could

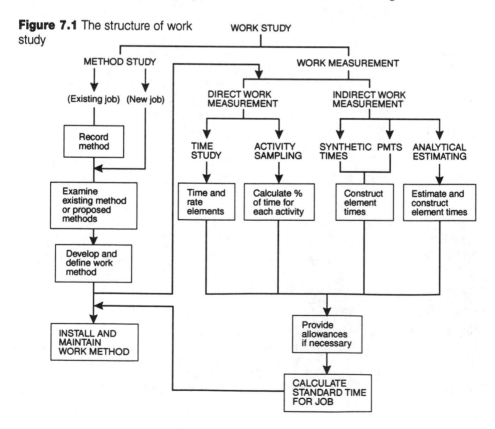

Figure 7.1 The structure of work study

also result from low machine utilization, excessive labour overtime, or idle time, complaints from workers, inadequate quality, high scrap or wastage rate, etc.

Figure 7.1 shows the structure of work study. Two aspects exist: *method study*, concerned with establishing optimum work methods; and *work measurement*, concerned with establishing time standards for those methods. Method study is normally conducted before work measurement.

METHOD STUDY

Method study is the systematic recording and critical examination of existing and proposed ways of doing work, as a means of developing and applying easier and more effective methods and reducing costs. Method study, when applied to an existing job, consists of a maximum of seven steps:

1. Select the work to be studied.
2. Record the existing work method and all other relevant facts.
3. Examine the method.
4. Develop the most efficient method of doing the work.
5. Define the method.
6. Install this method as standard practice.
7. Maintain this practice.

Step 1: Select the job to be studied

Maximum potential cost benefit is the normal objective. Direct costs of labour, materials and equipment are certainly the main components of total cost, but indirect cost, such as the cost of supervision, training, recruitment and welfare, is also relevant. Although work methods may affect each of these costs, there is a tendency to emphasize direct costs, and to develop work methods which minimize the cost of labour, machinery and materials. The elimination of work hazard, fatigue and stress may also be important objectives.

Step 2: Record the work method

The objective here is to obtain a record of the work method for subsequent examination. We must consider two interrelated aspects:

(a) the type of record which is to be obtained (the principal distinction being the amount of detail provided);

(b) the procedure by which this record is to be obtained, e.g. by direct observation or subsequent examination.

Types of record

We shall begin by considering records which provide relatively little detail of the work method: such records might be appropriate for a preliminary investigation of a work method. Later we shall look at more detailed records which might be appropriate for detailed critical examination of existing work methods. The more common methods are outlined below.

Flow diagram

A *flow diagram* shows the location and sequence of the activities carried out by workers and the routes followed by materials, components, or (in the case of service and transport systems) customers.

Multiple activity charts

This type of record is of value where the activities of one or more workers and/or pieces of equipment are to be examined. The activities and their duration are represented by blocks or lines drawn against a time scale.

Multiple activity charts are also valuable in studying jobs where work-loads are varied and uneven and where several products and machines are to be attended by one worker.

Process charts

These are the most common of the recording procedures. The sequence of events is represented by a series of symbols. They are shown in Table 7.1.

Table 7.4	Process chart symbols			
Symbol	**Type of process chart**			
	Outline	**Flow process chart**		**Two-handed (or operator)**
		Worker type	**Material type**	
○	Operation	Operation	Operation	Operation
◊	–	Transportation	Transportation	Transportation
□	Inspection	Inspection	Inspection	–
▽	–	–	Storage	Hold
D	–	Delay	Delay	Delay

Note. Operations are the main steps in a process method or procedure. Usually the part, material or customer in the system or product concerned is modified or changed during the operation.

Transportation indicates the movement of workers, materials, customers or equipment from place to place.

Storage indicates a controlled storage in which items for customers are received into or issued from stores under some form of authorization, or an item is retained for reference purposes.

Delay indicates a delay in the sequence of events, for example work waiting between consecutive operations, or any object or customer laid aside temporarily without record until required.

Inspection indicates an inspection for quality and/or a check for quantity.

Hold indicates the retention of an object in one hand, normally so that the other hand may do something to it.

An *outline process chart* is a record of the main parts of the process only (i.e. the operations and the inspections). It is often used as a preliminary step, prior to more detailed study. Alternatively, outline process charts are often used to record basic information for use during the arrangement or layout of plant, during the design of the product or specification of the service, or even during the design of equipment for the system. It is a simple record of the important 'constructive' and essential steps in a process, omitting all ancillary activities.

A *flow process chart* may be concerned with either *materials* (or customers in the system) or *workers* or both. It is an amplification of the outline process chart and shows, in addition, the *transportations, storages* and *delays* which occur. Figure 7.2 shows a simple worker-and-material flow process chart.

Figure 7.2 Worker-and-material flow process chart

Flow Process Chart

Method Present		Type	Worker and material
		Job	Inspection of component
		Begin	Worker in inspection department
			Material in goods receiving
		Finish	Worker in inspection department
			Material in stores

WORKER   MATERIAL

WORKER		MATERIAL	
1	To goods receiving department	1	Await arrival of worker
1	Locate component	2	Wait
2	Book out	3	Wait
2	To inspection department	1	To inspection
3	Set up on bench	1	Set up on bench
1	Visual inspection	1	Inspection
4	Measure and record length	2	Measured
5	Measure and record diameter	3	Measured
6	Stamp	4	Stamped
3	To stores	2	To stores
7	Book into stock	1	Stored
4	Return to inspection		

SUMMARY		
	WORKER	MATERIAL
○	7	4
⇨	4	2
□	1	1
D	0	3
▽	0	1

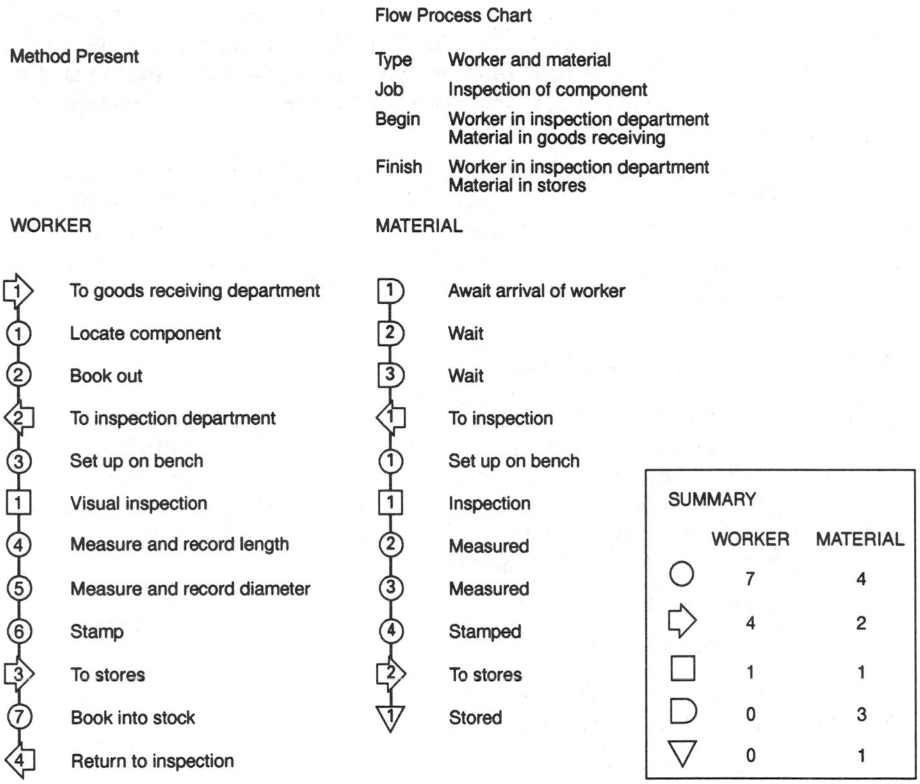

A *two-handed* or *operator process chart* is the most detailed type of flow process chart, in which the activities of the worker's hands are recorded in relation to one another. Unlike the previous recording methods, the two-handed process chart is normally confined to work carried out at a single place. The ordinary symbols are used, except *inspection* is omitted since this can be represented by movements of the hands, and the *storage* symbol is now taken to mean *hold*.

Simo (simultaneous motion cycle) charts

When it is necessary to study work in more detail than is possible using two-handed or flow process charts, a different notation and a different type of record are required. The recording method most frequently used is the SIMO chart which shows in detail the work method, usually for the worker's left and right hands. 'PMTS' notation is often used in such charts. PMT systems classify motions and provide codes to identify each type and class of motion. The notation can be used in recording and describing the method, especially where it is intended to use the record subsequently to determine a standard time for the job (See Chapter 8).

Recording procedure

The type of record to be obtained, in particular the level of detail to be incorporated, will in part determine the recording procedure to be used.

Direct observation of a work method will permit the development of most of the records outlined on p.106, but when more detail is to be obtained, the observer will need to watch several repetitions of the task. In these (and other) situations, filming is of value. If a video of a method is obtained, process charts can subsequently be developed in any level of detail.

Electronic portable 'data capture' terminals are often used in work study. These are of particular use in time study, where the objective is to record the times for the elements of a job in order to determine the time required. The terminals will store such information and then transmit it to a computer for analysis. Some such terminals allow the type of work elements to be recorded as well as the elapsed time (See Chapter 8).

Step 3: Examine the method

The purpose of recording the existing method is to enable subsequent examination and criticism with a view to improvement. The recording method used should be sufficient to show all the relevant information. Many procedures for examining and criticizing existing work methods have been suggested and adopted, but basically they simply involve asking six basic questions: Why? What? Where? When? Who? How? The purpose of this is to define what is accomplished, how and why:

Why was the process undertaken?

What purpose does it serve?

Where is it accomplished and why?

When is it accomplished and why?

Who is involved and why?

How is it accomplished and why?

The aim is to determine the effectiveness of the process as a whole, and to identify whether any of the following major changes would be beneficial:

(a) changes in material used;

(b) changes in the design of the product or service;

(c) changes in the nature or design of the process.

The activities in the process belong in one of two categories. Those in each category must be examined and considered for elimination or change. First are those in which something is happening to the material, the product, or the customer, i.e. it is being moved, inspected, or worked on. Second are those in which nothing constructive is happening, i.e. delays or storages.

The first category can be further divided into *make ready*, *do*, and *put away*. *Make ready* activities are required to prepare the material, workpiece, or customer and set it in position ready to be worked on; *do* activities occur whenever these are changed in shape, condition or composition; and *put away* activities occur when the material, or product or customer is moved away from the machine or work area. It is obviously beneficial to have a high proportion of *do* activities during the process and a low proportion of the others, since it is only *do* activities which carry things towards completion, and it is only during these activities that value is added.

Examination of these activities will question purpose, place and sequence, the person undertaking the activity and the means by which it is performed, in order to establish useful alternatives which subsequently can be examined and perhaps incorporated in an improved work method.

Step 4: Develop and improve work method

Now a *process improvement formula*, which consists of four steps—eliminate, combine, sequence, simplify—is applied to each separate activity in the job, i.e. to each meaningful group of work elements.

Complete *elimination* of unnecessary activities is the most important step that can be taken in developing an improved work method. An activity may have been retained because of custom, inertia, inadequate communications or even ignorance. Changes in materials, product/service design, process design, tools or the workplace may facilitate the elimination of activities. If elimination is not possible, then combination of activities should be considered. In many processes two or more activities may be usefully *combined*. Changes in the *sequence* of activities is the next possibility, and this may then facilitate elimination or combination. Should none of these three steps succeed in eliminating or combining the activity then the last, more expensive, step should be considered, i.e. attempting to *simplify* the activity by reducing the number of operations, reducing or eliminating delays and storage, or minimizing transportation. It may become necessary to conduct a more detailed motion study to obtain enough information to enable activities to be simplified, and again consideration should be given to changes in materials and to product/service and process design. The object of simplifying the activity is to permit the worker to complete the job more quickly and easily.

Step 5: Define the new method

It will be necessary to describe the work method to be adopted in sufficient detail for others to be able to install it or for subsequent use in training and instructions, etc. This definition comprises a statement of the nature of the work method and may be used subsequently in the case of any disputes or misunderstandings. It may be referred to when work method changes are contemplated or when changes are considered to have taken place.

Step 6: Install the new method

Clearly the first stage is to gain acceptance of the method from management, supervisors and workers. Then a programme for the installation of the method should be developed showing the main steps, those responsible for carrying them out, and the timetable involved. This will include time for training and learning (see below) and the rearrangement of equipment, tools, workplaces, etc.

EXAMPLE

Methods improvements at Salt River

The Salt River Project public power utility in Arizona developed an easy-to-use, do-it-yourself methods improvement kit. The kit enables a department to analyse its own work methods and simplify its procedures in order to increase productivity. It provides instructions and forms for implementing a 7-step task analysis procedure. Employees are instructed to list their major job tasks and activities and to select one for analysis. Employees are then asked to list all of the steps involved in performing that task or activity. The instructions encourage the employees to think of possible changes that would simplify the task or eliminate unnecessary steps. After a group discussion, the supervisor evaluates the suggestions and takes steps to implement those that have merit.

Source: Copp, E. Methods improvement kit uses IE techniques to simplify work. *Industrial Engineering* **20** (8) pp. 47–50.

Learning

In installing a new work method, appropriate training must be provided and a period of learning must be expected. We cannot examine this subject here in depth, and it will be sufficient for our present purposes to consider learning as the process by which an individual acquires skill and proficiency at a task which, in turn, has the effect of permitting increased productivity in his or her performance of that task. Here we shall be concerned only with worker task learning, the speed at which a task can be executed, the extent to which the learning can increase this speed, and the influence of various factors on the learning phenomenon. We shall consider the nature of the learning curve (sometimes called the Improvement curve or the progress function), but shall discuss the use of the curve in the next chapter.

The learning curve of the type shown in Figure 7.3 shows three features:

(a) The time required to complete a task or unit of work will reduce with repeated performance of that task.
(b) The rate of reduction will decrease over time.
(c) This reduction in time will follow a general pattern.

Figure 7.7 75% learning curve

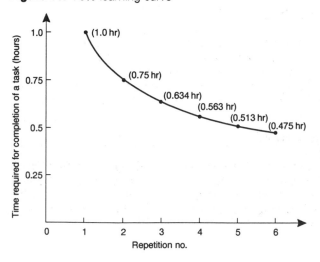

This learning curve represents a 75% rate of improvement. The curve shows a performance improvement resulting from learning equivalent to a constant rate of improvement of 75%, i.e. the first performance of the task requires one hour and thereafter every doubling of the number of performances or number of repetitions shows a 75% improvement. Thus the second performance requires 1×0.75, i.e. 0.75 hours, the fourth performance requires 0.75×0.75, i.e. 0.56 hours, etc.

Task learning is influenced by numerous factors. The most important for our purposes are as follows:

(a) Task length, i.e. the longer the task, in general the slower the learning, not only in terms of
the total time required to reach a particular level of performance, but also in terms of the number of repetitions required to reach that level of performance.
(b) Task complexity.
(c) The capability or skill of the worker and his or her familiarity with the type of work to be learned.
(d) Task similarity, i.e. the extent to which the task being learned is similar to that undertaken previously by the worker.
(e) Worker motivation and personal characteristics.
(f) External influences, e.g. physical conditions, etc.
(g) Learning methods and circumstances.

Step 7 Maintain the new method

Finally, once the method is installed, a period of maintenance is required. Unnecessary changes to the work method should not be allowed, and periodic reviews/checks should be carried out, to ensure that the method is satisfactory, that disputes do not arise, that earnings are maintained and that related activities do not compromise the work method.

COMPUTER APPLICATIONS (see also pp. 132–133)

Computer methods are now widely used in work study. They permit the rapid recording and analysis of data, storage of data for subsequent use, etc., and such applications benefit all aspects of work study, i.e. method study and work measurement. We shall look at some of these applications in the next chapter, but here we consider some *uses specifically related to method study*.

Methods development and analysis

Several programs are available to assist in the development or analysis of work method. Typically, information relating to the work required, the layout of the workplace and the tools and equipment employed is input, from which the program determines the most appropriate work method and provides a detailed work place layout.

This is useful not only for automatic development of work method but also for rapid comparison of alternative work methods. For example, by varying the input slightly different methods can be developed and compared.

Methods description

Less ambitious than methods development programs are those which seek only to provide detailed methods descriptions. These require as input a description of a work method in at least outline and coded form. Then, using stored information from which detailed element descriptions can be obtained, and using one of the PMTS notations, the program generates a description in, for example, SIMO chart format of the job (usually with element and operation times). In this type of application the computer is taking over the detailed, often time-consuming task of preparing printed work-method descriptions in a usable format, often also drawing upon filed data for standard or commonly used elements or sequences of elements.

Data storage and retrieval

Most of the computerized work study programs provide a facility to store information on work elements, sequences of work elements and complete work methods together with information on tools, equipment, layouts and time standards. Such data will be of particular relevance in the development of work standards for jobs, and this will be discussed in the following chapter. Additionally, in developing and specifying work methods for new jobs, it may be possible to 'build up' a method simply by fitting together appropriate sequences, etc. from the data file. With this type of facility it is possible to reduce considerably the time required to develop and specify the new work method. The method study analyst need only identify the major parts of the total job, and the computer program can then construct detailed methodology using the filed data.

KEY POINTS FOR CHAPTER 7

Work study

incorporates method study and work measurement.

Work study is a means to design and improve work methods and performance.

Method study

aims to design, or develop good work methods, whether for new or for existing jobs.

There are seven basic steps in method study, i.e.

    select

    record

    examine

    develop

    define

    install

    maintain

Select the job to provide high potential benefits.

Record the work method using an appropriately detailed technique, for example:

    Flow diagram

    multiple Activity chart

    process chart

    Simo chart

Examine the method critically.

Develop, i.e. improve, the method.

Define the improved method.

Install the new method.

Maintain the new method.

Learning is an important factor, i.e. an individual's ability to improve work performance through repetition.

Seven factors influence the extent and nature of learning:

    task lengths

    task complexity

    skill

    task similarity

    motivation

    condition

    learning methods

Computer applications are important, e.g. for:

    methods development and analysis

    methods description

    data handling

FURTHER READING

British Standards Institution (1977) *Glossary of terms used in Work Study and Organization and Methods* (BS 3138), BSI, London.

Doty, L.A. (1989) *Work Methods and Measurement for Management*, Delmar.

Niebel, B.W. (1988) *Motion and Time Study*, Irwin, Illinois.

CASE STUDY

The following case, from Part 9 of the book, is relevant to the topics covered in this chapter.

No.	Name	Country
6	Airport Building Project	India

QUESTIONS

7.1 Describe, with examples, the method study techniques you would use to investigate the work of:

(a)   a team of six workers in a hotel reception/cashier area;

(b)   a single worker on a short-cycle repetitive clerical task.

7.2 The Gobust Co. packs 'nick-nacks'. They are imported and weighed out in lots of $1/2$ kg. There are 12 'nick-nacks' to the kg. on average. The 'nick-nacks' must be inserted in a jar, to which a portion of 'nick-nack' juice is added. The jar is then sealed with a twist cap.

(a)   Analyse the job. Develop a good sequence of work elements.

(b)   Sketch the process flow and layout.

(c)   Use an operation chart to detail the work involved.

7.3 An electric plug is to be assembled manually in large quantities. Describe the plug and then develop a method of assembling the components of the plug and sketch the workplace layout. Use a two-handed process chart to indicate your method. You may approximate the element times.

7.4 What are the six important steps involved in performing a method study? Describe very briefly the principal techniques available for the execution of the second of these steps, and describe also the logical sequence or 'formula' which constitutes step 4.

7.5 Discuss the problems in human relations which are likely to occur during a method study exercise and indicate how they might be minimized. In your answer show how the problems differ at various stages of the investigation.

Chapter 8

Work measurement and work standards

ISSUES

Why do we need to measure work?
What are the basic work measurement procedures?
How accurate and objective is such measurement?
How do we deal with human differences?
What is the effect of the 'learning curve'?
Can work measurement be computerized?

Work measurement is defined in British Standard 3138 as the 'application of techniques designed to establish the time for a qualified worker to carry out a specific job at a defined level of performance'.

Work times are necessary for the comparison of work methods, for operations scheduling, capacity planning and for use in 'payment by results' schemes. The proper co-ordination of operations depends on the availability of accurate time estimates.

Standard times for jobs may be used to determine the operating effectiveness of equipment, workers, groups of workers or departments, and to determine standard costs of operations for pricing or estimating purposes.

EXAMPLE

Retail work

Four major UK retail companies developed staff deployment methods to meet customer demand with minimum costs and increased sales opportunity. The approach combined traditional work study techniques with computer modelling. The concept was based on several factors, including detailed work measurement at the store level, quantifying how staff spend their time, customer flow patterns, missed sales opportunities, and sales conversion rates. These and other factors are computerized to determine the staffing levels needed, relating prime resources to known customer flow patterns.

Source: Lee, M. Retain staff scheduling—The staff deployment concept. *Management Services* **37**(1) pp. 16–20.

WORK MEASUREMENT PROCEDURES

The conventional and traditional procedures for work measurement are discussed below.

Direct work measurement

Time study

We can break down the time study procedure into a series of simple logical steps, as follows.

Obtain all necessary information

As the objective in work measurement is to determine the time required for a job to be carried out under specified conditions, it is necessary to have a record of these conditions in case the exercise is referred to or used at a later date. This requires the recording of information about the worker, equipment, material, layout, output, method, quality standard, etc.

Divide the job into work 'elements'

This is necessary for the following reasons:

(a) to provide a better understanding of the nature of the job;

(b) to break a time study exercise up into manageably sized 'pieces';

(c) to permit a more accurate study;

(d) to distinguish different types of work;

(e) to enable 'machine' elements, i.e. machine-paced work, to be isolated from 'worker' elements;

(f) to enable detailed job descriptions to be produced;

(g) to enable time standards to be checked or modified;

(h) to enable times for certain common or important elements to be extracted and compared.

Jobs may consist of constant or variable, manual or machine, repetitive or occasional elements. Constant elements are of identical specification and have the same duration whenever performed, unlike variable elements, the times of which vary according to characteristics such as weight, size, distance, etc. Machine elements are often constant while worker elements are often variable. Occasional elements do not occur in every cycle but nevertheless are an essential part of the job.

The ease with which the study is conducted and data obtained is dependent on the definition of the job elements. Fortunately there are some general rules which can be used:

(a) The elements selected will be timed separately and repeatedly; consequently, it is essential that clearly-defined beginning and ending points should be available to identify the element.

(b) Elements should be as short as possible yet not too short to be conveniently timed.

(c) Elements should be as unified as possible. Whenever possible, elements consisting of a logical sequence of basic motions should be used.

(d) Worker and machine elements should be separated.

(e) Regular and irregular elements should be separated.

(f) Elements involving heavy or fatiguing work should be separated out.

(g) Finally, constant elements should be separated from variable elements.

Timing elements

A variety of devices are available to assist in the timing of work elements. Traditionally, analogue stopwatches were used, but digital stopwatches are more common now. In both cases the watches are usually mounted on an observation board to which are clipped record sheets on which the observer writes the element, time, ratings, etc.

More sophisticated electronic equipment is used in element timing. A variety of types of 'event recorder' are available which combine ease of use with accuracy and versatility. Electronic data capture terminals are also used. They are, in effect, alpha/numeric keyboard devices with some internal storage and a small LCD display. They can be programmed to 'prompt' the observer with element descriptions in code form so that the times can be recorded and then stored within the device. Summary calculations can be performed, and in some cases by interfacing the device directly with a printer a list of element times can be printed out for editing and for checking for missing observations, etc. In most cases such devices provide for interfacing with the computer so that the stored information can be 'downloaded' for subsequent analysis.

Some methods of timing elements involve filming. A video film can be made of the operation for subsequent analysis 'off the job'. The filmed record can incorporate a clock so that detailed timings can be obtained, or the film can be run at a known and constant speed.

The number of cycles to be timed

We must take enough readings to be reasonably confident of an accurate result. Direct time study is a sampling process, and the accuracy of the sample as a measure of the elements themselves is determined by the variability of the elements and the size of the sample. The number of observations required depends on:

(a) the variation in the times of the element;

(b) the degree of accuracy required;

(c) the confidence level required.

A 95% confidence level and an accuracy of $\pm 5\%$ or $\pm 10\%$ are usually adopted. This means that the chances are at least 95 out of 100 that the mean or average we obtain from the observations will be in error by $\pm 5\%$ or $\pm 10\%$ of the true element time.

Before the number of observations necessary to fulfil this requirement can be calculated, we must establish the variability of the element time by conducting a brief 'pilot' study. We can then use one of the following formulae to calculate the required number of observations.

95% confidence ± 5% accuracy:

$$N^1 = \left(\frac{40 \sqrt{N \sum x^2 - (\sum x)^2}}{\sum x}\right)^2$$

95% confidence ± 10% accuracy:

$$N^1 = \left(\frac{20 \sqrt{N \sum x^2 - (\sum x)^2}}{\sum x}\right)^2$$

where N^1 = required number of observations for given confidence and accuracy

N = actual number of observations taken in pilot study

x = each observed element time from the pilot study.

Rating the worker

So far we have been concerned only with the observed or actual times required by a worker to perform elements of work, but the object of work measurement is to determine not how long it *did* take to perform a job or elements of a job, but how long it *should* take. It is necessary, therefore, to compare the actual rate of work with a standard rate so that the observed times can be converted to basic times, i.e. the time required to carry out an element of work at standard performance. So every observation we make must be rated and the appropriate rating factor recorded.

Performance rating is the comparison of an actual rate of working against a defined concept of a standard rate. The standard rate corresponds to 'the average rate at which qualified workers will naturally work at a job, provided they know and adhere to the specified method, and provided they are motivated to apply themselves to their work'. On the British Standard Performance Scale, standard rating is equal to 100, i.e. a rating of 50 is equal to half the standard rate of working.

However, standard rate is really only a concept. In practice the standard rate of working is a function of the situation, e.g. the physical conditions, the type of labour, company policy, and may differ greatly between companies. Consequently, the company must train the time study analyst to recognize what the company or industry regards as standard performance.

Several systems of rating have been developed. *Effort rating* is concerned primarily with work speed, the worker being rated according to the speed of movement, with adjustments being made for the perceived difficulty of the job. *Objective rating* is similar, and depends on the consideration of two factors: speed and difficulty. The operator is rated first according to the speed of movement, irrespective of the nature of the job. After this rating, an adjustment is made depending on the nature of the job, particularly:

(a) how much of the body is used;

(b) the use of footpedals;

(c) the need for bimanualness;

(d) eye-hand coordination;

(e) the handling requirements;

(f) the weight of objects handled.

The Westinghouse Company devised a system in which four characteristics were considered: the skill used, the effort required, the conditions prevailing and the consistency required. A numerical scale is attached to each of these characteristics (Table 8.1). Unlike the two systems above, this is used to rate a job rather than the separate elements of the job. For this reason it is sometimes referred to as a *levelling system* rather than a rating system. A separate rating for each element is made for each area and the sum of the four figures represents the final rating factor for each element, e.g.

Observed (actual) element time = 0.45 minutes

$$
\begin{aligned}
\text{Element rating} \quad &= + 0.06 \text{ (skill)} \\
&+ 0.12 \text{ (effort)} \\
&+ 0.00 \text{ (conditions)} \\
&\underline{+ 0.01} \text{ (consistency)} \\
&+ 0.19
\end{aligned}
$$

Basic time for element = $0.45 \times (1.00 + 0.19)$

= 0.54 minutes

Whichever one of these or other methods of rating or levelling is used, the basic time corresponds to the observed time after rating, i.e.

$$
\text{Basic time for element or job} = \text{Observed time} \times \frac{\text{Rating}}{100}
$$

Table 8.1		Factors and point values in performance rating									
Skill			**Effort**			**Conditions**			**Consistency**		
+0.15	A1	Superskill	+0.13	A1	Excessive	+0.06	A	Ideal	+0.04	A	Perfect
+0.13	A2		+0.12	A2		+0.04	B	Excellent	+0.03	B	Excellent
+0.11	B1	Excellent	+0.10	B1	Excellent	+0.02	C	Good	+0.01	C	Good
+0.08	B2		+0.08	B2		0.00	D	Average	0.00	D	Average
+0.06	C1	Good	+0.05	C1	Good	−0.03	E	Fair	−0.02	E	Fair
+0.03	C2		+0.02	C2		−0.07	F	Poor	−0.04	F	Poor
0.00	D	Average	0.00	D	Average						
−0.05	E1	Fair	−0.04	E1	Fair						
−0.10	E2		−0.08	E2							
−0.16	F1	Poor	−0.12	F1	Poor						
−0.22	F2		−0.17	F2							

Allowances

It may be necessary now to provide allowances to compensate for fatigue, personal needs, contingencies, etc. The basic time does not contain any allowances and is merely the time required by the worker to perform the task at a standard rate without any interruptions or delays. Allowances are normally given as a percentage of the basic element times and usually include:

(a) Relaxation allowances:

    1. fatigue allowances to give the workers time to recover from the effort (physiological and psychological) required by the job;

    2. personal needs—to visit toilets, washrooms, etc.

(b) Contingency allowances given to compensate for the time required by the workers to perform all necessary additional and periodic activities which were not included in the basic time because of infrequent or irregular occurrence and the difficulty of establishing the times.

(c) Tool and machinery allowance to compensate the worker for the time necessary for adjusting and setting up equipment, and so on.

(d) Reject allowance, necessary where a proportion of defective items must necessarily be produced.

(e) Interference allowance to compensate for time unavoidably lost because of the stoppage of two or more machines, attended by one worker, at the same time.

(f) Excess work allowance to compensate for the extra work necessary because of unforeseen or temporary changes in the standard conditions.

Total allowances are often of the order of 15 to 20%, so inaccuracies are of some consequence. Nevertheless, whilst different methods are available, practice is again very much a function of the situation.

Calculate standard time

The standard time for an element or a job is calculated as follows:

$$\text{Standard time} = \left(\text{Observed time} \times \frac{\text{Rating}}{100}\right) \times \text{Per cent total allowance}$$

For example, where the worker is observed to be working at greater than the standard rate, the three element times may bear a relationship to one another, as shown in Figure 8.1.

Figure 8.1 Breakdown of the standard minute

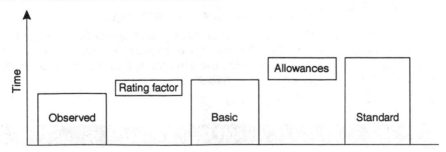

The *standard minute* is the unit of measurement of work, consisting partly of work and partly of relaxation. It represents the output in one minute if the work is performed at the standard rate. By means of work measurement we can express the work content of jobs in terms of single units—standard minutes (SMs)—irrespective of the differences between the jobs themselves.

Note that an SM is a measure of *work* and not a measure of time. It is connected with time only in that one SM of work will take one minute of time at 100 performance. SMs can therefore be used in calculating wages and performance. For example, performance can be measured by:

$$\frac{\text{Output of work in SMs}}{\text{Total labour time in minutes}}$$

Activity sampling

Direct time study, as above, is appropriate where we are concerned with short-cycle repetitive work. If, however, it is necessary to establish work standards in situations where long irregular-cycle work is conducted, or where many different jobs are performed, these techniques may be quite inappropriate.

It may be necessary to study the activities of several workers on several machines in order to establish the proportion of time each worker spends on various activities, or to determine the utilization of resources, space, etc., and in such cases some form of sampling procedure is invaluable.

The accuracy of our sample as a measure of the actual activity is dependent on the number of observations we take. If we are willing to take many observations, our confidence in the result can be high, but this will have been obtained only at higher cost.

Again, we must decide what confidence level and accuracy we require before we can decide how many observations to take. Furthermore, a pilot study must be conducted to establish the frequency of occurrence of the activity being studied; then for a confidence level of 95% the formula to determine the number of observations required is:

$$N^{1} = \frac{4p\,(100 - p)}{L^{2}}$$

where N^{1} = number of observations needed

p = percentage of total time occupied by the activity with which we are concerned, as obtained from a pilot study.

L = required limits of accuracy (expressed as a percentage).

Activity sampling is normally used to determine the percentage of the total time that a person or machine spends on certain activities. In the simplest case, the requisite number of random observations is taken to determine the percentage of total time spent by either a worker or a machine in working or not working.

EXAMPLE:

Texas Department of Human Services

The Texas Department of Human Services (TDHS) administers more than $8 billion in aid work each year. Much of this derives from federal programmes that specify how costs are to be divided between the federal and state governments. Most TDHS employees work across several programmes and how they distribute their time must therefore be determined in order to charge salary and overheads properly. To deal with this, TDHS experimented with a variation of traditional work sampling. A simple self-administered random survey was designed. Selected employees were issued a 'random reminder beeper', instructions, and survey sheets. When the beeper sounded, employees recorded the current time, the case they were working on and a code to indicate the programme being worked on at that moment.

Source: Ramsay, G.F (1993) Using self-administered work sampling in a state agency. *Industrial Engineering* **25**(2) Feb. pp. 44–45.

Indirect work measurement

Synthetic timing

As time studies are completed, the 'elemental' data are coded and stored. Periodically these data are examined to determine whether there is any consistency between times for similar elements. When enough consistent data have been gathered, the information can be compiled as a data base for future use.

The generation of data for 'machine' elements normally involves comparatively little trouble, since such times are often either constant or the functions of known variables. Similarly, constant 'worker' elements provide little difficulty, since an equal time will be required whenever the job or element is performed.

It is more difficult to deal with variable elements. First, we must examine the variations in time which occur in our accumulated data to establish whether the variation is a result of a difference in the nature of the element itself, or whether it results from the action of one or more variables. If the variations are particularly large there may be fundamental differences in the nature of the elements, in which case the data cannot be assembled together. The remaining variation can usually be attributed to variables such as distance, size and weight, and graphs or tables can then be constructed.

Such 'synthetic' data are reliable and consistent, since normally they have resulted from many studies over a period of time. They can be used to establish time standards for short-run work on which there would be insufficient time to conduct a direct time study, and to construct time standards for jobs not yet begun. It is normal to synthesize basic times to which allowances must be added. The need to rate the job under consideration is avoided and, since the synthetic data will probably have been derived from numerous studies, the consequence of inaccuracies in the original studies is reduced.

Predetermined motion time systems (PMTS)

PMTS can be defined as 'a work measurement technique whereby times established for basic human motions (classified according to the nature of the motion and the conditions under which it is made) are used to build up the time for a job at a defined level of performance'. A PMT system therefore consists of a list of all motions that a worker can use in doing a task, together with time values for these motions at a specified level of performance and in specified circumstances.

MTM-1

Methods time measurement (MTM) is the oldest and best known PMTS—and also the basis for many other PMTSs.

The first MTM system (MTM-1) provided times for basic motions, the argument being that, because such motions approximated to the 'lowest common denominators' of all work, it was possible, theoretically at least, to construct time standards for all jobs from a set of tabular data.

MTM-1 classifies all hand motions into basic units as follows:

Reach (R) — The basic element employed when the predominant purpose is to move the hand to a destination or general location.

Move (M) — The basic element employed when the predominant purpose is to transport an object to a destination.

Turn (T) — A movement which rotates the hand, wrist and forearm.

Apply pressure (AP) — The element employed whenever pressure is applied.

Grasp (G) — A hand or fingers element employed when an object is required for further operation.

Position (P) — The basic element employed to align, orient or engage one object with another, when motions used are minor and do not justify classification as other basic elements.

Release (RL) — The basic element employed to relinquish control of an object by the fingers or hand.

Disengage (D) — The basic element employed to break contact between objects.

Eye travel and *eye focus* (ET, EF)
Body, leg and foot motions

The times for various sub-groups of each of these units, and under various conditions, are shown in Figure 8.2. In addition, Table 8.2 shows how the MTM-1 notation is constructed.

The time units used in MTM are 'time measurement units' where:

1 TMU = 0.0006 min.

It should be noted that because MTM-1 was developed in America, TMU values do not necessarily correspond to 100 on the BS rating scale. It has been suggested that, for all practical purposes, job times derived using MTM values should be accepted as equivalent to a BS rating of 83.

Figure 8.2 MTM–1 application data in TMUs. Reproduced with the permission of the MTM Association of the UK

TABLE I – REACH – R

Distance Moved Inches	Time TMU				Hand in motion		CASE AND DESCRIPTION
	A	B	C or D	E	A	B	
3/4 or less	2.0	2.0	2.0	2.0	1.5	1.6	A Reach to object in fixed location, or to object in other hand or on which other hand rests
1	2.5	2.5	3.6	2.4	2.3	2.3	
2	4.0	4.0	6.9	3.8	3.5	2.7	
3	5.3	6.3	7.3	5.3	4.5	3.6	B Reach to single object in location which may vary slightly from cycle to cycle
4	6.1	6.4	8.4	6.8	4.9	4.3	
5	6.5	7.8	9.4	7.4	6.3	5.0	
6	7.0	8.6	10.1	8.0	5.7	5.7	
7	7.4	9.3	10.8	8.7	6.1	6.5	C Reach to object jumbled with other objects in a group so that search and select occur
8	7.9	10.1	11.5	9.3	6.5	7.2	
9	8.3	10.8	12.2	9.9	6.9	7.9	
10	8.7	11.5	12.9	10.5	7.3	8.6	
12	9.6	12.9	14.2	11.8	8.1	10.1	
14	10.5	14.4	15.6	13.0	8.9	11.5	D Reach to a very small object or where accurate grasp is required
16	11.4	15.8	17.0	14.2	9.7	12.9	
18	12.3	17.2	18.4	15.5	10.5	14.4	
20	13.1	18.6	19.8	16.7	11.3	15.8	
22	14.0	20.1	21.2	18.0	12.1	17.3	
24	14.9	21.5	22.5	19.2	12.9	18.8	E Reach to indefinite location to get hand in position for body balance or next motion or out of way
26	15.8	22.9	23.9	20.4	13.7	20.2	
28	16.7	24.4	25.3	21.7	14.5	21.7	
30	17.5	25.8	26.7	22.9	15.3	23.	

TABLE II – MOVE – M

Distance Moved Inches	Time TMU			Hand in Motion B	Wt Allowance			CASE AND DESCRIPTION
	A	B	C		Wt (lb) Up to	Fact–or	Con–stant TMU	
3/4 or less	2.0	2.0	2.0	1.7	2.5	1.00	0.0	
1	2.6	2.9	3.4	2.3				
2	3.6	4.6	5.2	2.9	7.5	1.06	2.2	A Move object to other hand or against stop
3	4.9	5.7	6.7	3.6				
4	6.1	6.9	8.0	4.3	12.5	1.11	3.9	
5	7.3	8.0	9.2	5.0				
6	8.1	8.9	10.3	6.7	17.5	1.17	5.6	
7	8.9	9.7	11.1	6.5				
8	9.7	10.6	11.8	7.2	22.5	1.22	7.4	
9	10.5	11.5	12.7	7.9				B Move object to approximate or indefinite location
10	11.3	12.2	13.5	8.6				
12	12.9	13.4	15.2	10.0	27.5	1.28	9.1	
14	14.4	14.6	16.9	11.4				
16	16.0	15.8	18.7	12.8	32.5	1.33	10.8	
18	17.6	17.0	20.4	14.2				
20	19.2	18.2	22.1	15.6	37.5	1.39	12.5	
22	20.8	19.4	23.8	17.0				
24	22.4	20.6	25.5	18.4	42.5	1.44	14.3	C Move object to exact location
26	24.0	21.8	27.3	19.8				
28	25.5	23.1	29.0	21.2	47.5	1.50	16.0	
30	27.1	24.3	30.7	22.7				

TABLE III – TURN AND APPLY PRESSURE – T AND AP

Weight		Time TMU for Degrees Turned										
		30°	45°	60°	75°	90°	105°	120°	135°	150°	165°	180°
Small	0 to 2 lb	2.8	3.5	4.1	4.8	5.4	6.1	6.8	7.4	8.1	8.7	9.4
Medium	2.1 to10 lb	4.4	5.5	6.5	7.5	8.5	9.6	10.6	11.6	12.7	13.7	14.8
Large	10.1 to 35 lb	8.4	10.5	12.3	14.4	16.2	18.3	20.4	22.2	24.3	26.1	28.2

APPLY PRESSURE CASE 1 16.2 TMU APPLY PRESSURE CASE 2 10.6 TMU

123

Figure 8.2 continued

TABLE IV – GRASP – G

Case	Time TMU	DESCRIPTION
1A	2.0	Pick Up Grasp – small, medium or large object by itself, easily grasped
1B	3.8	Very small object or object lying close against a flat surface
1C1	7.3	Interference with grasp on bottom and one side of nearly cylindrical object. Diameter larger than1/2"
1C2	8.7	Interference with grasp on bottom and one side of nearly cylindrical object. Diameter 1/4" to 1/2"
1C3	10.8	Interference with grasp on bottom and one side of nearly cylindrical object. Diameter less than 1/4"
2	5.6	Regrasp
3	5.6	Transfer grasp
4A	7.3	Object jumbled with other objects so search and select occur. Larger than 1" x 1" x 1"
4B	9.1	Object jumbled with other objects so search and select occur. 1/4" x 1/4" x 1/2" to 1" x 1" x 1"
4C	12.9	Object jumbled with other objects so search and select occur. Smaller than 1/4" x 1/4" x 1/2"
6	0	Contact, sliding or hook grasp

TABLE V – POSITION – P

CLASS OF FIT		Symmetry	Easy to Handle	Difficult to Handle
1 – Loose	No pressure required	S	5.6	11.2
		SS	9.1	14.7
		NS	10.4	16.0
2 – Close	Light pressure required	S	16.2	21.6
		SS	19.7	25.3
		NS	21.0	26.6
3 – Exact	Heavy pressure required	S	43.0	48.6
		SS	46.5	52.1
		NS	47.8	53.4

*Distance moved to engage – 1 or less

TABLE VI – RELEASE – RL

Case	Time TMU	DESCRIPTION
1	2.0	Normal release performed by opening fingers as independent motion
2	0	Contact release

TABLE VII – DISENGAGE – D

CLASS OF FIT	Easy to Handle	Difficult to Handle
1 Loose. Very slight effort, blends with subsequent move	4.0	5.7
2 Close. Normal effort, slight recoil	7.5	11.8
3 Tight. Considerable effort, hand recoils markedly	22.9	34.7

TABLE VIII – EYE TRAVEL TIME AND EYE FOCUS – ET AND EF

Eye Travel Time = $15.2 \times \frac{T}{D}$ TMU, with a maximum value of 20 TMU

where T = the distance between points from and to which the eye travels
D = the perpendicular distance from the eye to the line of travel T

Eye Focus Time = 7.3 TMU

Figure 8.2 continued   TABLE IX – BODY, LEG AND FOOT MOTIONS

DESCRIPTION		SYMBOL	DISTANCE	TIME TMU
Foot motion	Hinged at ankle	FM	Up to 4"	8.6
	with heavy pressure	FMP		19.1
Leg or foreleg		LM	Up to 6"	7.1
motion			Each add 1 inch	1.2
Sidestep	Case 1	Complete when	SS-C1	Less than 12"	Use REACH or
		leading leg			MOVE Time
		contacts floor		12"	17.0
	Case 2	Lagging leg must con-	SS-C2	Each add 1 inch	6
		tact floor before next		12"	34.1
		motion can be made		Each add 1 inch	1.1
Bend, stoop or kneel on one knee		B,S, KOK		29.0
Arise		AB, AS, AKOK		31.9
Kneel on floor both knees		KBK		60.4
Arise		AKBK		76.7
Sit		SIT		34.7
Stand from sitting position		STD		43.4
Turn body 45 to 90 degrees –		TBC1		
Case 1 – Complete when leading leg contacts floor				18.6
Case 2 – Lagging leg must contact floor before next		TBC2		37.2
motion can be made				
Walk		W-FT	Per foot	5.3
Walk		W-P	Per pace	15.0
Walk		W-PO	Per pace	17.0

Table 8.2   Examples of MTM-1 notation

Motion	Code	Meaning and TMU value
Reach	R7A	Reach, path of movement 17.5 cm, class A. Hand not in motion at beginning or end (7.4 TMU)
Move	M6A	Move, 15 cm, class A, object weighs less than 1.1 kg (8.9 TMU)
Turn	T90M	Turn, 90° object weighing 0.95 to 4.5 kg (8.5 TMU)
Grasp	G1C1	Grasp, case 1C1 (7.3 TMU)
Position	P2NSE	Position, close fit, non-symmetrical part. Easy to handle. (21.0 TMU)
Release	RL1	Release, case 1 (2.0 TMU)
Disengage	D1D	Disengage, loose fit, difficult to handle (5.7 TMU)
Eye travel	ET10/12	Eye travel, between points 25 cm apart, line of travel 30 cm from eye (12.7 TMU)

EXAMPLE

Tomato picking

Methods by which labour standards for a type of tomato production were examined. Both time study and predetermined time systems were used to determine standards for pruning and harvesting in a singletruss tomato production system. It was expected that a predetermined time system could be used to establish greenhouse labour standards, thus replacing the costly process of direct time study. The results indicated that, although the predetermined time values differed from measured time study by 6.12% to 23% for pruning and from 2.82% to 6.82% for harvesting, the predetermined time system can be used effectively to establish greenhouse labour standards for short cycle tasks without significant loss of accuracy.

Source: Luxhoj, J.T. and Giacomelli, C.A. (1990) Comparison of labour standards for a green-house tomato production system: a case study. *International Journal of Operations and Production Management* **10**(3), pp. 38–49.

MTM–2

MTM–2 was synthesized from MTM–1 data and consists of nine motions—Get; Put; Apply pressure; Regrasp; Eye action; Crank; Step; Foot motion; Bend and arise. Only Get and Put have variable categories, so the MTM–2 data card has only 39 time standards. As with MTM–1, the motions and their various sub-categories are closely defined and precise rules govern their use.

Get (G)	A motion with the predominant purpose of reaching with the hand or fingers to an object, grasping the object, and subsequently releasing it.
	Class A—no grasping motion required.
	Class B—grasping involving closing of the hand or fingers with one motion.
	Class C—complex grasping motion.
	Class W—*get weight*, the action required for the muscles of the hand or arm to take up the weight of an object.
Put (P)	A motion with the predominant purpose of moving an object to a destination with the hand or fingers.
	Class A—continuous smooth motion.
	Class B—discontinuous motion, but without obvious correcting motion (i.e. unintentional stop, hesitation or change in direction).
	Class C—discontinuous motion with obvious correcting motions.
	Class W—*put weight*, in an addition to a put action depending on the weight of the object moved.
Apply pressure (A)	An action with the purpose of exerting muscular force on an object.
Regrasp (R)	The hand action performed with the purpose of changing the grasp of an object.
Eye action (E)	The action with the purpose of either (a) recognizing a readily distinguishable characteristic of an object, or (b) shifting vision to a new viewing area.

Crank (C)	A motion with the purpose of moving an object in a circular path more than 180° with hand or fingers.
Step (S)	Either (a) a leg motion with the purpose of moving the body or (b) a leg motion longer than 30 centimetres.
Foot motion (F)	A short foot or leg motion the purpose of which is *not* to move the body.
Bend and arise (B)	Bend, stoop or kneel on one knee and subsequently arise.

The time standard, in TM units, for each of the motions is easily obtained from the MTM–2 data card (Figure 8.3). The values for the seven motions without variable categories are given at the bottom of the card, while the remaining figures on the card relate to Get and Put. The time standard for both of these is determined by the category of the motion and the distance involved. The left-hand column gives distance in centimetres. The time standards for GW and PW are shown on the card; in the case of the former, a time value of 1 TMU per kilogram applies, and in the case of the latter 1 TMU per 5 kilograms, i.e. the TMU associated with 'Getting' an object of effective net weight 10 kg (GW 10) is 10 TMU, whereas the time standard for PW 10 is 2 TMU.

Figure 8.3 The MTM–2 data card. Reproduced with the permission of the MTM Association of the UK

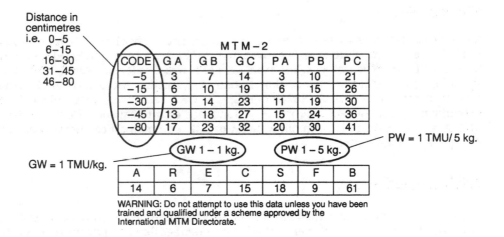

WARNING: Do not attempt to use this data unless you have been trained and qualified under a scheme approved by the International MTM Directorate.

Other MTM-derived PMTSs

MODAPTS

MODAPTS (Modular Arrangement of Predetermined Time Standards) and MODAPTS PLUS is now one of the best known systems for computer application.

4M

The 4M DATA system was also developed specifically for use in a computerized PMTS.

MOST

The MOST system was derived with the objective of simplifying and accelerating application without loss of accuracy. MOST identifies eight key activities.

EXAMPLE

McDonnell Douglas

McDonnell Douglas had to create standards for the assembly of fighter aircraft. A predetermined time system was needed and the MOST computer system was selected. The system had 3 basic attributes which attracted the Company: 1. ease and simplicity of elemental time development, 2. the ability to combine any frequent suboperations, and 3. a method of slotting time values using Occurrence Frequency Group Tables. (These tables are a part of the MOST system; they are designed to predict accuracy levels based on the occurrence of an activity within a given period of time). McDonnell Douglas engineers estimate that they saved 62% of the time they would have required using a conventional approach for setting standards.

Source: Mayo, W. and Horne, R.H. Considerations in developing standards for long cycle assembly *Industrial Engineering* **22** (3), pp. 38–42.

'Clerical' PMTS

Many of the PMTSs described above are of value in the study of most types of manual work. However some systems, also derived from MTM, have been developed specifically for use with office/clerical jobs. For example, PADS was developed around 1989. It is a simplified, predetermined method-time system that analyses the sequences of manual actions performed in clerical work and assigns to each sequence a data code and time determined by the method used in the performance of the sequence. PADS is a 3-level data system consisting of: 1. simplified MTM data, 2. common office motion sequences, 3. application data for specific tasks.

Analytical estimating

Analytical estimating may be described as 'a work measurement technique whereby the time required to carry out elements of a job at a defined level of performance is established from knowledge and practical experience of the elements concerned'.

In some circumstances there are often insufficient synthetic data available to allow time standards to be established, and consequently standards must be constructed using whatever data are available, plus estimates of the basic times for the remaining elements. Clearly a requirement in analytical estimating is that the estimator is completely familiar with, and preferably skilled and experienced in, the work concerned.

The procedure used is much the same as before, in that jobs are first divided into appropriate elements, synthetic data being used for as many of the elements as possible, while basic times are estimated for the remainder. Rather than applying allowances to individual elements, relaxation and contingency allowances are applied as overall or blanket figures for the whole job.

THE LEARNING CURVE

We noted the trend to provide training and to allow a period of learning following introduction of a work method, in chapter 7. We looked also at the nature of the learning curve. Now we must look again at this topic, for often it will be necessary for us to be able to calculate both learning times and performance during learning.

Learning curve calculations:

A 75 per cent learning curve was shown in Figure 7.7. The same 'curve' is shown, with others, on a logarithmic scale, in Figure 8.4. This type of presentation clearly shows one of the important characteristics of the learning effect—predictably. Tables of learning coefficients are also available—Table 8.3.

Figure 8.4 Learning curves (75–90%)

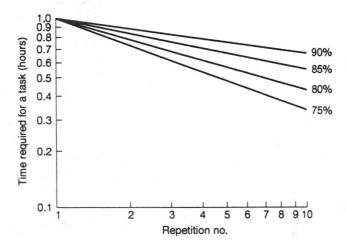

The following formula may also be used for calculating performance times:

$$y = ax^b$$

where y = time for xth repetition

x = number of repetitions

a = time for first repetition

$$b = \frac{\log \text{ of \% improvement rate}/100}{\log \text{ of } 2}$$

For example, the time required for the tenth repetition of a task which initially required one hour, given a 75% learning effect, would be:

$$1 \times 10^{-0.416} = 0.385 \text{ hours}$$

The following examples illustrate further types of learning curve calculations in which the coefficients in Table 8.3 are used.

| Table 8.3 | Learning curve coefficients | | | | | | | | |

Unit number	70% Unit time	70% Total time	75% Unit time	75% Total time	80% Unit time	80% Total time	85% Unit time	85% Total time	90% Unit time	90% Total time
1	1.000	1.000	1.000	1.000	1.000	1.000	1.000	1.000	1.000	1.000
2	0.700	1.700	0.750	1.750	0.800	1.800	0.850	1.850	0.900	1.900
3	0.568	2.268	0.634	2.384	0.702	2.502	0.773	2.623	0.846	2.746
4	0.490	2.758	0.562	2.946	0.640	3.142	0.723	3.345	0.810	3.556
5	0.437	3.195	0.513	3.459	0.596	3.738	0.686	4.031	0.783	4.339
6	0.398	3.593	0.475	3.934	0.562	4.299	0.657	4.688	0.762	5.101
7	0.367	3.960	0.446	4.380	0.534	4.834	0.634	5.322	0.744	5.845
8	0.343	4.303	0.422	4.802	0.512	5.346	0.614	5.936	0.729	6.574
9	0.323	4.626	0.402	5.204	0.493	5.839	0.597	6.533	0.716	7.290
10	0.306	4.932	0.385	5.589	0.477	6.315	0.583	7.116	0.705	7.994
11	0.291	5.223	0.370	5.958	0.462	6.777	0.570	7.686	0.695	8.689
12	0.278	5.501	0.357	6.315	0.449	7.227	0.558	8.244	0.685	9.374
13	0.267	5.769	0.345	6.600	0.438	7.665	0.548	8.792	0.677	10.052
14	0.257	6.026	0.334	6.994	0.428	8.092	0.539	9.331	0.670	10.721
15	0.248	6.274	0.325	7.319	0.418	8.511	0.530	9.861	0.663	11.384
16	0.240	6.514	0.316	7.635	0.410	8.920	0.522	10.383	0.656	12.040
17	0.233	6.747	0.309	7.944	0.402	9.322	0.515	10.898	0.650	12.690
18	0.226	6.973	0.301	8.245	0.394	9.716	0.508	11.405	0.644	13.334
19	0.220	7.192	0.295	8.540	0.338	10.104	0.501	11.907	0.639	13.974
20	0.214	7.407	0.288	8.828	0.381	10.485	0.495	12.402	0.634	14.608
21	0.209	7.615	0.283	9.111	0.375	10.860	0.490	12.892	0.630	15.237
22	0.204	7.819	0.277	9.388	0.370	11.230	0.484	13.376	0.625	15.862
23	0.199	8.018	0.272	9.660	0.364	11.594	0.479	13.856	0.621	16.483
24	0.195	8.213	0.267	9.928	0.359	11.954	0.475	14.331	0.617	17.100
25	0.191	8.404	0.263	10.191	0.355	12.309	0.470	14.801	0.613	17.713
26	0.187	8.591	0.259	10.449	0.350	12.659	0.466	15.267	0.609	18.323
27	0.183	8.774	0.255	10.704	0.346	13.005	0.462	15.728	0.606	18.929
28	0.180	8.954	0.251	10.955	0.342	13.347	0.458	16.186	0.603	19.531
29	0.177	9.131	0.247	11.202	0.338	13.685	0.454	16.640	0.599	20.131
30	0.174	9.305	0.244	11.446	0.335	14.020	0.450	17.091	0.596	20.727
31	0.171	9.476	0.240	11.686	0.331	14.351	0.447	17.538	0.593	21.320
32	0.168	9.644	0.237	11.924	0.328	14.679	0.444	17.981	0.590	21.911
33	0.165	9.809	0.234	12.158	0.324	15.003	0.441	18.422	0.588	22.498
34	0.163	9.972	0.231	12.389	0.321	15.324	0.437	18.859	0.585	23.084
35	0.160	10.133	0.229	12.618	0.318	15.643	0.434	19.294	0.583	23.666
36	0.158	10.291	0.226	12.844	0.315	15.958	0.432	19.725	0.580	24.246
37	0.156	10.447	0.223	13.067	0.313	16.271	0.429	20.154	0.578	24.824

Table 8.3 continued

Unit number	70%		75%		80%		85%		90%	
	Unit time	Total time	Unit time	Total time	Unit time	Total time	Unit time	Total time	Unit time	Total time
38	0.154	10.601	0.221	13.288	0.310	16.581	0.426	20.580	0.575	25.399
39	0.152	10.753	0.219	13.507	0.307	16.888	0.424	21.004	0.573	25.972
40	0.150	10.902	0.216	13.723	0.305	17.193	0.421	21.425	0.571	26.543
41	0.148	11.050	0.214	13.937	0.303	17.496	0.419	21.844	0.569	27.111
42	0.146	11.196	0.212	14.149	0.300	17.796	0.416	22.260	0.567	27.678
43	0.144	11.341	0.210	14.359	0.298	18.094	0.414	22.674	0.565	28.243
44	0.143	11.484	0.208	14.567	0.296	18.390	0.412	23.086	0.563	28.805
45	0.141	11.625	0.206	14.773	0.294	18.684	0.410	23.496	0.561	29.366
46	0.139	11.764	0.204	14.977	0.292	18.975	0.408	23.903	0.559	29.925
47	0.138	11.902	0.202	15.180	0.290	19.265	0.405	24.309	0.557	30.482
48	0.136	12.038	0.201	15.380	0.288	19.552	0.403	24.712	0.555	31.037
49	0.135	12.173	0.199	15.579	0.286	19.838	0.402	25.113	0.553	31.590
50	0.134	12.307	0.197	15.776	0.284	20.122	0.400	25.513	0.552	32.142
51	0.132	12.439	0.196	15.972	0.282	20.404	0.398	25.911	0.550	32.692
52	0.131	12.570	0.194	16.166	0.280	20.684	0.396	26.307	0.548	33.241
53	0.130	12.700	0.192	16.358	0.279	20.963	0.394	26.701	0.547	33.787
54	0.128	12.828	0.191	16.549	0.277	21.239	0.392	27.094	0.545	34.333
55	0.127	12.955	0.190	16.739	0.275	21.515	0.391	27.484	0.544	34.877
56	0.126	13.081	0.188	16.927	0.274	21.788	0.389	27.873	0.542	35.419
57	0.125	13.206	0.187	17.144	0.272	22.060	0.388	28.261	0.541	35.960
58	0.124	13.330	0.185	17.299	0.271	22.331	0.386	28.647	0.539	36.499
59	0.123	13.453	0.184	17.483	0.269	22.600	0.384	29.031	0.538	37.037
60	0.122	13.574	0.183	17.666	0.268	22.868	0.383	29.414	0.537	37.574

EXAMPLES

1. A worker is to repeat a job 20 times. It is estimated that the first time the job is done it will take 1.5 hours. It is estimated that an 80% learning effect will exist. How long will it take to finish all 20 jobs?

    Answer. For 20 units at 80% learning, total time = 1.5 (10.484) = 15.73 hours

2. It is known that the average time for a job over a 'run' of 15 identical jobs is 3 hours. What is the time required for the first and the last jobs if the learning rate is 75%?

    Answer. Total time for 15 units (for an initial time of 1 hour) = 7.319

    Average time for 15 units (for an initial time of 1 hour) = $\dfrac{7.319}{15}$ = 0.4879 hours

Hence:

Time for first unit $\dfrac{3}{0.4879} = 6.149$ hours

Time for last unit $0.325\,(6.149) = 1.998$ hours

In certain circumstances, particularly where work has begun on a particular task, it will be possible to estimate the learning percentage and thus to predict, using the formula above, the time required to complete a task or the performance level at some future date. Thus it will be possible to predict the relatively steady state performance, i.e. the work standard for a particular task. In other circumstances, especially where work has not begun on a task, it will be necessary to estimate the learning percentage in order to predict the 'relatively steady state' work standard. Prediction might be undertaken either by comparing the task to be completed with similar work undertaken in similar circumstances or by analysing the nature of the task by comparison with other tasks.

Because of this learning phenomenon, it will be unrealistic to assume that a constant time is required for the completion of particular tasks, i.e. that a particular work standard will always apply. Thus in direct time study it will be necessary to take some account of the level of learning accomplishment of the worker in order to 'correct' the work standard based on the observed time. Thus if the worker being observed during direct time study is inexperienced, it must be assumed that a more experienced worker will be able to perform the task in a shorter time. However, if a work standard is being determined for a new job, the learning effect must be allowed. Similarly, in establishing work standards for jobs some account must be taken of the 'life' of such jobs. If a worker is to perform a job for some considerable length of time then it is reasonable to assume that he or she will achieve a level of performance equivalent to the relatively steady state level. If, however, the task is to be performed for a relatively short time it might be assumed that learning will still be taking place when the last cycle is completed. In applying indirect work measurement, e.g. PMTS, an allowance must also be made for the learning effect. In general, PMTS times will provide work standards for fully trained, skilled and accomplished workers, i.e. steady state learned performances. Some allowances must be made in such times to provide for the learning effect during the start-up period.

COMPUTER APPLICATIONS
Computers in work measurement

Initially computer programs were used to analyse direct time study data. At a slightly more sophisticated level, programs attach element times to elements by reference to PTMS tables. Thus, if the elements are identified by appropriate code, reference can be made to a data base of element times and these can then be attached to the elements and standard times for the job can be calculated. This application is not far removed from a fully comprehensive computerized PTMS system. Here element and job times will be calculated, for a given job description, by reference to PTMS tables. In addition, by reference to filed data, the computer is able to print out a fully detailed statement of the job methods using full element description, PTMS code, etc. and also, perhaps by checking against certain rules or heuristics, is able to ensure that the method does not violate any of the rules and procedures for effective work methods, e.g. by checking that sequences of elements do not incorporate any difficult motion sequences. In addition, such a program might determine various indices as measures of the effectiveness of the method, e.g. the number of difficult motions used.

Computer applications in work study

We referred to computer applications in Method Study in Chapter 7. Now we can bring those comments together with the above, and consider computer applications which serve both aspects. Many broad-based systems are available. They provide for the following:

(a) preparation of detailed work methods descriptions;

(b) methods development and analysis (and workplace layout);

(c) storage and retrieval of data on work methods and times;

(d) development of workplace layout;

(e) analysis of direct time study data;

(f) determination of time standards;

(g) computerized PMTS.

KEY POINTS FOR CHAPTER 8

Work measurement

is concerned with establishing times for jobs performed in standard conditions.

There are two basic means to obtain times: direct and indirect study.

Time study

is the normal means for direct study.

There are six steps in a time study.

    obtain information

    divide into elements

    time elements

    rate worker

    provide allowances

    calculate standard time

Other methods

for direct time study include:

    activity sampling

Indirect work measurement

methods include:

    synthetic timing

    PMTS

    Analytical estimating

PMTS systems include:

    MTM–1

    MTM–2, synthesized from MTM–1 and based on 9 motions

The learning curve

describes how task times might reduce with increased repetition.

Computers

are widely used in work measurement.

FURTHER READING

Whitmore, D. A. (1987) *Work Measurement*, 2nd edition. Heinemann, London. (See also references as follows for Chapter 7.)

Hall, M. (1991) Computer work measurement systems, *Management Services* 35, 2, pp. 30–35.

QUESTIONS

8.1 The figures below are the observed times obtained during 25 observations of a single element of a manual task. Have sufficient observations of this element been made to provide an accuracy of ± 5% with a confidence interval of 95%?

Observation number (N)	Time for element (in 1/100 min)	Observation number (N)	Time for element (in 1/100 min)
1	40	14	41
2	45	15	43
3	43	16	44
4	42	17	46
5	45	18	43
6	47	19	42
7	40	20	42
8	48	21	44
9	47	22	43
10	42	23	40
11	40	24	42
12	39	25	45
13	42		

8.2 Using the data given on the sheet shown on p.135, calculate the output of a worker at standard performance for an eight-hour shift.

8.3 Assume that after the application of appropriate work simplification techniques you have taken a direct time study and you get the results shown on p.135 (time in minutes):

(a) Elements 2 and 4 are machine paced.

(b) You have a decision rule which states that any reading which varies by more than 25% from the average of all readings for an element will be considered 'abnormal'.

(c) The operator is rated at 120%.

(d) Allowances have been set at (for an eight-hour shift):

personal time	30 minutes
unavoidable delay	36 minutes
fatigue	5%

Table for Question 8.2					
Study		**Worker**	**Times**	**Date**	**Sheet**
		Male	1/10 min		1

Element number	Rating	Observed time	Ineffective time	Basic time	Element number	Rating	Observed time	Ineffective time	Basic time
1	110	0.45			1	105	0.45		
2	100	0.70			2	110	0.70		
3	110	0.35			3	115	0.40		
1	105	0.50			1	100	0.45		
2	110	0.65			2	100	0.80		
3	105	0.40			3	90	0.50		
1	100	0.45			1	95	0.52		
2	100	0.72			2	100	0.75		
3	100	0.42			3	110	0.45		
					1	100	0.45		
–			3.80		2	100	0.75		
					3	100	0.40		
1	100	0.47			1	110	0.52		
2	90	0.85			2	100	0.75		
3	110	0.50			3	100	0.38		
1	100	0.45							
2	100	0.75					Adjust jig every 25 cycles		
3	110	0.48							

Allowances: Fatigue 5%   Personal 10%   Delay 2%

(e) The operator, who is paid on a straight time rate, receives 50p per hour.

(f) Material costs are 3p per piece.

(g) Overhead costs are calculated at 80% of the sum of direct labour and material costs.

Table for Question 8.3					
Cycle number	**Element number**				
	1	2	3	4	5
1	0.15	0.62	0.33	0.51	0.23
2	0.14	0.58	0.20	0.50	0.26
3	0.13	0.59	0.36	0.55	0.24
4	0.18	0.61	0.37	0.49	0.25
5	0.22	0.60	0.34	0.45	0.27

How many pieces per shift should each operator produce and what is the production cost per piece? Discuss the appropriateness of these estimates for planning purposes.

8.4 'The principal benefit in using predetermined motion time systems to develop work standards is the avoidance of performance rating, and hence the avoidance of undue dispute over the resultant standards.' Discuss.

8.5 (a) An 80% learning effect is known to exist in a situation in which the first performance of a manual task takes 100 hours. What is the average performance time for the task after 32 task repetitions?

(b) How many hours are required for the eighth performance of the task?

(c) How many repetitions of the task are required before a target performance level of 41 hours is achieved?

Chapter 9

Workplaces, technology and jobs

ISSUES

How do we design an efficient 'worker/machine' system?
What are the requirements of a well-designed work place?
How do we design a VDU workplace?
How does technology impact on work?
How should tasks be divided between people and machines?
How should jobs be designed?
What is group working?

In this chapter, we concentrate on work and working conditions. The topics covered complement those in Chapters 7 and 8. They relate largely to the 'behavioural' dimensions in the design of work and work systems.

WORKING CONDITIONS

Ergonomics

In this section we focus on people at work and particularly on the design of workplaces and equipment.

The worker–machine system

Despite increasing automation people are still essential in most operating systems. Certainly the worker's role is changing—the worker being relieved of many routine and/or hazardous tasks. This trend will continue, but there will always be a need for some people. The emphasis will, increasingly, be on the design and management of worker–machine systems. Here we look briefly at the nature of worker–machine systems as a preliminary to further consideration of ergonomics. (NB: Throughout, our use of 'machine' implies equipment of all types.)

The efficiency with which the worker functions depends on environmental factors, on his or her own characteristics, such as motivation, training and experience, and on the efficiency with which the machine provides the information feedback and accepts control measures.

If we accept, for our present purposes, that workers and their characteristics are largely fixed, this leaves us with only three aspects of the worker–machine system to discuss:

(a) design of information displays;

(b) design of controls;

(c) environmental factors.

Design of information displays

The most common means of displaying or communicating information is visual. We can identify two categories of visual display: analogue and digital. We can further classify visual display as follows:

(a) Displays used without controls:

1. for quantitative measurement, e.g. clocks, meters, the purpose of which is to determine whether the correct value exists, or whether corrective action is necessary;

2. for check reading, i.e. to determine the proximity of a characteristic to a desired value, and not for obtaining a precise measurement;

3. for comparison, e.g. to compare the readings on two dials;

4. for warning; although warning systems often include audible devices, lights are also frequently used.

(b) Displays used with controls:

1. for controlling, i.e. to extract information and measure the effect of corrective action;

2. for setting, i.e. to use a control and display to ensure that a correct value is obtained, for example setting the running speed of an engine after starting up;

3. for tracking, i.e. to use a control continuously to correct movement or to compensate for external factors, for example keeping two indicators synchronized, or on target, by means of a control.

There are many sources of 'standards' and design data for visual displays. They are not identical in their recommendations, but the following covers most of the important points:

(a) Instruments should enable the worker to read information as accurately as necessary, but not more so.

(b) The scale used should be both simple and logical, using the minimum number of suitable divisions.

(c) The scale should provide information in an immediately usable form, and no mental conversions should be necessary.

(d) Scales that must be read quantitatively should be designed so that workers need not interpolate between marks.

(e) Vertical figures should be used on stationary dials and radial figures used on rotating dials.

(f) Scales should not be obscured by the pointer.

Also in the visual category are written or printed information and VDUs. Visual methods of communication involving permanent copies, such as printed output from computers, are particularly valuable where the message must be retained for future reference, where there is no urgency in the transmission of the information, and where long or complex messages are involved.

Instruments such as gauges and dials are of value where many sets of information are to be transmitted, and where the worker's job permits him or her to receive such information when it arrives.

Aural information 'displays', such as telephones, buzzers, bells and speech, are more appropriate where speed of transmission is important, where messages are short and uncomplicated, and where a record of the message need not be retained. Often aural communication is essential in industry, where visual channels are overloaded or where the environment does not permit visual communication.

Design of controls

The types of controls commonly used and their suitability for various tasks are shown in Table 9.1. The first and most important step is to select the type of control best suited to the requirements. This will involve answering the following questions:

(a) What is the control for?

(b) What is required, e.g. in terms of precision, force, speed, number of settings?

Table 9.1	Suitability of various controls for different purposes			
Type of control	**Speed**	**Accuracy**	**Force**	**Range**
Cranks				
small	Good	Poor	Unsuitable	Good
large	Poor	Unsuitable	Good	Good
Handwheels	Poor	Good	Fair/Poor	Fair
Knobs	Unsuitable	Fair	Unsuitable	Fair
Levers				
horizontal	Good	Poor	Poor	Poor
vertical (to–from body)	Good	Fair	{ Short Poor / Long Good	Poor
vertical (across body)	Fair	Fair	Fair	Unsuitable
Pedals	Good	Poor	Good	Unsuitable
Pushbuttons	Good	Unsuitable	Unsuitable	Unsuitable
Rotary selector switch	Good	Good	Unsuitable	Unsuitable
Joystick selector switch	Good	Good	Poor	Unsuitable

Source: Adapted from 'Ergonomics for Industry No. 7, Ministry of Technology, 1965, by permission of the Controller, HMSO

(c) What information must be displayed by the control, i.e. must the control be identified from the others, must it be picked out in the dark, and should the worker be able to tell how the control is set?

(d) How do environmental conditions affect or limit the use of the control?

Having selected the most appropriate types of controls to use, they should be logically arranged, clearly marked and easily accessible. They should suit the capabilities of the operator and should be positioned to distribute the loads evenly among them. Functionally similar controls may be combined; also, as far as possible, controls should 'match' the changes they produce in the machine or the system (e.g. clockwise rotation to 'increase' something, etc.). There should be consistency in the direction of movement of controls and they should be close to, and identifiable with, their associated displays.

EXAMPLE

Three Mile Island nuclear power plant

Poor information flow is judged to have contributed to the 1979 accident at the Three Mile Island nuclear power plant. Today, the facility is a model for the effective collection, analysis and distribution of critical data. As poor layout and a confusing labelling of instruments is judged to have contributed to the accident, the control room has since been redesigned to provide operators with more intelligible, reliable information. Now control room staff utilize high-speed colour-display monitors and instrumentation panels that have been marked to show normal ranges. Deficiencies outside of the control room became increasingly pressing and a range of new projects has also been implemented, including systems for on-line radiation-exposure monitoring, maintenance and work management. The plant performance monitoring system now automatically updates up to 1,000 of the 3,500 data points it monitors every 3 minutes, covering measurements of temperatures, pressures and flows.

Source: Buchanan, L. (1992) An information powerhouse *CIO* **6**(11) pp. 50–56

Environmental factors

The provision of good workplace lighting, heating, ventilation, etc. is often a statutory requirement, and is necessary, though insufficient, to motivate workers and provide job satisfaction.

Lighting

Good lighting is not achieved merely by adding extra lights, since the type of lighting should depend on the type of work being performed, the size of objects, the accuracy, speed and duration of the work, etc. An adequate lighting system should provide:

(a) sufficient brightness;

(b) uniform illumination;

(c) a contrast between brightness of job and of background;

(d) no direct or reflected glare.

Lighting should be arranged to avoid 'flicker' and to provide an acceptable amount of shadow. Notice that freedom from shadow is not always desirable, since in certain circumstances, e.g. inspection, shadows can be used to improve the visibility of details by accentuating surface details.

Noise

We can make the obvious distinction between continuous and intermittent noise. Both are to some extent inevitable, and both can have detrimental effects on behaviour and may even cause physical damage to the worker.

Noise levels and the effect on workers can be reduced by controlling noise at its source, by putting barriers between the worker and the source of noise, by providing protective devices for the workers, or by modifying work processes to reduce workers' exposure to noise. Prolonged exposure to continuous noise levels in excess of 90 dB (decibels) is likely to result in hearing loss; 40 dB is an acceptable maximum level for comfort.

Sudden noises greatly in excess of the background noise level can produce a reaction, shock or startling effect which could have disastrous consequences for workers employed on or close to machinery. Regular intermittent noise is a common feature where, for example, automatic machines are involved, but there is a danger of underestimating its effect by assuming an eventual adjustment by the worker to the situation.

Figure 9.1 Tolerance to heat. From Woodson, W. S. and Conover, D. W. (1964) *Human Engineering Guide for Equipment Designers*. Berkeley: University of California Press. Reproduced with permission

Temperature and ventilation

Figure 9.1 shows that the type of work and its duration determines the individual's tolerance to heat, and Table 9.2 indicates the relationship between space requirements and ventilation.

Workplace design

In many jobs the worker has to remain sitting or standing for long periods of time while performing a given series of tasks. Inadequate design of workplaces will inhibit the ability of the worker to perform his or her tasks and may result in injuries, strain or fatigue, or a reduction in quality or output.

Determination of workplace requirements will involve an examination of the work elements which constitute the work cycle and an examination of the body measurements, reach and movement capacities of the worker.

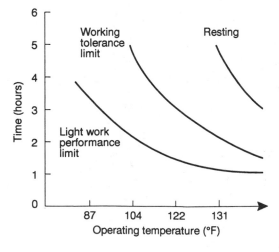

Table 9.2	Relationship between space requirements and ventilation

Net volume of space (cubic feet) Fresh air supply (cubic feet per minute)	Volume of space required per person (cubic feet)
1000	500
600	450
400	400
200	300
100	200
60	150
35	100
22	65

Source: Fogel, L. J. (1963) Biotechnology: Concepts and Applications. Englewood Cliffs, NJ: Prentice-Hall. Reproduced with permission

Table 9.3	Anthropometric data (mean dimensions, adult males and adult females) used in Figure 9.3

Measurement	Adult male (mean dimension, cm)	Adult female (mean dimension, cm)
1	175	162
2	90	85
3	48.5	45.5
4	58	55.5
5	36	34
6	55	51
7	9	8.5
8	178	162
9	107	101.5
10	87	79
11	59.5	56
12	47.5	46.5
13	47	43
14	22.8	–
15	27.5	24.5
16	44.5	39.5
17	33	34.5
18	9	8.8

Anthropometric data

Figure 9.2 and Table 9.3 give anthropometric data, in terms of mean dimensions in centimetres, for western adult males and females. The dimensions for males given in Table 9.3

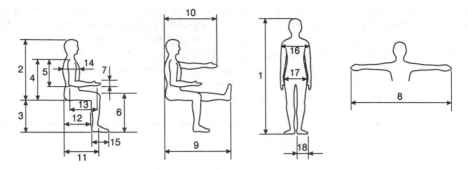

Figure 9.2 Anthropometric data (for dimensions see Table 9.3)

correspond to a 'nude' height of 175 cm, and those for females to a height of 162 cm. Corrections for different heights can be made by increasing or decreasing the given dimensions in proportion to the different heights.

Aetna Insurance

Aetna Life and Casualty has studied office ergonomics since 1979, when its facilities planning department examined data processing workstations. That study led to the replacement of traditional metal furniture with new furniture systems designed for computer use. In a study to determine if the ergonomic furniture was providing productivity benefits, managers said the new furniture and other changes had accounted for a 10% to 15% productivity boost.

Source: (1989) Aetna's edge in office ergonomics *Occupational Hazards* **51**(10), pp. 133–135.

VDU (visual display unit) and keyboard work

A substantial proportion of people now work with VDUs and keyboards. Increasingly this is a normal feature of working life in all types of organization. Both this importance and also the fact that there are particular issues relating to the design of such workplaces, justify our devoting some space to the subject.

There is evidence that VDU work gives rise to physical discomforts, especially visual fatigue, headaches, back and shoulder ache. Clearly, good ergonomic design of VDU workplaces is important. Much of the previous discussion is relevant here but there are additional factors, which in the case of some countries are covered by regulations or official guidelines, e.g. protection against glare, action to prevent repetitive strain, provision of rest periods, etc.

European Community directive

The directive passed by the Council of the European Commission in May 1990 deals with the minimum safety and health requirements for work involving visual display units (VDU). European Community member states were required to introduce the changes necessary to comply with the directive by 31 December 1992, and to report to the commission every 5 years on the implementation of the provision, giving the points of view of both employers and workers. The directive applies to employees who habitually use VDUs for a significant part of their normal work. Employers must analyse workstations to evaluate the safety and health conditions to which workers are exposed. In particular, risks to eyesight, physical problems, and mental stress must be considered. Minimum requirements were established with regard to: 1. the equipment, 2. the environment, and 3. the operator–computer interface.

The sections below outline some of the major considerations in the design of VDU workplaces.

Visual conditions

A major problem in designing VDU workplaces is the distribution of luminescences (light emissions) at the workplace. A compromise must be found between the low luminescence required of the display screen and the high luminescence required for reading the keyboard and printed documents.

Symbols on the VDU are produced by an electron beam which excites an emission of light in the phosphor coating of the screen. There is a choice of different phosphors, and this influences not only luminous intensity but also colour, flicker and the life of the screen. The legibility of symbols on the screen depends on the contrast, and it has been suggested that a contrast of 10:1 is near optimum, while the maximum and minimum values are 15:1 and 2.5:1 respectively. Depending on the level of illumination in the room the symbol luminescence of 90 cd/m² is near optimum, with maximum and minimum values of 160 and 20 respectively. Symbol colour is not considered to be of critical importance; however, 'flicker' is a major factor. A 'critical flicker frequency' is that at which the individual can just detect a flicker in a light source. This varies from person to person but is normally in the range 20 to 60 Hz. It is dependent also on the flicker area, the shape of the light source, its illumination, location in the visual field, etc. The closer the worker to the screen and the higher the luminescence, the higher the critical flicker frequency. The surface of VDUs can reflect surrounding features, and this can reduce symbol contrast and increase strain. Such reflections can be muted by surface treatment or the use of filters.

The cabinet surrounding the VDU screen should have a higher reflection factor than the screen itself to provide a smooth transition to the normally brighter surroundings. The luminescence of keyboards should not differ substantially from that of screens, which in most situations will necessitate the use of a dark-coloured keyboard. Concave keys can result in reflections.

Normally the level of illumination required for reading a manuscript will be higher than that required for other aspects of VDU work. However, substantial contrast with the level of illumination at the workplace is undesirable, so in most cases 'manuscript illumination' will be lower than that provided for normal office work; hence legibility must be good. Printed character size, character colour and paper colour will affect legibility.

Ambient lighting conditions in working environments where VDUs exist will often be influenced by the needs of other workers on different types of work. In such cases VDUs must be positioned and oriented to prevent glare and to minimize the contrast between screen, keyboard and manuscript illumination, and levels of background illumination. It has been suggested that the area surrounding the VDU workplace should have a horizontal illumination of 300 lx and a background luminescence of 20 to 40 cd/m².

Heat and noise

The power delivered to the VDU and associated equipment is partly converted to heat and can result in a higher temperature than is desirable unless adequate local ventilation is provided. The largest contributor to local heat production will be the control unit for the VDU; the heat output of such units, typically in the range 75 to 100 W, must be considered in determining the thermal balance for working environments. Convention effects which might produce draughts and humidity requirements must also be considered.

Several sources of noise are associated with the operation of a VDU: mechanical ventilation of a VDU can add considerably to the local noise level, and keyboard noise and the noise caused by printers can be substantial. A recommended noise level below 55 dB(A) has been recommended, while VDU tasks requiring high levels of mental concentration might be adversely affected by background noise levels greater than 45 dB(A).

Ergonomic considerations

The checklists below deal specifically with a VDU working environment comprising VDU screen, keyboard, manuscript or printed material (being read) and operator.

Desk

(a) Adjustable desk height is desirable. A height indicator to facilitate adjustment by different workers is beneficial.

(b) The desk top should be large enough to allow for all items used by the operator and for readjustment/repositioning of those items. The VDU, keyboard and documents should all be included in a range of 50 to 70 cm from the eyes.

(c) The desk top should consist of one piece with no gaps, joints, etc.

(d) The desk top should have a non-reflecting surface and a pleasant (not a cold) feel.

Keyboard

(a) The thickness/height of the keyboard should not exceed 20 mm including the second row of keys and it should be as narrow as possible.

(b) Keyboards with a height greater than 30 mm should be sunk into the desk (although this reduces the possibility of relocation, etc.).

(c) It should be easy to push or turn the keyboard.

(d) The keyboard should stand firmly.

(e) The keyboard should not be attached to the screen unit.

(f) The slope of the keyboard should be between 5° and 15°.

(g) The keyboard should not have more keys than are needed for the work in question.

(h) It will often be better to change from one keyboard to another to accommodate different types of work rather than have a comprehensive, over-large keyboard to accommodate all requirements.

Keys

(a) The force required to press a key should be 0.25 to 1.5 N.

(b) The distance of travel in key depression should be 3 to 4.8 mm.

(c) The length of a square key should be 12 to 15 mm.

(d) The distance from centre to centre of adjacent keys should be 18 to 20 mm.

(e) The function keys should be larger than, and a different colour from, other keys.

(f) The symbols should be engraved in the key surface or printed below a non-reflecting transparent cap.

(g) The keys should be concave but only enough to match the convexity of fingers and not so much as to cause undue reflection.

(h) Guide keys should be marked with a small raised dot for easier touch typing.

Screen unit

(a) It should be possible to adjust the height of the screen unit and to tilt (–3° to +20°) or turn it without tools.

(b) It should be possible to push the screen unit backwards and forwards on the desk. Distance markers will facilitate readjustment.

(c) The screen unit should stand firmly and not be too heavy to move.

Documents

(a) A manuscript stand should be stable and adjustable in height and sideways. Tilt (+15° to +20° when at side of VDU; +60° to +75° between VDU and keyboard).

(b) The best position for the documents is at the same distance from the eyes as the screen is, and as close to the screen as possible. Abrupt changes in luminescence and reflection must be avoided.

Work schedules

Views on the definition of fair rest periods for VDU workers are numerous. Collective agreements in industry have envisaged short breaks after rather longer periods, e.g. 15 minutes minimum after two hours' work at a VDU. Clearly the 'relaxation' allowance provided (see Chapter 8) in VDU work will be significant in most situations. This is an area in which legislation and collective agreements will undoubtedly have considerable impact.

Health and safety

Our discussion of working conditions and job design leads us to consider issues relating to health and safety at work—important aspects for operations managers who in many cases are legally responsible for the health and safety of their staff. Employees are of course required to carry responsibility for the safety of themselves and their colleagues through both the observance of safety practices and the adoption of those working methods in which they have been instructed. The employer or manager is required to provide an overall working environment, including adequate training, so that it is safe and healthy for employees to undertake their jobs. In effect, therefore, the safety of workers becomes the individual responsibility of managers responsible for departments as well as the responsibility of the employing organization.

In considering health and safety we are concerned in effect with the prevention of accidents or ill health. Such subjects should of course be considered in a preventive rather than a remedial sense, since it is in the interests of all parties to prevent the occurrence of illness or accidents, but in order to indicate the magnitude of the problem it will be appropriate to remind ourselves of the effects of accidents and the extent to which accidents have occurred in industry and commerce in the past.

Industrial accidents

In most industrialized countries, statistics reveal that accidents are one of the most significant causes of lost working days—in many countries an accident is defined as something which 'causes disablement for more than three days'.

In general, at least in factories, the major source of accidents is concerned with the handling of goods, e.g. lifting, placing, movement, etc., at the workplace and between workplaces. Falls, and accidents caused by machinery, are the next most important source of accidents. Most severe accidents occur as a result of individuals becoming 'involved' with machinery, while accidents occurring during the handling of goods comprise a major proportion of those accidents causing lesser or shorter periods of disablement. Fires and explosions are also a major source of accidents.

The economic implications to the employer resulting from an accident include:

(a) working time lost by the employee;

(b) time lost by other employees who choose to or must of necessity stop work at the time of or following the accident;

(c) time lost by supervision, management and technical staff following the accident;

(d) proportion of the cost of employing first aid, medical staff, etc.;

(e) cost of disruption to the operation;

(f) cost of any damage to the equipment or any cost associated with the subsequent modification of the equipment;

(g) cost of any compensation payments or fines resulting from legal action;

(h) costs associated with increased insurance premiums;

(i) reduced output from the injured employee on return to work;

(j) cost of reduced morale, increased absenteeism, increased labour turnover among employees.

This is just one side of the equation, since the injured person, his or her dependants, colleagues, etc. also incur some cost. Certainly it would be socially, morally and probably legally unacceptable to consider accidents only in terms of direct and indirect cost to the employers.

Preventive action

The prevention of illness and accidents requires efforts on the part of employees and management, the latter including those responsible for the design of the operating system and its staffing. Some of the steps which might be taken to reduce the frequency and severity of accidents are as follows:

(a) developing a safety awareness among all staff;

(b) developing effective consultation between management, workers and unions so that safety and health rules and procedures can be agreed and followed;

(c) giving adequate instruction in safety for new and transferred workers, or where working methods are changed;

(d) minimize materials handling and provide, as far as possible, for safe working and operation;

(e) ensuring a satisfactory standard for all equipment;

(f) good maintenance of all equipment.

Fire prevention and control represent a further area for preventive action. The main causes of fire tend to be associated with electrical appliances and installations. Smoking is a major source of fires in business premises. The Fire Protection Association (of the UK) suggest the following guidelines for fire prevention and control:

(a) Management should accept that fire prevention policies and practices must be established and reviewed regularly.

(b) Management should be aware of the possible effects and consequences of fires in terms of loss of buildings, plant and output, damage to records, effects on customers and workers, etc.

(c) Fire risks should be identified, particularly as regards sources of ignition, presence of combustible materials, and the means by which fires can spread.

(d) The responsibility for fire prevention should be established.

(e) A fire officer should be appointed.

(f) A fire prevention drill should be established and practised.

As for other sources of illness and accidents, there are detailed guidelines for fire prevention and checklists for use in assessing the adequacy of existing procedures and in designing new procedures.

EXAMPLE

Arley Merchandise

Arley Merchandise Corp. found that it needed to take a more comprehensive and proactive approach to both accident prevention and post-injury management. The process was based on a joint labour-management team that evaluated present safety practices and management systems and identified areas for improvement. Ergonomic-related training played a major part in the process. Workstation and seating adjustability were addressed first. The concept of substantial employee involvement in both the planning and execution stages of any project will increase the chances for success. By encouraging and empowering employees to take an active role in making improvements, morale and self-esteem were lifted, interest intensified and efficiency, productivity and quality improved.

Source: Costa, J. (1993) Better designs for the times *ISS* **34**(6), pp. 32–35.

TECHNOLOGY AND WORK

We have noted that because of technological developments workers' roles in all types of operating system are changing. It is appropriate now to look more closely at the nature and effects of such change. We will do so by focusing on 'automation.

The nature of mechanization and automation

One attempt to overcome some of the problems of defining automation suggests that, in general, automation means something significantly more automated than that which existed previously. Hence automation in one industry may contrast both in level of development and in characteristics with automation elsewhere. Other authors have taken the view that the elimination of direct manual involvement in *control* is the key feature of automation. In other words, mere elimination of work tasks (i.e. 'doing' tasks) is not automation but simply mechanization. It is reasonable, therefore, to view automation as a trend rather than a state. Mechanization is an aspect of, or component part of, automation; it is concerned with activities, while automation also implies the use of control procedures which are also largely dependent on human involvement. The two terms will be used in this manner throughout the remainder of this chapter.

EXAMPLE

Banking

New technology in banking is readily evident to the customer (automatic dispensers of cash, statements, etc.; automatic in-payments, telephone/computer banking, etc.). These are associated with new technology developments 'within' the banks and the banking system. Technology-related changes in the nature of the work of employees are also evident—and have been studied. Some of the principal findings of such studies for clerical type jobs in banking and insurance, are as follows:

Work level	Changes
Micro (i.e. tasks and jobs performed)	Increased load and complexity
	More stress
	Problems with workplace ergonomics
	Less control over work and work pace
	Changed skill requirments
	Less scope for decision-making
Macro i.e. work systems and relationships between jobs	Integration of previously separate tasks/jobs
	Increased technical communication between workers
	Reduced face-to-face/social contact between workers
Ecology i.e. contact, form and organization of work	Less contact with customers
	Changing working patterns (shifts, hours)
	Changing employment patterns (fewer female full-time jobs— more part-time work— more female part-timers).

Source: Wild R. (1991) Technology, work, and workplaces. *Management Decision* **29**(8), pp. 32–37.

The impact of automation

The relationships between technology and work are complex. Technological change, such as increasing automation, has both direct and indirect impacts on work.

We will look first at the broad context and then at specific 'cause and effect' type relationships.

The technological capability available to an organization will influence the strategy of that organization, i.e. what it seeks to do and how it aims to do it. This must influence the nature of the operations which are established, and thus the whole context, organization, arrangement and nature of the work associated with those operations. So, technology is an enabling factor making possible certain competitive strategies for organizations (see Chapter 2). So, also, technology makes possible certain types of work system and different forms of work, and working contexts. This is the biggest impact that technological change has on work. It is the indirect impact—and it opens up possibilities for the nature of jobs that might not have existed before.

But technology, and technological change such as automation, also has a direct impact on work—at the more 'micro' level. It can directly and immediately change the nature of the tasks which are undertaken, as well as the work cycles, skill requirements, and the interaction of groups of workers with one another and with others. This is, perhaps the level of the relationship of technology and work which is of greatest and most immediate interest to us here, so it will be appropriate to summarize some of the findings of studies of the impact of automation on work.

With increasing automation, jobs tend to become more demanding, varied, interesting and challenging for many workers, although in some cases such changes may be of a temporary nature—a result of a 'start-up' situation. Technical know-how tends to become more important and workers may expect increased job content together with increased demands on skills, knowledge and training. In general, greater job complexity and responsibility, and therefore greater intrinsic rewards, are associated with work in automated systems, but often at the expense of increased worker inactivity.

A further consideration is that of social interaction. Often the greater distance between workers in automated systems results in reduced social interaction. However, as full automation is approached, the central grouping of controls gives rise to grouping of workers. Up to a certain level, therefore, automation increases the ratio of working space to people and therefore inhibits social relationships. The relationship of workers and their supervisors is also affected by automation, the general view being one of increased contact and improved worker/supervisor relations. An increased separation of workers from both operations and their outputs is often found. Increased training needs are often associated with the wider responsibilities of automated jobs, while emphasis on vigilance and monitoring duties, the importance of minimizing process disruption, the consequences of breakdowns, and the comparative inactivity of workers are considered to lead occasionally to increased stress.

The above comments relate mainly to situations approaching full automation. The effects of lower levels of automation have received less attention; however, we can conclude tentatively that such developments tend to give rise to:

(a) the increasing isolation of workers and hence a reduction in social interaction;

(b) a reduction in the amount of physical effort required, largely due to reduced handling requirements;

(c) a loss of worker control of work pace and worker independence from the machine cycle;

(d) improved working conditions and increased safety;

(e) increased use of shift working.

In summary, therefore, although the manner and characteristics of the development of automation can be affected by other factors, in general at higher levels of automation, work becomes more varied and demands greater use of skills and knowledge, offset to some degree by physical inactivity coupled with the need for vigilance, which could give rise to a stressful situation. Equally, it is clear that what has generally been referred to as mechanization, because of continued dependence on manual intervention in control, offers few of these job characteristics.

Worker–machine systems

Full automation obviates the need for direct human intervention, except perhaps in a supervisory capacity, but semi-automation, or advanced mechanization, requires some human contribution in, for example, control. Semi-automation is commonplace. In these

Table 9.4	Skills and abilities of man and machines	
Functional area	**Man**	**Machine**
Data sensing	Can monitor low-probability events not feasible for automatic systems because of number of events possible.	Limited program complexity and alternatives; unexpected events cannot be handled adequately.
	Absolute thresholds of sensitivity are very low under favourable conditions.	Generally not as low as human thresholds.
	Can detect masked signals effectively in overlapping noise spectra.	Poor signal detection when noise spectra overlap.
	Able to acquire and report information incidental to primary activity.	Discovery and selection of incidental intelligence not feasible in present designs.
	Not subject to jamming by ordinary methods	Subject to disruption by interference and noise.
Data processing	Able to recognize and use information, redundancy (pattern) of real world to simplify complex situations.	Little or no perceptual constancy or ability to recognize similarity of pattern in spatial or temporal domain.
	Can make inductive decisions in new situations; can generalize from few data.	Virtually no capacity for creative or inductive functions.
	Reasonable reliability in which the same purpose can be accomplished by different approach (corollary of reprogramming ability).	High reliability may increase cost and complexity; particularly reliable for routine repetitive functioning.
	Computation weak and relatively inaccurate; optimal game theory strategy cannot be routinely expected.	Can be programmed to use optimum strategy for high-probability situations.
	Channel capacity limited to relatively small information throughput rates.	Channel capacity can be enlarged as necessary for task.
	Can handle variety of transient and some permanent overloads without disruption.	Transient and permanent overloads may lead to disruption of system.
	Short-term memory relatively poor.	Short-term memory and access times excellent.

Table 9.4 (continued)		
Functional area	**Man**	**Machine**
Data	Can tolerate only relatively low imposed forces and generate relatively low forces for short periods.	Can withstand very large forces and generate them for prolonged periods.
	Generally poor at tracking though satisfactory where frequent reprogramming required; can change to meet situation. Is best at position tracking where changes are under 3 radians per second.	Good tracking characteristics over limited requirements.
	Performance may deteriorate with time, because of boredom, fatigue or distraction; usually recovers with rest.	Behaviour decrement relatively small with time; wear maintenance and product quality control necessary.
	Relatively high response latency.	Arbitrarily low response latencies possible.
Economic properties	Relatively inexpensive for available complexity and in good supply; must be trained.	Complexity and supply limited by cost and time; performance built in.
	Light in weight, small in size for function achieved; power requirement less than 100 watts.	Equivalent complexity and function would require radically heavier elements, enormous power and cooling resources.
	Maintenance may require life support system.	Maintenance problem increases disproportionately with complexity.
	Non-expendable; interested in personal survival; emotional.	Expendable; non-personal; will perform without distraction.

Source: Beishon, J. and Peters, G. (eds) (1981) Systems Behaviour. London: Harper & Row. Reproduced with permission

situations there is some sharing of work between people and machines. A work system, whether manual, automated or a combination, will be established to fulfil certain job requirements. Certain tasks or activities must be performed. One requirement in the design of the system, therefore, is the allocation of these tasks to the active parts of the system, i.e. their division between man and machine. This allocation of functions must reflect the abilities of man and machine, i.e. their skills, capabilities and limitations, and, where a choice exists, the relative cost of performing a task by man and machine.

A general procedure for the allocation of functions is outlined below:

Step 1: *Job or task analysis*—identify jobs/tasks which must be undertaken by the work system.

Step 2: *Skills analysis*—identify the skills/abilities of the component parts of the work system, i.e. the worker(s) and the machines.

Step 3: *Allocation of tasks*—allocate tasks from 1 to the component parts of the system as far as possible to match 2.

A general skills statement for 'man' and machines is given in Table 9.4.

IBM (UK)

In 1989 IBM (UK) installed an automated robotic assembly line at its Greenock, Scotland factory for the assembly of PC monitors. At the time, the £6-million facility was one of the most advanced robot assembly lines in the world.

Late in 1993, the company threw out the line. It had decided that humans produced a better product with higher productivity. Now 50 workers make about 700 items each shift, i.e. compared to fewer than 25 people involved in managing the robotic line which produced 550 items per shift.

The key reasons for the change were the need for greater flexibility to deal with the far greater product mix of screen sizes, features, specifications, etc. now needed and related to this, the need to avoid having to shut down the line to reconfigure the robots for each major product change.

Source: Hallahan, S. (1994) All hands to the production lines. *The Times (London)* 29 July, pp. 29.

THE WORKER

Job design and work organization

No longer is the design of work and jobs simply to do with the application of method study, work measurement and ergonomics. There is a need to consider the behavioural aspects of work and job design.

Views about how work and jobs should be designed have changed considerably. Initially the design or specification of work made few assumptions about the capability of workers beyond considering them as programmable 'machines'. This *'Scientific Management'* approach, therefore, was concerned with identifying the single best way of working. Concern with the working environment and with fatigue and performance then began to focus on worker *psychology*. Later interest in the *social* aspects of the workplace grew, to be replaced in turn with a focus on worker *motivation*. Soon after, predominantly in Europe, the *Industrial Democracy* or workplace autonomy approach began to influence thinking about the design of jobs. At about the same time there was considerable interest in the *redesign* of existing repetitive jobs in order to introduce greater sources of *satisfaction*. All of this provides the foundation for present thinking, which as yet cannot be characterized or categorized.

We will pick up on these developments at around the 1980s with the *job redesign* or *restructuring* movement, which aimed to rectify some of what were seen to be the inadequacies of many current work and job designs resulting from the pursuit of scientific management and work study approaches. The aim was to design into new jobs and redesign into existing jobs more satisfying and motivating features.

Lloyds Bank

Lloyds Bank in the UK felt that one of the most significant threats to an organization's competitive advantage may lie as much within the organization as outside, since low levels of employee morale and motivation can lead to low productivity, increased absence rates, resistance to change, and a failure to capture the benefits of investment in new technology. The bank conducted pilot programmes in two regions. The programme set out to establish whether and how the higher employee involvement needed to remedy such a situation could be achieved. The study revealed that staff were not utilized properly; that work processes and facilities were key issues; that poorly designed existing jobs were demotivating staff; and that the concepts underlying the design of jobs were difficult to understand, but that staff had become committed to change.

Source: (1993) Employee Involvement through job redesign at Lloyds Bank. *Industrial Relations Review and Report* **550**. Dec., pp. 13–16.

Job restructuring

The job restructuring 'experiments' undertaken around this time involved one or of two basic approaches, i.e. the *enlargement* of work content through the addition of one or more related tasks, and job *enrichment*, involving the increase in the motivational content of jobs through, for example, the addition of different types of tasks or the provision of increased worker involvement and participation. Both approaches are concerned with the content of jobs. A different approach involves the way in which jobs are organized. The provision of job rotation, i.e. workers moving between jobs in either a self-organized or a scheduled manner, and the provision of some opportunities for workers to organize their own jobs are examples of this approach. We shall describe this approach as work organization. This two-part categorization is summarized in Figure 9.3. The distinction between job enlargement and job enrichment permits examination of the degree to which the changes employed are likely to increase the motivational content of jobs.

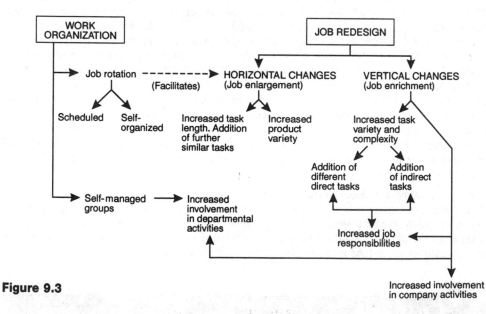

Figure 9.3

Our objective here is to develop a checklist which can be used in the redesign of jobs and in work organizations. For this we must look in more detail at the 'mechanics' of redesign and organizational changes (i.e. the means) and at the objectives (i.e. the ends) of such change.

Table 9.5	Desirable characteristics of jobs (for job satisfaction and motivation)

Job/Work
1. **Work content**
   - A   'Closure', i.e. complete module of work
   - B   Obvious relationship between tasks
   - C   New and more difficult tasks added
   - D   Increased variety of tasks
   - E   Make use of workers' valued skills and abilities
   - F   Include some auxiliary and preparatory tasks
   - G   Individual inspects own work
   - H   Worker repairs defective items
   - I   Operator sets up machines
   - J   Operator responsible for cleanliness of work area
   - K   Operator responsible for maintenance
   - L   Perceived contribution to product's utility
   - M   Work content such that job is meaningful and worthwhile

2. **Work method**
   - A   No machine pacing

Organization
3. **Work organization**
   - A   Give worker some choice of method
   - B   Worker discretion
   - C   Operator plans own work
   - D   Operator organizes own work
   - E   Self-regulation
   - F   Worker responsible for controlling own work
   - G   Operator sets own performance goals
   - H   Subgoals to measure accomplishment
   - I   Individual accountable for own work
   - J   Job responsibilities (generally)
   - K   Worker autonomy
   - L   Operator involved in solving problems
   - M   Workers participate in design and improvement of own job
   - N   Workers involved in decision-making concerning work
   - O   Workers receive performance feedback at regular intervals

4. **Job opportunity**
   - A   More than minimum required training provided
   - B   Worker able to learn new things about process
   - C   Promotion prospects for worker
   - D   Specific or specialized tasks enable worker to develop expertise
   - E   Increased challenge for worker

5. **Social conditions/relations**
   - A   Conversation either easy or impossible
   - B   Facilitates workers' movement about factory

Table 9.5 identifies most of the desirable job characteristics which have been advocated by authors, i.e. those characteristics which are considered to give rise to job satisfaction and worker motivation. These are further considered below.

Examination of the items listed in Table 9.5 suggests that some characteristics are in fact prerequisities for the existence of others, i.e. some must be provided in order that others might exist. In fact by re-organizing these characteristics we can develop a type of 'means' and 'ends' model. The model is summarized in Figure 9.4. This model does not necessarily provide a complete checklist; nor does the information reviewed above yield

Figure 9.4 Model relating the characteristics and attitudes of work and jobs. From Wild R. (1975) *Work Organization*. New York: Wiley.

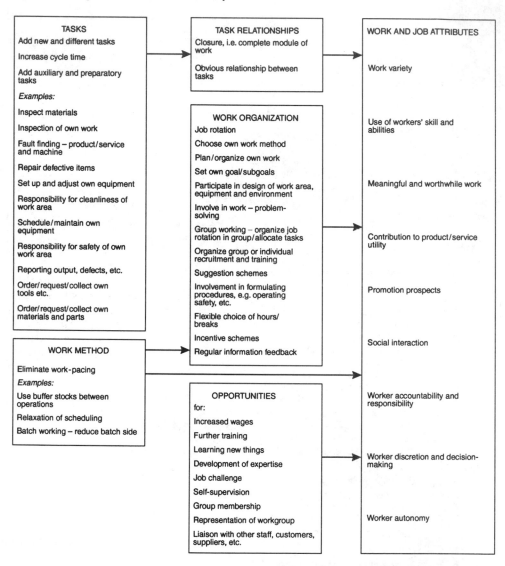

only to this interpretation. However, the structure is of value in that it helps to distinguish between those aspects of jobs which might be manipulated and those job features which result.

The model suggests that certain types of task and work methods should exist in order that particular task relationships might exist, and so that certain work organization changes can be made. These task relationships, methods of work organization and other opportunities can give rise to work and jobs which have the attributions necessary for the provision of job satisfaction and worker motivation.

Toyota

In 1984, General Motors and Toyota set up a joint-venture called New United Motor Manufacturing Inc. (NUMMI). The venture employs an innovative form of work study not only to create high productivity and quality but also to increase worker motivation and satisfaction. By the end of 1986 NUMMI's productivity was higher than that of any other GM facility and absenteeism was a steady 3–4% compared to 20–30% elsewhere in the industry. NUMMI shows that work structure and standardization can be used in a co-operative manner and not by enforcement.

The system has 2 features that distinguish it. It is committed to the social context in which work is performed but also it puts an intense focus on the standarization of work. Social concern is most evident in the no-layoff policy. With respect to work standardization workers themselves analyse jobs, design more efficient procedures, and create a consensus for the new standards.

Source: Adler, S. (1993) Time and motion regained *Harvard Business Review* **71**(1), pp. 97–108

Group working

The use of this approach to job design with its emphasis on work organization and worker autonomy will in many situations give rise to the creation of 'semi-autonomous work groups'. Such groups are usually quite small and comprised of interdependent workers, together taking responsibility for most of the activities involved in delivering a service or an item. The creation of such groups is increasing as organizations seek satisfactory solutions to job design problems in increasingly technology-dominated workplaces and in situations where change is constant and where organization-wide approaches are being used to try to achieve incremental and constant improvements in performance and in quality (see Chapter 19).

Thus some of the benefits of this approach, first popularized—albeit in somewhat different circumstances, in the 1970s—are

(a) increased employee satisfaction

(b) increased flexibility

(c) improved quality

(d) decreased need for supervision

The critical prerequisites for the successful implementation of this approach include:

1. Management support

2. Training

3. Adequate/appropriate structuring of work

4. Review/evaluation and development of workers.

Patient care jobs

Redesigning work patterns and jobs is becoming an important activity in nursing administration. Striking a balance between adapting jobs to people and adapting people to jobs is considered to be the best approach. There is increasing interest in the use of the sociotechnical systems approach which provides a framework, logic and method. It aims at work designs which neither compromise the integrity of people in order to achieve work efficiency, nor compromise productivity to satisfy people. Rather than seeking to reduce immediate tensions and errors, the approach encourages a broader perspective oriented towards the enterprise's long-term purpose. This helps designers see nursing as an integral part of the total patient care delivery system and to blend clinical and economic case management.

Source: Tonges, M. C. (1992) Work designs: sociotechnical systems for patient care delivery. *Nursing Management*, **23**(1), pp. 27–32.

KEY POINTS FOR CHAPTER 9

The worker–machine system

is an important element in most operations.

Efficient worker/machine operation requires good design of

> Information displays
>
> Controls
>
> Environment

Environmental factors

Include noise, lighting, temperature, ventilation.

Workplace design

involves consideration of workplace and worker dimensions.

The design of *VDU workplaces* raises special problems concerned with lighting, heat and ergonomics.

Health and Safety

issues are of concern to the Operations Manager. Accidents are a major source of loss to both employees and the organization. Preventative action is essential.

Technology

affects work and working conditions.

The allocation of tasks

as appropriate to people and to machines is essential.

The design of jobs

involves consideration of

> job/work content
>
> work methods
>
> work organization
>
> job opportunities
>
> social conditions

Group Working

is an aspect of job design which has particular potential and relevance in many situations.

FURTHER READING

Salvendy, G. (ed.) (1987) *Handbook of Human Factors*. Wiley, New York.

Wild, R. (1990) *Technology and Management*. Cassell, London.

Safizaden, M.H. (1991) The case of workgroups in manufacturing operations. *Calif. Mgt Rev* **33**(4) Summer pp. 61–82.

Schuring, R. (1992) Reasons for renewed popularity of autonomous group working. *Int J. of Ops and Prod. Mgt.* **12**(4), pp. 61–68.

CASE STUDY

The following case, from Part 9 of the book, is relevant to the topics covered in this chapter.

No.	Name	Country
12	Open Polytechnic of New Zealand	New Zealand

QUESTIONS

9.1 State, discuss and compare the principal requirements of displays used for the following purposes.

    (a)   indicating road speed of car to driver;

    (b)   indicating domestic oven temperature required (i.e. set) and actual temperatures;

    (c)   indicating time of day in an airport departure lounge.

9.2 State, discuss and compare the principal requirements of controls used for the following purposes.

    (a)   setting temperature required for a domestic oven;

    (b)   emergency 'off' control for metal-cutting lathe;

    (c)   controls for a hi-fi stereo radio receiver.

9.3 How might the following jobs be enriched:

    (a)   word-processor worker;

    (b)   bank teller;

    (c)   domestic appliance service repair worker?

Indicate any assumptions made about the jobs and their circumstances.

Chapter 10

Payment and incentives

ISSUES

What are the ingredients of remuneration?
What should a good payment system achieve?
How are jobs evaluated?
What is Payment By Results (PBR)?
What are the basic PBR schemes and how do they work?
What are the 'Gain share' payment systems?

In Chapter 8 we looked at work measurement, one application of which is in the design and operation of payment systems. Here we review the principles of payment and reward systems. We consider the context and objectives of payment systems, and look in more detail at job evaluation and at 'payments by results'.

PAYMENT AND REWARD SYSTEMS

Nature of remuneration

All work undertaken in the context of employment will be associated with some form of remuneration, the major element of which will be financial. We shall focus on financial rewards which might be classified as follows:

(a) wages, i.e. payment received by employees on a periodic basis, e.g. weekly or monthly;

(b) bonuses, e.g. lump sum awards, often provided on an annual basis;

(c) benefits, e.g. insurance benefits, pensions, allowances, non-monetary rewards such as the use of company cars, etc.;

(d) long-term rewards, i.e. lump sum rewards over a long period of time, typically five years and/or on termination of contract or on completion of contract employment period.

Our focus here will be on wages and wage-related factors, in particular the establishment of wage payment systems and structures, and forms of incentive wage payment. Adequate wages and acceptable wage systems are matters of importance to most working people. We must, however, distinguish between those factors which encourage an individual to work and those factors influencing satisfaction at work. Financial reward is undoubtedly a major factor in the former, although beyond a certain level and in certain circumstances job satisfaction may be influenced largely by factors other than wage. Certainly in many countries in recent years there has been a growing interest in non-wage aspects of remuneration, and increasing importance is now attached to such factors. However, without adequate wages and without the use of an acceptable and equitable wage payment system such interest would decline. Adequate wage levels and an acceptable wage payment system may therefore be seen as a foundation or 'platform' upon which other aspects of remuneration might be built and without which other aspects might not exist.

Payment of wages often represents a major cost source in many organizations. Not only do companies compete with one another as regards wage levels, but also their competition in the marketplace, being affected by price, is affected by wages as one factor affecting price and margins. The value added during operations is influenced by wage levels, and the ability to recruit and retain labour is also influenced by wage levels and the nature of payment systems. In these respects, therefore, the design and administration of wage payment systems are of relevance to the operations manager.

Payment structure and systems

The objectives of any payment system include the following:

(a) to enable the employee to earn a good and reasonable salary or wage;

(b) to pay equitable sums to different individuals, avoiding anomalies;

(c) to be understandable and acceptable to the employees and their seniors;

(d) to reward and encourage high-quality work;

(e) to encourage employees to accept transfers between jobs;

(f) to encourage employees to accept changes in methods of working;

(g) to discourage waste of materials or equipment;

(h) to encourage employees to use their initiative and discretion;

(i) to encourage employees to develop better methods of working;

(j) to reward and encourage high levels of output;

(k) to discourage and lead to a decrease in overtime working.

The design of a wage payment system to meet some or all of the above objectives will require some consideration of (a) pay structure and (b) pay systems.

The development of an adequate pay structure will require some consideration of the pay to be provided and the differentials between various jobs, i.e. the establishment of the 'relative worth' of different jobs in different circumstances. In most cases it will be necessary to establish some scale or grading of jobs based on some objective assessment and to relate jobs measured on this scale to pay rates or levels in

Figure 10.1 A pay/job structure

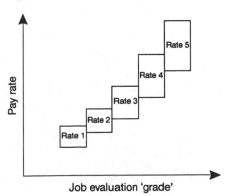

Job evaluation 'grade'

the manner shown in Figure 10.1. The establishment of such a scale will often provide some form of career or job structure for employees.

Various job evaluation schemes are available for the establishment of such structures; however, it should be remembered that in many cases the establishment of pay levels or pay bands for particular jobs will be a matter of negotiation between employees (often represented by trade unions) and employers. In some cases, of course, there will be national agreements between employers or employers' associations and trade unions. Such agreements may stipulate pay bands or minimum pay levels for particular jobs and conditions of service, etc.; in supplementing such national agreements there may be certain local negotiating and bargaining machinery to establish pay and wage structures at local or company level. Other factors, e.g. government intervention, may constrain companies' action; however, in most situations it will be appropriate to aim to develop and employ some consistent method of job evaluation if differentials are to be recognized and wage drift is to be avoided.

The design of the wage payment system will require the consideration of questions such as: 'To what extent will the wage be paid through some form of incentive payment system? How might such an incentive payment system operate? How will standards of performance be established and what control system will be introduced to monitor payment levels, earnings, etc?' In many cases some form of incentive payment system will be employed, although, as we have noted, in recent years there has been a move towards the introduction of non-financial incentives.

Job evaluation and incentive schemes are now examined in more detail.

Job evaluation

This is a term used to cover a number of methods of systematically measuring the relative worth of jobs, using yardsticks which are derived from the content of the jobs. A job evaluation scheme will enable new jobs to be placed in a proper relationship with existing jobs by the use of easily explained and acceptable facts and principles. Thus the principal purpose of job evaluation is to rank jobs as a basis for a pay structure. It aims, therefore, to compare all jobs under review using common criteria, to define the relationship of one job to another. It is essentially concerned with establishing relationships and not with absolutes. In comparing jobs it is the job content which is considered, and job evaluation is used primarily for establishing basic pay levels or wage bands.

Four methods of job evaluation are described below.

Job ranking

This is perhaps the simplest method. Job descriptions are prepared for each job to identify the duties, responsibilities and qualifications necessary for the job. Such descriptions may be developed jointly by management and worker representatives, and should be agreed by both parties. In some cases 'key' jobs are chosen which adequately cover the whole range of jobs and these are compared with one another in order to produce a ranking of jobs. Where few jobs exist it will be possible to develop a ranking for the entire list at the outset. Given this ranking of jobs on the basis of difficulty, importance to the firm, etc., job grades are established through an examination of the relative importance or merit of adjacent jobs on the scale. Thus grade boundaries may be established between jobs in the ranking which are agreed to have substantially different importance or difficulty ratings. Pay levels or ranges are then attached to each job grade.

The job ranking method is simple, straightforward and flexible. It does, however, suffer the disadvantage of relying heavily on judgement. In the use of this job ranking system there is a tendency to rank jobs to reflect current pay systems. Furthermore, the resultant ranking of jobs reflects only their rank order importance and does not provide for the quantitative assessment of differences between jobs.

Job classification

Using this procedure a number of job grades are first determined and then the existing jobs are allocated to these predetermined grades. Each grade will normally have recognizable characteristics, taking into account features such as the skill required in jobs, and their responsibilities. Each grade may be represented by a 'benchmark' job, which, taking into account the majority of factors, is most representative of the job grade. The job descriptions are then prepared for each of the existing jobs or each of the jobs to be allocated to the job structure. These jobs are then allocated to the existing grades through a process of comparison with the job grade descriptions or with the predetermined 'benchmark' jobs. Thus the procedure is much the same as in job ranking, except that jobs are allocated against an existing or required job structure. In both cases whole jobs may be treated and in both systems jobs may be evaluated on a variety of factors as agreed or as considered important within the particular circumstances. Skill and responsibilities are usually considered, and job difficulty and job-holder qualifications are also usually of some importance.

Points evaluation

This is one of the most popular job evaluation schemes. Unlike the others it relies on the identification and comparison of job factors rather than of the job as a whole. Factors, e.g. skill, effort, responsibility and working conditions, are selected which are common to all or most of the jobs in the organization. These 'compensatable' factors are defined. Each is then broken down into sub-factors which are again defined.

In evaluating jobs a weighting is attached to each of the general factors, i.e. those which apply throughout the organization. This represents the maximum points score which is achievable for that factor. This weight/score is then broken down amongst the sub-factors to indicate their relative importance. Then job descriptions are prepared for each job to be evaluated and each job (not the worker carrying out that job) is scored against the relevant list of sub-factors. This evaluation, or scoring, will normally be carried out by a committee responsible for examining all jobs in a department. A typical evaluation is given in Table 10.1. The total points score represents the evaluation or 'merit' of that job. Jobs are finally ranked according to points score, job grades are established, and pay scales or ranges are agreed.

Unlike the above systems, the points evaluation system provides a semi-objective means of job evaluation. Because of the detail which might be introduced through the identification and definition of sub-factors, the scheme might be employed consistently and agreement may be achieved relatively easily. The use of this scheme provides not only a means of establishing job rankings and a job structure but also a way of quantitatively identifying differentials between jobs and grades.

Table 10.1	Points evaluation of job: telephone 'help-line' operator for a computer software company		
Factors		**Points**	
	Weighting (i.e. maximum) for group	Normal maximum for factor	Actual for job
A. Skill	(60)		
1. Education		15	10
2. Experience		20	15
3. Initiative		25	20
B. Effort	(40)		
1. Mental		20	15
2. Visual		20	5
C. Responsibility	(70)		
1. Equipment		10	5
2. Subordinates		10	0
3. Environment		10	0
4. Financial		20	5
5. Customers		30	25
D. Conditions	(30)		
1. Surroundings		15	5
2. Working hours		15	10
	(200)		115

EXAMPLE

A wholesaler

A job evaluation scheme has been in operation for 3–4 years in a firm of wholesalers that provides six warehouse distribution points throughout the UK. Although there was a job structure of 16 grades, little thought had been given to the evaluation of the jobs within that structure, so some employees were apparently overpaid and some underpaid. Consultants were hired to: 1. establish an objective grading structure, 2. devise an appropriate salary scale, 3. introduce a means of rewarding merit, 4. calculate the cost of the changeover, and 5. recommend a programme of implementation. They adopted a conventional points system of evaluation against a number of criteria that reflected the characteristics of the various positions. The criteria to be used were defined and weighted, after which was selected the number of degrees into which each criterion should be divided.

Source: Wilde, E. (1992) A job evaluation case history. *Work Study* **41**(2), pp.6–11.

Factor comparison

This method is an extension of points evaluation and uses five factors:

(a) mental effort required in the job;

(b) skills required for the job;

(c) physical effort required for the job;

(d) responsibility of the job;

(e) job conditions.

A number of key jobs are selected and then a panel of 'experts' determines the proportion of the total wage paid for each constitutent factor. Each factor is given a monetary value for the key jobs. This allows a scale to be established for each factor and other jobs can then be compared with them, factor by factor, to yield a ranking of all jobs. Since the initial exercise is carried out in terms of monetary values, interpolation will yield wage rates for all jobs. This method is more complex and difficult both to describe and implement because it uses, in one process, job evaluation and the allocation of monetary values.

EXAMPLE

e.g. *Equal pay*

...ol district set out to investigate teachers' pay with a view to ensuring or implementing pay equality for men and women. A job evaluation approach was used. The approach emphasized the reaching of a consensus between employees, and the supervisors filling out the job-evaluation questionnaire. Major features of the job evaluation questionnaire included areas of supervision, contacts with others, and budget responsibilities. The new questionnaire described jobs in terms of instruction or training, with the lowest degree being service or support operations. Two other categories were added, one dealing with the amount of exposure to the risk of physical harm and the other relating to the employee's flexibility. To the usual categories of direct or indirect supervision were added ultimate authority, functional supervision and consultative supervision. Salaries fixed as a result of this exercise were then examined and no gender or race inequalities were found.

Source: Gray, M.W. (1992) Pay equity through job evaluation: a case study. *Compensation and Benefits Review* **24**(4), pp. 46–51

PAYMENT BY RESULTS (PBR)

We shall not comment directly on the merits of PBR schemes, but it is appropriate to describe some schemes so that their basic principles are understood. We shall deal with two types of scheme—individual and group incentives.

Individual incentives

100% participation or one-for-one schemes

This is one of the simplest and most widely used incentive payment systems. Under this system, increases in performance above a certain level lead to directly proportional increases in wages. In its simplest form, incentive payment is provided for throughput or output above 100 performance, there being a guaranteed payment of the base rate for performances at 100 or less. In other words, earnings are calculated on a time basis as follows:

Essentials of Production and Operations Management

$E = RH + R(S - H)$

where E = earnings for a given period

R = base pay rate

H = hours worked

S = standard hours allowed for job

= standard hours for each unit[1](s) × number of units (N) output or throughput.

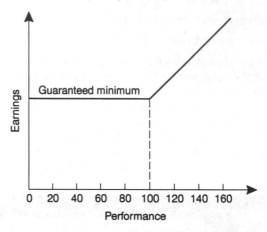

Figure 10.2 100% participation incentive payment scheme beginning at 100 performance

EXAMPLE

Base pay rate	= 250 pence per hour
Hours worked	= 8
Standard minutes (SM) per unit	= 20
Output/throughput	= 30 units

$$E = 250(8) + 250\left[\left(\frac{20}{60} \times 30\right) - 8\right]$$

$$= 2000 + 250(10 - 8)$$

$$= \ \ 2000 \ + \ \ \ 500$$

$$\text{(base pay)} \ \text{(incentive pay)}$$

$$= 2500 \text{ p (total pay)}$$

Often 100% participation or 'one-for-one' schemes begin at a level less than 100 performance, i.e. incentive payment is offered to workers who exceed a performance of perhaps 75 or 80. As with the previous scheme, it is usual to guarantee minimum base rate earnings. In this case earnings are calculated as follows:

$$E = RH + R\left(\frac{100S}{X} - H\right)$$

where X = the performance at which participation begins, e.g. 75 or 80.

---

[1] Each unit processed or produced, e.g. item produced, customer dealt with, etc.

Less than 100% participation or geared schemes

A large number of schemes have been developed which differ from those described previously in that they do not offer 100% increases in payment for 100% increases in performance. Such schemes differ mainly in the extent to which workers participate as a result of increased performance. The main benefit of such incentive payment schemes is that they provide some measure of safeguard for management in circumstances where allowed times may have been inaccurately estimated. An additional safeguard can, of course, be provided by applying an upper limit to incentive earnings.

The formula for calculating earnings for geared schemes without an upper earnings limit, and starting at a performance level of 100, is as follows:

$$E = RH + YR(S - H)$$

where Y = the extent of the gearing, e.g. 0.5 for a 50/50 plan.

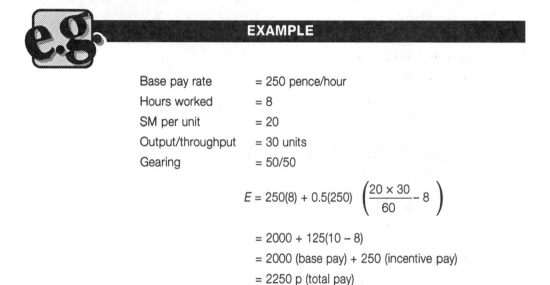

EXAMPLE

Base pay rate	= 250 pence/hour
Hours worked	= 8
SM per unit	= 20
Output/throughput	= 30 units
Gearing	= 50/50

$$E = 250(8) + 0.5(250) \left(\frac{20 \times 30}{60} - 8 \right)$$

$$= 2000 + 125(10 - 8)$$

$$= 2000 \text{ (base pay)} + 250 \text{ (incentive pay)}$$

$$= 2250 \text{ p (total pay)}$$

As before, participation may begin at a level below 100, in which case earnings are calculated by the following formula:

$$E = RH + YR \left(\frac{100S}{X} - H \right)$$

'Piece-work'

This is one of the oldest methods of incentive payment, under which workers are paid a fixed amount for each unit processed. In fact the piece-work system is very similar to the 100% participation or one-for-one system previously described, the principal difference being that in piece-work the standard is described in terms of money and not time. As with the previous systems, it is usual to operate the incentive payment system in conjunction with a guaranteed minimum payment level.

The piece-rate (P) is defined as follows:

$P = Rs$

consequently earnings (E) over a period of time are calculated by means of the following simple equations:

$E = RsN$ (where performance is above 100)

$E = RH$ (where performance is below 100).

EXAMPLE

Base pay rate   = 250 pence per hour

Hours worked   = 8

SM per unit   = 20

Output/throughput = 30

Piece-rate = Rs

$$= 250 \times \frac{20}{60}$$

$$\text{Performance} = \frac{\text{Standard hours produced}}{\text{Hours worked}} \times 100$$

$$= \frac{\dfrac{20}{60} \times 30}{8} \times 100 = 125$$

$\therefore$ Earnings (E) = RsN

$$= 250 \times \frac{20}{60} \times 30 = 2500 \text{ p}$$

It should be noted that certain practical complexities must be accommodated during the operation of any incentive payment method. For example, a certain amount of waiting time will be incurred throughout most working periods and, in addition, unmeasured work may be undertaken. It is usual to pay both of these at base rate or at day-work rate and, consequently, care must be taken to include them in the wage calculations.

EXAMPLE

Base pay rate   = 250 pence per hour

Total hours worked   = 9½

Hours worked on unmeasured work   = ½

Waiting hours $\qquad = 1$

SM per unit for measured work $\qquad = 20$

Output/throughput of measured work $= 30$ pieces

Using a 100% participation system above a 100 performance,

$$E = 250(9\tfrac{1}{2}) + 250 \left[\left(\frac{20}{60} \times 30 \right) - (9\tfrac{1}{2} - 1\tfrac{1}{2}) \right]$$

$\qquad = 2375 + 500$ (incentive pay) $= 2875$ p (total pay)

EXAMPLE

Exel Logistics

In 1987, Exel Logistics, one of the largest distributors in the UK, started a programme aimed at improving the effectiveness of the drivers engaged on one of its major store delivery contracts, as the customer was undertaking a review of its delivery policy. It was felt that the existing drivers' bonus incentive scheme was no longer appropriate. Working with consultants, Exel developed a new version of its own standard hour plan specifically to meet the needs of that particular contract. The new plan operates on the principle that driver earnings should be related solely to work done, and not the time spent doing it. As a result, there would be no overtime premium, since the plan operates on a single pay rate. Time standards on which earnings would be based were established and used to evaluate the work done by the driver. Subsequently the plan has been extended by Exel and now provides the basis of payment for over 300 drivers.

Source: Drew, R. (1992) Following the Exel route. *Work Study* **41**(3) pp. 25–26.

Measured day work

The use of the measured day work system avoids some of the problems normally encountered in the design and administration of the type of incentive wage systems described above. It avoids the need for continual measurement of performance and adjustment of wage levels based on such performance, yet it provides a form of incentive wage system. Measured day work offers a fixed rate of pay for a defined standard of performance. Work measurement is used to establish standard times for various jobs and to negotiate the pay rate for such jobs at different levels of performance. Workers are then guaranteed a regular weekly wage if they are able consistently to achieve a given level of performance. Having demonstrated the ability to maintain a level of performance over a minimum period, they are paid an appropriate wage. Subsequent failure to achieve this level of performance results first in some form of discipline or review by management, and subsequently in a reduction to a lower wage level. Measured day work therefore incorporates elements of normal incentive pay with some other benefits of a straight time rate system, in that wage levels do not fluctuate as much as in incentive pay, yet an incentive element remains.

Premium payment scheme

The approach here is similar to that of measured day work, but the time-scale is often extended so that performance reviews take place at long intervals; hence stability is high.

Multi-factor incentives

Increasingly, incentive payment schemes are based on multiple performance or achievement criteria. In particular, such schemes take into account factors other than the output-related or throughput-related criteria used in the schemes described above. At the simplest level, multi-factor schemes will also provide for the reward of quality, attendance and timekeeping achievements. At this level they can readily be applied to individuals, but in general multi-factor schemes are more appropriate for group incentive payment (see below). In these cases, factors such as output (or throughput) quality, resource utilization and customer service criteria can be accommodated. With this approach a high base rate is supplemented by an 'incentive' earning usually calculated on a 'points' basis, points being awarded for a level of achievement on each factor. Factors may carry different weightings to reflect their relative importance in the particular situation, and the total incentive earning may be obtained by adding the weighted points achievements for each factor and converting the total to a money equivalent, to be added to the base pay.

Such schemes offer the following benefits:

(a) The incentive has a broad base and can be designed more readily to reflect the organization's needs.

(b) Overall performance/achievement is rewarded, and the risk of high achievement on one factor at the expense of another is reduced.

(c) The setting and weighting of factors offer opportunities for the participation of all groups involved.

(d) Flexibility can be built into the scheme by allowing for changes in factor weighting.

EXAMPLE

Englewood City

Englewood City in Colorado has changed to an employee payment scheme that rewards employees who have mastered skills, who have demonstrated performance and who have met their targets. Previously the payment system was similar to those of other municipal governments. Employees were hired at a fixed initial payment level, and if their performance was acceptable, received 3 increases of 5% at 6-month intervals. Officials began to realize that this type of scheme not only tolerated mediocrity but encouraged it. Employees were not rewarded for acquiring additional skills, for accepting increased responsibility or for showing initiative. The new plan is successful in motivating and compensating talented employees at levels that will keep them from moving to other jobs purely for financial reasons. The increases in efficiency and productivity should also reduce operational costs.

Source: Woika, M. (1993) Pay play based on performance motivates employees. *H R Magazine* **38**(12), pp. 75–77.

Group 'PBR' Schemes

The schemes described above are *primarily* applied to individuals. Derivatives of them (in particular measured day work, premium payments and multi-factor schemes) may be applied to small groups of people employed in related tasks in a particular area, but in general other types of scheme, with a distinctive philosophy, are used to provide incentive pay to groups of workers. Many such schemes exist, ranging from those developed for a particular application to those based on general principles, which are relevant in a variety of organizations. Such group incentive schemes might be applied to small groups of workers engaged together on a task and working interdependently, to departments, and in some cases to entire organizations. In general the larger the group involved in such incentive pay the greater the problem of designing a scheme which has perceived *relevance* and *immediacy*. In other words, the larger the group and the more 'remote' the criteria for determining the amount of incentive pay, the greater the likelihood that individuals will see the factors which influence their incentive pay as being beyond their direct influence, and the greater the risk that the time lag in providing the incentive pay will limit the development of individuals' motivation. These, therefore, are the principal motivational obstacles of such schemes, but on the other hand such schemes do emphasize the sharing of achievements and productivity gains, and with that the need for team working, and perhaps the development of some greater identification with organizational goals, etc.

Group PBR schemes are being used, increasingly, in all types of business, whilst individual PBR schemes are seen to be of diminishing importance. Amongst the main reasons for this trend to group schemes are:

1. The increasing need for people to work together, e.g. on teams, rather than individually and independently;

2. The reducing importance of direct labour costs as a part of total cost;

3. The increased emphasis being placed on organizational approaches to improving efficiently and effectiveness, e.g. the use of Total Quality Management (see ch 19);

4. The increasing importance of non-price and non-cost factors in achieving competitive advantage (see ch 19).

These trends make it increasingly difficult to build effective and appropriate PBR schemes on simple, single criteria (e.g. time to do a job or task) for individual workers, so organizations have begun to pursue different means to link pay and performance.

Basically, group PBR schemes aim to achieve the following:

1. To encourage the continual improvement, by employees working together, of productivity/efficiency and effectiveness, i.e. to improve organizational 'performance';

2. To secure measurable financial benefits from increased performance, and to share these between employees and the organization.

The principal prerequisites for a successful scheme are as follows:

1. The scheme should be relatively straightforward, and should be readily understandable by all concerned.

2. There should be commitment to the scheme from all concerned.

3. There should be a clear measure of 'performance'.

4. Performance measurement, feedback on performance, and reward should be rapid and frequent.

5. There should be substantial and general management commitment.

6. Training, instruction, and education programmes are required for all involved.

7. The scheme should be introduced and then maintained, in a participative manner—not unilaterally.

EXAMPLE

Southern Company Services

Southern Company Services has organized a team incentive programme to improve productivity through better use of labour and materials. It is a group-based incentive programme that encourages employees to improve productivity through efficient use of labour, capital, materials, and energy. The value of the increased productivity is determined, and the dollar amount is split between the company and the team. In this way, the company and its stockholders see tangible benefits for their investment, and the employees receive bonuses for their work. Specifically organized around natural work groups and not individuals, the programme is administered by a steering committee composed of 7 staff personnel and 11 management personnel. The amount of money allocated to the payment 'pool' is based on gains over target rates and achievements related to system performance service-level objectives. Eligible participants receive payments equal to a certain percentage of their total annual wages.

Source: Davidson, R. L. (1988) Gain sharing incentive spurs productivity. *Transmission and Distribution* **40**(12), pp. 42–44.

Types of group PBR system

Traditionally there are two types of scheme, although the distinction between them is now blurred.

a) **Team profit sharing**—through which groups of employees and the organization share the financial benefits of increased profits;

b) **Team 'gainsharing'**—through which groups of employees and the organization share the financial benefits of reduced costs.

Profit sharing schemes tend to relate to total costs, whereas Gainsharing schemes relate to labour costs or, in the case of broader schemes, to operations costs. The difference, of course, is the range of costs covered. The broader the range the more likely it is that the scheme will be seen to be related, substantially, to profit.

In practice the term 'Gainsharing' is now generally used to cover the full range of schemes.

Implementation and operation

The essential steps in designing and introducing a 'Gain share' scheme are:

1. Identifying the measure of performance;

2. Identifying the size/scope (i.e. membership of the groups) to be covered by the scheme;

3. Establishing a representative and consultative process (to cover management, employees involved, and specialist personnel) through which to define and introduce the scheme;

4. Designing and defining the scheme and, if appropriate, incorporating in collective bargaining agreements;

5. Training and educating all involved and affected;

6. Establishing a representative committee to join the scheme;

7. Establishing a representative review/monitoring procedure;

8. Establishing a communications procedure to provide information on bonuses paid, sizes of bonus 'pools', trends, etc.

Experience with 'Gain share' schemes

Organizations which have introduced 'Gain share' type group PBR schemes have reported significant initial profit and productivity improvements. Figures around 5–15% in the first year and 25–35% overall (i.e. when a steady state is achieved) are typical. Other reported benefits include:

greater employee involvement in decision-making;

greater/better ideas generation;

higher morale;

improved absenteeism and reduced labour turnover.

EXAMPLE

Mosier Industries

Mosier Industries of Brookville, Ohio implemented a gain sharing programme in an effort to involve employees in improving company performance. A committee of three company officers monitors company performance and has full authority to resolve any issues connected with the 'Efficiency Reward Program.' At the end of each six-month bonus period, the committee allocates an amount of money which varies according to performance, to the efficiency reward fund. Eligible employees earn efficiency points based on seniority, job classification, and co-operation. Employees receive a cash award based on their number of efficiency points and the total amount in the fund. In the 18 bonus periods that have occurred since the programme was implemented, awards totalling nearly $250,000 have been paid out over only six bonus periods. The company has tied wage increases to the bonus formula to prevent workforce letdown at the end of a bonus period when it becomes apparent that a bonus will not be achieved.

Source: Owens, T. (1988) Case history—making Gain sharing work. *Small Business Reports* **13** (10), pp. 29–32.

KEY POINTS FOR CHAPTER 10

Remuneration can comprise

wages
bonuses
benefits
long-term rewards.

Payment systems which deal with wages and bonuses have multiple objectives.

Job evaluation is concerned with the measurement of the relative 'worth' of jobs.

The main methods for job evaluation include
job ranking
job classification
points evaluation
factor comparison.

Payment by Results (PBR)

Schemes seek to relate rewards to some measure of achievement.

There are several types of PBR scheme including

    individual incentives

    group schemes.

There are two interrelated types of Group PBR scheme:

    team profit sharing

    team gain sharing.

FURTHER READING

Friedman, B. (1990) *Effective Staff Incentives*. Kogan Page.

Gowen, C. R. (1990) Gain sharing programs: an overview of history and research. *Journal of Organizational Behaviour Management* 11(2) pp. 77–99.

QUESTIONS

10.1 Refer to Question 8.2. The worker on that job produces 2600 pieces during an eight-hour working shift. He is working on a 10% participation incentive scheme, in which the basic rate is £3 per hour and in which incentive payment is given for outputs in excess of 75. What are the worker's total gross earnings for the shift?

10.2 Show how any two of the job evaluation schemes described in this chapter would be used to evaluate:

(a)   the job of a supermarket 'check-out' worker;

(b)   your job.

10.3 A worker is capable of giving a regular 125 performance over a working week of 40 hours. If she is employed on testing work and if the standard hour (SH) per item tested is 0.75, what would the gross total pay per week be on a base rate of 270 pence per hour under the following systems of payment:

(a)   100% participation with incentive payment for performances over 100;

(b)   100% participation with incentive payment for performances over 75;

(c)   50/50 scheme with incentive payment for performances over 100;

(d)   50/50 scheme with incentive payment for performances over 75?

What piece-rate must be paid to the worker if her gross total weekly earnings under a piece-work system are to equal the largest gross total weekly earnings provided by one of the above incentive schemes?

10.4 What are the principal benefits, disadvantages and applications of a 'gain share' payment scheme?

Capacity Management

INTRODUCTION TO PART 5

In this chapter we deal in some detail with what is perhaps the most difficult, and certainly the most important, problem and decision area for operations management. Unless the capacity of the operating system is managed effectively, the operations manager is unlikely to achieve his or her twin objectives. Good decision-making and effectiveness in other areas are unlikely to compensate for or to conceal poor capacity management.

This is one of the 'principal' problem areas of operations management as defined in Chapter 1. The strategies which might be adopted for the management of capacity can be: (a) limited by feasibility constraints (associated mainly with the structure of the operating system) and (b) influenced by desirability factors (deriving from the objectives in the organization and operations managers).

Chapter 11

Capacity management

ISSUES

Why is the management of capacity a major strategic issue?

What is the capacity of a system?

How do we determine the future capacity required?

How do we deal with uncertainty, especially with variations in demand?

What are the basic strategies for managing capacity?

How do capacity decisions relate to operations objectives?

What capacity management procedures are available?

Capacity management is the critical strategic decision area of operations. Decisions on how to match the capacity of the operating system to the levels of demand which are to be met by that system will influence many other decisions, yet no other decisions can rectify wrong decisions in this area. The capacity of an operating system is a measure of the usable resources available to that system. Acquiring the wrong levels of resource must have direct consequences for either customers' service or resource utilization—the twin objectives of Operations Management. The reverse also applies, i.e. the importance to be attached to customer service or to resource utilization will influence the way in which capacity is managed, i.e. the capacity management strategy. We noted in Chapter 1 that this is the desirability constraint on capacity management. Also, the strategy used for capacity management will be influenced by the structure of the operating system. As we saw in Chapter 1, this is the feasibility constraint on capacity management.

In this chapter we look in detail at strategies, and then briefly at some procedures for capacity management. To set an appropriate context, we first consider the nature of operations planning and control.

OPERATIONS PLANNING AND CONTROL (see also Chapter 12)

We regard operations planning as a *pre*-operating activity, i.e. the determination of the facilities needed to provide the required goods or services and the construction of a schedule by means of which this will be achieved. Operations control we consider to be a *during*-operating activity involving the implementation of operations planning decisions. Our definition of the two areas is, therefore:

Operations planning is concerned with the determination, acquisition and arrangement of all facilities necessary for the future operations.
Operations control is concerned with the implementation of a predetermined operations plan or policy and the control of all aspects of operations according to such a plan or policy.

Notice, however, that operations planning and control are closely linked and interdependent. Decisions during planning will determine the problems, and often the nature, of control, and experiences during control will influence future planning.

The stages in operations planning and control

Figure 11.1 outlines the main stages in operations planning and control and identifies the area of responsibility of capacity management. They are described below.

Figure 11.1 Principal stages in operations planning and control

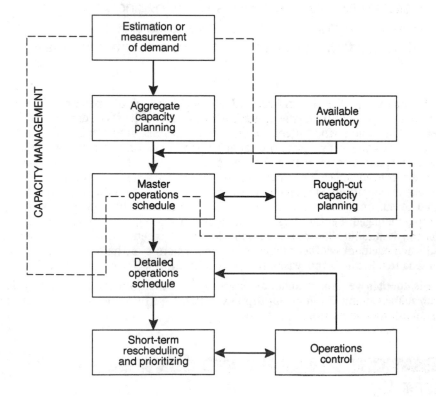

Demand estimation or measurement

A prerequisite of any purposeful planning is a statement of the demand which is to be satisfied. In most cases this will involve estimation or forecasting. Rarely will it be possible to measure future demand.

Aggregate capacity planning

(cumulative)

Here the objective is to develop a medium- to long-term statement of capacity requirements in aggregate terms, i.e. a plan indicating the amount of facilities needed to satisfy total expected demand, period by period.

Master operations schedule (MOS)

The master operations schedule is developed from the aggregate capacity plan. It is a breakdown of the aggregate plan showing when the major operations required for each expected item of demand are to be undertaken. Unlike the aggregate capacity plan, the MOS is time-phased, and identifies each major resource category and individual orders.

Rough-cut capacity planning

This involves the analysis of the MOS in order to identify time-phased capacity requirements for major resources or operations. It is, in effect, a means to test the feasibility of the MOS. If the rough-cut plan reveals that inadequate capacities are available for any major resource during any period, the MOS will be recalculated.

Detailed operations schedule (DOS)

Given a feasible MOS, the next requirement is the development of a detailed schedule for all operations for all jobs or orders to be completed in the planning period. The time horizon here will be less than that for the MOS.

Short-term rescheduling and prioritizing and control

Some short-term rescheduling will be necessary to accommodate changes in capacity demands or availabilities. For example, particular operations may require more time than anticipated or equipment may be unavailable through breakdown. The operations control activities will monitor such changes and modify the DOS.

Computer systems for planning and control

Until recently the above aspects of operations planning and control have been dealt with by separate systems. For example, the master operations schedule has often been developed and maintained by using a computer-based materials requirement planning system (see Chapter 12). Recently attempts have been made to integrate these separate systems. Mostly these developments have focused on manufacturing operations and one such system is Manufacturing Resource Planning (also known as MRP II—see Chapter 12).

Monsanto

A decision support system (DSS) was developed to optimize the production planning in the herbicide department at Monsanto in Antwerp, Belgium. With the highly seasonal demand pattern and the limited capacity, careful planning was needed to provide the desired service levels at a reasonable cost. The PC-based system balances the cost of alternative production resources against inventory-holding cost, taking into account production capacity constraints, storage limitations, and container available. In addition to being used for short-term planning purposes over an 18-month time horizon, the system is easily adapted to cover a longer horizon to deal with strategic decisions.

Source: Bloemen, R. and Maes, J. (1992) A DSS for optimising the aggregate production planning at Monsanto Antwerp. *European Journal of Operational Research* **61**(12), pp. 30–40.

CAPACITY MANAGEMENT

The management of capacity is the key planning responsibility of operations managers. All other operations planning takes place within the framework set by capacity decisions.

Capacity management is concerned with the matching of the capacity of the operating system and the demand placed on that system, i.e. those areas identified on Figure 11.1.

A system has capacity if it has at least some of *each* of the types of resource which are needed to perform its function. For example, a taxi service has capacity to transport a person if it has a vacant cab, a driver, fuel, etc., and a manufacturing system has capacity to produce if it has equipment, raw materials, labour, etc. Some of *each* of the necessary resources must exist if capacity is to exist. However, in measuring capacity we shall often refer only to the principal, or most costly, or most greatly used, or most commonly used resource in the operating system.

One approach to the capacity management problem is to try to plan the capacity required and then manipulate that capacity so that it matches the changing demands placed on it. If insufficient capacity is provided it will be possible to meet only some of the demand, and so some customers must wait or go elsewhere. If too much capacity is provided there will be some under-utilization of resources. Another approach is to try to manipulate demand to match the available capacity. Demand might be increased through advertising, increased promotion, lower prices, etc., and this might help avoid under-utilization of available capacity. However, if there is insufficient capacity available, demand may be allowed, or even encouraged, to fall.

In most cases an organization will seek to match capacity and demand by a combination of these two approaches. However, operations managers will be concerned mainly with the former, and in most cases they will see their task as that of trying to ensure that a forecast or given demand can be satisfied. From the operations manager's viewpoint, one of the major problems is uncertainty of demand. The existence of a stable and known demand would simplify the problems of capacity management considerably, and changing demand can be accommodated relatively easily providing changes can be predicted accurately. However, the expectation of changing demand levels without the possibility of accurate prediction gives rise to extremely complex capacity problems. We should note that this uncertainty of demand level may be caused by:

(a) uncertainty about the number of 'orders' to be received; *and/or*

(b) uncertainty about the amount of resources required for the satisfaction of customer orders.

Capacity management will involve the study of likely demand patterns for the medium to long term, the determination of the capacity required to meet such demand, and the development of strategies for the deployment of resources, in particular for accommodating changes in demand levels. Capacity management will involve the examination of alternative strategies. For example, it will be necessary to examine alternative methods of meeting demand-level fluctuations. Can and should the amount of resources (e.g. labour) be varied? It is desirable to maintain a steady level of activity and, if so, how can this be achieved? Can customers be expected or required to wait? What is the role of inventories and should the system attempt to meet all potential demand?

An objective of capacity management is the determination of the quantity of each resource required. Notice that some resources (e.g. labour and machines) may be stocked, used and re-used, while others (e.g. materials) will be acquired, i.e. input, and consumed. For the former, a decision must be made about the amount of each resource to have in stock, whilst for the latter the input rate must be determined. In many cases such decisions will reflect assessment of the *average* demand rate expected over a period of time. If resources are available to satisfy average demand, and if fluctuations about this level can be accommodated, then capacity is satisfactory. In some cases, periods during which demand exceeds average may be offset against periods below average. In others, demand above expectation may be lost, so there may be some justification in providing capacity in excess of expected requirements as a form of safeguard. In most cases demand levels lower than expected will give rise to either an under-utilization of capacity and/or a build-up of resources beyond expectations. Failure to satisfy either resource utilization and/or customer service criteria can therefore result from inaccurate assessment of average demand levels and hence the provision of too little or too much capacity, or failure to provide for adequate capacity adjustment.

Although it is convenient to consider capacity management as occurring in two stages—determination of normal capacity required and planning for meeting variations about this level—these two aspects are clearly interdependent. The capacity provided may be influenced by the manner in which adjustments may be made. Constraints on adjustment, particularly limitations on ability to accommodate short-term excess demand, may necessitate provision of 'excess' capacity.

THE NORMAL CAPACITY REQUIRED

The objective here is to determine the normal capacity required for the medium to long term. The decision will be based on demand forecast.

When future demand is being forecast for capacity planning purposes, fluctuations will be expected but to some extent ignored. The aim will be to get a general picture of future demand. Short-term fluctuations will usually be dealt with later, but knowing how demand fluctuations might be dealt with may influence the normal capacity which is provided.

DEALING WITH DEMAND FLUCTUATIONS—CAPACITY MANAGEMENT STRATEGIES

Faced with fluctuating and uncertain demand levels, there are two basic capacity planning strategies which might be employed: (a) providing for efficient adjustment or variation of system capacity; and (b) eliminating or reducing the need for adjustments in system capacity.

Strategy 1: Provide for efficient adjustment or variation of system capacity

In most situations it will be both possible and desirable to adopt this strategy. Usually system capacity can be changed within certain limits, perhaps not instantaneously but certainly with little delay. Temporarily, more useful capacity might be created by providing more resources and/or by providing for their more efficient or intense utilization. Temporary reductions in capacity might be achieved through the transfer of resources to other functions or the temporary reduction in the resources on hand or the input rate of resources.

In *supply* systems, e.g. supermarkets, such a strategy is employed as the principal means of accommodating inevitably fluctuating demand levels. Consider the supermarket checkout system. In periods of low demand some of the resources, i.e. the staff, can be transferred to other functions such as re-stocking shelves. During periods of high demand, staff resources may be increased temporarily by transfer from other functions to provide 'double-staffing', e.g. operation of cash register and wrapping and loading, in turn providing for more intensive utilization of the other resources, i.e. the cash register and the counter. Similarly in certain *manufacture* systems capacity released during periods of low demand might be employed on rectification or service work, while peak demand periods might be

Table 11.1	Means available for capacity adjustment (capacity strategy 1)	
Resources	**Capacity increases**	**Capacity reductions**
All	Subcontract some work	Retrieve some previously subcontracted work
	Buy rather than make (manufacture only)	Make rather than buy (manufacture only)
Consumed	Reduce material content	
Material	Substitute more readily available materials	
	Increase supply schedules	Reduce supply schedules
	Transfer from other jobs	Transfer to other jobs
Fixed	Scheduling of activities, i.e. speed and load increases	
Machines	Scheduling of maintenance, i.e. defer, hire or transfer from other functions	Scheduling of maintenance, i.e. advance
		Subcontract or transfer to other functions
Labour	Hours worked, i.e. overtime rearrangement of hours, shifts, holidays	Hours worked, i.e. short time rearrangement of hours, shifts, holidays
	Workforce size, i.e. staffing levels temporary labour transfer from other areas	Workforce size, i.e. layoffs, transfer to other areas

accommodated by temporary increase in resource levels through, for example, overtime working and more intensive use of equipment, perhaps through deferral of maintenance work. In some cases capacity might effectively be increased by subcontracting work. To some extent this strategy might be appropriate in the management of *transport* and *service* systems. In both cases maintenance and service work might be scheduled for periods of low demand, and flexible work shift patterns might be employed, overtime working introduced, etc.

Table 11.1 lists some of the means available for the adjustment of system capacity.

Strategy 2: Eliminate or reduce the need for adjustments in system capacity

In some cases it may be impossible, undesirable or time-consuming to provide for temporary adjustment in system capacity. In general it will be difficult to provide for temporary capacity adjustments in systems which employ large quantities of a large variety of resources, without incurring considerable expense and/or delay. Complex process plants which normally work around the clock present little scope for capacity adjustments to meet temporary demand increases, while reductions in demand will often give rise to under-utilization of major resources. Similarly, in systems which use highly specialized resources such as skilled labour, it may be desirable to avoid the need for temporary capacity adjustments.

In such situations a strategy of minimizing the need for system capacity adjustments will be more appealing. The adoption of such a strategy might involve the provision of excess capacity and therefore the acceptance of perhaps considerable under-utilization of resources, in order to increase the probability of being able to meet high or even maximum demand. Such an approach might be desirable where there is little possibility of providing temporary increases in capacity, and where customer service is of paramount importance. Examples of such situations might include an emergency ambulance service, power station or hospital emergency ward. The provision of some excess capacity, yet insufficient to meet maximum demand, necessitates the acceptance that during periods of peak demand either customers will be lost or they must wait or queue until demand levels fall. In practice such an approach is frequently adopted, for in many cases very considerable excess resources must be provided to ensure that peak demand can be satisfied.

In systems where output stocks can exist, the provision of inventories of goods is a conventional strategy for the smoothing of demand. Such inventories not only insulate the function from fluctuations in demand levels and thus facilitate the use of relatively stable resource levels and high utilization, but also enable customers to be provided with goods with little delay. Many systems operate in this fashion.

A similar situation exists where customer waiting or queuing is feasible. In such cases, despite a fluctuating demand rate, the rate at which customers are dealt with, i.e. the system capacity, might remain fairly stable. Bus and rail services are frequently intended to operate in this manner. Similar situations might exist at times of peak demand in both manufacture and supply, e.g. the bespoke tailor and the retail shop.

To summarize:

(a) It is possible to eliminate the need for adjustments in capacity if sufficient capacity is provided to deal with all future demand.

(b) It is possible to reduce the need for adjustments in capacity if

(i) the capacity level which is provided will be sufficient to cope with most demand situations but, when that capacity is insufficient, one or both of the following situations is accepted.

loss of trade

customer queuing/waiting

(ii) output stocks are provided to 'absorb' demand fluctuations.

This strategy for capacity management is outlined in Table 11.2. These four approaches can be used individually or in combination. Notice that in Table 11.2 only methods (b) (i) with customer queuing and (b) (ii) will enable us to deal with demand reductions without reducing resource utilization. Notice also that the provision of excess capacity alone is rarely a sufficient basis for accommodating demand fluctuations. In most cases it will be necessary to take some action aimed at reducing or smoothing the effect of fluctuations on the function, i.e. approaches (b)(i) and (b)(ii) above.

Table 11.2	Methods for eliminating or reducing the need for capacity adjustment (strategy 2)	
Method	**Relevance for:**	
	Dealing with demand increases	**Dealing with demand decreases**
(a) *Eliminate adjustment by:* Maintaining sufficient excess capacity	Yes	Not directly relevant
(b) *Reduce/minimize adjustment by:*		
(i) Some excess capacity, together with:		
Loss of trade *and/or*	Yes (ignore some demand)	Not directly relevant
Customer queuing	Yes (increase queue)	Yes (reduce queue)
(ii) Output stocks	Yes (reduce stock)	Yes (increase stock)

CAPACITY STRATEGY AND TYPE OF OPERATING SYSTEM

In many cases organizations would prefer to have demand level fluctuations eliminated or reduced. To some extent they may be able to smooth demand by offering inducements or by requiring customers to wait. Failing or following these efforts to reduce the effects of demand level fluctuations, operations managers will seek to accommodate fluctuations by adjusting capacity. However, the opportunities to adopt these strategies for capacity planning will be influenced or limited by the structure of the system. We shall consider only those structures in which resource stocks are maintained, since capacity planning as outlined above is needed only where resources are acquired in anticipation of requirements. In these cases capacity planning will aim to deal with uncertainty about the number of orders to be received and perhaps also uncertainty about the resources needed to satisfy the orders received. The feasibility of each strategy for each of the four structures is outlined in Figure 11.2 and discussed below.

Operating systems which provide for output stocks permit accommodation of fluctuations in demand level through the use of physical stocks, which not only protect the function against unexpected changes in demand level, but also permit a relatively stable level of function activity and thus high capacity utilization. The stock levels employed will often reflect the variability of demand and the 'service level' to be provided, i.e. the acceptable level of probability of stock-out situations with the consequent risk of loss of trade or customer waiting. Systems which are unable to operate with output stocks will in most cases have relatively fixed capacity, hence during temporary high-demand periods they will either require customer waiting or suffer loss of trade. Since some excess capacity will normally be provided, capacity utilization will often be low, especially when demand is highly variable.

Figure 11.2 Capacity planning strategies for systems with resource stocks. From Wild, R. (1977) *Concepts for Operations Management*. New York: Wiley. Reproduced with permission

STRATEGY / STRUCTURE	1. PROVIDE FOR EFFICIENT ADJUSTMENT OF SYSTEM CAPACITY	2. ELIMINATE OR REDUCE NEED FOR ADJUSTMENT OF SYSTEM CAPACITY			
		(a) Maintain sufficient excess capacity	(b) Reduce or smooth effect of demand level fluctuations		
			(i) Capacity limit with effect of		(ii) Use stock to absorb demand fluctuations
			Loss of trade	Customer queuing/waiting	
⇒▽⇒○⇒▽⇒C	Feasible and often desirable to supplement strategy 2b(ii)	Feasible, but not necessary	Feasible, but not normally necessary	Waiting teasible, but not normally necessary	Feasible and normally adopted
⇒▽⇒○⇒C	Feasible and often desirable to supplement strategy 2b(i)	Feasible and may be necessary in conjunction with or instead of 2b(i)	Feasible and normally adopted	Waiting feasible and normally adopted	Not feasible
⇒▽⇒ ○⇒ / C⟹	Feasible and desirable in conjunction with 2a	Feasible and normally adopted	Might be feasible depending on nature of function	Not feasible	Not feasible
⇒▽⇒ ○⇒ / C⇒▽⇒	Feasible and often desirable to supplement strategy 2b(i)	Feasible, but not necessary	Feasible and might be adopted	Queuing feasible and normally adopted	Not feasible

Transport and service systems do not permit function in anticipation of demand, hence either a relatively fixed capacity will be under-utilized despite efforts to maximize the ability of the system to adjust, or customer queuing will be required. The queue size will depend on relative levels and variabilities of demand and function capacity and, in some cases, through the use of scheduling (e.g. appointment) systems, customer queuing can be planned.

The relative values of strategy 1 (provide for efficient adjustment of system capacity) and strategy 2 (eliminate or reduce the need for adjustment in system capacity) are influenced by operating system structure feasibility. Other factors, however, will influence the choice of strategy. If, for example, there is a limit to the size of output stocks, then although strategy 2b (ii) is feasible it may not be possible to rely on this for meeting demand level changes. In most situations it will be desirable to consider providing effective capacity adjustment to meet demand level change, but in most cases effective capacity management will also depend on a preventive strategy, either through the absorption of fluctuation through stock or through customer queuing and waiting. Systems which permit function in anticipation of demand will normally use output stock to protect against demand level fluctuations. Hence the management of the finished goods inventory is of crucial importance. Other systems will normally rely on customer queuing and will, where possible, seek to schedule customer arrivals.

Examples of the types of approach which might be employed in managing capacity are outlined in Table 11.3.

| Table 11.3 | The nature of capacity: examples |

		Capacity management		
Example	Operating system structure	Determination of capacity required	Capacity planning strategy	Principal objectives
Builder (of 'one-off' houses)	→O→C	Demand is measured. Capacity is provided to meet each demand.	1 and/or 2b(i), i.e. Provide for capacity adjustment and/or some excess capacity.	Maximum customer service (in particular through minimizing completion time) + Maximum utilization of (consumed) resource
Fire service	→▽ →O→ C→	Expected demand is forecast. Capacity is provided to meet maximum or near maximum demand.	2a with some possibility of 1. i.e. Eliminate or reduce need for adjustment in system by providing excess capacity with further possibility of providing some capacity adjustment.	No customer queuing + High resource productivity
Furniture removal	→▽ →O→ C→▽	Expected demand is forecast. Capacity is provided to meet average or 'sufficient' demand.	2b(i) (with customer queuing and possibly loss of trade), with possibility of 1. i.e. Eliminate or reduce need for adjustment in system capacity by smoothing effect of demand-level fluctuations through fixing upper capacity limit and accepting loss of trade with the further possibility of providing some capacity adjustment.	Minimum customer queuing and/or loss of trade + High resource productivity

CAPACITY PLANNING

This section deals with procedures for two tasks: first, the determination of the capacity required and the factors affecting the choice of capacity, and second, meeting demand level fluctuations.

Determining the capacity required

The objective here will be the determination of required capacity through either measurement or estimation of the demand to be placed on the system. Estimation or forecasting of future demand will normally be necessary where resources and/or output are stocked. In other situations, since no output or resources are provided prior to receipt of customer order, demand can be measured, hence estimation is unnecessary and the capacity planning problem is considerably simplified.

EXAMPLE

Sport Obermeyer

The ski-wear market is very fickle. For Sport Obermeyer, the trick lies in realizing that although demand for each product can be highly uncertain, the distribution of demand follows a discernible pattern. Obermeyer found that demand data followed a normal distribution and that there are two critical components for accurate planning—assessing a probability distribution for demand and estimating the cost of stockouts and markdowns. The close fit which was found between actual and forecast demand provided a basis for determining which products were safe to produce before additional sales data became available and which were not. Using this information together with data on minimum lot sizes and other production constraints, an appropriate production was formulated.

Source: Coping with demand uncertainly at Sport Obermeyer. *Harvard Business Review* **72**(3), May/June p. 90.

Demand forecasting

The length of the forecast period will depend largely on the nature of system resources and the nature of the market. Capacity plans may involve periods in excess of five years where there is sufficient stability or predictability of demand. A long-term view may be essential where there is a long lead time on the provision or replacement of resources. In contrast, a shorter-term view would be appropriate where demand is less stable or less predictable, and where resources are more readily provided or replaced, or where the manner in which the function is accomplished may change through, for example, technological change.

Figure 11.3 A life-cycle curve for a single good or service

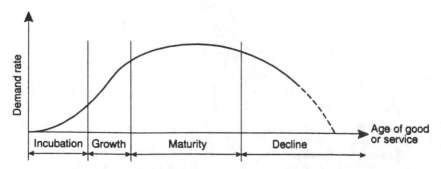

service. Various policies might be employed for the provision of capacity to satisfy such demand. At one extreme, sufficient capacity to meet all expected demand might be provided from the outset, with attendant benefits of economies of scale in ordering, acquisition, training, etc. Alternatively, capacity might be matched to demand by incremental change over time, with benefits in utilization, etc.

Aggregation

The term 'aggregate planning' is often employed in the capacity context. The implication is that such planning is concerned with total demand, i.e. all demands collected together. This is of relevance only where different goods or services are provided, and in such cases aggregate or capacity planning will seek to estimate or measure all demands and express the total in such a way as to enable sufficient total capacity to be provided. Demand for all outputs must therefore be expressed in common units such as the number of resources or resource hours required.

Resource improvement and deterioration

In determining the quantity of resources required to meet either forecast or measured demand, it should be noted that the capability, or capacity, of a given set of resources might also change with time. The reliability of machinery might change and the efficiency of labour might improve, due to the learning effect. (The effect of such learning is to increase the capacity of a given quantity of labour resource.) Such capacity change effects may be of considerable importance in capacity planning.

Economic operating levels

Figure 11.4 shows the relationship between the unit cost of processing and the throughput rate for a hypothetical situation. The economic throughput rate is p^1 since this is the rate at which the unit cost is least. The use of a higher throughput rate involves higher unit costs, as does a lower throughput rate. Such a situation will often exist, especially where an operating system has been designed specifically to process items or customers at a particular rate.

If, for the type of situation shown in Figure 11.4, it is now considered appropriate to increase the level of resources in order to provide for a greater throughput rate, then it may be possible to shift the entire curve as shown in Figure 11.5. This implies that the

Figure 11.4 Unit cost/volume relationship

Figure 11.5 Unit cost/volume relationships

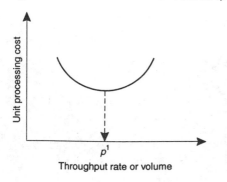

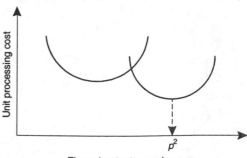

facilities have been rearranged or set up in a different manner so that the intended rate is now p^2. Again, departures from this throughput rate p^2 can incur increased unit costs.

This concept of an 'economic operating level' is relevant in many situations and is of value in capacity planning since, where curves such as those shown in Figures 11.4 and 11.5 are available or can be approximated, the cost of changing capacity through the adoption of capacity planning strategy 1 can be established for different magnitudes of change.

Notice that in some situations the cost/throughput rate relationship is not a 'smooth' one. For example, in some situations a throughput rate can be increased only incrementally. However, whatever the nature of the relationship, providing it is known or can be approximated, the economic level of operations can be found and the cost of capacity changes above or below a particular level can be obtained.

Cumulation

The capacity provided to satisfy estimated or measured demand will, as mentioned above, be influenced by the strategy employed for meeting demand fluctuations. The use of *cumulative curves* is a method of examining alternatives.

Table 11.4 gives the estimated monthly demand for a one-year period. The figures are plotted cumulatively in Figure 11.6, which also shows two possible cumulative capacity

Figure 11.6 Cumulative demand and capacity curves

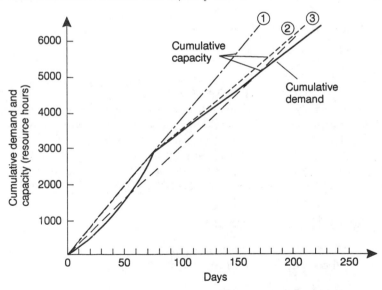

curves. Curve 1 corresponds to a capacity of 37.5 resource hours per day—the minimum required to ensure that capacity is always equal to or in excess of expected demand for this period. The adoption of a strategy of providing sufficient excess capacity to eliminate the need for capacity adjustment (strategy 2(a)), would lead to the provision of such capacity. The provision of approximately 30 resource hours per day—curve 2—might result from the adoption of a different strategy for the use of resources (strategy 2(b)). Such an arrangement would give rise to either increasing output stock or reducing cus-

Table 11.4	Estimated monthly demand			
Month	Working days	Cumulative days	Estimated demand (in resource hours)	Cumulative estimated demand
Jan.	20	20	500	500
Feb.	18	38	650	1150
Mar.	22	60	750	1900
Apr.	18	78	900	2800
May	21	99	700	3500
June	20	119	500	4000
July	20	139	300	4300
Aug.	10	149	300	4600
Sept.	20	169	450	5050
Oct.	21	190	500	5550
Nov.	20	210	550	6100
Dec.	18	228	300	6400

tomer waiting time during the period up to day 50 and after day 160, when capacity exceeds demand. Day 50 to day 160 would see:

(a) stock diminishing or depleted, and/or

(b) increased customer waiting time, and/or

(c) loss of trade,

since capacity would be lower than expected demand.

Both curves 1 and 2 require no capacity adjustment during this period. The adoption of an approach relying wholly upon or involving the strategy of providing for efficient adjustment in capacity (strategy 1) might give rise to the provision of capacity in the manner of curve 3, in which one capacity adjustment is made (at day 75) and which provides for the satisfaction of all forecast demand without the use of output stocks, customer queuing or loss of trade, yet with better capacity utilization than curve 1.

Meeting demand-level fluctuations

In this section we shall examine the procedures by which capacity management strategies might be implemented and the factors which will influence their relative merit and cost.

Adjustment of capacity

Some aspects and implications of the strategy of adjusting system capacity are considered below.

Make or buy/subcontract

An organization may find another willing to take some of the excess demand. This will often involve a higher cost per unit processed because of subcontractor overheads and profit and increased cost of inspection, administration, transport, etc. Such an approach is often least reliable, most expensive and least flexible when it is needed most, since a need for greater capacity is often associated with a general increase in total 'industry' demand. At such time, potential subcontractors will also be busy.

Workforce and hours changes

Not all system outputs will necessarily be subject to high demand simultaneously. If labour can move from one function/system to another and machinery is also flexible, high demand for one output may be offset by low demand elsewhere. Again this approach may be least reliable when most needed, for the reasons given above. The additional costs incurred derive from the time and effort invested in multi-job training and lower performance during learning periods.

Changes in labour force and working hours are the normal means of adjusting system capacity. The most used method for increasing labour capacity is overtime working. Overtime and shift premiums are added costs, and productivity may be lower, supervision and service costs higher, etc. Long hours may also lead to more accidents, more illness and greater absenteeism. Where layoffs are undesirable, overtime working is preferable to adding temporary workers. Adding workers to the payroll increases the costs of recruitment and training. Employment often can be reduced without formal layoffs. Normal labour turnover may help reduce labour capacity. Again this approach may be unavailable when most required. An alternative to layoffs is shorter work weeks or idle time. The latter requires the company to carry the cost of under-utilized capacity.

Deferred maintenance

In periods of temporary high demand it is possible to keep resources operating longer by not closing down as scheduled. Demand reductions will permit shutdowns earlier than originally scheduled. The costs involved in such an approach may derive from the difficulties of scheduling the use of maintenance facilities, earlier breakdowns, etc.

Activity scheduling

The selection of the appropriate activity schedules, including if possible the scheduling of customer arrivals, can contribute considerably to the ability of the system to meet demand fluctuations. Such changes, which will not affect capacity substantially, are relevant only for capacity increase. Costs incurred derive from the increased complexity of scheduling and control, perhaps to some extent offset by higher capacity utilization.

Avoidance or reduction of need for capacity adjustment

Some aspects and implications of this strategy are examined below.

Refusing business, reducing service and adjusting backlogs

An organization may decline an order when its capacity is fully utilized. If capacity is short throughout an industry the organization may be able to lengthen its deliveries, and therefore its customer queues, without loss of trade. In such cases the customer's order may simply be added to the backlog of work. In the opposite situation reduction of the backlog is desirable. Given customer queuing during periods of high demand, greater flexibility may exist in selecting orders to fill in the gaps in activity schedules. This may give better capacity utilization but poorer customer service, which may be tolerated if competitors offer similar delivery at a comparable price.

Adjustments in inventory levels

An output stock permits the utilization of capacity during low demand periods and relieves the congestion, helps avoid queuing, etc. during peak loads. In some cases partly completed output may be stocked, and finished on receipt of order. Customer service might be improved and this may bring an increased share of the demand, greater workloads and further capacity problems. The costs of inventory are related primarily to the opportunity costs of the capital invested and the risks of obsolescence. To maintain operations, prices can be manipulated, especially on goods and services where individual price quotations are offered subject to negotiation. When demand is high, prices can be increased to increase total contribution; and in low demand periods, prices can be lowered towards variable costs to help reduce the fall in demand placed on the system.

KEY POINTS FOR CHAPTER 11

Capacity management is the key strategic decision area for operations management.

Capacity management decisions are influenced by operations objectives (the 'desirability' constraint) and system structure (the 'feasibility' constraint).

Capacity management takes place within an overall operations planning and control context.

Capacity management is concerned with the matching of the capacity of a system with the demands placed on that system.

The main problem faced in capacity management is demand uncertainty.

There are two aspects to capacity management:

1. Determining the normal capacity required;
2. Dealing with fluctuations demand.

There are two basic strategies for dealing with demand fluctuations:

1. Adjustment;
2. Elimination or reduction of adjustment.

There are several means to implement each of these strategies.

The choice of strategy will be influenced by objectives and system structure.

The effectiveness of the strategy will influence resource utilization and/or customer service.

In deciding on the normal capacity required, and in selecting the strategy for dealing with fluctuations, the following will be of relevance:

forecasting;

demand aggregation;

economic operating levels;

demand life cycles.

FURTHER READING

Vollmann, T. E., Berry, W. L. and Whybark, D. C. (1988) *Manufacturing Planning and Control Systems*. Homewood, Ill.:

Irwin, Eilon S. (1975) Five approaches to aggregate production planning.

AIIE Trans. 7(2), pp. 118–31.

Jarrett, J. (1991) *Business Forecasting Methods*. 2nd edition. Oxford: Basil Blackwell.

QUESTIONS

1.1 What are the two basic capacity management strategies? Describe, with examples, the use of each and their use together.

11.2 Identify and discuss the relevance of the various approaches available for the adjustment of capacity. Indicate what factors or considerations might encourage or prevent the use of each.

11.3 What is aggregate planning? Show, using your own figures, how the cumulative graph method might be used to compare alternative capacity plans for a future one-year period given the forecast demand for the three products produced by a company.

11.4 A company has decided to set up an interior design consultancy. It will provide a service for individuals and organizations on the design of rooms, offices, furnishings, decorations, etc. What type of capacity planning problems might be encountered and how might they be dealt with?

PART 6

Operations Scheduling

INTRODUCTION TO PART 6

The scheduling of the activities within the operating system is another principal problem area of operations management, as defined in Chapter 1. As with capacity management (see Introduction to Part 5), the strategies employed in activity scheduling will again be influenced by:

(a) feasibility constraints (influenced mainly by the operating system structure);

(b) desirability factors (influenced mainly by the organization's and operations manager's objectives).

The nature of the activity scheduling problem will be influenced by the operating system structure, but equally, activity scheduling decisions can change that structure. Further, the objectives being pursued by the operations manager, in particular the relative importance of resource utilization and customer service, will influence the selection of an activity scheduling strategy but, given some freedom of choice, the operations manager may prefer to employ an approach which insulates the operating system from external uncertainties, e.g. demand changes.

Here we deal with the scheduling (or planning or timing) of the conversion activities of the operating system. We try first to identify the different types of scheduling problems which can be encountered, and then consider some techniques for their solution. Further details on some of the techniques and procedures are then dealt with in the other chapters in this part.

Chapter 12

Activity scheduling

ISSUES

What is the purpose of activity scheduling?
What are the basic types of scheduling problem?
What are the basic strategies for scheduling?
What is JIT?
What are the appropriate procedures for scheduling?

Activity scheduling is an aspect of operations management which has considerable strategic importance. Decisions in this area will be influenced by business strategy, and will in turn influence performance and effectiveness of the business as regards both service to customers and resource utilization.

The nature of the scheduling problems faced by operations managers will be influenced by the structure of the operating system. The system's structure influences what operations managers can feasibly do in scheduling activities. Also, the nature of the problems is influenced by operations objectives: these influence what, desirably, the manager should achieve.

Within these constraints of what can be done and what should be achieved, the operations managers will have preferences—that is, they may wish to deal with scheduling problems in particular ways, if possible.

This framework for decision-making was set out in Chapter 1. Within this framework, the operations manager must decide what general approach or strategy to use in dealing with activities scheduling, and then identify the most appropriate procedures to follow to implement that strategy. This two-stage approach will be used in this chapter. First we examine the nature of scheduling problems and the strategies that are available, then we examine scheduling procedures. These issues are relevant in all types of business.

EXAMPLE

English county cricket

Each team in the English County Cricket Championship plays against some other teams twice a year but against others only once. One main aim in trying to develop a new scheduling system was to overcome any inherent problems by producing a four-year schedule of opponents that was as fair as possible and that could clearly be seen to be fair, while still allowing for traditional rivalries between certain teams.

Source: Wright, M. (1992) A fair allocation of county cricket opponents. *Journal of the Operational Research Society* **43**(3), pp. 195–201.

STRATEGIES FOR ACTIVITY SCHEDULING

Here we are dealing with the activities which take place *within* the operating system. An activity schedule will show the times (or dates) at which all of these activities are to be undertaken. The fixing of such times determines the manner in which items or (in the case of service and transport systems) customers will flow through the operating system. The activity scheduling problem is concerned with the fixing of these times in advance. The manner in which the problem is tackled will depend largely on the situation in which activity scheduling is undertaken. For example, if an operating system is working in anticipation of demand, the scheduling problems will differ from those in an operating system which is working specifically to satisfy individual customers' 'due date' requirements. Other factors will influence the nature of the activity scheduling problem and therefore the techniques which might be appropriate for the solution of that problem. In order better to understand the nature of the activity scheduling problem, we shall first consider two factors:

(a) whether scheduling is to be 'internally' or 'externally' oriented;

(b) whether demand is 'dependent' or 'independent'.

Internally and externally oriented scheduling

Activity scheduling is concerned with the timing of activities, but these times must be fixed in relation to some other requirements. Consider as an example a situation in which products are manufactured against a specific customer order. Each customer order specifies exactly what is to be produced and when it is required—the 'due date'. Here the internal activities which create end products must all be scheduled so that each end product is available by the required 'due' or delivery date. A similar situation can exist in non-manufacturing organizations. Here those activities which are necessary to satisfy a particular service or transport requirement must be performed in time to satisfy a particular customer's request. In all such cases the customer has a *direct* influence on the timing of activities within the operating system, so activity scheduling can be seen to be *externally* oriented in that the timing of all activities is fixed to satisfy *particular* external customer timing requirements.

In contrast, consider a situation in which items are manufactured for stock in anticipation of future customer orders. Here there need be no *direct* influence from a particular customer on the internal activity schedule. Customers are satisfied from stock and the need to replenish this stock gives rise to the need to schedule activities within the operating system. A similar situation can exist in service and transport systems, where a system is 'buffered' from its customers by an input queue. In these circumstances the activity scheduling can be mainly *internally* oriented, and in such cases there can be more freedom in activity scheduling, so schedules can be fixed more easily to maximize resource utilization, etc.

Thus the nature of the activity scheduling problem can in part be defined by the *orien-*

tation of scheduling. Clearly, the structure of the operating system will have some influence on the choice of a scheduling strategy. In some cases an internal scheduling strategy seems likely to be more apparent. In other cases, it seems likely that an external strategy will be employed. It is not only a matter of feasibility, but also of desirability. In fact it is feasible to employ an internal strategy in all situations, but clearly in some cases the consequences of doing so, for customer service in respect of timing, will make that type of approach quite unattractive.

The systems which have a goods stock between the function and the customer, and those in which there is a customer queue (i.e. system structures SOS, DOS, DQO and SQO—using the notation from Chapter 1), permit the use of an internal scheduling strategy without risking customer service on timing.

In contrast, for the other system structures, in which there is no buffer between demand and the function, the adoption of an internal scheduling strategy, whilst feasible, seems likely to give rise to relatively poor customer service on timing. So, unless service on timing is unimportant the use of an external scheduling strategy is more likely.

Table 12.1 outlines some typical situations and suggests the approach which might be used for activity scheduling.

Table 12.1	Scheduling strategies – some typical situations				
Example	**Function**	**System structure**	**Operations objectives**	**Scheduling strategy**	**Comments**
Routine surgery ward in a large public hospital	Service	SQO	Resource utilization and customer service on specification	Internal	Waiting lists of patients will exist, and appointments will be given to ensure full use of facilities
Ambulance service	Transport	SCO	Customer service on timing and specification	External	Resource utilization will be low as ambulances stand by for emergencies
Bank cash machine or 'Auto Teller' providing 24-hour service	Supply	SOD	Customer service on specification timing	External	The aim is to enable customers to be supplied on demand Utilization of the machine will be low
Domestic appliance manufacturer	Manufacturer	SOS	Resource utilization and customer service on timing (and cost or specification)	Internal	Goods are made in anticipation of future orders, and held in stock in the distribution 'channel'

'JUST IN TIME'—EXTERNALLY ORIENTED SCHEDULING AND ITS IMPLICATIONS

The Just in Time concept is simple, but its adoption has widespread implications. JIT is the application of an externally oriented approach to activity scheduling, but its implementation—perhaps even more so than in other approaches to scheduling—has an impact on inventory and capacity management and other areas of responsibility of operations managers.

This is a convenient place at which to introduce some of the concepts of JIT, although some details will also be considered elsewhere (especially Chapters 16 and 17).

The philosophy

JIT was developed in manufacturing, but the philosophy has far more widespread application. JIT has been defined as involving 'the production of the necessary items in the necessary quantities at the necessary time'. In other words, with this approach, the materials and items required by a process are made available at that process as and when they are required, and not before. This seemingly simple idea in fact contrasts markedly with practice in many operating systems which depend upon substantial inventories. Thus, with the JIT approach, queues awaiting processing at an operation are minimal. Work-in-progress, therefore, is low. Throughput times are reduced, space requirements are reduced, and flow through the system is virtually continuous. Given the uncertainty which exists in most operating systems, it has been quite common to build inventories into the system to provide some degree of safety and to 'de-couple' processes. If an inventory exists between two processes then the failure of one does not immediately impact on the activities of the other. An inventory might also exist so that increases in demand can be met without the immediate need to change the rate at which the operating system works. Inventories of output items, work-in-progress and materials are commonplace in industry for these reasons. The JIT approach, however, completely reverses this principle. In JIT inventories are minimized, and work is not done until required. Items are not processed until required at the next process, and processes are interdependent.

JIT aims to create a zero or low inventory operating system. It is argued that the reduction in inventory is of considerable benefit in its own right, e.g. to reduce space requirements, reduce the amount of tied-up capital, reduce the risk of loss and damage and reduce handling requirements. In addition, the elimination of inventories is considered to have considerable managerial benefits. If, as is often the case, inventories have grown up in order to protect an operating system against uncertainties, then it can be argued that such inventories serve to conceal the real problems, whilst JIT aims to reveal them in order that they can be tackled at source. Thus for low inventory operation, problems must be identified and solved. If input stocks of materials have been held in order to protect an organization from disruptions in supply, then the use of JIT requires that those problems be overcome through, for example, the use of different vendors, and/or the establishment of different arrangements with suppliers. If work-in-progress stocks have been held to protect against the breakdown of equipment, the introduction of JIT requires that the causes of breakdown be identified and eliminated. Thus JIT has both system and managerial advantages.

JIT AS AN OPERATIONS POLICY

On the framework developed in Chapter 2, JIT is concerned with the pursuit of cost, speed and flexibility, as means to achieve competitive advantage. So the emphasis is on achieving customer service with an emphasis on cost and timing.

Elements of the JIT policy

There are six characteristics of JIT:

'Demand call'

The entire system is led or pulled by demand, i.e. the system is externally scheduled. The need to serve/supply a customer triggers activities throughout the operating system. Thus, where a customer places an order for a manufacturing operation, that order requirement flows back through the system triggering each stage of the overall process. This contrasts with the practice in many manufacturing systems where work is begun when materials become available. (This might be regarded as an input 'push' system.)

Reduced set-up times and smaller batch sizes

Excepting in systems where only one type of product or service is provided, it will be necessary to 'set up' processes in order that they can deal with a particular type of item. This is a basic characteristic of a batch processing system. The JIT aim of processing items only as and when required necessitates the processing of small batch sizes. It will be shown in Chapter 14 that reducing the cost of set-ups, which in turn is related to set-up time, reduces the economic batch size. JIT, therefore, is associated with small batch sizes and short, economical set-ups.

Efficient flow

The need for rapid throughput and the avoidance of substantial work-in-progress and thus the need for space necessitates—and enables—efficient flow systems to be established. The rapid movement of items between processes is an essential prerequisite. Rationalization of flows is therefore a requirement.

These three aspects are the essential characteristics of a JIT system. They are the necessary characteristics. However, in practice, because of the manner in which JIT is normally pursued, there are three additional characteristics:

Employee involvement

The interdependence of operations, the rapid flow and the absence of buffers necessitate smooth and efficient control. In practice this has been found to necessitate the active participation of all employees. In this way, possible disruptions can be seen and avoided, and operations scheduling and control improved also. In practice, however, in the introduction of JIT improved communications and participation is also one of the principal aims. It is pursued because of its intrinsic benefits. JIT in effect provides the opportunity to achieve participation in matters such as quality control, problem-solving work, etc. (See the discussion of quality circles in Chapter 19.)

Kanban

Kanban is a device used in the scheduling of activities in JIT systems. It is a Japanese name for 'card'. The Kanban system, and its derivatives, has become the standard means for achieving production control with JIT. This aspect will be considered in detail in Chapter 18.

Visibility

One of the principal objectives of JIT is simplicity. One means to achieve and sustain a simple system is by ensuring visibility, e.g. one of our objectives is to ensure that stocks are visible. The ability to see what is happening is an important characteristic of JIT.

Benefits of JIT

From the above, it will be clear that the benefits of JIT include:

(a) reduced inventories and work-in-progress;

(b) reduced space requirement;

(c) shorter throughput times;

(d) greater employee involvement, participation and motivation;

(e) smoother work flows.

To these can be added the following, also normally sought and achieved in good JIT systems:

(f) greater productivity;

(g) improved product/service quality;

(h) improved customer service;

(i) more uniform loading of facilities.

These benefits derive in part from the systems efficiencies of JIT, and also from the managerial/organizational benefits. Some are direct benefits whilst others are indirect.

EXAMPLE

Cummins Engine

Cummins Engine (UK) found itself falling behind its Far East competitors. At that time, Japanese competitors had 80 per cent lower inventory levels, more responsiveness to customers, and almost no scrap or rework. Cummins decided to implement just-in-time (JIT) manufacturing, which involves reducing non-value-added activities. At its Darlington plant, $25-million was invested in JIT tools, including automated assembly, automated guided vehicles, and a computerized assembly information-management system. JIT reduced overhead labour cost by 30 per cent, reduced floor space required by 31 per cent and reduced work in process by 97 per cent. Batch size was reduced from 25 to 6, time spent on large machine tools was reduced by up to 80 per cent. A Kanban system helped decrease inventory from a 29-day supply to an 8-day supply and eliminated some material shortages.

Source: Mullins, P. (1989) *JITs Competitive Edge Production*.**101**(7), July, pp. 62–64.

PREREQUISITES FOR EFFECTIVE JIT

1. Low variety of items being processed

2. Demand stability

3. Vendor reliability (to ensure reliable supply)

4. Defect-free materials (to avoid disruptions)

5. Good communications (to help ensure continuous operation and minimum disruption)

6. Preventive maintenance

7. Total Quality Control

8. Management commitment

9. Employee involvement

10. Worker flexibility

EXAMPLE

JIT in health care

The feasibility of using just-in-time (JIT) in the health care industry was examined through a study of several cases which used JIT as well as those that do not. The research revealed the different impacts that the introduction of JIT philosophy had had on the health care industry's inventory management, service quality, and competitiveness. The introduction of the JIT philosophy in the health care industry's material management system was seen to have improved that system and reduced implementation problems. It was found that great potential existed for the successful implementation of JIT for material management even though most of the JIT in the health care industry is still in its early stages of development.

Source: Kim, G. and Rifai, A.K. (1992) Efficient, approach to health care industry material resource management. *Hospital Material Management Quarterly* **13**(3), pp. 10–24.

Dependent and independent demand

Another way of describing the activity scheduling situation is to consider the relationship between demand for the outputs of the operating system (i.e. the products or services) and the need to perform the various activities which take place within the operating system. Consider as an example the manufacture of a complex product consisting of several components, parts, sub-assemblies, etc.

If in this case we know the parts and components which are required to produce a particular end product, and if we know the demand for that product, then we can, for a particular period of time, calculate exactly what activities must be performed within the system to satisfy that demand. Thus there is a completely *dependent* relationship between demand, which is known, and the activities required within the operating system. A similar situation can exist in the non-manufacturing organization where the satisfaction of a particular customer requirement, e.g. a service or transport, requires the performance of particular activities within the system and where demand for that service is known, and hence the particular activities which must be performed can be calculated and known with certainty.

Thus we can describe a *dependent activity demand situation* as one in which a knowledge of customer demand in terms of both *what* is required and *when* it is required permits us to calculate what activities must be performed within the operating system in a particular period of time.

In contrast, an *independent activity demand situation* exists where it is impossible to calculate exactly what activities are required within the operating system in a particular period of time. Such a situation can exist *either* where there is not enough knowledge about demand, i.e. customers' orders are not known in advance or there is a good deal of uncertainty about future customer orders, *or* where there is no clear relationship between the nature of the product, service, transport, etc., required by the customer and the nature of the activities which must be performed by the operating system to satisfy that customer requirement. In an independent activity demand situation, therefore, the activity scheduling problem is more complex since there are more uncertainties. In this type of situation it will often be necessary to estimate or forecast in some way the amount of activities required to satisfy some future, as yet unknown, demand, and then to schedule those activities to take place so that the end products are available at what is expected to be the right time, or so that the service or transport is available when customers arrive.

TYPES OF SCHEDULING PROBLEM

The distinction between the internal and external orientation of scheduling, and that between dependent and independent activity demand, are relevant in identifying different types of activity scheduling situations. These two factors are *interrelated* and normally those responsible for the scheduling of activities will find themselves dealing with a situation in which there is either dependent activity demand and externally oriented scheduling or, in total contrast, independent activity demand and internally oriented activity scheduling. These are the two normal and distinctive activity scheduling situations but a third situation is possible, as outlined in Table 12.2. These three situations are described in more detail below.

Externally oriented activity scheduling with dependent activity demand

Here the nature of the customers' demand on the system is known, whether for goods, services or transport. The customers have been identified and their requirements determined in terms of both the nature of the things required and the time when those things are required. There is a known relationship between the nature of products or services provided by the organization and the types of activities which must be performed within the organization so that these outputs or services are available. Thus given the knowledge of demand and given this relationship, the activities required by the operating system and the dates by which these activities must be completed can be calculated. Here the activity scheduling problem is that of determining when to do given activities such as to satisfy given customer due date requirements, while also satisfying certain internal requirements, e.g. capacity requirements.

Appropriate scheduling techniques for this type of activity scheduling situation will include:

(a) materials requirements planning (see this chapter);

(b) network analysis using scheduled project completion dates (see Chapter 13);

(c) line of balance (see Chapter 14);

(d) reverse or forward scheduling (see this chapter).

| Table 12.2 | Activity scheduling situations |

	Externally oriented activity scheduling	Internally oriented activity scheduling
	①	③
Dependent activity demand	*Situation* Customer demand known in terms of what is required, quantities and due dates. Hence the activities required to satisfy this demand can be calculated.	*Situation* Customer demand known in terms of what is required, quantities and due dates, but due dates not taken into account *or* demand stated only in terms of what is required and the quantities (i.e. no due date requirement). The activities which are needed can be calculated.
	Activity scheduling problems Determine when known activities must be done to satisfy given customer due dates while also satisfying internal requirements.	*Activity scheduling problems* Determine when known activities must be done to satisfy internal requirements.
	Appropriate techniques MRP (Chapter 12). 'Reverse' network analysis, i.e. with scheduled project completion dates (Chapter 13). Line of balance (Chapter 14). Reverse scheduling (Chapter 12) for production and supply. Forward scheduling (Chapter 12) for service and transport.	*Appropriate techniques* Forward network analysis (i.e. without scheduled project completion dates) (Chapter 12). Sequencing (Chapter 12). Batch scheduling (Chapter 14). Dispatching (Chapter 12). Assignment (Chapter 12). Forward scheduling for production and supply (Chapter 12). Flow scheduling (Chapter 15). Timetabling (Chapter 12).
	④	②
Independent activity demand		*Situation* Activities to be completed in a given time period must be *estimated*.
		Activity scheduling problems Determine when activities must be done to satisfy the estimated overall requirements for the period while satisfying internal requirements.
	Does not normally exist	*Appropriate techniques* Forward network analysis (i.e. without scheduled project completion dates) (Chapter 12). Sequencing (Chapter 12). Dispatching (Chapter 12). Assignment (Chapter 12). Forward scheduling for production and supply (Chapter 12). Batch scheduling (Chapter 14). Flow scheduling (Chapter 15). Timetabling (Chapter 12).

Internally oriented activity scheduling with independent activity demand

Here we have little information about customer demand. It is not possible to calculate actual activity requirements, so the nature and quantity of the activities which must be performed within the operating system will be obtained by direct forecasting of activity requirements. The activity scheduling problem in this situation therefore involves the timing of an estimated activity requirement in order to satisfy a period's estimated needs while also satisfying internal, e.g. capacity, requirements. In this situation there are no known customers and no definite due dates.

Appropriate techniques for use in this type of situation might include.

(a) network analysis without the use of schedule end dates (see Chapter 13);

(b) sequencing (see this chapter);

(c) dispatching (see this chapter);

(d) assignment (see this chapter);

(e) forward scheduling (see this chapter);

(f) batch scheduling (see Chapter 14);

(g) flow scheduling (see Chapter 15);

(h) timetabling (see this chapter).

Internally oriented activity scheduling with dependent activity demand

This situation will not occur often. However, it is possible to envisage such an approach where, even though knowledge of customer demand permits the calculation of the activities required within the system in terms of quantity, nature and due dates, it is nevertheless intended that scheduling of these activities is undertaken primarily to satisfy internal requirements. The situation therefore differs from ① in that the scheduling problem is not specifically concerned with due date requirements. It differs from ② in that the activities which are to be performed during a particular period of time are known with certainty rather than being a result of the estimates.

Such a situation might occur where it is necessary to manufacture goods against specific customer orders without a due date requirement, or where items are to be supplied to particular customers without any due date/dates being imposed by such customers. In transport or service industries such a situation may exist where it is necessary to deal with particular customers and their requirements over a period of time, but where the timing of this provision is not imposed by customers. The scheduling techniques which might be appropriate in this situation are similar to those for ②.

MANAGING DEMAND UNCERTAINTY

At the beginning of this chapter we noted that one purpose of scheduling was to deal with demand uncertainty, i.e. with uncertain timing of demand. Our initial analysis of scheduling strategies has shown that in some cases it is feasible to adopt an approach which enables schedules to be fixed without direct reference to individual customers' timing requirements. This 'internal strategy' eliminates the need to deal directly with timing uncertainties. An 'external strategy', however, brings operations managers face to face with the problem. This is often unavoidable—especially where output stocks of items or input queues of customers cannot or may not exist. In such situations attempts can be made to reduce scheduling problems by managing demand uncertainty. Rarely can this be done to such an extent as to eliminate *all* uncertainty about timing, but often *something* can be done—sufficient, that is, to influence the way in which we schedule the activities of the operating system.

The problem of 'random arrivals'

In many situations demand from individual customers is entirely random. Individuals may arrive at a transport or service system, or customers may arrive at a manufacturer or supply system at random intervals. The only method of dealing with such arrivals, if waiting is to be avoided, is 'external scheduling' coupled with the use of 'total' excess capacity (strategy 2a) for capacity management. (see Chapter 11)

In practice, since it will not often be possible to have excess capacity on all occasions, some waiting by customers will occur. A complementary approach is to try to reduce the randomness of the arrival pattern. If this can be done, arrivals can be anticipated, capacity requirements may be reduced, and scheduling could thus be made easier.

Appointments and reservations

This is the normal way to manage demand uncertainty. It is employed extensively in service systems such as hospitals, dental practices, professional services, etc. It makes arrival times and thus the arrival rate of customers more certain. If the 'work content' of customers—i.e. the extent of the demand that they will place on the system—is also known, it makes the level of demand more certain. By giving appointments to customers, i.e. by obliging them to arrive at the system at particular times, an internal scheduling strategy is in effect made possible where otherwise an external approach would have been employed. Similarly, by offering reservations, i.e. pre-committing activities, to customers, the same is achieved. Such an approach is often used in conjunction with the timetabling of activities (dealt with later in this chapter).

ACTIVITY SCHEDULING TECHNIQUES

The discussion above has identified which types of scheduling techniques might be appropriate in different activity scheduling situations. A third factor will influence which type of technique is employed in a particular situation: this factor is concerned with the nature of the process involved within the operating system. Let us take as an example a system in which the operating system provides services to satisfy different customer requirements. No two customers ever come to the system with precisely the same requirements, so the operating system must respond to quite different customer needs. This is a form of 'one-off' situation. A similar situation can exist in the manufacturing industry where items are to be manufactured against specific customer orders and where such orders are never repeated. In the manufacturing context this will be referred to as project production.

In contrast, there are manufacturing systems which produce one type of item only to satisfy the needs of a particular set of customers; this might be a form of repetitive production. A similar situation can exist in service or transport industries where an operating system exists solely to provide one particular service or transport for customers who require, or are prepared to accept, that service or transport. There are also intermediate situations in which jobbing or batch processes are employed.

The type of scheduling technique used in a particular situation will depend on the factors outlined in Table 12.2 (see p. 205), and in addition on whether the activities are to

| Table 12.3 | Activity scheduling techniques for project, jobbing, batch and flow systems | | | | | |

Scheduling technique	Brief description	Project	Jobbing	Batch	Flow	See Chapter:
A Reverse scheduling (Gantt charts)	A technique by which the durations of particular activities are subtracted from a required completion date, i.e. the schedules for all the activities required for the satisfaction of some particular customer requirements are determined by scheduling in reverse from the required due date.	√	√	√		12
B Forward scheduling (Gantt charts)	The opposite of reverse scheduling, where the scheduled times for a particular set of activities are determined by forward scheduling from a given date in order ultimately to obtain a date for completion of a particular set of activities or project.	√	√	√		12
C Sequencing	The determination of the best order for processing a known set of jobs through a given set of facilities in order, for example, to minimize total throughput time, minimize queuing, minimize facility idle time, etc.		√	?		12
D Dispatching	A technique by which it is possible to identify which of an available set of jobs to process next on an available facility in order to minimize, over a period of time, throughput times, lateness, etc.		√	?		12
E Assignment	A technique by which it is possible to assign or allocate an available set of jobs against an available set of resources (where each job may be undertaken on more than one resource), in order to minimize throughput time, maximize resource utilization, etc.	?	√	?		12

Table 12.3 continued

Scheduling technique	Brief description	Project	Jobbing	Batch	Flow	See Chapter:
F Timetabling	Techniques resulting in the development of a schedule, timetable or rota indicating when certain facilities or resources will be available to those wishing to use them.				√	12
G Materials requirements planning (MRP)	A technique by which known customer demand requirements are 'exploded' to produce 'gross' parts, components or activity requirements. These 'gross' requirements are compared with available inventories to produce 'net' requirements which are then scheduled within available capacity limitations. MRP is for scheduling and also for inventory management and capacity management.	?	?	√		12
H MRP II	A development of MRP, but far broader in concept and application.	?	√	√	?	12
I Network analysis (or critical path analysis)	A technique by which the various interrelated and interdependent activities required in the completion of a complex project can be scheduled, with any slack or free time being identified. The technique can be used in scheduling activities from a start date (forward NA) or by working backwards from a required completion date (backward NA).	√	?	?		13
J Batch scheduling	A technique involving the determination of optimum batch sizes and a schedule for the completion of such batches on a set of facilities. The batch sizes are determined by comparing set-up (or change) costs with holding or inventory costs. The schedule is determined by reference to these batch sizes. The technique is concerned with both scheduling and inventory management.			√	?	14

Table 12.3 continued		Project	Jobbing	Batch	Flow	See Chapter:
Scheduling technique	Brief description					
K Line of balance (LOB)	A technique which permits the calculation of the quantities of the particular activities or parts and components which must have been completed by a particular intermediate date, in order that some final delivery schedule might be satisfied. It is therefore a scheduling and a control technique.			√		14
L Flow scheduling	A technique for establishing appropriate facilities for the processing of items and customers where each item or customer passes through the same facilities in the same order. The technique is concerned primarily with meeting certain output requirements in terms of cycle time and balancing the use of the resources within the system.			?	√	15

be scheduled in a project, jobbing, batch or repetitive manner. This distinction is rather simplistic, since there are areas of overlap between the four categories; however, it is sufficient for our present purposes. Table 12.3 lists the activity scheduling techniques previously introduced in Table 12.2. Each technique is described briefly and some indication is given of whether the technique will be appropriate for project and/or jobbing and/or batch and/or repetitive processes.

Reference to Tables 12.2 and 12.3 will indicate which scheduling technique might be appropriate for a given situation. Some of the main techniques are described in the remainder of this chapter.

REVERSE SCHEDULING

External due date considerations will directly influence activity scheduling in certain structures. The approach adopted in scheduling activities in such cases will often involve a form of reverse scheduling.

One problem with such reverse or 'due date' scheduling is in estimating the total time to be allowed for each operation, in particular the time to be allowed for waiting or queuing at facilities. Some queuing of jobs (whether items or customers) at facilities is often desirable since, where processing times through facilities are uncertain, high utilization is achieved only by the provision of such queues.

Operation times are often available, but queuing times are rarely known initially and can only be estimated.

Schedules of this type are usually depicted on Gantt or bar charts. The advantage of this type of presentation is that the load on any facility or any department is clear at a glance, and available or spare capacity is easily identified. The major disadvantage is that the dependencies between operations are not shown. Notice that, in scheduling the processing of items or customers, total throughput time can be minimized by the batching of similar items to save set-up time, inspection time, etc.

FORWARD SCHEDULING

For a manufacturing or supply organization a forward scheduling procedure is the equivalent of that described above. This approach will be particularly relevant where scheduling is undertaken on an internally oriented basis and the objective is to determine the dates or times for subsequent activities, given the times for an earlier activity, e.g. a starting time.

In the case of service or transport organizations, the objective will be to schedule forward from a given start date, where that start date will often be the customer due date, e.g. the date at which the customer arrives into the system. In these circumstances, therefore, forward scheduling will be an appropriate method for dealing with externally oriented scheduling activities.

SEQUENCING

Sequencing procedures seek to determine the best order for processing a set of jobs, whether items or customers, through a set of facilities.

Two types of problem can be identified. First, the static case, in which all jobs to be processed are known and are available, and in which no additional jobs arrive in the queue during the exercise. Second, the dynamic case, which allows for the continuous arrival of jobs in the queue. In the static case the problem is merely to order a given queue of jobs through a given number of facilities, each job passing through the facilities in the required order and spending the necessary amount of time at each. The objective in such a case is usually to minimize the total time required to process all jobs: the throughput time. In the dynamic case the objective might be to minimize facility idle time, to minimize work-in-progress or to achieve the required completion or delivery dates for each job.

DISPATCHING

Some scheduling techniques described above offer optimum solutions to problems, but a question that should be asked is whether or not optimum solutions are necessary or even desirable. Clearly, if a solution to a problem can be obtained only after excessive computation or through over-simplification then there is little to recommend it.

Furthermore, many methods deal only with the static problem. When the dynamic situation arises there is no practical and general method of ensuring an optimum solution. If this fact is accepted, then it is reasonable to consider such problems in simpler 'dispatching' terms, i.e. to consider the immediate priority of jobs on one facility, rather than attempting explicitly to consider several facilities at once. The efficiency with which dispatching is performed determines to a large extent the overall operations, since it can affect resource utilization, etc. The principal procedure for 'dispatching' is the use of priority rules. Many such rules exist, some of which are described below. In all cases the aim is to use the rule to decide the order in which waiting jobs will be processed.

1. *Job slack (S)*. Give priority to the jobs with least 'job slack', i.e. the amount of contingency or free time, over and above the expected processing time, available before the job is completed at a predetermined date, i.e.

$$S = t_0 - t_1 - \Sigma a_i$$

where t_0 = future date (e.g. week number)

         t_1 = present date (e.g. week number)

         Σa_i = sum of remaining processing times (e.g. weeks).

Where delays are associated with each operation, e.g. delays caused by interfacility transport, this rule is less suitable, hence the following rule may be used.

2. *Job slack per operation*. Give priority to jobs with least 'job slack' per operation i.e. S/N, where N = number of remaining operations. Therefore where S is the same for two or more jobs, the job having the most remaining operations is processed first.

3. *Job slack ratio*, or the ratio of the total remaining time to the remaining slack time, i.e.

$$\frac{S}{t_0 - t_1}$$

In all the above cases, where the priority index is negative the job cannot be completed by the required date.

4. *Shortest imminent operation* (SIO), i.e. process first the job with the shortest processing time.

5. *Longest imminent operation* (LIO). This is the converse of (4).

6. *Scheduled start date*. This is perhaps the most frequently used rule. The date on which operations must be started so that a job will meet a required completion date is calculated, usually by employing reverse scheduling from the completion date, e.g.

$$x_i = t_0 - \Sigma a_i$$

or $x_i = t_0 - \Sigma(a_i + f_i)$

where x_i = scheduled start date for an operation

       f_i = delay or contingency allowance.

Usually some other rule is also used, e.g. first come, first served, to decide priorities between jobs with equal x_i values.

7. *Earliest due date*, i.e. process first the job with the earliest due or completion date.

8. *Subsequent processing times*. Process first the job that has the longest remaining process times, i.e. Σa_i or $\Sigma(a_i + f_i)$

9. *Value*. To reduce work-in-progress inventory cost, process first the job which has the highest value.

10. *Minimum total float*. This rule is the one usually adopted when scheduling by network techniques (see Chapter 13).

11. *Subsequent operation*. Look ahead to see where the job will go after this operation has been completed and process first the job which goes to a 'critical' queue, that is a facility with a small queue of available work, thus minimizing the possibility of facility idle time.

12. *First come, first served* (FCFS).

13. *Random* (e.g. in order of job number).

Rules 12 and 13 are random since, unlike the others, neither depends directly on job characteristics such as length of operation, value, etc.

Priority rules can be classified further, as follows:

(a) *Local rules* depend solely on data relating to jobs in queue at any particular facility.

(b) *General rules* depend on data relating to jobs in the queue at any particular facility and/or data for jobs in queues at *other* facilities.

Local rules, because of the smaller amount of information used, are easier and cheaper to calculate than general (sometimes called *global*) rules. All the above with the exception of rule 11 are local rules.

One further classification of rules is as follows:

(a) *Static rules* are those in which the priority index for a job does not change with the passage of time, during waiting in any one queue.

(b) *Dynamic rules* are those in which the priority index is a function of the present time.

Rules 4, 5, 6, 7, 8, 9, 10, 11, 12 and 13 above are all static, whereas the remainder are dynamic.

A great deal of research work has been conducted in an attempt to evaluate the merits of these rules. Perhaps the most effective rule according to such research is the SIO rule, and more particularly, various extensions of this rule. Simulation studies have shown that of all 'local' rules, those based on the SIO rule are perhaps the most effective, certainly when considered against criteria such as minimizing the number of jobs in the shop, the mean of the 'completion distribution' and the throughput time. The SIO rule appears to be particularly effective in reducing throughput time, the truncated SIO and the two-class SIO rules being perhaps the most effective derivatives, having the additional advantage of reducing throughput time variance and lateness.

The 'first come, first served' priority rule has been shown to be particularly beneficial in reducing average lateness, whereas the 'scheduled start date and total float' rule has been proved effective where jobs are of the network type.

EXAMPLE

Dresser Industries

The Jeffrey division of Dresser Industries supplies underground mining equipment largely to the coal mining industry. Gear manufacturing for such equipment is a high-volume activity, with demand associated with new orders, spare parts, and repairs. Since virtually every product contains gearing, both quality and performance against schedule are critical. As part of a study using due-date performance as the primary measure of effectiveness, a change in dispatching policy was tested, and it achieved 39% improvement over existing policy at the highest demand level.

Source: Hutchinson, J, Leong, G. and Ward, P. T. (1993) Improving delivery performance in gear manufacturing at Jeffrey Division of Dresser Industries. *Interfaces* **23** (2), pp. 69–79.

ASSIGNMENT

Sometimes, in attempts to decide how orders are to be scheduled on to available facilities, there are alternative solutions. For example, many different facilities may be capable of performing the operations required on one customer or item. Operations management must then decide which jobs are to be scheduled on to which facilities in order to achieve some objective, such as minimum cost or minimum throughput time.

TIMETABLING

The timetabling of activities is of particular relevance for repetitive functions. Bus, train and air services usually operate to a timetable. Similarly, the activities of certain service systems, e.g. cinemas, are timetabled. These are 'customer push' systems, so customers have to take advantage of the function at predetermined times. The function is not performed at other times, so customers arriving at the wrong time must wait, and of course, if there are no customers at the time selected for the performance of the function, or if not enough customers are available to utilize fully the facilities provided, there will be under-utilization of capacity. In many situations timetables are necessary, since common resources are deployed to provide a variety or series of functions. In many transport systems, for example, vehicles travel a set route providing movement for individuals between points along that route. In certain service systems, for example hospitals, common resources such as medical specialists provide a service in a variety of departments, or for a variety of types of customers, in a given period of time. Certain out-patient clinics operate in this fashion. In all such cases a timetable will normally be developed and made available to customers. Timetabling is an exercise in internally oriented scheduling, since no direct account is taken of individual customers' demands. The development of timetables will take into account the time required for, or the duration of, activities, and in many cases (e.g. transport systems) the required or preferred order or sequence.

Few quantitative techniques are relevant in the development of such timetables. 'Routeing', flow planning and vehicle scheduling procedures are of relevance in timetabling transport systems. In some cases the problem will resemble that of sequencing outlined above, while in others it may be convenient to use Gantt charts and simulation procedures in both the development and the evaluation of timetables.

MATERIALS REQUIREMENTS PLANNING (MRP)[1]

The principal applications of MRP are in manufacture, particularly batch manufacture. In this context it has some similarities with the line of balance technique. There are also similarities with group technology and the reverse scheduling method. MRP, however is in principle of relevance in other situations, both in manufacture and in service operations. Where an MRP approach is appropriate, it will often provide the framework within which all scheduling and also inventory decisions are made.

---

[1] MRP is an open-loop system. It deals only with a part of the planning and scheduling problem for demand-dependent systems. If, in the same computer system, we were able also to take account of some of the other decisions required in planning, scheduling and controlling activities and workflow in an operating system (e.g. the areas covered by Figure 11.1), we would have a more comprehensive, closed-loop system for operations planning and control. MRP II was developed for this purpose. Whilst its origins are in MRP, it is not just an extension of MRP but rather a computer-based system of which MRP is just one part. It was developed for use in manufacturing situations and is also known as manufacturing resource planning

The principles of MRP

Materials requirements planning is concerned primarily with the scheduling of activities and the management of inventories. It is particularly useful where there is a need to produce components, items or sub-assemblies which themselves are later used in the production of a final product or, in non-manufacturing organizations, where the provision of a transport or service for a customer necessitates the use or provision of certain sub-systems. For example, it may be used when a customer orders a motor vehicle from a manufacturing organization, which must first manufacture or obtain various components which are then used in the final assembly of that vehicle for that customer. Similarly, in treating a patient in a hospital, e.g. for a major operation, the hospital must, in order to satisfy this service requirement, provide accommodation for the patient, diagnostic tests, anaesthetics and post-care facilities as well as surgical facilities so that the patient's total requirements are satisfied. In these two cases the product or service requested by the customer can be seen to be the 'final' output of the system, which derives from certain lower-level provisions. These lower-level provisions are considered to be *dependent* on the customer's final requirement.

Given a measure or forecast of the total number of customers, the demand at lower levels can be obtained. The materials requirements planning technique is used for precisely this purpose. It takes as one of its inputs the measured or forecast demand for the system's outputs. It breaks down this demand into its component parts, compares this requirement against existing inventories, and seeks to schedule the parts required against available capacity. The MRP procedure produces a schedule for all component parts, if necessary through to purchasing requirements, and where appropriate shows expected shortages due to capacity limitations. The basic procedure is illustrated in Figure 12.1. The

Figure 12.1 Basic MRP structure

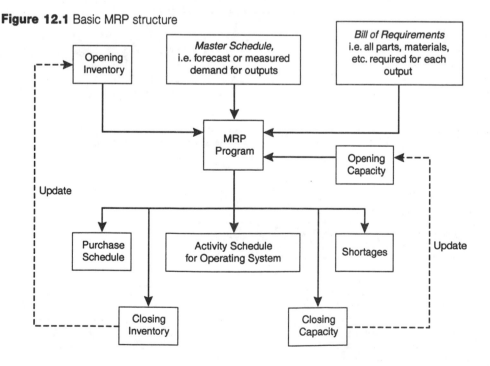

procedure will be undertaken on a repetitive basis, the 'explosion' and scheduling procedure being repeated at regular intervals, perhaps corresponding to the intervals at which demand forecasting is undertaken or as and when required as a result of changes in known demand. The use of this procedure involves considerable data processing, even for relatively simple outputs. The popularity of the MRP technique and its extensive use have resulted largely from the availability of cheap computing power within organizations.

The use of MRP

The manner in which MRP operates will be described by reference to a manufacturing situation. The principal *inputs* to the MRP process are as follows:

(a) The **bill of requirements**. This, in effect, identifies the component parts of a final output product. At each 'level' the different components, materials or subassemblies are shown, thus the bill of requirements shows not only the total number of sub-parts but also the manner in which these parts eventually come together to constitute the final product. The lead time between levels is also shown. The arrangement is shown diagrammatically in Figure 12.2. There are several different methods of structuring the bill of requirements data. In general, however, the final product level will be referred to as level zero. Below this, at level 1, are the principal subassemblies, etc. which

Figure 12.2 Bill of requirements structure (five levels)

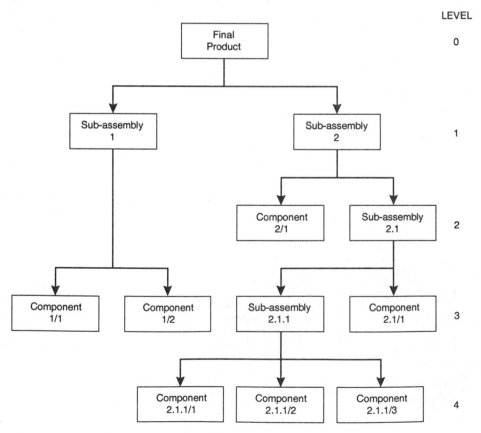

together make up the final product. At level 2 are the components, etc. of the principal subassemblies, and so on through as many levels as appropriate to reach the level of raw materials or bought-in items. Each item is assigned to one level only, and each item at each level has a unique coding. The different levels and/or branches may correspond to different design or manufacturing responsibilities. Where complex end products may be made in several different possible configurations from a large number of parts or subassemblies which may be assembled in different ways, it is common to use a 'modular' bill of requirements structure. Using this approach, even though there may be a very large range of end products differing in detail from one another, it will not be necessary to have a large number of different, unique bill of requirements structures, but sufficient to specify those modules from a composite bill of requirements structure which together constitute the required end product.

(b) The ***master production schedule*** is based on known or forecast demand for a specified future period. The schedule shows how much of each end item is wanted and when the items are wanted. It is in effect the delivery or the 'due date' schedule for each product expressed in terms of both quantity and timing. The period over which this demand is expressed will depend on the type of product concerned and the capacity planning procedures used by the organization. In general, however, the time period should allow enough time for the acquisition of all materials, the manufacture of all components, parts and subassemblies, and the assembly of the final product.

(c) ***Opening inventory***. This record will show the available inventories of all materials, components, subassemblies, etc. required for the manufacture of the end product. In general the file will show both total and free (i.e. unallocated) inventory. The latter is more important in the context of MRP, since the objective is to compare component or parts requirements against available stock (i.e. excluding those items already committed to the manufacture of other products), in order to determine purchase and manufacture requirements for items for a particular delivery schedule.

(d) ***Opening capacity***. If the MRP procedure is to be used to provide a production schedule it will be necessary to have available information on free capacity. The MRP programme will allocate component manufacturing requirements against this capacity so that the appropriate components at each level in the bill of requirements are available at an appropriate time, in order to ensure that the final product is available to the customer at the required time. In this respect the procedure is very similar to that used in the line of balance technique.

The basic procedure involves the 'explosion' of the final product requirements into constituent component and materials requirements. This procedure (sometimes referred to as 'netting') is performed level by level through the bill of requirements. The gross requirements for each item at each level are compared with available inventory so that the outstanding parts, components or materials requirements can be determined. This procedure determines how many units of each item are required to meet a given production schedule and also when those units are required, in order that manufacturing lead times might be satisfied. The result of this procedure will be the production of a schedule of purchase requirements, a schedule of manufacturing requirements (i.e. manufacturing activity schedule) and, if appropriate, a schedule showing the shortages that will occur as a result of there being insufficient capacity available to meet component/item manufacturing requirements.

Thus the principal *outputs* from the MRP procedure are as follows:

(a) purchase requirements, including which items are to be ordered, at what time, and in what quantities;

(b) manufacturing activity schedules indicating which items are to be manufactured, in what quantities and by what date;

(c) expected shortages (and/or items which must be expedited);

(d) resultant free inventory following satisfaction of the master schedule;

(e) available free capacity.

The above procedure will be undertaken repetitively. Basically there are two types of approach available. Using the *regenerative* approach the entire MRP procedure, as described above, is repeated periodically. The time period between repetitions will normally conform to the time period between demand forecasts, the two usually being undertaken on a regular basis, e.g. once a month. The approach using the regenerative system is in effect to undertake an entirely new MRP calculation on each occasion, i.e. to undertake each set of calculations as if there had been no previous MRP study. In such cases the inventory inputs to the system will assume that all current stocks are free and that none of the available capacity is committed. Thus each MRP repetition takes into account all known demand for the schedule period and, from the demand, bill of requirements, inventory and capacity data, calculates a new schedule. Such an approach may be appropriate where the output schedule changes to a relatively small extent. In such circumstances the amount of computation may not be too great and the differences between the schedules produced for successive calculations may not be substantial. An additional advantage of the regenerative approach is that data errors are not repeated or compounded.

Where there is considerable change in the output schedule, or where forecasts are subject to large margins of error, or where the bill of requirements details change, e.g. as a result of design changes, it may be more appropriate to adopt a *net change* approach to materials requirements planning. Using this procedure, only the alterations to the master schedule and/or the other input data are taken into account as and when necessary. These changes are considered and their effects on purchase and manufacturing schedules, inventories, capacity factors, etc. are considered. While the regenerative approach might be useful in a relatively stable situation, in a volatile situation the net change approach might be more appropriate. The net change system requires more processing and will not normally be used when the volumes are high.

EXAMPLE

Black and Decker

Having defined its key aims of flexibility and quick response, Black and Decker focused on its material requirement planning (MRP) system. The goal was to use MRP as a way to reduce the company's 8–10 week manufacturing time to just a few days. (Simply bringing this down to 2 weeks would reduce finished inventory by $40 million.) The company aimed to deploy an MRP system that within minutes could generate detailed schedules for every operation and every machine in the plant. In the event of equipment breakdown or material shortage, the system would be able to generate new schedules for every operation in the system within 5 minutes.

Source: Cosco, J. (1994) Black and Deckering Black and Decker. *Journal of Business Strategy* **15** (1), pp. 59–61.

BALANCING SCHEDULING AND CONTROL

In many situations it will not be feasible, and in some cases not desirable to attempt to develop optimal schedules. In such situations there will be some need to control things as they happen. The relative importance attached to scheduling (planning ahead) or control will depend to some extent on the type of situation and particularly the type of system structure.

In general, scheduling will be more complex in 'function to order' situations where scheduling decisions will be required to absorb external (i.e. demand) fluctuations directly. Furthermore, in such situations the degree of repetition may be less, therefore the need for control may be greater. In contrast, in 'function to stock' situations, scheduling will be somewhat easier, therefore the need for control somewhat less. In 'demand push' situations where stocks exist between function and customer, scheduling will tend to be easier and the need for control less.

Demand levels may also influence the relative complexity and importance of scheduling and control activities. In general, high demand levels will be associated with function repetition and the provision of special-purpose resources together with product or service specialization. In contrast, relatively low demand levels may be associated with relatively low function repetition, high product or service variety and the use of general-purpose resources; hence scheduling may be complex and there will be a relatively greater dependence on control. In situations where predictability of the nature of demand permits the provision, i.e. stocking, of resources, and where demand levels are high, the provision of special-purpose equipment may give rise to an emphasis on the provision of balance, the avoidance of interference and the consideration of learning or improvement effects. In such situations much of the internally oriented scheduling will be 'built into' the system. In contrast, in situations where demand predictability is low and where demand levels are also low, accurate scheduling will be impossible, hence low equipment utilization, high work-in-progress and/or customer queuing will be evident. In these situations the use of local dispatching rules, resource smoothing, allocation of jobs, etc., together with an emphasis on control, will be evident.

THE EFFECTIVENESS OF SCHEDULING

Criteria or measures of effective activity scheduling and control might include the following:

(a) the level of finished goods or work-in-progress (for systems with output stocks);

(b) percentage resource utilization (all systems);

(c) percentage of orders delivered on or before due date (for 'function to order' systems only);

(d) percentage stockouts/shortages (for systems with output stocks only);

(e) number of customers 'processed' (all systems);

(f) down time/set-ups, etc. (all systems);

(g) customer queuing times (for systems in which customers wait or queue).

In virtually all cases there will be a need to avoid sub-optimization. It may be easy in most cases to satisfy each of the above criteria individually but the objective of operations management, and therefore of activity scheduling, is to obtain a satisfactory balance between customer service criteria (for example c, d, g) and resource utilization criteria (for example b, f).

KEY POINTS FOR CHAPTER 12

Activity scheduling is a key strategic decision area for operations management. The purpose of scheduling is to determine in advance the time at which things will be done.

There are two basic strategies for scheduling:

Internal

External (or due date).

JIT is an example of external scheduling.

The choice of strategy will be influenced by operations objectives and system structure. Scheduling can take place in dependent or independent demand situations.

Taking scheduling strategy and demand situation, three types of scheduling problem can be identified. Of these, the following are the most common:

Externally oriented/Dependent

Internally oriented/Independent

Activity scheduling procedures can be identified, which are appropriate for these situations.

Occasionally it may be possible, and necessary, to try to manage demand uncertainty to help scheduling.

Appointments, reservation and timetabling methods are means to 'manage' demand uncertainty.

Some of the key scheduling procedures include:

Reverse scheduling

Forward scheduling

Sequencing

Dispatching

Assignment

Time tabling

MRP.

Where accurate scheduling is not possible, it is necessary to exercise control.

There are several criteria for measuring the effectiveness at activity scheduling.

FURTHER READING

Vollman, T. E., Berry, W. L. and Whybark, D. C. (1989) *Manufacture Planning and Control Systems*. 2nd edition. Homewood, Illinois: Richard Irwin.

Department of Trade (UK) (1989) *Managing into the 90s: Just-in-Time; Manufacturing Resources Planning; Computer Integrated Manufacturing; Optimized Production Technology*. Dept of Trade.

Morris, B. and Johnson, R. (1987) Dealing with inherent variability: the difference between manufacturing and service? *International Journal of Operations and Production Management* 7 (4) pp. 13–22.

Harrison, A. (1992) *Just in Time Manufacturing in Perspective*. Hemel Hempstead; Prentice Hall.

QUESTIONS

12.1 Distinguish between the sequencing and the dispatching problems. How important is the sequencing problem in activity scheduling and how useful in practice are the various algorithms which can be used to provide optimal solutions to such problems?

12.2 Ten jobs are waiting to be run through a medical analysis process.

(a) Given the information below, arrange these jobs in priority order (the one with highest processing or dispatching priority first) according to the following priority rules:

1. job slack;
2. job slack per operation;
3. job slack ratio;
4. shortest imminent operation;
5. longest imminent operation;
6. scheduled start date;
7. earliest due date;
8. subsequent processing time;
9. first come, first served.

Job	Schedule completion date (week no.)	Sum of remaining processing times (weeks)	Number of remaining operations	Duration of operations on this machine	Arrival order at this machine
1	17	4	2	1	1
2	15	6	3	2	10
3	17	3	4	1	2
4	16	5	1	3	4
5	19	7	2	0.5	9
6	21	4	5	2	3
7	17	2	4	0.5	5
8	22	8	3	3.5	8
9	20	6	2	2	6
10	25	10	1	2	7

N.B. The present date is week no. 12.

(b) Use the 'first come, first served' (FCFS) priority rule to resolve 'ties' given by the above rules.

12.3 Describe some of the activity scheduling problems which may occur and the techniques available for their solution in the following situations:

(a) an emergency ward in a hospital;

(b) a furniture removal company;

(c) a take-away food shop (e.g. a hamburger shop).

12.4 Holdtight Company Ltd have just received orders from four customers for quantities of different expanderbolts. Each order is to be manufactured over the same very short period of time, during which three machines are available for the manufacture of the bolts.

The table below shows the manufacturing time in hours/bolt for each of the three machines and the total available hours' capacity on each for the period in question.

Assuming that each order is to be manufactured on one machine only, how should orders be allocated to machines?

Order no.	Number of expanderbolts	Manufacturing time (hours/bolt)		
		M/c A	M/c B	M/c C
1	50	4	5	3
2	75	3	2	4
3	25	5	4	3
4	80	2	5	4
Total capacity (hours)		175	275	175

Chapter 13

Project management and network scheduling

ISSUES

What is a project?
How are projects managed?
What is the distinctive role of project managers?
What are the success factors in project management?
How are projects scheduled and controlled?
What is Network Planning and how is it done?
What is a PERT, and how is it used?
How are resources and costs managed?

We shall concentrate in this chapter on the scheduling of project type activities, i.e. of non-repetitive work. We shall deal in detail with network scheduling, but it will be appropriate, initially, to set this discussion in a broader context.

PROJECT MANAGEMENT

The nature of projects and project management

A project can be defined as an activity with a specific goal occupying a specific period of time. A project is a finite activity, not only in time, but also in the use of resources.

Project management, therefore, is concerned with the pursuit of a specific goal, using given resources over a defined time period. This will often require the planning and establishment of an operating system, the acquisition of resources, the scheduling of activities and evaluation/review of the completed activity. Project management is a distinctive activity requiring a different type of approach to that of managing ongoing repetitive operations.

The management of finite projects is a need not only in the engineering and construction industries—the focus of much of the literature on this subject—but also in areas such as:

Transport: planning and executing a major transport project, e.g. deploying military resources, major explorations and missions.

Supply: planning and executing projects such as the distribution of aid, the sale and distribution of equities during privatizations, etc.

Service: managing projects, such as emergency and disaster relief, mass immunizations, and major consultancy projects.

In many cases the focus, as above, will be upon major projects—often involving considerable resource, cost and time. Scale however, is not a part of our definition. Projects may be large or small.

Figure 13.1 outlines a typical project three-phase life-cycle. Some of the managerial activities associated with the seven stages are discussed below:

Project formulation and definition

In managing an activity such as research and development within an

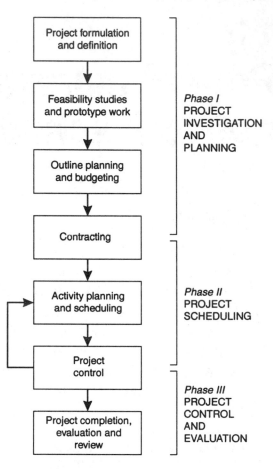

Figure 13.1 Typical project life-cycle

Project formulation and definition

Feasibility studies and prototype work

Outline planning and budgeting

Phase I
PROJECT INVESTIGATION AND PLANNING

Contracting

Activity planning and scheduling

Phase II
PROJECT SCHEDULING

Project control

Project completion, evaluation and review

Phase III
PROJECT CONTROL AND EVALUATION

organization, decisions will be required on the selection of projects for further work. Whilst the number of possible projects, for example those projects on which some initial exploratory work has been done, may be large, only a few of these may qualify for further development through prototype work to ultimate product development and marketing. Project selection, in such circumstances, is of crucial importance. The corporate objectives, in particular product/market policy (see Chapter 3), the availability of appropriate skills and resources, financial implications, and development cost estimates will be amongst the 'checklist' of items that might be used in an initial test of project feasibility or in the ranking of possible projects.

In contrast, in those types of organization which operate essentially in response to customer enquiries, project selection may be unimportant. The emphasis here will be upon the interpretation, definition and formulation of project requirements. The interpretation of tender conditions, the development of outline specifications, initial evaluation of alternatives and discussions with customers should lead to an agreed project formulation in sufficient detail to permit further work.

Feasibility studies and prototype work

Excepting in the case of small projects or activities undertaken by organizations against known customer requirements, further feasibility studies, possibly culminating in prototype work, will be required. Such work may, itself, be covered by a contractual arrangement between an organization and its customer. In the case of organizations involved in the development of projects in anticipation of demand, e.g. development of new products or services, prototype development may be required not only to test feasibility and performance, but also as a means to determine initial market reaction through pilot or test marketing exercises.

Outline planning and budgeting

Whether a project has been undertaken as part of a company programme with the intention of developing new products or services, or against a specific customer requirement, a project budget must be established in order that expenditure might be controlled, and so that an estimate might be made of the final product/service cost. Development of outline plans for the execution of the project indicating the total time required and the general level of resources to be committed to the project will be a prerequisite for such budget preparation.

Contracting

In the case of projects undertaken for a particular customer, the preparation and completion of legal contracts is an essential stage. Whilst the legal form and details differ the essential requirements will normally be for a written contract, covering details of specification, documentation, costs, project management, cancellation, modification, completion and delivery. A type of contracting may also be involved even for projects undertaken within an overall R&D framework within an organization. For example, the commissioning of projects from specific departments and the involvement of sub-contractors may necessitate contractual arrangements.

Activity planning and scheduling

The detailed plan or schedule of activities showing estimated start and finish times for all major work and the resource requirements of such work is an essential prerequisite at the start of any project. By definition all or a major part of any project will be new. Thus in developing a plan or schedule the project manager faces uncertainty. The amount of time required to complete jobs, the amount of resources required and the interdependence of jobs are all uncertain. The planning procedure must take account of such risk, and opportunities for modification/revision of schedules or the use of alternative methods/resources are necessary.

Project control

This, together with planning and scheduling, is the major ongoing task for project management. Since, by definition, planning cannot be exact, some emphasis must be placed upon project control. A principal characteristic of project management situations is the need for close monitoring and control of activities, for comparison of progress against plans, subsequent modification of schedules, redeployment of resources, and redirection of effort. Here, also, the project manager will be concerned with the management of project teams, the provision of leadership for such teams and the management of personnel. Team working is characteristic of project-type work and considerable attention must be given to the selection, training and development of individuals, the creation of effective teams and the management of work groups.

Project completion, evaluation and review

On project completion, final outcome costs will be calculated and compared to budget, the effectiveness of the project will be assessed, and project teams will be 'wound down'. The evaluation and review of the project provides information and opportunities for improvement in the management of subsequent projects, and permits the development of a database (e.g. of resource requirements, activity durations, learning times, etc.) to facilitate future project planning and control.

ROLE OF PROJECT MANAGEMENT

It is the role of the overall project manager to take responsibility for this whole project life cycle. Thus, frequently, project managers must operate within a matrix type organization, being responsible for co-ordinating specific activities across functions, each of which is headed by its own function manager. The success of a project—e.g. completion on time, to specification and to cost—is very dependent on effective project management.

Successful project management has been found to depend upon the adoption of an appropriate strategy designed to ensure that:

1   There exists an attitude for success;
2   The objectives by which success is to be measured are defined;
3   There is a procedure for achieving objectives;
4   The environment is supportive;
5   Adequate and appropriate resources are available.

Within such a strategy the most appropriate approach, or style, for project management will normally involve

(a) managing through a structured breakdown: the management system is built around a structured breakdown of the facility delivered by the project into intermediate products or results;

(b) focusing on results: what to achieve, not how to do it; the deliverables, not the work for its own sake;

(c) balancing the results between different areas of technology; and between technology and people, systems and organizational changes;

(d) organizing a contract between all the parties involved, defining their roles, responsibilities and working relationships;

(e) adopting a clear and simple management approach.

PROJECT SCHEDULING AND CONTROL

In the remainder of this chapter we deal in detail with the use of network (or critical path) techniques in activity scheduling and control. The topic was introduced in Chapter 12, where it was noted that this approach provides a means of establishing schedules for sequentially interdependent activities. It is useful for internally or externally oriented scheduling. Our description throughout will refer to projects, the planning of projects, etc., and it should be noted that such projects might relate to manufacture, supply, service or transport.

The rudimentary steps in operations planning by network analysis are as follows:

(a) Construct an arrow or network diagram to represent the project to be undertaken, indicating the sequence and interdependence of all necessary jobs in the project.

(b) Determine how long each of the jobs will last and insert those times on the network.

(c) Perform network calculations to determine the overall duration of the project and the criticalness of the various jobs.

(d) If the project completion date is later than required, consider modifying either the network and or the individual job durations so that the project may be completed within the required time.

This is the extent of the planning phase of simple network analysis; there are, however, subsequent steps concerned with the control of the operation and these will be dealt with later. Furthermore, this simple description of the procedure has omitted all considerations of costs and resources, and these will be dealt with later in this chapter.

EXAMPLE:

Scheduling maintenance at Weyerhauser

Weyerhauser Paper Company plan shutdowns for preventive maintenance to reduce and better control risks of unplanned and more costly major breakdowns. Each year, the Company's Springfield plant has two maintenance shutdowns. A project management system based on the critical path method scheduling technique is used to schedule the work. The CPM shows the interrelationships among project activities. The intention is also to determine the optimal sequencing of maintenance activities for better resource utilization.

Source: Roberts, S. M. and Mask, K. J. (1992) Shutdown management—five years of learning. *American Association of Cost Engineers Transactions* **2**, pp. U.3.1-U.3.7.

THE CONSTRUCTION OF NETWORK DIAGRAMS

Any project may be represented by means of an arrow diagram in which the arrangement of arrows indicates the sequence of individual jobs and their dependence on other jobs. Arrow diagrams consist of two basic elements: *activities* and *events*.

An activity is a time-consuming task and is represented by an arrow or line. An event is considered as instantaneous, i.e. a point in time. An event may represent the completion or the commencement of an activity and is represented by a circle. A sequence of events is referred to as a path.

Unlike bar charts, the scale to which activities are drawn has no significance. The length of an activity arrow on a network diagram is unrelated to the duration of that activity. It is normal to number events as in Figure 13.2 so that paths within the network can easily be described but, other than for identification, event numbers have no significance. Also for convenience we shall identify each activity with a letter and/or description.

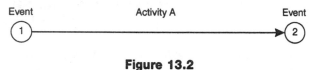

Figure 13.2

The network diagram is constructed by assembling all activities in a logical order. For example, the networks shown in Figures 13.3 and 13.4 relate to a decorating job.

No activity may begin until all the activities leading to it are completed. In Figure 13.3 only after the walls have been cleaned can they be painted. In Figure 13.4 starting to

Figure 13.3

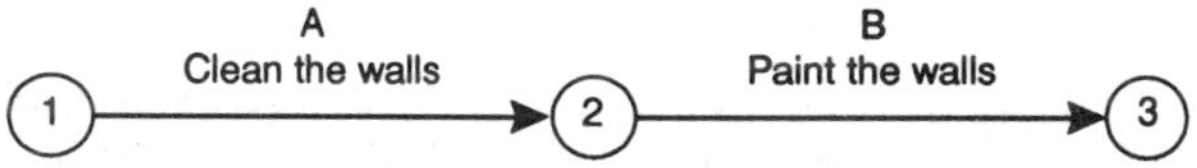

Figure 13.4

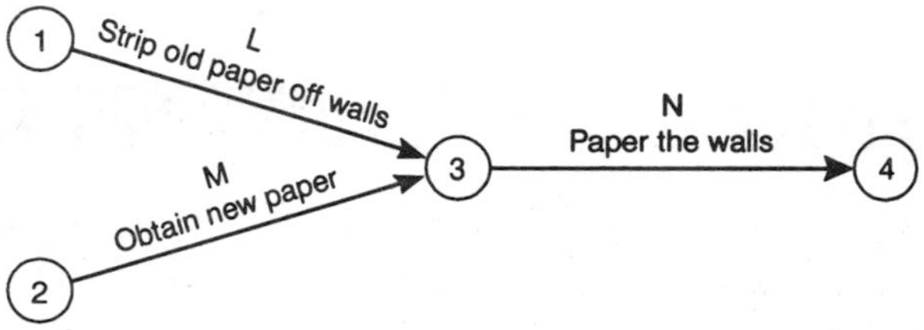

paper the walls is dependent not only on the old paper having been removed but also on the new paper being available.

Activities occurring on the same path are *sequential* and are directly dependent on each other. *Parallel* activities on different paths are independent of one another (Figure 13.5).

The convention in drawing networks is to allow time to flow from left to right, and to number events in this direction so that events on the left of the diagram have smaller

Figure 13.5

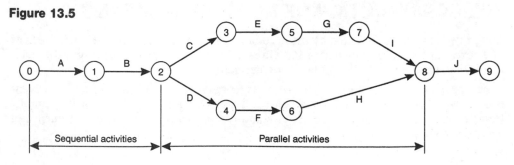

numbers than, and occur before, events on the right of the diagram.

It is not usually possible to use network diagrams in which 'loops' or 'dangles' occur; a loop such as that in Figure 13.6 may be a perfectly legitimate sequence of operations where, for example, a certain amount of reprocessing of materials or rectification takes place but, because of the calculations which must later be performed on the diagram, it cannot be accepted in network analysis.

Figure 13.6

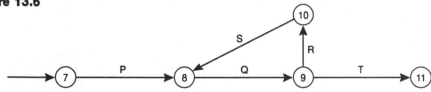

Although there are certain computer programs which will accept multiple-finish and multiple-start events on networks, it is not normally possible to leave events 'dangling' as in Figure 13.7.

Figure 13.7

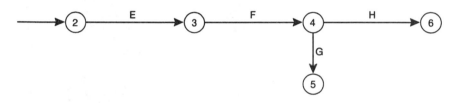

Dummy activities

The activities discussed above represent some time-consuming operation or job to be performed during the project. Dummy activities consume no time; they are of zero duration and are used solely for convenience in network construction. Dummy activities, represented by dotted lines, may be necessary on the following occasions:

1. To provide the correct logic in the diagram. In Figure 13.8 the completion of activities C and D is necessary before either E or F may begin. If in practice only activity E depends on the completion of both activities C and D, and activity F depends on D alone, then to represent this logic a dummy activity is required (Figure 13.9).

Figure 13.8

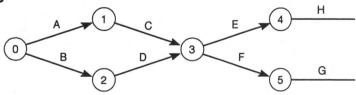

2. To avoid having more than one activity with the same beginning and end event (Figure 13.10). It is not usually possible to represent activities in this manner since activities B and C would be described from their event numbers as 3–4, so a dummy activity is necessary (Figure 13.11).

Figure 13.9

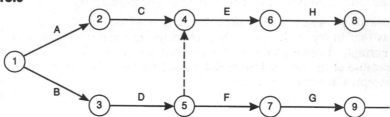

Figure 13.10

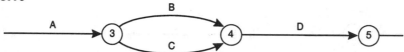

Figure 13.11

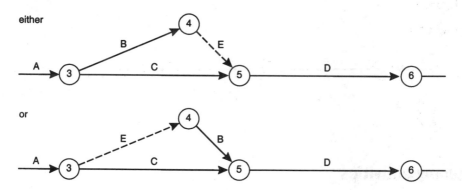

3. For convenience in drawing. The two networks in Figure 13.12 are equivalent, but the use of dummy activities facilitates representation. This is often necessary in complex networks.

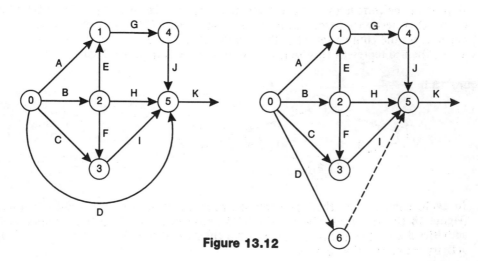

Figure 13.12

It may be necessary to use dummy activities when initially constructing networks to avoid complicated and untidy diagrams. Nevertheless, since the amount of subsequent analysis is dependent on the number of activities in a diagram, redundant dummies should be eliminated in order to save calculation time.

In drawing large networks for projects with many activities often it is easier to begin from the end of the project and work backwards. It is often helpful to consider large projects in separate parts, i.e. certain sections of the project or, if more appropriate, certain periods during the project, and then to piece together several smaller networks rather than trying to construct the complete network from scratch.

Except in the case of simple projects it is usually beneficial to construct the network around the important activities. Identify the important or major parts, locate the important activities on the diagram, then attach all the other, secondary activities to construct the complete network.

NETWORK CALCULATIONS

Dates

The objective of initial network calculations is to determine the overall duration of the project either so that a delivery date can be given to the customer or so that we can consider what alterations are necessary for the project to be completed on or before a date to which we are already committed.

To perform the network calculations two things are required: first an *activity network* representing the project, and second the durations of all the activities in that network. Network analysis is only a tool; its value depends entirely on the way in which it is used and the information on which it is based. Consequently, the collection of activity durations from records, or the estimation of durations, is an important part of the exercise.

If the activities have been performed previously, when, assuming the use of the same resources and procedures, the durations may be obtained from records. On the many occasions where the activities have no direct precedent some form of estimation is necessary. For the time being we shall ignore the possibility of using multiple estimates of activity durations and consider only the case in which each activity is given one duration.

Earliest start date for activities (ES)

The earliest start date for each activity is calculated from the *beginning* of the network by totalling all preceding activity durations (*d*).

Where two (or more) activities lead into one event the following activity cannot begin until both of the preceding activities are completed. Consequently, the last of these activities to finish determines the start date for the subsequent activity.

In Figure 13.13 the earliest start date for activity 1 is day 17 (assuming the project starts at day 0), since the start date of activity I will depend on the completion of the later of the two activities G and H, which is H.

Therefore, when calculating *ES* dates, work from the *beginning* of the network and use the *largest* numbers at junctions.

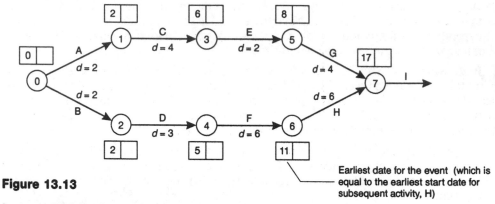

Figure 13.13

Earliest date for the event (which is equal to the earliest start date for subsequent activity, H)

Latest finish dates for activities (LF)

This is calculated from the *end* of the project by successively subtracting activity durations (*d*) from the project finish date.

Where two (or more) activities stem from one event the earliest of the dates will determine the latest finish date for previous activities.

In Figure 13.14 the latest finish date for activity A is day 3, since activity B must start at day 3 if the project is not to be delayed.

Therefore, when calculating *LF* dates begin from the *end* of the network and use the *smallest* numbers at junctions.

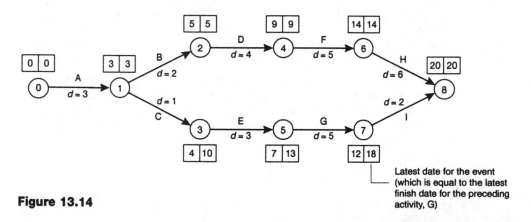

Figure 13.14

Latest date for the event (which is equal to the latest finish date for the preceding activity, G)

Earliest finish date for activities (EF)

The earliest finish date for any activity is determined by that activity's earliest start date and its duration, i.e. for any activity: $EF = ES + d$.

Latest start date for activities (LS)

The latest start date for any activity is determined by that activity's latest finish date and its duration, i.e. for any activity: $LS = LF - d$.

Float

In the previous example the earliest completion date for the project, i.e. the date of event 8, is determined by the *EF* dates for activities H and I. Activity I could finish at day 14 (the *EF* date for activity I is $ES + d = 12 + 2$), but activity H cannot finish until day 20 and it is the activity which determines the finish date for the project. In fact, it is the path consisting of activities ABDFH which determines the project's earliest finish date, rather than path ACEGI.

The earliest finish date for any project is determined by the longest path through the network; consequently, it follows that the shorter paths will have more time available than they require. The difference between the time available for any activity and the time required is called the *total float* (*TF*).

In Figure 13.14 the time required for activity I is 2 but the time available is 8 and hence the *TF* on activity I is 6.

$$\begin{aligned}
\text{Time available} &= LF - ES \\
\text{Time required} &= d \\
\text{Total float} &= LF - ES - d
\end{aligned}$$

i.e. for any activity (say G), using our notation the *TF* can be expressed as in Figure 13.15.

Figure 13.15

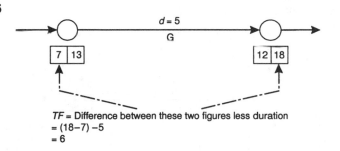

TF = Difference between these two figures less duration
= (18−7) −5
= 6

Total float is a characteristic of a path and not a characteristic of a single activity. For example, in Figure 13.14 the total float on activities A, C, E, G, and I is 6. If the total float is used up at any time by delays or lateness in one of the activities then it is no longer available to any of the other activities on that path.

The critical path

The critical path is the longest path through the network and is, therefore, the path with minimum total float (zero *TF* in the above example). Any delay in the activities on the critical path will delay the completion of the project, whereas delay in activities not on the critical path will initially use up some of the total float on that path and not affect the project completion date.

EXAMPLE 13.1

The table below lists all the activities which together constitute a small engineering project. The table also shows the necessary immediate predecessors for each activity and the activity durations.

1. Construct an activity network to represent the project.

2. Determine the earliest finish date for the entire project, assuming the project begins at day 0.

Activity	Immediate predecessors	Activity duration (days)
A	–	2
B	A	3
C	A	4
D	A	5
E	B	6
F	CD	3
G	D	4
H	B	7
I	EFG	2
J	G	3

Answer

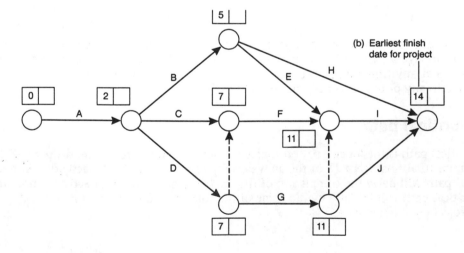

(b) Earliest finish date for project

EXAMPLE 13.2

For the project described in Example 13.1 determine:

(a)   the total float on each activity;

(b)   the critical path;

(c)   the latest start date for activity B;

(d)   the earliest finish date for activity F;

(e)   the effect on the project duration if activity I were to take three days;

(f)   the effect on the project duration if activity F were to take six days.

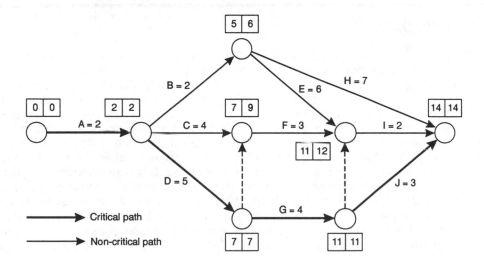

(a)   *Activity*   A B C D E F G H I J

    TF   0 1 3 0 1 2 0 2 1 0

(b)   Critical path = A D G J

(c)   Latest start date for B $= LF -$ duration
                                        $= 6 - 3$
                                        = day 3

(d)   Earliest finish date for F $= ES +$ duration
                                          $= 7 + 3$
                                          = day 10

(e)   No effect, but since increase in duration is equal to total float on activity, this activity would become critical.

(f)   Project would be delayed by one day since only two days *TF* are available on activity.

EXAMPLE

Rockwell International

A simulation system to model Space Shuttle ground processing activities and resourcing was developed for Rockwell International. The activities modelled were those on the critical path for completing turnaround operations between Shuttle flights. The model was necessary in order quickly to evaluate facilities requirements to support various proposed flight rates for future years. The purpose of the study was to help determine what combination of facilities and resources was required to support Shuttle flight rates ranging from one to ten launches per year. The study showed how this type of critical path simulation can be used to determine facilities and resources combinations that support desired Shuttle flight rates before detailed schedule planning is begun.

Source: Heileman, D., Linton, D. G. and Khajenoori, S. (1992) Simulation study aids space shuttle flight rate planning. *Industrial Engineering* **24**(3), pp. 58–59.

Schedule dates

At the beginning of this section we indicated that one objective of network calculations is to calculate the earliest completion date for the project and to compare this with the desired completion date. We may be committed to completing a project by a certain date and, if the calculated earliest finish date for the project occurs after this scheduled finish date, it will be desirable to try to reduce the project duration. If we had used the schedule completion date in the calculations, then we would have obtained negative total float values, the greatest negative values occurring on the critical path and indicating the minimum amount by which the project would be late unless some alterations were made. Schedule dates may also be placed on intermediate events. If it is necessary to complete one of the intermediate activities by a given date, e.g. so that the customer or the main contractor may inspect or test the partly completed product, then an *intermediate schedule date/late* may be used. If this date is earlier than the *LF* date for that activity it would be used in the network calculations instead of the calculated *LF* date. If one of the intermediate activities cannot be started until a given date for some reason, e.g. because of the

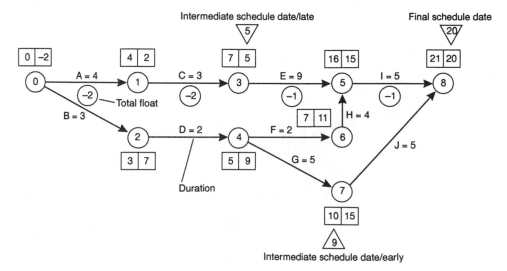

Figure 13.16

delivery of materials, then an *intermediate schedule date/early* may be used. If this date is later than the *ES* date for that activity it would be used instead of the calculated *ES* figure.

In the example in Figure 13.16 the final schedule date, day 20, is earlier than the calculated finish date for the project and therefore replaces the calculated *LF* date. The same applies to the intermediate schedule date/late for the completion of activity C. The intermediate schedule date/early for the start of activity J has no effect since this date is earlier than the calculated *ES* date for that activity.

Using schedule dates it is possible to obtain not only negative values of total float but also different values along the critical path. In the example in Figure 13.16 the *TF* on activities A and C is –2, and on E and I it is –1, but all four activities form a critical path.

MULTIPLE TIME ESTIMATES (PERT)

We have previously assumed that a single time can be given for the duration of every activity. There are many occasions, however, when the duration of activities is not certain or when some amount of variation from the average duration is expected. For example, in maintenance work unexpected snags may occur to increase the activity duration, or failures may be found to be less serious than had been expected and the activity duration reduced. In construction work jobs may be delayed because of unfavourable weather, etc.

In such cases it is desirable to be able to use a time distribution rather than a single time for activity durations to represent the uncertainty that exists.

In network analysis uncertainty in durations can be accommodated and the following notation is usually used:

m = the most likely duration of the activity

a = the optimistic estimate of the activity duration

b = the pessimistic estimate of the activity duration

These three estimates can be used to describe the distribution for the activity duration. It is assumed that the times are distributed as a 'beta' distribution (Figure 13.17).

Figure 13.17

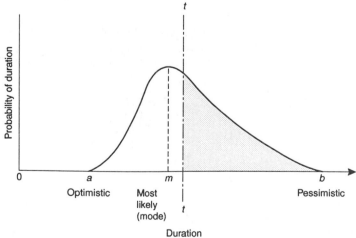

237

t = the expected time (the mean of the distribution)

σ = the standard deviation (which is a measure of the spread of the distribution)

$\approx$ the range between the extreme values divided by 6

$$\equiv \frac{b-a}{6}$$

If certain assumptions are made about the distribution, the mean (t) and the variance σ^2 can be expressed as follows:

Mean (the expected time) $t = \dfrac{a + b + 4m}{6}$

Variance $\qquad\qquad \sigma^2 = \dfrac{(b-a)^2}{36}$

Probability of achieving scheduled dates

Suppose we have two sequential activities, A and B, for which the durations are:

$a_A = 0.5$ days $\qquad a_B = 4$ days

$b_A = 3.5$ days $\qquad b_B = 12$ days

$m_A = 2$ days $\qquad m_B = 8$ days

Using these formulae, for activity A the expected duration t_A is 2 days and the variance σ^2 is 0.25 days, and for activity B the expected duration t_B is 8 days and variance is 1.75 days. Assuming activity durations to be independent, the expected duration for the pair of activities is 10 days and, since the variances may be added together, the variance for the pair is 2 days. It is usually assumed that the distribution for the duration of a series of activities corresponds to the 'normal' probability curve; consequently, in this case, the probability that the two activities will be completed in a minimum of 10 days is 50 per cent, since the normal distribution is symmetrical about the mean (Figure 13.18) and consequently the probability is given by the proportion of the area to the left of the mean of 10 days (50 per cent).

Suppose we have three activities which represent the critical path in a network, as in Figure 13.19. If we assume that these durations are independent, i.e. that the duration of activity A does not affect that of B, and so on, and that the normal distribution applies for the project duration, then we can calculate the probability that the project will be

Figure 13.18

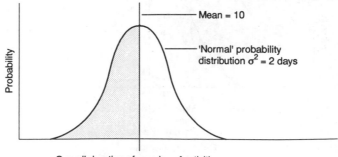

Overall duration of a series of activities

completed on or before the required schedule date.

Expected project duration $(t) = 2 + 8 + 5 = 15$

$$\sigma^2 = 3$$

Figure 13.19

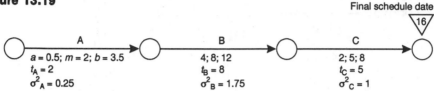

Final schedule date

A		B		C	
$a = 0.5; m = 2; b = 3.5$		4; 8; 12		2; 5; 8	
$t_A = 2$		$t_B = 8$		$t_C = 5$	
$\sigma^2_A = 0.25$		$\sigma^2_B = 1.75$		$\sigma^2_C = 1$	

Figure 13.20

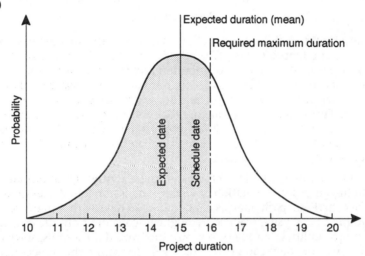

In the distribution shown in Figure 13.20 the probability of meeting the schedule date is represented by that portion of the area under the curve to the left of the 16-day ordinate. This area can be obtained from normal distribution tables if the diagram is first converted to a standardized scale.[1] In this case the probability of completing the project by day 16 is 0.72, since the area to the left of the 16-day ordinate is 72 per cent of the total area.

---

[1] The standardized scale is used solely for convenience. The standardized normal distribution has a total area of 1.00, a mean value of 0, and variance of σ^2 of 1 (Figure 13.21(a)):

where s = schedule date

t = expected date

σ = standard deviation

x = standardized value for the ordinate required, i.e. the schedule date

$$x = \frac{s - t}{\sigma} = \frac{16 - 15}{\sqrt{3}} = 0.58$$

When this value is located in normal distribution tables (Figure 13.21(b)) the area to the left of this value is found to be 72%.

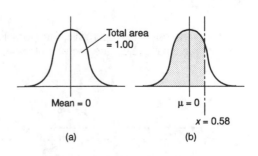

Figure 13.21

Figure 13.22

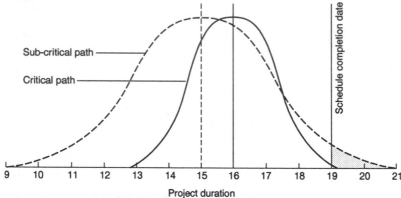

Project duration

The assumptions underlying the use of probabilities in this way in network analysis are, to say the least, of doubtful validity. The assumptions that the distribution for each activity duration corresponds to a 'beta' distribution and that the distribution of the duration of a sequence of activities can be regarded as 'normal' are not based on thorough research and should be regarded only as empirical rules which, over a period of time, have been found to work. Furthermore, in calculating the probability on project end dates only the critical path is used, but where the duration of each activity in the network is uncertain any path through the network has a certain probability of being critical and we should perhaps examine more than one path.

Suppose that in a network in which most of the activities' durations are uncertain the critical path has an expected duration of 16 days and a standard deviation of 1 day. In the same network there is a path of expected duration 15 days with a standard deviation of 3 days. According to the usual practice we ought to consider only the critical path in calculating our probabilities, but to do so in this case would mislead us, since there is a possibility that it will be the second path which will determine the project duration (Figure 13.22).

Had our scheduled completion date been day 19 then, considering the critical path only, we would be almost certain of meeting it, but the probability would be less if we considered the sub-critical path since, although the expected duration of this path is shorter, it is subject to greater variance.

EXAMPLE 13.3

The three time estimates (optimistic, likely, pessimistic) for the duration of the individual activities which form a small project are shown on the network diagram below.

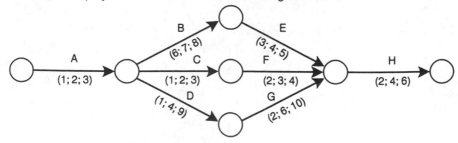

(a) Calculate the expected project duration.

(b) Determine the probability of finishing the project by day 18 or earlier.

Answer:

(a)

Activity	t days	σ^2	Activity	t days	σ^2
A	2	4/36	E	4	4/36
B	7	4/36	F	3	4/36
C	2	4/36	G	6	64/36
D	4.33	64/36	H	4	16/36

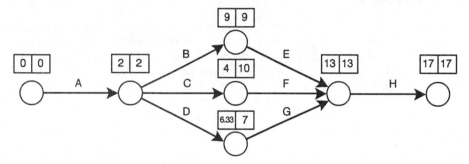

Expected project duration = 17 days

(b) Considering critical path ABEH:

$$t = 17$$
$$\sigma^2 = 4/36 + 4/36 + 4/36 + 16/36$$
$$= 0.776$$
$$x = \frac{s - t}{\sigma} = \frac{18 - 17}{\sqrt{0.776}}$$
$$x = 1.14$$

From normal probability tables x = 87.3%

Considering sub-critical path ADGH:

$$t = 2 + 4.33 + 6 + 4$$
$$= 16.33$$
$$\sigma^2 = 4/36 + 64/36 + 64/36 + 16/36$$
$$= 4.1$$
$$x = \frac{s - t}{\sigma} = \frac{18 - 16.33}{\sqrt{4.1}}$$
$$x = 0.825$$

From normal probability tables x = 79.6%

In using three activity duration estimates to calculate the probabilities of completing projects or parts of projects on or before given scheduled completion dates, it is important to consider sub-critical paths. This is particularly important when the length of such paths approaches the length of the critical path, and also where the duration of the activities on such paths is subject to comparatively large variance.

Unless jobs have been done before, it is often difficult to obtain accurate estimates of activity durations. One advantage of using multiple estimates is that it encourages people to commit themselves to estimates when they might be reluctant to give a single estimate. But if this method is used principally for this reason, then there is little to be said for using these figures and subsequently calculating project durations and probabilities to several places of decimals. In such cases it may be sufficient merely to take the average of the three estimates; in fact many computer programs provide this facility.

RESOURCES

Our treatment of network analysis so far has assumed that only time is important in executing tasks. There are certainly many situations where time is indeed the only or the most important factor, but in the majority of cases other factors affect our ability to do the job. We have assumed, for example, that the correct facilities have been available and in the correct quantities. The availability of such facilities as labour, plant, etc. determines not only our ability to do the job but also the time required to do it. Estimates of activity duration will rely implicitly on our capability to undertake those activities, so it is a little unrealistic to speak of activity durations in the abstract.

An estimate of the duration of an activity may differ substantially depending on the time at which the activity is undertaken. When very little other work is being undertaken an activity duration is likely to be shorter than when facilities are already heavily loaded or committed.

Each estimate of durations is based on the assumed use of a certain amount of resources, and consequently, when the project duration is initially calculated, we may also calculate the forward resource utilization, e.g. Figure 13.23.

Figure 13.23

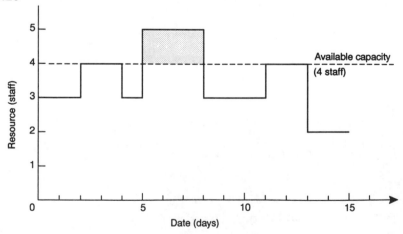

In this example an overload occurs from day 5 to day 8; consequently, unless we arrange to either subcontract this work or obtain additional resources, we cannot expect to meet our project completion date. The only remaining alternative is to reschedule some of the jobs which constitute this overload. We can, for example, delay three work-days of work from this period until days 8–11 and avoid overloading the resources.

Consider the part of a network shown in Figure 13.24. To be completed in four days, activity C requires six workers and four machines; activity D requires eight workers and

Figure 13.24

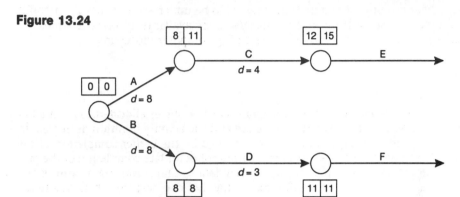

five machines for three days. The total resources available are eight workers and six machines, therefore activities C and D cannot occur together. The solution is to:

(a) Subcontract one of the activities, or

(b) Obtain additional resources, or

(c) Reschedule one or both of the activities.

Solutions (1) and (2) are particularly suitable where large overloads would occur and where this occurrence can be predicted well in advance. Often rescheduling is undertaken, and certainly where the overload is small and has occurred unexpectedly this is perhaps the only solution. The question is how we can reschedule the project to avoid overloading the resources and yet incur a minimum delay in completion. Activity D is on the critical path (it has a total float of 0) and the total float of activity C is three days, so activity D should be undertaken before C and this results in no additional project delay (Figure 13.25).

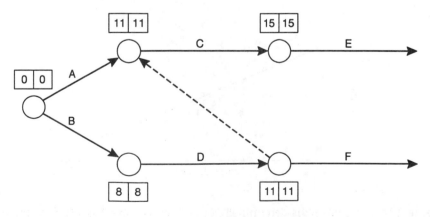

Figure 13.25

Resource aggregation, i.e. calculating the total resources necessary in any period to complete the project as in Figure 13.23, is a straightforward job, but resource allocation, as in Figure 13.25, can involve extensive computation for a large project. Networks involving more than a few hundred activities are normally processed on a computer, but the use of one of the numerous computer/network analysis programs is still economic for networks of fewer activities if resource allocation is to be undertaken. Although methods of resource allocation suitable for manual processing are available, in practice almost all resource allocation in network analysis occurs during computer processing.

COSTS

The duration of an activity depends on the quantity of resources allocated to it. At additional cost more resources can usually be acquired and the activity duration decreased. In many cases this additional expenditure can be justified by the earlier completion of the activity and of the project. If a heavy penalty clause applies for late completion of the project, or if the project must be completed by a given date so that it can begin earning revenue (e.g. a hotel ready for the beginning of the holiday season), then additional expenditure may be economically justifiable. In network analysis it is assumed that cost is linearly related to activity duration, and that as duration decreases the cost increases (Figure 13.26).

When it is possible to reduce an activity duration by engaging extra resources at additional cost, two extreme cases are assumed to exist:

(a) *Normal* activity duration at normal cost, utilizing the normal quantity of resources.

(b) A shorter *crash* activity duration at crash cost, utilizing additional resources.

Where the difference between normal and crash durations results from the use of a different method or process, no intermediate duration may be possible. For example, an estate of houses built by conventional techniques may require 50 days and cost £200 000 but an estate of 'industrialized' buildings may require 25 days and cost £330 000. Since two entirely different resources are used no compromise state exists on the same cost/duration function, whereas where the difference between normal and crash duration results from the use of additional similar resources, the two extremes may be interpolated, as in Figure 13.26.

Figure 13.26

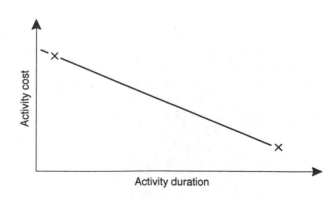

The total cost of a project is determined not only by variable costs such as production resources, but also by fixed or overhead costs such as rent for buildings, insurance, power, and administration. Consequently the project duration involving minimum total cost is not necessarily the duration with minimum cost of resources.

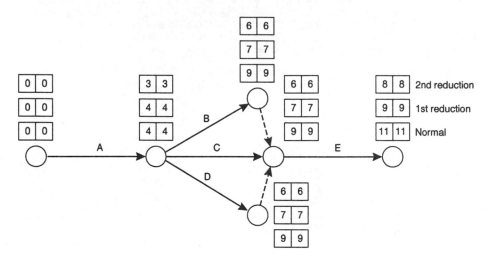

Activity	Normal		Crash	
	Duration (days)	Cost (£)	Duration (days)	Cost (£)
A	4	30	3	40
B	5	12	2	18
C	3	10	2	20
D	5	10	3	12
E	2	15	1	30
		Total 77		

N.B. Indirect fixed cost – £5/day.

Figure 13.27 Network diagram and comparison between cost of normal and crash activities

The network diagram for a small construction project, activity cost data and network dates are shown in Figure 13.27. Only the activities on the critical path affect the project duration, therefore reduction in project duration must be sought on the critical path and from those activities offering time savings at least cost. Initially there are two critical paths—ABE and ADE—and the least cost time saving is two days from both activities B and D. After activities B and D have been reduced from five to three days all three paths are critical and, since no further reduction is possible on activity D, savings must be obtained from activities A and E. Activity A can be reduced by one day at a cost of £10, then activity E by one day at a cost of £15. This procedure for reducing the project duration is given in the table in Figure 13.28, which also shows the construction of the total cost/project duration curve. The least cost project duration is nine days.

Normal duration = 11 days
Normal cost = £77

Job	Cost/day saved	Reduction (days)	Total reduction (days)	Additional cost (£)	Duration (days)
Initial critical paths = { A B E, A D E					
					11
Least cost saving occurs on B and D					
B }, D }	2 + 1	2	2	6	9
Now three critical paths = { A B E, A C E, A D E					
Least cost saving on A					
A	10	1	3	16	8
Least cost saving on E					
E	15	1	4	31	7

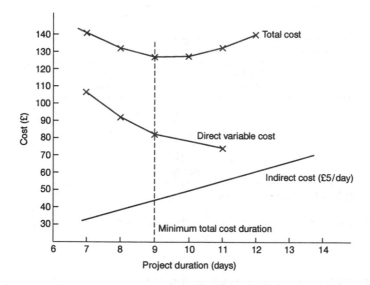

Figure 13.28 Activity variable cost/duration relationships for Figure 13.27

COMPUTER-BASED PROJECT MANAGEMENT

Most of the early software packages for use in project management provided primarily for network construction and analysis, together with schedule production. Procedures for resource allocation and for dealing with multi-project situations were then developed.

These early, somewhat limited, network analysis packages were valuable for project planning and control when more than 200 or 300 activities were involved, and where regular updating was unnecessary. The inputs required for such network analysis programs were typically.

(a) List of activities, described by the beginning and ending event number.

(b) The duration(s) for each activity.

(c) Schedule dates on intermediate and/or finish events.

(d) The description of each activity. This is not necessary for the program but forms part of the output so that the information is meaningful and activities can easily be recognized.

(e) The *responsibility code* for each activity, i.e. whether it is performed department A, B, and so on, so that, if desired, the output can be broken down into separate lists showing the plan for each department.

(f) Description of the work week and the holidays, etc., so that the work will not be scheduled during holidays and so that activity durations in hours or days can be used to calculate project durations in weeks or months.

(g) The resource levels normally available, i.e. normal work and machine hours per week.

(h) Additional resources available due to overtime, etc.

(i) Maximum activity delay which, if necessary, can be tolerated because of the rescheduling of activities to conform to resource availability.

Many, more comprehensive, and sophisticated software packages for Project Management are now available. Current estimates suggest that there are about 250 on the market. Table 13.1 provides a categorization of such software and outlines capabilities/features.

Table 13.1 Types and capabilities of computer software packages

1. Simple: Single project planning
Limited analysis (e.g. no rescheduling)
Simple, easy to use and understand

2. Single: Single project management (planning, scheduling control, monitoring)
Comprehensive analysis (with progress reports, re-scheduling, etc.)

3. Multiproject: Multiproject management (planning, scheduling control, monitoring)
Comprehensive analysis and reports
Uses common database

Typical capabilities

1. Formats (activity on arrow or on mode)
2. Bar or Gantt chart displays/outputs
3. Schedule dates
4. Updating (e.g. with revised durations, schedule dates, etc.)
5. Sorting (i.e. listing of activities with dates, by department)
6. Resource Aggregation and Allocation
7. Cost controls and calculations
8. Calendar dates (i.e. internal calendar used to apply calendar dates to activities)
9. Reports (i.e. choice of report formats)
10. PERT calculations
11. Cost/duration comparisons
12. 'What if?' calculations (e.g. calculate effects of changes in durations, resources, etc.)

EXAMPLE

Gibraltar Savings

Gibraltar Savings installed a microcomputer-based project management system, to manage the conversion from one manufacturer's computer system to another, following acquisition of another savings company. The project management system created a conversion system detailed to task level. It was used to schedule the execution of the weekend-long conversion, indicating at what points the conversion process should stop for data verification and when to undertake full-production file testing, etc. Because of the success in this application the system was adopted by Gibraltar as a standard for major conversions and for regular operations.

Source: Skylar, J. (1988) 'Macro project, macro manager. *Computer Decisions* **20**(11), pp. 76.

KEY POINTS FOR CHAPTER 13

Project management

Is concerned with the management of activities which are finite in respect of both time and the use of resources.

There are three phases in the project life cycle.

  Project investigation and planning

  Project scheduling

  Project control and evaluation

Project scheduling and control is often undertaken using network techniques.

Network analysis involves

  Network diagram construction

  Determination of activity times

  Network schedule calculation

  Network/Time modification (if necessary)

Multiple estimates of activity times can be used to investigate schedule date probabilities and risk. This is traditionally known as 'PERT'.

Resource aggregation and allocation is often necessary.

The duration of an activity is often a function of the resources devoted to it and hence cost.

Project duration and cost are often interrelated.

Most project management with network analysis employs computer procedures.

FURTHER READING

Turner, J. R. (1993) *The Handbook of Project Based Management.* London: McGraw Hill.

Kerzner, H. (1992) *Project Management: A Systems Approach to Planning, Scheduling and Control.* New York: Van Nostrand Reinhold.

East, E. and Kirby, J. (1990) *A Guide to Computerized Project Scheduling.* New York: Van Nostrand Reinhold.

CASE STUDIES

The following cases from Part 9 of the book, are relevant to the topics covered in this chapter.

No.	Name	Country
10	Linden Christian Nursery A	South Africa
11	Linden Christian Nursery B	South Africa

QUESTIONS

13.1 Construct a network diagram for the following activities:

Activity	A	B	C	D	E	F	G	H	J	K	L	M	N	O
Necessary preceding activities	–	–	A	AB	C	C	D	D	E	EF	GH	H	JK	LM

13.2 Draw an activity network for the following activities. Assuming that the project starts at day 0, calculate the earliest start and latest finish dates for all activities, and the project earliest completion date. Calculate also the total float on all activities and identify the critical path.

Activity	A	B	C	D	E	F	G	H	I
Immediate predecessors	–	–	A	AB	BC	CD	CD	EF	EGF
Activity duration (days)	3	5	6	2	4	7	3	4	5

13.3 The following table describes the various activities of a small project. What is the probability that the project will be completed in 22$\frac{1}{2}$ days or less?

Activity	Immediate predecessor(s)	Estimates of activity duration (days)		
		Optimistic	Likely	Pessimistic
A	–	2	4	6
B	A	1	5	9
C	A	–	9	–
D	C	5	6	7
E	B	5	7	9
F	B	4	10	16
G	DE	–	7	–
H	F	6	9	12

13.4 A small civil engineering project consists of 15 activities and can be represented by the network diagram below:

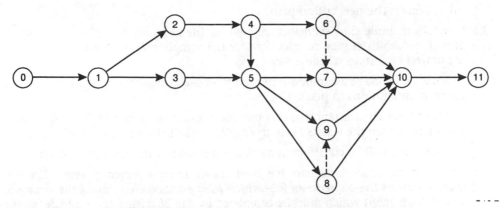

The duration of each of the activities is given in the following table.

Activity		Duration (days)
Begin event	End event	
0	1	10
1	2	5
1	3	6
2	4	3
3	5	4
4	5	3
4	6	8
5	7	4
5	8	5
5	9	9
6	7	Dummy
6	10	7
7	10	2
8	10	3
9	8	Dummy
9	10	6
10	11	9

(a) If the project is to start at, say, day 0 and is to end as soon as possible, calculate the total float (TF) on each activity and identify the critical path.

(b) Activity 3–5 is 'lay 150 mm pipe'.

Activity 6–10 is 'lay 250 mm pipe'.

The project is begun on day 0 but the supplier of the pipes informs the company that the 150 mm pipe will be delivered on day 18 and the 250 mm pipe on day 34.

(i) What effect do these deliveries have on the earliest completion date of the project?

(ii)   What is the new critical path?

13.5 If certain multiple time estimates are used for the duration of individual jobs in a project, probabilities may be calculated for the completion of the project or part of the project by certain schedule dates.

What are the basic assumptions necessary for such calculations, and how justified are such assumptions in practice?

Under what circumstances is this procedure likely to be beneficial, and in what circumstances are the results likely to be either inaccurate or unrealistic?

Wherever possible, construct numerical examples to illustrate your answer.

13.6 The following network diagram has been drawn up by a project planner. The diagram represents the sequence of jobs which will be undertaken during the service of a large component which must be completed by day 35. Using the estimates of the job durations given by the managers of the various departments, the project planner has calculated event dates which indicate that the project will be completed one day before the scheduled completion date.

The information given on the diagram has been submitted to you, the project executive, for approval prior to being distributed to the various departments. What are your reactions and why?

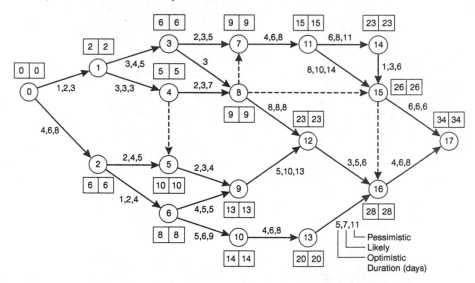

13.7 From the information given below construct a network diagram.

(a) Neglecting resource considerations, what is the earliest finish date for the project?

(b) Assuming that each activity begins as early as possible, construct a graph showing the amount of resources used during each period.

(c) The maximum number of resources available is 19 workers. Again, assuming that activities are begun as soon as possible, redraw the network so that the resources used at any time do not exceed 19 workers, and so that a minimum project delay is incurred.

(d) What project delay is incurred through this adherence to the resource limit?

Activity	Immediate predecessor	Duration (days)	Number of workers used
A	–	8	4
B	–	7	8
C	A	6	5
D	B	8	4
E	B	4	8
F	B	8	6
G	CD	5	5
H	E	6	4
I	F	6	5
J	GHI	10	6

Table for Question 13.7

N.B. Because of the nature of the work, jobs cannot be interrupted and must be finished once begun.

Chapter 14

Scheduling for batch processing

ISSUES

Is batch processing desirable or just unavoidable?
How does batch processing work?
Is batch processing still relevant when there is a desire to operate with low inventories?
What are the key decisions in batch processing?
How are batch sequences and schedules determined?
Why are batch sizes important?
How can batch processing be avoided?
What is Group Technology?
What is an FMS and what does it achieve?

In the previous chapter we discussed planning in relation to project or 'one-off' type operations. In the next chapter scheduling for repetitive operations will be discussed. Both types of system are comparatively easy to describe since, in both cases, reference can be made to their 'pure' forms, i.e. the processing of unit quantities of different types of item or customer and the continual processing of a single type of item or customer respectively. Here we shall deal with the situation which exists between these two extremes. It is more difficult to envisage and describe. It is unlike flow processing, since the operating system must deal with a variety of types of item or customer and the processing rate is not normally equal to the demand rate; it is unlike project systems since a greater variety of types of item or customer must be dealt with. For convenience we will use the traditional terminology, and refer to this as the 'batch' processing system.

DEALING WITH BATCHES AND AVOIDING THEM

There are two parts to this chapter. First, we shall discuss how batches are dealt with, and second, we shall look at how to minimize or even avoid the problems of batch processing.

Batches and inventories

Typically, if items or customers are processed through systems in batches, inventories will exist. For example, in processing a batch of items to meet subsequent demand we often build up an output stock. That stock is used to satisfy demand during a period in which that item is not being processed. Also, stock is usually created 'in process' as batches await completion at individual operations in the complete process. Batch processing of customers in a service or transport system usually necessitates input queues (i.e. stocks) of customers.

We have noted in Chapters 2 and 12 that organizations are now seeking to reduce, even to eliminate inventories, e.g. through the use of Just-in-Time systems. The effect of this is to reduce batch sizes, since lower batch sizes involve lower inventories.

With this approach the ideal is to operate with batch sizes of one. We shall see that batch size is, in effect, a function of two costs: inventory holding costs which increase with increased batch sizes, and set-up costs which reduce with increased batch sizes. So the use of small batch sizes—perhaps approaching unity—in order to minimize in-process inventory would be justified where unit holding costs were high, and where process set-up costs were low. In practice, therefore, in seeking to implement low inventory, operations management will seek to reduce set-up costs. This can be achieved in two ways: by reducing the difference between the processing requirements of the items which are being dealt with (i.e. increasing their processing similarity) and by improving the inherent flexibility or adaptability of processing equipment. The processing similarity of items might be improved through design changes and the use of common parts. Additionally, families of similar items might be identified, and processing systems set up to deal with each such family. This is the Group Technology approach discussed later in this chapter. Improvements in the inherent flexibility of processes can be achieved through the use of standard tooling, changes in equipment design, or the use of more sophisticated equipment which provides for automated set-up re-configuration. This latter is the principal characteristic of the flexible manufacturing systems (FMS) which are now being introduced into traditional batch manufacturing situations. We shall look at these means to reduce batch sizes in the second part of this chapter. First, however, we shall look at how batch processing is managed.

MANAGING BATCH PROCESSING

Examples of batch processing

Batch processing can exist in all four types of operations, i.e. supply, service, transport and manufacture.

A batch flow system might exist in *supply* in that the function might seek to transfer items from input stock to customers in batches rather than in unit quantities. For example, where the cost of supply, i.e. transfer from input stock to customer, is high there may be some benefit in dealing with several customers at one time given the possibility of accumulating 'customers' for particular types of item. Equally, in supply systems which operate without input stocks, i.e. in which items are acquired for particular customers, there may be benefits in operating on a batch processing system.

In *service* systems customers may be processed in batches. For example, certain entertainment services operate in this way in that the service is provided when a given number or minimum number of customers are available. Such a situation might exist in systems in which resources are stocked, as in certain entertainment facilities or in situations which must acquire resources to satisfy customer needs.

Likewise certain *transport* systems might operate on a batch processing arrangement. Transport, for example, might be available only when a certain number of customers have presented themselves. Thus a function might be triggered by the growth of the queue of customers to or beyond a certain minimum limit.

In *manufacture*, batch processing might be employed in systems which have output stocks, i.e. batches of items are produced in anticipation of demand. Also the batch processing method might be employed in the manufacture of items to order, providing, of course, orders are received for sufficiently similar items. (See 'Group Technology in Manufacture' later in this chapter.)

Normally, batch processing involves the use of inventories or queues. It was for this reason that we drew attention to low inventory systems above. In manufacture, batch processing often, but not always, gives rise to output stocks. For transport and service systems it is likely that batch processing can be employed only where customer input queues exist, since it is unlikely that batches of customers will present themselves to the organization but rather that they will be allowed to accumulate over time. In these cases, the use of batch processing at the expense of customer waiting or queuing time is feasible only in certain market situations. However, the use of batch processing to provide a stock of items in anticipation of demand will be appropriate in circumstances where customer waiting or queuing is to be minimized. The main benefit of batch processing is higher resource utilization than might otherwise be possible. Customer service, except on cost, does not normally benefit in comparison to what otherwise might be achieved.

Batch processing decisions

In general the planning of batch processing[1] requires the solution of three problems:

(a) *batch sequencing*, i.e. the determination of the order in which batches of different items (or customers) will be processed;

(b) the determination of *batch sizes*, i.e. the quantity of each type of item (or customer) to be processed at one time;

(c) *batch scheduling*, i.e. the timing of the processing of batches of items (or customers).

BATCH SEQUENCING (see also Chapter 15)

It is possible that the cost of setting up, i.e. preparing, a set of facilities for the processing of a batch of items (or customers) will depend not only on the type of items (or customers) to be processed in that batch, but also on the type in the batch which was previously processed on the same facilities. In these circumstances, total set-up cost is also a function of the sequence of items, and it is appropriate to try to determine the appropriate sequence in order to minimize set-up cost. Thus if four types of item, A, B, C and D, are to be processed in batches on a common set of facilities, and the set-up cost for each batch is influenced by the type of item which was previously processed, where that cost

---

[1] Much of what will be discussed in this chapter will relate to and overlap with that introduced in Chapter 17 on inventory management. Many of the problems of planning for batch processing are similar to those involved in inventory management, and in general, detailed treatments, particularly of more sophisticated aspects, will be covered in Chapter 17.

is known an optimum sequence of batches can be determined. The assumption here, of course, is that each batch must be processed the same number of times, i.e. that a repetitive sequence involving one batch of each item can be established. This is the normal situation, and a solution can often be found using the assignment method of linear programming. (The problem is identical to that of determining the optimum sequence for batches of items to be processed on a mixed-model repetitive/flow processing system. This is described in Chapter 15.)

Processing 'families' of items

A situation might exist in which several different types of item (or customers) each require a similar, but not identical, set-up. In this situation those items may be seen as a 'family' of similar items. It will be sensible when setting up the facilities to process a batch of any one of the items in the family to take advantage of that set-up and process a batch of all the other items within the family, especially where the cost of the set-up is relatively high.

For example, in the situation shown in Table 14.1, the set-up costs incurred between the processing of items B, C and D are small whereas the cost of setting up the process between either A or E and any of the family B, C and D is relatively high. In this case, therefore, there will be some merit in processing the 'family' of items B, C and D in succession, (possibly in the order C, B, D) with the other two items produced at another time (possibly in the order A, E). In fact the sequencing problem shown in Table 14.1 is an example of the type of situation which *cannot* be solved using the assignment method referred to above; this is because of the configuration of the cost within the matrix. In such cases, particularly where a 'family' of items exist, an alternative approach will be required.

One approach to the solution of the 'family' sequencing problem is as follows:

(a) Identify the items within a 'family'.

(b) Determine the 'processing cycle' for these items (i.e. the time interval between the successive processings of the family) together with the batch quantity for each item.

(c) Determine the optimum sequence for the remaining items and process these items as required between families.

The procedure for determining the optimum processing cycle for a set of items is given later in this chapter.

(Notice that the 'family' processing problem has some similarities with the approach discussed in the section on group technology later in this chapter.)

Table 14.1					
Preceding item	**Succeeding item**				
	A	B	C	D	E
A	0	100	90	110	60
B	105	0	10	5	60
C	95	20	0	25	70
D	100	15	10	0	80
E	70	75	80	75	0

Determination of batch sizes

Batch quantities which are too large will result in high stock levels and cause a large amount of capital to be tied up in stock which might otherwise be invested elsewhere. Additionally, unduly high stock levels will incur other costs, such as the cost of stock-keeping, insurance, depreciation, etc. On the other hand, batch quantities which are too small will result in both low stock levels, which may be insufficient to meet large fluctuations in demand, and the frequent processing of small batches, each time incurring costs associated with set-up, ordering, etc.

The problem, then, is to determine the batch size which minimizes total costs; consequently we must consider the following:

(a) stock holding;

(b) processing;

(c) set-up and preparation of machines and equipment.

Minimum cost batch size

The minimum cost batch size can easily be determined providing, of course, that the assumptions made in deriving the formula are justified in practice, and providing also that the various costs can be determined accurately.

We shall consider first a simple *static* and *deterministic* situation, i.e. one in which both processing and consumption rates are *known* and *constant*. Let us assume that items are delivered into stock as a complete batch at the end of the processing period. In other words we are considering the type of batch processing system shown in Figure 14.1.

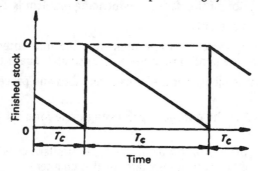

Figure 14.1 Batch processing in a 'pure' inventory system

Our notation is as follows:

Q = Process batch quantity

C_S = Set-up or preparation cost/batch

C_1 = Stock-holding cost/item/unit of time

r = Consumption rate/unit of time

q = Processing rate/unit of time

Then:

Average stock level = $Q/2$

Minimum cost batch size $= Q^* = \sqrt{\dfrac{2C_s r}{C_1}}$

Total cost/unit of time $= C$

$\therefore C^* = \sqrt{2r C_s C_1}$

Processing cycle time, $t^* = \dfrac{Q^*}{r}$

$\therefore t^* = \dfrac{Q^*}{r}$

EXAMPLE

Watertight Ltd

Watertight Ltd are the manufacturers of a range of plastic overshoes. The complete range consists of 14 different types (i.e. sizes and styles). Type BB (Big and Black) is sold in the largest quantities, demand being reasonably stable at 4500 pairs per month.

All overshoes are manufactured in batches, the production process being such that the entire batch is completed at the same time.

(a) Given the following information, use the formulae above to determine the economic batch production quantity:

Machine set-up cost per production batch	= £150
Stock-holding cost per pair	= £3.75 per annum

(b) The present production policy is to manufacture BB overshoes in batch sizes of 3000 pairs at regular intervals. How does the actual production cycle time compare with the optimum production cycle time?

(a) $r = 4500$ per month
$C_S = £150$

$C_1 = 3.75 \times \dfrac{1}{12} = £0.313$ per month

$\therefore Q^* = \sqrt{\dfrac{2C_S r}{C_1}} = \sqrt{\dfrac{2 \times 150 \times 4500}{0.313}}$

$= 2077$ pairs

(b) $t^* = \dfrac{Q^*}{r} = \dfrac{2077}{4500}$

$= 0.46$ months

Actual $Q = 3000$ pairs

$\therefore$ Actual $t = \dfrac{Q}{r} = \dfrac{3000}{4500}$

$= 0.67$ months (46% longer interval than optimum policy)

We can extend this simple model to include the possibility of stock shortages or 'stock-outs'. This introduces an additional cost factor, the cost of shortages, C_2. The model, which still assumes known and constant demand, is depicted in Figure 14.2. The areas below the horizontal axis, i.e. periods t_2, represent demand which would have been satisfied had adequate stock been available. The cost of such shortage, in terms of loss of profit, etc., must be introduced into the formula, since it will influence the choice of batch size.

Using the previous notation, plus C_2 = shortage cost/item/unit of time:

$$Q^* = \sqrt{\frac{2rC_S}{C_1}}\sqrt{\frac{C_1 + C_2}{C_2}}$$

$$C^* = \sqrt{2rC_1C_S}\sqrt{\frac{C_2}{C_1 + C_2}}$$

$$t^* = \frac{Q^*}{r}$$

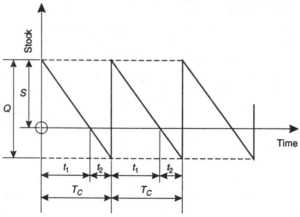

Figure 14.2 A stock/batch processing model allowing shortages.

EXAMPLE

A shoe wholesaler

r = 9500 per month
C_1 = £5 per item per annum
C_S = £1 250
C_2 = £2 per item per month

Compare the optimum processing quantities for:

(a) a policy in which stock-outs are permitted;
(b) a policy in which stock-outs are not to occur.

(a) $\quad Q^* = \sqrt{\dfrac{2C_s r}{C_1}} \; \sqrt{\dfrac{C_1 + C_2}{C_2}}$

$\quad\quad = \sqrt{\dfrac{2 \times 1\,250 \times 9500}{5/12}} \; \sqrt{\dfrac{5/12 + 2}{2}}$

$\quad\quad = 7550 \times 1.1$

$\quad\quad = 8305$

(b) $\quad Q^* = \sqrt{\dfrac{2C_s r}{C_1}}$

$\quad\quad = 7520$

Now instead of considering the total processing batch to be delivered into stock at the same time, we shall consider a situation in which the items which constitute the batch are delivered into stock continuously throughout the process period. Such a situation is depicted in Figure 14.3.

Figure 14.3

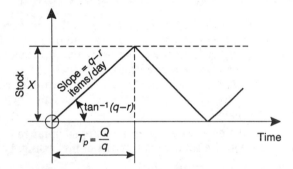

We can again calculate optimum batch quantities, etc., as follows (adopting the notation used above):

$$\text{Average inventory} = B + \frac{Q}{2}(1 - r/q)$$

$$Q^* = \sqrt{\frac{2C_s r}{C_1(1 - r/q)}}$$

$$C^* = \sqrt{2rC_s C_1} \; \sqrt{1 - (r/q)}$$

$$t^* = \frac{Q^*}{r}$$

EXAMPLE

Express Drinks Company (1)

A product is sold at a constant rate of 600 per day, the processing rate for the item being 2000 per day. It is known that set-up costs are £10 per batch and that stock-holding costs, including notional loss of interest on capital, are £0.5 per item per year. If a buffer stock of 500 items is maintained, what is the minimum cost processing batch quantity?

$C_S = £10$

$B = 500$

$q = 2000$

$r = 600$

Assuming that there are 250 working days per year:

$$C_1 = \frac{0.5}{250} = £0.002 \text{ per item per day}$$

$$Q^* = \sqrt{\frac{2 \times 10 \times 600}{0.002[1 - (6/20)]}}$$

$$Q^* = 2925$$

The 'production' range (or processing range)

Because of the frequent difficulty of accurately establishing costs such as C_1 and C_S it is fortunate that the total cost curve is fairly flat at the point of minimum cost, since this means that the total variable cost is not very sensitive to deviations from optimal batch size. It is possible, therefore, to adopt a batch size which differs slightly from the optimal without incurring substantially increased costs. This feature of the total cost curve gives rise to the 'production range' concept (see Figure 14.4). Batch quantities within this range are considered as acceptable.

The procedure for the determination of an acceptable range is dependent on knowing the allowable increase in the total variable costs of processing; i.e. let:

$$c = \frac{\text{Actual variable costs per unit}}{\text{Minimum variable costs per unit}}$$

$$q = \frac{\text{Actual batch size}}{\text{Minimum cost batch size}}$$

then:

$$q = c \pm \sqrt{c^2 - 1}$$

Figure 14.4 Economic batch size

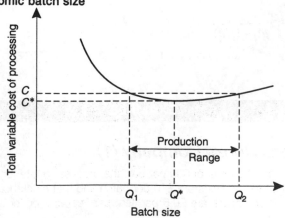

and the two limits of the range are:

$$Q_1 = Q^* (c - \sqrt{c^2 - 1}) = Q^*q$$
$$Q_2 = Q^*(c + \sqrt{c^2 - 1}) = Q^*q$$

The values of q_1 and q_2 can be found from the curve given in Figure 14.5 and consequently the production range can be calculated.

Figure 14.5

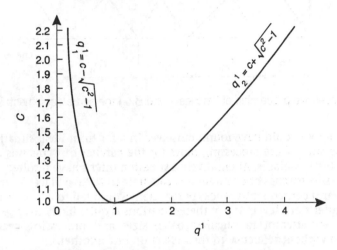

EXAMPLE

Express Drinks Company (2)

In our previous example the optimal batch size was 2925 units. A policy of an allowable increase in cost per unit of 10 per cent has been adopted, i.e. $c = 1.1$. From Figure 14.5:

$q^1 = 0.65$
$q^2 = 1.55$
$Q_1 = Q^*q_1 = 2925 \ (0.65) = 1901$
$Q_2 = Q^*q_2 = 2925 \ (1.55) = 4533$

SCHEDULING FOR BATCH PROCESSING

Having decided the optimal size of the batch for each item which is to be processed, we must consider when these batches are to be processed. Here we shall focus on one particular aspect of the scheduling problem which is peculiar to batch processing and then on one further technique which is of relevance in this area. Previously we have considered each item in isolation, whereas now we must consider how these batches are to be processed on the available equipment and how they affect one another.

As an illustration of the batch scheduling problem, consider a situation in which only two items (A and B) are to be processed successively on the same equipment. The economic (minimum cost) batch quantity for each item has been calculated by use of one of the previous formulae and the processing schedule is shown in Figure 14.6. In this case there is no idle time on the equipment and the optimum and individually calculated processing policies for the two batches do not clash, so we must think ourselves particularly

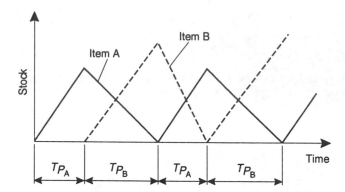

Figure 14.6 Successive processing of batches A and B on the same equipment: ideal situation.

lucky. Quite easily we could have found ourselves in a far from ideal situation in which, for example, the sum of the processing times for the batches of items was either greater or less than the time available. Alternatively a situation might have resulted in which processing of successive batches of one item was constrained to take place at greater than the desired interval and consequently stocks of that item would fall to a level below the desirable safety or buffer stock level. Any of these situations is quite likely to arise if, in a multi-item situation, we attempt to calculate batch sizes and processing cycles for items individually and without reference to their effect on one another.

The problem is to find the most economical cycle, i.e. that which minimizes set-up and holding or inventory costs. As before, the set-up costs increase and the holding costs decrease as the number of cycles increases, but to obtain a satisfactory solution the cycle time for all items must be set simultaneously.

The line of balance technique

Our discussion has taken for granted the fact that batch processing proceeds in a series of steps. For example, we have assumed that in a process consisting of several operations, 1, 2, 3, etc., the entire batch is completed on operation 1 before being passed to operation 2 and so on. This type of situation is attractive, since it provides easier operations control. On the other hand there are disadvantages in this iterative type of procedure. For example, the throughput time for any batch will be high, the work in progress will be high and, consequently, a large amount of storage space will be required. Ideally, therefore, we must look for a procedure in which batches of items might be divided, i.e. processing begun on subsequent operations before the complete batch has been processed on previous operations, and yet a procedure which enables adequate control of operations to be exercised. Such a situation might be desirable in manufacture, supply or service systems in certain conditions.

When batches are kept complete during processing and when an activity schedule for each batch on each operation is available, it is an easy matter to determine whether processing is proceeding according to plan. If the dividing of batches is allowed then the situation is more complex and it is often quite difficult both to establish an activity schedule and to determine whether progress is satisfactory or not. It is difficult, for example, to determine whether, at a given time, sufficient items have completed sufficient operations.

For example, consider the completion schedule shown in Table 14.2. Twelve finished items must be completed at the end of week 1, another fourteen at the end of week 2, and

Table 14.2	Job completion requirements	
Week no.	**Delivery of finished items required**	**Cumulative completions required**
0	0	0
1	12	12
2	14	26
3	8	34
4	6	40
5	10	50
6	12	62
7	14	76
8	16	92
9	18	110
10	22	132

so on. It is clear from this that, at the end of the fifth week, forty items should have completed the final operation. What is not clear, however, is how many items should have passed through the previous operations at this date so as to ensure completion of the requisite quantity of items in later weeks.

The 'line of balance' technique was developed to deal with precisely this type of situation. The technique is an example of 'management by exception' since it deals only with the important or crucial (exceptional) operations in a job, establishes a schedule or plan for them and attracts attention to those which do not conform to this schedule (those about which something must be done if the progress of the entire job is not to be jeopardized). It is particularly useful where large batches of fairly complex items requiring many operations are to be delivered or completed over a period of time.

The technique can be regarded as a slightly more sophisticated form of the Gantt chart, the objective being to study the progress of jobs at regular intervals, to compare progress on each operation with the progress necessary to satisfy the eventual delivery requirements, and to identify those operations in which progress is unsatisfactory.

We can best describe the technique by means of a simple example. Two pieces of information are required: first the completion requirements and second an operation programme, i.e. the sequence and duration of the various operations. Four stages are involved in the use of the technique:

(a) the completion schedule;

(b) the operation programme;

(c) the programme progress chart;

(d) analysis of progress.

The completion schedule

Construction of the completion schedule is the first step. The cumulative complete

265

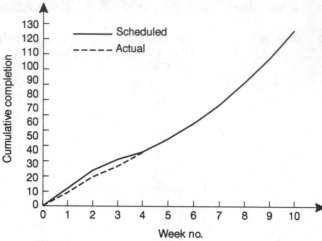

Figure 14.7 Cumulative completions

requirements must be calculated and presented as either a table (Table 14.2) or, and this is more useful later, a graph (Figure 14.7), which may also be used to record deliveries in the manner shown.

The operation programme

The operation programme depicts the 'lead time' of the various operations, i.e. the length of time prior to the completion of the final operation by which intermediate operations must be completed.

In a simple job it is possible to show such information for *all* operations in the job, but in more complex jobs we concern ourselves only with those operations which are important or critical to the progress of the job and the satisfaction of the schedule.

The operation programme is best depicted as a chart, with the final delivery date as zero. Figure 14.8 is such an operation programme. The final completion date (completion of operation 15) is zero and the time scale runs from right to left. This programme shows that items B and C must be combined (operation 14) two days before completion. Item C, prior to this combination, undergoes two conversion operations; the second must be finished five days before final completion, and the first two days before that. Purchase of the material for item C must be completed by ten days before final combination. The item with longest lead time, 17 days, is B.

These two pieces of information—completion schedule and operation programme—are prerequisites for use of the line of balance technique. They need to

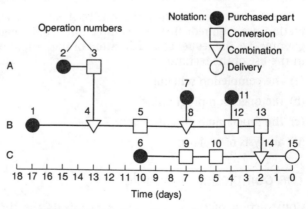

Figure 14.8 Operation programme

be constructed only once for any job, unlike the following documents, which must be constructed each time the schedule and progress are examined.

The programme progress chart

This chart shows the number of items which have been finished at each of the critical or important operations at a given date. Suppose, for example, the review date is week 4, by which, according to the completion schedule, 40 items should have been completed, i.e. 40 items should have passed operation 15 of the operation programme. The number of items that have completed this and each of the other operations can be obtained simply by checking inventory levels. The results can then be depicted by means of a histogram. Figure 14.9 shows the programme performance at week 4.

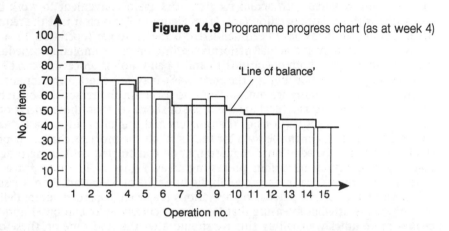

Figure 14.9 Programme progress chart (as at week 4)

Since the object is to compare actual progress with scheduled or planned progress, the information given in Figure 14.9 must be compared with required progress. This is done by constructing a line on the programme progress chart which shows the number of items which should have been finished at each operation at the time of review. This line—the line of balance—can be constructed analytically or graphically. The line of balance shows the total number of items which should have been finished at each operation. Since a

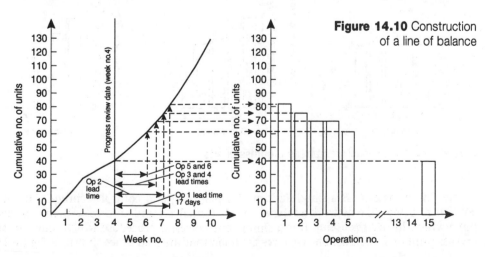

Figure 14.10 Construction of a line of balance

cumulative completion of 40 items is required for week 4, a total of 40 items must have completed operation 15 by this date. Operation 14 has a lead time of two days, consequently at week 4 sufficient items must have completed operation 15 to ensure that completion requirements two days later are satisfied. From the completion schedule the delivery for week 4 plus two days is 44 units (assuming five working days a week). The longest lead time, operation 1, is 17 days, so at week 4 enough items to satisfy the delivery requirements for week 4 plus 17 days, i.e. 82 units, should have been finished. The graphical procedure shown in Figure 14.10 is a convenient way of performing these calculations.

Analysis of progress

In comparing required with actual progress it is again convenient to work backwards, beginning with the last operation (15). From Figure 14.9 it is clear that the required number of completed items have been delivered to the customer (operation 15 = 40), a fact which is reflected by the actual performance line on the completion schedule. Clearly there is a shortage on both operations 13 and 14 and, unless processing can be expedited in some way, completion during the next week may fall short of requirements. When shortages occur, obviously we must attempt to ascertain the reasons. If operations other than those considered as critical are the cause of shortages then those operations must be included in subsequent versions of the progress and line of balance charts. As an aid to control, colour codes might be used for the 'bars' on the progress chart to depict responsibility; alternatively, additional charts might be constructed containing progress information on operations in various processing areas. Figure 14.11 shows three additional programme progress charts, each containing one type of operation. From these it is clear that performance on the purchasing operations may well jeopardize future deliveries. We must therefore attempt to ensure that items, particularly on operations 1 and 2, are purchased more quickly, or failing this we should alter the lead time on these operations. Charts such as these might be issued to and used by departmental managers or production controllers.

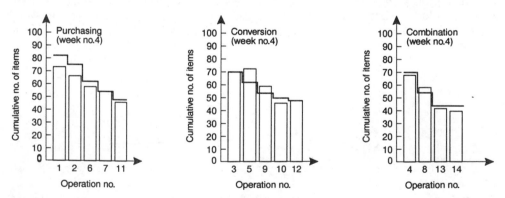

Figure 14.11 Additional programme progress charts

The line of balance is a simple and useful planning and control technique, its main advantage being, like network analysis, that it formalizes and enforces a planning discipline which in itself is useful. It is a simple but powerful procedure which relies on several assumptions. For example, we have assumed that the lead times shown in Figure 14.8

are constant, and that the type and sequence of operations are independent of production quantities. Such assumptions are very often justified in practice and consequently the technique as it has been presented here is of direct value.

REDUCING BATCH SIZES—MANAGING WITHOUT BATCHES?

We identified ways in which batch sizes might be reduced towards unity at the beginning of the chapter. Now we look more closely at two tactics which promise the possibility of smaller batches than would otherwise be necessary, and thus the advantages of lower inventories.

Group technology

Group technology or 'cellular' processing was developed in manufacturing. The aim was to get away from traditional batch manufacture. The approach adopted was to concentrate on components or parts rather than end products. The logic was that even though the end products differed and therefore could not be processed through common facilities and at the same time, some of the component parts were often quite similar, and if grouped together they could be put through the same facilities together—so avoiding the need for batch processing and the change of facility set-up between batches.

Adopting a group technology method, the following stages are achieved:

1. The parts of each of the items processed are examined and placed into logical classes or families and the operations sequence for each class of parts is determined and specified.

2. Groups of facilities suitable for the processing of these classes of parts are specified using the operations planning details and forecasted demand for the items and hence the components.

3. The sequencing of each class of parts for each group of facilities.

For purposes of implementing group technology, two types of family or group and three methods of processing can be identified. The two types of family are:

1. *Type A*, consisting of parts which are similar in shape and which have all or the majority of processing operations in common.

2. *Type B*, consisting of apparently dissimilar parts which are related by having one or more processing operations in common.

The three methods of processing using group technology are therefore as follows:

1. *Method 1*—processing of a type-A family on a group of different conventional machines.

2. *Method 2*—processing of a type-A and/or type-B family on one or more similar and conventional machines.

3. *Method 3*—processing of a type-B family on a group of different machines.

In conventional terms the processing of a large quantity of type-A parts by method 1 corresponds to flow processing, which is, of course, an efficient method since it maximizes machine utilization. It is the object of group technology, by identifying common features in parts, to extend this type of application and to obtain increased efficiency in processing by adopting one of the three methods described above.

Formation of parts families

On occasions the selection of the parts for inclusion in a family may be relatively simple; hence the use of one of the more rigorous techniques will be unnecessary. Such a situation may occur when the item range is fairly static, when there are large numbers of parts with similar shapes, and when several obviously exclusive categories of parts exist.

Classification in this context refers to the assignment of parts into predefined groups or classes, while *coding* is the allocation of identities to these groups. The type and amount of information contained in the code depend on the potential uses of the system. A designer may wish to retrieve designs to obtain relevant information and to use existing parts in new items, while retrieval is also necessary in connection with costing, planning, variety reduction, etc. For this reason the design of a classification and coding system is normally a compromise that attempts to satisfy as many potential demands as possible.

The demands made on the system require not only that it should establish what types of parts are being processed, but that it should also facilitate the arrangement of parts into groups suitable for manufacture by the group method. The size of some groups formed will be such that their process is not economically feasible, but by merging such groups together their group processes may become economic.

A different type of approach relies on the classification of operation or process routes for parts to identify families which use the same group of facilities, or which can be readily re-routed to do so. In production flow analysis a progressive form of analysis is used, consisting of three basic steps as follows:

(a) *Factory-flow analysis.* The objective of this is to identify the best division of facilities into departments. The operations routeings for all parts (obtained from route cards) are coded to indicate the department visited by each item and then sorted by this code to create groups of parts with the same interdepartmental routeings.

(b) *Group analysis.* The route cards for all parts processed in each department are analysed to identify the best division into groups. This is achieved by sorting cards into packs containing items with the same operation routeing, these packs then being combined to form viable facility/operation groupings.

(c) *Line analysis.* The objective here is to obtain the best sequence of facilities in groups through study of the flow patterns within these groups. This is the layout problem in group technology, which will be discussed more fully in the next section.

Facilities grouping

The facilities necessary to perform all operations on the parts family, and the expected load on each piece of equipment, can be listed for each family identified. It may be necessary at this stage to eliminate certain parts from families, or to add others to avoid low or uneven machine utilization. Rarely, however, will it prove possible to achieve full utilization of all machines in a group, and some flexibility of labour is probably required—a characteristic which distinguishes group technology from classic flow processing.

Several techniques suitable for assisting in the determination of the arrangement of facilities in a group-technology system have been developed.

Travel or cross charts are of some value in developing layouts (see Chapter 6). Such a chart can show the nature of inter-operation movements for all parts for a given period of time. The row totals on the chart show the extent of movement from an operation, and the column totals show movement to an operation. Each cell of the chart shows the relative frequency of movement between two operations; an ideal movement pattern suitable for use on a flow line is indicated when all the entries in the matrix appear in the cells immediately above the diagonal. Such travel charts can be used to help develop a sequence of operations. For example, operations with a low 'to/from' ratio (i.e. row-total/column-total ratio) receive parts from relatively few sources but distribute work to a large number of destinations. Hence, if in-sequence movement is to be maximized and backtracking is to be minimized, such operations should be placed at the beginning of the sequence of operations. Conversely, operations with a high 'to/from' ratio should be placed towards the end of the sequence, since they receive work from a large number of sources but distribute to comparatively few destinations. This heuristic approach is simple and attractive, and clearly has considerable practical merit.

Sequencing

The determination of the sequence in which batches of parts are loaded on to a group-technology cell or 'line' will be influenced by the desire to reduce setting cost and minimize throughput time. The problem is entirely congruent with the multi-model line batch sequencing problem and can be approached in the same way (see Chapter 15). If component batching is not adopted, individual components will be launched into the cell in much the same manner as in mixed-model line production. However, in this case, launch discipline and model sequence are unlikely to be important, because of the far greater throughput time and component idle time.

EXAMPLE

Northern Telecom

The Switching Division of Northern Telecom took a major step in its effort to reach its manufacturing goals with the introduction of cellular manufacturing for the circuit pack assembly and test part of its operations. The project gave more than $2 million in annual cost savings from the reduction of overhead and work-in-process inventory, as well as improvement in throughput and quality.

Source: Taheri, J. (1990) Northern Telecom tackles successful implementation of cellular manufacturing. *Industrial Engineering* **22**(10), pp. 38–43.

Flexible manufacturing systems

If the inherent flexibility of the individual processes in a system and the linkages between these processes can be increased, then smaller batch sizes can be justified. In this way the 'low inventory' processing associated with just-in-time (JIT) can be achieved. In practice, attempts to increase inherent process flexibility will go hand in hand with attempts to minimize the differences between the processing requirements of the types of item which the system is required to deal with. Thus the implementation of design changes, the use of common items and the grouping of similar items into families for processing through a 'common' system are also associated with the use of flexible manufacturing systems (FMS).

A flexible manufacturing system can be described as a computer-controlled arrangement of work stations, each with automated load and unload facilities, connected by an automated materials handling system, supplied by, and supplying to, an automated storage area. The essential ingredients of an FMS are therefore:

(a) computer-controlled work stations with automated load/unload facilities;

(b) automated materials handling system;

(c) automated storage facilities;

(d) control computers.

A true FMS will operate largely as an unmanned facility, requiring intervention only for maintenance and repair work. It will be capable of processing a range of different types of item in unit batch quantities and in random sequence. Work-in-progress, throughput times, queuing time at facilities and machine and facility idle time will all be low. The capital investment required in such facilities is, however, substantial—typically being 60% for hardware and 40% for software.

In a manufacturing application, complex 'machining centres' will be the principal components of an FMS. These will be served by automatic tool change facilities and automatic pallet loading and unloading of components to be machined. Such facilities will be linked by automated conveyors, or by AGVs (automatically guided vehicles). A supervisory computer will schedule work through an FMS comprising up to a dozen such machines, and provide also for instructions for tool changes at machines, etc. Automated inspection and measurement will be incorporated, as well as the monitoring of machines to detect tool wear and tool breakage. A tool supply system will schedule the delivery of cutting tools to each machine, and an automated swarf and waste removal system will be in use. The FMS will be linked into an overall scheduling and inventory control system, and such an arrangement might operate, essentially unmanned, for 24 hours per day, so that with a sophisticated FMS 'lights out' operation is feasible with minimum human intervention.

In practice many systems have been established to deal only with a limited range or family of components, and virtually all systems are concerned with machining work. At the present time, therefore, an adequate volume requirement for a limited range of quite similar items are the prerequisite conditions. The rate of development is such, however, that more sophisticated systems will soon be employed providing for a combination of machining and assembly work, and themselves forming part of a more extensive computer-integrated manufacturing (CIM) environment. In such applications data drawn directly from a computer-aided design database will be used to configure and equip machines for the manufacture of particular items which will automatically be checked against design specification before being passed on for subsequent operations. A CIM system will also handle design changes, scheduling and inventory control, order book details, quality control and quality records, and machine performance monitoring.

EXAMPLE

Rover

Rover, the motor vehicle manufacturer, developed a flexible machining and assembly line for cylinder head and cam carriers for the 16-valve engine used in its 800 model. One feature of the system was that it could handle heads for the company's diesel engines, along with batches of 16-valve cylinder heads. The line had nine computer numerical control (CNC) machining centres, each with a 40-tool magazine. Each machine also had local intelligence, to check parts before machining starts and to make sure the component was held securely in the fixture. The line included a washing cell and inspection station that cleared a part from a 'quarantine' system before it could go into assembly.

Source: (1998) A showplace FMS. *Production* **100**(1), pp. 69–70.

KEY POINTS FOR CHAPTER 14

Batch processing (or 'lot' processing) is common and complex.

A characteristic of batch processing situations is inventories.

The three main batch processing decision areas are

    sequencing

    batch sizes

    scheduling.

Batch sequencing involves determination of the order in which batches of different items will be processed through a set of facilities.

The determination of batch sizes involves consideration of costs, i.e.

    stock holding costs

    processing costs

    set-up/change-over costs.

There are minimum ('optimum economic') batch size formulae for most processing situations.

Scheduling for batch processing involves the timing of the processing of batches.

The Line of Balance technique is of value in scheduling.

There is merit, in some situations, in reducing batch sizes. This requires the use of procedures which reduce the set up/change over cost.

Group technology and Flexible Systems (e.g. FMS) are means to reduce batch sizes.

FURTHER READING

For books on techniques, particularly analytical techniques relating to batch size, schedules, etc. see Further Reading in Chapter 17.

Snead, C. J. (1989) *Group Technology*. New York: Van Nostrand Reinhold.

QUESTIONS

14.1   What circumstances necessitate the use of batch processing in manufacture, supply, transport and service systems? What are the principal characteristics of this method of processing and what are the principal managerial problems involved?

14.2   (a) Calculate:

        (i) the optimum processing batch quantity;

        (ii) the processing cycle time, given the following information:

            Set-up cost per batch   = £17

Stock-holding cost per item per month   = £0.05

Buffer stock required   = 25 items

Demand rate per year   = 12 000 (stable)

Process rate per month   = 1500

Processing cost per item   = £25

The process is such that all items in a batch are completed at the same time.

(b) Because of deterioration in the processing facilities, the processing rate per month drops from 1500 to 900. How does this change affect the economic batch quantity?

14.3   Experimental Brewers Ltd are the sole manufacturers of 'Instant Beer'. Because of the market potential for this new style of beverage, an entirely new manufacturing facility has been established, the capacity of which is 5000 litres (equivalent) per day. At the moment demand for 'Instant Beer' is stable at 3000 litres (equivalent) per day. The product is manufactured intermittently, set-up costs for the facility being £250, and storage costs per day per 10 000 litres (equivalent) being £100.

The company is prepared to tolerate the occasional stock-out, which it estimates to cost £500 per 10 000 litres (equivalent) per day.

In what batch quantities should 'Instant Beer' be manufactured?

14.4   The assembly section of a factory uses a certain component at a rate of 200 units per day. The associated set-up cost is £100, the manufacturing cost is £5 per unit, and the inventory holding is £0.1 per unit per day.

If the management is prepared to tolerate an increase of up to 1 per cent in the minimum total cost per unit, what flexibility does this give in the choice of batch quantities and what is the total cost per unit of the cheapest solution if, for technical reasons, production batches are restricted to multiples of 50 units?

14.5   Discuss the advantages, disadvantages and limitations of the line of balance planning and control technique. Compare and contrast it with any other planning and control technique, such as network analysis, with which you are familiar.

14.6   The delivery schedule of items and the operation programme for the manufacture of these items are given below.

Week no.	Delivery required	Cumulative delivery	Week no.	Delivery required	Cumulative delivery
0	0	0	7	15	89
1	12	12	8	10	99
2	15	27	9	27	126
3	12	39	10	15	141
4	20	59	11	20	161
5	5	64	12	17	178
6	10	74			

Construct the line of balance for weeks 3, 6 and 10. Indicate how you would use the line of balance to analyse production progress in the several different departments involved in the production of the items.

Operations programme for each item

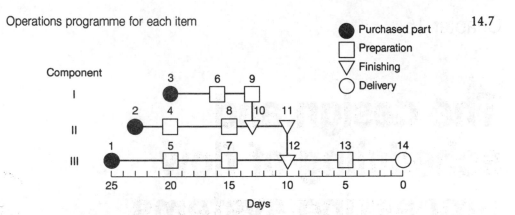

- ● Purchased part
- ☐ Preparation
- ▽ Finishing
- ○ Delivery

14.7

What is group technology, and what benefits are likely to be obtained by introducing group technology, if appropriate, into a manufacturing company?

What steps would be followed during an investigation to determine whether group technology is appropriate in a given manufacturing situation?

Describe briefly the principal methods of component classification, designed for use in group technology.

Chapter 15

The design and scheduling of flow processing systems

ISSUES

What is 'flow processing'?
What is a flow Line?
Are flow lines used only in manufacturing?
How do we design a simple flow line?
Can flow lines cope efficiently with variety?
How do we deal with worker variability?

In this chapter we concentrate on the design and scheduling of flow processing systems. There is perhaps a temptation to think that such systems exist only in manufacturing. This is not the case. Certainly flow processing and flow technology was first developed, in a sophisticated way, for mass production, and our discussion here will make some reference to that, but we should note that the basic principles have far wider relevance.

THE NATURE OF FLOW PROCESSING

Fundamentally, most types of operating system provide a form of flow processing, i.e. customers, materials or products arrive into the system and proceed through several departments or facilities before emerging from the end of the system. For example, each of the following could be considered as a form of flow processing:

(a) passage of paperwork through an office;

(b) passage of patients through a hospital;

(c) passage of children through classes and schools in an educational system;

(d) passage of a car down a vehicle assembly line.

The manner and nature of 'flow' in these cases differ. In some cases items or customers will flow through a system by different *routes*, i.e. visiting different departments or facilities (e.g. (a) and (b) above). In some cases the *flow rate* will be low and/or the *throughput time* high (e.g. (b) and (c) above). In some cases the consistency of routes, the flow routes and the desire to minimize throughput times will justify a 'product'-type arrangement of facilities, e.g. as a 'line' (as in (d) above), but in others a functional/process layout will be appropriate.

We will be concentrating on those types of system in which the flow characteristic is a distinguishing feature. So, some consistency of routeing through the system and relatively high flow rate will usually exist, whether the things which are flowing are products or customers being treated. The classic example is the manufacturing flow line, but even that will be evident in different 'guises'.

EXAMPLE

Mama Mia Pasta

This pasta restaurant is at 160 Michigan Ave, Chicago. The manner in which it operates is best described by considering the passage of a customer through the system.

On entering the restaurant the customer first sees a large menu giving the day's selection for starters, main courses, and deserts. The customer then enters the serving process. The arrangement is shown in the diagram in Figure 15.1. Customers place their order at the start of the 'line', i.e. they specify their full meal requirement. This is entered on to a form (by checking certain boxes)

Figure 15.1 Layout of Mamma Mia Pasta restaurant

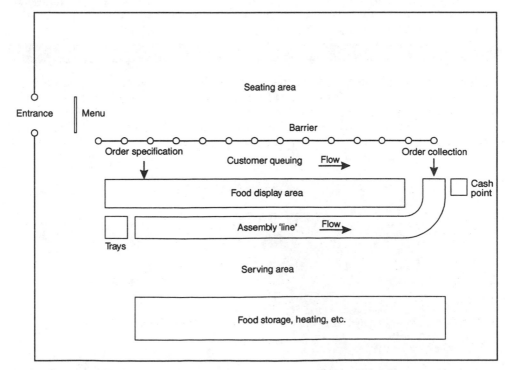

by a member of staff, and the form is placed on a tray, which is then dispatched down the line. Customers move through their queuing area at the same speed as their trays. As the trays are moved along the assembly line the required meal is assembled by staff, each manning one or two adjacent stations concerned with a particular type of menu item. The trays are pushed through all stations but receive items at only some of them. Occasionally serving staff interact with customers, e.g. to identify the required size of portions (e.g. dressings, sauces, etc.). When both the fully assembled tray and the customer reach the end of the line the meal is paid for, collected and taken away.

We will focus on the 'flow line' as in(d) above and in the Case Example. This provides a good basis for an examination of the most important aspects of flow processing system design and operations.

FLOW LINE PRINCIPLES

Although details differ, the basic flow line principles remain the same: items are processed as they pass through a series of work stations along a line. Generally, raw materials, items, customers or components are fed in at the beginning of the line, and output is delivered from the end of the line.

Flow lines which are engaged, essentially, in product assembly are often referred to as assembly lines, while those which use automatic material transfer between the automatic machining 'stations' are normally referred to as transfer lines. Given these two classes of flow line, we can now identify various subdivisions (Table 15.1). Both classes can be used for the processing of one or more products. The processing of one product or model on either class of line can be accomplished without the need to alter the 'set-up' of the line, i.e. without the need to change tools or work allocations, etc. The processing of more than one product, however, gives rise to more complex situations. In such cases two alternative strategies are available.

Table 15.1	Classes and varieties of flow line				
Flow line description		**Number of products**	**Product changes**	**Flow of items**	**Setting of equipment and allocations of work**
Class	**Variety**				
Transfer line	Single model	1	None	Regular	No changes required
	Multi-model	>1	Batch changes	Regular batches	Changes of equipment setting and/or work allocation required on change of batch
Assembly line	Single model	1	None	Irregular[a]	No changes required
	Multi-model	>1	Batch changes	Irregular[a]	Changes of equipment setting and/or work allocation required on batch change
	Mixed model	>1	Continual[c]	Irregular	Changes of equipment setting and/or work allocation normally required[b]

[a] Because of variable work station times – characteristic of manual flow lines.
[b] Alternatively, as in 'group technology', tools and equipment might be permanently allocated a specific group of components.
[c] At any time the line contains a mixture of product types.

(a) The processing of the two or more products in separate batches. This we shall refer to as the multi-model situation, and it necessitates the rearrangement of the flow line between batches.

(b) The processing of the two or more products simultaneously on the line. This we shall call the mixed-model situation, which gives rise to rather complex design problems and will be discussed in some detail later. ('Mama Mia Pasta' was a simple example of a mixed model line.)

Whichever strategy is adopted, if more than one model or product is to be processed on the line, the models must have similar work contents. The greater the similarity, the easier it will be to provide either multi-model or mixed-model processing. More flexibility is normally available on assembly lines; in contrast, transfer lines are far less flexible. They are normally confined to single-model, or occasionally large-batch multi-model, operation.

THE DESIGN OF 'SIMPLE' FLOW LINES

We begin by considering the nature and design of 'simple' flow lines, which consist essentially of a series of work stations.

The total work content of the product or item, i.e. the total time required to complete the item, is divided among these stations so that, as the item travels down the line, it becomes incrementally more complete at each station.

One objective in designing flow lines is to attempt to allocate equal amounts of work to each station, i.e. to divide the total work content of the job as evenly as possible between the stations. This is known as *line balancing*. Without such balance, a certain amount of inefficiency or loss must inevitably occur, since some stations will have more work to perform than others but all stations will normally be required to process the same number of items within a given period of time.

The time required to complete the work allocated to each station is known as the *service time*. The time available at each station for the performance of the work is known as the *cycle time*—the cycle time normally being longer than the service time. The cycle time at a station is the time interval between the completion or the starting of work on successive items, and therefore includes both productive and non-productive work as well as any idle time. Non-productive work will include the transfer of the product between stations, and may also include a certain amount of handling, movement, etc.

Cycle time = Service time + Idle time or loss

$$= \frac{\text{Productive}}{\text{work time}} + \frac{\text{Non-productive}}{\text{work time}} + \text{Idle time or loss}$$

The total work content of the job consists of the total productive work plus the total non-productive work.

Total work content = Total productive work + Total non-productive work

The manner in which work can be allocated to stations on the line is influenced by certain constraints. Each job will consist of certain work elements, and normally the order in which some of these elements of work can be performed will be influenced by technological or *precedence* constraints, e.g. one operation must be completed before another one can be started. Such precedence constraints will limit the ability to achieve balance in allocating work (i.e. work elements) to stations.

The allocation of elements to stations may also be limited by *zoning* constraints. Such constraints will necessitate or preclude the grouping of certain work elements at certain stations. For example, it may be essential that two work elements are not allocated to the same station if they might in some way interfere with one another. Such a constraint is known as a negative zoning constraint. In contrast, a positive zoning constraint necessitates the grouping of two or more work elements at one station, as might be the case when the maximum utilization of a single expensive piece of equipment is to be achieved.

Because of such constraints, perfect line balance is rarely achieved in practice, and a certain amount of *balancing delay* or *balancing loss* is normally inevitable. Balance delay is the difference between the total time available for completion of the job and the total time required. For example, at any one station the balance delay is the difference between the cycle time and the service time. The percentage balancing loss for any station is given by the difference between the cycle time and the service time, expressed as a percentage of the cycle time. Similarly, the balancing loss for a complete line is given by the difference of the total time available (e.g. the sum of the cycle times) and the total time required (i.e. the sum of the service times), expressed as a percentage of the total time available.

The cycle time can be calculated, at least theoretically, from the required output. For example, if N items are to be produced in T minutes, then the cycle time (C) should be:

$$C = \frac{T}{N}$$

Furthermore, given these two figures and knowing either the total work content or each of the element times (t), the minimum number of work stations (^{n}min.) can be calculated.

$$^n\text{min.} = \frac{N\Sigma t}{T}$$

In fact, since we must have a whole number of work stations, ^{n}min. will be the integer equal to or greater than $N\Sigma t/T$.

The average work station time ($\bar{c}$) is simply the total work content (Σt) divided by the actual number of stations, n:

$$\bar{c} = \frac{\Sigma t}{n}$$

Almost invariably, this figure is less than the cycle time (C). Hence:

$$\text{Balancing loss (\%)} = \frac{C - \bar{c}}{C} \times 100$$

$$\text{or (\%)} = \frac{n(C) - \Sigma t}{n(C)} \times 100$$

Although we have spoken of and depicted idle time resulting from imperfect line balance, in practice periods of idleness caused by the difference between cycle time and work station times may not exist because the work to be done may be undertaken more slowly to occupy the time available. Nevertheless, the consequences are precisely the same because an under-utilization will result.

The objective of line balancing is that, given a desired cycle time or output rate, the minimum rational work elements and their standard times and other constraints, one should attempt to assign work elements to work stations in order to:

(a) minimize idle time or balancing loss;

(b) minimize the number of work stations;

(c) distribute balancing loss evenly between stations;

(d) avoid violating any constraints.

Methods of simple line balancing

The first analytical treatments of the line balancing problem were developed in the 1950s. They aimed to secure optimum solutions and depended upon many simplifying assumptions. Because of the nature of the problem and the inadequacy of these treatments, several authors then developed 'heuristic' methods of line balancing. Whilst other approaches are available, two of these methods only will be dealt with here.

The Kilbridge and Wester method[1]

This simple heuristic method of line balancing is best described by means of an example.

Assembly of a simple component requires the performance of 21 work elements which are governed by certain precedence constraints, as shown in Figure 15.2. This precedence diagram shows circles representing work elements placed as far to the left as possible, with all the arrows joining circles sloping to the right. The figures above the diagram are column numbers. Elements appearing in column I can be started immediately, those in column II can be begun only after one or more in column I have been completed, and so on.

The data shown on this diagram can now be represented in tabular form as shown in Table 15.2. List (c) of this table describes the lateral transferability of elements among columns; for example, element 6 can be performed in column III as well as in column II

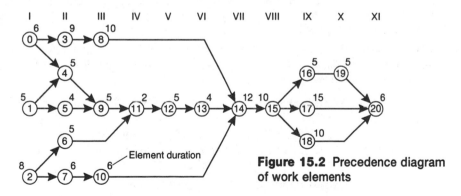

Figure 15.2 Precedence diagram of work elements

without violating precedence constraints. Element 8 can also be performed in any of the columns IV to VI, as can element 10. Element 3 can also be performed in any of the columns III to V provided element 8 is also transferred, as can element 7.

Suppose it is our objective to balance the line for a cycle time of 36. In this case we would proceed as follows:

1. Is there a duration in list (f) of the table equal to the cycle time of 36? *No.*

2. Select the largest duration in list (f) less than 36, i.e. 19 *for column I.*

---

[1] Kilbridge, K. and Wester, L. (1961) A heuristic method of assembly line balancing. *Journal of Industrial Engineering*, **11**(4), p. 292.

Column no. in precedence diagram (a)	Element no. (b)	Transferability of element (c)	Element duration (d)	Duration for column (e)	Cumulative duration (f)
I	0		6		
	1		5		
	2		8	19	19
II	3	III–V (with 8)	9		
	4		5		
	5		4		
	6	III	5		
	7	III–V (with 10)	6	29	48
III	8	IV–VI	10		
	9		5		
	10	IV–Vi	6	21	69
IV	11		2	2	71
V	12		5	5	76
VI	13		4	4	80
VII	14		12	12	92
VIII	15		10	10	102
IX	16		5		
	17	X	15		
	18	X	10	30	132
X	19		5	5	137
XI	20		6	6	143

Table 15.2   Tabular presentation of data in Figure 15.2

3. Subtract 19 from 36 = 17.

4. Do any of the elements in column (II), either individually or collectively, have a duration of 17? *No, the nearest is, 16 for elements 4, 6 and 7, which will give a work station time of 35 for station 1.*

5. Select the smallest duration from (f) which is larger than 36, i.e. 48 *for columns I and II.*

6. Can one or more of the elements in columns I and II be transferred beyond column II so as to reduce the duration as near as possible to 36? *No, but element 3 (with 8) plus 6 can be transferred to give a work station time of 34.*

7. Select the next largest duration from (f), i.e. 69 *for columns I, II and III.*

8. Can one or more of the elements in columns I, II and III be transferred beyond column III so as to reduce the duration to 36? *No, the nearest are elements 3, 7, 8 and 10, which would give a duration of 38, which is too large.*

9. Will an improved allocation of elements for this station be obtained by considering a large duration from column (f)? *No.*

10. Adopt the best allocation found previously, *i.e. step 4, which gave a work station time of 35.*

11. Rewrite the table to show this allocation and calculate new cumulative figures for (f) (Table 15.3).

12. Is there a duration in (f) of the new table equal to 36? *Yes, for columns III and IV.*

Column no. in precedence diagram (a)	Element no. (b)	Transferability of element (c)	Element duration (d)	Duration for column (e)	Cumulative duration (f)
I	0		6		
	1		5		
	2		8		Station 1
II	4		5		
	6		5		
	7		6		(35)
III	3	III–V (with 8)	9		
	5		4		
	9		5		
	10	IV–VI	6	24	24
IV	8	V–VI	10		
	11		2	12	36
V	12		5	5	41
VI	13		4	4	45
VII	14		12	12	57
VIII	15		10	10	67
IX	16		5		
	17	X	15		
	18	X	10	30	97
X	19		5	5	102
XI	20		6	6	108

Table 15.3

13. Allocate the elements in these columns to the second work station and redraw the table showing new figures for (f) (Table 15.4).

14. Is there a duration in (f) of the new table equal to the cycle time of 36? *No.*

15. Select the largest duration in (f) which is less than 36, *i.e.* 31 *for columns V, VI, VII and VIII.*

16. Subtract 31 from 36 = 5.

17. Does one or more of the elements in the next column (IX) equal 5? *Yes, element* 16.

18. Allocate the columns concerned and that element to the work station and redraw the table (Table 15.5).

19. Is there a duration in (f) of the new table equal to 36? *Yes, for columns IX, X and XI.*

20. Allocate the element in these columns to the work station.

All 21 (including element 0) elements have now been assigned to four work stations in the manner shown in Figure 15.3 the balancing loss involved being:

$$\frac{n(C) - \Sigma t}{n(C)} \times 100$$

$$= \frac{4(36) - 143}{4(36)} \times 100$$

$$= 0.7\%$$

Table 15.4

Column no. in precedence diagram (a)	Element no. (b)	Transferability of element (c)	Element duration (d)	Duration for column (e)	Cumulative duration (f)	
	0					Station 1
	1					
	2					
	4					
	6					
	7			35	(35)	
III	3		9			Station 2
	5		4			
	9		5			
	8		10			
	10		6			
IV	11		2	36	(36)	
V	12		5	5	5	
VI	13		4	4	9	
VII	14		12	12	21	
VIII	15		10	10	31	
IX	16		5			
	17	X	15			
	18	X	10	30	61	
X	19		5	5	66	
XI	20		6	6	72	

As can readily be seen from the example, this heuristic method is rapid, easy and often quite efficient. The allocation of elements is basically determined by precedence relationships, lateral transferability of elements being used to aid allocation when necessary. The originators of this method offer the following comments to aid in the application of the method.

(a) Permutability within columns is used to facilitate the selection of elements (tasks) of the length desired for optimum packing of the work stations. Lateral transferability helps to deploy the work elements (tasks) along the stations of the assembly line so they can be used where they best serve the packing solution.

(b) Generally the solutions are not unique. Elements (tasks) assigned to a station which belong, after the assignment is made, in one column of the precedence diagram can generally be permuted within the column. This allows the line supervisor some leeway to alter the sequence of work elements (tasks) without disturbing optimum balance.

(c) Long-time elements (tasks) are best disposed of first, if possible. Thus, if there is a choice between the assignment of an element of duration, say, 20 and the assignment of two elements of duration, say 10 each, assign the larger element first. Small elements are saved for ease of manipulation at the end of the line. The situation is analogous to that of a paymaster dispensing the week's earnings in cash. He will count out

Table 15.5

Column no. in precedence diagram (a)	Element no. (b)	Transferability of element (c)	Element duration (d)	Duration of column (e)	Cumulative duration (f)	
	0					Station 1
	1					
	2					
	4					
	6					
	7			35	(35)	
	3					Station 2
	5					
	9					
	8					
	10					
	11			36	(36)	
V	12		5			Station 3
VI	13		4			
VII	14		12			
VIII	15		10			
IX	16		5	36	(36)	
IX	17		15			
	18		10	25	25	
X	19		5	5	30	
XI	20		6	6	36	

Figure 15.3 Allocation of 21 elements to four work stations

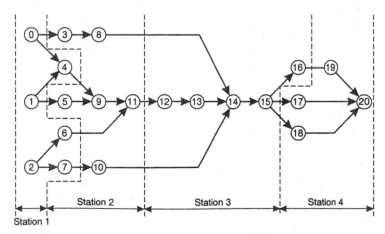

the largest bills first. Thus, if the amount to be paid a worker is $77, the paymaster will give three $20 bills first, then one $10 bill, one $5 bill and two $1 bills in that order.

(d) When moving elements laterally, the move is best made only as far to the right as is necessary to allow a sufficient choice of elements for the work station being considered.

In view of point (c) above, the *ranked positional weight (RPW)* method of line balancing, described next, might be considered a logical extension of the present method, since in the RPW method a heuristic procedure is used which allocates elements to stations according to both their position in the precedence diagram and their duration.

Ranked positional weights[2]

The ranked positional weight procedure is a rapid, but approximate, method which has been shown to provide acceptably good solutions quicker than many of the alternative methods. It is capable of dealing with both precedence and zoning constraints. The procedure is best illustrated by considering a simple example.

Assembly of a very simple component involves 11 minimum rational work elements. There are constraints on the order in which these elements are to be undertaken, but there are no zoning constraints. Figure 15.4 is a precedence diagram in which the circles depict work elements. Element 2 must follow elements 0 and 1 and must precede element 5, etc. The standard element times (hours) are also shown in Figure 15.4. In Figure 15.5 this same information is listed: in the first column the element number is given, and in the second its standard time. The middle of the table shows the element precedences; for example, element 0 is immediately followed by element 2, which in turn is followed by 5, which is followed by 6 and 7, and so on. A single mark indicates the element which follows immediately and crosses indicate elements which follow because of their relationship with other elements. The final column of the table gives the *positional weight (PW)* for each element. This is calculated by summing the element's own standard time and the standard time for all following elements. Thus, in the case of element 0:

$$
\begin{aligned}
PW = \text{element } \;\;0 &= 0.32 \\
+ \text{element } \;\;2 &= 0.20 \\
+ \text{element } \;\;5 &= 0.23 \\
+ \text{element } \;\;6 &= 0.20 \\
+ \text{element } \;\;7 &= 0.05 \\
+ \text{element } \;\;8 &= 0.32 \\
+ \text{element } \;\;9 &= 0.10 \\
+ \text{element } 10 &= 0.30 = 1.72
\end{aligned}
$$

The positional weight is therefore a measure of the size of an element and its position in the sequence of elements.

Figure 15.4 Element precedence diagram

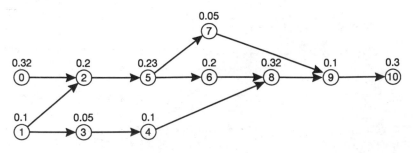

[2] Helgerson, N. B. and Birnie, D. P. (1961) Assembly line balancing using the ranked positional weight technique. *Journal of Industrial Engineering*, 12(6), p. 394.

Figure 15.5 Precedence and positional weights table

Element number	Element time (hours)	0	1	2	3	4	5	6	7	8	9	10	Positional weight
0	0.32		I			+	+	+	+	+	+	+	1.72
1	0.1			I	I	+	+	+	+	+	+	+	1.65
2	0.2						I	+	+	+	+	+	1.40
3	0.05					I			+	+	+		0.87
4	0.1								I	+	+		0.82
5	0.23							I	I	+	+	+	1.20
6	0.2								I	+	+		0.92
7	0.05									I	+		0.45
8	0.32										I	+	0.72
9	0.1											I	0.40
10	0.3												0.30

In Table 15.6 the elements, their times and the immediate predecessors are given in order of decreasing positional weights.

Table 15.6		Elements in order of positional weights										
Element no.	0	1	2	5	6	3	4	8	7	9	10	Total
Element time	0.32	0.1	0.2	0.23	0.2	0.05	0.1	0.32	0.05	0.1	0.3	1.97
PW	1.72	1.65	1.4	1.2	0.92	0.87	0.82	0.72	0.45	0.40	0.30	
Predecessors (immediate)	–	–	0, 1	2	5	1	3	4, 6	5	7, 8	9	

We are required to design a line with the minimum number of stations to provide a cycle time of 0.55 hours (i.e. an output of 1.82 per hour). Using Table 15.6, elements are allocated to work stations in order of decreasing positional weights and without violating precedence constraints. Element 0, with the highest PW of 1.72, is allocated first to station 1. This allocation is acceptable because element 0 has no immediate predecessors, and furthermore its element time is less than the spare time available in station 1 (see Table 15.7).

Element 1 is the next to be allocated since it has the next highest PW. It is acceptable in station 1 since no precedence constraints are violated and there is sufficient unassigned cycle time left to accommodate it.

The next highest PW belongs to element 2, but this cannot be assigned to station 1, even though its immediate predecessors have been assigned, because the unassigned station time remaining (0.13) is less than the element time (0.2).

Element 5 cannot be allocated because it must follow element 2; nor is there enough time available.

Element 6 cannot be allocated to station 2 for the same reasons.

Element 3 can be allocated to station 1 since its immediate predecessor is already allocated and there is enough time available.

Of the remaining elements only 7 is short enough for accommodation in station 1, but

Table 15.7	Element allocation for cycle time of 0.55 hours					
Work station	Element	PW	Immediate predecessor	Element time	Cumulative station time (Z)	Unassigned station time (C – Z)
1	0	1.72	–	0.32	0.32	0.23
	1	1.65	–	0.1	0.42	0.13
	3	0.87	1	0.05	0.47	0.08
2	2	1.4	0, 1	0.2	0.2	0.35
	5	1.2	2	0.23	0.43	0.12
	4	0.82	3	0.1	0.53	0.02
3	6	0.92	5	0.2	0.2	0.35
	8	0.72	4, 6	0.32	0.52	0.03
4	7	0.45	5	0.05	0.05	0.50
	9	0.4	7, 8	0.1	0.15	0.40
	10	0.3	9	0.3	0.45	0.10

$C = 0.55$

Balancing loss $= \dfrac{4(0.55) - 1.97}{4(0.55)} \times 100 = 10.4\%$

it cannot be allocated here because it must follow element 5.

The same procedure is now repeated for the remaining stations.

Four work stations are required for this line, and the initial allocation gives a balancing loss of 10.4%. Notice that there is unassigned time at each station, the largest work station time of 0.53 hours occurring at station 2.

For the specified output required (1.82 per hour) there is no better solution than the one given above, but, if other considerations permit, the cycle time could be reduced to 0.53 hours with a corresponding increase in output to 1.89 per hour and a reduction of balancing loss to 7%. A reduction of the cycle time to less than 0.53 hours would necessitate the use of five work stations.

There is really little point in retaining a cycle time of 0.55 hours in this case, since to do so is merely to introduce inefficiency into the system for the sake of obtaining a given output. Here, as in many cases of line balancing, it is desirable to modify output in order to minimize balancing loss. In this case, therefore, the assembly line balancing procedure would be first to seek a balance for a given cycle time *C*, and then to minimize the cycle time for the same number of work stations.

EXAMPLE

Assembly line balancing in a bank

Assembly line balancing (ALB) techniques can be applied to bank processing functions that produce homogeneous products having fairly deterministic demand and processing time. An example of such a processing function is an instalment lending, documentation operation. ALB techniques are used to determine the optimal staff level and job assignment scheme for this operation. In this case the Assembly Line Balancing Module of a proprietary decision support software package is used to show how substantial cost savings can result.

Source: Levary, R.R. and Renfro, M.D. (1991) Applications of assembly line balancing techniques to instalment lending operations of commercial banks. *Computers and Industrial Engineering* **20**(1), pp.105–109.

Multi-model and mixed-model line design

The use of flow-line techniques certainly leads to highly efficient operation when product variety is small, but any increase in the variety of items to be accommodated on the line not only leads to more complex design and management problems but will often result in reduced operating efficiency. Multi-model or mixed-model lines must be used in such circumstances.

(a) *Multi-model line*. Again assuming a simple line design problem, this approach requires the following major decisions to be made:

1. How will the line be 'balanced'?

2. What will be the batch sizes of the models?

3. In what order will the batches be processed? (The batch sequencing problem.)

(b) *Mixed-model line*. Here the major decisions are:

1. How will the line be balanced?

2. In what order will the models be launched into the line? (The model sequencing problem.)

Multi-model lines

The multiple models may be either different items or different versions of the same item, but in either case the different models will have similar, though not identical, processing requirements, since otherwise there would be little justification in processing them on the same basic line. In practice the line is set up for one model, then adjustments are made to the line prior to the processing of a batch of the second model, and so on. We can therefore consider the problem as a succession of separate line design problems, hence decisions (a) and (b) above may be treated in the manner outlined previously. Decision (b), batch sizes, was dealt with in detail in Chapter 14.

The optimum sequence for the batches of different models is clearly influenced by the cost of setting up the line. The total cost of setting up the line comprises the cost of tool and machine changeovers, tool and machine resetting, machine and labour idle time, etc., and is clearly influenced by the nature of the preceding and succeeding models. The problem, therefore, is to determine the sequence order of the model batches to minimize the total setting-up cost over a given period of time. It is highly unlikely that line set-up costs will be constant, but, of course, if this were the case the sequence order of model batches would be immaterial.

Mixed-model lines

The advantage of this type of processing is that, unlike multi-model lines, a steady flow of models is produced in order to meet customer requirements, theoretically without the need for large stocks of finished goods. The major disadvantages arise from the differing work contents of the models, resulting in the uneven flow of work and consequent station idle time and/or congestion of semi-finished products.

Line balancing for mixed-model lines might be considered merely as several single-model balancing problems, i.e. each model could be considered separately and the total work content divided as equally as possible between the work stations. Consider a case where a line is built for two similar models A and B. The work elements of model A are allocated to the work stations so that during the periods in which A is being processed, balancing loss is minimized. Similarly, the work elements of B are allocated to work stations in order to minimize balancing loss during the processing of model B. Such a procedure is often adopted and is fairly satisfactory when the models to be produced are of a similar nature, i.e. when the processing of each model involves similar work elements to be undertaken in a similar order or when the processing of all models merely involves the repetition of similar work elements. When such circumstances apply, the workers at each station will be required to do the same type of work irrespective of which model is being processed. If, on the other hand, basically dissimilar models are to be processed, then independent line balancing for each will often result in dissimilar work elements, e.g. work involving different skills, necessitating different training, etc. being allocated to each station. In circumstances such as these, balancing should be undertaken in such a way as to ensure that similar work elements are allocated to the same work stations or groups of stations, irrespective of which model is being produced. A method by which this might be achieved (not described here) is to assign elements to stations on a total time rather than a cycle time basis.

The efficient design and operation of mixed-model lines depends also on the solution of the model sequencing problem. The problem (not dealt with here) is concerned both with the time interval between the 'launching' or starting of models on to the line and also with the *order* in which models are launched on to and flow along the line. The objective of such sequencing is to provide for the best utilization of the assembly line, high utilization being associated with minimum station idle time and minimum congestion of work along the line (item waiting).

THE DESIGN OF 'COMPLEX' FLOW LINES
Human aspects of assembly line design

Work element or service time variability is the fundamental difference between lines involving human operators and those depending exclusively on machines, i.e. fully automated lines. It is not invalid to assume that machines at stations require a constant time for elements of work, but it certainly is quite unrealistic to make the same assumption about human beings. The procedures described above are adequate by themselves for the design of automated lines, but insufficient for the design of lines involving people.

Clearly, if we were to design lines in which workers were allowed a fixed standard time, neither more nor less, in which to complete an operation, we might find that on some occasions the worker would easily complete the task within this time, while on other occasions he or she would be prevented from doing so. This type of situation is referred to as *rigid pacing*. There is no 'freedom' for workers, since they are confined to perform each and every operation in a given time. This rigid pacing causes both worker idle time and incompleted work.

These losses or inefficiencies, often referred to as *system loss*, can be reduced only by reducing or eliminating the pacing effect. There are two ways in which we can attempt to do this; both involve making the items available to the worker for a longer period of time. Take, for example, a line consisting of workers sitting at a bench above which jobs travel by means of a conveyor belt. The workers must take the job off the belt, perform the operation and replace it on the belt, which carries it to the next station. Jobs spaced at 5 m intervals on a belt moving at 5 m/min will produce an output of 60 products/hour. The same output will result from a spacing of 10 m and a belt speed of 10 m/min, or a spacing of 2.5 m and a belt speed of 2.5 m/min. But each of these different arrangements has different consequences for the seated workers, who can reach only a certain distance either side of their work stations. If they can reach 2.5 m either way, then in the first case each job will be within their reach and available to them for one minute only, in the second case for half a minute, and in the last case for two minutes. Clearly the greater the time the job is available to the worker the lower the pacing effect, and system loss is reduced.

On lines where jobs pass directly from one worker to the next, every worker, except the one at the first station on the line, is dependent on the previous worker. Under such conditions the work must be strictly paced in order to avoid excessive labour idle time. If, for example, because of faulty material, a worker at one station takes longer than the cycle time to complete the operation, then the worker at the next station on the line will probably have to wait for work. This coupling or interdependence of stations necessitates pacing, but if the stations could be decoupled in some way the pacing effect, and also system loss, could be reduced.

The way in which this is done is to introduce buffer stocks of several jobs between stations, so that temporary hold-ups or delays at stations do not immediately result in idle time at subsequent stations. There are certain disadvantages of using buffer stocks on lines. Work-in-progress stock and hence tied-up capital will be increased, and additional space will be required. In fact, in many cases, because of the size of the items, it may be quite unrealistic to consider using buffer stocks. However, in many situations buffer stocks are an important feature of line operation.

KEY POINTS FOR CHAPTER 15

Flow processing systems exist in most types of business. (In manufacture they are often in the form of assembly lines or transfer lines.)

In flow processing, the work to be done on an item is achieved incrementally, through a series of 'stations'.

To design a simple (single type of item/product) line the following must be achieved:

allocate work to stations

minimize imbalance between stations

achieve appropriate output rate, or cycle time.

There are several methods for Line Balancing, but the most useful are heuristic procedures.

Where different items are to be processed along a line it is necessary to provide for

either

multi model operation, or

mixed model operation.

Multi model line design requires

line balancing

batch size determination

batch sequencing.

Mixed model line design requires

line balancing

model launch decisions.

In practice line design and operation is complex because of the need to deal with human aspects, in particular variable work times.

Variable work times can give rise to system loss which is caused by worker pacing.

FURTHER READING

Wild, R. (1972) *Mass Production Management.* New York: Wiley.

Ghosh, S. Gagnou, R. J. (1989) A comprehensive literature review and analysis of the design, balancing and scheduling of assembly systems. *International Journal of Product Research* 27(4), pp. 637–670.

CASE STUDY

The following case study from Part 9 of the book is relevant to the topics covered in this chapter.

No	Name	Country
5	Pokhara Weavers	Nepal

15.1 A multi-station line is to process a minimum of 6000 items per 40-hour working shift. The processing of one item consists of 25 elements of work together constituting a total work content of 11 minutes.

What is the minimum number of work stations for this line and what will the cycle time (C) ideally be?

15.2 What will be the balancing loss of the line, the requirements of which are given above?

15.3 The diagram indicates the necessary precedence requirements of 12 work elements which together constitute the total work content of a simple assembly task.

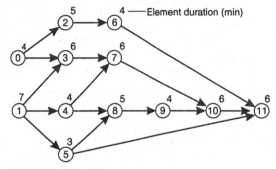

Using the line balancing technique devised by Kilbridge and Wester, design a line (i.e. assign work elements to the required number of work stations) to produce as near as possible to, and no less than, three items per hour.

What is the balancing loss for the line that you have designed?

15.4 The work involved in assembling a small component can be described in terms of 11 minimum rational work elements whose element times are as follows:

Certain precedence constraints apply to the work; these are shown diagrammatically.

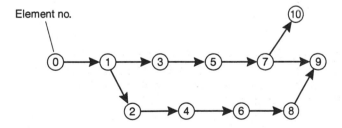

Furthermore, because of the nature of the work it is necessary to ensure that elements 0 and 3 *do not* occur at the same work station, elements 3 and 5 *do not* occur at the same work station, and the elements 8 and 10 *do* occur at the same work station. Two assembly lines are to be designed (without buffer stocks), one producing components at a rate of 4.61 per hour and the other components at a rate of 5.0 per hour.

Element	Time (min)
0	4
1	3
2	3
3	3
4	7
5	5
6	4.5
7	9.5
8	5
9	7
10	7

Use the ranked positional weight method to assign work elements to work stations in order to minimize the number of work stations and the balancing loss on each line. Calculate the balancing loss in both cases.

Describe the heuristic device you are using to solve this problem and justify its use as a method of assembly line balancing.

15.5 What is 'system loss', how is it caused, and how can it be reduced?

15.6 Analytical line balancing procedures are sufficient for the successful design of 'transfer lines' but are they adequate themselves for the design of systems in which human operators are involved in executing the work?

What are the 'human' problems associated with the design and operation of flow lines?

PART 7

Materials Management

INTRODUCTION TO PART 7

Here we deal with the management of items, products and customers throughout the operating system, from inputs to outputs. We first identify different approaches to this task of 'materials management', and then consider those topics which are of particular and direct relevance to the operations manager.

Again, especially when dealing with inventory management in Chapter 17, we shall consider 'principal' or 'characteristic' operations management problem areas, i.e. problems which are influenced by the operating system structure and where the approaches employed are influenced by the operations objectives.

Chapter 16

Materials management and supply chains

ISSUES

What is materials management?
What are the relationships of materials management, inventory management and logistics?
Should materials management be a centralized activity?
What is supply chain management?
How is effective purchasing managed?
What is the impact of JIT on purchasing?
How does an organization manage its distribution 'channels'?

Materials management can be defined as the methods and principles by which we endeavour to plan, organize, co-ordinate, control and review the flow of materials throughout an organization. It offers therefore a means for the overall control of materials throughout an organization.

In the absence of a materials management approach within an organization, the management (i.e. the planning, organization, co-ordinating, controlling and reviewing) of materials, materials stock, materials flows, parts stocks, materials in progress and where appropriate, the flow of customers will be the responsibility of several departments or individuals. This is the more decentralized approach.

Materials management can be subdivided into three main areas:

(a) *purchasing* or *procurement*, i.e. responsibility for obtaining and managing incoming materials through to input stocks;

(b) i.e. the *management of in-process materials*, items, and where appropriate, customers through the transformation process (see also Chapters 12–15);

(c) 1. in the case of manufacture and supply systems: *distribution/logistics* for the transfer of items, products, etc. and to the customer from the system or from output stock;

2. in the case of transport and service systems: *customer handling*, i.e. the management of customers joining the operating system or its input queue.

INTEGRATED MATERIALS MANAGEMENT

Whether the management of the entire flow into, through, and from the operating system should be treated as a single integrated function, or as separate activities, has been a matter of considerable debate.

Initially the focus was on the merits of centralized and decentralized materials management. The benefits of a centralized (i.e. controlled from a single, central function, with little delegation of authority, or local autonomy) approach were seen to use:

(a) avoidance of problems of divided responsibility;

(b) avoidance of possible conflicting objectives and priorities;

(c) avoidance of duplication of effort;

(d) ease of communications throughout the organization;

(e) ease of, and better representation of, the materials management function at board/policy level;

(f) better career/developmental opportunities;

(g) economies of scale.

A more decentralized approach might be seen to offer the following potential benefits:

(a) greater opportunity for functional specialization;

(b) greater flexibility;

(c) greater opportunity for materials managers to act as integral parts of geographically dispersed organizations (rather than being seen as separate head office/personnel staff).

The type of approach employed within an organization will depend on the relevance of the above advantages and the circumstances in which the organization is to work. For example, it might be argued (see Chapter 3) that a centralized approach might be more appropriate in 'static' situations subject to few uncertainties. In such situations the organization will face fewer changes in markets, demand, customer behaviour, supplier behaviour, technological change, etc., and thus it may be possible to implement and stick to relevant rules, procedures, etc. for materials management throughout the organization. Where there is a greater degree of uncertainty, for example because of demand changes, product changes, changes in the nature of the service and technological changes, particularly where these affect different parts of the organization in different ways, then there may be some merit in a decentralized approach which facilitates rapid response to their changing circumstances from different parts of the organization.

There are, however, other factors to consider. The approach to materials management must, for example, be influenced by strategic objectives; thus for many organizations the integrated management of flows into, through and from the operation is a prerequisite for achieving high quality, rapid and low cost provision for customers. Managing the **supply chain** is now, therefore, a major concern for organizations working in a 'Just in Time' (see Chapter 12) and 'Total Quality Management' (see Chapter 19) framework.

SUPPLY CHAIN MANAGEMENT (SCM)

There is increasing recognition that good supply chain management provides a major opportunity for organizations to improve efficiency and increase customer service. Supply chain management focuses on the organizing, integrating and operation of the complete materials management function. To this end an organization must:

1. define its strategy
2. select an implementation framework
3. resolve how to manage change
4. identify the critical success factors that will measure SCM performance across the organization.

EXAMPLE

Du Pont, Australia

Du Pont (Australia) consists of many customer-focused operating departments. Printing Systems, one of these departments, supports a manufacturing facility at Girraween in Sydney that is one of the most technically advanced and cost-efficient plants in the company. The plant was under-utilized in servicing Australia and some small-scale exporting. It was appropriate therefore to consider a more integrated international strategy for film and chemistry, the products for the plant. The proposal to supply Southeast Asia with film and chemistry from Australia was the outcome of looking at the 'larger picture'. Using an integrated approach to the supply chain has meant that the system has been managed more closely. Customer service, manufacturing, and distribution have not been considered in isolation from strategic planning. The information chain running alongside the supply chain and reporting back on the logistical function is the key to Du Pont's success.

Source: Blackshaw, D. (1989) Graphics arts film and chemistry to South East Asia: a case study. *International Journal of Physical Distribution and Materials Management* **19**(10), pp. 27–33.

The nature of the supply chain

The supply chain is the complete flow system into, through, and from the organization. Notice, however, that there are two flows—physical and information. In general, information flows in the opposite direction to the physical flow.

Managing this chain will normally involve dealing directly with the following:

(a) purchasing and supply;

(b) inventory management;

(c) operations schedules;

(d) distribution and logistics.

This, in turn, indirectly brings SCM into contact with other areas, e.g.

(e) facilities location and layout;

(f) capacity management.

All of this will be undertaken against a set of strategic and operational objectives which will involve achieving the necessary levels and securing the appropriate balance between resource utilization and customer service.

Developing a supply chain strategy

A three-stage process can be identified[1] for developing an SC strategy, i.e.

1. **Evaluation of the competitive environment**

    This will normally involve:

    (a) understanding the market characteristics;

    (b) examining current strategies;

    (c) deciding on market-winning strategies (i.e. the policy options referred to in Chapter 2).

2. **Review of existing SC operations**

    This will normally involve:

    (a) developing a cost model;

    (b) identifying those activities which can have a significant impact on customers;

    (c) listing improvement techniques for these activities.

3. Development of the supply chain. The aim here is to develop an integrated supply chain to achieve the market-winning strategies, concentrating if appropriate on those key elements identified during 2. above.

To develop an integrated supply chain requires consideration of functional, internal and external integration, i.e.

(a) Functional integration: the aim will be to diminish/or remove the separation between functions within the organization, e.g. by merging previously separate activities such as purchasing and receiving, and sales and distribution.

(b) Internal integration: the aim now will be to improve the interfacing of the remaining activities, e.g. by reducing or eliminating inventories.

(c) External integration: finally, the objective will be to improve the input and output side interfaces of the organization, e.g. by removing inventories and improving information flows.

EXAMPLE

McDonalds

Quality, service, cleanliness, and value are the cornerstones of the McDonald's business, and the success of the supply and distribution functions can be attributed to this focus. Strict guidelines are applied to delivered quality and temperature, along with on-time performance, order reliability, etc. McDonald's logistics approach includes the following principles: 1. the recognition that the end performance of delivering satisfaction to customers will only be as good as the weakest link in the supply chain; 2. the need to ensure that each link clearly understands the expectations of performance and why McDonald's has those expectations; 3. a constant monitoring or measur-

[1]See Stevens, G. C. (1990) Successful supply chain management, *Management Decision*, **28**(8), pp.25–30.

ing of each critical element of the logistics function in accordance with predetermined criteria; and
4. the need to keep flexibility in the system to allow for growth and changing needs.

Source: Ritchie, P. (1990) McDonald's: awinner through logistics. *International Journal of Physical Distribution and Logistics*, **20**(3), pp.21–24.

We can now examine the elements of the supply chain. Here the focus will be on purchasing/supply and on distribution/logistics, as scheduling and inventory management are covered in detail in other chapters.

PURCHASING AND SUPPLY

Although rarely the sole responsibility of operations managers, the purchasing or procurement function clearly touches on their responsibilities. Operations managers are responsible for providing goods or services of the right specification and quality, at the right time, in the right quantity and at the right price, and purchasing or procurement managers are, in the same terms, responsible for purchasing materials and items of the right specification and quality, at the right time, in the right quantity, from the right source and at the right price. Theirs, in other words, is the responsibility of obtaining those items required by the operating system. They are concerned with the input to the operating system, i.e. the flow of physical resources to the operating system.

The objectives of purchasing

The main objectives of purchasing are as follows:

(a) 1. to supply the organization with a steady flow of materials and services to meet its needs;

2. to ensure continuity of supply by maintaining effective relationships with existing sources and by developing other sources of supply either as alternatives or to meet emerging or planned needs;

(b) to obtain efficiently, by any ethical means, the best value for every unit of expenditure;

(c) to manage inventory so as to give the best possible service at lowest cost;

(d) to maintain sound co-operative relationships with other departments, providing information and advice as necessary to ensure the effective operation of the organization as a whole;

(e) to develop staff, policies, procedures and organization to ensure the achievement of the foregoing objectives.

Reference (c) to the management of inventories raises the question of the relationship of purchasing to inventory management. Purchasing will, in some cases, be responsible for the provision of goods to input inventories (i.e. in those system structures in which inventories exist). In some cases, this responsibility for supplying items and materials to input inventory will be linked with some responsibility for the maintenance of such inventories. In other situations, inventory replenishment needs will be identified, to provide purchase requirements to be executed by the purchasing function. We shall assume the latter, i.e. separate purchasing and inventory responsibilities. We shall deal with inventory management in Chapter 17. The topics covered there are of relevance in purchasing, as indeed the topics covered here are relevant to inventory management.

Deriving from the above objectives, we can identify the following as being the principal benefits to be gained from the effective management of the purchasing process:

(a) lower prices for materials and items used;

(b) faster inventory turnover;

(c) continuity of supply;

(d) reduced replenishment lead times;

(e) reduced transport cost;

(f) reduced materials obsolescence;

(g) improved vendor relationships;

(h) better control of quality;

(i) effective administration and minimization of organization effort;

(j) maintenance of adequate records and provision of information for the operations managers.

The purchasing process is concerned primarily with obtaining physical items for use in, and conversion through, the operating system. Most operating systems need such items. Hospitals, for example, need a regular reliable supply of consumable items such as medicines and sterile equipment. Transport operations are dependent on an adequate supply of consumable materials such as fuel and tyres. Supply organizations naturally are dependent on an adequate, reliable and efficient supply of those items which are to be passed to customers, while manufacturing organizations are entirely dependent on the supply of consumable and non-consumable materials and items.

The organization of purchasing

One major issue is the degree to which purchasing as a function should be centralized. In recent years there has been a trend towards the establishment of centralized purchasing functions. This has been particularly noticeable in health services and in local and central government supply, as well as in manufacturing. The principal benefits associated with central purchasing are summarized below:

(a) the possibility of standardizing specifications and establishing common needs, as regards quantity, quality, specification, etc.;

(b) the possibility of more economic purchase through, for example, larger batch quantities;

(c) the reduction in administrative cost through the purchase of larger quantities on few occasions, possibly from fewer sources;

(d) the possibility of purchase staff specialization and thus increased knowledge of sources and supplies;

(e) the possibility of the use of more effective, detailed and accurate purchase information and records;

(f) the possibility of more detailed accurate and rapid budgetary and financial control procedures;

The principal advantages derive from the possibility of increased purchase volumes, from standardization and from specialization. Disadvantages of centralized purchasing, however, might include:

(a) difficulties of communication within the organization, deriving perhaps from geographical separation;

(b) slow response to new or unusual supply needs from the organization;

(c) possible increased dependence on a smaller number of suppliers resulting from increased volume and from standardization.

Thus the merits of centralized purchasing will depend on the possible financial savings through volume and variety considerations as against the possibility of reduced response times and flexibility.

EXAMPLE

Hospital Inventories

Many small to medium-sized hospitals face stable or declining operating revenues and increasing costs. For them the idea of 'stockless inventory systems' is of containing costs. The approach involves shifting some of the materials management functions further up the supply chain. The overall purpose is to eliminate inventory completely in the central storeroom, with the benefits of 1. reduction in costs, 2. eliminating the costs of running a storeroom or warehouse operation, 3. reducing costs of obsolescence, and 4. achieving economies for purchasing and materials management. Studies in three hospitals have shown that such an approach can result in significant reductions in inventory levels and related costs.

Source: Wilson, W., Cunningham, A. and Westbrook, W. (1992) Stockless inventory systems for the health care provider: three successful applications. *Journal of Health Care Marketing* **12**(2), pp. 39–45.

JIT purchasing

Summarizing (from Chapter 12), JIT (Just-in-Time) can be defined as the processing of items or customers in the quantities required, when required. JIT, therefore, involves processing only as and when required rather than in anticipation of needs. One of the prerequisites for the effective implementation of JIT is vendor reliability. JIT involves the pursuit of low or zero inventory, so incoming goods and materials inventory is of particular importance. This inevitably affects the relationship between an organization and its vendor/supplier organization. Unless regular timely supplies of the requisite items with consistent quality can be assured, JIT is impossible. Some features of JIT purchasing are listed in Table 16.1.

Organizations which have pursued the JIT philosophy have identified the need to establish special relationships with vendors, the principal characteristics being:

(a) close relationships with few vendors/suppliers;

(b) long-term relationships with few suppliers;

(c) the establishment of an interdependence in the vendor/consumer relationship.

Effective JIT within an organization depends therefore on the organization's suppliers also adopting the JIT philosophy. The willingness to supply smaller quantities of items more frequently with assured quality is the principal requirement. To this end, organizations have often found it necessary to help their suppliers develop JIT systems of their own, even to the extent of helping them develop their process technology, scheduling systems and management systems. In effect, organizations have, in many cases, come to regard vendors simply as extensions of their own organization. These issues will be of relevance here and also in our discussion of quality in Chapters 19 and 20.

Sourcing and suppliers

An important function of purchasing is the identification of suitable sources of supply. The systematic investigation and comparison of sources, the evaluation and monitoring of the performance of supply sources and the development of appropriate procedures with suppliers are therefore of importance. Vendor rating is discussed briefly below and in

Table 16.1 Some features of JIT purchasing

Suppliers
Few suppliers
Nearby suppliers
Repeat business with same suppliers
Active use of analysis to enable desirable suppliers to be price competitive
Cluster of remote suppliers
Competitive bidding mostly limited to new items
Suppliers encouraged to extend JIT buying to their suppliers

Quality
Minimal product specifications imposed on supplier
Help suppliers to meet quality requirements
Close relationships between buyers' and suppliers' quality assurance procedures
Suppliers encouraged to use control charts (see Chapter 18)

Quantities
Steady output rate
Frequent deliveries in small lot quantities
Long-term contract agreements
Minimal paperwork
Delivery quantities variable from release to release but fixed for whole contract term
Little or no permissible 'overage' or 'underage' of receipts
Suppliers encouraged to package in exact quantities
Suppliers encouraged to reduce their production lot sizes

Deliveries
Scheduling of inbound deliveries
Gain control by use of company-owned or contract delivery and storage where possible

Source: Based on material from Schonberger, R. J. and Gilbert, J. P. (1983) Just in time purchasing: a challenge for US industry. California Management Review, 26(1), pp. 54–68

more detail in Chapter 20. Although market research will not be discussed in detail here, it will be appreciated that supplier market research is of importance in obtaining adequate supply sources for the organization.

Figure 16.1 outlines the procedure normally involved in selecting suppliers. The model suggests that the buyer, on receipt of a request to purchase, first checks whether the organization is currently committed to the particular supplier for the supply of such items and, if not, whether an existing source might satisfy the requirement. Repeat ordering with an existing source would be normal, unless there are reasons for review. Such reasons might include recent price increases, recent extensions in supplier supply lead time, failing to meet specifications, decline in vendor rate performance, etc. Buyer source loyalty is a well-documented phenomenon, and clearly offers benefits in terms of reduced administrative difficulty, improved vendor/buyer understanding and relationship. In fact, benefits accrue both to supplier and to vendor. Vendors tend also to give preference to existing customers.

Figure 16.1 Outline of procedure for selecting a supplier

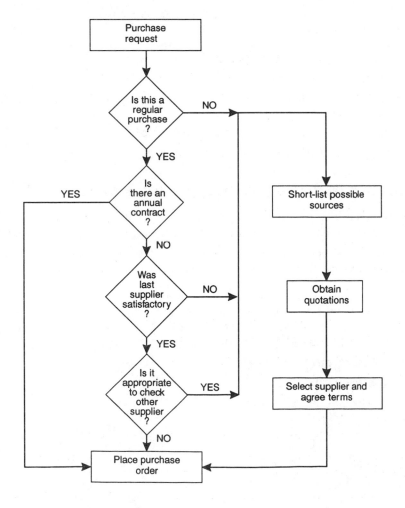

Often an investigation of possible sources for the supply of new items and materials will reveal several alternatives, hence the question of single or multiple sourcing often arises. Factors to be considered in this respect include the following:

(a) *Effect on price*, i.e. single sourcing of increased quantities may reduce purchase price. Alternatively, in certain circumstances, multiple sourcing may in fact reduce price as a result of supplier competition for orders.

(b) *Effect on supply security*, i.e. while organization of supply will be simpler with a single source, the organization will be dependent and thus at great risk as a result of any disruptions through, for example, strikes.

(c) *Effect on supplier motivation*. Although the security resulting from regularly supplying large quantities to an organization might increase supplier motivation, and thus increase willingness to improve specifications, etc., undoubtedly in some circumstances increased motivation might also result from a competitive situation.

(d) *Effect on market structure* of single sourcing may in the long term result in the development of a monopolistic situation with the eventual elimination of alternative sources of supply.

The process of identifying and determining supply sources will often involve obtaining competitive bids and analysing such bids and proposals. The latter will often involve price and delivery comparisons, but in most cases more detailed analysis will be necessary. The following factors may be among those considered:

(a) price and cost factors, i.e. cost, delivery costs, insurance costs, price breaks etc.;

(b) delivery factors, including delivery lead times, delivery quantities and delivery frequencies;

(c) specifications factors and quality control/assurance practices;

(d) legal factors, e.g. warranty, in terms of condition etc.

Considerations in purchasing policy and procedures

Table 16.2 provides a checklist for the make or buy decision. Such decisions can be complex and therefore past, present and future market conditions will normally be analysed.

Documentation procedures for purchasing will not be considered here; however, it should be noted that, because of the often considerable amount of money involved in purchase and purchase decisions, adequate records must be maintained, and because of the often complex situations which exist, computer-based records and control procedures are normally essential. Such a system should cover all purchases including bought-out equipment, standard parts, raw materials, subcontract work, repairs, services, commercial equipment and stationery. It should assist in the following functions:

a) accumulation of the requirement to buy;

b) printing of purchase orders;

c) recording the progression of the purchase order;

d) receipts;

e) inspection;

f) accumulation of the purchase history;

g) supply analysis.

Table 16.2   A make or buy checklist

If currently purchased from an outside source

(1) Does capacity exist within own company?

(2) If so, is such capacity likely to be available for the planning period involved?

(3) Is the necessary raw material available now at economic rates?

(4) Will that material continue to be available at economic rates for the planning period?

(5) If tooling is involved: (a) what is the cost? (b) what is the expected life? (c) what is the delivery?

(6) Are we satisfied that the current suppliers are the most economic source?

(7) Is there a patent involved and thus the possibility of royalties to be paid?

(8) Is VAT chargeable (e.g. printing)?

(9) Are the current suppliers doing development work towards an improved version of the item?

(10) Have the current suppliers had difficulty with quality, quantity or time factors, and have their costs escalated as a result, thus affecting their selling price?

(11) If their quality has been affected: (a) has the suppliers' quality system been vetted? (b) what has been the extent of quality failures? (c) is our production department confident that the specified quality can be economically maintained in internal production? (d) are we over-specifying?

(12) If their other costs are escalating: (a) what are the reasons? (b) are we confident that we will not be affected in the same way?

(13) If the item is currently being imported, what is the cost breakdown? If duty is payable, what rates are applied? What duty, if any, will be payable on the relevant raw materials/components if they are imported?

If currently being manufactured within the company

(1) Is there a matter of secrecy to be considered?

(2) If the item is withdrawn from production, would redundancies result?

(3) If 'yes', what action would need to be taken by management regarding these redundancies?

(4) If tooling is involved, what is its condition? Can it be used by the prospective source?

(5) Will the machinery involved on current manufacture be fully utilized for alternative work if the part is withdrawn?

(6) Is there a possibility of development work being done on the part? If so, can this be done satisfactorily in conjunction with an outside supplier?

(7) Will the quantities involved interest an outside supplier?

(8) Do we know the true cost of alternative supply against manufacture (e.g. transport and handling costs)—present and forward?

(9) Is the item part of an integral production route involving several stages of manufacture? If so, can outside manufacture be satisfactorily co-ordinated with production schedules and machine loading in our shops?

(10) What is the forward market position for the item concerned for the relevant planning period?

(11) Are all drawings current?

(12) Is there any advantage in our supplying raw materials/components if a decision to buy is made?

(13) Can we indicate to the potential supplier the remaining life of the product?

(14) Can the potential supplier suggest ideas for taking cost out of the product?

Source: Baily, R. and Farmer, D. H. (1985) Purchasing Principles and Techniques. *London: Pitman. Reproduced with permission*

EXAMPLE

Edwin Gould Academy

In order to revamp the Academy's overburdened purchasing system, its Director enlisted the help of the President and the Purchasing Director of Ark Restaurants. It was discovered that the school had problems in food management and that it had been making unnecessary purchases. One of its first steps was to persuade the school administrators to order more frequently. The school was also brought into Ark's purchasing system, so an immediate improvement in the price and quality of its food was achieved. According to the school, it had been receiving overpriced generic products but now it is enjoying high-quality, name-brand items and paying 20% less.

Source: McLaughlin, J. (1993) The easy mark. *Restaurant Business* **91**(11), pp. 74–6.

Materials requirements planning

Although developed primarily for use in batch manufacturing situations, materials requirements planning (MRP) has potential in other manufacturing and non-manufacturing situations. The procedure is discussed in detail in Chapter 12 and will only be summarized here.

In batch manufacture, particularly assembly, certain components may be required in large quantities at infrequent intervals, i.e. to suit the batch assembly schedule. In many such situations, there will be little benefit in maintaining stocks of all parts and items at all times, since at most times these stocks will not be drawn upon. If a procedure can be developed by which those items required for assembly are available at the times required and stocks of these items are not maintained, or are maintained at a far lower level at other times, the high cost of maintaining unnecessary stock is avoided, but items will still be available when required. Materials requirements planning provides such a procedure. It is based on the use of a 'bill of materials' file and a production or assembly schedule. The bill of materials file provides information on all parts and materials required for all finished products and the production schedule provides information on the production or assembly schedule for all finished products.

Co-ordination of this information together with a knowledge of supply lead times permits the procurement of parts as and when required by the production/assembly schedule. MRP aims to keep inventories low in order to facilitate purchasing, to ensure a supply of parts and materials when needed and to highlight exceptions and priorities.

In non-manufacturing situations the MRP procedure may be of relevance, particularly when the system requires the acquisition of inputs specific to particular operations, jobs or outputs, i.e. when a batch processing procedure is employed. In, for example, certain supply operations where items are acquired against particular customer orders, MRP may be of value in providing an effective means of planning, controlling and monitoring the purchase of large quantities of a large range of items, to satisfy the requirements of a large number of customers each of whom has particular delivery or due date requirements.

PHYSICAL DISTRIBUTION AND LOGISTICS

In manufacturing and supply systems the responsibility of distribution is that of getting goods *to* the customer. A similar responsibility exists in 'customer input' type systems (i.e. service and transport), where the responsibility is to get customers, whether they be people or things, into the system: *customer handling*. In the simplest situation these responsibilities involve the direct relationships of the organization with the customers. In more complex cases there will be intermediate stages.

In this section we shall deal with the management of both situations. The term 'customer channels' will be used to remind us that we are concerned with flows from or to customers.

EXAMPLE

Benetton

Benetton Group, one of the world's leading fashion retailers and manufacturers, ships 80 million items each year directly to 7,000 stores in 100 countries with an order cycle time of as short as 7 days. Most items are shipped from a single automated warehouse. Making use of technology the company's logistics, manufacturing and information systems tie together the stores, 80 company agents, 200 suppliers, 850 subcontractors, major carriers, and an in-house forwarder. The system has helped the company achieve near-perfect customer service levels and no excess stock in-process or in the distribution 'pipeline'.

Source: Foster T. A. (1993) Global logistics Benetton style. *Distribution* **92**(10), pp. 62–66.

Physical distribution management (PDM)

PDM, concerned with the dynamics of distribution and with customer channel behaviour, may be defined in our context as the process by which appropriate quantities of items or customers are passed through the distribution channel to or from customers. This definition suggests that, given certain channels, the task of PDM is to make them work. However, it begs the question of 'influence' or 'control'. An enterprise may have a one-stage customer channel, i.e. dealing directly with its own ultimate customers, perhaps through a stock or customer queue over which it has some direct control. The manner in which it operates, i.e. its stock-holding, the service level provided to customers and its coverage of the market, can therefore be determined entirely by itself. If, however, more stages exist, e.g. there are intermediaries between the organization and its end customer, then each party may have some influence over such decisions.

Ideally an enterprise would like to influence all stages in the distribution channel between itself and the final customer, and this is easily achieved for organizations with one-stage customer channels. The extent of the influence or the 'reach' of the enterprise along the customer channel will affect its PDM decision. An enterprise which controls its entire distribution channel to or from the final customer will make decisions affecting all stages in that channel, whereas an enterprise with less influence may make decisions affecting only a part of of the channel.

PDM decisions

The principal interrelated decision areas in PDM are as follows:

(a) the choice, design and implementation of a channel of distribution;

(b) the 'level of service' to be provided to customers;

(c) inventory decisions.

These are outlined in the following section, which can provide only an introduction to this subject. Notice that for single-stage channels the PDM decisions are principally (b) and (c) above, and in such cases the problem can be seen largely as one of inventory management. We shall be dealing with inventory management in this context in Chapter 17, so here we shall concentrate on the more complex PDM case of multi-stage channels where the approach required is somewhat different because of both (a) above and the more complex situations in (b) and (c).

Channel decisions

We can identify four important questions:

(a) the question of *level*—the number of levels or stages which should exist in the channel;

(b) the question of *type*—which type or types of intermediary should be employed once the level has been decided;

(c) the question of *intensity*—how many of each type of intermediary are to be used;

(d) the question of *control*—what degree of control should the organization seek to exercise, and where appropriate what degree of control should it accept from others.

Level (or stages)

Here we are concerned with the length of the customer channel, which to some extent will be influenced by the nature of the operation. For example, perishable items, those whose processing requires close liaison with customers, those delivered in bulk, those with high unit value, those which are urgent and those requiring particular services will all best be dealt with through short channels.

Markets which are temporary or which have limited potential will rarely justify the establishment of long channels, and small markets are often best served through short channels. Where communication and/or transportation is difficult or expensive, or where there are numerous 'sources' and 'destinations', an intermediary in the customer channels can reduce the total number of contracts. Where one customer represents a large proportion of total demand there will be pressure to establish relatively direct channels to that customer; conversely, where total demand is spread relatively thinly over many customers, the merit of intermediaries in reducing contact complexity is clear.

Type

Which types of intermediary are most suited to particular channels? The nature of the 'end' market of customers should influence the choice of 'type' rather than vice versa. Items, transports or services must be available to 'end' customers where they expect to find them. It will therefore be difficult to break with tradition unless service to the end customer is clearly improved, although there are obvious examples of successful innovation, e.g. in new forms of retailing and in direct selling.

Intensity and control

At one extreme there is the possibility of limited distribution through an exclusive channel, and a move from this situation will involve an organization in dealing with a greater number and range of intermediaries. This, however, may be justified where greater market coverage or 'presence' is required yet where the organization does not aspire to maintain close control over all intermediaries. The increased 'coverage' of the market might justify the use of more intensive distribution through multiple intermediaries at each stage with increased PDM costs. However, the use of a greater number of 'contact' points with the market will influence the stock levels required in order to provide a given level of service (see below).

Service level decisions (see also Chapter 17)

The level of service provided to end customers might be expressed in terms of:

(a) percentage of customer orders satisfied in a given period of time;

(b) average delivery or waiting time before a customer order is satisfied;

(c) percentage of customer orders which are satisfied after a quoted delivery or waiting time;

(d) percentage of total demand satisfied in a given period.

The type of measure employed in setting objectives for, and then in monitoring, customer service will depend on the type of organization, and in particular the type of product or service which is being provided. For example, (a) above will be relevant in a 'manufacture to stock' situation where the customer is normally to be satisfied from stock. Measure (b) above will be relevant where goods or service are provided against a specific order, i.e. where customers will normally expect to wait to be served, or where capacity is insufficient to create output stocks of goods or avoid input queues of customers, even though the nature of customer needs is known in advance.

Whatever the measure of customer service, normally the provision of higher levels of service will incur greater costs to the organization.

Clearly there is a cost penalty in providing high customer service, so the justification for aiming for high service must be demonstrable. The obvious reason is the need to conform to what customers expect, i.e. what competitors provide; indeed this will be essential unless some compensatory satisfaction is provided, e.g. through lower price. Equally, inability to compete in the market through price or specification will necessitate the provision of better service through better delivery, short waiting times, etc. (see Chapter 1).

Inventory decisions (see also Chapter 17)

Where inventories of items exist, service-level decisions can influence inventory decisions in terms of not only the levels of inventory to be provided, but also their location throughout the customer channel.

Chapter 17 will deal in detail with inventory management decisions. The emphasis there will be on the management of 'single-stage' inventories (e.g. the managment of each stock in an operating system). Here we must consider inventories *throughout* customer channels. For example, in a three-stage distribution channel there may be three levels of inventory of the same type of items, with several different stock-holdings at each level.

Among other purposes, inventories provide service to the next stage in the channel. For example, an input stock of raw materials in a hospital helps to ensure that the medical activities of the hospital are not held up. An output stock in a manufacturing company helps to ensure that those directly served by that organization are able to get what they want when they want it. In other words, for each stock there is an immediate customer and a purpose of the stock is to provide service to that customer. We shall see in Chapter 17 that where demands on stock are uncertain, as is often the case, or when the time required to replenish stocks is uncertain, it is necessary to provide some buffer or safety stock to ensure that most customers get what they want most of the time, i.e. that 'stock-outs' are normally avoided. Two related PDM questions, themselves related to the service-level question, are therefore: what stock levels to provide and where to provide them.

The determination of safety (or buffer) stock levels to provide given levels of service will be dealt with in detail for the 'single-stage' problem in Chapter 17. These single-stage methods can be modified to deal with stocks in multi-stage systems. Here we shall consider only the basic principles to be remembered in making inventory decisions in multi-stage systems.

The number of stock locations at a given stage

If one stock location is established from which demand throughout a given market is to be satisfied, then a safety stock must be provided in addition to a base stock. The base stock is that amount of inventory necessary to satisfy average demand during a given period of time, while the safety stock is that extra amount provided to protect against uncertainties. The way in which this safety stock can be determined is explained in Chapter 17. If we establish several stock locations *each* for a given sector of the market, e.g. a region, then base stock and safety stock must be provided at each. The sum of the base stocks for each stock location will be the same as the original single base stock, but the sum of the safety stocks at each location to provide the original level of service will exceed the safety stock required for the single location.

The general relationship between the sum of the safety stocks required for *n* stock-holdings and that required for a single holding can be shown to be as follows:

$$B_n = \frac{B_1(n)}{\sqrt{n}}$$

Figure 16.2 Safety stock v. number of stock locations at a given stage or level

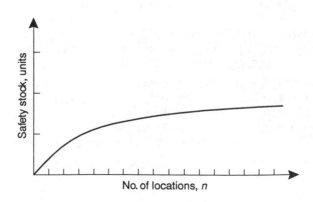

where B_n = total safety or buffer stock for n locations

B_1 = safety or buffer stock for 1 location

n = number of locations

The general nature of the relationship is shown in Figure 16.2.

[fig 16.2]

Stock-holdings at different levels

In considering safety stock provision it should be noted that less total safety stock will be needed to provide a given level of end customer service if that stock is provided at a 'higher' level in the customer channel, providing of course that when required it can quickly be deployed to the end customer. For example, in a customer channel which has a wholesale and several retail stocks, safety stock provided at the wholesale level can protect against uncertain demand at all retail outlets, but since high demand at one can be offset by low demand at another, the safety stock-holding at the warehouse level will be less than the total safety stock required by all retailers if each is required to operate entirely separately in its own market sector.

The existence of stocks at 'higher' levels in the customer channel should not simply permit the duplication of stocks held at 'lower' levels, but should complement lower-level stocks. For example, low-usage and/or high-cost items should be stocked at higher levels to reduce cost, while high-usage/low-cost items should be concentrated in lower-level stocks since this permits high customer service at low cost.

EXAMPLE

Channel integration

K-mart, Kodak, and Lee Apparel adopted a new approach to inventory management to co-ordinate the flow of product from the warehouse to the store floor. Known as 'channel integration', this process depends on retailers sharing information on sales at the store level with suppliers. This exchange of information enables suppliers to manufacture at the level of actual demand for a product and dispatch only the product needed. Channel integration allows both the supplier and the retailer to carry the minimum inventory in their warehouses. Both retailers and the manufacturers benefit from channel integration by reducing inventory levels and lowering handling and transportation costs.

Source: Cooke, J. A. (1992) Supply chain management—1990s style. *Traffic Management* **31**(5), pp. 57–59.

KEY POINTS FOR CHAPTER 16

Materials management

is the planning, organizing, co-ordination, control and review of the flow of materials throughout an organization.

Materials management comprises:

  purchasing and procurement

  in-process materials management

  distribution/logistics or customer handling.

Decisions are often required on whether materials management should be a central-ized function or not.

Supply chain management

focuses on integrating the operation of the complete material function, comprising:

  purchasing and supply

  inventories

  scheduling of activities

distribution and logistics.

The integration of the supply chain requires:

  functional integration

  internal integration

  external integration.

Purchasing deals with inputs

The objectives of purchasing relate to the security/continuity, cost, co-ordination.

Purchasing may be centralized.

JIT implementation requires effective co-ordi-nation with purchasing.

Sourcing and supply decisions are a main responsibility of purchasing.

Physical Distribution Management (PDM) and Logistics deals with outputs.

PDM decisions relate to channels and inventories.

FURTHER READING

Baily, P. and Farmer, D. H. (1985) *Purchasing Principles and Techniques*, 5th edn, London: Pitman.

Busch, H. F. (1988) Integrated materials management. *International Journal of Physical Distribution and Materials Management* 18(7), pp.28–39.

Schonberger, R. Gilbert, J. (1983) Just in time purchasing: a challenge for US industry, *California Management Review* 26 (1), pp.54–68

Christopher, M. (1992) *Logistics and Supply Chain Management*. London: Pitman.

QUESTIONS

16.1   Discuss the merits of centralized purchasing procedure for a series of small retail domestic hardware stores.

16.2 What factors might influence the make or buy decision for a manufacturing organization, and how might similar considerations operate in a transport or service organization?

16.3 'Materials requirements planning is little more than the extension of reverse scheduling from operations to the purchasing function.' Discuss.

16.4 Give examples of one-stage and two-stage customer channels for:

   (a) a manufacturing organization;

   (b) a supply organization;

   (c) a transport organization;

   (d) a service organization.

Explain why such channels are employed in these cases.

16.5 Select *one* of the following organizations and outline and explain the types of decision likely to be required in PDM in that organization (i.e. in the planning, management and control of flows through the customer channels):

   (a) a book publisher dealing with college books;

   (b) a microcomputer manufacturer.

Chapter 17

Inventory management

ISSUES

What types of stock are there and where do they exist?
What are 'consumed items' stocks?
How are stocks controlled?
What inventory management decisions are required?
What is the value and relevance of 'Order quantity'
    formulae?
How do we deal with uncertainty?

We discussed the management of inventories in the context of materials and supply chain management in Chapter 16. There we concentrated on multi-stage systems and the management of inventories throughout such systems.

Here we shall concentrate on the management of single-stage inventories. All of what we shall discuss will be relevant in the management of the supply chain, as in some cases it will be appropriate to manage each stock-holding as a separate entity, and in other cases each stock-holding will be the property or responsibility of a different organization, so there will be little opportunity for co-ordinated control of inventories at different levels.

For our purposes we can consider stocks to compromise either *consumed* or *non-consumed* items. Consumed items (e.g. materials or products) are utilized by the operating system or taken by the customer and must therefore be replaced. Non-consumed items (e.g. capital equipment and labour) are used repeatedly by the system and need repair and maintenance. In this chapter we deal only with consumed items, and therefore with three types of inventory:

(a) *system output inventory* (in manufacturing and supply systems), e.g. goods produced or provided by the operating system;

(b) *system input resource inventory* (in manufacturing, supply, transport or service systems), e.g. materials which will be consumed by the operating system;

(c) *customer input queues* (in transport or service systems), i.e. the input stocks of customers that will be processed through the system. (They are a resource which is input to the operating system, since the system cannot operate without them.)

Notice that 'work-in-progress' inventory, i.e. partially processed items or customers, is really the output stock of one part of the operating system and the input to the next. It is therefore contained within categories (a) and (b) above.

Inventory management is concerned essentially with the use and control of inventories. The need for inventory management is influenced by capacity management decisions, since the existence of inventories will, in part, be determined by the capacity management strategies which are to be employed. If inventories exist, they should serve some useful purpose, and therefore must be carefully managed. These 'purposes' might include:

(a) *For output stocks* (in manufacture and possibly supply systems):
 1. to provide good service to customers;
 2. to protect the function from uncertainties in demand, e.g. permitting stable level of operating of function despite fluctuating demand;
 3. to permit manufacture or supply of items in economic quantities.

(b) *For input resource stocks* (in manufacture, supply, transport and service systems):
 1. to permit favourable purchase/provision arrangements, e.g. price discounts and economic order quantities;
 2. to protect the function from uncertainties in supply, e.g. permitting stable/undisrupted operation despite fluctuating/interrupted supplies.

(c) *For customer input queues* (in transport and service systems): to protect functions from uncertainties in demand, e.g. permitting stable level of operating of functions despite fluctuating demand.

INVENTORIES OF CONSUMED ITEMS
Output stocks

Certain operating system structures provide for output stocks. Customer demand is satisfied from such stocks, which in turn are replenished from the function. The information flows in the opposite direction to the physical flow; hence, in the case of intermittent stock replenishment, customer orders will be received at output inventory, depletion of which will give rise to the dispatch of replenishment orders to the function.

Stocks may be replenished *intermittently* or *continuously*, although in some cases the distinction is more evident in the type of inventory management decisions that are required than in the physical flow into stock.

For our purposes we can consider the nature of customer demand to be given; however, a knowledge or estimate of the nature of demand, in particular the demand level and fluctuations, will influence inventory management. The stock levels maintained and/or the amount of buffer (or safety) stock provided will reflect expected demand levels and fluctuation.

The complexity of the inventory management problem and the likely effectiveness of inventory management depend on the variability or unpredictability of stock input and output levels and also on the opportunities for, and the extent of, control. Thus in certain systems, inventory management is likely to be more effective than in others simply because there is the opportunity for the exercise of closer control.

The classic stock control problem is that of establishing an inventory policy based on some *control over stock inputs* to satisfy unpredictable demand or output. Given a forecast output or usage rate per unit time and the variability of that output rate, the following inventory parameters might be established:

(a) For intermittent stock replenishment:

    1. either reorder level *or* interval; and

    2. order quantities.

(b) For continuous replenishment:

    1. input rate; and

    2. average stock level required.

Input resource inventory

Certain systems require input stocks. The problem of managing the stocks of input resources closely resembles that of system output inventory management. Here the function is the customer for input resource stocks. So, as with output stocks, demand is satisfied from stock, which in turn is replenished from supply. The activity scheduling function will be responsible for the manner in which the input stocks are depleted. Either consumable resources will be scheduled intermittently through the function or a regular throughput rate will have been fixed. In either case we can again consider the nature of demand on stocks to be given; however, a knowledge or estimate of the nature of demand, in particular demand level and fluctuations, will again influence input inventory management. As with output stocks, the amount of buffer (or safety) stock provided will reflect expected demand levels and fluctuation as well as the predictability and degree of control available over *inputs to stock*.

Again the following parameters might be established:

(a) For intermittent stock replenishment:

    1. either reorder level *or* interval; and

    2. order quantities.

(b) For continuous replenishment:

    1. input rate; and

    2. average stock level required.

Customer input queues

Two operating system structures require input queues (or stocks) of customers (see Chapter 1). Here, customers, or items provided by them, are consumed resources. They are an input which differs from other consumed resources only in being beyond the direct control of system management. In other words there is little or no control over the input or arrival of such resources, i.e. their input is unpredictable. Since there is little opportunity for control over inputs, such inventory is mainly managed through *control over the output*.

Given an estimate of the input rate and the variability of that rate, the following inventory parameters might be established:

(a) For intermittent depletion:

    1. output intervals *or* the stock levels at which output is to occur; and

    2. output quantities.

(b) For continuous depletion:

1. output rate; and
2. average stock level required.

The strategies available in inventory management, from above, are summarized in Table 17.1.

Table 17.1	Inventory management decisions (consumed items)	
Nature of flow	**Location of flow control**	
	On stock inputs	**On stock outputs**
Intermittent	Determine stock replenishment level *or* interval	Determine stock levels *or* intervals at which output is to take place
	Determine input quantity	Determine output quantity
Continuous	Determine average (or safety) stock levels required	Determine average stock levels required
	Determine stock replenishment (input) rate	Determine stock output rate

COSTS IN INVENTORY MANAGEMENT

Two sets of costs are of immediate relevance in inventory decision-making: inventory costs and customer service costs.

Inventory costs

Items held in stock incur costs. *Holding costs* comprise the costs of storage facilities, provision of services to such facilities, insurance on stocks, costs of loss, breakage, deterioration, obsolescence, and the opportunity cost or notional loss of interest on the capital tied up. In general, an increase in the quantity of stocks held will be reflected in an increase in holding costs, although the relationships may not be linear. For example, costs of increasing stock-holdings may be in the form of a step function, since increased space is required when stocks reach certain levels. The cost of capital, insurance, etc. may also be discontinuous through the effect of price breaks or quantity discounts. Stock-holdings of a certain level may permit replenishment in quantities sufficient to attract quantity discounts. Other things being equal, higher costs of holding will result in lower stock quantities and vice versa. Certain stock-change costs apply particularly in intermittent flow systems; e.g. in input control systems change costs will consist of the cost of *ordering* replenishment and in some cases the cost of delivery of replenishment items and the cost of receipt, inspection, placing in stock, etc. In output control systems change costs will consist of the cost of ordering or initiating depletion and the cost of dispatch, etc.

Customer service costs

Customer service considerations influence inventory decisions in operating systems in which output stocks exist. Here customer service might be measured in terms of the number of occasions over a given period on which orders cannot immediately be satisfied from stock, i.e. the number of 'stockouts'. Equally, the *probability* of such stock-outs might also provide a measure of customer service. In such a situation customers are in effect being starved by the system. In transport and service systems, customer service may be measured by the occurrence or duration of queuing. Where queuing is required, customer service may be measured by the average time spent in the queue or the number of items in the queue. Where queuing is not normally required, customer service may be measured by the probability that queuing will occur. In such situations customers are in effect being 'blocked' by the system. This customer service, whether in input or output control systems, has inventory cost implications, e.g. costs of shortage, loss of trade.

WHICH ITEMS TO CONTROL

Many companies subject all items, purchased or produced, irrespective of their value, usage or quantity, to the same type of stock control procedure. Such a policy can be a waste of time and effort.

Although high usage rate does not necessarily mean high stock levels, fast-moving items, i.e. those for which the usage rate is high, and expensive items are likely to incur greater stock costs than slow-moving, inexpensive items. Consequently we should aim to control the 'fast-moving/expensive' items, since by doing so greater potential savings are possible. The Pareto or ABC curve can be used in this context (see Figure 17.1 below). It helps show that a small proportion of the stocked items accounts for a large proportion of inventory cost or value. Their relationship is often referred to as the 80/20 'law', i.e. up to 80 per cent of the firm's total inventory cost or value is accounted for by about 20 per cent of items. This relationship encourages us to categorize inventory items into three classes, A, B and C. Category A would be those relatively few types of item which account for a relatively large proportion of total inventory cost or value, category B would be the slightly larger number of items which account for a smaller percentage of total cost, and category C would be that large proportion of items which account for a very small proportion of total cost.

Category A items should be closely controlled. Category B items should be subject to less control, whereas for category C items a simple control procedure is probably sufficient.

EXAMPLE

Tampa General Hospital

Tampa General Hospital in Florida lost some $12 million in 1983. In 1984 organizational adjustments were made in materials management. The aim was to provide the basic foundations of efficiency, simplification, close interaction with finance, and a commitment to serve and support all areas of the institution. A master plan was developed that focused on the high departmental inventories, the numerous goods receiving areas and the slow turnaround of orders, among other problems. A new system was introduced through which supplies were delivered to theatres, etc. The aim was to improve control and stock utilization. By 1989, there had been a dramatic turnaround. For example inventory turnover, a measure of the efficiency of the use of inventories, had improved from 2.2 in 1987 to 4.3 in 1989.

Source: Richardson, I. (1990) Material management in the operating room: a case study. *Hospital Mat. Mgt. Quarterly.* **12**(2) pp.44–48.

Figure 17.1 ABC chart for stock items

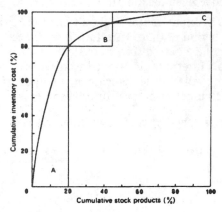

Figure 17.2 Input control inventory: types of control

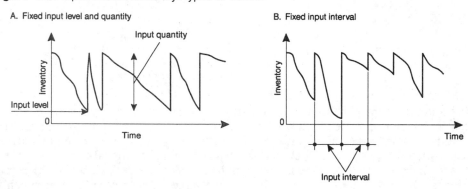

INVENTORY MANAGEMENT SYSTEMS

We can now look more closely at the types of problems posed by the adoption of the inventory management strategies outlined in Table 17.2. We shall focus on the more usual case of intermittent flow/input control.

Intermittent flow/input control

Most published treatments of inventory management deal with input control of intermittent flow systems, with the objective of satisfying a given output need or criterion. There are two basic approaches that might be adopted (see Table 17.2):

(a) fixed input level;

(b) fixed input interval.

The two approaches are compared in Figure 17.2.

Fixed input level control relies on the replenishment of stock by a given input quantity, actuated at a given inventory level. In other words, inventory will fall to a reorder level when replenishment is initiated or takes place. This approach is sometimes known as the 'maximum–minimum' or 'two-bin' system.

The fixed input interval approach relies on the replenishment of inventory at fixed intervals of time. The replenishment quantity in such situations is often determined such as to replenish inventory to a given maximum level.

Replenishment of stock in input control/intermittent flow systems might take place instantaneously or over a period of time. The stock level 'traces' on Figure 17.2 rely on instantaneous replenishment, i.e. replenishment of stock by a whole quantity at one time. Figure 17.3 compares (a) intermittent input/instantaneous with (b) intermittent input/with usage. The latter relies on replenishment of stock intermittently yet over a period of time during which usage or output continues to occur.

Figure 17.3 Input control inventory – types of intermittent replenishment

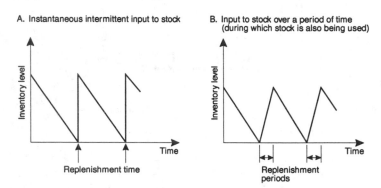

The input level approach to inventory control is in effect a form of *perpetual* inventory management. Stock is replenished when it falls to a particular level, so it will be necessary to maintain some 'perpetual' monitoring of the inventory in order to ensure that action is taken when the appropriate stock level is reached. The input interval system is in effect a *periodic* inventory control system. There will be no need to check stock level except at the times when the replenishment order is to be placed. The type of system which is employed will depend largely on the circumstances. In some situations it will be very difficult, or expensive, to maintain a perpetual check on inventory levels in order to be able to operate the order level approach. However, where the number of transactions, i.e. the number of times the stock is depleted, is low compared with the annual usage, or where the unit cost of items is high, it may be more appropriate to use the perpetual inventory control system.

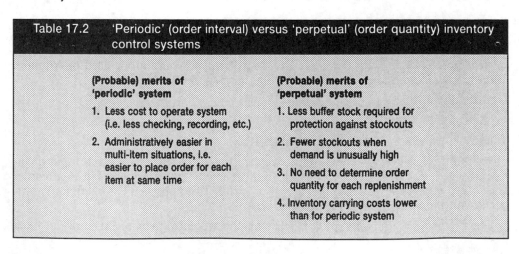

Table 17.2   'Periodic' (order interval) versus 'perpetual' (order quantity) inventory control systems

(Probable) merits of 'periodic' system	(Probable) merits of 'perpetual' system
1. Less cost to operate system (i.e. less checking, recording, etc.)	1. Less buffer stock required for protection against stockouts
2. Administratively easier in multi-item situations, i.e. easier to place order for each item at same time	2. Fewer stockouts when demand is unusually high
	3. No need to determine order quantity for each replenishment
	4. Inventory carrying costs lower than for periodic system

Table 17.2 compares the two systems. In many cases the cost of running a perpetual inventory control system (order level approach) will be greater than that of running a periodic inventory control system (order interval approach). However, the cost of carrying inventory may be less with the perpetual system than with the periodic system, especially where the periodic control system involves the replenishment of stock by a fixed quantity. As a guide, the order level approach, i.e. the perpetual inventory control system, may be more appropriate where:

(a) the number of transactions (i.e. stock depletions) is low compared with the annual usage;

(b) the processing cost of transactions is low compared with the ordering cost;

(c) the unit price of items is high;

(d) the required service level or degree of protection against stockouts is high;

(e) sales fluctuations are high and difficult to predict;

(f) inventory carrying costs are high;

(g) the use of a computer-based system permits frequent stock level updating (e.g. after every transaction), thus minimizing the disadvantage of the high operating cost of 'perpetual' inventory control.

Where demand is constant and replenishment is instantaneous or where the replenishment lead time is known, the fixed input level approach will resemble the fixed input interval approach. Only where either replenishment lead time or demand is uncertain will the adoption of each approach lead in practice to different inventory behaviour (e.g. Figure 17.2, in which the diagrams show the effect of each policy against the same demand pattern.)

Virtually all inventory control quantitative models deal with intermittent flow and input control, i.e. batch ordering, and in most cases the objective is cost minimization, i.e. the minimization of the total of holding and inventory change costs. Most such models are deterministic, i.e. they assume a known constant demand and either known input rate with no lead time or instantaneous input and known lead time. In such deterministic situations (which rarely, if ever, occur) there will be no need for provision of buffer or

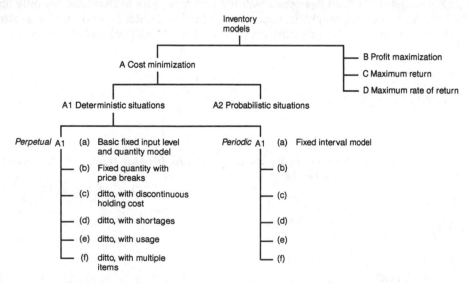

Figure 17.4 Intermittent flow/input control inventory models (N.B. Letters refer to text)

safety stocks. Such stocks will be provided only to protect against uncertain demand and/or lead time (see below). Probabilistic models are available, as are models aimed at profit maximization, etc. Figure 17.4 provides a taxonomy of intermittent flow inventory models (models B, C and D are not discussed in the text).

EXAMPLE

Hilton Hotel

A large Hilton Hotel complex decided to introduce a specially designed linen-management and inventory control system that was expected to save the 1,620-room property between $70,000 and $100,000 annually. The hotel had a laundry facility that processed about 13.2 million pounds weight of linen and clothing annually for the three Hilton properties in the area. The new system eliminated the need to sort manually linen from the three different properties. In addition, because the system provided for perpetual inventory control, needs could be better anticipated and over-time costs for housekeeping staffs be minimized.

Source: Bard, S. M. (1991) Linen-management system may save a bundle. *Hotel and Motel Management* **206**(11), pp. 27–28.

A1 Deterministic models: perpetual control

The order quantity approach

As we have already pointed out, the act of replenishing inventories is costly. Such replenishment costs are normally proportionate only to the number of orders placed and not to the size of the orders.

The ordering cost is equivalent to the set-up cost considered during our discussion of batch quantities in Chapter 14.

The order quantity decision involves the determination of the most economical order quantity—the quantity which minimizes total variable costs. Various economic order quantity (EOQ) models have been developed over the past fifty years so that now not only formulae but also tables, graphs, charts, etc., are available for calculating optimum order sizes in a variety of situations. The following are those commonly adopted and of most value.

Model A1(a)

1. Known constant demand
2. Complete deliveries
3. No shortages

The derivation of the economic order quantity formula for this model is unnecessary, since it was presented in Chapter 14.

The notation adopted is:

Q = Order quantity

C_S = Ordering cost/order

C_1 = Holding cost/item/unit of time

r = Usage rate

$$EOQ = Q^* = \sqrt{\frac{2C_S r}{C_1}}$$

Model A1 (d)

As Model A1(a) *except shortages allowed.*

Notation as before.

Plus C_2 Shortage or stock-out cost per item per unit of time

$$EOQ = Q^* = \sqrt{\frac{2rC_S}{C_1}} \sqrt{\frac{C_1 + C_2}{C_2}}$$

The total variable cost associated with this ordering policy is:

$$C^* = \sqrt{2rC_1C_S} \sqrt{\frac{C_2}{C_1 + C_2}}$$

Model A1(e) for fixed quantity with usage

1. Known constant demand
2. Delivery of order at a known and constant rate
3. No shortages
4. Buffer stock

Notation:

Q = Order quantity

C_S = Ordering cost

C_1 = Holding cost/item/unit of time

q = Delivery or production rate

r = Usage or consumption rate

$$EOQ = Q^* = \sqrt{\frac{2C_S r}{C_1\left[1 - \dfrac{r}{q}\right]}}$$

$$C^* = \sqrt{2C_S r C_1} \sqrt{1 - \frac{r}{q}}$$

A wine retailer

A company which uses a maximum–minimum stock-ordering policy orders 2500 of purchased item A at a time. They wish to determine what annual saving might be made by ordering this item in different quantities. An examination of previous stock records indicates that the annual usage of these items is constant at 7000. They further find that the cost of making an order, which is independent of the order size, is £10. The purchase price of the items is £0.5 and the cost of holding stock is 7 per cent of item price per item per year. The supplier undertakes to deliver the items at a constant rate of 50 per day.

$q = 50 \times 250$/year (assuming that there are 250 working days per year)

$r = 7000$/year

$C_S = £10$

$C_1 = 0.07 \, (0.5) = £0.035$/item/year

$$EOQ = Q^* = \sqrt{\frac{2 \times 10 \times 7000}{0.07 \, (0.5) \times \left(1 - \dfrac{7000}{12\,500}\right)}}$$

$Q^* = 3015$ units

Total annual variable cost associated with this policy C^*:

$$= \sqrt{2 \times 7000 \times 10 \times 0.07 \, (0.5)} \; \sqrt{1 - \frac{7000}{12\,500}}$$

$= £46.4$ p.a.

Total annual variable cost associated with present policy:

$$= \frac{C_1 Q}{2}\left[1 - \frac{r}{q}\right] + \frac{C_S r}{Q}$$

$$= \frac{0.035 \times 2500}{2}(0.44) + \left(10 \times \frac{7000}{2500}\right)$$

$= £47.25$ p.a.

Potential annual saving on item A = £0.25

The re-order level approach

We decided earlier that in the fixed quantity (two-bin or order quantity) ordering system, two questions must be answered: what is the fixed order quantity (Q) and what is the re-order level? We have decided how, in a few typical situations, the fixed order quantity can be determined and we must now look at the problem of re-order levels.

If the usage or consumption of items is perfectly constant and accurately known and if stock replenishment time is zero, then the stock order level may be zero and orders for stock replenishments can be placed when stock falls to this level. Thus in a deterministic situation the order level decision is easily made.

Unfortunately such an ideal situation rarely, if ever, exists. In practice two complications can arise. First, the usage rate may be absolutely constant and consequently there is the risk that stock may be prematurely exhausted. Even so, if replenishment of stock is instantaneous, no problems arise because exhausted stock can immediately be replaced. The second complication concerns replenishment. If this is not immediate, it becomes necessary to place orders some time prior to the items being needed and replenishment times may fluctuate. The occurrence of both these complications necessitates the maintenance of buffer or safety stocks.

If both of these complications arise in any magnitude then we cannot reasonably use any of the ordering models discussed in the previous section, since all of those assume a static and deterministic state. However, if these fluctuations are not excessive then these models can be used, since only a slight, and usually tolerable, error is introduced.

To summarize, then, the need to consider order levels other than zero arises because of uncertainty, i.e. the probabilistic nature of demand and/or replenishment lead time. Such uncertainty is alien to the ordering models we have discussed but they can nevertheless be used, with only minor error, provided demand and lead time vary only marginally. The approaches which might be employed are outlined under a discussion of probabilistic models later in this chapter.

A1 Deterministic models: periodic control

If, to begin with, we again assume that usage or demand is constant and known, then this sytem of ordering is, in both practice and theory, identical to the maximum–minimum or order quantity system. In the maximum–minimum system, when stocks fall to a predetermined level (which can be zero if order delivery is instantaneous), a further predetermined quantity of items is ordered. In the order interval system, at predetermined intervals, a quantity of goods sufficient to restore stock to a given level is ordered. In the ideal conditions the results of using the order quantity and the order cycle systems would be the same. Consequently, for such cases the answers to our two basic questions—when to order and how much to order—can be found in the previous section, i.e.

$$\text{Order interval} = \frac{\text{Order quantity}}{\text{Usage rate}}$$

$$\text{Optimum order interval} = \frac{\text{EOQ}}{\text{Usage rate}}$$

i.e.

$$t^* = \frac{Q^*}{r}$$

For the models we examined in the previous section the optimum order intervals are given by the following formulae:

Model A1(a)

$$t^* = \sqrt{\frac{2C_S}{rC_1}}$$

Model A1(d)

$$t^* = \sqrt{\frac{2C_S}{rC_1}} \sqrt{\frac{C_1 + C_2}{C_2}}$$

Model A1(e)

$$t^* = \sqrt{\frac{2C_S}{rC_1 \left(1 - \dfrac{r}{q}\right)}}$$

It is only during conditions of uncertainty that these two methods of ordering differ. The fundamental characteristic of the order interval system is that the stock status of each item is examined at regular and fixed intervals, at which time the following questions are asked:

1. Should an order be placed to replenish stock now?
2. If so, how many units must be ordered?

The order interval system is administratively more convenient than the maximum–minimum system. Since stocks are reviewed and orders placed at regular intervals, the stock control department can more easily plan their activities and make better use of their time; however, the penalty for this administrative convenience is that, generally, the use of such a system involves the adoption of higher stock levels. The system is particularly suitable where stocks consist of a larger number of different products, since in such cases the ordering cost is often less than the equivalent cost for variable interval (maximum–minimum) ordering.

Continuous flow/input control

Conventional inventory control theory also largely ignores the case of continuous, as opposed to intermittent, input flow. In this case input control is again a means for the management of inventory to satisfy expected output needs, and one problem for inventory management is the determination of an input rate (or average rate). Other problems will generally relate to the determination of average, minimum or safety inventory levels, and inventory capacity. Given deterministic output (or full control of output) and full control of input, input rate can be matched to output, and inventory problems are obviated. Here, therefore, we must deal with problems deriving from probabilistic output and/or incomplete control of input.

The problem can be considered to be one of matching two probability distributions (i.e. for input and output rates). A mismatch may give rise to:

1. *Output starving*, i.e. depletion of stock due to excess of demand over input (i.e. shortage, etc.).

2. (a) ***Input blocking***, i.e. insufficient space or capacity for inputs due to excess of input over output; or

    (b) ***Excess stock-holding***, if inventory capacity is not limited.

The required average inventory capacity will be influenced by input and output rate variability (mean input rate must equal mean output rate). The higher the variability, the greater the stock capacity required to accommodate short-term differences in input and output sales. Hence, as a general rule of thumb, the greater the possible short-term difference between rates (i.e. assuming symmetrical distributions, the upper end of one distribution minus the lower end of the other), the greater the stock capacity required. For a given (known or forecast) output rate distribution, inventory levels can be determined for alternative input rate distributions, and vice versa. Simulation techniques will normally be employed.

KEY POINTS FOR CHAPTER 17

Inventory management

is an aspect of materials management, but is concerned with single-stage inventories.

Single-stage inventories exist as:

    system outputs

    system inputs

    customers' queues.

Inventory management

is concerned with the management of stocks of consumed items.

Inventory management decisions are concerned with:

    replenishment levels or times

    replenishment quantities

    average stock levels

    safety stock levels.

Such decisions are influenced by costs, including:

    stock holding costs

    customer service costs.

Not all items require the same degree of control. An ABC or Pareto analysis can identify categories requiring close/loose control.

The main types of inventory management system are:

    intermittent flow/input control

    continuous flow/input control

    intermittent flow/output control

    continuous flow/output control.

Intermittent flow/input control is the 'classic' concern of inventory management.

There are two basic approaches to intermittent flow/input control inventory management:

    fixed input level control ('perpetual' control)

    fixed input internal control ('periodic' control).

Economic (minimum total cost) quantity models are used in determining order/replenishment quantities.

FURTHER READING

Barker, T. (1989) *Essentials of Materials Management:* McGraw Hill. (An introductory practical text, relevant to this chapter and also Chapter 16.)

Waters, C. D. J. (1992) *Inventory Control and Management.* Chichester: Wiley.

17.1 Describe the principles of maximum–minimum and order cycle systems of stock control. In what circumstances is the use of each of these types of system appropriate? In what circumstances would the use of either system give rise to basically the same stock control system (i.e. the same ordering decision)?

17.2 In a certain situation, demand for goods is both known and stable. The goods are ordered from an 'outside' supplier, they are delivered in complete batches and no quantity discount arrangements apply. No buffer stock is to be maintained. Determine:

  (a) the economic order quantity, given:

ordering cost per order	= 20
holding cost per item per annum	= £0.05
demand per annum	= 10 000
price per item	= £15

  (b) the economic order quantity, given:

ordering cost per order	= £20
holding cost per item per annum	= 5% of item price
demand per annum	= 10 000
price per item	= £15

  (c) the regular economic ordering interval, given:

ordering cost per order	= £50
holding cost per item per annum	= 5% of item price
demand per annum	= 15 000
price per item	= £25

17.3 Refer to Figure 17.4. In comparison with model A1(a) what additional factor(s) must be taken into account in determining the economic batch size for model A1(b)? Comment on how the economic batch size might be determined in such a situation.

17.4 Using the following information determine the approximate economic order quantity. NB. In obtaining your answer either use a graphical approach, i.e. plot the 'change' and the 'holding' cost curves, and thus obtain the total cost curve and therefore the minimum total cost batch, or develop your own numerical approach.

$$r \ = 2500 \text{ units/year}$$
$$C_1 = 10 \text{ per cent of unit price/unit/year}$$
$$C_2 = £100$$

Order quantity	100–499	500–2499	2500–4999	≥ 5000
Unit price/unit	£5	£4.75	£4.6	£4.5

PART 8

The control of operating systems

INTRODUCTION TO PART 8

This section deals with control. The principal topics covered are the management of quality and thus, the control of the quality of the goods or services provided by the operating systems and the reliability of those goods and services; the maintenance and/or replacement of the system, and its constituent parts; and the control of the system through performance monitoring.

The introductory chapter sets the scene for chapters on the three principal topics, quality; maintenance and reliability; and performance measurement. Two chapters are devoted to quality—the first dealing with important principles, and the second with controls.

Chapter 18

Operations control principles

ISSUES

What is the relationship of operations planning and
   control?
Where and when is control important?
What are the requirements for effective control?
How are operating systems controlled?
What is Kanban?

We have noted (in Chapter 11) that the general purpose of control is to ensure, as far as possible, the implementation of plans. Thus those involved in control, and those procedures established for the purposes of control, will in general seek to monitor activities with a view to ensuring that these activities correspond to some intended situation or state. Control derives from this process of monitoring activities and the comparison of actual and intended states. The need for control derives from the fact that rarely is it possible to ensure in advance that certain things will happen in a particular way at a particular time, etc. Control is necessary because of the existence of uncertainties. A purely deterministic situation is unlikely to necessitate control since, in such circumstances, planning in itself is sufficient. In practice such deterministic situations will rarely exist and thus control is an essential link in the circle or cycle which begins with planning and involves monitoring, action and correction, and possibly revision of planning for future events.

OPERATIONS CONTROL
Importance and emphasis

The relative *emphasis* on planning and control in operations management will, to a large extent, be determined by the nature of the operating system. Consider, for example, the contrasting case examples discussed below.

Case 1 This is the big 'one-off' planning project in a highly uncertain situation. Here planning cannot be perfect, and there will be little opportunity to replan. The emphasis, therefore, will be on the controls involved in using a given set of resources efficiently for different purposes. (Similar situations will exist in managing most one-off 'project' type situations, e.g. in the construction industry, hospital accident wards, expeditions, military operations.)

Case 2 This is the repetitive situation where the (annual) requirements of the operating system(s) are known and where planning can therefore be accurate and certain. Here considerable effort will be put into establishing the system, and the subsequent problems of control will be minimized. If the system is properly planned there will be little need for decision-making in control, since there will be few exceptions to the norm. (Similar situations exist in managing most repetitive/process-type operating systems, e.g. mass production, regular/scheduled transport systems, customer banking services, routine medical and surgery services.)

CONTROL CONCEPTS: REQUIREMENTS

The essential prerequisites for effective control are:

1. The purpose or objectives of the system to be controlled must be known.

2. Appropriate (level of detail, relevance and timeliness) information on system performance must be available.

3. A choice of actions must be possible and criteria for choice must exist.

4. There should be adequate (speed, appropriateness and accuracy) system response.

Diagrammatically a control system may be represented in the manner shown in Figure 18.1. (This is an 'output' control system where output is monitored in order to assess the performance of the operation.) It will be seen that there are four components:

Figure 18.1 Feedback and control system (closed) (output control)

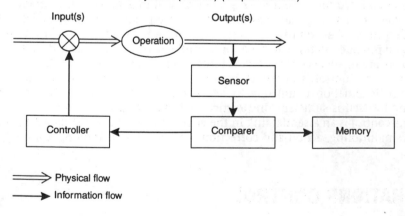

(a) a means of sensing output;

(b) a means of comparing actual output with intended output;

(c) a means of recording intended output (memory);

(d) a means of exercising control.

A *closed system*, as shown in Figure 18.1, is directly influenced by its own past behaviour. Its own outputs are monitored or observed in order that some purposeful control might be exercised over its inputs. The operation of the system is dependent on direct feedback of information.

In contrast, an *open system* exists where outputs have no direct influence over earlier parts of the system. In other words an open system does not react to its own performance. Its past actions have no influence over current or future actions. There is no direct feedback of information on its outputs for the control of its inputs.

In practice most operations control will be of the closed system type, although the mechanism by which systems are closed will differ and will vary in their degree of sophistication. For example, in process control (i.e. the control of flow processes such as chemical processes using computers) several types of application exist, their principal differences being the manner in which information is fed back and control is exercised. In a simple data logging system, a computer is used to scan rapidly and frequently the information secured from instruments connected to the process, e.g. flow meters, transducers, thermometers, etc., this information being recorded, processed and displayed, and used to calculate performance indices or guides which subsequently might be used by those concerned with the manual control of the process. Alarm systems are often incorporated, so the computer will signal the occurrence of faults or other unusual conditions in the process and also carry out simple diagnostic procedures using the input data to determine and indicate the cause of such conditions.

In contrast, a full control system will provide automated closed loop control of the system. The efficiency of such systems depends on their being fed with the correct information, i.e. efficient data logging, and on the speed with which the control system works. Such systems must be carefully designed to accord with the characteristics of the process. The nature of the inputs must correspond to known and foreseeable disturbances of the process, and the speed of the system to the nature of the process.

It is inappropriate here to enter into a detailed discussion of control theory. However, it is worth noting that in the development of feedback control systems, whether manual, automatic or mixed, it is essential that the feedback mechanism be matched to the characteristics and capability of the process. It is essential also that control be exercised at appropriate stages within the process and that each of the important variables be monitored for control purposes. In practice, therefore, control systems will often be complex, multi-stage and multi-level.

CONTROL OF OPERATING SYSTEMS

Most control actions are *information dependent* in that they derive from the acquisition and use of information on the nature or state of the operating system. In Chapter 1 we modelled operating system(s) entirely in terms of physical flow. We should now note, however, that such systems are in effect 'covered' by information links so that, together, there is adequate information available for the control of activities and events at all stages in the system. For example, the control of physical flows in operating systems is exercised through a combination of activity scheduling and inventory control decisions. This situation can best be illustrated in the manner shown in Figure 18.2. The diagrams in this figure show the principal points in the system at which control of flow is exercised and the decision loops associated with such control. Thus in a 'function from stock to stock system', (1), information in terms of order or delivery requirements goes from the customer

Figure 18.2 Operations control relationships

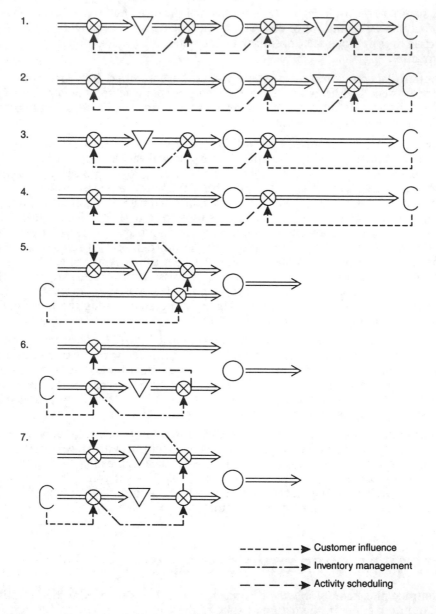

to a point equivalent to inventory output. Flow at this stage is monitored and information, through the inventory management system, passes to the flow control point on inventory input, from where, through the activity scheduling system, information passes to a flow control point on function input, and so on through to resource supply. A similar chain of information loops and a similar series of control points exist for all systems. For example, in a 'function from stock from customer queue' system (7), the customer influences the input to customer queues, which are monitored in order to ensure that appropriate decisions are made in respect of flow from customer queues through to the system. The flow into the system is monitored through the activity scheduling system so that the flow of resources to the system is appropriate. The flow in turn is monitored through the inventory management system in order to ensure that flow into (i.e. replenishment of) resource stocks is appropriate.

Flow control is an essential responsibility of operations management. Such flow control is associated with the inventory management system(s) and the activity scheduling system. Supplementing this flow control there will be a need to consider the *nature* of the items or customers which are flowing in the system, in order to ensure, for example, that intended quality levels are maintained and resources are utilized in the intended fashion. Chapter 17 dealt with control decisions relating to inventory management. In this part we shall consider control associated with activity schedules and quality control and also controls associated with resource utilization, i.e. with resource maintenance, replacement and repair. Finally we shall take a broader approach and consider performance measurement, i.e. the way in which the performance of the whole operating system might be monitored for both planning and control purposes.

THE KANBAN SYSTEM

The Kanban system developed by Toyota in Japan as part of their JIT philosophy (see Chapter 12) provides a simple visible means of feedback control in the manner outlined in Figure 18.2. The system provides a basis for both operations and inventory control through simple manual/clerical procedures. Kanban is a simple flow control system, serving the purposes identified above.

Kanban principles

The simplest Kanban system utilizes pairs of cards (Kanban is the Japanese for card). The cards are used to trigger movements between operations in flow systems where standard items are made in small batches against customer orders. More sophisticated systems can be developed for multi-product systems, but in all cases the flow through the system is triggered by demand from, or on behalf of, the customer as outlined in Figure 18.2.

A simple example will illustrate the principles of a two-card Kanban system. Figure 18.3 shows how the system would work between two sequential processing operations. Operation 4 which supplies the customer is in turn supplied by operation 3. Operation 3 has input and output stocks. Operation 4 has input stocks only and supplies directly to the external customer. The figure shows the two intermediate stocks. Items are held in stock in standard containers—in this case each containing six items for processing. Each container has attached to it a Kanban: either a *movement* Kanban, or a *processing* Kanban. Stage 1 shows a full container in both stocks, with their associated Kanbans. The receipt of an order at operation 4 for completed parts gives rise to the following sequence of activities:

Stage 1

The processing order is placed on operation 4.

Stage 2

The items held in the container in the operation 4 input stock are transferred to operation 4.

Figure 18.3 The operation of a two-card Kanban system

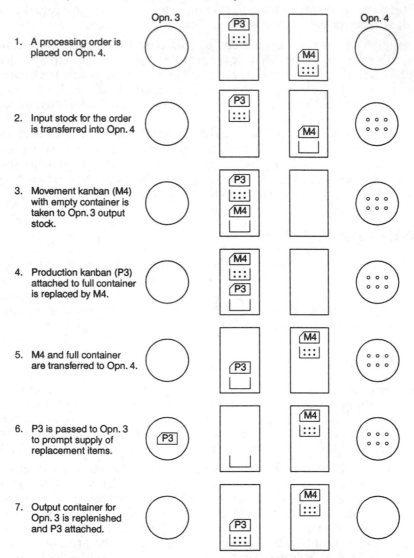

1. A processing order is placed on Opn. 4.

2. Input stock for the order is transferred into Opn. 4

3. Movement kanban (M4) with empty container is taken to Opn. 3 output stock.

4. Production kanban (P3) attached to full container is replaced by M4.

5. M4 and full container are transferred to Opn. 4.

6. P3 is passed to Opn. 3 to prompt supply of replacement items.

7. Output container for Opn. 3 is replenished and P3 attached.

Stage 3

The fact that a movement Kanban is attached to an empty container gives authorization for the movement of items from the preceding stage, so the empty container with the movement Kanban is moved to the output stock area of operation 3.

Stage 4

The two Kanbans are exchanged, thus the operation 4 movement Kanban is attached to the full container, and operation 3 processing Kanban is attached to the empty container.

Stage 5

The movement Kanban together with the full container is transferred to operation 4 input stock.

Stage 6

The fact that a processing Kanban is attached to an empty container in operation 3 output stock gives authorization for the processing of items through operation 3 for the replenishment of the container. In order to trigger this action, the production Kanban may be placed in an appropriate rack or display at operation 3.

Stage 7

Items processed through operation 3 are used to replenish the empty container in operation 3 output stock and the processing Kanban is attached to the full container.

There are alternative means for operating this visual flow control system. Some companies use a simpler system employing only one card. Other 'signalling' methods can be used instead of Kanban cards, for example coloured clips can be transferred between containers within stores, or flags can be attached to containers, etc. An alternative method is to mark out areas on racks or on the floor within store areas such that an empty area can operate as a trigger for the production of replacement items. The essential feature, however, of all such systems is that activities, e.g. the processing of items, are triggered only on demand. Requests, in effect, *pull* items through the sequence of operations.

Kanban-type flow control systems are an important part of JIT. The concept of processing only as and when required, coupled with the 'pull' system, are essential ingredients of JIT. The visibility of the system, e.g. the visibility of the movement of processed Kanbans, is a further important characteristic of JIT.

Since the number of Kanban cards operating within a system is directly proportional to the amount of work-in-progress in that system, changes in the number of cards will result in changes in in-process inventory. Thus operations management can control overall in-process inventory levels by the addition to or the subtraction of cards from the system. If, for example, management judge that a system can operate with less in-process inventory, then this is achieved simply by withdrawing Kanban cards. Since such cards (or other 'triggering' devices) are readily visible, this has an immediate impact upon operations, so the system is highly responsive.

EXAMPLE

Kanban at Schlegel Corp.

A Kanban-based production control system was designed for a batch flow manufacturing facility for woven products at Schlegel Corp. The firm produces its products in more than 450 varieties. The main characteristic of the production process is that the weaving stage involves batched production with significant setup and changeover times. Setting and maintaining the minimum finished inventory levels must accommodate the need to meet the target service levels for the customer. The production control system provides a framework for production planning and scheduling in addition to performance tracking and process improvements. One key element of the production control scheme is that the inventory at each part of the process is controlled.

Source: Groenevelt, H. and Karmarker, U.S. (1988) A dynamic Kanban system case study. *Prod. and Inv. Mgt.* **29**(2) pp.46–51.

ACTIVITY CONTROLS

The control of activities associated with activity scheduling is one aspect of flow control within a system. Inventory control, the complementary aspect of flow control, has been dealt with in Chapter 17. Here, therefore, we shall deal briefly with the elements of activity control. Essentially there are three steps necessary in achieving control of activities:

(a) monitoring and recording flows or activities;

(b) analysing flows and/or progress by comparison with plans or schedules; and

(c) control, that is, modification of plans or a rearrangement of schedules in order to conform as nearly as possible to original targets.

To some extent the manner in which these steps are accomplished will depend on the nature and manner of activity scheduling and the nature of the activity schedules. Thus if schedules have been developed in order to achieve a particular flow or particular state at certain points in the system at particular times, then performance will be recorded and monitored by reference to these same points. The manner in which plans and schedules have been expressed and drawn up will influence the way in which step (b) above is achieved, i.e. the analysis of progress by comparison with plans and schedules. The extent and nature of control will of course depend on the variance identified between actual progress or flows and intended progress or flows. The manner in which this control will be achieved will depend to some extent on the nature of the system and the opportunities for the exercise of control. Thus, for example, if a particular procedure has been established for scheduling purposes then control will be linked to the use of the same procedure. If bar charts have been used then progress and monitoring will utilize such charts. If network analysis has been used then similar calculations and procedures will be employed for purposes of control.

KEY POINTS FOR CHAPTER 18

Operations control

is necessary since plans can rarely be perfect.

There is a need to 'balance' planning and control—the more/better the planning, the less the need for control, and vice versa.

The requirements for effective control, are:

known objectives

appropriate information

choice of actions

appropriate response speed.

The components of a control system are:

sensor

comparator

recorder

activator.

Operating systems comprise physical flows and also information flows. The information flows are used to permit control of the physical flows.

The Kanban is a simple control device, used extensively in Just in Time systems.

FURTHER READING

Cleland, D. I. and King, W. R. (1972) *Management: A Systems Approach.* New York: McGraw-Hill.

Eilon, S. (1971) *Management Control.* London: Macmillan.

Singh, N. Kwok, Nung, Shek and Meloche, D. (1990) The development of a Kanban system—a case study. *International Journal of Operations and Production Management* **10**, pp. 28–36.

QUESTIONS

18.1 Show diagrammatically, in the manner of Figure 18.2, the principal control 'loops' which will be used for the control of flows through the following systems.

(a) a small 'jobbing' engineering production works;

(b) a restaurant;

(c) a specialist retail delicatessen store.

18.2 Explain the main features of, and identify the difference between, a closed and an open loop feedback control system.

18.3 Consider one of the scheduling procedures outlined in the chapters in Part 6 and show how a related control system might work.

Chapter 19

Management of quality

ISSUES

Who defines quality?
What is quality and how is it achieved?
Why are attitudes and expectations important?
What are the main dimensions or elements of quality?
What are the main quality costs?
How do these costs relate to levels of quality?
Is quality expensive?
What is TQM?
What are quality standards and why are they
    important?
Why are 'behavioural' and 'organization' considerations
    important?
What are quality improvement programmes?

All customers will have some expectation of the quality of the goods or services which have to be provided. There will be an agreed specification. Agreement will have been reached within the organization. They will have accepted the specification which has been offered, or there will be agreement from discussion and negotiation. Given an acceptable specification, customers will expect the product or service which is provided to conform to that specification.

These two factors—specification, which is to do with the 'design quality' of an item or service, and conformity, which is to do with the 'process' quality which is achieved—are of particular importance to customers. Ultimately they are the two factors which determine the quality levels provided by an organization to its customers. These two factors however are themselves determined by other factors, as shown in Figure 19.1. Consider first the specification. This will have been determined as a result of an organization's policy, which in turn resulted from decisions on its market policy, which in turn resulted from its consideration of the market or customer needs and requirements, and the activities of competitors. This is the process of designing quality into the product or service.

Figure 19.1 Factors influencing the quality of items/services as provided to customers

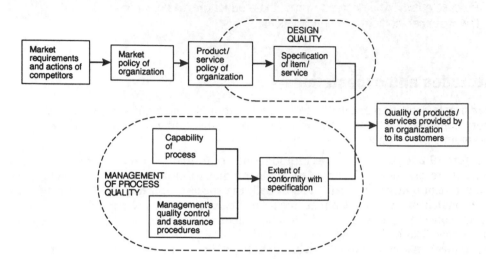

The degree to which the product or service conforms to the specification will be influenced by the capability of the conversion process. If the conversion process is incapable of providing products or services at the level specified, then it must follow that the products or services provided will be inferior. However, the fact that a conversion process is inherently capable of producing or providing products/services according to a specification will not in itself ensure that all products or services are of an acceptable standard, for some management control will be required to ensure that the conversion process is used in the appropriate fashion in order to ensure that the specification is achieved. This is all to do with the *management of process quality*, a topic which will be examined in detail in the next chapter, which deals with control and assurance protection.

THE NATURE OF QUALITY

Quality, cost and reliability are generally interrelated. Higher quality is usually associated with higher reliability and, where items are produced or where services are provided efficiently, some additional cost is usually incurred in attaining higher levels of quality, but some other costs are reduced.

Definitions

For our purposes we will begin with the following definitions:

Quality. The quality of a product or service is the degree to which it satisfied customers' requirements.

This is influenced by:

Design quality. The degree to which the specification of the product or service satisfies customers requirements.

> *Process quality.* The degree to which the product or service, when made available to the customer, conforms to specifications.

Attitudes and expectations

Our simple definition of quality, whilst useful, should not be allowed to conceal a rather more complex reality. In fact, perceptions of quality differ. Customers' and suppliers' viewpoints might differ.

Figure 19.2 looks again at specifications and conformance. It offers a simple model to illustrate several points. First, we are reminded that specification must be related to customers' requirements. Basically, and overall, the specification that is offered may fail to meet, match or exceed customers' requirements. Second, we are reminded that conformance concerns the extent to which what is actually provided to customers corresponds to the specification which was offered. Again basically, the extent of conformance might fail to meet, match, or exceed specification. It will be of interest now to consider the attitudes of customers and suppliers to the nine possible situations shown in Fig 19.2.

Figure 19.2 Possible attitudes to specification and conformance

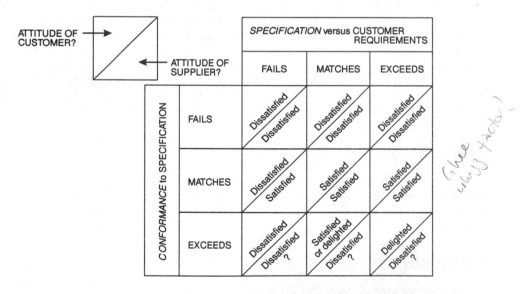

From the *customers'* viewpoint, *dissatisfaction* will be caused by the following:

(a) Failure of specification to meet requirements (irrespective of subsequent degree of conformance to that specification);

(b) Failure of conformance with a specification which matches requirements.

But in addition, dissatisfaction might also result when:

(c) What is provided fails to conform to a specification which exceeded requirements.

This latter situation might be the result of failure to receive items or services which meet new expectations, even though the specification was higher than would have been necessary, *or* failure to receive items or services which meet original requirements because of the extent of failure to conform to an even higher specification.

Customers will be *satisfied* if what is provided:

(d) matches an acceptable specification;

(e) matches a specification which exceeded requirements.

Where items or services actually exceed prior expectations, something stronger than satisfaction, e.g. *delight*, may result, i.e.

(f) provision of something which exceeds a specification, which exceeded initial requirements, or even

(g) provision of something which exceeds a specification which matched initial requirements.

Table 19.1	Some 'dimensions' of quality	
	Goods	**Services**
A. Functional dimensions	1. Utility (i.e. what it does)	1. Utility (i.e. what it provides)
	2. Reliability	2. Reliability
	e.g. Continuity of operation	e.g. Availability
		Accessibility
	Availability for use	Consistency of operation
	Consistency in use	
	Maintainability	
	3. Usability	3. Serviceability
	e.g. Safety	e.g. Safety
	Convenience	Convenience
	Comfort	Duration
B. Non-functional dimensions	1. Design	1. Processes
	e.g. Appearance	(i.e. nature of interactions of system and customer)
	Performance	
	2. Symbolic characteristics	2. Symbolic characteristics
	(i.e. affecting image or self-image of user)	(i.e. affecting image or self-image of user)
	e.g. Availability/exclusivity	e.g. Exclusivity
	Novelty/rarity	Novelty/rarity
	Modernity	Modernity
	Price	Customer group
		Price

One point worth emphasizing, from the above, is that customers will have *expectations*, even to the extent of expecting a specification which exceeds their original requirements, if that is what is offered. Failure to meet these expectations will cause dissatisfaction; matching these expectations will give rise to satisfaction, and exceeding them may result in 'delight'.

From the *suppliers'* (operations) viewpoint, we should be *dissatisfied* if:

(a) what is actually provided fails to meet a previously declared specification which has been accepted by the customer.

But, in addition, we might for different reasons have some cause for concern if:

(b) what is provided exceeds a previously agreed specification.

This concern might relate to the fact that to achieve this higher standard has incurred additional, unexpected cost. However, in a competitive situation the possibility of exceeding specification, and therefore customer expectations, might be a deliberate (if undeclared) intention in order to secure delighted and therefore loyal customers.

We will, of course, be satisfied if:

(c) what is provided matches specification.

Taken together, the above observations reveal two somewhat different sets of attitudes to quality. They are not congruent. Relatively few 'outcomes' will satisfy both parties. Customers' expectations are not fixed, and they are affected by experience, so even with the ability to provide items or services which exceed specification, it becomes progressively more difficult to secure a delighted customer.

Fitness for purpose implies that a product or service can perform its intended function. This term is often used in defining quality. Notice that fitness for purpose results only when the specification is appropriate and when conformity to specification is achieved. Notice again, however, that perceptions of customers and suppliers might differ. Four of the nine situations given in the matrix of Figure 19.2 may be seen to correspond to fitness for purpose, i.e. those situations in which specification matches or exceeds requirements, and where conformance matches or exceeds specification. Alternatively, just one cell (right at the centre of the matrix) might be regarded as the intention. Customers may tend towards the first view, whereas suppliers might have the second in mind. Whichever the view, it is of course essential that agreement be reached if the concept is to be of value in the management of quality.

The dimensions of quality

Quality, as perceived by customers, is a multi-dimensional concept. We look for a variety of things in the products or services we receive, as 'specification' can encompass many things.

Table 19.1 provides a simple set of 'core' dimensions which will be of interest to customers and to suppliers. Each of these dimensions can be elaborated for particular types of product or service, but in most situations these five basic dimensions will be evident.

Determination of quality level

Quality may be a policy option through which an organization seeks competitive advantage (see Chapter 2). Decisions relating to quality and consequently to cost will therefore be influenced by the policy of the organization and by the policy and behaviour of competitors in the market. Before launching a new product or service, a company will investigate the quality and the reliability of others already on the market, and their objective may then be to better their quality and/or their price. There are circumstances in which such a procedure for establishing quality levels is unnecessary; for example, certain products must be manufactured to national or international standards. Adherence to such standards is often mandatory. Except on such occasions, price and quality decisions are often made empirically. Furthermore, both price and quality will often change as a result of market pressures.

The specification of the project or service will be established first. The operations manager must then seek to ensure conformity with this specification. Clearly, process capabilities should influence specification decisions, since there is little point in specifying something that cannot be achieved. Process capability is therefore of importance in determining quality levels. Similarly, the cost of ensuring conformity with specification must be taken into account.

QUALITY COSTS

We must now look more closely at the nature of quality-related costs and then at the relationship of these costs to quality levels.

Cost types and categories

Figure 19.3 shows, diagrammatically and in approximate sequential order, the principal quality-related costs. Three *types* of cost are identified:

Figure 19.3 Quality-related costs

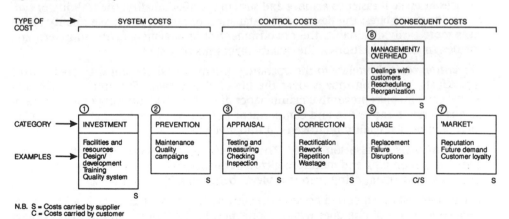

(i) *System costs*, associated with setting up the operating system to aim to provide goods or services of appropriate quality;

(ii) *Control costs*, incurred in monitoring checking and correcting activities during the operations;

(iii) *Consequent costs*, incurred after completion of operations, i.e. after delivery of the goods, or completion of the services.

Beware of 'over-quality'

Two *categories* of cost are identified for each cost type, and in addition one category, that of management/overhead costs, is identified as being incurred during control, and also after completion of operations.

We will examine these costs in more detail below, but some key points can be noted immediately, i.e.

(a) *sequential relationships.* There is a general sequential relationship between these costs. The greater the effect of or the benefit gained from system costs, the less the need for control costs. The greater the combined benefit of system and control costs, the less the consequent cost implication.

(b) *Cost responsibilities.* Most of these costs will fall on the supplier. Certainly all of the costs of investment, prevention, appraisal, and usually all of the correction costs must be borne by the supplier, as also the consequent cost implications. Customers will normally bear some but perhaps not all of the usage costs, some of which may have to be met by the supplier.

The nature of costs

Each of the cost categories can now be explained more fully.

1. *Investment costs* are incurred before operations begin. They are, essentially, concerned with the provision of appropriate facilities and systems, and also the design/development of the product or service. All this work will always be required, but here we are concerned with the additional costs which are incurred at the outset to try to ensure that an adequate quality level can be achieved and maintained. This expenditure therefore is intended to make 'life easier later'. Some examples of 'one-off' costs incurred in advance are these: the design of products or the specification of services to make it easier to achieve and sustain specified quality; the training of staff in quality procedures; the design and installation of facilities to make quality objectives more easily obtainable; the establishment of arrangements with suppliers; and the design and installation of the quality management system.

2. *Prevention costs* also relate to the operating system as a whole, but they are incurred repetitively, if not continually over the life of that system. Examples of such 'on-going' costs include: preventive maintenance of facilities; the running of quality campaigns to retain interest in and commitment to quality; the maintenance of supplier links; and regular quality improvement initiatives.

3. *Appraisal costs* are also 'on-going'. They include all costs associated with activities aimed at determining and monitoring current quality levels, including checking, testing, inspecting, monitoring customer views, benchmarking activities, etc.

4. *Correction costs* are incurred because the costs outlined above generally fail to ensure completely that nothing goes wrong. Correction involves doing things again (to get them right); replacing things which, when found to be wrong, cannot be rectified; repetition of operations; recycling of items or customers, etc. There are also costs of wastage, loss, scrap, and so on. These are often referred to as the 'internal costs of defects'.

5. *Usage costs.* These are the principal costs associated with individual failures. If, despite all of the activities referred to above, an operating system fails to deliver goods or services to the specified quality, then subsequent costs will be incurred. For example, if a defective item is passed to a customer, then it may fail in service, so there will

be a cost of disruption, referral, replacement—even compensation under warranty arrangements. On occasions disputes may arise, so there will be legal costs. The same can apply to a service which fails to meet specification: whilst this may not be evident immediately on completion of the service, so that neither the supplier nor the customer may be aware of it, failure to meet the specified quality standards may result in subsequent losses. For example, something may be damaged in transport, and only noticed later. Treatment in a hospital may be inadequate, resulting in recurrence of an illness. The food provided in a restaurant may be identified subsequently as having given rise to food poisoning, etc. In all such situations, costs will be incurred for the customer and/or the supplier. These are often called the 'external costs of defects'.

6. *Management/overhead costs.* This category has been included in order to remind us that there are many more indirect costs associated with failure to achieve quality standards. Management may have to devote considerable time to customer relations in order to offset the effects of poor quality. Persistently poor quality or major quality failures, even infrequent, may cause loss of morale, motivation and commitment of staff, which must then be re-established. Activities may need to be rescheduled. Organizational changes may need to be introduced. Management and others may be distracted and other activities may be neglected or delayed. All of these are the indirect managerial consequences of quality failures.

7. *'Market' costs.* Finally, the ability of an operating system to provide consistently goods or services at the required quality, or its inability to do so, will influence its reputation in the market. That reputation, or image, will in turn affect customer loyalty, and will influence future demand. A high reputation will facilitate and complement other marketing/promotional activities and make them more cost effective. A poor reputation will be an obstacle which may require extra effort, and thus extra cost, to compensate.

Quality costs and quality levels

The relationship of these costs to quality levels is far more complex than has traditionally been assumed. Each cost may relate differently to quality in different situations. Furthermore, the costs themselves are inter-related. Simple cause and effect/cost, and quality relationships may have little practical relevance. Despite this, it will be appropriate to initially consider each cost independently.

Cost/quality relationships

With reference once more to the categories shown in Figure 19.3, the following can be noted.

1. Increased *investment* should result in higher and consistent quality. Initially the 'returns' on investment may be great, but as the system becomes more sophisticated, it will become increasingly difficult to achieve higher quality. In other words, it will cost more to make a good system better than it will to make a poor system good. Since this is a 'one-off' cost, the greater subsequent volume through the system over its working life, the lower the investment quality cost per unit.

2. Increased *prevention* cost should also increase quality levels and/or consistency. Again, there may be diminishing returns as the system gets better, and of course in this case, since these are repetitive costs there are no volume benefits.

3. Increased *appraisal* effort and cost will result in increased quality in certain situations. If the system is unstable/or unsophisticated, then without on-going checking and monitoring quality might suffer. More frequent or more widespread checking, measuring, inspection and monitoring will probably contribute to quality improvement, by drawing attention to weaknesses, areas in which performance is deteriorating or where special attention is needed, etc. Without such appraisal, quality is unlikely *at this stage* to get better, and with less appraisal, it will probably get worse. Beyond a certain level, however, additional/further checking may contribute little, since it may simply draw attention more frequently to what is already known. Again therefore a 'diminishing returns' situation will apply.

4. *Correcting* things that are found to be wrong should improve the quality eventually delivered to customers. Greater expenditure here, therefore, will increase 'output' quality. Initially, if the system is unsophisticated, a linear relationship may exist, i.e. proportionally: correction cost will give rise to greater quality. Eventually however, saturation may occur. More and more correction effort may make it very difficult to organize such work adequately, so mistakes may occur, the level of attention may fall, and the benefit will be diluted.

5. The cost of inadequate quality, or quality failure during *usage*, will have a negative relationship to quality level. Higher costs will be associated with lower quality.

6. The same will apply to *management/overhead* costs. They will be higher if quality is lower.

7. The cost implication associated with the *market*, customer loyalty, subsequent demand, etc. is borne by the supplier. Lower quality will result in lower or reduced reputation; lower, or the loss of, customer loyalty; and lower future demand. The cost implications for the supplier result from the need to compensate for these effects, e.g. by spending more on advertising, etc. So, 'market' costs to the supplier are inversely related to quality levels.

'Spending' and 'saving' on quality

We noted earlier that the quality costs are inter-related and that there is a 'sequential' relationship between them. Thus there is often a choice to be made as to how best to 'spend' in order to achieve required quality levels. One approach would be to place emphasis on system cost expenditure, so that as expenditure here increases, the need for expenditure on control is reduced. This might be appropriate for large and complex systems providing complex products or services over long periods of time. A different approach would emphasize control expenditure to achieve higher quality as with less system expenditure. This might be appropriate where facilities are unsophisticated, where change is frequent, and where volumes are low.

Greater effort to achieve quality (i.e. greater expenditure on control costs plus system costs) should result in reduced consequential costs (i.e. usage, management and market costs). As 'spending' on achieving quality increases, so the 'savings' by reducing the costs consequent upon inadequate quality should also increase. Given these 'contradirectional' costs (one increasing and one reducing), it is possible that there exists a quality level at which the sum of the costs is at a minimum and, if so, then it might be argued that this is the optimal quality level. The type of relationship is shown in Figure 19.4a and b.

In Figure 19.4a, a minimum total cost quality level X is achieved. In comparison, for figure 19.4b the minimum cost quality level is higher: at Y. The only difference between the sets of costs in the two figures is in respect of 'consequential costs'. In 19.4a such costs

Figure 19.4 'Spending' and 'saving' on quality – the effect of cost levels

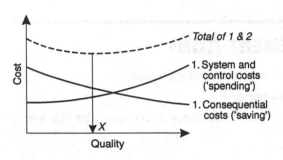

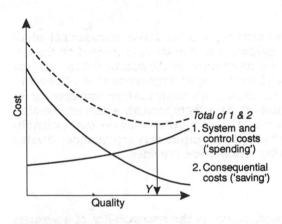

are relatively low, but reduce slowly. In 19.4b such costs are initially higher, but reduce more quickly as quality goes up.

These figures illustrate two important points.

1) It is not the *level* of the cost curves which influences the minimum total cost quality level, but rather the *shape* of these curves. In other words it is the relationship of the cost to quality that matters, not whether costs are generally high or low.

2) Other things being equal,

• If the consequential costs of higher quality reduce rapidly, *higher* quality levels are appropriate.

• If the costs of securing higher quality increase rapidly, *lower* quality levels are appropriate.

Given the above, we should aim for a higher quality level, where major savings can be achieved through reduction in the costs, to us, of quality failure. Where the costs of achieving higher quality levels increase steeply, we could aim for a lower quality level. Within this framework we can identify the quality levels up to which 'savings' outweigh 'spending' on quality. Up to that level quality is, in effect, free. Beyond that level costs are incurred.

But this is a static view. In practice, attitudes to quality will change. We have noted that it is customers' expectations which influence their attitudes to the quality they receive. In general, as higher quality levels are achieved, expectations will increase; so as higher quality levels are provided, the cost of subsequently failing to repeat those levels also increases. In other words the 'consequential' cost curve is not static.

So taking this view to the extreme, quality is a moving target: the best level is usually higher, but expenditure to achieve higher quality can always potentially be matched by greater returns. In other words, potentially, quality is alway free.

EXAMPLE

Xerox

As part of its 'Cost of Quality' Study, Xerox (USA) defined three categories of quality costs: 1. the costs of conformance (prevention and appraisal), 2. the costs of nonconformance (failure to meet customer requirements and exceeding customer requirements), and 3. the costs of lost opportunities. Lost opportunity costs are directly influenced by the other two cost categories. Eleven teams were then established to tackle Xerox's 1989 list of top quality problems. In its first year, the programme reduced the cost of quality, by $53 million.

Source: Carr, P. (1992) Applying cost of quality to a service business. *Sloan Management Review* **33**(4), pp. 72–7.

TOTAL QUALITY MANAGEMENT (TQM)

There are, in fact, two distinctive dimensions to the TQM philosophy—

(a) product/service *'life cycle' quality management;*

(b) commitment to and involvement in quality assurance and control by the *whole organization.*

The 'life-cycle' dimension

A 'life-cycle' approach to quality management requires the active management of all stages which influence the quality of the product or service which is received by the customer, followed by continued interest in the maintenance of the quality of items and services whilst 'in use' by the customer through service, repair, improvement, etc. The active management of quality in this 'longitudinal' manner is a major strategic commitment for the organization. It is a competitive instrument, an activity through which an organization competes with others. The recognition of this fact, together with the major commitment of resources which are required for TQM should ensure that organizations develop policies for and then plan their total quality management activities.

Organizational commitment

With the TQM approach we cannot regard quality as the responsibility of a separate department. Quality is the responsibility of all: it is an organization-wide commitment, even to the development of a 'quality culture' within the organization. We shall return to some of these issues later in this chapter under 'Behavioural and Organizational Factors'.

The Introduction of TQM

Seven steps have been identified for the introduction and adoption of a TQM approach.[1] They serve to remind us, before we begin to discuss details, that the effective management of quality requires an organization-wide approach and commitment, and that TQM has an organization-wide impact.

1. *Leadership*

   Make quality leadership a fundamental strategic goal to ensure that management energy is committed to the task. This requires a commitment throughout the organization and all of its activities.

   Recognize that quality levels are not permanent. The competitive stance of organizations, in relation to the changing customer perception of quality, creates a moving (upward) target.

---

[1] From Hill, T. (1991) *Production/Operations Management*. Prentice-Hall.

2. *Corporate-wide introduction*

   Quality should first be defined in terms of all aspects of a product/service package, all benefits and supporting facilities. The next step is to implement all the necessary actions throughout the organization (not just in quality functions/departments).

3. *Changing corporate orientation*

   Reorient the corporate approach to quality, i.e.

   (a) Product/service orientation: Move from a traditional 'control' type approach which accepts, implicitly, that defects will occur.

   (b) Process orientation: Use appropriate statistical process control procedures and do not depend on checking outgoing items. (see later in chapter)

   (c) Systems orientation: Establish a quality structure which embraces all parts of a business and not just quality functions.

4. *Motivation, education and training*

   Create continuous motivation to achieve quality improvements, supported by appropriate education and training. Place emphasis on education to affect attitudes and motivation to achieving quality improvements.

   Support improvements with adequate resources to ensure that they are achieved within appropriate timescales.

5. *The robust function*

   Recognize the need to built quality into the product/service at the specification stage.

6. *Cost orientation*

   (a) Optimizing product/service and process/delivery system design for improved quality and lower costs.

   (b) Use of the 'quality loss function' to quantify quality improvements in terms of cost and for use in design/specification. (see later in chapter)

7. *Customer orientation*

Apply quality control principles to design/specification activities to formalize the mechanism for ensuring that customer requirements are incorporated.

EXAMPLE

TQM at St Luke's Medical Center

St. Luke's Medical Center (Chicago) is using a TQM process to improve its operations. In addition to its principal urban, 983-bed facility, there are also two suburban hospitals, a health sciences university, a home health nursing service, a 'for-profit' subsidiary that markets health care products to corporations and other health case settings, and six occupational health clinics. To make the programme work, the organization is committing $100 000 a year in direct operating expenses for the TQM programme. Another $60 000-$100 000 was initially spent on customer research to determine areas in need of improvement. The organization is already seeing a return on its investment—TQM has been credited with department improvements such as:

1. decreasing the x-ray repeat rate in diagnostic radiology and reducing the department's absentee rate by 22.7% from 1987 to 1988

2. reducing laboratory result turnaround time by an average of 25%, resulting in a $10 000 sav-

ings and

3. reducing the number of checks manually typed by the accounts-payable department by 25%.

Source: Koska, M. T. (1990). Case study: quality improvement in a diversified health center. *Hospitals* **64** (23), pp.38–39.

QUALITY STANDARDS

National standards exist for many aspects of quality control and assurance, from specific statistical techniques through to the management of complete quality systems within organizations. In many cases these standards derive from those prescribed by governments for use in the defence industries.

British Standard 5750 was first introduced in 1979, replacing various others which by that time had begun to proliferate. BS 5750 was designed as the single base standard for quality systems. In 1987 the International Organizations for standards introduced ISO 9000 for the same purpose, and based very much on BS5750.

The existence of such standards not only helps organizations design and implement effective quality management systems, but also the accreditation of an organization under such a standard provides assurance to customers, reduces their own control and assurance needs and simplifies their procedures.

BS5750 and ISO 9000 standards

Both the British standard, now renamed BSEN ISO 9000and ISO 9000 are concerned with *Quality Systems*. They aim to define all relevant aspects of an organization's operations, procedures and systems concerned with identifying and meeting customers' requirements for quality products and services. Thus the standards aim to give customers an assurance that the quality of goods and services supplied to them meets their requirements, by specifying and regulating all the procedures which contribute to or affect quality.

The standards are of value in assisting organizations develop quality systems for use by organizations to help ensure quality inputs from suppliers, and as means for assessment for use by 'third parties'. Both standards were developed initially for engineering and manufacture, so the terminology relates to products, materials and items. However both now find widespread use in service organizations and, increasingly use of them and accreditation under these standards are being taken up by the customers of such organizations. The principal 'contents' of the two standards are outlined in Table 19.2.

Implementation and benefits

The benefits claimed for the use of such standards for a quality system relate to:

(a) Customer response: e.g. better relationships, fewer complaints, greater co-operation;

(b) Interval management: e.g. improved control, better discipline, reduced costs, greater awareness and commitment, improved working environment;

(c) 'Third party' relationships: e.g. less need for external audits and monitoring.

However to achieve such benefits implementation must be comprehensive and effective. This requires substantial and sustained effort over a period of time. Typical guidelines for the introduction of the standards indicate the nature of the implementation task.

1. Implementation should be managed as a major project.
2. The full reasons for implementation must be clear.
3. A receptive environment for implementation must be created.
4. Broad quality systems audit should be undertaken to identify the amount of work required in implementation.
5. A management committee should be established.
6. Training should be provided at all levels.

Table 19.2	BS5750 and ISO 9000 standards

British standard	ISO standards
	ISO 8420
	Quality vocabulary
BS5750 Part 0, Section 0.2	ISO 9004
Principle, concepts and applications	Quality management
Guide to quality management and quality system elements	Quality system elements
BS5750 Part 0, Section 0.1	ISO 9000
Principle, concepts and applications Guide to selection and use	Guidelines for selection and use of standards
BS5750 Part 1	ISO 9001
Specification for design/development, production, installation and servicing	Model for design/development, installation and servicing
BS5750 Part 2	ISO 9002
Specification for production and installation	Model for production/installation
BS5750 Part 3	ISO 9003
Specification for final inspection and test	Model for final inspection and test
	ISO 9004 Part 2
	The services standard
BS5750 Part 4	
Guide to the use of Parts 1, 2 and 3	

EXAMPLE

Avant Hotel

The Avant Hotel in Oldham in the UK was the first hotel to receive BS 5750. The BS 5750 certificate required management to establish quality specification for each product, to determine assignable causes of error, and identify ways of improving product performance. Initial work by the management, and a consultant, aimed at identifying operational objectives and quality standards. A Quality Manual was then developed and BSI assessors visited the hotel to determine whether the manual is a true representation of the standard of operation within the hotel. Routine assessments will take place about every six months. The benefits of BS 5750 include a keener focus on staff training, reduced staff turnover, waste reduction and beneficial publicity.

Source: Callan, R. J. (1992). Quality control at Avant hotels—the debut of BS5750. *Service Industries Journal* **12**(1), pp. 17–33.

BEHAVIOURAL AND ORGANIZATIONAL FACTORS IN QUALITY MANAGEMENT

We have noted the importance of organizational and related factors in the implementation of TQM. Here we will consider some more specific factors.

The impact of lower batch sizes

The implementation of JIT leads to a reduction in batch sizes and inventory levels. One intention is to make the system more responsive by cutting waiting times and through-put times. One effect of this is that disruption at any stage in the system quickly has an impact on the subsequent stage—because there is less 'buffer' between them. A flow stoppage will lead quickly to a starvation at a subsequent stage when the intermediate buffer of inventory has been used up. Control of flow is therefore very important. Similarly the production of a defective item at one stage, if noticeable at all, is soon evident at the next stage. It follows therefore that with an appropriate inspection and feedback system the production of defective items at some part in a system can more quickly be halted when a JIT approach is being used.

EXAMPLE

(a) A two-stage processing system operates with a batch size of 10 units. The cycle time for each unit is 1 minute at each stage. All 10 units must be completed at the first stage, before work can commence on any of them at the next stage. Items are processed in random order.

Time for processing batch through one stage = 10 mins.

Average inter-stage buffer stock ≥ 5 units.

Minimum time lag from production of one defective in a batch:

Stage 1 to identification at stage 2 ≈ 0 mins.

Maximum time lag ≈ 9 mins.

Average time lag ≈ 4.5 mins.

(b) As (a) but batch size = 2 units. Hence:

Minimum time lag ≈ 0 mins.

Maximum time lag ≈ 1 min.

Average time lag ≈ 0.5 mins.

An examination of the extent of quality improvement in Japanese industry associated with the introduction of JIT gives some measure of the importance of this *rapid feedback* characteristic. The earlier recognition of defectives enables early rectification of the problem, reduced wastage and reduced cost. This is especially important where there is a risk that defective items might otherwise pass through several subsequent stages of processing, each adding cost, but with the likelihood that at the end of the process the output will be scrapped or costly to rectify.

This is just one of the quality benefits of JIT. Potentially more important is the *motivational* effect. The fact that poor quality or defective items and their source are more immediately evident encourages those involved to strive for more consistent quality. There is, therefore, a greater motivation to do something about quality problems.

So, the JIT approach, whether in manufacture or service type industries, offers benefits for quality management through quicker identification and rectification of quality problems and greater awareness/involvement of staff. For this reason JIT is often accompanied by TQM characterized by a 'whole organization' approach to quality embracing techniques such as quality circles (discussed later).

People as inspectors

Inspection is an important activity in appraisal (see Figure 19.3). Despite the fact that increasing use is being made of automatic devices, the principal method of inspection, and hence of quality control and assurance, is still often the human inspector. What sort of decisions are inspectors asked to make? Essentially, there are two types: first, those connected with the inspection of variables (i.e. measurement); and second, those connected with the inspection of attributes (i.e. assessment).

In measurement, an inspector compares a characteristic of the item with a defined standard. Often this involves the use of a gauge or instrument against or within which the item is placed. Greater opportunity for error or mistake exists as the ease of comparison of characteristic and standard decreases.

A similar situation exists with respect to assessment. It is not too difficult to make decisions about the acceptability of certain noise levels, and of attributes such as brightness, because the inspector, conceptually at least, is able to compare such attributes with a known standard. In fact these could be considered as only slightly more difficult problems of *measurement* since it is possible to use decibel meters to measure noise levels and light meters to measure light levels. More difficult is the assessment of colour quality, since it is more difficult to define colour standards. The assessment of smell and taste is even more difficult because such characteristic standards are virtually impossible to define.

The more remote and ill-defined the standard the more difficult the comparison of characteristic and standard and, consequently, the more difficult and the more equivocal the decision. It should be clear, therefore, that in order to ensure adequate and consistent inspection procedures, instruments should be used which ensure easy and accurate comparison of characteristic and standard. Furthermore, standards for which instruments cannot be used should be clearly defined, e.g. colour shade cards might be used and inspectors could be trained and retrained to recognize standard noise levels, brightness levels, etc. in much the same way that time study practitioners are trained to recognize a notional concept of standard performance. Workplaces should be designed to permit and, preferably, emphasize the comparison of characteristic and standard.

The following notes will illustrate how the equipment and the situation might be designed to facilitate accurate and consistent inspection.

(a) Ideally the standard itself should be used during the inspection process as, for example, in the physical comparison of dimensions while using Go/No-go gauges.

(b) The standard, if not used during inspection, should be prominently displayed so that comparison of characteristic and standard is easy or, alternatively, so that inspectors might regularly refer to the standard in order to 'recalibrate their perception'.

(c) Where possible, inspection procedures might be 'reconstructed' as pattern recognition procedures. For example, in the design of instrument displays, dials are often arranged so that when each instrument is reading correctly all pointers appear horizontal or vertical. Consequently, when one instrument shows an unusual or wrong reading, the pattern is disrupted and recognition of the fact is made easier. In such a case the acceptable standard has been redefined, acceptability now being associated with consistency of appearance.

(d) Wherever possible the workplace conditions should be arranged to emphasize the characteristic being measured or assessed. For example, lighting might be arranged to emphasize irregularities or roughness of surfaces.

QUALITY IMPROVEMENT PROGRAMMES

'Zero defects' programmes

The original 'zero defects' programme was established by the Martin-Marietta Corporation in the USA around 1962. It was introduced to augment the established statistical quality control programme in order to try to improve product quality beyond that level which might economically be achieved by the statistical procedures. The programme was in large part a 'motivational' device which sought to organize and motivate direct and indirect workers to achieve higher levels of quality in their work. The slogan 'zero defects' was an important part of this motivational exercise.

This original zero defects programme was considered to be highly successful, and the company was able to demonstrate significant improvements in product quality as a result of its introduction. This in turn led other companies in similar industries, e.g. defence and aerospace, to adopt this motivational/organizational approach to quality assurance and, in time, 'zero defects' programmes became well established. It has been suggested that the principal features of such programmes were as follows:[2]

1. A motivational package aimed at reducing individual operator controlled defects. The contents of this package were such things as the 'Big Meeting Rally', 'Pledge Cards', 'Posters', 'Attention getters', 'Scoreboards', etc.

2. A prevention package aimed at reducing management controlled defects. This package centred around 'error cause removal' (ECR) suggestions to be made by employers for subsequent analysis and action by supervisors. These suggestions were submitted to the supervisor on ECR forms which defined the probable error cause and proposed action.

3. Procedures to provide for prompt feedback to the worker.'

Basic behavioural science principles and practices are the foundation of 'zero defects' programmes. Such programmes are based on efforts to motivate workers, and the approaches employed, e.g. providing clear objectives, participation in decision-making and positive

---

[2] Juran, J. M. and Gryna, F. M. (1980) *Quality Planning and Analysis*, 2nd edn. Maidenhead: McGraw-Hill.

feedback on performance, are established principles which have widespread use in other applications. Thus the development of zero defects (ZD) programmes demonstrates a sensible application of established theories in a relatively new field.

Effective ZD programmes would probably involve the following:

(a) some method of establishing agreement on the quality problems, or quality goals to be achieved, or the reasons behind these problems and/or goals;

(b) the use of a well-structured approach to establishing a motivational programme aimed at solving these problems and/or achieving these goals;

(c) the participation of all those involved, i.e. all those who might in some way contribute to the solving of quality problems/achievement of quality objectives, in both the establishment and running of the programme;

(d) the setting of clear targets against which to measure improvements;

(e) the establishment of formalized, regular, simple procedures for reporting achievement on goals;

(f) the establishment of procedures for reinforcing effort in connection with the above;

(g) the organization of jobs, e.g. of workers, quality controllers, supervisors, management, etc. in such a way as to facilitate the above.

EXAMPLE

Zero defects at Lavelle Aircraft

Lavelle Aircraft Company (Philadelphia) initiated a new 'Zero Defects' programme. They believe that, unlike such programmes in the past—which often relied largely on 'hype'—the new programme is solidly based on goals, measurements, and cash incentives for employees and management. It also has some aspects of quality circles. Lavelle realized that, in order to make the programme work, they had to take into account the fact that today's younger workers were brought up in an instrumental and materialistic society. The 'Zero Defects' programme includes separate programmes for:

1.   direct workers and 2. indirect workers, who are eligible for suggestion awards (maintenance, material handlers, etc.), and 3. indirect workers who are not eligible for suggestion awards (engineers, accountants, foremen, etc.). Since implementing the programme, Lavelle has found absenteeism to be down 31 per cent compared to the same period in prior years. Lateness has been reduced 66 per cent from the previous year and the number of direct workers eligible for suggestion awards has increased about 55 per cent from any prior year.

Source: Sklarow, G. (1989) Zero defects: old theme—new twist. *Industry Week* **238**(14), pp. 35–38.

'Quality circles'

The quality circle approach to quality assurance was widely established in Japan before being adopted in Europe and North America. Wherever employed the QC approach rests upon the motivation of individuals and the organization of efforts to improve quality through error reduction, etc., and as such the procedure is designed to supplement conventional quality control procedure as discussed in this chapter and the next.

A quality circle comprises a group of workers and supervisors in a single area or department within an organization, which meets regularly to study ways of improving quality and to monitor progress towards such goals. Thus it is a participative device, perhaps fundamentally more in tune with Japanese culture than with Western culture. A company will seek to establish quality circles largely on a voluntary basis. Those volunteering will often be up to half of the direct and indirect workers involved in the activities of a particular department. They are offered training in the analysis and identification of quality problems and problem-solving procedures. Once this training is completed the circle is formed and is invited to tackle particular quality problems nominated by management or identified by the circle itself. Each quality circle will normally tackle a series of projects, one at a time, identifying quality problems and means of eliminating such problems and establishing targets (often financial targets) to be achieved through quality improvement.

There will be numerous quality circles within an organization and their work will be monitored and co-ordinated by company management, who will be responsible for establishing overall objectives and monitoring the progress towards the achievement of these objectives. Thus the quality control effort within the organization is diffused through all levels rather than being seen as the responsibility of managers or indirect, often specialist, staff.

The *original* concept of QC may be of relevance only in a Japanese type of culture. For example, originally most of the training for those involved in QC and the meetings of the circles themselves took place out of working hours and on a voluntary and often unpaid basis. Normally there was no financial incentive in the improvement of quality except that obtained indirectly through improvements in the performance and financial status of the organization as a whole. The only major incentive was that of obtaining further training and of recognition within the organization. This analysis, however, conceals the fundamental nature of the programme, i.e. that of motivating individuals through participation in decision-making and reinforcement by positive feedback of results. Fundamentally such an approach is 'culture free' and can possibly be employed with benefit in other situations where quality performance is largely a function of individual effort and attention. Certainly the use of QC in Europe and North America does not follow exactly the pattern established in Japan, and interest in this type of approach to quality 'assurance' is increasing.

Quality circles have some similarity to ZD programmes; however, the former is essentially a group approach and the latter individual. The QC methodology (which is almost a ritualistic approach in Japan) probably requires considerable effort to establish and sustain, and it is perhaps for this reason that those companies which have adopted the approach, especially in Japan, have tended to concentrate on this one concept, rather than trying to sustain several different types of programme or campaign.

EXAMPLE

Quality circles in education

The Quality Circle process introduced in the South Huntington School District on Long Island in New York, early in the 1980s, has gradually evolved and changed the schools from a relatively autocratic management system to a far more participative one. Initially, staff identified work-related problems, put problem-solving techniques to work, researched data, reviewed findings and proposed solutions to the next higher level of management. Following the success of these first quality circles, joint decision-making groups were started for food-service workers, elementary-level teachers, and students. Student quality circles have completed presentations on several subjects, including: 1. improving relations between students and bus drivers, 2. improving menu selection in the cafeteria, and 3. helping young people deal with peer pressure.

Source: Wilson, J. (1990) Investing in our futures: quality and participation for students and school staff. *Journal of Quality and Partn*. July/Aug, pp. 78–81.

Taguchi method

Taguchi developed the concept of the 'Quality Loss Function' (QLF). The QLF is a measure of the economic loss or penalty suffered by the customer when he or she receives an item (or service) which fails, in any way and to any extent, to meet the target specified quality. Such losses would normally include increased maintenance costs, increased operating costs, adverse environmental costs, etc. Use of the QLF approach reminds us that any variation from a target specification incurs unexpected and unwelcome costs for the customer. In general, the greater the variation, the greater such costs. It is conceivable that an item could be judged to be satisfactory in that it exceeded a minimum required specification; however, failure to meet a higher target level imposes costs on the customer. So the QLF of two items may be different, even though both may have been judged acceptable.

The QLF provides a means to quantify quality improvements and thus to decide on where and how best to seek improved quality. (This is part of a broader approach which focuses the design of inputs rather than the traditional approach of controlling outputs from the system.)

Ishikawa (Fishbone) method

Kaoru Ishikawa developed the quality circles approach described above. He also introduced the term Company Wide Quality Control (CWQC) for he felt that the Total Quality Management approach laid insufficient emphasis on the inputs on non-specialists within the organization. Ishikawa is also credited with the development of the 'Fishbone' diagram: it is a cause and effect diagram showing the various possible causes of a quality problem and their interrelationship.

KEY POINTS FOR CHAPTER 19

Acceptable *Quality* is defined, primarily, by the customer.

Actual Quality is a function of original/intended specification, and the degree of conformity to that specification.

Attitudes and expectations of quality are important.

Fitness for purpose, a common definition of quality, exists when an item or service achieves or exceeds customers' expectations.

The two basic dimensions of quality are:

Functional, i.e.	utility
	reliability
	usability/serviceability
Non-functional, i.e.:	design
	symbolic factors

Quality-related costs influence the intended specified quality level. Such costs are:

system

control

consequent

Investment in certain costs reduces exposure to others, e.g. more spent on system and control costs reduces the consequent cost of inadequate quality.

Theoretically, an *optimal quality* level can be identified at which total cost is lowest. In practice, *our expectations change*, so do the cost functions, and the appropriate quality level increases.

Total Quality Management (TQM) is about the management of 'life cycle' quality through the use of an organization-wide approach.

Effective TQM requires:

leadership

corporate commitment

motivation and training

customer orientation.

Quality standards aim to ensure the existence of adequate procedures. The main standards are:

BSEN5750 ISO 9000

ISO 9000.

Effective TQM requires consideration of *behavioural and organizational* factors.

Quality improvement procedures exist, e.g.

zero defects

quality circles

Taguchi

Ishikawa.

FURTHER READING

Dale, B. G. (1994) (Ed.) *Managing Quality*, 2nd Ed. Prentice Hall.

Zeithaml, V. A., Parasuraman, A. and Berry, L. L. (1990) *Delivering Service Quality*. Free Press.

Dale, B. and Cooper, C. (1992) *Total Quality and Human Resources*. Oxford: Blackwell.

King Taylor, L. (1993) *Quality—Sustaining Customer Service*. Century Books.

Robson, M. (1982) *Quality Circles—A Practical Guide*. Gower: Aldershot.

CASE STUDY

The following case, from Part 9 of the book, is relevant to the topics covered in this chapter.

Case No	Name	Country
8	The Shire of Corio	Australia

QUESTIONS FOR CHAPTER 19

19.1 Why do some quality-related costs, incurred after delivery of goods or after completion of service, fall on the provider rather than on the customer? Give examples and explanations.

19.2 'Quality is Free': explain and discuss. Give examples.

19.3 What does 'Total' mean in TQM?

19.4 Why are Quality Improvement campaigns sometimes necessary, and how can they be integrated with a TQM programme in an organization?

Chapter 20

Quality control and reliability

ISSUES

What are the 3 stages of process quality control and
  assurnace?
What procedures can be used in these 3 stages?
What are the roles of inspection and sampling?
What is acceptance sampling?
What are control charts?
What is reliability?

In this chapter we outline some of the procedures which are available for controlling quality. We are in effect dealing with the implementation of one part of the quality management activity identified in Figure 19.3 in the previous chapter. Figure 20.1 shows the link. We are dealing with control activities and costs, in particular with Appraisal but also, to some extent, with Correction. We shall refer to the activities in this area as Quality Control and Assurance, because it is necessary for us to make a distinction between two types of activities. Notice, however, that the assurance activities to which we shall refer are not the same as those mentioned when we discussed investment and prevention costs in the previous chapter.

To a large extent, the emphasis is on statistical procedures. These procedures have been in use for many years. They have not changed much, but what has changed is their role within the overall framework of the management of quality. These are the important but subsidiary procedures which are used as part of the implementation of an overall or total managerial approach to delivering product or service quality. In the final part of this chapter we shall briefly consider the nature of reliability.

QUALITY CONTROL AND ASSURANCE FOR ITEMS

We shall concentrate now on systems for ensuring conformity to specification, i.e. the management of process quality. Throughout we shall refer to items—i.e. physical entities—whether they be materials, parts, products or customers. Such items are the things which

Figure 20.1 The link between quality control costs and control and assurance procedures

⑥
MANAGEMENT

① INVESTMENT   ② PREVENTION   ③ APPRAISAL   ④ CORRECTION   ⑤ USAGE   ⑦ MARKET

SYSTEM COSTS   CONTROL COSTS   CONSEQUENT COSTS

⬇

QUALITY CONTROL
AND ASSURANCE
RELATING TO:

INPUTS

↓

PROCESSES

↓

OUTPUTS

flow into, through and from conversion systems. We shall assume that the specification of the output, i.e. the item of primary interest to the customer, has been established and that an appropriate process is available and hence it is now our aim to ensure conformity to such specification.

To achieve this objective, three stages can be defined. We must first ensure that only items which conform to the given specifications are accepted as inputs. Second, we must implement control procedures to attempt to ensure that, during the conversion of these items, only outputs which conform to the specifications are produced. And finally, we must ensure that only those items which conform to the specifications are actually allowed to exit the system. These procedures are outlined diagrammatically in Figure 20.2, and are discussed below.

Control of inputs

An organization may adopt one or (usually) both of the following procedures in an attempt to ensure that it uses only items which fully conform to the required specifications and standards.

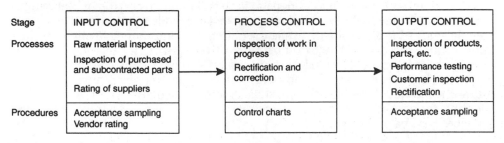

Stage	INPUT CONTROL	PROCESS CONTROL	OUTPUT CONTROL
Processes	Raw material inspection Inspection of purchased and subcontracted parts Rating of suppliers	Inspection of work in progress Rectification and correction	Inspection of products, parts, etc. Performance testing Customer inspection Rectification
Procedures	Acceptance sampling Vendor rating	Control charts	Acceptance sampling

Figure 20.2 The stages, processes and procedures of quality control and assurance

365

1. The items which are supplied will normally have been subjected by the supplier to some form of quality control. The purchasing firm will often monitor the quality controls conducted by the supplier. It may ask to be supplied with regular information about the quality of the items as they are prepared, ask for copies of all the final inspection documents to be supplied, or ask a third party (e.g. an insurance company) to ensure that the items conform to the required minimum quality. However, despite such precautionary steps, inspection of purchased items will normally also be conducted on receipt, and before use. One or both of the following procedures will normally be adopted:

   (a) exhaustive inspection of every item received;

   (b) an inspection of a sample of the items received—this procedure, which is commonly adopted, is referred to as *acceptance sampling* and is discussed in some detail later in the chapter.

2. The organization will purchase only from those suppliers which are known to be likely to provide acceptable items. To ensure this the purchaser may undertake some form of *vendor rating* (VR), i.e. a comparative rating of suppliers taking into account quality-related factors such as:

   (a) percentage of acceptable items received in the past;

   (b) quality of packaging;

   (c) price;

   (d) percentage of warranty claims which can be traced to defective items provided by the vendor.

   The commonest VR procedures will be discussed below.

Control of process

Inspection of items between operations is undertaken, not only to ensure that faulty or defective items do not proceed to the subsequent operations, but also in order to predict when the process is likely to produce defective items so that necessary preventive adjustments can be made. Quality control during the process often involves the use of *control charts*, which will be discussed in some detail shortly. The number and location of inspections should reflect both the probability of faults or defectives occurring and the consequences of such occurrences, as well as the cost of conducting inspection. Frequently, technical considerations determine the position and number of inspection operations, but nevertheless, within certain limitations, operations management is usually able to design the inspection procedure.

Well-defined procedures should be established for the selection and inspection of the items, for the recording and analysis of data, for reprocessing, rectifying or scrapping of defectives, and for the feedback of information. We have tended to assume that a group of people attached to a separate department within the organization is involved in these quality control procedures, but two other alternatives exist. First, automatic 'on-line' inspection or gauging could be used. Such procedures are increasingly used for automatic inspection and checking of variables (dimensions); often the equipment involves a 'feedback' to the machine, which is self-correcting. A second alternative is for workers to be responsible for checking and inspecting their own work. In such cases appropriate time allowances must be provided.

Control of outputs

Quality inspection of output items is essential because unless defective output is identified by the producer it will be passed on to the consumer. Final inspection is unfortunate, since the purpose of all previous inspection has been to ensure that defective or faulty output is not produced. However, it is not a reflection on the ineffectiveness of earlier inspection, since items can be damaged at any time during the entire process.

Final inspection may involve only a sampling procedure, or exhaustive checks. Suitable procedures must be designed for the collection and retention of inspection data, for the correction, replacement or further examination of faulty items and, if necessary, for the adjustment or modification of either previous inspection or processing operations to ensure that faulty items do not continue to be produced—at least not for the same reasons.

Inspection of output is normally conducted in a similar manner to the inspection of input items, the procedures being referred to as *acceptance sampling*.

QUALITY CONTROL PROCEDURES

We have identified three basic stages in quality control (Figure 20.2), i.e.

1. Control of quality of input items.

2. Control of quality during operations.

3. Control of quality of output items.

These three stages are complementary. Inadequate control at one stage will necessitate greater effort at subsequent stages. In the remainder of this chapter we shall focus on quality control procedures, and shall discuss three procedures:

1. Vendor rating

2. Acceptance sampling   involving the *inspection* of items.

3. Control charts

Vendor rating is concerned with the monitoring of the performance and the selection of suppliers. Acceptance sampling is of relevance for the control of input and output quality. Control charts are of relevance for the control of quality during operations.

Vendor rating

The supplies received by an organization are normally evaluated and used in purchasing decision-making. In vendor rating, this evaluation process is formalized to provide a quantitative measure of 'vendor quality'. Such ratings are meant primarily to provide an overall rating of a vendor for use in reviewing, comparing and selecting vendors. Vendor rating is therefore an integral part of a rigorous purchasing procedure, and an aspect of quality assurance for use alongside, or in some cases instead of, acceptance sampling.

It will often be difficult to create a single numerical quality/rating score because of the different factors which must be taken into account. These may include:

(a) the 'lot quality' (number of lots rejected);

(b) the 'parts quality' (percentage of items defective);

(c) the 'characteristic quality' of items (e.g. percentage active ingredient, performance, etc.).

Because such factors differ in importance in different companies and for different items, the vendor rating method employed must be tailored for specific applications. However, in general such methods will fall into one of the following four categories:

1. Categorical plan: a non-quantitative system in which those responsible for buying hold a periodic meeting to discuss vendors and rate each one, usually only as 'plus', 'minus' or 'neutral'.

2. Weighted point plan: each vendor is scored on quality, price and service. These factors are weighted and a composite rating is then calculated for each vendor. An example is shown in Table 20.1.

Table 20.1	Example of a 'weighted point' vendor rating plan. A hospital purchases sterile supplies from three companies. Data are collected over a one-year period so that the three suppliers can be compared		
	Supplier A	**Supplier B**	**Supplier C**
1. Lots received[a]	60	60	20
2. Lots accepted[a]	54	56	16
3. Percentage accepted[b]	90.0	93.3	80.0
4. Quality rating $((3) \times 0.4)$[b]	36	37.3	32
5. Net price[a]	0.93	1.12	1.23
6. $\dfrac{\text{Lowest price}}{\text{Net price}} \times 100$[b]	100	83	75.6
7. Price rating $((6) \times 0.35)$[b]	35	29	26.5
8. Delivery promises kept[a]	90%	95%	100%
9. Service rating $((8) \times 0.25)$[b]	22.5	23.8	25
10. Total rating $(4) + (7) + (9)$[b]	93.5	90.1	83.5

[a] Data
[b] Calculations
Note. Here the relative importances of quality, price and service have been judged to be 0.4, 0.35 and 0.25.

3. Cost ratio plan: compares vendors on the *total* cost involved for a specific purchase. This will include:

   (a) price quotation;

   (b) quality costs (e.g. repair, return or replacement of defectives);

   (c) delivery costs.

4. Quality only rating plans: the first three types of plans above recognize item quality in the rating of vendors but in no case is the rating restricted to quality alone. In the fourth type of plan *only* quality is taken into account.

Many such vendor rating systems exist. In selecting a system for a particular situation, a basic decision must be whether the rating will be based solely on quality performance or on additional considerations such as cost and delivery.

True vendor ratings (for the purpose of making decisions on retaining or dropping vendors) are published infrequently. These ratings are not to be confused with monthly publications of 'vendor performance', which serve mainly as product rating rather than vendor rating.

It is important that vendor ratings be used as an *aid*, and not as the sole criterion in vendor decision-making. It should be remembered that:

1. A single index will often hide important detail.
2. The specific purpose of the rating should be kept in mind.

Most vendor rating plans involve some degree of subjectivity and guesswork. The mathematical treatment of data in the plans often tends to obscure the fact that the results are no more accurate than the assumptions on which the quantitative data are based. In the final analysis, therefore, supplier evaluation must represent a combined appraisal of facts, quantitative computations and value judgements. In most cases vendor rating will be used along with an acceptance sampling plan.

Vendor rating is an important defect prevention device if it is used in an atmosphere of interdependence between vendor and customer. This means that the customer must:

(a) make the investment of time, effort and special skills to help the poor vendors to improve;

(b) be willing to change the specifications when warranted (in some companies 20 to 40 per cent of rejected purchases can be used without any quality compromise).

Finally, in cases of consistently poor vendors who cannot respond to help, the rating highlights them as candidates to be dropped as vendors.

EXAMPLE

ICL

The UK-based computer company ICL has been using performance measurement under its vendor accreditation framework for partnership sourcing for several years. The effectiveness of performance measurement is based around agreed measurable objectives and the monitoring of likely indicators of success. An immediate benefit to ICL was to distinguish between service problems caused by supplier process failure and those rooted in ICL's own internal processes. Defining the requirement and agreeing objective measurement gets both partners to focus on what is jointly required from the relationship.

Source: Mannion, D. (1994) Performance measurement: people, purchasing, partnership. *Purchasing and Supply Management*, Jan., pp. 34–6.

Inspection

In this section we shall consider both acceptance sampling and control chart procedures. Both procedures will involve the *inspection* of items so that a decision can be made on whether an item, or the batch from which a sample of items is drawn, is acceptable or not. The planning of inspection may involve deciding *where* to inspect. These problems will be considered before we look at acceptance sampling and control chart techniques.

The location of inspection

There will normally be some choice for the location of quality inspection points in operating systems. For example, we may choose to locate inspection before or after the inventories which exist in operating systems, or between an operation and its supplier, and its customer. This will provide a wide choice of locations but, additionally, since most businesses are multi-stage, it will usually be necessary to decide where to inspect within a sequence of operations. Rarely will items be inspected formally after every stage in the system, since to do so would be expensive. The problem, therefore, is to locate inspection operations, taking into account the cost of inspection and the benefits of inspecting (or the risks of not inspecting).

In practice such decisions are often based on empirical and quantitative rules. For example, good 'rules of thumb' are:

1. Inspect before costly operations in order to avoid high processing costs for defective items.

2. Inspect before any series of operations during which inspection will be difficult and/or costly.

3. Inspect after operations which generally result in a high rate of defectives.

4. Inspect before operations which would conceal defects previously caused.

5. Inspect before a 'point of no return', i.e. after which any rectification is impossible.

6. Inspect before points at which potential damage may be caused, i.e. before the use of equipment which would be damaged through the processing of faulty items.

7. Inspect before a change in quality responsibility, e.g. between departments.

Acceptance sampling

Inspection of each critical feature of every item received may be a very desirable procedure in that, by so doing, no defective items would pass unnoticed, except by a mistake or error in the inspection procedure. There are, however, several reasons why such a procedure may be uneconomical or even impossible:

1. Inspection may cause damage or even complete destruction of the items.

2. The accuracy of inspection may be diminished after frequent repetition. For example, an inspection task may take only a few seconds to complete but if this is undertaken continually over a long period, it may be excessively fatiguing and boring for the inspector, whose accuracy and judgement might then be affected.

3. Handling of the item may result in deterioration, or, alternatively, items may naturally deteriorate rapidly prior to use, and lengthy inspection procedures may be undesirable.

4. Inspection may be a particularly expensive procedure involving the unpacking or dismantling of items, the use of special machines, etc.

5. Inspection may be a hazardous, even dangerous procedure.

For these reasons, some form of *sampling inspection* is often required. In acceptance sampling, decisions about the quality of batches of items are made after inspection of only a portion of those items. If the sample of items conforms to the requisite quality levels then the whole batch from which it came is accepted. If the sample does not conform to the requisite quality level, then the whole batch is rejected or subjected to further inspection. Adopting this procedure, decisions about the quality levels of items can be made fairly quickly, easily and cheaply. However, a certain amount of risk is involved, since there is the possibility that the sample taken will not be of the same quality as the batch from which it came. A greater proportion of defectives in the sample will lead us erroneously to attribute a lower quality level to the batch and vice versa.

Several types of acceptance sampling plan may be used. For example, some necessitate taking a *single* sample lot from a batch, upon which a quality decision is made, while others may necessitate the use of *multiple* samples from the same batch. Plans will also vary in the types of measurement that are involved. The most common, and simplest, type of inspection decision involves classifying items as good or bad, as acceptable or unacceptable. This is referred to as acceptance sampling by *attributes*. Less often, acceptance sampling by *variables* is used, in which the purpose of inspection is to obtain exact measurements for dimensions. We shall concentrate on the more usual procedure, which is *single acceptance sampling by attributes*.

Acceptance sampling by attributes is suitable not only for items whose critical features cannot easily be measured, such as the quality of finish of furniture, the power of light bulbs, etc., but may also be used where inspection is concerned with dimensions, since such dimensions ultimately are either acceptable or not. For example, the size of a hole in a component will either fall within the upper and lower tolerance specified, and hence be acceptable, or if it does not then it will be rejected. In such cases Go/No go gauges are often used to check the acceptability of variables.

Customers would ideally like 100 per cent of the products which they obtain to be acceptable but this, as we have pointed out previously, is impractical. Therefore some lower quality level must, of necessity, be agreed. Even so only by 100 per cent inspection (and even then, only if there are no errors during inspection) can we be absolutely certain that a batch conforms to this agreed standard. In Figure 20.3 100 per cent inspection has been used, so we can be 100 per cent certain that batches do, or do not, conform to the agreed quality level, which is a maximum of 20 per cent defectives per batch (again assuming no mistakes during inspection).

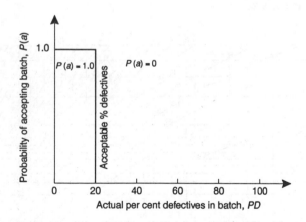

Figure 20.3 The probability of accepting batches, with 100% inspection (acceptable percentage defective 20%)

A curve such as this is known as an *operating characteristic* curve and shows the probability of accepting batches with various percentage defectives. Operating characteristic (OC) curves can be calculated and drawn for any sampling plan if we specify:

(a) the sample size n;

(b) the acceptance number, i.e. the maximum allowance number of defects in the sample c.

An example for a sampling plan with $c \leq 1$ and $n = 10$ is shown in Figure 20.4.

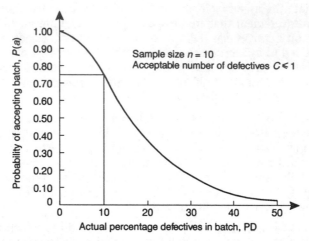

Figure 20.4 Operating characteristic curve ($n = 10$; $C \leq 1$)

For simplicity, the calculations may be performed with the assistance of the *Thorndike chart*. This chart, as shown in Figure 20.5, gives the probability of *c* or less defectives (*P(a)* on the vertical axis) for given values of PD×*n*/100 (on the horizontal axis)

where *PD* = actual per cent defectives in a batch or lot

    n = sample size

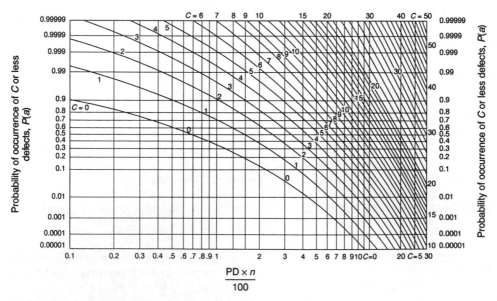

Figure 20.5 Thorndike chart. Adapted with permission from Dodge, H. F. and Romig, H. G. (1959) *Sampling Inspection Tables*, 2nd edn. London: Wiley.

EXAMPLE

Use the Thorndike chart to construct an operating characteristic curve for

$n = 100$ sample size

$c \leq 3$ allowable number of defects

Answer

Actual percentage of defectives in batch (PD)	$\dfrac{PD \times n}{100}$	P(a)
1	1	0.98
2	2	0.86
3	3	0.65
4	4	0.44
5	5	0.26
6	6	0.15
7	7	0.08
8	8	0.04
9	9	0.02
10	10	0.01

These figures can now be used to plot an OC curve of the type shown previously.

The ability of a sampling procedure to distinguish between good and bad batches is primarily a function of the sample size. If three sampling processes are designed to test the quality level of batches of components for which the acceptable quality level is 1 per cent or less defectives, then the procedure using the largest sample will be more accurate than those using smaller samples, particularly where the actual percentage of defectives in the batch is high. Figure 20.6 shows three such OC curves, each of which is fairly accurate up to a percentage defective level just below the acceptable level but, above that point, curve 3 is superior. As the sample size is increased, the curves become steeper and begin to approach the perfectly discriminating OC curve given in Figure 20.3.

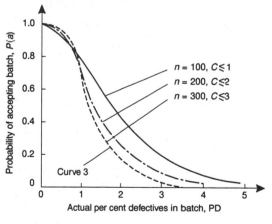

Figure 20.6 Operating characteristic curves

The design of single acceptance sampling plans

The merit of any sampling plan depends on the relationship of sampling cost to risk. As the cost of inspection decreases and the cost of accepting defective items increases, then the merit of inspection increases and the more willing we are to use larger samples. The OC curve shows, for any plan, both the probability of accepting batches with more than the acceptable number of defectives and the probability of rejecting batches with fewer than the acceptable number of defectives.

It is the consumer's desire to reduce the probability of accepting batches including too many defectives and the producer's desire to minimize the probability of rejecting batches including an acceptable number of defectives. These are called respectively the *consumer's risk* (β) and the *producer's risk* (α). These two values are used in order to design acceptance sampling plans and, in addition, two further points are used:

1. *Acceptable quality level (AQL)*—the desired quality level, at which probability of acceptance should be high.

2. *Lot tolerance per cent defective (LTPD)*—a quality level below which batches are considered unacceptable, and a level at which probability of acceptance should be low.

These four values are shown on the OC curve in Figure 20.7. The consumer's risk (β) is often specified at about 10 per cent and the producer's risk (α) at approximately 5 per cent. Acceptable quality level is often around 2 per cent and lot tolerance per cent defective around 10 per cent. These four figures are specified in designing the sampling plan. All that then remains is to construct an OC curve which passes through the two points (*AQL*; α) and (*LTPD*; β). This can be done by trial and error, selecting various values for the sample size (n) and acceptable number of defectives (c) and substituting into the binomial probability formula until an acceptable curve is obtained, or by use of the Thorndike chart. The OC curve constructed in this way determines the sample size n and the value of c to be used in the acceptance sampling procedure.

Defective items found in the *samples* will always be either rectified or replaced. If, during inspection, samples are drawn from the batch which include more than the acceptable number of defectives, then two alternatives are available:

Figure 20.7 Operating characteristic (OC) curve and points specifying a sampling plan

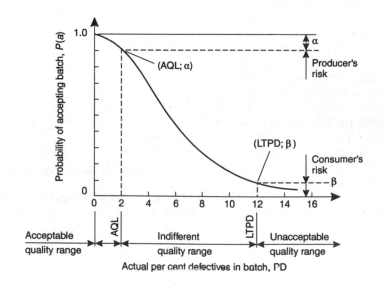

1. Reject and scrap the complete *batch*.

2. Subject the complete *batch* to 100 per cent inspection and replace or rectify all faulty items found in it.

The choice of alternative (1) or (2) will depend on the value of the items concerned and the cost to replace or rectify them, but often, in order to obtain a high-quality level for batches with a minimum of inspection, the second alternative is adopted.

Double and multiple sampling

The total amount of inspection required to obtain a certain output quality level can be reduced if *double* or *multiple sampling* is used.

In single acceptance sampling as described above, the decision to accept or to reject the batch of items is dependent on the inspection of a single random sample from that batch. In *double* sampling there exists the possibility of delaying that decision until a second sampling has been taken. A random sample of *n* items is drawn from the batch, each item is inspected and the number of defectives (*c*) is counted. If this number is less than or equal to a given acceptance number (*c*1) then the batch is accepted. Alternatively, if it is greater than a larger given acceptance number (*c*2) the batch is rejected. If, however, the number of defectives in the sample falls between these two levels, then the result is inconclusive and a second sample is drawn from the same batch. Again, the number of defectives is counted and this number is added to the number of defectives found in the first sample. If the total number is less than *c*2, the batch is accepted, but if the total number is greater than *c*2, the batch is rejected.

Multiple sampling is a similar procedure, but here there is the possibility of taking more than two samples from the same batch. An initial sample is drawn from the batch and, depending on the number of defectives found, the batch is accepted (*c*≤*c*1), rejected (*c*>*c*2) or a decision is deferred (*c*1<*c*<*c*2). The number of defectives in the second sample is added to the number found in the first and the total is compared with two further acceptance numbers, the batch being accepted or rejected or the decision deferred as before. This procedure is repeated until a decision can be made. A multiple sampling plan is depicted diagrammatically in Figure 20.8.

Sequential sampling is a similar procedure but involves taking one at a time from the batch and basing acceptance or rejection decisions on the number of defectives accumulated.

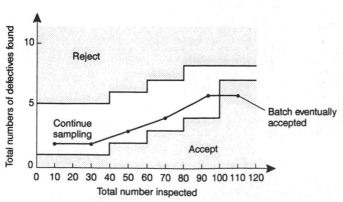

Figure 20.8 Multiple sampling plan (for batch sizes of 500 to 799 for 3% AQL)

Double or multiple sampling permits smaller-sized samples to be taken. Consequently, on the occasions when the items or material inspected are well within, or well beyond, acceptable quality levels, fewer items need to be inspected. In such cases double or multiple sampling is more economical than single acceptance sampling.

Control charts

Irrespective of how well designed or maintained manufacturing equipment is, or how skilfully it is used, the items produced by such equipment will inevitably be subject to some variation. This variation might be caused by numerous factors, but we can classify types of variation into two categories:

(a) **usual** *or* **chance** variations, which are likely to occur in a random manner and about which comparatively little can be done;

(b) **unusual** *or* **assignable** variations, which occur less frequently and which can normally be traced to some 'external' cause, such as wear on tools or faulty materials.

'Usual' variations are normally of a lesser magnitude than 'unusual' variations and, since they result from some inherent process variability, they occur randomly and can be described by the normal probability distribution. Quality controllers define *limits* within which variations are acceptable and beyond which they are either unacceptable, or necessitate some examination. Such limits are called *control limits*. For example, for a normal probability distribution, 99.73 per cent of all chance or usual variations would be expected to occur within limits placed three standard deviations larger and smaller then the mean value of the variable. Therefore any variation occurring beyond such limits would probably have resulted from some other unusual or assignable cause and would merit some investigation.

For example, after a pilot investigation of the length of rods produced by a cropping press, we discover that the mean length $(\bar{x})$ is 100 cm, and that after excluding the faulty rods that were produced when the setting on the press was accidentally altered, the standard deviation (σ),[1] which is a measure of the variability of the rods produced, was 2.1 cm. We could then set up a control chart with a mean of 100 and control limits of plus and minus three standard deviations. Such a chart (Figure 20.9) might then be used to test the quality of rods produced by this press. Rather than examine every rod, we take a sample rod every hour and examine it, then plot our result on the control chart, and by so doing we are able to discover that the process, while initially 'in control', is now running 'out of control' and often producing items which are too long.

A process is considered to be statistically 'under' or 'in control' if it regularly produces items whose attributes or variables fall within the acceptable or tolerable range, whereas a process is said to be 'out of control' if items are produced whose attributes or variables are beyond the acceptable or tolerable range. In this case (Figure 20.9) the process appears to have gone out of control because of the change in the mean value $(\bar{x})$

Figure 20.9 A simple control chart for the lengths of rods

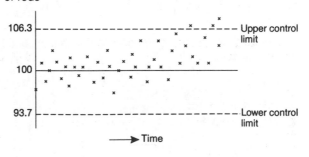

---

[1] The standard deviation (σ) is calculated using the formula:

$$\sigma = \sqrt{\frac{\Sigma(\bar{X} - X^2)}{\bar{N}}}$$

where X = length of individual bar
$\bar{X}$ = mean length of all bars measured
$\bar{N}$ = number of bars measured

This is only one of the three possible types of change which might occur in a process, i.e. in Figure 20.10, (1) has resulted from a change in the value of the mean, (2) has resulted from a change in the standard deviation, and (3) has resulted from a change in both of these characteristics. Each of these changes or disturbances in the process might lead to the production of defective items, but in each case the use of a control chart to monitor output will enable such items to be observed and action to be taken to prevent the production of defective items.

Figure 20.10 Frequency distribution showing types of change which might occur in a process

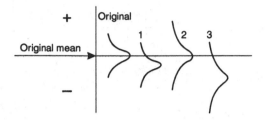

Control charts would therefore be used as follows:

Step 1 Decide which characteristics of the items are to be controlled.

Step 2 Conduct a pilot study of the process to determine the mean and the standard deviation of the characteristics.

Step 3 Design the control chart(s) using these data.

Step 4 Check these control limits to ensure that they are economically feasible and realistic.

Step 5 Take samples of the process output and plot the characteristics on the control charts.

Step 6 Whenever points fall beyond the control limits:

    (a)   investigate causes;

    (b)   take corrective action;

    (c)   inspect remainder of batch if necessary.

Control charts for variables

Control charts for variables are usually based on the normal probability distribution and are most frequently designed to test the *means* of samples rather than individual measurements. In practice, therefore, the dimensions of individual components are not plotted separately on control charts; only the *mean*, or average value of the dimensions in the sample, is plotted.

Two upper and two lower control limits are normally used, these being referred to as the *upper and lower warning limit* and the *upper and lower action limit*. If points fall beyond the warning limits, this is taken to indicate that the process may be going out of control and that careful observation or additional sampling is required. Points falling beyond the action limits indicate the need to take immediate steps to establish and eliminate the causes. Action limits are normally set so as to exclude only 0.2 per cent of the points through usual or random variations. Warning limits are set so as to exclude 5 per cent of the points through usual or random variation.

The following formulae are used

where σ = standard deviation of individual items

$\bar{w}_x$ = mean range of several samples

d_n = a constant depending on the sample size

$$\sigma = \frac{\bar{w}_x}{d_n}$$

Upper action limit $\quad = \bar{X} + \dfrac{3.09(\bar{w}_x/d_n)}{\sqrt{n}}$

Upper warning limit $\quad = \bar{X} + \dfrac{1.96(\bar{w}_x/d_n)}{\sqrt{n}}$

Centre (= process mean) = $\bar{X}$

Lower warning limit $\quad = \bar{X} - \dfrac{1.96(\bar{w}_x/d_n)}{\sqrt{n}}$

Lower action limit $\quad = \bar{X} - \dfrac{3.09(\bar{w}_x/d_n)}{\sqrt{n}}$

(where $\bar{X}$ = overall process mean value).

To simplify such calculations even further, tables for $3.09/\sqrt{n}d_n$ and $1.96/\sqrt{n}d_n$ can be used (see Table 20.2).

Even though the mean value is constant, we have seen how the process might produce defective items by an increase in variability (Figure 20.10). Consequently, a process cannot be said to be fully under control unless *both* mean and standard deviation are under control. We should, therefore, also construct a control chart on which to plot standard

Table 20.2	Factors for calculating control limits for control charts for means		
Sample size n	Constant d_n	Factors (m) for warning limits $1.96 = \dfrac{1.96}{\sqrt{n}d_n}$	Factors (m) for action limits $3.09 = \dfrac{3.09}{\sqrt{n}d_n}$
2	1.128	1.23	1.94
3	1.693	0.67	1.05
4	2.059	0.48	0.75
5	2.236	0.38	0.59
6	2.334	0.32	0.50
7	2.704	0.27	0.43
8	2.847	0.24	0.38
9	2.970	0.22	0.35
10	3.078	0.20	0.32

Note: To calculate control limits, multiply w_x by factor (m) and add or subtract from $\bar{X}$.

deviations, but, for the same reasons as before, it is found to be easier to use the range as a measure of variability. In much the same way as for control limits for means, factors can be calculated from which control limits for ranges can be established. These are shown in Table 20.3.

Table 20.3	Factors for calculating control limits for control charts for ranges			
Sample size n	Factor (R) for warning limits		Factor (R) for action limits	
	Upper	Lower	Upper	Lower
2	2.81	0.04	4.12	0.00
3	2.17	0.18	2.98	0.04
4	1.93	0.29	2.57	0.10
5	1.81	0.37	2.34	0.16
6	1.72	0.42	2.21	0.21
7	1.66	0.46	2.11	0.26
8	1.62	0.50	2.04	0.29
9	1.58	0.52	1.99	0.32
10	1.56	0.54	1.94	0.35

Note: To calculate control limit, multiply w_x by the appropriate factor (R)

EXAMPLE

Again referring to a cropping press on which bars are to be cut continually to a length of 12 cm, a random sample of five bars is taken from each hour's production, and for each sample the mean and range are calculated, i.e.

Sample (size $n = 5$)	Sample mean ($\bar{X}$)	Sample range (w_x)
9.00 a.m.	12.005	0.007
10.00 a.m.	12.001	0.008
11.00 a.m.	11.993	0.010
12.00	11.991	0.003
1.00 p.m.	12.001	0.006
2.00 p.m.	12.003	0.015
3.00 p.m.	11.995	0.011
4.00 p.m.	12.004	0.008
5.00 p.m.	12.003	0.009
6.00 p.m.	12.000	0.010
7.00 p.m.	11.999	0.006
8.00 p.m.	11.997	0.013
9.00 p.m.	11.999	0.011
10.00 p.m.	12.000	0.010
Total	167.991	0.127

From an earlier pilot study the overall mean ($\bar{X}$) and average range ($\bar{w}$) have been found to be:

$$\bar{X} = 11.9994; \quad \bar{W} = 0.0091$$

Now using the factors from Table 19.2 and Table 19.3, control limits for means and ranges can be calculated.

Mean
$$
\begin{cases}
\text{UAL} & = 11.9994 + 0.59(0.0091) = 12.0048 \\
\text{UWL} & = 11.9994 + 0.38(0.0091) = 12.0029 \\
\text{Centre} & = 11.9994 \\
\text{LWL} & = 11.9994 - 0.38(0.0091) = 11.9959 \\
\text{LAL} & = 11.9994 - 0.59(0.0091) = 11.9940
\end{cases}
$$

Range
$$
\begin{cases}
\text{UAL} & = 0.0091 \times 2.34 & = 0.0213 \\
\text{UWL} & = 0.0091 \times 1.81 & = 0.0165 \\
\text{Centre} & = 0.0091 \\
\text{LWL} & = 0.0091 \times 0.37 & = 0.0034 \\
\text{LAL} & = 0.0091 \times 0.16 & = 0.0015
\end{cases}
$$

The control charts can now be constructed using these figures and the individual sample means and ranges plotted (Figure 20.11). The charts indicate that the process is beginning to settle down. The mean lengths from early samples were probably unacceptable, but towards the end of the day the process was under better control.

Figure 20.11 Control chart for means and for range

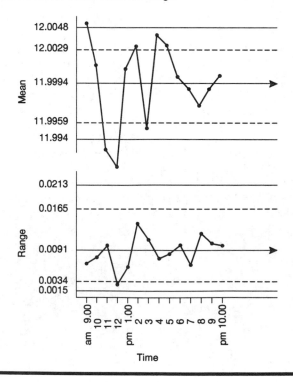

Design limits and control limits

The control limits we have discussed do not necessarily bear any relationship to the design limits, since in constructing the control charts no account was taken of the dimensional tolerance specified for items. It is possible then, using the control charts, to accept items which are *not* manufactured to design specifications. To avoid such a situation the design limits, i.e. the tolerances on a dimension, must fall outside the action limits of the control chart, i.e. the dimensional tolerance should be a minimum of 6.18σ. During design it is important, therefore, to ensure that manufacturing equipment is capable of producing parts to the required tolerance so that (say) 99.8 per cent of the items should be within such tolerances. During the design of the control charts it is essential to ensure that the limits constructed after a pilot study are within the design limits.

Control charts for attributes

Often, as was the case in acceptance sampling, it is possible after inspecting items to classify them only as 'good' or 'bad', as 'acceptable' or 'not acceptable', and it is for reasons such as these that control charts for attributes have been devised. Such charts are developed in much the same way as were control charts for variables.

Two types of chart are most popular:

1. Control chart for *proportion* or *per cent* defective.
2. Control chart for *number* of defects.

The method of using the charts is similar to that outlined previously, except that, in this case, rather than calculating the mean and range of all the items in each random sample, only the number, or the percentage, of defective items in the sample is calculated.

Control charts for *proportion* or *per cent defective* are known as *p-charts*. Control limits are constructed after a pilot investigation and if, during production, the proportion of defectives in a sample falls within these limits the process is considered to be 'under control', whereas, if the proportion of defectives in a sample falls beyond these limits, this is taken to be a good indication that the process is, for some reason, out of control and that some investigation and corrective action are required.

An estimate of the proportion defective produced by the process $(\bar{p})$ is obtained after a pilot study consisting of several samples, i.e.

$$\bar{p} = \frac{\text{Total number of defectives in 10 to 20 samples}}{\text{Total number inspected}}$$

0.2 per cent (and less frequently 5 per cent) control limits are set in the usual way, using the following formulae.

$$\text{Upper action limit: } \bar{p} + 3.09 = \sqrt{\frac{\bar{p}(1 - \bar{p})}{n}}$$

$$\text{Lower action limit: } \bar{p} - 3.09 = \sqrt{\frac{\bar{p}(1 - \bar{p})}{n}}$$

where n = sample size

EXAMPLE

Time of sample	Sample size (n)	Numbers in defectives in sample	p
9.00 a.m.	205	12	0.0585
10.00 a.m.	206	14	0.07
11.00 a.m.	195	12	0.0615
12.00	200	15	0.075
1.00 p.m	210	14	0.0665
2.00 p.m.	195	12	0.0615
3.00 p.m.	200	15	0.075
4.00 p.m.	200	16	0.080
5.00 p.m.	205	13	0.0635
6.00 p.m.	195	14	0.0715
7.00 p.m.	200	15	0.075
8.00 p.m.	195	14	0.0715

Output for previous week = 10 000
Number of defectives included in this output = 370

The proportion defective produced by the process can in this case be estimated from the figures given for the previous week's production, i.e.

$$\bar{p} = \frac{370}{10\ 000} = 0.037$$

Therefore, upper action limit is: $\bar{p} + 3.09 \sqrt{\dfrac{\bar{p}(1 - \bar{p})}{n}}$

$$= 0.037 + 3.09 \sqrt{\frac{0.037(0.963)}{200}}$$

$$= 0.079$$

Figure 20.12 *p*-chart

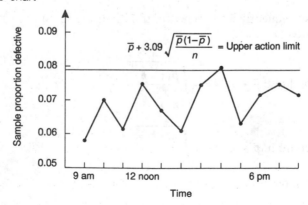

This action limit is shown on the *p*-chart in Figure 20.12. The proportion defective in each of the 12 samples is plotted on the chart, from which it can be seen that, compared with the previous week's production, the proportion of defectives in the batches has increased, and the process is almost 'out of control'.

Since the control limits for a *p*-chart are a function of *n* (the sample size), when the sample size changes the control limits must also change (e.g. Figure 20.13). In the above example, the sample size was nearly constant, hence a mean *n* = 200 was taken.

Figure 20.13 A proportion defective control chart (*p*-chart) in which the sample size, *n*, has changed

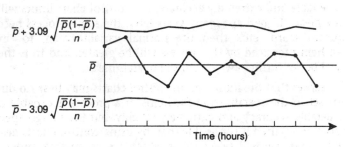

$$\bar{p} + 3.09 \sqrt{\frac{\bar{p}(1-\bar{p})}{n}}$$

$$\bar{p}$$

$$\bar{p} - 3.09 \sqrt{\frac{\bar{p}(1-\bar{p})}{n}}$$

Time (hours)

Control charts for *number* of defects are known as *c-charts* and are of particular value for controlling the number of defects in, or on, a particular unit, i.e. a single item, a group of items, or a part of an item. For example, the *c*-chart might be used to control the quality of cloth by counting the number of defects in a roll, to control the quality of a riveted structure by counting the number of faulty rivets, etc. Conditions such as these enable the Poisson distribution to be used. The symbol $\bar{c}$ is the average number of defects per unit obtained after a pilot investigation. The standard deviation of the Poisson distribution is given by $\sqrt{\bar{c}}$; consequently, the control limits are set at:

Upper action = $\bar{c} + 3.09 \sqrt{\bar{c}}$

Lower action = $\bar{c} - 3.09 \sqrt{\bar{c}}$

The manner in which *c*-charts are constructed and used is very similar to the construction and use of *p*-charts.

EXAMPLE

Empire-Detroit Steel

Empire-Detroit Steel of Ohio uses statistical process control techniques through a computer package called SQC/3. The quality control system audits the 2 000 tons of steel shipped daily throughout each of the many production steps. The plant comprises 787 acres, employs 1 350 workers, and, along with one other plant, produces carbon, silicon, stainless flat-rolled steel, and galvanized steel for use in consumer and industrial products. All control charts are automatically updated and instantly accessible to the entire network whenever new data is entered into the quality management system. Supervisors can recall a plant-wide status screen to summarize the data of all updated control charts.

Source: Software system speeds concrete answers. *Iron Age* **8**(9), Sept. 1992, pp. 45–6.

PROCESS CAPABILITY
Control limits and design limits

The use of control charts permits us to determine whether a process is 'statistically' in control or not. By establishing action limits and plotting observations on a chart we can determine when to take appropriate remedial action or, using warning limits, appropriate preventive action. The positioning of these limits, however, is based on observations of the actual items received, or items output from a process. If we consider the latter, i.e. items produced by a process, then the establishment of the control chart involves us in considering the normal performance of the processes in order to establish limits beyond which output can be considered to be abnormal for those same circumstances. Thus if a process is highly reliable and extremely accurate, the control chart limits will be set relatively close to the mean. If, perhaps many years later, the same process becomes unreliable, the equipment worn, etc., then the normal variability in, for example, the dimensions of an item produced by the process will be greater, and thus the action and warning limits will be set further away from the overall mean.

We have noted earlier that the limits set on control charts may bear no direct relationship to the limits set in the specification for items. If a process is capable of producing items with considerable accuracy and extremely reliably, but the design specification for those items is very 'loose', then it is possible that, by using control charts designed in the manner described above, we will reject items which are acceptable under the original design specification. Conversely, if a process is not consistently capable of producing items to fine tolerances, yet the design tolerances for the item are very narrow, then it is possible, in using a control chart, to accept items which are not acceptable against the original design specification.

For these reasons we must consider the relationship between control chart limits and design or specification limits, and in doing so we must consider the question of *process capability*.

The use of the mean and range charts shows us whether a process is in statistical control or not, but does not necessarily give any adequate indication of whether individual items are acceptable within specification limits. Organizations are concerned primarily with ensuring that items are within the intended specification tolerance rather than being under 'statistical' control overall.

It will be recalled that in discussing the design of control charts for items we chose to use charts for mean values for reasons of convenience. Ideally we would have liked to set up control charts for individual observations in the manner shown below:

$$\text{UAL}_{individuals} = \text{Overall mean} + 3.90\sigma$$

$$\text{LAL}_{individuals} = \text{Overall mean} - 3.09\sigma$$

We chose instead to set up a control chart for mean values as follows:

$$\text{UAL}_{means} = \text{Overall mean} + 3.09\ \frac{\sigma}{\sqrt{n}}$$

$$\text{LAL}_{means} = \text{Overall mean} - 3.09\frac{\sigma}{\sqrt{n}}$$

In fact the action limits for a control chart based on mean values are somewhat narrower than those that would be established for the same population of individuals. It follows, therefore, that if in using control charts based on mean values we are to be sure that individual items conform to design specifications, the design limits must be placed well beyond the action limits of a mean control chart. This relationship is shown in Figure 20.14. If the design limits are within the action limits for the mean chart, or even just beyond those limits, then it is possible that, using the means chart, individual items will be accepted which do not conform to the specification limits.

Figure 20.14 Comparison of action limits and possible specification limits

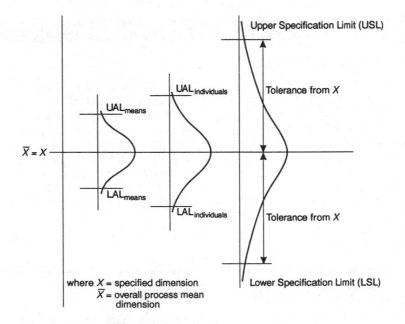

Process capability measurement

In studying process capability we shall be concerned with the extent to which a process is capable of processing items which correspond to the design specification limits.

A measure of process capability can be obtained as follows:

$$PC = \frac{USL - LSL}{\sigma}$$

where PC = Process capability

    USL = Upper specification limit

    LSL = Lower specification limit

    σ = Standard deviation of individual items

Strictly, this measure of process capability applies only where the specification tolerances are distributed symmetrically about the intended dimension, and where the overall mean dimension produced by a process is the same as the intended dimension. In these circumstances, where the value of PC is less than 6, more than 2 per cent of defective items will be produced, hence either the process variability must be improved or the specification tolerances must be increased. For a value between 6 and 11 the process may be controlled in the manner described above using a mean control chart. Where the value is greater than 11 then the use of a mean control chart may imply the use of a quality control procedure which is far tighter than is actually required. In these circumstances it may be appropriate to use modified action limits in the manner described later. Alternatively it may be appropriate, or indeed necessary, to retain action limits which are very much narrower than the specification limits in order to allow some 'drift' in the mean value.

EXAMPLE

General Dynamics

Multilevel inspection sampling plans adopt the strategy that as the level of achieved quality increases, the sampling activity decreases. General Dynamics' Air Defense Systems Division in California incorporated such multilevel sampling into a programme called the systematic process observation technique (SPOT). SPOT is used to audit individual part characteristics for conformance. With SPOT, a personal computer randomly selects a fraction of the available features for audit based on the sampling level that the process has achieved. A spreadsheet program is used to administer the sampling plans. With this approach, quality control resources are more effectively and efficiently utilized. SPOT has reduced tedious 'output' inspection, replacing it with more effective in-process quality control audits. It has also improved quality feedback of process performance.

Source: Glaccum, J.F. (1991) Combining multilevel sampling plans and personal computers. *Quality Progress* **24**(9), pp. 75–78.

RELIABILITY OF ITEMS

The reliability of items has been considered above in connection with the specification and achievement of quality. We have seen that quality, reliability and cost are linked, higher quality being associated with higher reliability and normally higher cost. In Chapter 21 we shall consider the maintenance and replacement of facilities. Here, again, consideration of reliability is relevant, since the higher the reliability the less the need for replacement and maintenance. We shall also have cause to mention reliability in a slightly different context in discussing performance measurement in Chapter 22.

Clearly, therefore, the reliability of items, products and facilities is an important consideration during design. It is of relevance to the user, and is a factor to consider in quality management and in maintenance and replacement.

The curve in Figure 20.15 shows the classic 'bath tub' pattern. It shows the failure rate, i.e. the number of failures per unit time, expressed as a fraction of

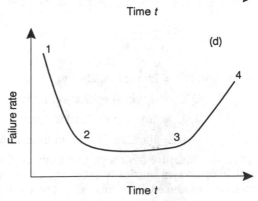

Figure 20.15 Reliability distributions

the number of survivors. Three phases are evident:

1–2 'burn-in' or 'infant mortality' or 'early life' failures;

2–3 'random' or 'normal operating' or 'middle life' failures;

3–4 'wear-out' or 'old age' failures.

In analysing item reliability we must consider each of the three phases of reliability. Following a period of low but improving reliability during the 'infant mortality' period, reliability would be expected to be relatively high during 'middle age' and to reduce again during the 'old age' period. Analysis of reliability during these periods necessitates the use of appropriate formulate to describe these three essentially different curves.

System reliability

The characteristics discussed above apply both to single items or components and to products comprising several components. The latter may fail if any one of their component parts fails unless the failed part is redundant, i.e. is not required for effective system operation. This of course raises the possibility of deliberately introducing redundant components as a design feature. Thus it may be possible to design a product such that, initially, certain components are redundant and are brought into operation only when other components fail.

The reliability of complex products, or systems of components, is clearly a function of the number and the reliability of their components. Thus in a system without redundancy, which fails when any of its components, A, B, C and D, fail:

$$R_{SYSTEM} = R_Z \times R_B \times R_C \times R_D$$

For example, in a system comprising ten components, each essential for satisfactory system operation (i.e. without redundancy), if component reliability is 0.99:

$$R_{SYSTEM} = 0.99^{10}$$

$$= 0.904 \text{ approximately}$$

Now if in this example, because of built-in redundancy, five of the components would instantly be replaced by parallel components if they fail, the system might be shown as in Figure 20.16.

Figure 20.16 Diagrammatic representation of a ten-component system with redundancy

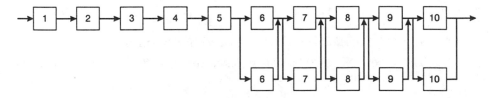

The reliability of components 1–5 = 0.99; the reliability of components 6–10 = 0.99; but since these are each arranged in parallel, the reliability of each pair is:

$$1 - (1 - R_{6,7 \text{ etc.}})^2$$

$$\text{Thus } R_{SYSTEM} = 0.99^5 \times (1 - (1 - 0.99)^2)^5$$
$$= 0.950$$

Such system reliability considerations are relevant in design and in planning maintenance and replacement.

KEY POINTS FOR CHAPTER 20

Quality Control and Assurance focuses on control costs, i.e.

    costs of appraisal;

    costs of correction.

Control and Assurance procedures are largely statistical, and deal with:

    input control;

    process control;

    output control.

Input control uses vendor rating and acceptance sampling.

Process control uses control charts.

Output control uses acceptance sampling.

Vendor rating provides a means to monitor and control suppliers.

Acceptance sampling uses inspection of samples to monitor overall acceptability of items.

The nature of an acceptance sampling procedure is defined by:

    sample size;

    acceptable number of defects in the sample;

and whether sampling is by

    single sample; or

    multiple samples.

Control charts are used to monitor on-going processes through a form of sample inspection.

The nature of control charts is defined by:

    whether attributes or variables are being inspected;

    action and warning limits.

Process capability defines the limits of capability of a process. Such limits should conform to the intended quality standards.

Reliability is a measure of liability or propensity to failure.

Reliability can be measured for items or systems.

FURTHER READING

Oakland, J. S. (1986) *Statistical Process Control*. London: Heinemann.

Lloyd, D. K. and Lipow, N. (1990) *Reliability: Management, Methods and Mathematics* (3rd edn.). American Society of Quality Control.

CASE STUDY

The following case from Part 9 of the book, is relevant to the topics covered in this chapter.

Case No	Name	Country
2	Jograni Handicrafts	Bangladesh

20.1 (a) What is the purpose of acceptance sampling?

    (b) What is an operating characteristic curve?

    (c) Use the binomial probability expression to calculate the probability of finding two or fewer defectives in a sample of size 12, if the actual percentage defectives in the batch from which the sample was drawn is 20 per cent.

20.2 Construct an operating characteristic curve to show the probability of accepting batches of varying percentage actual defective levels, if sample sizes of 80 items are drawn from the batches and if batches are accepted when two or fewer defectives are found in the samples.

20.3 Distinguish between and describe double acceptance sampling and multiple acceptance sampling.

20.4 (a) Distinguish between quality assurance and quality control.

    (b) Distinguish between quality control as regards the 'attributes' of items and the 'variables' of items.

    (c) Distinguish between design limits and control limits.

    (d) Distinguish between usual or chance variation and unusual or assignable variation, in respect of quality control.

    (e) Distinguish between warning limits and action limits in respect of control charts.

20.5 (a) A machine produces components at a rate of 100 per hour. Every hour a random sample of five components is taken and their lengths are measured. After ten hours the data given below have been collected. Use these data to design control charts for the sample mean and range of the dimension concerned.

Sample number	Measurements (cm)				
1	9.00	9.10	9.00	9.05	8.95
2	9.10	9.10	9.00	9.05	9.05
3	9.00	9.05	9.00	9.05	9.00
4	9.00	9.00	8.95	9.00	9.05
5	9.00	9.05	9.05	9.05	9.00
6	9.00	9.10	9.10	9.05	9.00
7	9.00	9.10	9.05	9.15	9.05
8	9.00	9.10	9.10	9.00	9.05
9	9.00	9.00	8.95	9.00	9.00
10	9.00	9.05	9.00	9.10	8.95

    (b) Following the construction of the charts, the same sampling procedure is followed and the data shown below are obtained. Plot these data on the control charts and comment on the quality 'performance' of the process.

Sample number	Mean length (cm)	Range	Sample number	Mean length (cm)	Range
1	9.020	0.100	11	9.040	0.150
2	9.030	0.100	12	9.040	0.125
3	9.025	0.050	13	9.035	0.100
4	9.030	0.100	14	9.040	0.055
5	9.035	0.025	15	9.030	0.100
6	9.040	0.105	16	9.025	0.050
7	9.020	0.050	17	9.030	0.125
8	9.030	0.100	18	9.025	0.100
9	9.040	0.050	19	9.025	0.150
10	9.035	0.065	20	9.030	0.150

Number of blemishes per product: 6, 7, 6, 5, 6, 7, 7, 6, 8, 7, 7, 7, 6, 8, 9, 8, 7, 8, 9, 8, 8, 7

20.6 Phragyle Products Ltd supply imitation glass decanters to the hotel trade. Because of the delicate nature of the manufacturing process, each decanter is expected to have some minor blemishes, most of which are completely invisible to the naked eye. These very minor blemishes may occur almost anywhere on the product and are not usually sufficient to lead to the rejection of the item. Nevertheless, the sales manager of Phragyle Products is anxious to investigate the effects of recent efforts that the manufacturers claim to have made to improve the manufacturing process and the quality of the products supplied to Phragyle.

Prior to the modifications to the process, each decanter had an average of five almost imperceptible blemishes. The table below shows the number of blemishes on every fifth decanter for a short period after the claimed improvement in manufacture. Comment on the success of the supposed adjustments to the manufacturing process.

20.7 (a) Even if 100 per cent acceptance sampling is adopted, it is likely that a certain number of defective items will be accepted. Discuss.

(b) What measures can be taken, and in what circumstances, to decrease the error of human inspectors?

20.8 Three phases are often evident in the reliability of items. Describe them and explain the reasons for their existence. Use examples.

Chapter 21

Maintenance and replacement

ISSUES

What is the relationship of maintenance, repair and replacement?
What is the role and purpose of maintenance?
Which items should be maintained?
How is maintenance organized?
What is preventive maintenance?
How can a replacement policy be established?

Our discussion of item quality in the previous chapter led us to consider the question of reliability. We noted that quality and reliability were related: in general, higher-quality items were likely to be more reliable. We noticed also that quality level and cost were related, so higher reliability is often associated with higher cost. Since few purchases are made irrespective of cost, most products or items in use will have less than perfect reliability. At some time most items will cease to function satisfactorily. On such occasions they will have to be repaired or replaced. To some extent, however, the need for repair or replacement may be reduced through effective servicing and maintenance. Thus:

(a) Most items will be inspected regularly, in order to detect any signs of reduced effectiveness or impending failure. And additionally:

(b) Items will normally be serviced regularly, also to try to ensure continued effective operation.

(c) Preventive maintenance will often be provided on a regular basis in order to try to sustain satisfactory operations of items or equipment. During preventive maintenance, items or parts which are liable to failure may be changed prior to the end of their working life. But nevertheless:

(d) Breakdown maintenance (i.e. repair) will normally be required so that items and equipment might be returned to satisfactory operation. And eventually:

(e) Replacement of items and equipment will occur when they are no longer capable of satisfactory operation and are beyond economic repair.

The relationship of these five activities is outlined in Figure 21.1—(a) to (d) above can be seen to be part of the maintenance function, while (e) is concerned with replacement. Initially in this chapter we shall consider maintenance, and then the problem of replacement.

MAINTENANCE

Equipment of whatever type, however complex or simple, however cheap or expensive, is liable to breakdown. Thus in manufacture, supply, transport and service not only must procedures exist for equipment maintenance, but also the possibility of breakdowns and disruption of operation must be considered during capacity planning and activity scheduling. The effective operation of any system is dependent on the maintenance of all parts of the system, e.g. machines, buildings, services. In this chapter we shall not deal with the maintenance of human facilities although, in concept at least, the maintenance requirement also applies to workers. Indeed, company welfare or personnel practice may be designed partly as a maintenance activity, e.g. training and retraining to maintain the availability of appropriate skills, medical facilities to maintain human capacity, counselling to maintain interest and motivation. Here we deal only with the maintenance of inanimate items, e.g. equipment.

Large sums of money are wasted in business and industry, each year, because of ineffective or badly organized maintenance. However maintenance is just one element which contributes to effective operation during the life cycle of a piece of equipment. It has an important part to play, but must be co-ordinated with other disciplines. Taken together, this approach, aimed at achieving economic life-cycle cost for an item, has been called 'tetrotechnology', and defined as:

Figure 21.1 Maintenance and replacement activities

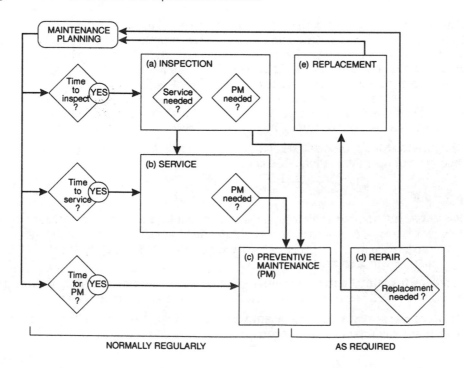

the multidisciplinary approach to the specification, design, installation, commissioning, use and disposal of facilities, equipment and buildings in pursuit of economic life-cycle costs.

Figure 21.2 shows a typical life-cycle for a facility. The diagram indicates those activities required in conceiving, creating, providing, operating, maintaining and disposing of a physical facility. Taking maintenance from this set, it will be seen that many decisions and activities will affect the nature and amount of maintenance required. The design of the facility, both with regard to its design 'for function' and its design 'for maintenability and reliability', will influence operation, as will its installation and commissioning. The effectiveness of maintenance will influence the time available for and the time spent in operation. Thus the need for maintenance and the nature of the maintenance required are determined by a variety of factors. The maintenance function within an organization is therefore influenced by many other activities within the organization.

Figure 21.2 The operating life-cycle of a facility

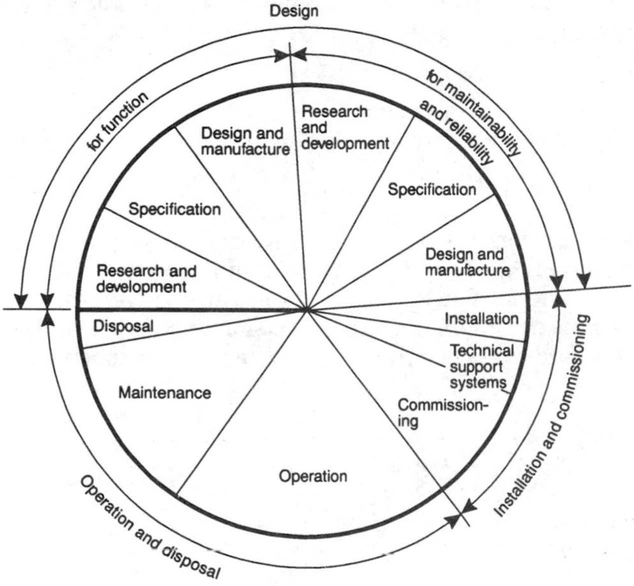

The objectives of maintenance

The purpose of maintenance is to attempt to maximize the performance of equipment by ensuring that such equipment performs regularly and efficiently, by attempting to prevent breakdowns or failures, and by minimizing the losses resulting from breakdowns or failures. In fact it is the objective of the maintenance function to maintain or increase the reliability of the operating system as a whole.

Many steps can be taken to ensure that such an objective is achieved, but only a few of these are normally considered to be the responsibility of the maintenance department. For example, each of the following will contribute to the reliability of the operating system:

(a) improvement of the quality of equipment and components through improved design and or 'tighter' manufacturing standards;

(b) improvements in the design of equipment to facilitate the replacement of broken items and inspection and routine maintenance work;

(c) improvements in the layout of equipment to facilitate maintenance work, i.e. providing space around or underneath equipment;

(d) providing 'slack' in the operating system, i.e. providing excess capacity so that the failure of equipment does not affect the performance of other equipment;

(e) using 'work-in-progress' to ensure that the failure of equipment is not immediately reflected in a shortage of materials or parts for a subsequent piece of equipment;

(f) establishing a repair facility so that, through speedy replacement of broken parts, equipment downtime is reduced;

(g) undertaking preventive maintenance, which, through regular inspection and/or replacement of critical parts, reduces the occurrence of breakdowns.

These points may be summarized in two overall objectives, which are:

(a) to attempt to ensure that breakdowns or failures do not occur ((a) and (g) above);

(b) to attempt to minimize the disruption or loss caused by the breakdowns which do occur ((b), (c), (d), (e) and (f) above).

Excluding the influence of improvements in equipment design and layout, discussion of which is not appropriate to this chapter, it is clear that two distinct facets of maintenance may contribute to the increased reliability of the operating system: preventive maintenance and repair.

We can, of course, draw the familiar total cost curve as shown in Figure 21.3, which demonstrates that increased effort in preventive maintenance should reduce the cost of repair maintenance. Were we able to define both of these curves, then it would be a simple matter to determine the minimum, cost maintenance policy. However, the problem is not as simple as this, and consequently maintenance policy is substantially more difficult to determine.

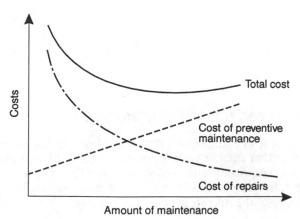

Figure 21.3 Maintenance costs

MAINTENANCE DECISIONS

It will be seen from the above that several decisions are required in the establishment of a comprehensive maintenance policy for any set of facilities. We can consider the establishment of a maintenance policy as comprising three necessary and interdependent decisions:

(a) Which items, facilities, etc., are to be maintained?

(b) What kind of maintenance will be applied in each case?

(c) How is this maintenance work to be organized?

What is to be maintained?

Any maintenance activity incurs some cost. Inspection is costly in that it involves some-one devoting some time to looking at an item or a facility, and that may mean that the operation of that facility has to be interrupted. Service work will be expensive and will not normally be possible while the facility is operating. Preventive maintenance will normally be undertaken while the facility is out of operation. To some extent all this work can be planned to take place at a time when the disruption caused by the inoperation of the facil-ity is minimized, but of course breakdown maintenance can occur at any time and can be very disruptive, and can therefore be expensive in terms of both the direct effort involved and the time lost while the facility is repaired.

If the cost of any of this maintenance exceeds the cost benefits obtained, then it may be cheaper simply to dispose of items when they eventually break down. Indeed in some situations the way in which the items work and the conditions in which they are employed necessitate such an approach. There will, therefore, be situations in which it will be decided that some items will not be maintained, except perhaps through regular inspection and service to avoid safety and health hazards. Furthermore, the manner in which items break down or are subject to failure may make it difficult to develop an effec-tive preventive maintenance strategy. And, if the cost per unit of time of undertaking pre-ventive maintenance is greater than the cost per unit of time of repair, then there will be a tendency to rely on the latter.

Although in some cases preventive maintenance and even breakdown maintenance, i.e. repair, may not be employed, in most cases facilities will require one or both of these approaches in addition to inspection and service. In these situations we must decide on the size of 'unit' to be maintained. Here there are three possible approaches:

(a) A large system comprising several interdependent facilities can be considered as one 'unit' for maintenance purposes.

(b) Single facilities can be considered to be the 'unit'.

(c) Parts or subsections of a particular facility can be considered to be the 'unit' for which maintenance must be planned.

For example, in transport an entire system may comprise all the independent and inter-linked parts of a complete vehicle, whereas the single-facility approach may involve the development of a maintenance plan for each separate part of that system, e.g. engine, transmission, etc. The third approach would involve the planning of maintenance for appropriate parts of these separate parts, e.g. electric items.

The extent to which the facilities within a larger system are interdependent, i.e. the extent to which the breakdown of one can cause disruption of the others, will influence the approach which will be employed. A system comprising similar facilities all installed at around the same time would perhaps be treated as an entire unit for maintenance pur-poses, whereas a system in which items, although linked together in some interdependent way, were installed at different times and have quite different reliability characteristics might encourage us to adopt the second approach. If an entire configuration of facilities operates continuously, then the entire system must be stopped when any part requires maintenance, and again there will be a tendency to see the entire system as the 'unit' for maintenance. On the other hand, where facilities operate intermittently, different facilities being idle at different times, then there will be a tendency to see each facility as a 'unit' for maintenance, since this provides the greatest opportunity for scheduling maintenance work. Where a system comprises several facilities, and where each facility has similar component parts, e.g. electric motors, and where the reliability and/or breakdown characteristics of these parts are known, the third approach above may be appropriate.

Types of maintenance

Inspection

Facilities will normally be inspected at intervals in order to determine whether service and/or preventive maintenance is required, or likely to be required soon. Such work may involve visual inspection or the measurement of certain physical characteristics of a facility. Inspection may involve the whole facility or simply those parts which are known to be liable to failure. One of the problems in planning inspection is to decide on the *inspection interval*.

Service

This will involve the routine readjustment of equipment. Such work will often be undertaken, if seen to be required, alongside inspection.

Preventive maintenance

Preventive maintenance is precautionary and is undertaken to try to prevent or delay breakdowns, and therefore the need for repair. Preventive action may be undertaken according to a predetermined and regular schedule or when required. A regular schedule can be established for items which have known and fairly predictable reliability or breakdown characteristics. Preventive maintenance can be undertaken as and when required in circumstances where there is some evidence of deteriorating efficiency or impending breakdown. One of the problems, therefore, in planning preventive maintenance is to identify the type of approach which will be suitable in particular circumstances.

Repair

Breakdown maintenance or repair is remedial, taking place after an item has ceased to operate satisfactorily. The need for repair is not necessarily the result of inefficient or insufficient inspection, service and preventive maintenance, since in some cases the cost of repairs will be less than the accumulated cost of preventive work. One of the major problems in planning repair work is to decide on the amount of resources to be made available, since the larger the repair 'team' the shorter the repair time, but also the larger the amount of repair team idle time.

Seattle City Lighting

In Seattle, a typical maintenance area has about 5 000 ducts, terminal poles, and transformers for street lighting. Comprehensive maintenance is essential to avoid interruptions in the system. The programme covers inspecting, recording, maintenance and repairing. By determining the total number of items that must be inspected on a four-year cycle, the Authority found it a simple matter to prepare a rolling schedule to cover ¼ of the inspections every year. With priorities set, the preventive maintenance inspections schedule is determined by the computer system, which provides an easy way to manage and track all the information that is generated by the maintenance programme. The system also supplies information in response to queries and requests from engineers and management.

Source: Kirkpatrick, D. (1990) Preventative maintenance programme is a three-step process— inspection, recording and repairing. *Transmission and Distribution* **42**(7), pp.58–60.

The organization of maintenance

Maintenance work can be performed by:

(a) the personnel who normally use the equipment:

(b) staff employed in a maintenance department by and within the organization;

(c) external maintenance personnel, e.g. under certain service contracts from equipment suppliers.

The first approach will often be employed for inspection and sometimes for service work. It may also be appropriate where preventive maintenance activities are relatively straightforward and are undertaken as and when required, i.e. where some urgent preventive action is required without prior warning. It may be employed for repair work where the facility operator has specialist skills and knowledge, perhaps acquired through the use of the facility, which are not available to other personnel.

More often an organization will maintain a specialist 'maintenance department'. The resources of this department will be employed in inspection, service, preventive maintenance and repair work, some of which can be undertaken on a scheduled basis. The main problems in organizing maintenance in this way are to decide on the size of the maintenance 'crew', the range of skills required, the amount of stocks to be held, the amount of standby equipment to be held in stock, etc.

Maintenance will be the responsibility of an external organization either where specialist equipment is involved or where a service or maintenance contract has been provided as a compulsory or normal part of the purchase contract for that equipment. This is normal for computer installations, etc. It may also be appropriate where maintenance work is highly specialized or hazardous, but infrequent, e.g. the maintenance of complex installations or underwater installations.

The planning of effective maintenance, however undertaken, will require collection and maintenance of certain data. For example, a complete list of all facilities in use, their date of purchase and their maintenance history to date will normally be kept. Statistics on operating life between failures, the time required to perform repair operations, etc., will be held so that decisions can be made about the scheduling of preventive work and the merits of preventive compared with repair maintenance.

The 'data base' of information on each facility will be updated regularly so that appropriate statistics, etc., can be extracted. Often such data will be held on a computer-based system, such a system being used to schedule maintenance, allocate maintenance resources, etc.

PREVENTIVE MAINTENANCE

Preventive maintenance is used to delay or prevent the breakdown of equipment, and also to reduce the severity of any breakdowns that occur. Two aspects of preventive maintenance can be identified:

1. *Inspection.* Inspection of critical parts will often indicate the need for replacement or repair well in advance of probable breakdown. (Inspection forms an important part of motor vehicle maintenance, regular inspection of tyres, radiator, battery, brakes, etc., being called for by all maintenance schedules.) Regular inspection, conducted either by the equipment operator or by the maintenance department, is the most important direct means of increasing equipment reliability.

2. *Servicing.* Routine cleaning, lubrication and adjustment may reduce wear significantly and hence prevent breakdowns. Frequently such duties belong to the equipment operator rather than being the direct responsibility of the maintenance department; however, irrespective of responsibility, servicing or routine preventive maintenance must be conducted regularly according to schedules constructed from both operating experience and manufacturers' recommendations.

No matter how much preventive maintenance is undertaken, failures will still occur, if only because of the use of defective or sub-standard parts, or the misuse of equipment. It will always be necessary, therefore, to provide breakdown maintenance. Repair policy may involve the use of subcontractors, the repair of equipment immediately upon breakdown or later, the replacement of parts or subassemblies, or even the replacement of whole pieces of equipment. Repairs may be conducted on equipment in situ or equipment may be removed to a more appropriate situation. Standby equipment may be available for permanent or temporary replacement in cases of breakdown.

EXAMPLE

Northwest Airlines

A manual system for scheduling maintenance at Northwest Airlines was overtaxed when the company joined with Republic Airlines, in effect doubling its fleet to 360 aircraft overnight. In looking for a computer based system, Northwest's aim was to increase the time between maintenance visits, taking into consideration the constraints of labour, parts, and facilities. The system chosen enables planners to run various 'what-if' scenarios for long-range planning. The system creates a 'macro job list' for each aircraft. The planner can then determine what needs to be done and enter into the computer the required labour hours, parts and facilities.

Source: Menagh, M.(1973) Maintaining the jet set. *CIO* **7**(1), p. 96.

REPAIRS

Consider now the situation in which several machines of the same type are to be maintained. Furthermore, let us consider a policy which provides only for repair maintenance and not preventive maintenance (a policy which might have been adopted because of large variability in breakdown time distributions).

Providing appropriate assumptions are made about the nature of breakdowns and repair time, the design of a maintenance system for such a situation can be accomplished by using conventional queuing theory.

Clearly, machine idle time caused by waiting for service by a maintenance team currently engaged on another machine can be reduced if the time needed to repair machines is reduced. Reduction in machine repair time, can normally be achieved by devoting more resources to maintenance, i.e. by increasing the size of the maintenance team. Such action, however, will increase costs; consequently the problem is one of achieving an acceptable balance between, on the one hand, the cost incurred by machine idle time due to breakdowns, and on the other hand the cost of the maintenance facility.

REPLACEMENT

Replacement policies for items subject to sudden failure

When a machine stops because of the failure of one component, then the maintenance team may simply go along to the machine and effect a repair by replacing the broken component. An alternative strategy is to replace not only the broken component but also all other similar components, on the assumption that since they have all been in service for some length of time, because one has already failed, the others are also likely to fail in the near future. A third strategy might be adopted, namely the replacement of the broken component and *certain* of the other similar components.

As an example, consider the problem faced by someone whose job it is to replace, when necessary, the bulbs in the lights of every room of a multi-storey building. The replacement strategies may be as follows:

1. Replace only those bulbs that fail. Such a strategy may involve an excessive amount of work, since replacing a bulb takes an average of 30 minutes erecting a ladder, obtaining new bulbs from stores, etc. Because of the difference between the comparatively low cost of a new bulb and the comparatively high cost of replacement, an alternative strategy may be preferred.

2. When one bulb fails, replace *all* bulbs in that room, or on that floor.

3. Alternatively, as a compromise, replace the bulb that has failed *and* a proportion of other bulbs, say those that have been in service for longer than six months, in other words those that are expected to fail fairly shortly.

The problem then is to decide which of these strategies to adopt, a decision which must, of course, be made on a basis of cost considerations. The cost involved in replacement is dependent on the probability of component failure. In the case of strategy 1 the total cost of maintenance over, say, a year is given by the following:

$$\text{Cost of making a single replacement} \times \text{Probable number of failures during year}$$

In the case of strategy 2 the total cost is determined by the number of components replaced each time and the number of 'first failures' during the period. In the final strategy (3) the cost would depend on the number of 'first failures' and the number of components at every replacement period which have been in service longer than a given time.

Although it is possible to develop formulae for the replacement problem in which items are subject to sudden failure, such formulae are often inadequate for the practical situation; consequently the choice of replacement strategy is often made with the aid of a simulation exercise.

Replacement policies for items which deteriorate

The cost of operating equipment and machinery normally increases with the increasing age of the equipment. Such increasing cost may be caused by: (a) the increasing cost of the maintenance necessary to obtain continuing reliability of the equipment, and (b) the obsolescence of the equipment, making its continued operation comparatively more costly in relation to that of the equipment which might be used to replace it. There comes a time, therefore, when it is not economically justifiable to replace the present ageing equipment, but economically beneficial in order to obtain equipment which has greater output, reliability, etc.

Our present problem, then, is to decide at what time such equipment should be replaced. Such a decision must obviously be made on economic grounds, by a comparison of the net economic benefit of retaining present equipment and the net economic benefit of replacing present equipment.

As regards *present* equipment we must consider the following:

(a) its life;

(b) its current and future salvage or sale value;

(c) the revenue produced throughout the rest of its life;

(d) the expenditure incurred throughout the rest of its life.

As regards the *proposed* replacement equipment we must consider:

(a) the purchase price of the equipment;

(b) its life;

(c) the salvage or sale value at various times in its life;

(d) the revenue produced by the equipment;

(e) the expenditure incurred throughout its life.

In considering the replacement of equipment it is important to remember that money has a time value. For example £100 is of more value to us now that it would be next year. The evaluation of the economic worth of equipment therefore depends on both its earning potential and time considerations. We must therefore make our replacement decisions by considering the *present value* of the net revenue associated with its use.

If i = annual rate of interest, then £100 now is worth

$$\frac{100}{(1 + i)^n} \text{ in } n \text{ years time}$$

e.g. £100 is worth $100/1.1^2$ = £82.6 in two years' time.

Suppose that the investment of £10 000 in a new piece of equipment results in a net income of £5000 for each of the following three years. If we assume that the 'cost of capital', or the rate of interest which might have been achieved had the £10 000 been invested, is 10 per cent, then the *present value* of this income is £12 434, i.e.

$$\frac{5000}{(1.1)} + \frac{5000}{(1.1)^2} + \frac{5000}{(1.1)^3}$$

$$= £12\ 434$$

The calculation of present values in this way, by *discounting* future sums of money at a given rate, is the basis of the *discounted cash flow* technique for investment appraisal.

Table 21.1	Compound interest table ($1/(1 + i)^N$)								
n	**i = 1%**	**2**	**3**	**4**	**5**	**6**	**7**	**8**	**9**	**10**
1	0.9901	0.9804	0.9709	0.9615	0.9524	0.9434	0.9346	0.9259	0.9174	0.9091
2	0.9803	0.9612	0.9426	0.9246	0.9070	0.8900	0.8734	0.8573	0.8417	0.8264
3	0.9706	0.9423	0.9151	0.8890	0.8638	0.8396	0.8163	0.7938	0.7722	0.7513
4	0.9610	0.9238	0.8885	0.8548	0.8227	0.7921	0.7629	0.7350	0.7084	0.6830
5	0.9515	0.9057	0.8626	0.8219	0.7835	0.7473	0.7130	0.6806	0.6499	0.6209
6	0.9420	0.8880	0.8375	0.7903	0.7462	0.7050	0.6663	0.6302	0.5963	0.5645
7	0.9327	0.8706	0.8131	0.7599	0.7107	0.6651	0.6227	0.5835	0.5470	0.5132
8	0.9235	0.8535	0.7894	0.7307	0.6768	0.6274	0.5820	0.5403	0.5019	0.4665
9	0.9143	0.8368	0.7664	0.7026	0.6446	0.5919	0.5439	0.5002	0.4604	0.4241
10	0.9053	0.8302	0.7441	0.6756	0.6139	0.5584	0.5083	0.4632	0.4224	0.3588
11	0.8963	0.8043	0.7224	0.6496	0.5847	0.5268	0.4751	0.4289	0.3875	0.3505
12	0.8874	0.7885	0.7014	0.6246	0.5568	0.4970	0.4440	0.3971	0.3555	0.3186
13	0.8787	0.7730	0.6810	0.6006	0.5303	0.4688	0.4150	0.3677	0.3262	0.2897
14	0.8700	0.7579	0.6611	0.5775	0.5051	0.4423	0.3878	0.3405	0.2992	0.2633
15	0.8613	0.7430	0.6419	0.5553	0.4810	0.4173	0.3624	0.3152	0.2745	0.2394
16	0.8528	0.7284	0.6232	0.5339	0.4581	0.3936	0.3387	0.2919	0.2519	0.2176
17	0.8444	0.7142	0.6050	0.5134	0.4363	0.3714	0.3166	0.2703	0.2311	0.1978
18	0.8360	0.7002	0.5874	0.4936	0.4155	0.3503	0.2959	0.2502	0.2120	0.1799
19	0.8277	0.6864	0.5703	0.4746	0.3957	0.3305	0.2765	0.2317	0.1945	0.1635
20	0.8195	0.6730	0.5537	0.4564	0.3769	0.3118	0.2584	0.2145	0.1784	0.1486
21	0.8114	0.6598	0.5375	0.4388	0.3589	0.2942	0.2415	0.1987	0.1637	0.1351
22	0.8034	0.6468	0.5219	0.4220	0.3418	0.2775	0.2257	0.1839	0.1502	0.1228
23	0.7954	0.6432	0.5067	0.4057	0.3256	0.2618	0.2109	0.1703	0.1378	0.1117
24	0.7876	0.6217	0.4919	0.3901	0.3101	0.2470	0.1971	0.1577	0.1264	0.1015
25	0.7798	0.6095	0.4776	0.3751	0.2953	0.2330	0.1842	0.1460	0.1160	0.0923
26	0.7720	0.5976	0.4637	0.3607	0.2812	0.2198	0.1722	0.1352	0.1064	0.0839
27	0.7644	0.5859	0.4502	0.3468	0.2678	0.2074	0.1696	0.1252	0.0976	0.0763
28	0.7568	0.5744	0.4371	0.3335	0.2551	0.1956	0.1504	0.1159	0.0895	0.0693
29	0.7493	0.5631	0.4243	0.3207	0.2429	0.1846	0.1406	0.1073	0.0822	0.0630
30	0.7419	0.5521	0.4120	0.3083	0.2314	0.1741	0.1314	0.0994	0.0754	0.0573

where *i* = annual interest rate
n = number of years

When concerned with equipment replacement, this discounting procedure can be expressed by the following equation:

$$NPV = \left(\sum_{n=1} \frac{I_N - E_N}{(1 + i)^N} \right) + \frac{S_N}{(1 + i)^N}$$

where NPV = net present value

I_n = income for year n

E_n = expenditure for year n

i = discount rate

N = life of equipment or number of years being considered

S_N = sale or scrap value at end of life, i.e. year N

Clearly, to be economically beneficial the net present value (NPV) must be equal to or greater than zero.

To assist discounted cash flow calculations, tables for 1 have been prepared (see Table 21.1).

The replacement decision normally takes the following form: whether to replace existing equipment now, or at a later date, up to and including the last year in the life of the existing equipment. The problem, then, is one of comparing, at *present value*, the cash flows associated with the use of the present and the proposed equipment over the common period, from the present time to the end of the life of the present equipment. Naturally cash flows that have already occurred do not enter into the decision, for example past operating costs of present equipment. We are concerned only with the cash flows that will result from the decision to retain the equipment and the decision to replace it, i.e. the operating costs, the revenues and the changes in disposal values.

KEY POINTS FOR CHAPTER 21

The need for repair can be reduced through effective maintenance.

To manage maintenance requires consideration of

    preventive maintenance

    replacement

    service

    inspection.

The aim of maintenance is to improve the operating life cycle of an item or facility.

Maintenance decisions include

    what to maintain

    what kind of maintenance

    how to organize maintenance.

The types of maintenance are

    inspection

    service

    preventive

    repair/breakdown.

Replacement can follow breakdown or be used as a means to avoid breakdown.

Replacement policies relate to risk of failure, timing of replacement/frequency.

Tombari, H. A. (1982) Designing a maintenance management system. *Production and Inventory Management* **23** (4), pp. 139–147.

Cordero, S. T. (1987) *Maintenance Management Handbook*. Englewood Cliffs: Fairmont Press.

Kimmel, P. S. (1992) From a maintenance to a management system. *Facilities Design and Management* **11**(7).

Kelly, A. Harris, M. J. (1993) *Uses and limits of total productivity maintenance. Professional Engineering* **6**(1) pp. 9–11.

QUESTIONS

21.1 Define and differentiate between preventive maintenance and repair. What are the objectives of maintenance? In what circumstances is preventive maintenance particularly appropriate?

21.2 Describe briefly how you would collect and analyse data in order to assist in the determination of a maintenance policy for a small jobbing machine shop.

Having determined the policy, what data would you collect regularly in order to ensure that the maintenance procedures were adjusted to conform to changes in the characteristics of the equipment in the shop?

21.3 What are the principal factors which contribute to the effective operation of a facility throughout its entire life-cycle? In what way might decisions on or the management of certain of these factors reduce the need for maintenance of the facility during its operating life and/or delay the need for its replacement?

21.4 Show, by a simple numerical example, how the present value of future costs and revenues can be taken into account in comparing alternative replacement and maintenance policies for a facility.

Chapter 22

Performance measurement

ISSUES

What is the purpose of performance measurement?
What should be measured?
How do we measure customer service?
How do we measure resource utilization?
What is integrated productivity measurement?
What is Kaizen?
How is benchmarking used?

Two basic objectives for operating systems and operations management were identified in Chapter 1, i.e. the provision of customer service and resource utilization. If operating systems are intended to achieve certain objectives in respect of both customer service and resource, it is appropriate that system performance should be measured against both objectives. Performance measurement in respect of resource utilization is common in operations management. The measurement of performance in respect of customer service is less common.

Here we shall again consider the nature of both customer service and resource utilization and the manner in which objectives in each area are established and performance against them is measured.

CUSTOMER SERVICE PERFORMANCE

The items, movement or treatment provided by the operating system must match customers' needs if these customers are to be satisfied. The provision of customer service and the creation of customer satisfaction is a multi-dimensional problem, three principal factors having been identified in Chapter 1.

The measures of customer service: specification, cost and timing

These three customer service factors are general factors only; they each comprise several dimensions and in most cases it will be more practical and appropriate to assess or measure performance on these narrower dimensions.

1. The *specification* of goods may be considered in terms of their design features and performance characteristics. Together these dimensions define what the item is and how it is intended to perform its purpose. Similarly, the specification of a transport may be expressed in terms of its 'design' and performance. In this context design, i.e. the nature of the transport, movement may be expressed in terms of the origin, destination and route of movement. The performance can be considered synonymous with 'means', i.e. the means or method by which the movement is achieved. A service treatment may be defined in similar terms. The nature of the treatment can be considered to be the design characteristic or dimension, and the means by which the treatment is provided can be considered to be the performance characteristic. Two main dimensions can therefore be identified for the specification of items, movement or treatment. They are the 'what' and 'how' dimensions. In designing an item, a movement or a treatment an organization will define these two characteristics. In assessing the performance of an organization the customer will again consider these two dimensions. They are summarized in Table 22.1.

Table 22.1 The specifications of items, movement and treatment			
Dimensions for specification	**Items**	**Movement**	**Treatment**
Design, i.e. *what* is the item, movement/ treatment?	e.g. comprising: *Appearance* and dimensions *Material* specifications Design and manufacture quality	e.g. comprising; *Source, destination* and route	e.g. comprising: *Nature* of treatment
Performance, i.e. *how* is the purpose achieved? – the means or method employed	e.g. comprising: *Operating* characteristics or *performance* characteristics or operating principles or means	e.g. comprising: *Means* of transport	e.g. comprising: Means of treatment or *procedures* employed, or *form* of treatment

Source: Wild, R. (1979) Operations Management: A Policy Framework. *Oxford: Pergamon. Reproduced with permission*

2. The general dimension of *cost* identified above may similarly be broken down into important components. The customer—theoretically at least—will evaluate an item of a given specification in terms of its total expected costs, i.e. acquisition price plus any necessary additional expenses associated with an item, e.g. installation, running and maintenance costs, all discounted to the present time in order to take account of cash flows over a period of time. Similarly the cost of a transport movement or service may be expressed in terms of the original price of acquisition plus any additional and necessary costs or expenses. We can therefore distinguish, for our purposes, two aspects of costs, i.e. price and expenses. In seeking to provide customer service an organization will consider these two dimensions. In evaluating an organization, customers will

consider or respond to these two dimensions. These cost dimensions of customer service are summarized in Table 22.2.

Table 22.2	The cost of items, movement and treatment		
Dimensions for cost	**Items**	**Movement**	**Treatment**
Price, i.e. intended or quoted cost	e.g. comprising: *Purchase price*, or initial cost of good	e.g. comprising: *Cost of journey or fare*	e.g. comprising: *Cost of treatment or charge*
Expenses, i.e. expected additional costs	e.g. comprising: Cost of installation Cost of maintenance and replacement Running costs	e.g. comprising: Additional costs such as insurance, etc.	e.g. comprising: Additional costs such as insurance, etc.

Source: Wild, R. (1979) Operations Management: A Policy Framework. *Oxford: Pergamon. Reproduced with permission*

3. The third factor identified above—*timing*—may also be subdivided. Consider first the cost of goods. A customer will take into account the delay or wait involved between the expression of a want and the subsequent satisfaction of that want. This delay or wait will normally be evident as the period of time between placing an order and receiving the goods. This is clearly an important dimension of customer service, since delay greatly in excess of that which is acceptable will give rise to reduced overall customer satisfaction and loss of customers. Again this is a dimension which is, to some extent, within the control of the organization. It can, for example, set out deliberately to provide goods virtually on demand, or alternatively might choose to provide goods for which customers are expected to wait, perhaps for some considerable time. This delay dimension is also relevant in the provision of both transport and service. However, a further dimension is also important in these two functions. Both transport (i.e. movement) and service (i.e. treatment) are time consuming. In both cases, therefore, the customers will consider their likely duration or the time required for their performance, i.e. to move from source to destination, or to be treated or accommodated. In assessing an organization the customer will therefore have regard to this dimension, and equally, in seeking to achieve customer service, an organization will seek to provide an appropriate or acceptable duration for its transport or service. The timing factor can therefore be subdivided into the dimensions of delay and duration, summarized in Table 22.3.

Table 22.3	The timing of the provision of items, movement and treatment		
Dimensions for *timing*	**Items**	**Movement**	**Treatment**
Delay i.e. intended or quoted delay or waiting time	e.g. comprising: *Delivery time* or waiting time for delivery of goods	e.g. comprising: Time spent waiting for transport	e.g. comprising: Time spent waiting for treatment
Duration, i.e. intended or quoted duration		e.g. comprising: Travel time or duration of journey	e.g. comprising: Treatment time or duration of treatment

Source: Wild, R. (1979) Operations Management: A Policy Framework, *Oxford: Pergamon. Reproduced with permission*

Customers, in appraising the specification of an item, will be aware that it may perform differently in practice than had been intended at design. Design and performance characteristics may therefore be seen as intended features. There will be some probability that items will perform unsatisfactorily. An item may fail to function as intended, i.e. to achieve its intended purpose. It may function for some time and then fail, i.e. break down. It may function, but not at a desired level of performance. The customer must therefore consider the probability of an item satisfactorily achieving its intended purpose or continuing to achieve that purpose, i.e. its reliability. An organization must recognize this as a dimension of customer service and a characteristic of the product. The manner in which this reliability might be measured will depend on the nature of the item. It could, for example, be measured in terms of mean time between failures, or average operating life, or simply the probability that it will work at all. Similarly, in the specification of a transport or service, it is necessary to consider reliability, namely the probability of the required destination being reached and the probability of the movement being achieved as intended. The cost factor will also be seen in terms of its reliability. Price and expenses, as outlined above, can be considered to be quoted or intended costs. In practice, actual costs may differ, hence the probability of such changes will be an important customer service dimension and characteristic.

In considering the timing of goods, transport and service it is necessary to consider reliability issues. Both delay and duration, as discussed above, can be considered as intended times. The customer must consider the likelihood of the quoted or intended delay occurring and the likelihood of the quoted or intended duration occurring. In many cases in the provision of goods a delivery time is quoted, but both parties realize that there is a probability that in practice a longer delay will occur. Similarly, in the provision of transport, both parties will realize that, while the normal intended or quoted duration for a journey may be x hours, due to a variety of factors the actual duration may be greatly in excess of x hours. In this case, therefore, it is necessary again to consider reliability, i.e. the probability that the intended or quoted duration will in fact be achieved and the probability that the intended delay will in fact occur.

These three reliability dimensions (reliability of specification, cost and timing) are of major concern to operations management. The reliability of intended specification, cost and timing will depend to a considerable extent upon the effectiveness of operations management. Inadequate management of capacity, inventories, and poor scheduling may give rise to cost, timing and specification changes. Poor resource utilization will add to costs, bring delays, and increase durations. Inadequate execution of design intentions may give rise to poor performance. Since the responsibility for achieving customer service in these three areas is primarily the responsibility of operations management, operations management must have a major influence on the formulation of objectives on these three reliability dimensions.

Nine basic customer service dimensions can therefore be identified (Table 22.4). The intended specification, cost and timing of goods, transports and services will be largely determined by policy decisions within the organization. In some cases organizations will seek to maximize customer service on each of the six main dimensions, but in most cases different importance will be attached to each of these six dimensions. For this reason there can be no valid absolute measure of the performance of operations on design, performance, price, expenses, delay and duration. It is relevant only to measure the extent to which intended objectives are achieved, i.e. specification, cost and timing reliability.

Table 22.4	The principal dimensions of customer service	
Factors	**Dimensions**	
Specifications	i.e.	
of goods, movement	1. *Design*	7. *Specification reliability*
or treatment	2. *Performance*	
Cost	i.e.	
of goods, movement	3. *Price*	8. *Cost reliability*
or treatment	4. *Expenses*	
Timing	i.e.	
of goods, movement	5. *Delay*	9. *Timing reliability*
or treatment	6. *Duration*	

EXAMPLE:

Royal Bank of Scotland

The Royal Bank of Scotland began its process of service quality improvement with the aim of becoming more competitive, keeping customers, winning more repeat business, and taking more business from its competitors. It takes the view that service is sales, and that a higher quality of service must bring improved sales. The Bank has developed a service management system, which relies on a comprehensive measurement process, but is also about providing support through communication, training, etc. as well as ensuring that the environment is right for continuous improvement. The first stage of the process was to define customer needs and priorities. This led to the establishment of clear and agreed service standards against which performance would be judged. From that followed the development of measurement techniques.

Source: Crawford, R. (1993) Service you can bank on. *TQM Magazine* **5**(1) pp. 53–56.

RESOURCE UTILIZATION PERFORMANCE

Here we are on more familiar ground, for in most situations the intensity of the utilization of resources will be accepted as a legitimate measure of the performance of the operating system.

A useful approach to the discussion of resource productivity as a concept is the identification of the manner in which various interested parties might apply measurement. From the engineer's standpoint, productivity and efficiency are synonymous and efficiency is the measure of the amount of energy supplies converted into useful work. Productivity would be seen as the quotient obtained by dividing output by a factor of production, whether capital or raw material. Input generates output, and in a physical sense at least the quotient cannot exceed unity, although in a financial sense it must do so if the business is to secure a profit to survive.

An economist might take a different approach and might emphasize labour rather than capital productivity. Emphasis on the former encourages one to express inputs in terms of labour or labour equivalent, with attendant risks of estimation, averaging, etc. In an attempt to overcome this, we can employ the idea of net output per employee as a productivity measure, i.e.

$$\text{Net output per employee} = \frac{\text{Added value per annum}}{\text{Total number of employees}}$$

'Added value' represents the value added to materials by the process of production and from which wages, salaries, rent, rates, tax reserves and dividends, selling distribution, and advertising costs have to be met.

An accountant might take yet another view. Many contemporary productivity measures are financially oriented because many firms evaluate the worth and effectiveness of their enterprise by using 'financial ratio analysis'. A variety of ratios might be developed, but it is essential that those adopted be seen to be useful and relevant. The following are among those commonly employed:

(a) profit/capital employed;

(b) profit/sales;

(c) sales/capital employed;

(d) sales/fixed assets;

(e) sales/stocks;

(f) sales/employee;

(g) profits/employee.

In such an approach an emphasis is placed on sales revenue and profit; however, it is possible that both are affected by market supply and demand factors as well as being influenced by the efficiency of operations.

Integrated productivity measurement

Each of these approaches to the measurement of productivity may be seen as parts of a composite or integrated productivity model. Such a model has been developed and

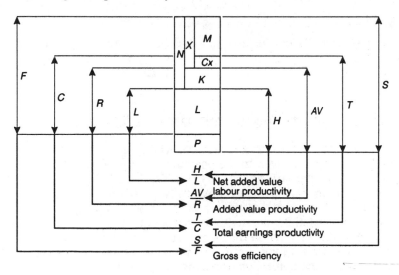

Figure 22.1 Integrated productivity measurement model. Adapted with permission from Norman, R. G. and Bahiri, S. (1972) *Productivity Measurement and Incentives*. London: Butterworth

presented by Norman and Bahiri (see 'Further Reading'). Figure 22.1 presents an integrated productivity model through which can be identified various means for the measurement of the productivity of operating systems. The notation is given in Table 22.5. All inputs and outputs are measured in financial units, and while the model is particularly relevant in the measurement of resource productivity in conversion or creation systems, it can be modified for use in service, and even non-profit, systems. Referring back to the above, the engineer's measure of efficiency might be seen to be equivalent to a measure of total earnings productivity, i.e. T/C in Figure 22.1. The economist's measure may be seen to be equivalent to added value productivity, i.e.

AV/R, while the accountant's measure of productivity may be seen to be equivalent to the measure of gross efficiency shown in Figure 22.1, i.e. S/F.

Table 22.5	Notation for integrated productivity measurement model
S	= Sales revenue or gross output
T	= Total earnings
AV	= Added value or net output
H	= Net earnings
M	= Materials throughput
Cx	= Indirect external expenses
X	= Total external purchase
K	= Capital charges
N	= Non-labour factorial cost
L	= Employment or labour charges
P	= Profits
C	= Operations costs
F	= Total factorial inputs
R	= Internal expenses

Source: Adapted with permission from Norman, R. G. and Bahri, S. (1972) Productivity Measurement and Incentives. London: Butterworth

The 'physical' dimensions of resource utilization

The above integrated approach takes a largely financial approach to resource productivity measurement. Returning, however, to the operations management objectives developed in Chapter 1, we might alternatively logically consider three dimensions of resource productivity, and in so doing take a largely 'physical' approach to the measurement of productivity. In Chapter 1 we identified three principal types of operating system resource: machines, labour and materials. We shall now consider these dimensions of productivity measurement. They offer another means for productivity measurement. Capital or money will often be considered, as above, although since all resources can be measured and expressed in financial terms it may, on occasions, be logical to consider money as a common denominator resource, and as a unit for the measurement of productivity for each resource and overall productivity.

Each of our three main physical resources must be used effectively, hence we must consider productivity on each of these three 'dimensions'. Table 22.6 outlines some objectives for each resource and some means of measuring productivity against these objectives. In each case the achievement of high productivity can be considered in terms of maximizing resource utilization or, of course, minimizing loss or waste. The precise objectives and hence also the performance standards employed will depend on the nature of the resource in each area, as will also the amount of detail necessary in both stating and measuring the achievement of objectives in these areas.

Table 22.6   Resource utilization and measurement

Resource	Utilization objectives	Utilization measures
Machines i.e. all physical items, e.g. equipment, tools, buildings, space, directly and indirectly used by the system.	e.g. *Maximize* Output/distance/throughput/ machine hour Proportion of total available time utilized Effectiveness of utilization (e.g. capacity utilized) Occupancy/space utilization	Output/distance/throughput/ machine hour Time(s) used or percentage Capacity used or percentage Occupancy/space utilization or percentage
	Minimize Idle time and downtime Under-utilized/unoccupied space Machine cost content	Idle time and/or downtime or percentage Percentage utilized/occupied space Machine cost content or percentage
Labour i.e. those people who directly or indirectly necessarily provide or contribute to the operation of the system, e.g. manual labour, supervision, etc	e.g. *Maximize* Output/distance/throughput/ work hour Proportion of total available time utilized Effectiveness of utilization (e.g. capacity utilized)	Output/distance/throughput/ work hour Time(s) used or percentage Capacity used or percentage
	Minimize Idle and ineffective time Labour cost content	Idle and/or ineffective time or percentage Labour cost content or percentage
Materials i.e. those physical items directly or indirectly consumed or converted by the system.	e.g. *Maximize* Yield (i.e. output/distance/ throughput) per unit weight/ volume, etc.	Yield quantity, weight, etc.
	Minimize Wastage, losses or scrap Material cost content	Wastage, losses or scrap quantity or percentage Rework/rectification quantity or percentage Material cost content or percentage

IMPROVEMENT AND BENCHMARKING

Much of what has been discussed in the previous chapter has relevance to performance improvement in operations. Many of the procedures presented there, if effectively used, should contribute to improvements in operating performance. Now it is appropriate in the final chapter to reinforce the notion that operations managers, in all that they do, aim to contribute to continual improvement in system performance. We shall deal briefly with two specific aspects: continual improvement and benchmarking.

Continual Improvement

The Japanese have a term for the continuous systematic effort to improve business, or system performance: *Kaizen*. It means the gradual unerring improvement, and thus the setting and achieving of ever higher standards. There are two prerequisites for the effective use of this type of approach, i.e.

1. setting demanding but achievable objectives;

2. feedback of achievements against these objectives.

These, in turn, require other actions and/or conditions, e.g.

For 1: Objectives must relate to business strategies;

         Objectives must be agreed by all parties;

         Objectives must be relevant to the tasks of employees.

For 2: Feedback must be frequent and regular;

         Opportunities for examination and analysis of achievements must exist.

In addition, generally, the following will also be required:

         Remuneration will be related to performance;

         High achievement will be recognized by awards;

         Operations problem solving procedures are required, so that obstacles to improvements in performance can be removed;

         There will be a participative process-oriented management style.

Kaizen is a philosophy and, of course, has much in common with total quality management (Chapter 19).

Benchmarking

Finally and logically, we turn to Benchmarking: a technique which enables organizations to compare performance to relevant and achievable standards and thus help secure continual improvement.[1]

Arguably intermittent heat measurements of operations performance, such as output/throughput performance, provide little value to managers; but by measuring performance over time, managers can establish a record of performance and measure the rate of improvement. In order to judge the performance of operations effectively, therefore, managers should compare, i.e. benchmark, performance with the outside world (see Figure 22.2) A benchmark can be an historical reference point that has already been

---

[1] Miller, J.A. (1992) Measuring Progress through Benchmarking. *CMA Magazine*, **66**(4), May, p. 37.

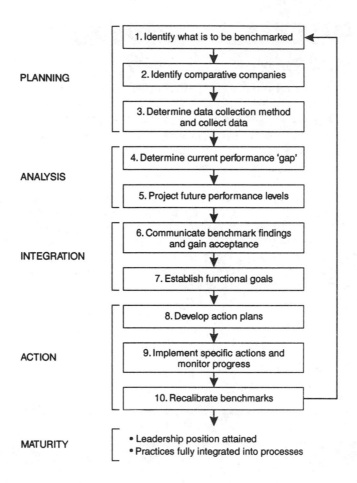

Figure 22.2 Benchmarking process steps. Reproduced, with permission, from Camp, R. C. (1989) *Benchmarking.* Milwaukee, Wis.: Quality Press (Am. Soc. for Qual. Control).

passed or, more appropriately, a goal not expected to be reached for some time. Usually the benchmark reflects best known actual performance for a sector, or the performance of a respected competitor. Obtaining benchmark data needed to create an external-based comparison of performance and improvement can be difficult, since most organizations are secretive about internal measures of performance. However, procedures exist, using for example consultants, or survey organizations, to enable market-oriented measures to be obtained, against which an organization can measure its own performance.

Thus, there are two basic complementary aspects of performance measurement: internal, against company norms and standards; and external, against competitors standards.

Rank Xerox

Competitive benchmarking is closely tied to the RX 'Leadership Through Quality' programme. The elements are as follows:

1. *Planning.* Decide what is going to be benchmarked, and how to find out information about that company. Care must be taken in securing information. Direct contact with competitors is not allowed. All information-gathering must be open. Systematic questioning of customers (of both RX and/or other suppliers) is the normal way, e.g. through surveys, questioning by service engineers, etc.
2. *Analysis.* After the data are gathered, they must be analysed. The following questions would be relevant. 'Is the competition really better?' 'How much better?' 'What seems to make them better—what are they doing that we are not?' 'Could we do it?' 'Should we do it?'
3. *Integration.* This step is to do with gearing up for change, i.e. on the basis of the data analysis, deciding what changes are going to be made in the way work is done. If the changes involve other people, this step includes communicating to them what has been learned and what needs to change. Together, a list of functional goals can be established that take advantage of what has been learned from the competition.
4. *Action.* In this step, action plans to achieve goals are developed, implemented and evaluated. Evaluation asks the question: 'Are we doing better as a result of this than we were doing before?'

If evaluation shows that there is still a gap between RX practices and those of the competitor, it will be necessary to go back and repeat the process.

Source: *Leadership through Quality.* Rank Xerox (UK) Ltd. Circa 1991.

KEY POINTS FOR CHAPTER 22

Operations performance should be measured against operations objectives, i.e.

  Customer Service

  Resource Utilization.

Customer service performance should cover:

  specification/quality

  cost/price

  timing/availability.

The measurement of resource utilization performance often takes the form of:

  output

  input.

Continual improvement is a corporate policy, often supported by benchmarking.

Benchmarking is a means to compare performance against that of others.

FURTHER READING

Chew, W. B. (1988) No nonsense guide to measuring productivity. *Harvard Business Review*, Jan-Feb, pp. 110–118.

Didis, S. K. (1990) *Kaizen Internal Auditor*, **47**(4), pp. 64–69.

Wisner, J. D., Fawcett, S. E. (1991) Linking firm strategy to operating decisions through performance measurement *Prod & Inv Mgt*, **32**(3), pp. 5–11.

Camp, R. C. (1989) Benchmarking: the search for industry best practices that lead to superior performance *Quality Progress*, **22**(4), pp. 62–69 (also, book of same title, pub 1989 by Quality Press, Wisconsin).

QUESTIONS

22.1 Describe and compare the customer service objectives which might be expected to influence the operation of the following systems:

   (a) a small bespoke (i.e. 'made to measure') gents' manufacturing tailor.

   (b) a dentist's practice;

   (c) a city bus service.

   How might system performance in respect of these objectives be measured in each case?

22.2 Show how (a) added value productivity (b) gross efficiency and (c) total earnings productivity would be measured in a small batch production to stock manufacturing organization.

22.3 Compare the notion of reliability introduced in this chapter with that discussed in Chapter 21. How might measures of item performance reliability and techniques for maintenance management be of value in performance measurement?

PART 9

International Case Studies

N.B. These cases are not intended to illustrate effective or ineffective management or decision making. They are intended only as a basis for student work and 'classroom' discussion.

INTRODUCTION TO PART 9

The material in this part of the book is intended to support that in Parts 1–8. These international cases are included here for use as study aids, as 'vehicles' for group discussion, and as bases for assignments, presentations, assessments, etc. Together they cover most of the topics dealt with in the previous chapters; however, as they deal with real, often complex situations, they do not in general focus exclusively on any single topic, and it is for this reason that they have been grouped together here rather than included at the end of chapters.

ACKNOWLEDGEMENTS

I am grateful to the following in the preparation of these cases:

Sheena Orr	For the preparation of the material on which the 'Jograni Handicrafts' case study is based, and for writing much of the case study;
Geoff Buxey	For writing and providing 'The Shiro of Corio' case study;
Henrique Correa	For writing and providing the 'American Burger and Past' case study;
Roy Snaddon	For writing and providing the 'Linden Christian Nursery A' and 'B' case studies;
Nevan Wright	For writing and providing the 'Open Polytechnic of New Zealand' case study;
Tow Khee Kin	For writing and providing the 'Food Concept' case study.

Case study 1

Carreras SL

CARRERAS SL is involved in making, packaging, distribution and the sale of wines, in the Levante region of Spain, i.e. the area around and inland from Valencia and Alicante on the Mediterranean coast (see Figure CS1.1). It is an old-established organization which has grown substantially, and now faces decisions about its future development in the context of a rapidly changing Spanish wine industry.

THE SPANISH WINE INDUSTRY

Spain has about 1700 hectares (1 ha = 2.47 acres) of vineyards, the largest of any country world wide. This compares for example with Italy 1400 and France 1300. However, Spain only produces about 33 million hectolitres of wine per annum or approximately 20 hl/ha which compares to 70 million hectolitres for Italy—the world's largest producer, and 66 million hectolitres for France.

Spain has a wine consumption per capital less than that of other large producer areas. Table 1 makes comparisons.

More than 50 per cent of Spain's vineyards (approximately 1050 ha) are designated 'Denominacion de Origen' under the quality control system established in 1972 (compared to 12 per cent DOC in Italy and 15 per cent Appellation Contrôlée in France). There are 39 DO areas. They produce approximately one-third of the total wine output. Some of the DO areas are listed in Table CS1.2.

The largest producing region is La Mancha (4 DOs). The second largest is Levante (6 DOs). Table CS1.3 shows outputs for domestic use and for export by wine type for several of the 32 DO areas.

The best known and highest quality wine is considered to be Rioja (excluding Jerez—Sherry, a fortified wine). Approximate comparative trade price indices for some Spanish wines (Rioja = 100) are shown in Table CS1.4.

Spain presently exports about 25 per cent of total production (compared to 20 per cent for Italy and 9 per cent for France). Traditionally most wine has been exported in bulk, and has been used in countries such as France, Germany and Italy for blending and fortification purposes, partly because of the traditionally high alcoholic strength of Spanish wines (typically 13–14 per cent compared to 10 per cent and 11 per cent in Italy and France) but also because of their relative cheapness and the lack of a substantial market for Spanish wines per se (excepting Rioja and Sherry). However, in recent years things have begun to change, exports have increased and the proportion of exports in bottles has grown substantially: Table CS1.5.

THE WINE-MAKING PROCESS

The process

All that is required to convert grapes to wine is fermentation, which is the chemical process of changing sugar into alcohol and carbon dioxide brought about by yeasts: micro-organisms in the grape skins. This process can take place naturally provided the grape skins are broken. But left entirely to nature, fermentation will convert all the sugar, and so the wine will be dry and high in alcohol (e.g. about 15 per cent by volume). So often fermentation is stopped by neutralizing the yeast or by filtering it out.

By using different grape varieties and by controlling the fermentation, different types of wine can be produced.

The basic steps typically involved in wine making are:

1. Grapes harvested (approximately October);
2. Grapes crushed and (usually) de-stemmed;
3. Grapes pressed and (for white wine only) skins removed;
   (October/November)
4. Fermentation in vat (up to 15 days);
5. Wine run off and filtered into barrels or larger containers (racking);
6. Re-racking and storage in barrels/tanks;   (November–June or longer for wine to be matured)
7. Blending of wines (if appropriate);   (June year 2)
8. Bottling (if appropriate);   (June year 2)
9. Ageing in bottles (if appropriate).   (June year 2 onwards)

Wine types and terminology

vino de mesa	table wine
vino corriente	ordinary wine (not usually bottled)
blanco	white
tinto	red
rosado	rose
seco	dry
dulce	sweet
espumoso/cava	sparkling
Reserva	mature quality wine
Denominaciones de Origen	area with 'regulated' output based on maximum yield, content, etc.

CARRERAS SL

The organization began as a small business located in Requena, 70k west of Valencia, the home town of the Carreras family who have been involved in wine-making for 35 years.

Originally they made mainly red wines from their own vines in their own vinery, for sale locally and in Valencia. Over the following years, under the control of Sr Carreras, the business grew, mainly through certain key developments:

1. 1970   The extension and modernization of the family's wine making facilities at Requena to create a modern 'Cooperativa' with a capacity of 30 000 hl per annum. It was set up to serve not only the family's requirements but also the needs of the local growers in the Utiel–Requena area, many of whom could not afford nor were big enough to justify the investment in more modern wine-making and storage facilities.

2. 1975   The establishment of a road freight company to transport both bulk and bottled wine from the Requena Cooperativa.

3. 1975–85 The acquisition of a controlling interest in 5 Cooperativas in neighbouring DO areas, i.e.

    Valencia

    Jumilla

    Alamansa

    Yecla

    Alicante

    together, after modernization and extension, having a capacity of 200 000 hl per annum.

4. 1978–88 The development of a chain of 'bodegas' providing retail outlets for wine in major towns and tourist regions in the Valencia and Alicante provinces, mainly through acquisition from private operators.

5. 1983   The commissioning of a blending and bottling, packaging and warehouse facility in Valencia.

Through this development, the business (which was established as Carreras SL in 1985) grew into the largest of its type in the region, comprising, by 1991, the following:

Las Cavas Levante—a company operating 8 Cooperativas (in the 6 DO areas);

Bodegas Carreras—a company operating 15 retail wine stores;

Transportes Vinos Levante—the transport company, comprising 10 vehicles;

Industria Carreras—the packaging and warehousing business.

The business overall is profitable, and still controlled entirely by the Carreras family. Carreras SL, the holding company, is headquartered at Requena. Las Cavas and Bodegas Headquarters are also at Requena. Transportes and Industria are based in Valencia. All four companies operate under their own management, each having a Director and relevant staff. The four businesses as they are now are described below:

Las Cavas Levante

All Cooperativas operate in a similar manner. They differ in scale, in produce/product mix and in the number of growers they serve.

All grapes are provided by local growers who, if they choose to deal with the Cooperativa, must opt annually for one of two contractual relationships.

1. Sale of grapes to the Cooperativa at the time of delivery, at the prevailing price deter-

mined by the Cooperativa management for the relevant type, quality and quantity.

2. Contract, at a price agreed with the Cooperativa for the processing of the grapes for the production of wine which remains the property of the grower, who may, by July the following year, choose to remove the wine, sell it on to a third party, or sell it to the Cooperativa at the prevailing price determined by the Cooperativa management.

   NB Contract price for processing paid 50 per cent on delivery of grapes and 50 per cent by July the following year.

Negotiations between growers and the Cooperativa typically take place in July, after prices are announced. Until such negotiations are finished, the Cooperativa does not know how many suppliers it will have that September/October. The extent of the harvest, and thus the quantity and quality of grapes to be provided by contracted growers, is not known until September/October. The busy period in the Cooperativa is from September through to early November.

Each Cooperativa has facilities to produce the wines appropriate for its area. In doing so, wine produced from different growers' grapes are not separated. Their rights to the wine are determined in relation to their portion of the tonnage of the grapes used.

The Cooperativa supplies wine in bulk from vats either into the customers' own containers or into the Cooperativa's own bottles or cubitainers (large plastic containers) labelled with the Cooperativa's own label, or left blank. The customers for such wine are:

> The local growers (contracted under 2. above);
>
> Local retailers (e.g. shops, restaurants, etc.) and individuals;
>
> Industria Carreras.

Traditionally several of the Carreras Cooperativas also processed other crops, mainly olives and almonds, but such work has been largely phased out as the Company invested in the modernization and extension of the wine-making facilities.

Whilst growers without their own facilities are not obliged to use their local Cooperativa (they can transport their grapes to other Cooperativas in other towns), they are usually loyal to their local Cooperativa providing the price they receive/pay is competitive.

The relationship of growers to the Cooperativa, i.e. whether they chose 1 or 2 above, is influenced by the demand for their local wines and their ability to sell their own brand wines. In general, demand for local wines is higher in the higher quality areas.

Some details on each of the Cooperativas is given in Table CS1.6.

Bodegas Carreras

The 15 retail wine stores, whilst located throughout the region, are in general located in the larger or tourist towns, e.g. Alcoy, Gandía, Benidorm, Alicante, Denia, Valencia, Oliva, Jávea, Algemesí. They are all now owned freehold by the Company, and managed by local managers employed by the Company. Each outlet stocks a full range of spirits, beers, soft drinks, waters, juices, milks, oils, fortified wines, table wines and certain foodstuffs (e.g. nuts and snacks). The wines stocked, whilst including the full range from Carreras, also include other brands. The Carreras wines are supplied by Industria Carreras and not directly from any of the company's Cooperativas. The same Carreras wines are stocked by each bodega. A typical profile of a bodega is shown in Table CS1.7.

Trade tends to be higher during the summer period, especially in the tourist areas, with other peaks around Easter and Christmas/New Year. In addition to 'over the counter' retail custom, all of the bodegas have trade customers (e.g. local hotels, bars, restaurants etc.) In some areas this part of the business has grown substantially. However each bodega deals only with such customers in its own area (i.e. there is no 'trade' competition between the 15 bodegas). Long-term large-scale supply contracts for large trade customers can be established directly between such customers and Industria Carreras (see below).

Transportes Vinos Levante

The transport company is based in Valencia. Currently the main vehicle fleet (excluding cars, service vans, etc.) is:

2 Ebro 'L80', 4-wheel rigid open truck with canvas cover

TARA (unladen weight) 3730 kg

PMA (vehicle gross weight) 8000 kg

3 same, as tanker vehicle: 4000-litre capacity

2 Pegaso, 6-wheel rigid open truck with canvas cover

TARA 11 000 kg

PMA 26 000 kg

3 Nissan 'Trade 2.8', 4-wheel rigid van

TAR 2310 kg

PMA 3500 kg

Occasionally additional vehicles are hired and/or major transport jobs sub-contracted.

The vehicles are engaged on the following principal tasks:

Deliveries from Industria Carreras to:

Las Bodegas Carreras (bottled and cubitainers)

Local retailers and trade customers (bottled)

Wine exporters (bottled, cubitainers and bulk wines)

Deliveries from Carreras Cooperativas to:

Industria Carreras (cubitainer and bulk wines)

General transport activities, e.g. of equipment, materials, etc.

The work of Transportes Vinos Levante is the responsibility of a Director, based at the Valencia headquarters.

Industria Carreras

The company is responsible for the blending, bottling, packaging and warehouse facilities at a single site location in Valencia. The activities undertaken are as follows:

Receipt of wine in containers or in bulk (tanker) from the Company's Cooperativas (June–September);

Storage of such wine;

DO wine blending to the extent permitted by the regulations in order to provide Carreras branded wines for each of the DO source areas;

Table wine blending (non-DO) to provide Carreras branded table wines;

Bottling, labelling and casing of wines;

Supply of wines (bottle or container) to the company's Bodegas;

Supply of wines (bottle) to other local (Levante region) retailers, wholesalers and other large trade customers (e.g. hotels);

Supply of wines (bottle or container or bulk) to exporters;

Storage of wines (bulk, container or bottle) for stock and/or maturing.

The capacity available is currently as follows:

Blending/bottling/packaging	120 000 hl p.a.
Bulk storage	100 000 hl
Bottle/cubitainer storage	50 000 hl

The Company is managed by a Director based at Valencia.

THE MANAGEMENT OF CARRERAS SL

The company is controlled by the family. The President is still Sr Carreras. Other members of the family hold senior management roles. The Directors responsible for Las Cavas Levante and Industria Carreras are members of the family. Recently a new Director General was appointed to run Carreras SL. This appointment attracted considerable interest in Spain. For example, translated extracts from an interview in the national news section of a leading regional daily paper are given below.

You were appointed to the new post of Director General by the President of Carreras SL two months ago. However, you haven't worked in the family company, or in Spain, for nearly five years. Are you well prepared for this new job?

Sra Carreras

I worked for what is now Carreras SL for four years after finishing at University in Madrid and before going abroad for postgraduate study. I married at the end of my course and we worked together for three years in the wine industry in France until we both decided to come here earlier this year. So I feel that I have relevant knowledge and experience for the job, and may be able to bring some different views.

Do you believe that a new approach is needed in the Company now?

Sra Carreras

Certainly. The Spanish wine industry has changed dramatically since our entry to the EEC in 1986, but in both quality and efficiency we still lag far behind other European countries as well as the new world producers. There is a growing awareness of and market for Spanish wines in Northern Europe, but the output of many parts of Spain, including our region, are still largely unknown. We are still essentially a domestic industry struggling to modernize.

But what approach will you adopt with your Company which is already, in some respects, the dominant wine business in this region, and what are the main problems you now face?

Sra Carreras

One of our main problems is the lack of specialist and management skills. This is not a well-developed region with strong industry and business. It is difficult to find good managers and

---

technical people here, or to tempt them to come here. That is not likely to change, indeed it may get worse, so we need to have a better understanding of how we must manage each of our four businesses, each of which in many respects is quite different to the others. If, for example, there are major similarities, then we can perhaps develop our own management talent or organize the businesses in such a way that we can manage with fewer people. However, if each of the four businesses needs a different type of approach, then we may have to decide whether we should be doing so many different things. This company has just grown. We must now ask ourselves whether, managerially, we are in one business or four. Only then can we decide how to develop in the future and take advantage of the rapid changes which will undoubtedly continue in this industry. This will be my first priority.

Yours was a very unusual appointment, especially in a country like Spain. How do you feel about it now that you have seen some of the critical reaction from elsewhere in the industry?

Sra Carreras

Well I certainly do not agree with Cervantes's statement that 'An honest woman and a broken leg are best at home', and I aim to prove my critics to be wrong.

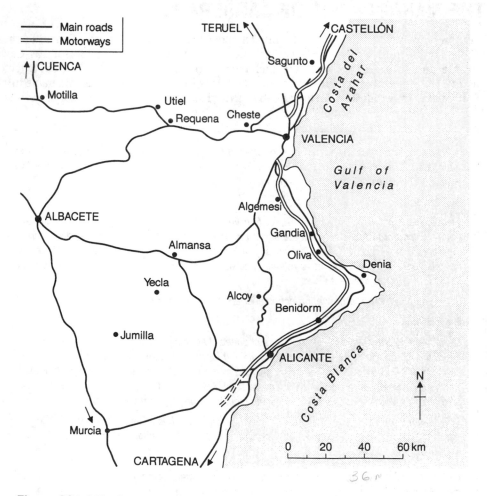

Figure CS1.1 The Levante region

Table CS1.1 Per capita wine consumption (litres/person/year)

	1990	1969
France	74	112
Italy	62.1	114
Luxembourg	58.3	31
Portugal	58	93.2
Argentina	55.8	87.5
Switzerland	49.9	38.6
Spain	47.4*	62.5
Chile	35	48.9
Austria	32.9	32
UK (26th by rank order)	11.4	2.8

N.B. Rank order by 1990 figures.

*50% white, 25% red, 25% rosé.

Table CS1.2 Some DO regions—area

DO	Area (000 ha)
Mancha	485
Tarragona	–
Rioja	44
Jerez	11
Cariñena	22
Penedes	–
Motilla-Moriles	–
Navarra	23
Huelva	19
Utriel Requena	50
Valencia	–
Almansa	8
Jumilla	25
Alicante	–
Yecla	26
All 32 DO areas	1050

(Utriel Requena, Valencia, Almansa, Jumilla, Alicante, Yecla bracketed as **Levante**)

Table CS1.3	Some DO regions—outputs (hl 1988–1989)				
DO		**White**	**Rosé**	**Red**	**Others**
Motilla-Moriles	Domestic	4	0	0	225
	Export	93	0	34	–
La Mancha (4 DOs)		702	27	687	0
		56	3	80	0
Rioja		107	104	618	0
		40	19	284	0
Jerez		0	0	0	194
		0	0	0	841
Navarra		13	126	94	0
		7	17	89	0
Huelva		97	0	6	31
		0	0	0	12
Penedes		362	37	50	0
		54	30	40	0
Cariñena		79	65	150	0
		1	1	5	0
Valencia		78	10	51	6
		110	28	103	9
Almansa		0	5	19	0
		0	0	1	0
Utiel Requena		2	22	33	0
		0.6	29	56	0
Jumilla	Levante	16	148	228	0
		4	15	117	0
Yecla		1	1.5	3	0
		0	1.5	3	0
Alicante		6	61	1	0
		0	0	20	0
Tarragona		289	8	37	3
		10	4	29	1
Total (32 DO areas)		2059	685	2288	1165
		446	149	8631	1260

N.B. 0 = zero or negligible.

1188.6

Table CS1.4   Wine trade price indices

DO	Approximate price index	
Rioja	100	(xx)
Rioja 'reserva'	125	(xxx)
Rioja 'gran reserva'	200	(xxxx)
Navarra	90	(xx)
Mancha	80	(x)
Jerez	125	
Motilla-Moriles	120	(xxx)
Cariñena	80	(x)
Penedes	100	(x–xxx)
Tarragona	100	(x–xxx)
Huelva	100	(x–xx)
Alicante	60	(x)
Valencia	50	(x)
Jumilla	70	(x)
Yecla	60	(x)
Utiel Requena	50	(x)
Almansa	60	(x)

Alicante, Valencia, Jumilla, Yecla, Utiel Requena, Almansa } Levante

N.B. ( ) = Quality rating from recent wine guide (x–xxxxx).

Table CS1.5   Spanish wine exports

	1981	1991 (approx.)
Table wine exports in bottle	16%	50%
Table wine exports in bulk	84%	50%

Destinations (1990) (% of total exports)

Germany	22
UK	19
Netherlands	13
France	4
Denmark	4
Belgium	3
All EC	66.5
Switzerland	12
All EFTA	19
USA	4

Table CS1.6 Profiles of Las Cavas Levante

Cooperativa No.	DO Area	Processing capacity p.a. (hl)	Typical no. of growers p.a.	Approx. % of throughput under contract type (1)	(2)
1	Utriel-Requena	33 000	120–170	85	15
2	Utriel-Requena	28 000	80–140	75	25
3	Valencia	100 000	180–240	75	25
4	Jumilla	85 000	100–150	30	70
5	Jumilla	70 000	90–140	35	65
6	Almansa	8500	30–40	60	40
7	Yecla	5500	30–40	60	40
8	Alicante	27 000	170–220	70	30

Table CS1.7 Profile of a typical Carreras bodega

Product		Number of different brands or types	% of total turnover
Spirits		15	12
Beers		3	9
Soft drinks		15	8
Waters		4	3
Juices		10	3
Milk		3	2
Oils		4	2
Fortified wines		10	12
Table wines			
	Carreras	10	18
	Others	10	21
Other items			10

Jograni Handicrafts

JOGRANI is a medium-sized handicrafts co-operative based in Dhaka, Bangladesh. Its main function, at present, is to market the various items produced by its 53 member societies. The relatively few male societies concentrate mostly on wood-based products, whilst the women use their sewing, weaving and basket-work skills. Most of the societies comprise poor rural women or men.

JOGRANI currently has a turnover of 90 000 per annum. It runs two marketing outlets itself but more than 50 per cent of its stock is sold through other outlets.

Product supply

In some cases member societies will request a design input. More often than not this is prompted by Jograni staff who are more in touch with the market place and the need to provide variations on traditional products.

Once items have been made in any reasonable amount they are sent immediately to the central marketing warehouse, as few societies have any secure storage facilities. Also, they have very little capital, so a watchful eye must be kept on their cashflow.

Goods are stocked at the central warehouse after being given a brief check for flaws and tagged with a JOGRANI tag. They are held in stock to await being made up into orders for dispatch to retail outlets.

Present markets

JOGRANI's market at present has three main segments:

(a) foreign tourists, who pay premium price for items to be exported;
(b) local 'ex-patriates', who pay above average price for items mainly for use in Bangladesh;
(c) middle/upper class Bangladeshis, who pay lower 'local' price.

The objective from the start has been to focus on the tourist and ex-patriate markets but, as this requires a significant degree of quality control as well as relevant design work, the task has been long and arduous. With help from consultants, JOGRANI has, however, partly achieved its objectives. Currently, 6 per cent of products are sold to tourists, 44 per cent to local ex-patriates and the remaining 50 per cent to Bangladeshis.

FUTURE MARKETS?

JOGRANI is now having to consider future policy, particularly as the handicraft market becomes more competitive. Present government restrictions on the number of missions and aid agencies working in Bangladesh have raised the question of a diminishing market amongst ex-patriates

The organization has grown steadily over the past 15 years but is now at a point where it needs to plan for the next 10 years. It has seen some of its stronger competitors go into the export business and is considering whether this is a viable option, given the problems that presently exist in producing quality items for the tourist market (where the quality demanded is virtually the same). On the one hand it is seen as the next logical step—simply an extension of current activities. Others argue that it will lead to some fundamental changes in the way in which the organization works, not least by altering the principal operational objectives which at present are dominated by resource and cost considerations, possibly to the detriment of aspects of customer service.

The tourist market has already shown JOGRANI that it needs to produce better quality items. At present only 6 per cent of turnover is derived from tourists, despite premium prices. A decision to export would mean new markets as well as better quality goods with more emphasis on customer service.

Scheduling has been largely a function of how much producers send to the warehouse. With little way of controlling these arrivals, inventory levels can vary enormously and tend to peak dramatically around (Muslim) festival times when producers are desperate for money. Trying to produce 'seasonal' items for non-Muslim festivals, such as embroidered Christmas cards, thus becomes a rather hit-and-miss affair.

FUTURE OPERATING PROCEDURES?

If Jograni is to achieve what is set out above, it is clear that certain changes will be necessary in the ways in which the organization operates. Amongst the implications of these changes are the following, which must now be considered by the management.

For *design* the current ad hoc system will probably have to be replaced. Systematic training and design input will probably be needed.

Local manufacture will still take place but some centrally supplied raw materials may be needed.

Distribution will perhaps undergo the biggest change. Research has shown that foreign buyers are particular in their orders and often specify minute changes to ensure originality. The implication is that a unique set of goods is produced for each overseas customer. In some cases raw materials may be supplied by the buyer to ensure adequate quality.

Overall *capacity* will probably have to increase in order to provide the volumes required for bulk ordering by overseas buyers. There is known to be some underemployment of facilities at present. However, estimating supply as well as forecasting future demand will be important tasks. Further, since at present output stocks absorb some demand fluctuations, the move towards supplying against customer orders will necessitate a different approach to capacity.

Stocks will still be important for two reasons:

1. The home market will still be the 'cash cow' of the business and improvements in inventory management may help to improve this part of the business;

2. Foreign buyers often like to take back large samples with which to test their market. Competitors already have showrooms backed up by a wide range of stock. This enables a quick response to buyers' initial requests.

At present, each group procures its own materials. Central *purchasing* of some materials has, however, been considered, mainly for reasons of quality control (e.g. batik work, where it is difficult to know the quality of the dye being bought beforehand). Reduced cost through bulk buying would be an added advantage. But, for JOGRANI, it would mean additional storage space.

There are expected to be some major implications for *scheduling*. To a larger extent customers' requirements will determine the delivery dates, rather than internal production schedules. This, in many ways, is seen to be the key to success in the export market, for even if the right quality of goods is produced, the delivery time, which will be linked to a 'movement' time (e.g. shipping arrangements), will be crucial to the whole process.

As a cultural aside it is worth pointing out that 'time' is much more 'fluid' in Asian cultures and while the more westernized Asian may appreciate the concept of a delivery date, conveying this idea to the rural producer is not just a question of introducing a new business concept but a whole new cultural viewpoint. Also, rural producers are rarely 'full-time' craft producers and will typically have many commitments. The priorities for them may not necessarily coincide with those of JOGRANI centrally, despite the fact that JOGRANI is attempting to work in their interests. In this respect it is also worth noting that those handicraft producers who have succeeded in breaking into the export market have all got the following in common:

1. centralized production centres near or in the capital city;
2. vertical integration of all activities to ensure schedules are met;
3. centralized purchasing of raw materials to some degree (usually more rather than less);
4. close ties with member groups including additional services such as literacy, health and community development;
5. substantial design and technical input (invariably by foreigners).

Thus in the Bangladesh context, the handicraft market cannot be divorced from the wider cultural and societal values and norms. Overcoming and developing these are additional challenges on top of the operational ones.

Quality is considered to be the key to successfully establishing a position in the export market. For this reason, a number of 'options' must be considered, i.e.

1. *Specifications* for items will be more rigorous than for the home market. Fashion and colour considerations will also be important. The ability of producers to incorporate specific design features into the process will for most handicraft producers be a new concept. The emphasis for some products may change from making what comes 'naturally' to making for a market. In the initial stages special training will be important.

2. The variability and sub-standard quality of some *inputs* such as dyes for batik work raises the question of central purchasing. This is one way of introducing more control over the input materials.

3. Learning to *inspect* work at each stage will be an integral part of this. (In batik work, for instance, it is important to check for 'spotting' or 'cracking' wax which can ruin the desired effect. As dyeing is expensive, checking at the pre-dyeing stage can save costly errors. Likewise, checking the results of the dyeing before the wax is removed allows redyeing if necessary.)

If the above is effective, the need for inspection of products arriving at the central distribution centre should, in theory, be minimized. However, in the Bangladesh context, it will take a number of years to get consistent quality, and cultural differences will play a large role in the change process. Having to make changes to what local people see as perfectly functional items will at first be difficult to understand. Concepts of quality will also vary. What is regarded as quality to a rural group may not be the same as the quality required by foreign buyers.

Case study 3

The Sahil Tea Garden

The Sahil Tea Garden (Sahil Çay Bahçezi) is at Kas — a small harbour village on the Mediterranean coast of southern Turkey. Kas has a normal population of 5000 but a 'seasonal' population of double that figure, for whilst it is undeveloped, unsophisticated and located a $3^1/_2$ -hour, difficult drive from the nearest airports (Dalaman and Antalya), it attracts holiday makers, mainly from Europe, through from June to September, and is a 'stop-off' for passing yachts and the occasional small cruise ship.

The Sahil Tea Garden, even by local standards, is a simple cafe/bar located along the pathway which runs immediately behind the rocky beach, to the west of the harbour. It is no more than an arrangement of tables under the vines and oleanders, together with a small kitchen, freezers, bar, chill cabinets, etc. It has seating for approximately 120 people around small tables. The layout is approximately as shown in Figure CS3.1.

The Tea Garden is open for the full day during the period June–September inclusive and closed for the rest of the year. It provides breakfast from around 8 a.m. to late morning, lunch from 11 a.m. (approximately) to 4 p.m. (approximately) and then drinks and snacks for the remainder of the day. Breakfast typically comprises fruit juice, coffee, çay (tea), pastries, etc. Lunch offers a broader menu (see below) and thereafter the service is only soft drinks, beer, çay, coffee, ice cream, cakes, etc.

The most distinctive feature of the Tea Garden – well known to both locals and visitors — is evident at lunchtimes. Then the Tea Garden offers freshly made gözleme — a traditional Turkish nomad dish, being a cross between a pancake and a French crepe.

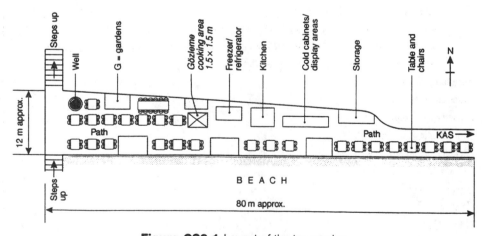

Figure CS3.1 Layout of the tea garden

The gözleme preparation process is outlined in Table CS3.1. One person—normally the owner's wife, Hatice—is responsible for all the cooking for the entire 4–4.5 hour period. This is undertaken in the open in one area in the middle of the Tea Garden (see Figure CS3.1) where the process attracts the attention of customers and passers-by alike. Whilst salads, bread, snacks and other dishes are served at lunchtimes, most customer order the gözleme with either herb and cheese, or herb and meat filling. With it they will often have beer, soft drinks, coffee or çay.

The staff of the Tea Garden at lunchtime typically comprises the manager (owner), wife/gözleme cook, another kitchen worker and two or three waiters. Staffing is much the same in the morning but fewer are involved in the evening.

The Sahil Tea Garden is a gathering/meeting place. In the morning customers take breakfast and read their newspapers. At lunchtimes, they meet friends and/or catch upon their reading or paperwork (e.g. letter writing) and in the evening it is a place to meet, drink and smoke before going on to somewhere for a meal or going home.

Table CS3.1   Gözleme – preparation process

A Pre-work

1. Prepare dough and store in basin, covered with cloth (keep in refrigerator until needed).
2. Prepare two fillings and store in dishes (keep in refrigerator until needed).

B Preparation and cooking

1. Small quantity of dough is rolled into a ball by hand, placed in centre of circular, floured, rolling board (approximately 0.7 m in diameter), sprinkled with flour and rolled to a 0.5 m diameter, very thin pancake with a round piece of wood (approximately 40 mm diameter and 0.8 m long).

   Approximate time required = 2 minutes.

2. Pancake is folded to approximate rectangle, filling is sprinkled on pancake, pancake is folded to a square (approximately 0.2 m) and edges sealed by pressing with fingers.

   Approximate time = 0.7 minutes.

3. Gözleme is placed on grill (approximately 0.5 m diameter, slightly convex, hot-plate, heated by gas burners), turned frequently (typically four times) and sides oiled with a brush dipped into bowl of oil, until cooked.

   Approximate time = 2.5 minutes.

4. Gözleme is removed to one of two plates awaiting serving.

5. Gözleme is removed from plate and placed on plate brought and taken by waiter as required.

   N.B. Times for (1), (2) and (3) allow interruptions for (4) and (5).

Equipment used

Circular rolling board

Round rolling wood

Hot-plate (and gas bottle/burner)

Spatula to turn gözlemes on hot-plate, move off plate, serve, etc.

Containers with dough and two fillings

Container for oil

Brush for oil

Two plates for storage

Average table occupancy in July–August is as follows:

Morning   =   30%
Lunch   =   45%
Afternoon and evening   =   35%

Typical prices are shown in Table CS3.2.

Table CS3.2 Prices (Turkish lira, 1992)	
Gözleme	6000
Beer – glass	6000
Beer – bottle	7000
Salad (tomato)	6000
Çay (tea)	1000
Meze (starters)	6000–8000
(e.g. Russian salad, stuffed tomatoes, etc.)	

This is one of 30 or so eating places in Kas, but is unlike many of the others in concentrating on lunchtime trade. Like all of the others, it is subject to some national regulations as regards health, etc. These regulations are enforced through inspection and the allocation of licences — renewable annually. The Sahil does not have a full restaurant licence but rather a bar/snacks licence, which permits the serving of all types of drink throughout the day and the preparation and serving of a limited range of 'snack'-type dishes.

Cold meze dishes (starters) are pre-prepared and served from a cold cabinet. The gözleme are cooked on site as required. Dishes such as salads are prepared on site as required. Coffee, tea, fresh fruit squashes, etc. are prepared on site as required also. The dough and fillings for the gözleme are prepared in the kitchen on site during the morning. Sufficient dough and filling are prepared for the day — dough left unused is thrown away. Any unused filling can be kept in the refrigerator and used the following day.

The renewal of the Sahil licence is due at the beginning of the summer season. A form must be filled out giving details of storage, serving and cooking facilities. A drawing showing the nature and layout of any cooking area must be included. Regulations are minimal but stipulate that food cannot be cooked where it can easily be touched by customers and that pre-prepared food awaiting serving must be behind glass, etc. The arrangement of the kitchen, cold cabinet, etc. is rarely changed. The main interest therefore is in the arrangement of the gözleme cooking area.

Case study 4

Bourg Breton

Bourg Breton is a rural leisure centre located near the edge of the town of Châteaulin (population 6000), which is near the Atlantic coast of Brittany in North West France.

Five years ago it was a small farm. Now it is a 'Centre d'Equestre' and 'Centre d'Accueil' providing facilities for local people and for visitors, mainly from other parts of Northern France. Many of the previously unused and in some cases derelict/buildings have been converted. Some have been extended. Other buildings have been added. The access road, the original farm yard, and the surrounding paths and grounds have been improved. No farming activities now take place, although a great deal of the type of work associated with farming is still needed, e.g. the maintenance of fences, grass, hedge and tree cutting, and so on.

FACILITIES

General layout of the Centre is shown in Figure CS4.1. The Centre presently comprises the following main facilities:

The **Original farmhouse**. This two-storey building is now unoccupied and unrenovated. It is used mainly for storage.

Main buildings. This is the largest facility. It comprises on the ground floor a large reception area, meeting rooms, offices, a large kitchen, two large dining rooms (with views over the countryside), services, etc. On the first floor there are mainly dormitory-style bedrooms (for 40 persons) and a small number of single bedrooms.

Indoor arena. This is a large enclosed barn now used for horse riding and jumping.

Outdoor arena. This open area at the side of the stables is set out as a horse jumping area.

Stables. There is stabling for 18 horses.

Games area (etc). This comprises the reception/booking area for the mini-golf, a games room, café, locker room and similar facilities.

Cottages. The smaller cottage (1) is occupied by one of the full-time staff. The larger cottage (2) is occupied by the owners of Bourg Breton.

Gîtes. The two gîtes are both converted farm outbuildings. They provide self-contained accommodation, each for up to four people.

Storage building. This open building is where the farm machinery, hay, etc. are stored.

Games room 2. This is simply an open-sided building used for table tennis, etc.

Changing rooms. This modern wooden building provides the main changing rooms, toilets, etc. outside of those in the other main buildings.

Unconverted buildings. There remains one original as yet unconverted farm building.

ACTIVITIES

The principal present activities of the Bourg Breton are as follows:

Centre d'Equestre

The stabling at the Centre is presently sufficient for 18 horses (in residence). Stabling care and maintenance (*pension*) is provided for horses owned and used by others; currently there are eight such horses at the Centre. Additionally the Centre owns and stables its

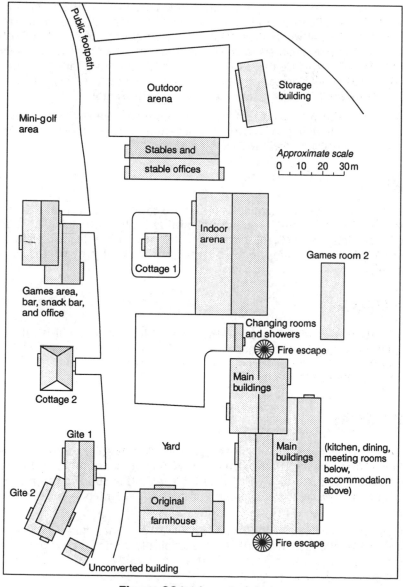

Figure CS4.1 Layout of centre

own horses (currently). These are used by the Centre to provide riding lessons, horse riding and horse jumping for its clients, either individually or in groups.

Horse riding and jumping tuition is also provided for those who stable their own horses at the Centre. For the serious rider, tuition can take people up to examination/competition level. The Centre occasionally organizes horse jumping competitions for its own clients and visitors.

Centre d'Accueil

This is the basis for the principal residential use of the Centre. Clients are mainly young people (15–18 years) who come in groups often organized by schools or community organizations. They stay at Bourg Breton using it as their *colonie de vacances* in the French tradition, usually for several weeks depending on the length of the school holidays. They come mainly from more urban areas in Northern France, often as far away as Paris, and use the full facilities of the Centre, as well as other facilities in Châteaulin and the surrounding area. They are accompanied by supervisors (often their teachers), and in general these are the only adults who stay for long periods at the Centre.

In addition to its main residential facility Bourg Breton rents out two cottages—*gîtes ruraux*—i.e. farm outbuildings converted into self-contained cottages. These are used by families on holiday, usually foreigners.

Mini-golf

Whilst advertised (e.g. on the signposts pointing to the Centre) as such, this is no more than a small 'crazy golf' course, i.e. a novelty putting facility with about 12 short 'holes' featuring hills, ramps, tunnels, obstacles, etc. It is used by residents, occasionally by tourists staying in the hotels in the town and, less occasionally, by youths and families living locally.

Other activities

The Centre occasionally rents out its meeting rooms (the largest of which will accommodate 45 people), with or without meals, and will also, occasionally, cater (i.e. provide meals and dining-facilities) for social, family or commercial events. The largest dining room can accommodate 50 people.

RESOURCES

The Centre is owned and managed by M. and Mme Penneueac'h. There is one full-time employee who lives on site. He has some supervisory responsibilities and deals mostly with the Centre d'Equestre activities. There are three other full-time employees, all of whom live in the area: two groundsmen and building maintenance workers, and one stableman.

All other employees are part- or full-time and temporary. Their numbers depend on the season, and the level of activity of the Centre. Typically, during a busy period, they will comprise

2   Stable workers

2   Cleaners

2   Dining room workers

1   Horse riding instructor

1   Horse riding 'attendant'

1   Labourer

2   Cooks

SEASONS

The Centre is open for the whole year, but not for all activities.

The Centre d'Equestre operates for the full 12 months.

The mini-golf is open from March to October inclusive.

The residential facility is open from March to October inclusive.

The principal facilities associated with the Centre d'Accueil are open from March to October inclusive (although meeting rooms and dining facilities can be hired 'out of season').

The gîtes are available for hire for the whole year.

Tariffs and fees

The currently advertised (1993) tariffs and charges for the Centre's services are summarized in Table CS4.1. They are in all cases 5 per cent above 1992. All charges are inclusive of TVA (value added tax). It is normal to have to provide a commission of between 5 per cent and 7 per cent of the advertised rate for agency booking of large groups.

Wages and costs

Table CS4.2 summarizes the principal operating costs of the Centre for 1992.

PROPOSED DEVELOPMENT

Bourg Breton has developed gradually over recent years to its present scale and form. It has in effect been an extension to the 'hobby' interests of M. and Mme Penneueac'h, especially the Centre d'Equestre. In developing the facilities, e.g. in converting previously unused farm buildings, advantage has been taken of government grants. Some assistance has also been available from the Département (Finistère) Administration, as this is designated as a development area with high unemployment, rural depopulation, etc.

The principal physical developments of the Centre have been funded by M. and Mme Penneueac'h from revenues and from their own capital. A new project is, however, under consideration for which a loan will be required. Essentially it comprises the conversion of the original farm house to provide a small *auberge* (or small hotel), the intention being to use the rather better accommodation and facilities provided to support the equestrian activities by attracting people who would wish to stay in the hotel in order to horse-ride, etc.

Table CS4.1	1993 Tariffs and fees (Francs)		
		Season	
	Low	**Mid** **(8 weeks)**	**High** **(8 weeks)**
Gîte rental (per week, per property)	1500	2000	2500
Centre d'Equestre			
Stabling of horse (per month) (6 months minimum)		600	
Riding lesson (per hour) Group (of four) Individual		100 300	
Horse 'trekking' (per hour) Group (of four) Individual		100 300	
Horse jumping (per hour) Supervised use of facilities Instruction		200 350	
Mini-golf			
Per person, per hour	25	35	50
Centre d'Accueil			
Accommodation (dormitory) (with use of all facilities excepting Centre d'Equestre) per person, per week—full board	1300	1600	2000
Accommodation (individual) (for persons accompanying groups of six minimum only) at above rates + 20% (N.B. half board: subtract 60F per day)			
Riding lessons for residents and horse trekking for residents: at above group rates less 10%			
Conferencing/events: Catering: from 70F to 250F per person Meeting rooms, from 150F to 500F per hour			

Plans have been drawn up and approved by the Planning Authority to create a six-bedroom facility in the farm house without substantially altering its character. The total cost of conversion and fitting out (including furnishing) is estimated at F550,000.

Table CS4.2 1992 Costs (Francs)	
Impôts/Taxe d'habitation	6500
Depreciation of assets[a]	70 000
Other fixed costs	7500
Salaries (inclusive of pension contributions, ins.)	
For gîtes	50 000
For Centre d'Equestre	590 000
For Mini-golf	50 000
For Centre d'Accueil	
Accommodation	480 000
Conferences/events	150 000
Other	140 000
Non-attributed salary costs	400 000
(excluding 'salary' for M. and Mme Penneneac'h	
Consumables	
For gîtes	30 000
For Centre d'Equestre	140 000
For Mini-golf	10 000
For Centre d'Accueil	
Accommodation	150 000
Conferences/events	50 000
Other	13 000
Non-attributables	50 000
Insurance	80 000
	2 467 000

[a] Includes all maintenance and repair work but not major new buildings. Excludes labour (excluding external contractors) and consumed materials.

M. Penneneac'h has already had discussions on his plans with the manager of his bank in town (Crédit Agricole, Quai Jean Moulin). The manager was supportive of the proposals in principle but a decision to lend the amount required would need the authority of the regional manager in Quimper. In preparation for a meeting in Quimper the Châteaulin branch manager sought more information from M. Penneueac'h, for he wanted to know how his business as a whole was going, and to get some idea of its future prospects. He was interested in the profitability of the various activities, bookings for the coming year, etc. He wanted to be sure that, if funds were to be advanced, they were best spent on adding a new facility rather than further developing the existing amenities.

Now M. and Mme Penneaueac'h are prepared for their meeting at Crédit Agricole in Quimper. They have in front of them the additional material shown in Table CS4.3.

Table CS4.3 Usage 1992 and 1993 (as at 1 April 1993)

	1992 (actual)			1993 (actual to date plus projections/reservations		
	Low	Mid	High	Low	Mid	High
Gîte weeks	8	6	7	10	7	7
Centre d'Equestre						
Stabling (horse months)		85			96	
Riding lessons and trekking						
Total hours (groups)		930			1100	
Total hours (individual)		350			390	
Horse jumping						
Facilities (total hours)		450			550	
Instruction (total hours)		250			300	
Mini-golf						
Total person hours	100	170	280	60	190	300
Centre d'Accueil						
Dormitory accommodation (person weeks)	290	300	376	340	380	400
Individual accommodation (person weeks)	27	32	35	25	33	36
Use of Centre d'Equestre (total hours)		1050			1100	
Conferences/events (total)						
Catering (no. of persons)		2200			2400	
Average price/person		150			170	
Meeting rooms:						
Total hours		280			350	
Average price/hour		350			360	

Case study 5

Pokhara Weavers

Pokhara is a large lakeside town in Central Nepal. Although its population is only 60 000 it is second in size and significance only to Kathmandu, the capital, 200 km to the East. The main crossroads in Pokhara is known as Prithvi Chowk. There, located virtually at the junction, is a group of people creating a variety of woven bamboo products. They occupy a piece of land about 10m × 10m at the side of the road. In addition, they have a small area to display finished goods at the side of the road, at the junction. Goods, materials, etc. are stored, where necessary, in a hut at the rear of the main site.

The goods produced are mainly baskets of various sizes and floor mats. Except for the final weaving operation, all operations are common, irrespective of the end product. The common operations together convert long pieces of bamboo into the raw materials for the final weaving process.

The description below focuses on the weaving of large floor mats approximately 3m square.

THE OPERATIONS

Bamboo poles, cut locally, are brought to the site by hand or cart. They are typically 2.5m long and 12 cm in diameter.

Usually it is necessary to cut off the solid end of the pole; this is done on the floor with a large heavy knife used as a hatchet.

The poles are then split, lengthwise. They are first cut in half with a heavy knife driven down by blows from a piece of wood until the pole splits into two. Each half is then split further by the same process, but now the knife can usually simply be pushed down the split pole. The number of splits determines the width of the final weaving material. Splitting each half into six (i.e. twelve pieces in total) produces pieces approximately 2.5 cm wide.

The next operation involves the cutting of thin flat strips from the split poles. Again this is done with a knife which is run along the poles but at right angles to the previous cut—i.e. producing strips at right angles to the radius—along the natural laminations of the bamboo. The material 'peels' quite easily in this way, but not always over the full pole length, so the strips produced are of different lengths. All but the strips from the outside of the pole are the same yellowish colour on both sides. The outer strip is green on one (the outer) side. All strips are approximately 2 mm thick.

The material is now ready for weaving. This, for mats, is done horizontally on the floor with considerable speed and dexterity, new strips being joined into the weave in either direction (along or across) as required, until a full mat is obtained. The green strips are used to introduce a squared pattern into the mat. Each mat is woven one quarter at a time, i.e. the first quarter is woven, then the second is added to make a half mat, then the third and finally the last quarter to complete the square. Finally the strips are trimmed off, and all edges are bound.

There are other occasional operations, i.e. occasional sprinkling of water on to the waiting strips to keep them flexible; removal of finished products; removal of waste material; measuring of mats during weaving; and sharpening of knives.

MANNING

When busy, five people undertake the above operations, as follows:

1 Trimming ends and splitting poles

1 Making strips

2 Weaving products

1 Supervising; helping out; moving materials between workers and occasional jobs.

During quiet times, all operations are undertaken by two or three people. With full manning, and making no other items in the site area, approximately five or six large mats could be made in one day.

Case study 6

Airport building project

The terminal building of a small rural airport at a town in the north of the Indian sub-continent is being extended. The present single storey L-shaped building has four rooms. A new room is now being added on to one end of the building.

The new single-storey room is approximately 6 × 8 metres. So far the foundations have been laid, the concrete floor laid, two of the three main walls have been built, and all the preparatory work for the roof has been done. The next job is to finish the roof and then the final (non-load-bearing) wall can be put in place and all the finishing work done.

The roof is to be of reinforced concrete. The preparatory work has involved the erection of wooden scaffolding from the floor of the building to support the timber 'formwork' onto which the concrete will be poured for the roof. Above this formwork the steel reinforcing rods have been placed.

Timber scaffolding has also been erected at one corner of the new building to provide access for workers to the roof. Moveable 'walkways' made from wooden planks are used to allow workers to move about on the roof, above the steel reinforcements.

The ingredients for the concrete have already been delivered to the site, i.e. sand, gravel, and cement. The sand and gravel are in two adjacent piles on the ground beside the building. The cement is in bags close by. Additional materials will be delivered when required. Water is available from a tap about 15 feet from the building.

The layout of the site prior to finishing the roof is shown in Figures CS6.1 and CS6.2.

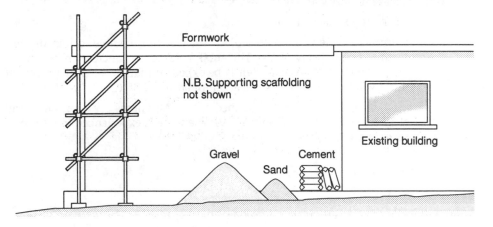

Figure CS6.1 Front elevation

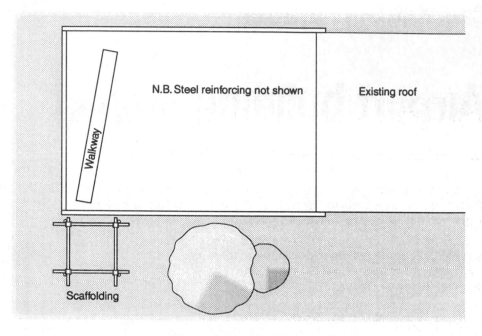

Figure CS6.2 Plan view

The immediate task now is to finish the roof. This will involve the following:

(a) Mixing the dry ingredients for the concrete;

(b) Adding water to mix the wet concrete;

(c) Transporting concrete to the appropriate place on the roof;

(d) Pouring concrete onto the roof formwork;

(e) Pushing/knocking the concrete into place to ensure that it fills all corners, fully surrounds the steel reinforcement, etc.;

(f) Smoothing off the top surface of the concrete.

This whole job must be done as a single project, for it is not possible to join up new concrete to that which has already dried. The total volume of concrete to be laid is approximately 10 cubic metres. It can confidently be expected that, at the present time of the year, the weather will be dry with a mid-day temperature of 25°C.

Plans are now to be made for the work described above. Any necessary equipment and labour must be obtained. The person responsible for the work is experienced in such projects, and has adequate access to the necessary resources.

Case study 7

Fotoprint Pronto

Grazia Ceri has obtained the franchise to open and operate the only FotoPrint Pronto shop in her town—if she can convince the franchiser that she has found a commercially attractive site. She needs at least 75 square metres. There is plenty of space to let in the town. (A comparison of rents is given in Table CS7.1.) Grazia has decided to take one of the shop areas in a new building soon to be opened on the Avenida Garibaldi, the main road which runs North to South through town from near to the railway station to the sports stadium. Whilst some of the shops in the building are already let, there is still a choice left for her. She aims to choose the best shop for her purposes and then present her final proposals to the regional director of FotoPrint Pronto.

Further details of a typical FotoPrint Pronto operation are given in Table CS7.2. The location of Grazia's chosen building is shown on the map (Figure CS7.1). The layout of the three floors is shown in Figure CS7.2. Further details on the building are given in Table CS7.3.

Table CS7.1 Comparison of property rentals	
Area	**Rentals (compared to most expensive area)**
Downtown retail area (around Avenida Garibaldi and north of the cathedral)	(most expensive area)
Industrial area 1 (north of autostrada)	30%
Industrial area 2 (south and adjacent to autostrada)	45%
Commercial area	60%
Government area	60%

For locations see Figure CS7.1.

449

Table CS7.2　A profile of a FotoPrint Pronto shop

Services offered

A. *Photographic*

　1. Development and printing of colour photographic film
　2. Enlargements from colour prints or negatives

B. *Printing and binding*

　1. Black and white photocopying (all sizes)
　2. Colour photocopying from customers' originals (all sizes)
　3. Binding (several methods)

C. *Other services*

　1. Laser colour copying of originals (with enlargement/reduction, etc.)
　2. Mounting and framing pictures, documents, etc.
　3. Design and production of business cards, invitations, posters, etc. (black and white and colour)

D. *Retail items*

　1. Sale of frames and framing materials
　2. Sale of stationery
　3. Sale of photographic film

Typical activity profiles

Typically, sales revenue is generated as follows:

A (above)	25%
B	40%
C	20%
D	15%

Typical customer profiles are as follows (by sales volume):

	Commercial/business customers	Individual/personal customers
A	10%	90%
B	85%	15%
C	65%	35%
D	10%	90%

Table CS7.3   Building details

Floor area

Shops		
Shops	1.2–5; 1.8; 1.9; 2.2–6; 2.0–2.13; 3.2–6; 3.9–3.13 }	= 80 m²
Shops	1.1; 2.1; 2.14; 3.1; 3.14	= 100 m²
Shops	2.7–8; 3.7–8	= 115 m²
Shops	1.6–7; 1.10	= 240 m²

Rental charges are quoted

The cheapest shops are the single 80 m² units on the top floor. Comparative charges for all other units are as follows:

Shops	Rental (if the cheapest)
3.1; 3.14	+10%
3.7; 3.8	+20%
2.2–6; 2.9–13	+10%
2.1; 2.14	+29%
2.7; 2.8	+30%
1.2–5; 1.8–9	+30%
1.1	+40%
1.6–7	+380%
1.10	+330%

Shops already let

Shops	Purpose/Nature
3.4	Travel agent
3.11	Insurance agency
3.2	Clothes (women)
3.13	Clothes (men)
2.4	Coffee shop
2.5	Pottery/ceramics
2.6	Hardware
2.9	Gifts (general)
2.10	Music
2.11	Sports goods and wear
2.13	Decorating
1.1	Bank
1.2	Toys
1.3	Clothes (women)
1.6	Fashions/clothes
1.7	Restaurant
1.9	Books/papers/stationery
1.10	Food

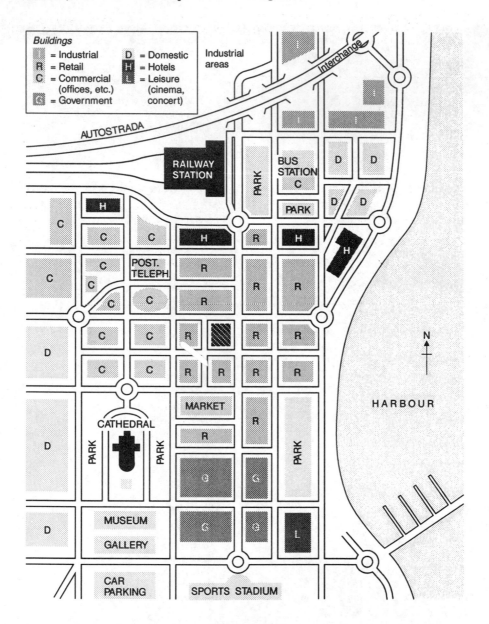

Figure CS7.1

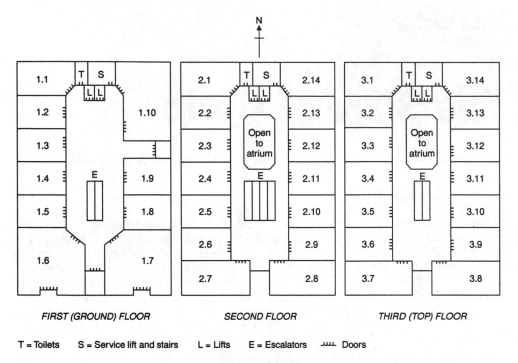

FIRST (GROUND) FLOOR　　　**SECOND FLOOR**　　　**THIRD (TOP) FLOOR**

T = Toilets　　S = Service lift and stairs　　L = Lifts　　E = Escalators　　 Doors

Figure CS7.2

Case study 8

The Shire of Corio

General background

This municipality is 80 km from Melbourne in Victoria, Australia, and takes in the northern ('blue collar') suburbs of Geelong, Victoria's second biggest city. With a heavy concentration of industry, companies of note are Ford (engines and body parts); Pilkington's (automotive glass); Henderson's Industries (vehicle seats); Shell (oil refinery); Australian Cement; BHP Steel Wire Products; Aerospace Technologies of Australia (a recently-privatized Federal Government facility which assembled and maintained FA/18A fighters for the RAAF and now has several contracts to provide major overhaul services for large international carriers); and Candy (a subsidiary of Pacific Dunlop making ladies' shoes). The Port of Geelong Authority operates several docks along the foreshore of Port Phillip Bay. However, more than two-thirds of the 700 square km area is rural, producing wheat, oats, barley, other cereals, and livestock, besides being home to five vineyards. Figure CS8.1 shows the wide range of property types.

Table CS8.1	Distribution of property types	
	Type	Number
	Residential	18 000
	Industrial	875
	Shops/commercial	445
	Small acres	1339
	Farms	341

The shire's population is 57 000 compared to 150 000 for the whole of urban Geelong. There are many low-income families and migrants from non-English-speaking countries, and during the current recession unemployment has reached 35 per cent in some districts. Geelong region comprises by the local government organizations. Corio is the largest with a budgeted annual recurrent expenditure for 1992/3 of A$29.9 million, whereas Geelong City's is A$15 million and Queenscliff's (a small coastal town) only A$2.7 million. Amalgamation is a hot political issue, following a recent change of State Government, and proponents claim that it would allow rationalization of resources and economies of scale.[1]

---

[1] Corio spends $18 million p.a. and has been prominent in the establishment of a purchasing syndicate (the Geelong Local Government Supply Group). The number of suppliers has been cut to 500 and increased buyer power has brought significant savings, e.g. A$21 000 per year on fuel costs alone.

© 1995, Geoff Buxey.

The Geelong Regional Commission exists to foster economic growth and co-ordinate the necessary activities, but has often been at loggerheads with the various Councils.

The organization

The Shire Council consists of 12 councillors elected from four wards for three-year terms, and acts as a sort of Board of Directors, establishing policies, setting priorities, and allocating resources via the budget. There are 290 full-time staff, 260 part-time and 100 volunteers (mainly working in community services), of whom only 120 are based at headquarters (Osborne House). They represent over 50 different professions, and provide a diverse range of more than 200 services for residents and the general community. A list of the most important premises/sites under Council management is given in Figure CS8.2.

Table CS8.2 Main premises and sites

Osborne House[a] (Shire headquarters)

Operations Centre (newly constructed depot for fieldwork support)

Shopfront (at Corio Village shopping centre)

Leisuretime Squash and Sports Centre[b] (three stadiums, eight squash courts, eight outdoor courts, and several multi-purpose rooms)

Norlane Waterworld[c] (swimming pools and gymnasium complex)

Lara swimming pool

Elcho Park Golf Course

Deppeler Park pitch and putt (par 3) course

Libraries (three) and a mobile unit[d]

Tourist Information Centre

Community halls (five), neighbourhood centres, community health centres (two)

Parks, passive gardens, nature reserves and playgrounds (61)

Major football/cricket sports reserves (six)

[a] Australia's first naval college, now incorporating a naval museum and a National Trust historic building.

[b] 300 000 visits in 1991.

[c] 330 000 visits in 1991.

[d] More than 250 000 books and magazines.

The various departments are assigned to one of five distinct programmes, whose principal activities/functions are listed in Figure CS8.3, along with incomes and expenditures for 1990/91 (Figure SC8.4). Rates are the dominant sources of funds, and whilst Corio can adjust this levy on its 23 000 rate-payers or cut certain services in order to balance the books, these are politically sensitive issues.

In fact, it is the sole Victorian council to keep annual percentage rate rises below inflation for the past five years (the last two adjustments were 1 per cent and 0 per cent). Notwithstanding, the variety and quality of services has increased. This period coincides with Brian Payne's appointment as General Manager (GM) in 1988. He came from a

Table CS8.3 The five programmes, principal activities, and executive responsibility

Management and development
Collect rates and administer budget allocations
Invest funds
Develop and promote commercial activities and tourism
Quality
Training
Purchasing
Asset management (including plant maintenance and replacement)
Foster community relations (annual report, newsletters, calendars, etc.).
Conduct council elections, hold civic functions
Maintain (computerized) records office

Community services
Neighbourhood watch
Maternal and child health service (home visits, play groups, capsule hire, etc.)
Family care and children's services (day care,[a] four child care centres, kindergartens, after-school care)
Youth services (Youth Centre activities, vacation activity programmes)
Home care (assistance for the aged and disabled and emergency cases)
Senior citizens (clubs, 'meals on wheels', transport)
Neighbourhood centres (further education classes, community group activities, etc.)

Health and environment
Environmental Health Service (immunization,[b] head lice eradication,[c] pest control, food handlers' inspections)
Animal control (dog registrations, ranger and dog control, cattle pound)
Urban development (street sweeping, public toilets, rubbish and sanitary pan collections, recycling, tip operation[d])
Urban planning and control (issuing town planning permits[e] and processing building approval applications,[f] enforcing town planning regulations)

Leisure
Swimming (Waterworld, Lara pool)
Indoor sports (squash, racquetball, netball, basketball, soccer, volleyball, badminton, karate, aerobics, etc.)
Public halls (sports, functions, meetings)
Arts (libraries and naval museum)
Outdoor sports (sports ovals, golf and pitch and putt courses)
Playgrounds and passive gardens, nursery, landscaping, tree maintenance

Transport
Roadworks and line marking
Foot and bicycle paths
Traffic control (school crossings supervision, parking and street signs, traffic wardens)
Street lighting (installation and surveillance)
Drainage construction and maintenance
Works and services for ratepayers, clubs and organizations on a 'user pays' basis
Depot operations and administration

[a] In homes of registered care givers.
[b] 2000 schoolchildren and 6200 infants in one year.
[c] 15 000 children inspected by council's nurse in one year.
[d] Caters for most of Geelong, 230 000 m^3 deposited per year.
[e] 247 planning permit applications plus ten appeals in one year.
[f] 1197 building approvals granted in one year.

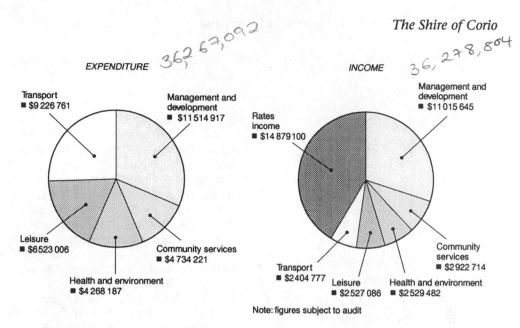

36267,092   36,278,804

Figure CS8.4 Shire expenditure and income for year ended 30 September 1991

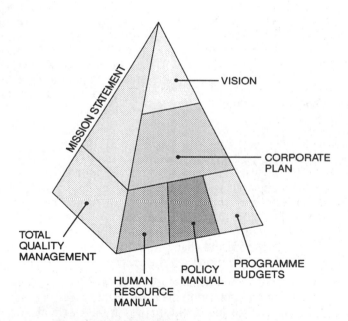

Figure CS8.5 The corporate philosophy

Melbourne council and it was his first time in the top job. Since then a corporate philosophy has been developed (see Figure CS8.5), along with a mission statement (Figure CS8.6) now prominently displayed in the Council chamber, in the reception area at Osborne House, etc., and on the Annual report and all job advertisements. Basically, Council determines the corporate plan, after being presented with several options.

SHIRE OF CORIO

Committed to delivering
Local Government
services of which our
community can be proud

☑ Excellent in quality

☑ Efficient in cost

☑ Effective in application

Figure CS8.6 The mission statement

The GM is in charge of overall operations and acts as senior adviser to Council. There are four functional divisions, headed by a Director, completing the Corporate Management team (Figure CS8.7). Departmental allocations correspond closely to the five major programmes (see Figure CS8.3), except that 'Leisure' is largely subsumed into the 'Environmental Services' portfolio and the 'Management and Development' programme is more or less split between the executives responsible for 'Administration and Community Services' and 'Corporate Services'. Logically, the Shire Engineer is responsible for 'Technical Services', which is mainly 'Transport' but includes the maintenance of all buildings and plant plus outdoor facilities. This is not the conventional structure where the Town Clerk and Shire Engineer run two separate halves and report directly to Council. There are even plans afoot to rotate executives, in the interests of innovation and teamwork, and it is fairly unique to have a Marketing Manager and an Economic and Quality Manager (Evan Sutton).

Total Quality Management

When Brian arrived he engaged an academic to give a session on teamwork and brainstorming to six management groups. Afterwards, a delegation suggested to him that supervisors were actually stifling ideas for improving operations. At the Geelong Business Club he heard a speaker from Enterprise Australia (Sydney) on TQM, and was then determined to build a Quality culture and change the shire from a bureaucracy to a customer-oriented service. Corio has since pioneered the concept in Australian local government.

TQM commenced in 1989 when the executive visited Ford to get ideas and then advertised for a co-ordinator. After appointing their own Data Processing manager they looked for a suitable consultant. One job applicant was from Gas and Fuel Corporation of Victoria, also in the public sector, which had had good experiences with TQM, and their contribution has since proven invaluable.

Even went to Enterprise Australia for two weeks and the executives attended a four-day course, whence a TQM committee was formed comprising the GM, two directors and three managers. It selected (transitional) *cross-functional* teams, from different hierarchical levels, so that 'outsiders' would play devil's advocate. The teams received two days' training and were asked to generate potential improvement projects via 'brainstorming', but the committee made the final choice(s). There were some teething difficulties because

COUNCIL

GENERAL MANAGER

Brian Payne   Strategic planning

**ADMINISTRATION AND
COMMUNITY SERVICES**

Richard Metcalf   General administration
                         Community services
                         Child care services
                         Maternal and child health

ENVIRONMENTAL SERVICES

John Quirk   Building
                         Town planning
                         Health
                         Local laws
                         Leisure services
                         Community development

CORPORATE SERVICES

John Coggle   Finance
                         Data processing
                         Risk management
                         Marketing
                         Training
                         Quality control

TECHNICAL SERVICES

Roger Marsden   Engineering
                         Construction and drainage
                         Waste management
                         Parks and gardens
                         Maintenance of council
                         properties

Figure CS8.7 The executive structure

the tasks tended to be too big for a 12-weeks completion target. For instance, 'parks maintenance' was only tractable when reduced to 'roundabouts' (there are 100). The successful groups tended to have strong leaders, so it was decided to train 12 'facilitators' who could be assigned to subsequent projects.

According to Brian the greatest obstacle was middle management. He said that generally they were products of the 1950s–70s who had received no formal management education. Their modus operandi was to check on people so as to catch them out, but now they must act as coaches, planners, facilitators and resource providers. After a TQM meeting supervisors would infer that team members had been 'bludging'. To combat this, 96 staff, in groups of 16, participated in a five day, in-house, 'management course' which was TQM in disguise. The GM introduced games and exercises he had obtained while studying for Melbourne University's MBA (he particularly enjoyed the TQM unit). This unearthed people with management potential. For example, a garbage truck driver became a TQM team leader and later a supervisor. Other measures included setting up a Quality Committee for each division incorporating all its managers, and, taking account of subordinates' contributions to TQM projects in their performance reviews. It is no longer sufficient to run a department efficiently—innovations and improvements are expected.

As TQM evolved, the emphasis switched to voluntary membership of Quality Circles. These are natural work groups, which must have full control over processes they aim to improve, or gain the necessary co-operation. Once savings had been demonstrated (over A$1 million in 1990/91 and A$4 million in total) Brian instigated two council-approved incentive schemes. Supervisors are empowered to give A\$50 in gifts, tickets or vouchers to individuals (once per person per year) for a good idea, and Quality Circles can apply for another award worth up to A\$5000 per team. All projects conclude with a report to Council at a presentation dinner and the receipt of a framed certificate.

A representative sample of TQM projects appears as Figure CS8.8. Two of these, 'water usage' and 'recycling', are discussed at greater length in Appendices CS8A, CS8B. They are both very topical subjects, related as they are to environmental concerns, so the teams were in effect breaking some new ground rather than merely trying to improve existing operations. The accounts illustrate how members of the general workforce can, when given the training and opportunity, collect and analyse data, calculate the costs of operations, and evaluate alternative strategies, technologies, and methods. Above all though, such exercises confer 'ownership' of the new work practices, and therefore facilitate the necessary but often thorny processes of change.

Table CS8.8   A sample of TQM projects

• roundabout maintenance	• depot relocation
• commercial garbage collection	• induction of new staff
• domestic garbage collection	• purchase order system
• recycling	• archiving
• street sweeping (Corio Village)	• disabilities and leisure
• water usage	

Customer focus

Ratepayers are encouraged to submit ideas for better services, and letter drop cards are distributed to particular zones asking for comments and suggestions to facilitate long-term planning. This tends to reveal major problems (e.g. inadequate drainage), whereas other statistics refer to symptoms (e.g. requests to unblock drains).

Amongst the new services is 'Corio Community Contact' available throughout the region to aged or disabled residents who live alone. It operates round the clock via a home unit connected to the telephone network. In an emergency the user squeezes a small pendant worn around the neck and the unit dials a switchboard at Shire Offices. After hours calls are diverted to the Vital Call National Monitoring Centre in Sydney. Voice-to-voice contact is provided, which is especially reassuring when waiting for help to arrive. All Geelong's councils support the initiative and a sponsorship campaign proved very successful. The costs of subscribing are further curtailed by using trained volunteers to man the switchboard, Lions club members to install the units, and friends and neighbours to respond to calls whenever it is appropriate.

On the industrial side, Evan runs a self-help programme for the embattled Textiles, Clothing and Footwear sector, advocating TQM as a way of competing with cheap Asian imports. Better networking has resulted in transport-sharing for deliveries to and from Melbourne, switching to local suppliers, etc. There has also been a 'TCF awareness day' to promote local manufacturers. The public can be a resource too. Corio's 'adopt a park' scheme covers 61 reserves, and by providing free materials to community groups a higher standard of maintenance is achieved for the same cost.

A radical step occurred in 1991 when Corio Village Shopfront opened to make services more accessible. It is in the municipality's big shopping mall, whereas Osborne House is somewhat isolated and bereft of public transport. Links to the Council's mainframe computer give terminals access to information on rates, property, electronic mail, diaries, etc. and the software relays customer requests and monitors response times. Shopfront now collects more rates payments than the main offices, the majority of postal votes in elections are lodged there, and there has been a general increase in inquiries.

Initially, over 80 staff (including the GM, gardeners, etc.) volunteered to man the shop, and even worked Friday evenings and Saturday mornings without pay for the three month trial period. They undertook five days training to familiarize themselves with the shire's operations and services. Once demand was established (90–150 customers per day) the hours were set at 9 a.m.–5 p.m. on weekdays plus 9 a.m.–1 p.m. on Saturdays, and Joanne Fields was appointed manager. A casual employee comes in two hours per day to give her assistance and a lunch break, and some of the original volunteers put in one rotating four hour shift per month. The shop advertises on local radio stations and in newspapers, emphasizing that Corio is the first council to introduce extended business hours.

A computerized payments system is used for rates, dog licences and parking fines, although most other transactions are manual. Joanne has learnt to cope with a great variety of demands and even redirects many clients to outside bodies such as the Commonwealth Employment Service, State Electricity Commission of Victoria, etc. Much of the required information is contained in brochures and leaflets, but if necessary keywords are input on a PC and text downloaded from central files and laser-printed. However, certain areas, such as building applications, are sometimes difficult and the system user leaves an electronic message for the staff member responsible (an answer is expected within 24 hours). A similar procedure handles specific service requests, of which more than one-third relate to street tree maintenance, and by entering the appropriate urgency code number the next level of management is automatically notified in the case of non-compliance with the corresponding target response time. For an actual complaint a formal reply is expected within five working days. About five queries/requests per day are processed this way and a register maintained so that if any department is the subject of too many complaints an investigation will be carried out.

Information Technology

Corio has been quick to adopt the latest technology, even though the old maxim 'roads, rates, and rubbish' still applies. In 1989, the implementation of a computerized Land Information System began, based on the GIS (Geographical Information System) package, to provide a database on people and their properties. The raw mapping data were supplied on tapes by the SECV, and files have subsequently been created for each address. When this header is entered at a workstation's keyboard a menu appears on the screen covering 'owner'; 'titles'; 'classification' (usage); 'rates'; 'certificates' (building/planning); 'licences' (e.g. dog); 'requests'; and 'works carried out'. The system can automatically project the right subdivision chart as it knows which properties are adjacent. This is particularly useful because ratepayers' 'requests' often concern neighbours' fences, overgrown gardens, building applications, and such like. However, for other purposes it is better to be able to use (flexible) smaller scales and now different layers (features) can be superimposed at the touch of a button. These include a blue inundation (flood) chart, the sewer network, and Shire-owned land. Recently, a lot of people have asked about a proposed new waste disposal site in Staceys Road, and staff were able to call up a plan, hatched in red, overlaid on a suitable map.

Many departments deal with property but the old manual systems meant that they had to store and maintain their own paper maps even though much information was common. There was always a compromise between quality (currency) and the cost of making updates, and considerable time was also wasted trying to reconcile maps with subdivision charts. Now property services, rates, customer inquiries, engineering and accounting share the same database, and, apart from ensuring consistency; it facilitates one person's rapidly obtaining all the details he or she (or a ratepayer) wants, and means not having to leaf through piles of charts, and still having to request documents from other functions. Even then there were difficulties in matching up information from different sources, including numerous cases where it straddled two adjacent maps. A microwave link, with satellite dishes, connects the central computer to terminals at the Operations Centre, Shopfront, Waterworld and Leisuretime. Without such modern technology these dispersed locations would have created yet more duplicate maps and records.

Richard Phillips, LIS Officer, has been developing decision support systems, based on extracting the appropriate data and displaying its sparial characteristics. As 'requests' are logged against properties, it is easy to highlight a service's 'blackspots'. For example, if drainage pipe failures are perceived to be excessive, the software allows the lengths of troublesome sections to be measured and estimates of the replacement costs made. The amounts spent on repairs are held in the database too, so the financial implications of these alternative maintenance procedures are clear. Similarly, the property file will soon contain details on trees. Then, complaints about street trees can be analysed to see if particular species are unsuitable and should have others substituted, or, whether some neighbourhoods are too bare and need planting. Routeing/scheduling is another class of applications. New garbage collection rounds, 'home help' assignments, and 'meals on wheels' rounds can all be designed more efficiently, by trial and error, on screen. If a volunteer driver for the latter service is absent his or her clients can quickly be reallocated because times for the proposed additional journeys are instantly supplied.

A separate package is used for engineering survey, design, and drafting because they require greater precision, although the files are fully compatible. Field measurements are recorded electronically and then transferred to the computer which automatically plots a survey plan. A drafting officer would use AutoCAD to superimpose a road design, and after completion produce a set of plans for use in the field.

THE FUTURE

Despite a recent history of notable achievements the Shire of Corio still faces an uncertain future. Not only is its very existence under threat as the Victorian Government awaits a consultant's report on council amalgamations for the Geelong region, but also, in the current political climate, its monopoly position in regard to the provision of many services is likely to be challenged by privatization. Jobs will certainly disappear under an enlarged and, one hopes, more efficient local government authority, and entire functions may vanish too unless they can beat commercial organizations when quoting for tenders. The task that the GM must now undertake is to keep all the staff motivated in their dealings with the ratepayers, and focused on the long-term goals of the Shire, notwithstanding these elements of insecurity, and to prevent any reversion to a 'public service' mentality. At the same time, he will be required to represent their best interests in the formation of any fledgling 'super-council', without losing sight of the economic rationale behind such a radical step.

Appendix CS8A

The recycling Ragers (service improvement programme team): Irene Van Rooyen (Leader), Boris Schanjko (Facilitator), Gary Bowyer, Enzo Bruscella, Kevin Flynn, Anna Hughes, Les Vaughan.

Purpose: To provide Lara with a house-to-house recycling service suited to its needs.

This group convened in February 1992 and adopted the above task. Lara is a country town with 2400 tenements and 7400 inhabitants. At the time it had just two drop-off recycling centres (Kees Road Kindergarten for paper and the Scouts in Rennie Street for glass), whereas the Shire's city districts had a regular collection carried out by contractors. The Lara area was defined by its domestic garbage collection service, which takes place on Thursdays when three compactors and crews (one driver and two pick ups) arrive from Corio suburb after finishing their rounds there.

The Ragers used brainstorming (about recycling), a herring-bone diagram, several flow charts, field trips to look at other systems, and a customer survey. A questionnaire and pre-addressed envelope were distributed to 2415 dwellings and returns were accepted by post or at Osborne House, Shopfront or the Operations Centre. The ten questions covered present practices, awareness of current facilities, perceived needs and ideas for improving the recycling service and there were 897 replies (27 per cent). The major findings were that 45 per cent of households used the existing (Lara) centres, the majority making monthly visits; 90 per cent saw a need for a better recycling service; 93 per cent preferred any upgrading to be based on a regular domestic collection; and 69 per cent favoured a *free* bag over alternative containers. In addition, respondents generally required monthly or fortnightly uplifts of the main categories of materials.

The principal recommendations were:

(i) a weekly house-to-house collection of all recyclables, coinciding with the Thursday waste removal, in order to simplify matters for residents;

(ii) to collect steel cans, aluminium products, plastics, glass, and milk and juice waxed containers commingled in a bag, and separate bundles of cardboard and paper;

(iii) to supply a free 1.2 m × 0.6 m bag with Velcro seal, and to discourage putting it out half-empty. A seal should eliminate spillages, but decreases the usable volume. So, the bag is double the normal size to reduce incidences where it is filled and thereafter recyclables are thrown in the rubbish bin;

(iv) use the Council's direct labour force, not contractors;

(v) sell the commingled product for now, but examine the feasibility of operating a sorting facility;

(vi) retain and promote the existing drop-off centres as the relevant community groups rely on this income;

(vii) decision (iv) rests upon amounts sold and the operation should be reviewed at the end of the financial year.

The proposed method calls for the Parks department to loan two tray trucks and trailers, plus two staff (their drivers) and 16 cages. They would start to recycle Lara's *five-acres lots* at 6 a.m. whilst the Shire's compactors work in Corio. After, each truck joins up with a compactor and commences their urban rounds. A team of five which tackles the *densely housed areas* consists of one compactor with its driver and two pick ups, and, one recycle truck with a driver and one pick up. Another team of four is assigned to lower density areas and needs just one driver and pick up per vehicle. The remaining compactor and crew of two remove garbage from the five-acre lots.

Firms were asked to quote for Lara and 7¢ per household per week was the lowest tender, an annual fee of A$8736. The cost of 3000 bags per year, which allows for some loss and damage and then replacement for sanitary reasons, amounted to A$2,450; a promotional leaflet for each property added a further A$1200 to the cost of contracting out the job. If Corio's resources are used, the hourly hire rates for labour and equipment are known and the equivalent annual outlay was readily calculated. Estimating revenue from recyclables was not so straightforward, so three comparisons were made. The optimistic scenario assumed a 50 per cent mean weekly household participation rate, from which quantities of commingled and paper could be extrapolated and multiplied by the relevant sale price. A figure of 25 per cent, based on the current collection from urban areas of Geelong, was taken as worst case, and the break-even point (36 per cent) found to be more or less midway between. The shire faced a deficit in all cases, but initial confidence that the in-house option was cheapest stemmed from the facts that 74 per cent of survey respondents already undertook some form of recycling and 45 per cent used the drop-off centres.

Appendix CS8B

The H20 team (service improvement programme team): Barry Smith (Team Leader), Fran Norley (Facilitator), Mick Jaensch (Secretary), John Van Parreren, Andrew McInnes, Tony Wood, Milan Osolnik, Boris Lettis, Peter Joynson, Jim Garlinge (Guest).

A (fluctuating) team was established to address the rising costs of water usage due to the Water Board's impending switch to 'user pays'. It began by calculating the impact of this policy and found that an *extra* A$89,000 per year would be incurred, split more or less between new service fees (based upon connection sizes) and increases to actual consumption charges. Those accounts covering the council's golf courses, swimming pools and recreation reserves were particularly hard hit, generating a series of smaller projects.

Elcho Park Golf Course

In year 1991/92 more than 75 000 rounds were played at this popular public course, which used 80 000 kilolitres of water costing A$52 000. The TQM team aimed to retain sufficient water on site to meet total requirements, as it believed that in winter there is enough flow over and around the course to fill any catchment areas. A connection between the course dams and Gibbons Road was vital in this respect, and potential savings were as illustrated below.

Kilolitres (town water)	Connection size (mm)	Cost (A$)
100 000	100	66 100
90 000	100	59 900
80 000	100	53 700
60 000	50	38 225
40 000	50	25 825
20 000	32	12 820
10 000	32	6610
0	25	164

Shire engineers estimated the existing reservoir's capacity at 17 000 kl, and the first proposal was to take in a tract of unused land going towards the 18th tee on one side and the driving range on the other and simultaneously increase the average depth from two to four metres, giving a revised volume of 72 000 kl. The preliminary costing was A$150 000 for the excavation of 42 000 m³ of soil and its removal to the tip, plus A$60 000 for piping runoff from Gibbons Road underneath the course. However, a private contractor suggested a figure of A$130 000 for the complete earthworks, and the group considered that a spoon drain to the dam could be constructed for only A$5000 and would be adequate for the first few years, so the minimum total outlay came to A$135 000. For just A$50 000 the drain could be completed and the dam extended in one direction after removing 12–15 000³ of earth, by spring, to give some quick payback over the first (dry) summer.

A strategy was also drawn up for commissioning two further dams, each of 15 000 kl capacity. The second priority was a new dam beside the 6th fairway because table drains already ran there from the main one and it could be filled from the overflow. After installing a pump there would be an option to either water the surrounding holes directly or send it back as necessary for centralized distribution from the 18th. The lowest priority was to create a reservoir next to the 12th tee. A marked water hazard existed there, although its state varied from marshy for most of the year to a dry cakebed in summer. Furthermore, it was the closest dam to Gibbons Road so tunnelling would be relatively easy. The negative aspect was the difficulty of linking it with the other sites, but the work was deemed essential to improve the course's appearance.

The team held discussions with the Golf Course Committee and gained their approval. They then obtained A$25 000 from the Elcho Park Reserve fund and another A$25 000 from the Parks Capital Works budget in order to schedule the initial stage for 1992/93.

Computerized watering solutions

All the shire's watering was (originally) carried out by Parks staff moving sprinkler hoses over a reserve, park, etc. This is labour intensive, and was done in normal working hours—a practice which often wastes water. The H20 team investigated the possibility of converting to automatic watering. This needs underground reticulation, and accordingly A$10 000 worth of equipment was trialled at Windsor Park (an Australian Rules football/cricket oval), but has already been extended to include the golf course, Deppeler Park, and the Operations Centre's lawns.

The control system essentially consists of a central PC controller at the Operations Centre, a radio link, and satellite controllers, numerous valves, sprinklers, and water sensors distributed around the various grounds. The software enables an unlimited number of spray programs to be initiated, depending on the weather (wind and rain), soil conditions, and local turf requirements, and satellites can be subject to manual overrides if desired. Sprinklers are normally activated in the middle of the night when it is cool and still, which also avoids interfering with recreational users. Different zones, such as greens, aprons and fairways on the golf course, or the forward pocket and centre-half forward patches on the 'footy' oval, can be both monitored and programmed independently.

During summer months staff used to manually operate 180 hoses on the golf course. The new automatic system cost A$300 000 in total and has 491 sprinklers linked to six satellite centres and makes use of rainwater. Elcho Park Golf Club made a joint financial contribution and members also helped by filling in and seeding trenches. The on-going labour savings here and at the other sites allows more time to be spent on general parks maintenance.

Solar watering systems

The Shire had some median strips and roundabouts which were watered either by hand or by manually connecting a sprinkler, and many which received no watering at all. It is not practical to join them all to the electricity grid, so the group recommended that A$5000 be spent on a pilot in-ground irrigation system for the Cox Road/Anakie Road roundabout to be activated by a solar-powered control box. This still triggers automatic watering at the optimum time of day, but as there are no ground sensors it is necessary to actually visit the site in order to change the set watering pattern.

Case study 9

America Burger and Pasta

The partners in the Brazilian AMERICA BURGER and PASTA venture seemed to have the main characteristics it takes for a group of entrepreneurs who intend to start a successful restaurant chain. Helio Mattar got his PhD in Industrial Management and Engineering from Standford University, USA. He is a former academic with a career in the fields of operations research, economics and strategic planning, having worked for some of Brazil's most prestigious business institutions. Dr Mattar is managing director. Artur Guimaraes and his wife Maria Helena were both considered to be 'cuisine artists', and have previous experience in the restaurant business including years working for prestigious restaurants and studying with important 'chefs' in Europe. Luis Guelpi and Paulo Maluhy, both have previous experience in the restaurant and other businesses.

Unlike many other restaurant chains which were originally planned to be a single restaurant and eventually, given their success, became chains, AMERICA was from the beginning planned and created to be a chain of restaurants.

The inspiration for the creation of AMERICA came from the 'American diners' which serve quick meals, frequently working in refurbished old train wagons or caravans. The partners noticed that this type of restaurant had no equivalent in Brazil. On top of that, they also wanted to fulfil the needs of a very promising market niche in São Paulo, the young professionals.

According to Dr. Mattar, the 'meal caterers' in São Paulo could be classified in five categories:

1. *Fast-food* which seek to serve the customers in the fastest, cheapest and most consistent (in terms of taste and service) way. They offer a limited variety of standard products. The great concern with cleanliness and service standardization, which this type of restaurant usually emphasizes, seeks to reinforce the customer's perception that 'he knows exactly what he will get'. Broadly speaking, one of the important features of fast-food restaurants is that the food is sold 'off the shelf', i.e. is ready waiting for the customer to consume it.

2. *Sandwich shop* where the emphasis is also with quick meals, mainly sandwiches, but the variety of products is normally much broader, and customization (small changes in the way the products are made) is generally possible. The cycle times involved in the service are also more variable than in fast-food systems and the consistency of the taste is not considered as such a critical aspect.

3. *Quick service* restaurants do not especially emphasize the speed of the service and do not sell only or mainly sandwiches. They also serve complete meals on the plate. The variety of products is usually larger than that of the sandwich shop. The service cycle times are also normally longer, but this is not regarded as a problem given that the

typical 'quick service' customer is not necessarily interested in the fastest service, but rather a service which takes the appropriate time; this should be sufficient for him to enjoy the ambience of the restaurant, which is therefore important. Normally quick service restaurants take more care with this aspect than do the sandwich shops. Here the service dimension is similar to that of the traditional restaurants.

4. *Traditional*. Most of the restaurants in São Paulo are in this category. The menu is varied and the customer is able to specify the way in which the dishes are prepared. This makes the service cycle times longer and more variable than in quick service restaurants. As customers are expected to wait longer in the site, the restaurant usually takes greater care with the ambience, and also provides some mechanisms to 'amuse' or occupy the customer (e.g. bar), in order that his perception about the delay is reduced. Italian and Indian restaurants are good examples of this category.

5. *Luxury* here ambience has maximum importance. Service is normally quite formal and the environment is designed to give an impression of sophistication, which requires that equipment (furnishings, etc.) are carefully chosen. Concern with service speed becomes secondary, since customers come for a pleasant time and a sophisticated environment.

AB & P-ORIGINAL STRATEGY

It is not always easy to classify a restaurant, because these categories are not completely self-contained. In fact they represent stages of a continuum. However, AMERICA's partners noticed that there was a gap in the continuum in São Paulo at the 'quick service' stage. They also reckoned that the quick service type restaurant would serve well the aim of establishing a restaurant chain rather than a single restaurant.

The partners noticed that to be in the quick service category, AMERICA should have some of the characteristics of fast-food, e.g. care with cleanliness and hygiene, and relatively quick service but with great consistency in both quality of the products and service time. AMERICA should also have some of the characteristics of the conventional restaurants, such as the higher quality of the food (deriving from special care with the quality of ingredients, the production process and the appearance of the dishes), the variety of the dishes served and the ambience.

The partners decided that, as distinctive or critical factors of AMERICA's competitive strategy, they would emphasize the following:

1. *Quality of the products served* – They would have a distinctive taste and appearance, always creating the perception of 'quality food'.

2. *Ambience* the emphasis would be on the 'modernity' of the ambience which should always reflect 'AMERICA's distinctive atmosphere'.

By analysing these strategic objectives, Dr. Mattar decided that some critical operational factors should be emphasized:

1. *The architectural and interior design of the shops*. This would always emphasize 'modernity'. The interior design and decoration should always be 'clean', i.e. without unnecessary details. The decoration would always have style references to the train wagons, because of the original concept based on the American diners. Every piece of equipment and every object, such as plates, cutlery, chairs, table mats, etc. should also emphasize the concepts of 'modernity' and quality, even if this should mean higher costs. The partners were conscious that this would require an extra creative effort (e.g. finding sponsors to buy space for publicity in the menus) in order that they could achieve the project at the desired quality levels.

2. *The quality of the recipes, ingredients and process*. This would be distinctive. All the recipes would be developed in-house. The ingredients should also be of extra quality, and only supplied by previously tried and certified suppliers. As to the production process, as far as possible the dishes should only be 'finalized' in the shops. The components which most influence the perception of quality (e.g. pasta sauces and hamburgers) would be made in a central kitchen, where process control methods should be used to keep quality and methods standard.

3. *Hygiene and cleanliness*. Emphasis would be put on employee training with regard to hygiene and cleanliness. They would be extremely important in establishing and consolidating the AMERICA brand, as meaning *reliable quality* in all respects.

4. *Informality, speed and consistency of service*. Waiters would not be as formal as in a conventional restaurant, but would be cordial, professional and very polite. This restricted, for example, the employment of 'part-time' staff. Priority would be given to professional waiters and maitres. The need for speed and consistency led to the development of a computerized service cycle time control system, and also to investment in the development of 'teamwork' and commitment among the employees.

From the beginning the partners knew that they would face some of the usual problems in similar service activities in São Paulo and that some could jeopardize the achievement of their objectives. The main expected problems would be poorly qualified people in the labour market and the lack of consistency and quality of supplies.

To safeguard against these factors, Dr. Mattar established rigorous criteria for selecting and hiring people. An intensive new employee training programme was established and special attention was given to the search for and approval of suppliers, together with the development of a quality control system for the bought in ingredients. Eventually in practice worries about the difficulties with the human resources were justified. During the first three months of operation of the first shop, 50 per cent of the employees had to be replaced because they proved to be inadequate (despite training) to AMERICA's needs. With regard to supplies, great managerial effort was always required to keep the product quality consistent.

THE AB&P HISTORY
The opening of the first shop: the start-up of the chain

The first AMERICA restaurant opened in December 1985 on an important avenue in São Paulo, in a district where mainly upper middle class and young urban liberal professionals live. The choice of the site was based on visibility and on the type of local population.

In the first phase, the marketing strategy emphasized the restaurant as a 'trendy' place, aiming at establishing and developing the AMERICA 'brand'. AMERICA hired the service of experts in press and public relations in order to devise strategies to attract São Paulo's 'trend-setters'. This was successful, but Dr Mattar knew that 'trend-setters' are not necessarily loyal to places and brands, so a second phase was necessary. This would aim to broaden the range of customers. During this phase the image of 'modernity' would be consolidated eventually to replace the 'fashion' image.

The 'cruzado' governmental plan

In March 1986, when the second phase of AMERICA's marketing strategy had just started, President Jose Sarney's government decreed the 'cruzado' economic plan (or 'package').

This froze all prices and salaries at a time when inflation was at more than 20 per cent per month. The price freeze helped AMERICA keep its prices at a relatively low and stable level and helped attract new customers, cheered with the momentary economic growth (which would later be seen only as a deceiving demand 'bubble' rather than sustained economic recovery).

AMERICA's turnover grew at the impressive rate of 150 per cent in the first six months of operation. The management became worried then about the risk of losing consistency of quality, and decided to establish AMERICA's first centralized industrial kitchen. It had 150 m² of space and capacity for the production of 32 different products, of those used in the menu. It was to start operating at the time of the opening of the second restaurant. The main objective of the central kitchen was to achieve tighter control over the products which most influenced customer perception of quality, and also to achieve scale economies in production through industrial scale processing.

AMERICA grew at the rate originally planned by the partners, making it possible to achieve their original goal of opening a new restaurant every year. The second was opened in November 1987 (together with the start-up of the central kitchen), the third opened in October 1988 and the fourth in March 1989.

Late in 1988 management noticed that the first central kitchen would reach its capacity limit at the time the fourth restaurant started operation, so they drew up plans to establish a new and larger kitchen. They decided to move on to a new location, a 800 m² plant, with modern and versatile equipment, capable of preparing 68 different products and with a capacity sufficient to support the operation of 20 restaurants. With the new kitchen, the original objective of only finishing the dishes in the restaurant sites could be achieved, thus ensuring levels of quality consistency of products and also improving the levels of consistency in the service cycle time, since fewer operations should be performed in the restaurants, following customer order.

The Collor economic plan

Everything was going well for the chain (despite the recession in the country) when in March 1990 the first freely elected President in 30 years, F. Collor, took power.

One of the first measures taken by the President, who inherited an inflation, then reaching 80 per cent per month (the freezing of prices and salaries of the 'cruzado' plan had been gradually relaxed since 1986), was a series of decrees (then called 'provisional measures') which became known as the 'Collor economic plan'. These included a new freeze of prices and salaries and also the 'arrest' of most of the means of payment of the economy, including current accounts, deposit accounts and investment accounts of companies and individuals. (The arrest would last 18 months, during which the major part of the means of payment were unavailable to the owners. From the 19th month on, the funds would be given back in 18 monthly instalments.)

The plan caused an initial euphoria which soon turned into a nightmare affecting most of the sectors of the Brazilian economy: the final result was a severe deepening of the recession and high levels of unemployment. For example, it resulted in reductions in AMERICA's market (Table CS9.1).

Given the new scenario, the partners were determined to reposition the AMERICA chain, as profit margins could not support such a dramatic reduction in income. Additionally, some competitors, most of them single restaurants, were struggling to survive by competing, frequently in an unfair or at least uneven way. Many of them operated and dealt with their suppliers and employees in an 'informal' way, by not paying all the due taxes.

Table CS9.1		
Reduction in the:	**AB&P**	**All restaurant businesses**
Number of customers	20%	25–30%
Consumption per customer	10–15%	10–15%
Total turnover	approx. 35%	approx. 45%

As well as being 'irregular', such practices were impossible for an organization such as AMERICA, because of the tighter controls the government kept on larger organizations.

AB & P's response to the deepening recession

AB & P's management decided to tackle the problem on three fronts:

1. By *increasing productivity* to reduce the break-even level. They did not consider reducing their prices because the demand was not very price-elastic (sufficiently to influence demand, the reductions in price would have to be of around 30 per cent which would make AMERICA unviable).

2. By *adjusting the market strategy* to win market share. This would be mainly through promotions and by increasing the product line flexibility to secure new market niches such as the professional public (for the day-to-day lunch) and children (who would, obviously, bring their parents along).

3. By *restructuring* the chain management. Such restructuring would also to achieve greater economies of scale. This would be by centralizing suitable operations. Such restructuring would also establish better management and financial control procedures (of paramount importance during high inflation).

Some of the managerial actions now taken by AMERICA's management in order to try to achieve these objectives and, where known, the results obtained to date, are listed below:

Increasing productivity

Productivity of the ingredients

A thorough study was done on the required quantity of each ingredient per dish, to fix 'standard' portions, so that standards of 'productivity' per ingredient could be established. Also, a work study was carried out on the operations for preparing dishes, in order to eliminate waste. Standard containers for sauces and other ingredients were designed. Measures to standardize the meat-cutting operation were adopted, and amongst others, exact measures for salads, chips and other side dishes were established and implemented.

Simultaneously, a computer system was developed to *control* the quantity of ingredients actually used, with the predetermined standards. The largest discrepancies could be identified and the appropriate actions to achieve productivity gains could be prioritized and performed. One of the findings of the system, was that AMERICA used twice as much sauce as it should have done (compared to standard portions). This increased costs and reduced margins.

Workforce productivity

Analysis of the jobs and tasks

The aim was to reduce the amount of labour per restaurant. This analysis, together with a persistent drop in demand, gave the possibility of substantial reductions in personnel.

New compensation and reward policy

The aim was to motivate the work force to fight waste. Here an unexpected phenomenon was identified. According to Dr Mattar:

'When we did the first analyses of the use of ingredients based on the standard portions, we found out that the levels of waste in the use of the premium meat we use to prepare the grilled rumpsteak was approximately 20 per cent, caused either by careless cutting, misuse or theft. In other words, AMERICA was spending 20 per cent more on meat than was needed to make the grilled rumpsteak dishes. We then tried to introduce a new reward scheme, based on a positive reinforcement technique. In order to motivate the employees to reduce waste we offered the kitchen team 10 per cent increased salaries if they were successful in fighting waste. At the end of one month of this policy, the new levels of waste were measured and disappointingly, we found the same 20 per cent. We then thought that maybe the level of increase in salary was not enough to motivate the team, so we decided to offer them 15 per cent instead. At the end of the following month we again measured the level of waste: once again we found 20 per cent. Given the unchanged level and after double checking the standard portions we decided to change the policy. We decided therefore to try a negative reinforcement policy this time. AMERICA would reduce the salaries of the kitchen team at the end of the month by the value found to be wasted with no reasonable explanation.'

Development of multiple skills for kitchen employees

Through a system of training and reward, the aim was to develop a different approach to the usual Brazilian restaurant practice which, generally, has dedicated employees for specific tasks. By training the kitchen employees to perform several tasks, it would be possible to maintain fewer people in the kitchen during off-peak hours. The adoption of the multi-skills policy, according to AMERICA's management, would not be easy, again because of the low level of skills of the work force.

Productivity of the facilities

The 'free home delivery' service

Through this, meals would be sold without the customer occupying AMERICA's physical facilities. Additionally, AMERICA might win a share of the market of those who usually prefer to eat at home. A measure was taken in order to try to guarantee that customers get the quality they expect when ordering dishes to be delivered. A simplified menu is given to customers to use for their phone orders. This gives information regarding which dishes are more or less subject to their taste/appearence being affected by the delivery. In this way, AMERICA aimed to manage the levels of expectation of the customer (who otherwise would tend to expect the dish at home to be exactly the same as that in the restaurant).

Industrial catering

With the objective of increasing the utilization of the central kitchen, Dr Mattar is also considering going into the 'industrial catering' market. His concerns, however, relate to the possibility of losing the focus of the business, because competition in 'industrial catering' would be based on criteria which are substantially different to those with which AMERICA is accustomed to operate. Although a different brand would be used for the new 'industrial catering' line, both lines of products would have to share the same facilities and most of the workforce. This could cause a whole new set of managerial problems.

Coffee served in a separate restaurant area

The traditional short strong coffee after the meal (a preference of nine out of ten Brazilians), which normally accompanies long and relaxing chats (which can last up to 30 minutes), will be served in a pleasant small and cosy 'winter garden' next to the main meal room. Thus customers should leave the table quicker, freeing it for the use of other customers and therefore possibly increasing dining capacity or levels of utilization of the facilities.

Discounts

The aim is to try to level up the demand by attracting people in the off-peak periods in the day, and at the same time alleviating peak hour load when either sales can be lost or the service level can drop (e.g. in terms of waiting time).

Work methods and procedures in the dining room

The objective here is to increase the consistency of the 'waiting to be served' time, for two main reasons. On the one hand, increased consistency will improve customer perception of service quality. Also, an improved consistency will help keep the customer turnover within the planned limits. According to Dr Mattar, the work methods used by AMERICA would make it possible to reduce customer waiting time substantially; but this is not necessarily desirable because, from assessment of customers' views (AMERICA assesses customer satisfaction continuously, through questionnaires and direct contact), it was discovered that they do not want to be served quicker than a specific time (20 to 25 minutes, between ordering and receiving the order). If the service is quicker, the customer feels as if someone wants to get rid of him. This has focused management on the consistency of the service cycle time and has prompted the implementation of a computer system which follows up the times of the events (e.g. being seated, ordering, receiving the order, asking for the bill, receiving the bill, paying and leaving) for each customer during his stay in the restaurant. One aim is to operate between a lower control limit for ordering time—the minimum the customer requires (20 to 25 minutes)—and an upper control limit influenced by the need for high customer turnover and, consequently, a high level of capacity utilization. With regard to the consistency of the service cycle time, AMERICA innovated in the distribution of tasks among the staff who work in contact with the customer. A new function was created, called 'marchador', responsible for the liaison between the kitchen and the table. So, in future it will no longer be the waiter who takes the dish from the kitchen to the customer table, but the 'marchador'. In this way, the finished dish should not be kept waiting for the waiter to be free of his other tasks of seating customers and taking orders, making suggestions and checking customer satisfaction.

Marketing strategy

In order to broaden the range of customers and also to recover possible lost customers, AMERICA made attempts to innovate in its marketing policies as follows.

Promotions

A marketing professional was hired to be in charge of promotions. Some which are to be tried are: the sponsorship of theatre plays and shows, and advertising on radio/TV and in cinemas. A promotion was planned in which the customer could choose one of several AMERICA postcards, write a message to someone and address it, and AMERICA would send it to anywhere. Another promotion will be a competition where the customers are invited to suggest a new slogan for the restaurant. The winners will win prizes and trips.

AMERICA also intend to reduce the price of one dish of each menu section (pasta, grilled, salads and so on) during one month. This discount would not affect all the dishes (which might affect viability) but it should allow the 'professional' customer to spend less on his day-to-day lunch.

Menu flexibility

The aim is to enable some dishes to be 'assembled to order' for the customer, from a variety of pasta, meat, salad and side dish types. The aim is to reduce the price paid by the customers and possibly to attract those customers who would otherwise consider AMERICA to be too expensive for their day-to-day lunch. AMERICA will also create a self-service buffet of salads, with a fixed price, cheaper than most of its dishes. They will also try to secure a new market niche represented by children through promotions (e.g. simple puzzles printed in the children's dish paper mats), lower prices ('kids' menu') and simpler dishes more adequate to children's tastes. The idea behind this promotion is that there is always an adult accompanying a child and he/she will pay regular prices for his/her meal.

Role of the waiters in suggesting dishes

The aim is to give waiters a more positive role but with the necessary subtlety in order to suggest dishes and drinks which result in higher profit margins (e.g. natural fruit juices instead of sparkling drinks). This way AMERICA aims to try to increase the margins per dish in order to offset the reduction in turnover.

Restructuring

After the fourth restaurant was inaugurated, AMERICA was restructured, by centralizing and where possible computerizing personnel control and payroll, accountability, stock control and management control systems. The objective was to reduce the overhead burden and improve efficiency. So, for example, for the opening of the fifth restaurant in November 1990, the process was much smoother than with the first four restaurants, because 50 per cent of the personnel for running the fifth restaurant were taken from the first four, and only 50 per cent were newcomers recruited in the market. The problem with turnover during the first months of operation was much simpler and easier to overcome.

AB & P—FUTURE PLANS

AMERICA opened its sixth restaurant in August 1991, so the original plan of growing at a rate of one new restaurant per year has been broadly achieved so far. Following the original plans, the capital for the opening of the last restaurants was attracted from the market, by admitting new partners, mainly 'capitalist' partners with no administrative role. The introduction of new partners bringing in capital is seen to be important as AMERICA's management has decided not to use the 'franchise' system because they are afraid of losing control over their critical competitive aspects such as quality.

The plan now is to pursue vigorously the actions taken since 1990, to build on successful actions and to look again at those which are less successful, and to try, therefore, to follow the original expansion plan.

In the operation of the chain the emphasis will be on reducing waste of all kinds; to automate and centralize administrative activities for economies of scale; to refine the computerized management control system, and continuously to seek productivity gains without jeopardizing the desired levels of quality, service and product flexibility. On the marketing side, the intention is continuously to reassess and reposition AMERICA' marketing strategy, in order to be able to respond well and quickly to the constant changes in the market.

Case study 10

Linden Christian Nursery School – A

A sub-committee of the board of management of Linden Presbyterian Church (LPC) was meeting to consider tenders received for a contract. Roy, who chairs this sub-committee, recalled the history of the nursery school.

LPC is a small suburban church in the north western suburbs of Johannesburg, largest city of South Africa. It serves a congregation of about 500 members.

Over the past few years LPC has bought two adjacent properties which are now consolidated on a single property. The whole property is about 4500 m² in extent at the corner of 5th avenue and 8th street in the suburb of Linden. (See Figure CS10.1.) On the north-western portion of the property there are a sanctuary, halls and offices. On the

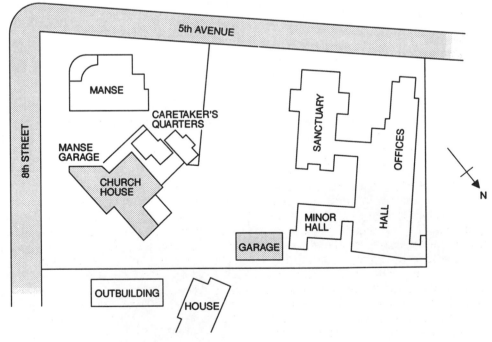

Figure CS10.1 Plan of LPC property

remainder of the property there are the two houses and out-buildings. Doug Crawford, the minister, uses the house at the south corner as a residence (called a manse). On the east, 'Church house' as it is called, and the associated garage are shaded in Figure CS9.1, and are used on Sundays only. Some members spotted the low level of utilization of 'Church house' and suggested setting up a nursery school there. At that stage one member suggested that R10 000 would convert 'Church house' to a nursery school.

The market for a nursery school depends on the demand by people who live in, commute through, or work in the area. Linden historically consists of detached residences. The congregation's home addresses are given in Table CS10.1 and a map of the catchment area is in Figure CS10.2. The public transport in this section of Johannesburg is indifferent and most people use cars.

Table CS10.1 Distribution of congregation relative to LPC		
Area	**Suburbs**	**%**
Central	Linden, Roosevelt Park, Northcliff, Montgomery Park	26.6
N to NE	Blairgowrie, Bordeaux, Robindale, Robinhills, Ferndale, President Ridge, Malanshof, Bromhof	26.8
N to NW	Randpark, Windsor, Fontainebleau, Aldara Park, Darrenwood, Cresta	12.2
W	Fairland, Valeriedene, Berario	8.3
Far W	Roodepoort, Weltevreden Park, Randparkridge	5.9
SE	Greenside, Emmarentia, Parkview, Parktown	4.6
S	Westdene, Auckland Park, Melville	2.9
Far N	North Rand	2.7
	other areas	10.0

Key: N. = North; E. = East; W. = West; S. = South; Central = Near Linden Church

In outlying areas people are moving into the north and west as the south and east is already settled and serviced. For example there is a large Presbyterian church in Parkview. Developers are starting to erect flats (apartment blocks) and cluster (or town) houses in Linden that will lead to higher-density living. Flats and cluster houses are associated with young married couples and retired people.

In April the board of management commissioned a sketch plan and budget from John Duncan, an architect who has had considerable experience in church work. This showed that the original estimate of R10 000 was a gross under-estimate, both because of the state of the building and municipal requirements for converting 'Church house' to a nursery school. John's budget for alterations to 'Church house' was R108 000. As some members of the church felt strongly about the need for a nursery school, a meeting was held to attempt to cut the budgeted conversion costs. This meeting included the architect, John, likely teachers for the nursery school including Monica, and selected members of the board of management including Ernest, the chairperson, and Roy. During this meeting members cut the budgeted expenditure on 'Church house' from R108 000 to R73 300 by omitting anything not absolutely essential. The decision to proceed with the nursery school depended on special consent in terms of planning regulations. As some people objected, there was a hearing and special consent was given to proceed with a nursery

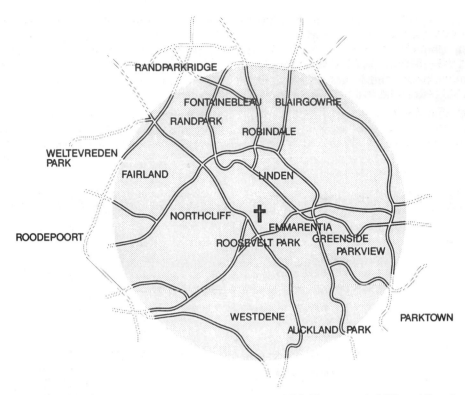

Figure CS10.2 Some suburbs and major roads near to LPC. The cross is LPC and the shaded circle designates a 5-km radius from the church

school. In addition, the decision depended upon a plan to move the Church or to stay in Linden. Both of these delayed the decision on the nursery school.

Some members of the LPC are qualified teachers and active in nursery school education. There are a few nursery schools in the area. A well known nursery school for approximately 40 children is about half a kilometre away at a Methodist Church. Informal discussion with the leader of this nursery school yielded the following information. Nursery school attendance had usually been strong with demand always exceeding supply. During the past year, demand at this nursery school had slackened and one factor contributing to this is the changes in formal schooling. (See Figure CS10.3)

Note on Formal Schooling

In South Africa nursery schools provide a service for children up to six years of age when formal schooling starts. The academic year starts in January, just after the long summer holidays.

Formal education in South Africa is undergoing changes. Changes imply that parents pay much more and have greater say in their children's education. Increases in fees of 50 per cent with the changes are common. (One example of the fees increase is R850 in the year before changes, R1200 in the year of changes and R2000 the year after changes; the inflation rate was about 15 per cent p.a. in these years.)

Figure CS10.3

On 10 August the board of management decided to convert 'Church house' and the associated garage to provide a nursery school, to open at the beginning of the following year. As builders take their holidays in December, the deadline for undertaking such work was tight. Ernest asked Roy to chair a sub-committee which, amongst others, would manage providing physical facilities for the nursery school. Monica would head the day-to-day running of the nursery school with assistants and a capacity of 54 pupils.

During the next two weeks John worked at getting the plans and specification into a format acceptable to the municipality. This involved gaining acceptance from many branches such as the fire prevention committee, the sewerage branch, etc. He also had to make sure that the revisions would provide an adequate service for the Nursery School. Part of the plan is given in Figure CS10.4.

John had to add extra work into the plan. The changes are listed below with the budgeted costs in brackets:

1. The caretaker's quarters had to be altered to provide privacy from the Nursery School. (R6000)

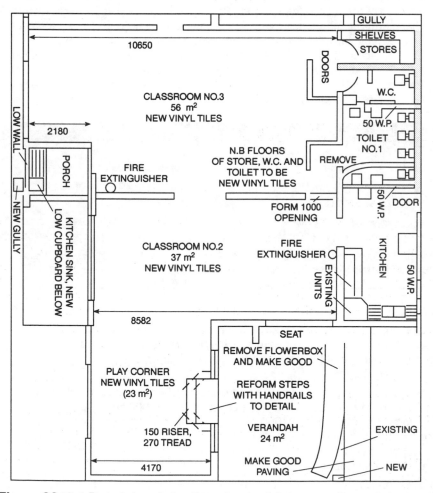

Figure CS10.4 Part of plan of alterations showing toilets, w.c., store and classrooms

2. Parking had to be provided with an extra entrance and driveway. (R9300)

3. Extra ablution facilities and washing up was required. (R4150)

4. Fire-fighting regulations had changed and extra work was required. (R6200)

John managed to lessen costs slightly in other areas by reduced painting, using standard gates at entrances, etc. John negotiated with officials in the various branches of local government required to approve the design, talked with Roy, and got quotes from suppliers. Monica pointed out that, to attract children, parents wanted to see what they were getting. For this she wanted completion by the end of October.

By 31 August John had finished the specification for a contract. The specification included alterations to the caretaker's quarters and extra ablution facilities but excluded fire-fighting and work for the driveway. It called for completion on the last day of October provided that the acceptance was on, or before 10 September. Three firms were willing to tender and were known to have performed well in the past. Their names were Ferromont (Pty) Ltd., Sinclair C.C. and Vogue Construction C.C.

Roy set up a meeting for the evening of 7 September as tenders closed at noon of that day. He spoke to Ernest, the Chairperson. They agreed that it was important to make an early decision and the sub-committee was empowered to make a decision. However Ernest was going to Angola until 9 September, and could not attend the meeting. Roy discussed setting up a sub-committee and the agreement was to have Barry and Eric. Barry is a senior executive from a large building society and Eric is the LPC treasurer. Just after the closing time on 7 September, Roy contacted John, and as all tenders were in, they opened the tenders. The tenders are given in Figure CS10.2.

Table CS10.2 Tenders received

Name	Tendered price (rand)
Ferromont (Pty) Ltd.	74 500
Sinclair C.C.	88 500
Vogue Construction C.C.	*

* Vogue Construction hand-delivered a letter of apology on 7 September, stating they could not quote on this task. The letter was dated 4 September.

Both tenderers intimated that they would finish at the end of October.

The meeting got under way at Roy's home on the evening of 7 September with Barry and Eric. John was invited to present the tenders. He did so and was perturbed by the apology from Vogue. Had he received this apology four or five days earlier another quote could have been sought.

Roy asked for comments and there was some clarifying discussion. Barry commented that, as bond (mortgage) cost about R15 per month per R1000 borrowed, and with current building costs running at over R1000 per m² of floor area, there was little chance of anyone else building a nursery school. Even as things stood, the break-even situation at the Nursery School, based on the alterations, set-up costs and a bond over 20 years was estimated at about 40 pupils.

Two questions faced the committee. What are the options? What should be done?

Case study 11

Linden Christian Nursery School – B

This case follows and must be read in conjunction with Linden Christian Nursery School, A.

The tender of Ferromont (Pty) Ltd was accepted subject to an OK by the chairperson, Ernest. When he arrived on 9 September, Roy saw him and secured approval. John, the architect, negotiated the usual financial terms of the contract.

On 10 September Ferromont started moving equipment on site ready to start work on 14 September. Immediately problems occurred. Standard materials such as window-and door-frames were difficult to obtain. The building recession and the approaching Christmas break meant that stockists were running their stocks as low as possible. The caretaker was aggrieved because he had been told that the builder would not start building until he had been informed. However by 14 September both the caretaker and the builder were ready for the start. The contract explicitly stated that the caretaker would be in occupation during the work and would use the bathroom and kitchen of 'Church house' until the caretaker's quarters were ready. In addition, the conversion of 'Church house' into classrooms two and three had to be given priority for marketing of the nursery school. Lastly, it was important to keep most of the site available, and safe, during Sunday activities. The complete area of caretaker's quarters, 'Church house' and garage was rapidly taken over as the builder proceeded, people became available, and material was delivered to the site. The unskilled work of demolition and excavating proceeded relatively quickly but other work, e.g. plumbing and electrical, was only undertaken when skilled labour was on site and when suitable materials were delivered.

The Annual General Meeting of LPC took place on 23 September and during this meeting the subject of the Caretaker's quarters was raised as an area of concern. It was apparent that the caretaker was going to be without washing and toilet facilities at his quarters.

Roy alerted Eric, the treasurer, on 30 September that the builder would be likely to ask for his first progress payment on 1 October. Eric had facilities of up to R35 000. The builder handed his first progress payment request for R19 800 to John on 5 October. John discussed it with Roy. It was difficult to reconcile the progress payment to the budget for work done, because of part work complete. (See Appendix CS11A for part of the budget and the architect's certificate for the provisional final account.) Substantial discussion followed. It included comments about the differences between the budget, which is estimated according to areas, and the building, according to skill and resource availability. Finally the amount was agreed as being reasonable. Roy passed the request and Eric paid the builder on 6 October. (R19 800 less 10 per cent retention = R17 820.)

By 8 October, demolition was complete but rubble was still to be removed. Inside 'Church house', internal brickwork and plastering was complete. The plumber had completed laying external pipes but trenches were still to be closed. The contractor was alerted to the length of time of open trenches. Open trenches jeopardized safety and so Sunday activities were relocated. The plumber had to start internal work. In 'Church house', there was no start on the flooring. At the caretaker's quarters, brickwork was in progress. In the garage, brickwork, plastering and glazing was completed. No electrical work was started.

By 16 October internal plumbing work was ready to start as the material was on site. Plumbing was not satisfactory, as the caretaker was without adequate washing and toilet facilities at his quarters. Backfilling of external trenches was still not complete as the plumber tended to get people on site and then withdraw them. Fencing work commenced on 16 October and by 2 November the major part of the contract work was completed. On 2 November backfilling was complete and the rubble removed. Vinyl flooring was being installed. By 6 November, the contract was complete except for a list of defects and variations to contract. Defects included doors which did not close, and water drainage problems.

On 14 November church members cleaned the walls and on 21 November about 35 members of the church painted the Nursery School. The next day the dedication service for the Nursery School took place. This comprised speeches by John, Monica and the minister, Doug Crawford. After this the builder asked for final payment less retention moneys for maintenance and defects. The nursery school was on track to open on 6 January. However, Roy wondered whether there were any lessons to be learned, and whether the project had been undertaken well. There had been no accidents reported to Roy and the contingency amount of R1800 had not been exceeded. John mentioned that the quality had been 'as good as you are likely to find these days'.

Appendix CS11A

Part of the budget and the architect's certificate for the provisional final account.

Table CS11.1 Budget—toilet no. 1, w.c. and store		
Items	**Rand**	**Rand**
Internal wall	2800	
Internal doors (four off)	800	
W.C.s (five off)	4000	
Basins (five off)	3500	
Floor tiling (14 m² at R42 per m²)	588	
Skirting (13 m at R5 per m)	65	
Subtotal		11 755
Other		71 695
Total—contractual budget		83 450

Telephone :

E. John Duncan
Architect No. 483

Postal address:

LINDEN PRESBYTERIAN CHURCH
NURSERY SCHOOL

PROVISIONAL FINAL ACCOUNT

Contract sum				R74 500–00
DEDUCT	Contingencies	R 1800–00		
	Vinyl floor tiles	7200–00		9 000–00
			Subtotal	66 500–00
ADD	Vinyl floor tiles	R 5900–00		
	Vinyl tiles to caretaker's bathroom	150–00		
	Topping to concrete outside caretaker's quarters	140–00		
	Masonite covering over lower glass panels of double doors in lieu of plastic adhesive	N/C		
	Plumbing extras (i) new manhole, (ii) new pressure valve, (iii) replace defective water main	R 1463–00		7 653–00
			Subtotal	R73 153–00
			Less previous payment	47 995–20
				R25 157–80
			Less 5% retention	1 257–89
			Penultimate certificate	R23 899–91

Figure CS11.2 Architect's certificate for provisional final account

The budget is undertaken in terms of areas, e.g. play corner and classroom no. 2, kitchen, external finishes, etc. The area for which a partial budget is given is the toilet no. 1, W.C. and store. It is given in Figure CS11.1. (Part of the alterations are shown in a plan of 'Churchhouses' conversion in Case Study 10, Figure CS10.5.) The architect's certificate is in Figure CS11.2.

The Open Polytechnic of New Zealand (TOPNZ) – 'The writing process'

THE BACKGROUND

Appendix CS12 A details the external environmental changes The Open Polytechnic has had to face in recent years. It is based on an address given by Shona Butterfield, Chief Executive Officer of The Open Polytechnic of New Zealand to the Australian Open Learning Conference of Australia held at Northern Rivers, New South Wales in September 1992.

The scenario

It is now 1989 and *you* are the newly appointed Principal and Chief Executive of TOPNZ. The Deputy Principal (Learning and Resources) is sitting opposite you. He has given you the writing plan for your approval. You note that he wants 379 new assignments to be written in 1989. Although you have not long been with TOPNZ you know that the teaching process revolves around assignments. An assignment consists of 30 to 40 pages of student learning material. Assignments also include exercises and assessment tests to return to tutors for marking and comment. It is important that assignments are well written and that the information given in them is current and technically correct.

You are surprised that such a large number, 379, need to be written. This seems to be an awful lot of writing, and you wonder whether the Polytechnic has the capacity to cope and just how the work is to be allocated. You glance at the plan again and say 'OK, Fred you want approval to write 379 assignments for 1989. How many did we write in 1988?'

Fred refers to his file and replies '309 against an approved target of 355. That was pretty good under the circumstances.'

You think to yourself 'There will always be circumstances.' Aloud, you say 'Yes, but that is quite a shortfall; have there been shortfalls in previous years?'

Fred replies 'There is always a shortfall. In 1987, the plan was to write 359 and only 314 were completed.'

You then ask 'For those not completed—for example, in 1987, 45 were not completed—were these assignments no longer required or did we just fall behind? And if they were still to be written, would they be included in the 1988 writing plan?'

Fred says 'Each year we fall behind by a similar amount. However, the courses still have to be completed. In some cases, most of the work has been completed and the writer is in the process of finishing off. The plan does not include assignments already approved in previous years.'

'This raises another question,' you say, 'How many of the 355 new assignments approved in the plan for 1988 were actually completed in 1988?'

Fred doesn't have this information, but he promises to provide it 'tomorrow'.

Next morning, Fred is again sitting in your office.

'These are the figures. In 1987, our plan was to write 355 new assignments in 1988. In 1988, we actually completed 309. Only 210 of these were 1988 assignments; the balance were the leftovers from 1987.'

You do some quick arithmetic and say 'That means that if we completed 210 out of a target of 355, we had a shortfall of 145!'

Fred nods assent.

'What has it been like in previous years—1987, for example?'

When you get the 1987 figures, you find that although the plan was for 359 assignments to be written, in fact, only 215 of these were completed in 1987, a shortfall of 144. Admittedly, 314 were completed in total, but 101 of these were for previous years.

You recheck the figures. Something doesn't add up. If, in fact, there was a shortfall of 144 in 1987, surely the shortfall would have been carried over into the next period and completed in 1988. If so, of the 309 completed in 1988, then 144 really belonged to 1987. This would mean that only 165 of the 355 approved for 1988 had been completed in 1988. If you are right, there is now a balance of 190 to be carried forward to 1989. You explain these figures to Fred.

Fred thinks for a moment. Then he says 'Yes, but some of the 1987 assignments had been withdrawn, and so the number to be carried forward is only 145.'

You could have asked Fred why assignments were put forward for writing if within 12 months they were no longer required. And what is the point of a writing plan if it is never achieved? You don't bother to ask these questions or several others that spring to mind. You now have enough information to know that a fully study is needed.

YOUR ANALYSIS

After Fred leaves your office, you make the following notes on the present situation (March 1989).

What is to be done?

A plan was agreed in 1988 by your predecessor for the writing of 379 new assignments in

1989. There is still a backlog of 145 assignments from 1988 to be completed. However, some of these may not now be needed.

If none are withdrawn, the writing requirement for 1989 becomes 524 (379+145). For the last 2 years, the numbers of completed assignments were 309 and 314. Therefore, with the same number of staff, unless something drastic is done, the backlog by the end of 1989 will be over 200.

How is the writing plan determined?

Tutors/supervisors recommend that assignments be written. These recommendations are considered for approval by the Head of Department. There are 14 heads of department. The Head of Department, after discussion with supervisors and tutors, prepares a list of new assignments for action by the Deputy Principal (Learning and Resources). This happens in September each year.

The Deputy Principal, who is responsible for vetting the list, actually does little more than add up all the requests and pass it to the Principal for approval. The previous Principal always approved the plan. In the past, the plan has been for about the same number each year and each year the target is almost achieved (that is, if you don't look too closely at the accumulating backlog).

Who does the writing?

Tutors do the writing. Tutors are employed as subject specialists but also have to pass a writing test before being employed.

Tutors who are marking have a target of twelve assignments a day. The turnaround time aimed for is three days from the time of receipt for each assignment. In addition to writing, many tutors are expected to carry some of the marking load as well as doing some technical editing. The target for writing is ten assignments a year.

Once writing of a new assignment is approved, each writer is assigned a technical editor. The Technical Editor works in tandem with the writer to make certain that the content is technically correct.

No tutor is expected to work more than 34 hours a week. Tutors keep time sheets and record their work in six-minute units. Tutors who work more than 34 hours in one week are encouraged by their union to take time off in the next week. This practice is known as 'glide time'. For many tutors, taking work home or working above the mandatory 34 hours just doesn't happen. Moreover, the buildings are locked at 5.30 p.m. on weekdays and closed over the weekends.

What is an assignment?

A course usually consists of eight to ten assignments. Each assignment contains 30 to 40 pages, but some are longer (up to about 60 pages). Assignments include study material, self-assessment questions, and assessment tests to be returned to the tutor for marking and comment. In many courses, students need no further material—they can complete the course by studying the assignments. Some assignments are thinly disguised plagiarisms, with few acknowledgements of the original.

Why is there such a need for new assignments each year?

Each year in August, tutors are urged to put forward a list of new assignments for writing.

However, the rewriting is not meant to start until the next February. (Tutors have leave from the beginning of December until the beginning of February.) It is easy to be optimistic when planning for something you might start in six months' time, especially when you are looking forward to a two-month break before you begin! Also, at the time of the year (August) when tutors are being asked to put forward their writing plans, they are conscious of being assessed for promotion. Writing capabilities are an important factor in promotion considerations.

How is progress of writing monitored?

Although there are strict guidelines as to how assignments are to be written—their style, layout, and self-assessment test questions, for example—there is no budget and no serious monitoring of progress. Once rewriting of a course (eight to ten assignments) has begun, it is expected to be completed in twelve months. The lapsed time for writing an assignment is, at best, four weeks, but the whole process from writing to final printing always takes several months. Appendix CS12B shows the process in flow chart form.

The writer/supervisor follows the assignment through all the stages of the process. The first delay faced is related to the availability of technical editors who, like writers, are expected to give marking first priority. Likewise, at every stage delays will be experienced. Considerable rewriting or retyping are often required.

How is the cost of an assignment calculated?

There is no mechanism for calculating the costs of delays or reworks. The cost of each assignment is not known.

Your objective

You are now determined to examine the writing process for new assignments with a view to improving efficiency. You intend to present your recommendations in a report which will analyse the present situation and make recommendations about:

Organizational structure;

The production process;

Job design;

Motivation;

Control system(s).

(N.B. You can assume that the information given in the address in Appendix CS12A was known to you in 1989. The address also gives an indication of some of the changes being contemplated at that time.)

Appendix CS12A: The Open Polytechnic of New Zealand
A brief history

Our institution was set up in 1946 as The New Zealand Technical Correspondence Institute. It began with the amalgamation of the Army's Overseas Education Service and correspondence courses for country apprentices which had been developed by the Wellington Technical College. Distance education was seen as suitable only for students in remote locations and was very much a second-best option. The NZTCI's national functions soon expanded as it became the primary provider of vocational education for the rural sector—a role it still performs today.

During the 1970s, the Institute increasingly provided apprenticeship, trades and technician training throughout the country. The 1980s saw rapid growth in professional courses, for example, in Accountancy, Management, Banking and Legal Studies. Other developments included the provision of flexible continuing education options for skills upgrading for re-entry to the workforce and for high school students taking 'taster' courses or first level vocational courses.

By the end of the 1980s, NZTCI offered 8500 different study units in over 900 different courses. The institution had over 500 full-time staff, 400 of whom were teachers, and it serviced approximately 35 000 students. Tuition was virtually all by correspondence with very little other student support.

The structure of the organization was very similar to that of a secondary school, with a Principal, First and Second Deputies, 14 Heads of Teaching Departments and a Registrar, who was accountable for monitoring expenditure against budgets set by the Department of Education. All salaries, capital work and so on were managed directly by the Department, not by the Institute.

By 1989, there were many in the Department and in other institutions who felt that the TCI, as it was then known, had not 'kept up with the times', that other institutions could easily take on distance education functions, and that there may be no need for such a national institution. In May 1989, the Minister of Education announced a review which challenged our right to exist as an institution.

A number of reforms were being carried through by the Government at that time which would allow considerably greater autonomy for tertiary institutions with, of course, accompanying increased accountability. As well as justifying our existence, we had to prepare to be successful in the market place from 1 January 1990.

We had been funded for 45 years to teach the courses that were not viable because of tiny numbers in any one geographic area. Now we would have to survive on the same funding formula as other institutes. Of the over 800 courses on offer at that time, fewer than ten were really economically viable even with Government funding. Thankfully those few had large enrolments and have provided the base to get us through the transition. Needless to say, they are predominantly business and management courses.

To give you some idea of the magnitude of the change, in 1989 our institution had a budget of around $2 million, most of which was spent on paper and postage. None of the Heads of Department had any budgets, yet from 1 January 1990 we had to be capable of managing a $30m. budget and operating as a business. We had no central systems in place for management, and certainly not computerized ones—not even for enrolment. We knew how many students we had by asking teachers to do a manual 'headcount' three times a year.

Another contrast—while under the Department of Education we had a protected status in that other institutions were not funded to offer distance education courses. However, we were not permitted to enrol any student who lived within 16 km of another polytechnic without the written permission of that polytechnic's Principal; nor would the department provide any budget for advertising. The result of this was that although we serviced larger numbers of students than any other polytechnic, the institution did not have a high public profile or image at a national level which would support it in a competitive environment.

From this brief introduction, you will understand that our institution had to change. What I want to paint for you now is a picture or our organization as it is at this point of time. It is very different from just three years ago!

The Open Polytechnic of New Zealand in 1992
Shared beliefs

Our stated values are excellence, equity, responsiveness, integrity and professionalism. These are the base from which we operate and they certainly give us plenty of challenge in trying to live up to them.

Strategy

The first thing is to put clients first. From an independent survey of all enrolled students last year, we learned that over 95 per cent are satisfied with the service we offer and we now have a benchmark against which we can monitor progress.

We have a strong vision of what Open Learning means and how we want to be the leaders in the that field. We say we want to be the client's FIRST STOP SHOP. We don't set out to be all things to all people. Our first commitment is to ensure they get what they need or want. If we can provide only part of that, we FIND A PARTNER who can help us meet the full requirement, or we recommend another provider. We want people to come back to us again and again, and they will only do that if we serve them well.

We are trying to follow the tenets of Open Learning and provide our services when and where the clients want. We are not putting investments into buildings—we are INVESTING HEAVILY IN UPSKILLING STAFF, in ensuring QUALITY COURSE PRODUCTION AND LEARNING SUPPORT, and in management and quality control systems which enable us to RESPOND FLEXIBLY to client need.

We have DIVERSIFIED OUR BASE OF PRODUCTS AND SERVICES. From being only a correspondence teaching institution, we have moved to being an open learning business. The last word is important, because moving more towards a BUSINESS ORIENTATION has been crucial for our survival. A key issue for staff is ensuring that this orientation does support EXCELLENCE IN EDUCATIONAL TERMS—we cannot compromise our standing as an academic institution. Profit is NOT our objective, but staying in business most certainly is.

While we are trying to get more people wanting our existing products and services, we are also DEVELOPING NEW ONES but always within our core business of provision of open learning. For example, we now offer use of exam centres, management of external examinations, training needs analysis, workplace training, and student record systems for open learning, all on a commercial basis. One of our major 'earners' is our Instructional Design Unit, which is now providing services for outside organizations, including other polytechnics.

We have also put considerable investment into developing technologies for increasing delivery options. We offer freephone access for tutor help, audio conferencing, and audio and video letters; we are piloting audiographic teleconferencing; and we are producing videos as well as buying in when appropriate. At present we do not use broadcast TV, since for our students it is still cheaper for us to pay for postage of the video cassette than pay for broadcast time.

In eight other polytechnics, we have student Learning Support Centres for our students, and we are now developing regional Open Learning Access Centres, beginning in Auckland next year.

All of these activities demonstrate our commitment to client choice. We have to provide the options.

Style

It has been difficult to obtain commitment from staff to what is currently a highly centrally-controlled system. Greater freedom will come as our systems are more robust.

In my view, there is probably a cycle through central control and autonomy which is recurring—or at least a spiral, which does mean you do progress with each swing.

With major changes, we do try to employ the key components of change management. While we have certainly used outside consultancy help, particularly where objectivity has been required, we have created our own future. We have not waited to have change imposed on us. It is our own staff who have made all key decisions and determined how these should be implemented. This has ensured that they understand better why and what is happening and is probably the major reason we have been able to achieve what we have.

Structure

Our structure is now functionally derived with a strong Management Team comprising three Deans, five Directors and me. We have three Faculties—Commerce, General Studies and Technology. Directors cover Planning and Development, Marketing, Human Resources, Corporate Services and Education Services. This team leads the Polytechnic. Although the accountability is mine, I believe that if I tried to implement any decision which did not have the support of this team, that decision is unlikely to succeed. We need the collective wisdom of each of the perspectives on that team.

As well as their responsibilities for contributing to Polytechnic management, each member of the team leads and is accountable for the negotiated outputs for his or her Faculty or Branch.

Within Faculties and Branches, each Dean or Director can develop a structure that is most appropriate for them, providing that there are clear lines of accountability and that the span of control of each Manager is not less than five and not more than twelve.

Teachers have now begun to accept that there is a management role in each work area in the Faculty—and that is a major change from the situation in 1989.

Systems

We have developed disciplined systems and processes to help achieve our goals. These ensure we assess our situation appropriately, plan well, focus people on doing things right the first time, give clear feedback on progress and performance, and evaluate the effectiveness of the system we use.

APPENDIX CS12B:
Production flow chart with essential responsibilities

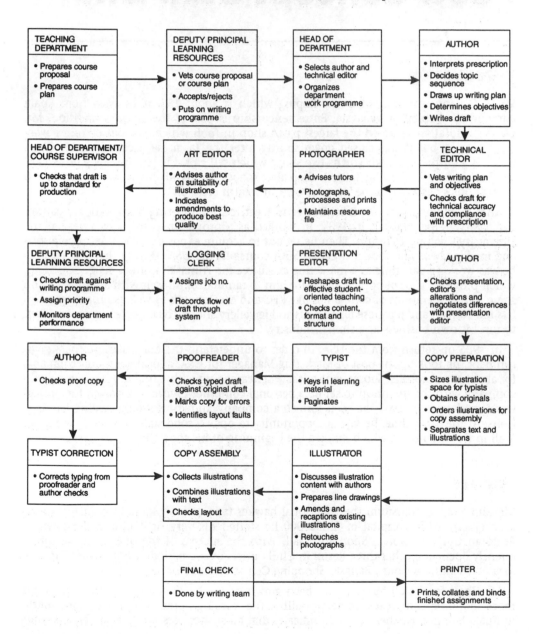

Food Concept Sdn. Bhd.

Introduction

Mr C. G. Cho was brought up in Taiping which is about 150 miles away from Kuala Lumpur, the capital of Malaysia. Entrepreneurship is part of the family's tradition. Mr. Cho's grandfather operated the largest pawn shop in Ipoh which is about 60 miles away from Taiping but it was closed down shortly after the Japanese occupation. Mr Cho's father is a businessman who owns two shops which sell clothing. During his school days, Mr Cho used to work in his father's shop after school. He recalls his father saying that to control one's destiny is to be 'on your own in wealth creation'.

After graduating with the B.Sc. Degree in Electrical Engineering from National Taiwan University, Taipei, Taiwan in 1981, he worked as a programmer for over a year at the University's computer centre. Then he set out to acquire exposure in business operations and management and took a two-year MBA course in the USA. During that programme, he was working part-time as a marketing executive for Trimark in direct mail advertising, which provided a lot of opportunities for him to familiarize himself with and understand some of the operations of companies like KFC and McDonald's as well as proprietary outlets like Korean and Japanese restaurants and jewellery shops. His experience inspired him to run his own business in a similar industry.

In 1985 on return from the USA, in order to understand the Malaysian business environment, he took up the post of Marketing Manager for CSA, a local computer company, for about nine months. Subsequent to that, he teamed up with a friend in an engineering company with the intention to set up a personal computer division; however, the project was abandoned. In 1987, he then formed a company known as Prolog, selling PC solutions. At the same time, he saw an opportunity to open a food stall in Yaohan Shopping Mall in Kuala Lumpur, which marked the beginning of his food chain businesses.

History

Mr Cho aims to transform the traditional hawker type of food stalls into an integrated food chain. With a capital of RM30 000 he started his very first food stall known as Restoran Chili in Yaohan Shopping Mall. With the success of the operation, he subsequently opened another three Restoran Chili outlets over a period of four years. They are located at Mutiara Court, Bangsar Shopping Centre and Lot 10 respectively.

Mr Cho's food stall business has been growing rapidly. At the same time, more and more shopping complexes are being built as the working population grows, particularly in Kuala Lumpur. Further, research indicates that most shoppers would also like to savour a variety of foods whilst shopping at their convenience. Mr Cho's aim is to establish his Food Concept Sdn. Bhd. business to incorporate Restoran Chili and other types of outlet—for example, the first Chili Food Court was opened at Lot 10 in October 1990. It is also planned to open another one at Dataran Merdek in mid-1993.

The overall vision is to operate an integrated food business. Having accomplished the first step, he has also ventured into the concept restaurant business with Cafe Galerie and Chili Restoran and Bar. The former was established in 1991 and located at Metrojaya Shopping Complex, while the latter was established in late 1992 and located at Jalan Ampang.

C. G. Cho's business philosophy and trade concept

'Business must grow and expand; if not, it will die.' On the basis of this maxim, Mr Cho has built his business to its present size. In line with his long-term vision, he has planned to open as many food stalls and food courts as possible in new and popular shopping complexes in order to recoup his investment within a short period, leveraging on the peak of the shopping complexes' business cycle and at the same time sustaining profitability and maintaining market share.

With the success of the Cafe Galerie and Chili Restoran and Bar, he is now also looking into the expansion in the niche markets. Thus a Sogo Cafe is scheduled to be opened in January 1994.

To control and monitor his business closely, Mr Cho has centralized the following:

Purchasing and inventory control

Preparation, cooking and quality control

Distribution

Administration and accounting.

He aims to ensure a net profit of 20 per cent.

Product Lines Development

As at May 1993, there are three main product lines:

Fast Food Chain—Restoran Chili

Food Courts—Chili Food Court, Lot 10 and Dataran Medeka

Concept Restaurants and Cafes—Cafe Galerie, Chili Restoran and Bar, and Sogo Cafe.

With the centralized kitchen facilities, an outdoor catering service unit has also been established to cater for parties/functions etc.

Mr Cho also wishes to venture into other types of restaurants such as Korean, Japanese, Vietnamese and Chinese restaurants, and also entertainment outlets like discotheques and bars. For long-term product development, he wishes to invest in hotels and resorts, food processing and trading.

Organizational Framework for Operations Control

Restoran Chili, Cafe Galerie and Chili Restoran and Bar are wholly owned subsidiary companies of Food Concept Sdn. Bhd. They are all managed by Food Concept Sdn. Bhd.

Figures CS13.1 and CS13.2 show the Corporate Profile and Group Organizational Structure as at May 1993.

The Group's operation consists of six major areas where the aims are as follows:

1. *Services*: To offer best customer services in the following areas:

    (a) attention to customer requests

    (b) prompt service in order-taking and dispensing of foods.

2. *Production*:

    (a) to ensure availability of all items on the menu at all times

    (b) to maintain consistency of quality foods at all times

    (c) to ensure only fresh and quality foods are served at all times

    (d) to ensure clean and hygienic preparation of all foods

    (e) use of sophisticated equipment to cut down preparation time and hence increase productivity

    (f) continue proper training and exposure for chefs to maintain leadership

    (g) all new items in menu being fully tested before introducing to the public.

3. *Distribution*:

    (a) timely and efficient delivery of goods from central kitchen to all outlets

    (b) optimization of scheduling and delivery.

4. *Purchasing, inventory control and cost control*:

    (a) centralization of purchase for all outlets

    (b) tendering exercise to ensure best pricing for bulk purchase

    (c) optimization of stock level

    (d) primary and secondary suppliers policy to ensure a continued supply of all goods

    (e) prompt, on-the-dot payment according to terms to ensure best services from suppliers.

5. *Promotion and advertisement:*

    (a) ensure that corporate image and identity are always being considered and followed on all P and A exercises

    (b) centralized co-ordination and planning for all outlets within the Group.

6. *Staffing:*

    (a) to provide on-going training and exposure to staff by having them visit other establishments (local and overseas)

    (b) total trust is given when any staff member is employed to ensure confidence/high motivation in work performance

    (c) participative and flexible management style is being practised at all outlets

    (d) internal promotion takes precedence to outside hiring

(e) provide better working environment, and office politics discouraged.

The organizational structure is shown in Figure CS13.3

The operating structure is shown in Figure CS13.4 (both as at May 1993)

Financial highlights are presented in Figure CS13.5

A look to the future

The Group has grown to such a stage that the management feels that it is high time to organize the business to optimize the operations and maximize profitability for future business expansion and diversification.

Better planning and control is also required in the six areas of the business.

Appendix CS13A: Company profile

Food Concept Sdn. Bhd. was founded in 1989, primarily to plan, design and manage the Chili Food Court (currently the most successful in Malaysia) at Lot 10, which opened on 10 October 1990. However, from its initial inception as a specialist in Food Court Design and Management, it soon ventured into other related businesses as a natural extension of skills acquired and opportunities identified. These include the chain of local fast food restaurants, food courts and concept restaurants.

The Company now employs a team of highly competent professionals in various aspects of marketing, finance, operations, personnel development and training.

Food Concept Sdn Bhd is a holding company with special focus on Food and Beverage operations. It is well established and positioned in three major areas:

1. Fast food chain – local fast food restaurants strategically located at:
    Yaohan
    Mutiara Court
    Lot 10
    The Bangsar Shopping Centre

2. Food courts – innovative concept of food courts serving both local and international food fare:
    Chili Food Court, Lot 10;
    14 000 ft^2, 16 stalls

    Chili Food Court, Dataran Merdeka (mid-1993);
    10 000 ft^2, 12 stalls

3. Concept restaurants and cafes – Cafe Galerie Sdn. Bhd. Metrojaya;
    first of its kind, combining cafe and art gallery
    Chili Restaurant and Bar, 35 Jalan Ampang;
    located in an old colonial building more than 100 years old, the restaurant is tastefully decorated in the 1930s and 1940s style, with an ambience to complement the fine Malaysian cuisine

    Sogo Cafe (January 1994);
    a vibrant, contemporary cafe combining Eastern and Western cuisine

The Group of Companies which together cover these areas of activity are:

1. Food Concept Sdn Bhd
2. Restoran Chili Sdn Bhd
3. Cafe Galerie Sdn Bhd
4. Restoran Chili (Jalan Ampang) Sdn Bhd

Group Turnoever: RM 5 millions

Total Staff Strength: 150 persons

Company	Date of Incorporation	Principal activities
1. Food Concept Sdn. Bhd.	1989	Independent management and consultancy company specializing in food court management
2. Restoran Chili Sdn. Bhd.	1987	Local fast food chain
3. Cafe Galerie Sdn. Bhd.	1991	Concept restaurant
4. Chili Restoran and Bar	1992	Concept restaurant

Appendix CS13B: Corporate structure

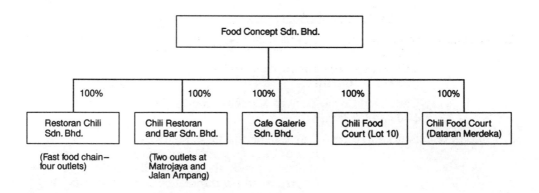

Appendix CS13C: Organizational structure

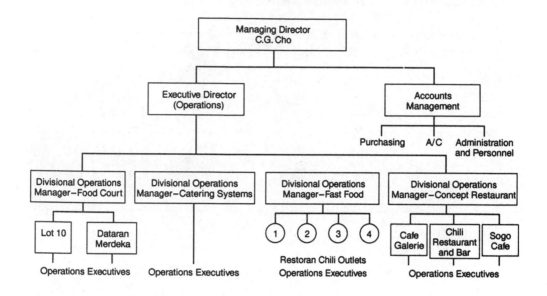

Appendix CS13D: Operational structure

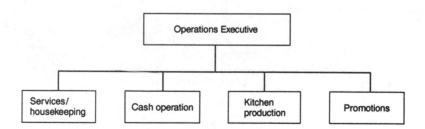

Appendix CS13E: Financial highlights: number of establishments and revenue summary

	1987	1988	1989	1990	1991	1992	1993
Fast food chain	1	2	4	4	4	4	5
Food courts			1	1	1	1	2
Concept restaurants					1	2	2
Total	1	2	5	5	6	7	9
Revenue (000s M$)	200	400	1000	3000	4000	4500	5500

Appendix

Appendix

Answers to analytical questions

Chapter 4

4.2 Break-even sales = 16 500 p.a.

Chapter 5

5.2 Select A.

Chapter 6

6.1

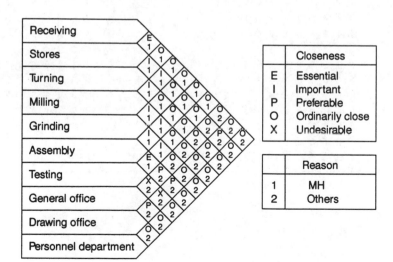

Chapter 8

8.1 $N^1 = 4.9$, therefore sufficient observations have been made.

8.2   2262 pieces.

8.3   Output per shift at standard performance = 200.
      Production cost per piece = 9p

8.5   (a) 45.9 hours

      (b) 51.2 hours

      (c) 16

Chapter 10

10.1 2530p

10.3 (a) 13 500p
      (b) 18 000p
      (c) 12 150p
      (d) 14 000p

Chapter 12

12.2

(a) Job	Priority rule									(b) Job	Priority rule (+ FCFS)								
	1	2	3	4	5	6	7	8	9		1	2	3	4	5	6	7	8	9
1	4	4	4	3	7	4	3	7	1	1	4	4	4	3	7	4	3	7	1
2	1	1	1	5	3	1	1	4	10	2	1	2	1	8	6	1	1	4	10
3	5	4	8	3	7	5	3	9	2	3	5	5	8	4	8	5	4	9	2
4	2	1	2	9	2	2	2	6	4	4	2	1	2	9	2	2	2	6	4
5	3	3	3	1	9	3	6	3	9	5	3	3	3	2	10	3	6	3	9
6	10	8	9	5	3	10	8	7	3	6	10	8	9	5	3	10	8	8	3
7	8	7	10	1	9	8	3	10	5	7	8	7	10	1	9	8	5	10	5
8	5	6	4	10	1	5	9	2	8	8	7	6	5	10	1	7	9	2	8
9	5	8	7	5	3	5	7	4	6	9	6	9	7	6	4	6	7	5	6
10	8	10	6	5	3	8	10	1	7	10	9	10	6	7	5	9	10	1	7

12.4

		Machine					
Order number	Number of products	A		B		C	
		I	Hours	I	Hours	I	Hours
1	50	0.33		0.67		0	150
2	75	0.5		0	150	1.0	
3	25	0.67		0.33	100	0	
4	80	0	160	1.5		1.0	
			175		275		175
			(91%)		(91%)		(86%)

Chapter 13

13.1

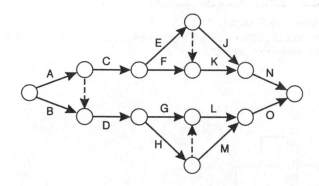

13.2

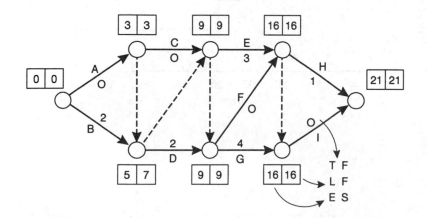

13.3 Critical path = A, C. F, I

Critical path = A, B, F, H, for which $t = 28$ and $\sigma^2 = 7.23$. From tables $p = 2\%$, i.e. considering critical path only, probability of finishing on or before 22.5 days = 2%. *But* minimum duration for path A, C, D, G = $2 + 9 + 5 + 7 = 23$. Therefore actual probability = 0.

13.4 (a)

Activity	TF	Activity	TF
0–1	0	5–8	7
1–2	0	5–9	0
1–3	1	6–10	3
2–4	0	7–10	9
3–5	1	8–10	3
4–5	0	9–10	0
4–6	3	10–11	0
5–7	9		

(b) (i) Delay project by 5 days.

(ii) The new critical path is 6, 10, 11, since these are the only activities in which delay will delay the project.

13.7 (a) 31 days

(b)

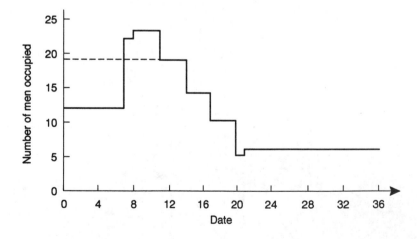

(c)

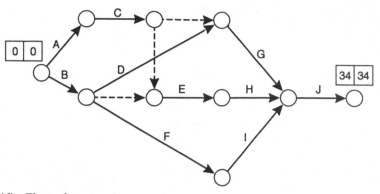

(d) Three days

Chapter 14

14.2 (a) (i) 1435

(ii) 1.4 months

(b) Since demand rate now exceeds processing rate, processing rate must be continuous and even then all demand cannot be satisfied.

14.3 21,000 litres (equivalent)

Chapter 15

15.1 $n_{min.} = 28$
$C = 0.4$ minutes

15.3 Cycle time = 20 minutes
Balancing loss = zero

15.4

Station	Work elements	Station time
1	0, 1, 2, 4	20min
2	3, 5, 7, 8	20min
3	6, 9, 10, 11	20min

	Station					
	1	2	3	4	5	6
4.61 per hour C = 13 minutes	0, 1, 2	3, 4	5, 6	7	8, 10	9
Balancing loss = 25.7%						
5 per hour C = 12 minutes	0, 1, 2	3, 4	5, 6	7	8, 10	9
Balancing loss = 19.6%						

Chapter 17

17.2 (a) 2830
(b) 633
(c) 0.64 months

17.4   Q* = 2500 units

Chapter 19

19.1 (c) 0.56

19.5

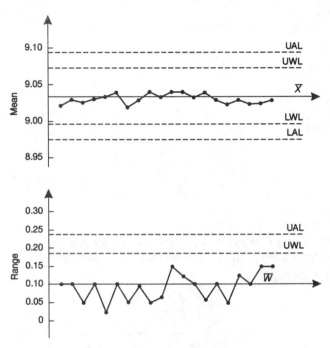

19.6

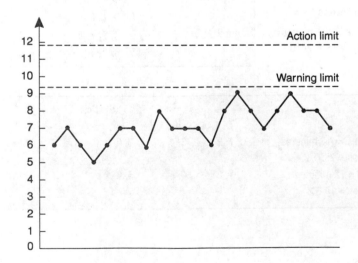

Author index

Subject index